Experimental Psychology
and Human Aging

EXPERIMENTAL PSYCHOLOGY AND HUMAN AGING

Donald H. Kausler
University of Missouri, Columbia

1807 1982
175 YEARS OF PUBLISHING

John Wiley & Sons
New York • Chichester • Brisbane • Toronto • Singapore

Library of Congress Cataloging in Publication Data:

Kausler, Donald H.
    Experimental psychology and human aging.

    Includes bibliographical references and indexes.
    1. Aging—Psychological aspects.   2. Adulthood—
Psychological aspects.   3. Middle age—Psychological
aspects.   4. Aged—Psychology.   5. Psychology,
Experimental.   I. Title.

BF724.55.A35K38   155.67   81–21972
ISBN 0–471–08163–9   AACR2

Printed in the United States of America

10 9 8 7 6 5 4 3 2 1

Preface

This book is intended for courses on the psychology of aging, particularly those that emphasize extensions of the content areas of experimental psychology to the psychology of aging. These content areas consist of the study of the processes governing sensory behavior, perception, information processing and pattern recognition, attention, learning, and the related phenomena of transfer and retention, memory, and the higher mental activities of concept formation, problem solving, and reasoning. Their extensions are concerned both with the detection and assessment of adult age differences and age changes in basic psychological processes and with the discovery of the reasons for those differences and changes. Understanding the nature of adult age differences/changes in basic psychological processes is essential for understanding changes in the adaptability of people to their environments as they progress from early to late adulthood. My survey of each content area has attempted not only to summarize the many laboratory studies relevant to that area but also to indicate the everyday implications of what has become known about that area.

Of course, the study of adult age differences and age changes in human behavior has by no means been restricted to those behaviors that concern experimental psychologists. Many studies have contributed substantially to our understanding of how intelligence, personality, and social behavior are affected by aging. To broaden the overall coverage of the psychology of aging, extensive reviews of aging research in these important nonexperimental content areas have been included.

Two additional features distinguish this book from those that offer surveys of the experimental content areas. First, each survey of the aging research in a content area is preceded by a thorough introduction to the basic concepts and theories indigenous to that area. Such introductions are usually too brief in other books on the psychology of aging to be of great value to students whose backgrounds in psychology are somewhat limited. My objective has been to provide these students with sufficient mastery of basic content areas so that they may readily follow their extensions to problems relevant to human aging. Second, I have given detailed analyses of the methodological designs guiding research in the psychology of aging and the methodological issues that are characteristic of aging research. The identification of true age changes in behavior from early to late adulthood as well as the causes of those changes is complicated by the potential presence of many confounding factors. To fully comprehend the results obtained in studies on the effects of aging we need considerable understanding of the means by which these potentially confounding factors are controlled. Many of the methodological issues inherent in research on adult development are also inherent in research on other components of human development. Consequently, the familiarity gained by students with the methodology of aging research should transfer considerably to methodology as it applies to developmental research in general. This book may therefore be useful in courses dealing more generally with developmental phenomena.

It is my pleasure to express my appreciation to the many individuals who contributed professionally to the completion of the present book. An early, but nevertheless important, contributor was the late Dr. Charles V. Lair. Nearly 20 years ago he stimulated my interest in the psychology of aging. Through his encouragement, I added an intense interest in aging research to a long-standing interest in basic experimental psychology. Among the more recent contributors have been Drs. Malekeh K. Hakami, William Kessen, Russell J. Ohta, and Ruth E. Wright. They served as highly competent reviewers of the entire manuscript at various stages of its completion. In addition, Dr. Timothy A. Salthouse provided valuable comments and reactions to several chapters. I am also grateful to Jill Kausler for her contributions to the more mundane, but equally important, task of typing my manuscript. Of course, the completion of a book calls for much more than the completion of a manuscript. The transition from an author's manuscript to a finished book has been accomplished most skillfully in this case by the editorial and production staffs of John Wiley.

My remaining pleasant task is to acknowledge the many indirect contributions made by members of my family as they endured what must have seemed at times to be an endless endeavor on my part. Heading the list is my wife Marty; her patience and support have been indispensable aids. Just a step behind are the similar contributions of my children and their spouses: Renee and Ranjan Ratna, Kathy and Don Kausler, Jr., Jill Kausler, and Barry Kausler. Finally, a very special thanks goes to my grandchildren, Neil and Tara Ratna. Their visits during the years of working on this book provided a delightful change of pace to the tedium of writing.

DONALD H. KAUSLER

Contents

Experimental Psychology and Human Aging

CHAPTER 1

Human Aging and Its Study

Most organisms age—including, most certainly, human beings. What makes the human organism unique, however, is that it alone possesses awareness of its own aging, thus aging joins death and taxes as one of life's inevitabilities. With this awareness comes the realization that someday you will be different from what you are now. In other words, you, too, will have become old.

Such awareness has probably been part of human consciousness throughout most of human history. However, awareness alone does not assure a true understanding of how we differ behaviorally as elderly adults from what we were like as young adults. The understanding most young adults have of age changes in behavior is likely to be based more on myth than on reality. Aging, in fact, is a phenomenon that is shrouded in myths. One of these myths, a familiar one, holds once vigorous adults become sexless, in terms of both the capacity for sexual intercourse and in the interest of maintaining sexual activity, and that this occurs when some undefined point in the lifespan is reached. This is clearly not true. Masters and Johnson (1966) found that many healthy elderly people are perfectly capable of engaging in sexual intercourse and experiencing orgasms well beyond the age of 80. Others (e.g., Pfeiffer, Verwoerdt, & Davis, 1972) have discovered through survey research that some degree of interest in sexual activity is present for most people beyond the age of 65.

Another familiar myth is that people grow more conservative politically and socially as they grow older chronologically. This myth originated through the failure to distinguish between an age difference in behavior and a true age change in behavior (Cutler & Schmidhauser, 1975). Consider, for example, allegiance to the Republican Party as a general index of a person's politically

conservative attitude. Not surprisingly, the proportion of our elderly population confessing membership in the Republican Party exceeds the proportion of
our young-adult population. Thus, there is an age difference in party allegiance
and, therefore, in political attitude as well. However, this does not mean that
today's elderly people were more liberal politically when they were young and
then changed as they grew older. Instead, most elderly adults presently considered to be politically conservative were probably just as conservative when they
were young adults. Conservatism was the reigning political mood at the time
our current elderly citizens were growing up. Accordingly, many of these people adopted it as their political philosophy by the time they were old enough to
vote, and they have simply held on to that philosophy ever since. By contrast,
liberalism had replaced conservatism as the dominant political mood by the
time today's young adults were born. Consequently, many of them have grown
up reflecting that mood, and they are likely to remain relatively liberal as they
become older. Thus, the age difference in political attitude stems mainly from a
generational change, or cohort effect, rather than from a true age change in
ideology. We will have more to say about cohort effects in later chapters.
Interestingly, there is evidence (Cutler, Lentz, Muha, & Riter, 1980) to indicate,
at least for certain attitudes (e.g., the attitude toward legalized abortion), that,
as society at large moves toward a more liberal position, the elderly members of
society move in step.

The final myth we will examine is one that is especially damaging to the
welfare of elderly people. It holds to the belief that age changes over the adult
lifespan serve, in effect, to de-differentiate elderly people, that is, age makes
people increasingly alike as they grow older. The nature of this myth was aptly
described by Maddox and Douglass, "With death being the end point of life, it
is implied, individuals become increasingly alike as they approach this common
denominator. Mean performance among the elderly decreases, and there is an
apparent regression toward a progressively lower mean" (1974, pp. 555–556).
Carried to its extreme, the de-differentiation myth implies that aging eventually
reduces virtually everyone to the common denominator of senility. Actually,
less than 3% of the people over age 65 in the United States develop behavioral
symptoms of true senility (e.g., loss of temporal orientation) (Busse & Pfeiffer,
1977). Moreover, for most behavioral tasks, individual differences in performance scores are greater for elderly adults than for young adults. Thus, increased
differentiation rather than de-differentiation with increasing age appears to be
the more general rule. Finally, the myth ignores the fact that throughout history
there have been elderly people whose great achievements clearly belie the existence of a universal massive decline in overall competence. Remember that
Arthur Fiedler conducted a major orchestra at age 84, that Margaret Mead
analyzed social mores as penetratingly at age 75 as she did at age 35, and that
some of the brightest and wittiest lecturers on a college campus are professors
whose accomplishments will soon earn them "promotion" to the rank of emeri-
tus professor.

What makes the de-differentiation myth especially harmful to the welfare
of elderly people is the fact that it translates readily into a negative stereotype

of old age. Surprisingly, young adults are not the only ones making this translation—the elderly themselves are equally guilty (Bennett & Eckman, 1973). A
negative stereotype means an overall unfavorable impression of an entire class
or group of people. To the possessor of that stereotype, each member of the
class is perceived and evaluated in terms of the unfavorable impression rather
than in terms of the member's actual competencies and skills. The manifestation of such prejudiced behavior is commonly referred to as the practice of
ageism (Butler, 1969, 1975).

A number of recent studies demonstrate quite convincingly the operation
of the stereotype in the evaluations given by young adults to elderly people in
general. For example, Weinberger and Millham (1975) had college students
rate a representative 25-year-old and a representative 70-year-old on a number
of categories, such as their possession of negative personality characteristics,
their possession of positive personality characteristics, their adaptability, and
their general satisfaction with life. The results indicated that college students
viewed the representative 70-year-old, relative to the representative 25-year-old,
as possessing more negative personality characteristics and fewer positive personality characteristics as well as being less adaptable and less satisfied with
life. In a similar vein, O'Connell and Rotter (1979) had college students rate the
personal acceptability of representative 25-year-old, 50-year-old, and 75-year-
old stimulus objects. Separate ratings were made for men and women as the
stimulus objects. Their results, expressed as mean ratings on a 7-point scale (7
equals high acceptability) are shown in Figure 1.1. It can be seen that perceived
acceptability decreases progressively with the increasing age of the stimulus
object, but this is truer for men than for women. In fact, a representative 75-
year-old woman was rated as being as acceptable as a representative 50-year-

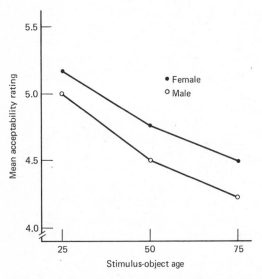

Figure 1.1. Mean acceptability ratings as affected by the age of the stimulus object being
evaluated. (Adapted from O'Connell & Rotter, 1979, Figure 2.)

old man. Interestingly, the ratings given by young adults to specific individuals identified as being either young or old are more complex. In some cases, an older individual may actually be perceived as being more competent than a younger individual when the same information is used to describe both individuals (e.g., a listing of daily activities). Further studies that deal with person perception will be reviewed in detail in Chapter 11.

The potential harm to the welfare of elderly people that is created by a negative stereotype is accentuated greatly by the fact that members of the so-called helping professions are far from free of its presence. Medical students commonly express a negative attitude toward their future treatment of elderly patients, even after they have completed a course stressing the problems associated with aging (Cicchetti, Fletcher, Lerner, & Coleman, 1973); psychotherapists have been reported to spend less than 2% of their time with elderly clients (Schofield, 1974). Even members of the clergy are not completely free of what has been called the YAVIS syndrome (the preference for young, attractive, verbal, intelligent, and successful—therefore, affluent—clients) (Longino & Kitson, 1976).

The negative stereotype of old age held by many people is probably acquired through their steady diet of the descriptions of elderly people found in folklore, literature, movies, and on television. These descriptions usually convey an exaggerated negative picture of the physical, psychological, and social competence of elderly people. Consider the many contributions of folklore to this unflattering picture. They include such adages as "You can't teach an old dog new tricks" and "There's no fool like an old fool," and then there are derogatory terms, such as old geezer and dirty old man. Even the preponderance of jokes about old people emphasize their physical, mental, or social deficits (Richman, 1977). The elderly have fared little better in literature (Beauvoir, 1972). In fact, the epitome of the de-differentiation myth is found in Shakespeare's famous description (in *As You Like It*) of old age as "sans teeth, sans eyes, sans taste, sans everything." As to the movies, two recent films nicely illustrate our point. In *House Calls,* the elderly director of a hospital is made to appear a complete idiot; in *10,* an elderly housekeeper is made to appear feeble to the point of ludicrousness.

Television has been especially unimpressive with its negative portrayal of the elderly. In commercials, elderly performers are commonly seen as members of the pathetic laxative generation, rarely as members of the fun-loving Pepsi generation. On regular television programs, the elderly people are often treated as if they do not even exist. For example, a survey of the 1969–1971 television seasons revealed that less than 5% of the characters appearing in comedies, dramas, and so on, were elderly people, a proportion well below the level of actual representation of elderly people in our total population (Aronoff, 1974). Perhaps the absence of elderly characters should be encouraged however. When elderly men and women do appear in television shows, the men are usually cast in the role of bad guys and the women are usually cast in the role of crime victims. Even when the spotlight is on an elderly person, as with Johnny Carson's Aunt Blabby, it shines on an invidious caricature of an older person. As observed by R. H. Davis, "Television perpetuates myths of old age through stereotypic characterization. The 'dirty old man' and 'little old lady from Pasadena' both have earned places in our story-telling repertoire along with the Irish cop and farmer's daughter" (1975, p. 322).

Fortunately, our knowledge of true age changes in behavior during adulthood can transcend the level of myths and stereotypes. Human awareness is accompanied by the capacity to analyze the contents of that awareness. A number of scientists have used this capacity for the study of human aging. Experimental psychologists have played a major role in such studies. Through their efforts, we have learned a great deal about age differences and age changes in sensation, perception, attention, learning, memory, concept identification, problem solving, and other cognitive activities. They have discovered that proficiency does decrease over the course of the adult lifespan for most of the tasks employed in experimental psychology. However, the decline in many instances is modest and relatively unimportant with regard to practical significance. In other instances, the decline is larger and of greater practical significance. Knowledge of these deficits is essential for the consideration of appropriate corrective and compensatory actions that involve elderly people. There are also tasks for which proficiency seems to be remarkably insensitive to change over the adult lifespan. Unfortunately, knowledge of this fact can lead to counterproductive myths that take the pollyanna position that virtually all aspects of human cognition are immune to aging deficits. Our position in this book is that our ability to combat the effects of human aging on important psychological processes and behavior can best be enhanced through a realistic appraisal of what those effects actually are.

In the remainder of this chapter, we will take a closer look at the nature of experimental psychology and its relationship to other areas of psychology and other areas of research on human aging. We will also discuss two more general topics that enter into all areas of research concerned with human aging. The first deals with the problems inherent in defining old age, the second deals with the demography of elderly people. We will end this chapter with a brief overview of the content found in Chapters 2 through 11.

Why an Experimental Psychology of Aging?

The skills and behaviors brought into the laboratory by experimental psychologists are by no means trivial ones. Indeed, these skills and behaviors enter into a wide variety of activities in the real world that exists outside the laboratory. Knowledge about adult-age differences and changes in these skills and behaviors is indispensable for our understanding of the capabilities and limitations of an elderly population. In addition, research by experimental psychologists often provides valuable insights into the reasons for age deficits in skills and behaviors. Knowledge about causative factors is a critical first step in the eventual discovery of means of retarding, modifying, or even eliminating an age-related deficit in behavior. Without due consideration of the findings derived from experimental research on aging, the lives of our senior citizens may continue to be regulated by rules that, at one extreme, force retirement from work at an arbitrary age, whether that age be 65 or 70 years, and, at the other extreme, permit operation of a lethal weapon, namely the automobile, by any slow-reacting octogenarian capable of passing a simple visual test and paying a small license fee.

By contrast, the effective use of the findings from experimental research on aging should enable elderly people to capitalize over their adult lifespan on those skills demonstrated in the laboratory to be relatively insensitive to deterioration with increasing age as well as to avoid tasks for which their likely deterioration in skill jeopardizes them and others. It is also conceivable, that experimental psychologists in their studies of aging will discover the means of retarding the deterioration of certain skills, the means of compensating for the loss of other skills, and even the means of reversing the loss of still other skills. Certainly, our older citizens deserve every opportunity to enrich their lives through the findings that the scientific community can provide. As stated recently by Senator Dewey F. Bartlett, a former member of the Senate Special Committee on Aging, "They [older people] have interests, skills, talents, and appetites—an undiminished zest for living. They deserve fullness of opportunity" (1978, p. 1).

The value of extending experimental psychology to human aging is not without its critics however. For example, in a review of the historical development of psychological research on aging, Riegel (1977), a prominent gerontological psychologist, commented on the abstract nature of experimental psychology and expressed the view that it represents the human being as a fictitious point in a developmental-historical vacuum. That is, experimental psychology tends to ignore both the individuality that occurs in development and the influence of historical-cultural changes on development.

Riegel's comments about the abstract nature of experimental psychology are generally true. Experimental psychologists do concentrate their efforts on the discovery of the laws of behavior, including those that relate to aging, and on the identification of the structures or processes that underlie these laws. Abstraction in the form of an "average" subject is a common step in these efforts; this abstraction is accomplished by expressing the outcomes of experiments in terms of the variation of the mean scores obtained on dependent variables by groups of subjects performing under different levels of independent variables. Each mean score is an average value that best represents the performance on a task by an entire group of subjects. Individual differences about that mean are often treated as nuisances that constitute a potential source of error in detecting lawfulness as abstracted from the differences among all of the means reported in an experiment. However, this is less often the case for experimental psychologists who work in the field of aging than it is for experimental psychologists who conduct basic research with young-adult subjects. Individual differences tend to increase over the adult lifespan for many of the tasks that are carried over from traditional experimental psychology. Assessment of adult age-level differences in variability is often made by the experimental aging psychologist. These assessments are vital parts of a descriptive research project in which age norms for behavior on a particular task are to be established and then used to interpret the competence of individual subjects of a given chronological age (to be described in Chapter 2).

Riegel's developmental-historical vacuum points to the frequent failure of experimental psychologists to consider the effects on behavior of (1) the individual subject's past lifespan development, both in terms of that subject's unique past experiences and in terms of experiences shared with members of the subject's generation (experiences that may not be shared by members of other generations), and (2) the cultural-social context extant at the time the behavior is evaluated (a context that may vary considerably from one time of evaluation to another time of evaluation). For some aspects of human behavior, particularly those related to social behavior and personality (remember our earlier example of attitudes regarding political and social issues), failure to consider developmental-historical effects probably creates serious distortions of our understanding of age differences in behavior and the causative factors underlying those differences. However, such distortions are likely to be far less serious for the aging phenomena studied by experimental psychologists. We will discuss these issues in depth in Chapters 2, 3, and 4, and we will examine the evidence relating to them at that time.

From the Laboratory to the Real World

Most of the research on aging conducted by experimental psychologists is basic, in the sense of dealing under highly controlled conditions, with the investigation of age differences in the performance of a task that involves a relatively small segment of behavior. The emphasis on basic research, however, does not mean that the results of these investigations have no practical implications. In fact, the knowledge emanating from basic experimental aging research often has considerable relevance for the real world of the elderly. Three examples should serve to demonstrate this relevance (others will be given in later chapters).

Learning: In the Laboratory and Away from the Laboratory. Our first example comes from the area of learning and memory. Specifically, it involves the task of learning a paired-associate list, a task that has been used by experimental psychologists since the 1890s. In paired-associate learning, the subject is asked to link together pairs of items (e.g., the words, *apple* and *king*) to the point where the second item of each pair *(king)* is recalled correctly as soon as the subject sees (or hears) the first item of that pair *(apple)*. Over the years experimental psychologists have found that imagery provides a potent means of relating paired items together, at least for young adults. For example, *apple* and *king* may be integrated into a compound image in which a royal figure who is a man is chomping away on a juicy red apple. Because this image includes a royal figure who is a man, its retrieval at the time of recall assures retrieval of the word *king* as well.

Elderly adults generally find it more difficult to learn a paired-associate list than do young adults (this will be elaborated on in later chapters). Research evidence strongly suggests that this difficulty is brought about by the frequent

failure of elderly adults spontaneously to use imagery as a mnemonic for learning paired items (Hulicka & Grossman, 1967). The question may be raised as to
whether the failure to engage in such mnemonics stems from a true loss of an
imaginal skill in elderly people. Alternatively, the failure may be only at the
level of performing a skill that is otherwise intact. That is, imagery may be an
example of those skills that become rusty through their disuse (Thorndike,
Bregman, Tilton, & Woodyard, 1928) once people find themselves removed
from formal educational settings. (The distinction between competence and
performance is an important one and will be elaborated on in Chapter 3.) If the
failure to use imagery effectively is due entirely to a loss of the relevant skill
(i.e., a loss of competence), then nothing can be done to enhance proficiency in
paired-associate learning for many elderly people. This does not seem to be the
case however. A number of researchers have demonstrated that proficiency in
paired-associate learning can be improved markedly by instructing and encouraging elderly subjects to make use of self-generated images in relating paired
items to one another. This may be seen in the study by Hulicka and Grossman
(1967). A portion of their results are illustrated in Figure 1.2. It may be seen
that elderly subjects encouraged to use imagery recalled 53% of the pairs in
their study list. By contrast, the control elderly subjects (i.e., those given no
special instructions or encouragement as to the use of imagery) recalled only
35% of the pairs. At the same time, the study warns us not to be too optimistic
about the possibility of eliminating completely the age difference in the proficiency of paired-associate learning that clearly favors young adults. As indicated in Figure 1.2, the young subjects in this study were superior paired-
associate learners under the instructed condition as well as under the control

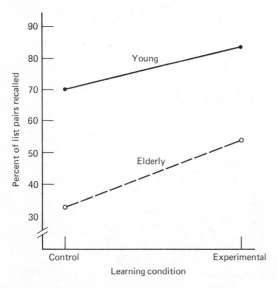

Figure 1.2. Age differences reflected in paired-associate learning under neutral instructions
(control) and experimental instructions (stressing the use of imagery to relate paired stimulus-response elements to one another). (Adapted from Hulicka & Grossman, 1967, Table 1.)

condition. The implication is that elderly subjects experience at least a partial loss in imaginal competence as well as a performance decrement in the use of their remaining competence. However, this implication has been challenged by Treat and Reese (1976) who were successful in eliminating the age difference in paired-associate-learning proficiency under special training and practice conditions. We will discuss their study more thoroughly in Chapter 8.

Paired-associate learning should not be regarded as an esoteric task that is encountered only in basic laboratory research. It has its definite real-life counterparts, such as learning a foreign language vocabulary (i.e., a foreign word and its English equivalent make up paired items). Atkinson and Raugh (1975) have offered convincing evidence for the value of an imaginal mnemonic in foreign language acquisition by young adults. This mnemonic should be equally important for the efficient learning of a foreign language vocabulary by elderly adults. Consequently, knowledge about imaginal deficits by elderly people and the means of overcoming these deficits can become an important contribution for improving the welfare of elderly people. Many elderly people with large blocks of leisure time to fill look forward to travel in a foreign country, but they may fear initiating that travel in view of their anticipated difficulty in mastering a sufficient vocabulary for getting by in the foreign country. It would certainly be worthwhile for Berlitz teachers and other teachers of foreign languages to become familiar with the literature of aging and visual mnemonics in paired-associate learning.

Paired-associate learning is not the only learning-memory task that elderly people find more difficult to master than do young adults. In fact, memory loss overall is one of the main concerns about the adverse effects of aging expressed by elderly people (Lowenthal, Berkman, Beuhler, Pierce, Robinson, & Trier 1967). Training programs for the elderly that promise to be effective in compensating for, or even overcoming, this loss are certainly to be encouraged. The success obtained by Treat and Reese (1976) in enhancing the use of imaginal mnemonics for more proficient learning by elderly people offers a portent of the eventual rewards to be reaped by an applied experimental psychology of aging. It should be noted that guidelines for conducting intervention programs for treating the learning-memory problems of the elderly have already been set forth by Poon, Fozard, and Treat (1978) and Treat, Poon, Fozard, and Popkin (1978). Full implementation of such intervention programs at various centers readily accessible to elderly people is likely in the foreseeable future. Moreover, there is impressive evidence to indicate that the effectiveness of intervention programs is by no means limited to healthy, cognitively alert elderly people. Langer, Rodin, Beck, Weinman, and Spitzer (1979) demonstrated that nursing home residents considerably improve their memory for people, objects, and events in their environment when they are rewarded for exerting greater effort to attend to such environmental information (e.g., the names of nurses and attendants).

Speech Perception: Understanding a Message. Our second example focuses on age differences in speech perception. In general, elderly adults are slower than young adults in the processing of aurally presented information, including spoken communications. The adverse effect of this slower processing may not be readily apparent as long as a spoken message is delivered at a normal conversational rate and is free of background noise. That is, the verbatim content of that message is as likely to be comprehended by elderly listeners as by young-adult listeners. However, even at a normal rate of delivery, elderly listeners have greater difficulty than young listeners in making inferences that are derivable from the content of a message.

The extent of this age difference may be seen in the results of a study by G. Cohen (1979). In this study, well-educated young-adult and elderly subjects received a series of messages presented by means of a tape recorder at a relatively slow rate (120 words per minute). The following is representative of the messages:

> Mrs. Brown goes to sit in the park every afternoon if the weather is fine. She likes to watch the children playing, and she feeds the ducks with bread crusts. She enjoys the walk there and back. For the last three days it has been raining all the time although it's the middle of the summer and the town is still full of people on holiday. (G. Cohen, 1979, p. 416)

Following each message, the subjects were asked two questions. One was a verbatim question that simply required reproduction of some fact embedded within the message (e.g., "What does Mrs. Brown give the ducks to eat?"). The other required an inference to be drawn from the factual content of the message (e.g., "Did Mrs. Brown go to the park yesterday?"). The results, expressed in mean percentage of incorrect answers, are shown in Figure 1.3. Although the

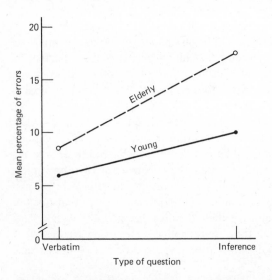

Figure 1.3. Age differences reflected in response to verbatim and inference questions that test comprehension of aural messages. (Adapted from G. Cohen, 1979, Table 1.)

age difference was slight and statistically nonsignificant for verbatim questions, it was considerably larger and statistically significant for inference questions.

In addition, there is evidence (Bergman, Blumfield, Cascado, Dash, Levitt, & Margulies, 1976) indicating that elderly listeners have greater difficulty than young listeners in comprehending the content of sentences when they are read at an accelerated rate or when they are distorted in some way (e.g., they are heard against a background of another message). Bergman et al. discovered that age deficits in both cases become appreciable in the fifth decade of life and accelerate greatly in the seventh decade.

The problems encountered by elderly people in speech perception are great enough to warrant alerting any speaker charged with communicating information to an audience that is diversified with respect to age. With elderly adults no longer strangers in college classes, professors are among those who should be alerted. A rate of lecturing that seems comfortable for the young members of a class may be too fast for the elderly members. To compensate for the auditory problems of their elderly students, professors could make written outlines and notes of their lectures available to their students. Written materials can be examined and studied by elderly adults at their own pace, and, of course, they can be gone over again and again to assure full comprehension. Consequently, the slower visual processsing of elderly readers, relative to young adult readers, does not present a problem under these conditions. In fact, it is highly unlikely that G. Cohen would have found an age deficit for answers to inference questions if the messages had been presented in written form and the subjects proceeded through them at their own pace. Alternatively, elderly students in large college classes could be encouraged to tape lectures and play them back as often as necessary for full comprehension.

Among those already alerted are advertising executives. Phillips and Sternthal (1977) warned them about the use of aurally oriented commercials on radio and television when the objective is to sway an elderly audience. That is, the spoken content of a message may not be fully comprehended by that segment of the audience for which it is primarily designed. Instead, Phillips and Sternthal recommended reliance largely on advertisements in newspapers and magazines. As with the consumer of a lecture's content, the potential consumer of an advertised product can process the written message at a self-paced rate.

Driving and the Concept of Functional Age. Our final example is concerned with age differences in the driving of an automobile. As shown in Figure 1.4, elderly drivers have a higher accident rate than young drivers who, in turn, have a higher accident rate than middle-aged drivers (Birren, 1964; McFarland, Tune, & Welford, 1964; Marsh, 1960). The increased accident rate of elderly drivers becomes a problem of considerable practical significance when it is realized that nearly 60% of our elderly citizens possess a valid driver's license (Aiken, 1978). Not surprisingly, it has often been proposed that rigorous annual tests be given for renewal of a driver's license when a person passes some critical age, such as 60 or even younger (e.g., Butler, 1975). Such tests do make sense,

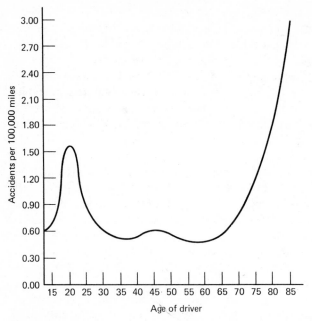

Figure 1.4. Automobile accident rates as a function of driver's age. (Adapted from Birren, 1964, Figure 6.1; original data in Marsh, 1960).

provided they assess skills known to be relevant to driving competence. Recommendation of their use is an admission of the fact that oldness per se does not cause increased accidents. Evidence of the kind illustrated in Figure 1.4 is only correlational. As such, it merely indicates some degree of covariation between chronological age and number of accidents.

The main causative factors for automobile accidents are deficiencies in those physical and psychological skills that are essential for good driving. The greater probability of an accident by an elderly driver is indicative of a greater probability, relative to younger drivers, of deficiencies in these skills. At the same time, a number of elderly drivers, as defined by chronological age alone, are likely to possess greater proficiencies in these skills than many younger drivers. What really matters, therefore, in any decision regarding renewal of a driver's license is a driver's functional age, which is defined by level of competence on those basic skills that determine overall driving skill. The distinction between chronological age and functional age is equally important when decisions have to be made about the retirement or the work reassignment of older commercial drivers. To force reassignment to some other work activity just because a person has reached some arbitrary age, such as 60 years, makes little sense when that individual's functional age for driving is, say, 45 years (i.e., in terms of the underlying basic skills, the person's performance corresponds to that of an average 45-year-old driver).

The feasibility of substituting functional age for chronological age as the basis for both license renewal and reassignment decisions is demonstrated in a study by Barrett, Mihal, Panek, Sterns, & Alexander (1977). As a first step, Barrett et al. analyzed the accidents over a 5-year period for a group of utility-company drivers who ranged in age from 25 to 64 years. Although the correlation between chronological age and number of accidents was found to be positive, its magnitude was, at best, moderate ($r = .36$). Thus, by no means were all of the accidents involving these utility-company drivers limited to the oldest members of the group. The second step taken by Barrett et al. consisted of bringing the drivers into the laboratory and having them perform on a variety of perceptual and motor tasks. Proficiency on some of these tasks, such as one involving choice reaction time, was found to be relevant to driving competence. Relative standing in performance on these tasks, therefore, offers the potential means of assessing a driver's functional age. Moreover, Barrett et al. believe that deficiencies on some of the underlying basic skills can be largely overcome through the use of various training programs suggested by basic research in experimental psychology. Most important, functional age, unlike chronological age, offers the hope of being modified.

Relationship of the Experimental Psychology of Aging to Other Areas

Psychology of Aging and Gerontology. Experimental psychology of aging is part of a broader psychological discipline that deals, on the one hand, with age-related changes in *all* behaviors, and, on the other hand, with the unique problems of elderly people and the resolution of these problems. This broader discipline is called either the psychology of aging or gerontological psychology. It is with age-related differences and changes in certain behaviors that the experimental psychology of aging is mainly concerned. The behaviors in question are those that enter into the traditional content areas of experimental psychology, such as sensation, perception, and learning. However, there obviously are other kinds of behaviors that may undergo age-related changes. Included here are behaviors that are related to personality, adjustment, attitudes, and so on. Certainly, these changes are of great interest to psychologists of aging. Investigations of these changes are ordinarily accomplished outside the experimental laboratory and with standardized paper-and-pencil tests rather than with laboratory-based experimentation. This kind of psychometric research extends human aging into the individual-differences tradition pioneered by Sir Francis Galton, James McK. Cattell, and Alfred Binet. The result is the assessment of age differences and changes over the adult lifespan by the use of such tests as the Wechsler Adult Intelligence Scale (WAIS), the Minnesota Multiphasic Personality Inventory (MMPI), and so on.

Even the behaviors that are excluded from the traditional content areas of experimental psychology can, under certain conditions, be considered to be part of the experimental psychology of aging. The reason is that experimental psychology itself may be defined in the "classical sense of experimentation" (Birren & Renner, 1977) as well as in terms of specific content areas. The reference here is to the use of the experimental method. This method involves the manipulation by an experimenter of one or more independent variables under carefully controlled conditions. The effect of this manipulation on a dependent variable, or behavioral index, is then observed. Given this methodological conceptualization of what defines experimental psychology, any aging study employing the experimental method qualifies as an experimental aging study. Consequently, the content areas entering into the experimental psychology of aging are not necessarily limited to the content areas of traditional experimental psychology. Some aging studies dealing with intelligence, personality, or social behavior merit inclusion in the experimental psychology of aging on the basis of this conceptualization. For example, an experimenter may attempt to determine if the performance of elderly adults on a particular intelligence test can be modified by an appropriate training program. Accordingly, two comparable groups of elderly subjects are selected. One group is given no special training, whereas the other group receives the training regimen. The two groups are then contrasted in their performance scores on the intelligence test in question. With respect to the methodological criterion for membership in the experimental psychology of aging, this study certainly passes. There is an independent variable (no training versus training) and a dependent variable (score on the intelligence test), thereby qualifying the study as a true experiment. The similarity of our present example to our earlier example involving imagery training in pair-associate learning should be obvious. The difference is that the present behavior, unlike behavior on a paired-associate learning task, is not ordinarily considered to be a component of one of experimental psychology's content areas.

Not all psychologists of aging are involved in the study of age-related changes in behavior. Instead, their endeavors are directed toward enhancing the adjustment of elderly people to the environmental and social stresses commonly associated with old age, such as those produced by retirement, reduced income, and so on. The emphasis is now on the methods of clinical psychology and counseling psychology rather than on either experimental or psychometric methods. Aging research as it is conducted by this group of psychologists becomes applied research, with its objectives being the discovery of more effective procedures for the therapeutic treatment of elderly people, rather than basic research, with its emphasis on the description and explanation of age-related changes in behavior.

The psychology of aging has become an important part of contemporary psychology. A number of journals are now devoted exclusively to aging research, and many of these journals, such as the *Journal of Gerontology* and *Experimental Aging Research,* publish several psychological studies in each issue. In addition, psychological journals devoted primarily to prematurity development, such as *Developmental Psychology,* often include articles dealing with gerontological research. Intensive interest and activity in gerontological psychology, however, are fairly recent phenomena. Riegel (1977) has counted the number of articles and books dealing with some psychological aspect of aging that appeared each year from the early 1870s to 1972. Until the late 1920s, published studies in the psychology of aging were few and widely scattered. This early lack of interest by psychologists in adult development contrasts sharply with the intense interest in child development that was already manifested by the early 1900s. Since the 1920s, however, the rate of increase in publications in gerontological psychology has been phenomenal, with the number eventually reaching over 200 per year by the early 1970s. Research in the experimental psychology of aging has been an integral part of this boom, although the absolute number of experimental contributions to the aging literature falls well below the number derived from the psychometric and clinical counseling approaches to aging research.

The psychology of aging, in turn, is part of a still broader discipline called gerontology. Gerontology is a very broad field of study that is concerned with every aspect of human functioning in late adulthood. It is not to be confused with geriatrics, the special branch of medicine devoted to the study of old age.

In other words, gerontology is concerned with the many facets of aging—sociological, biological, and psychological. Thus, the sociology of aging and the biology of aging join the psychology of aging as major components of gerontology. One of the main areas of research in the sociology of aging, or social gerontology, deals with the demographic characteristics of elderly people, some aspects of which we will examine shortly. Other major areas of research are concerned with the family life of elderly people, the services available for elderly people, and so on (Ward, 1979). Much of the research in the biology of aging is directed either at discovery of the mechanism responsible for aging (Shock, 1977) or at determining the nature of age-related changes in various physiological functions (Timiras, 1972). We will have occasions later to touch on both of these areas of research. Research production has expanded in recent years for both the nonpsychological components of gerontology and the psychological components. Research in all components has been greatly facilitated by the establishment of major omnibus research centers, such as the Andrus Gerontology Center at the University of Southern California, and, especially, by the creation in 1974 of the National Institute on Aging as part of the National Institutes of Health.

Developmental Psychology and Lifespan Developmental Psychology. Although less apparent than its membership in the psychology of aging (and, therefore, in gerontology), the experimental psychology of aging is also part of developmental psychology. In fact, all of the psychology of aging may be subsumed under the rubric of lifespan developmental psychology, thereby giving this area a somewhat unique dual membership in two broad disciplines, lifespan developmental psychology and gerontology. The nature of the overall hierarchical organization of disciplines and areas incorporating experimental psychology of aging is illustrated in Figure 1.5.

It is often not immediately apparent why the psychology of aging is subsumed under developmental psychology simply because the concept of development itself is often thought of only with regard to budding, unfolding, or expanding, and it is, therefore, seemingly antithetical to aging. However, a more appropriate conceptualization of psychological development is in terms of any and all behavioral changes that are associated with age increments. As

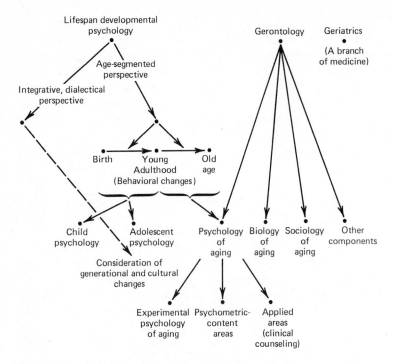

Figure 1.5. The dual hierarchical organization of the psychology of aging.

indicated by Reese and Lipsitt, "Ontogenesis is the development of behavior within an individual organism" and "the study of behavioral ontogenesis is usually called developmental psychology" (1970, p. 2). Behavioral change simply means intraindividual variability in behavior. The organism's behavior at an older age level is likely to show differences from its behavior at an earlier age level, regardless of the age levels being contrasted. The differences are likely to be in the positive direction (i.e., greater proficiency) when the contrast involves later childhood with early childhood and in the negative direction (i.e., decreased proficiency) when the contrast involves later adulthood with early adulthood. In either case, we are dealing with ontogeny and, therefore, with the proper subject matter of developmental psychology.

   The point is, development is not confined to any one segment of the lifespan—it is continuous over the lifespan. Thus, the study of ontogenesis from early to late adulthood is just as relevant to the objectives of developmental psychology as is the study of ontogenesis over any other age range within the lifespan. Traditionally, for purposes of studying development systematically and scientifically, the lifespan has been separated into at least three age ranges, with each segment yielding its own unique specialized content area. The three age ranges are those of childhood, adolescence, and adulthood; the resulting content areas are those of child psychology, adolescent psychology, and the psychology of aging (see Figure 1.5). Each age-range area may, in turn, be divided further into content areas based on still more limited age ranges. Thus, we may have a psychology of early adulthood, with the age range extending from the late teens to the late 20s, just as we may have a psychology of infancy. At any rate, the existence of a psychology of aging—and, therefore, an experimental psychology of aging—is perfectly consistent with the traditional age-segmented approach to developmental psychology. The consistency is made even more apparent by the many commonalities in methodology and explanatory issues found across the age-segmented areas. For example, the cross-sectional method has been as much a mainstay for researchers in child psychology as it has been for researchers in the psychology of aging. Similarly, the need to distinguish between maturational and environmental causative factors determining age changes in behavior is as much a part of child psychology as it is a part of the psychology of aging.

There is an alternative, however, to an age-range, or age-segmented, approach to developmental psychology. The alternative is offered by what is called lifespan developmental psychology. There are, however, differing views concerning its scope and objectives. At a superficial level, a developmental study could be considered lifespan simply by virtue of extending the age range covered from childhood through late adulthood. There are, in fact, occasional experimental studies on aging (e.g., Laurence, 1966) that can be termed lifespan because of their inclusion of age levels prior to adulthood as well as age levels along the adult portion of the total lifespan continuum. However, these studies are unlikely to be accepted as being truly part of lifespan developmental psychology as that area is defined by most of its advocates. Most important, these extended age-range studies are directed toward the analysis of age differences and changes for a limited segment of behavior (e.g., free-recall learning in the Laurence study). Isolation of behavior into limited components and then examination of each component separately under carefully controlled laboratory conditions has been a fundamental characteristic of experimental psychology throughout its history. Not surprisingly, this characteristic is preserved when experimental psychology combines its forces and traditions with those of the psychology of aging. The combination generally yields a methodology in which proficiency on a given task is contrasted among adults of different chronological-age levels. The standard approach of the experimental psychology of aging is, therefore, both segmental behaviorally and cross-sectional procedurally—even when the cross-section is extended to prematurity age levels. By contrast, the approach preferred by most devotees of a "true" lifespan developmental psychology is one that is integrative behaviorally (i.e., a number of interacting behaviors are studied simultaneously) and longitudinal procedurally (e.g., Baltes & Goulet, 1970). That is, development is seen as a multidimensional process that is strongly influenced by cultural-social changes as well as by biological changes in the organism per se.

Of course, there is nothing about the experimental psychology of aging that rules out the use of a longitudinal rather than a cross-sectional methodology (to be discussed in Chapter 3) when age-related changes in sensory, perceptual, and learning skills are being examined, for example. Nevertheless, its use does little to qualify the typical longitudinal experimental aging study as being

truly part of lifespan developmental psychology. Missing in the typical longitudinal study, just as it is in the typical cross-sectional study (see Riegel, 1977), is
the view of aging as a multidimensional process that is strongly influenced by
cultural-social changes occurring over the individual's lifespan. The main thrust
of lifespan developmental psychology as a separate entity within psychology is
that of dialectical interpretation, in the sense that this term is used in episte-
mology to refer to Kantian philosophy. A dialectical interpretation views the
individual organism "in terms of uncertainties, crises or conflicts" rather than
in terms of "an abstract entity within an equally abstract system of traits and
abilities" (Riegel, 1977, p. 86). The contrast between the traditional approach
to developmental psychology, as exemplified in the abstract nature of experimental aging psychology (with its use of mean performance scores on a seg-
mented behavioral task to represent "average" individuals of different
chronological ages), and the dialectical approach has been nicely summarized
by Riegel:

> In recognizing the codetermination of experience and action by inner-biological
> and cultural-sociological changes, dialectical theory deemphasizes individual-psy-
> chological development in the traditional, abstract sense. Instead it focuses upon
> concrete human beings and the gradual modifications (neurological, physiological)
> or sudden shifts (accidents, diseases) in their biological make-up that force them to
> change constructively their individual-psychological operations and, thereby, also
> the social conditions under which they live. At the same time, a dialectical interpre-
> tation focuses upon gradual modifications (increase in available time) or sudden
> shifts (births of children, promotion, loss of friends) in the cultural-sociological
> conditions that force the human beings to change constructively their individual-
> psychological operations and, thereby, their inner-biological state. Thus, individ-
> ual-psychological development is seen in its intimate and mutual determination by
> inner-biological and cultural-sociological shifts and changes. (1977, pp. 87–88)

A fair statement seems to be that neither lifespan developmental psychology nor the dialectical approach indigenous to that broad area have had much
of a direct impact on aging research in the experimental-content areas of psychology, although attempts are currently underway to promote greater application of the dialectical approach, particularly with respect to memory (e.g.,
Kvale, 1977; Meacham, 1977). Nevertheless, the issues raised by the dialectical
approach have had at least two important indirect effects on the experimental
psychology of aging. The first is the necessity of considering contextual factors
in determining the reasons why elderly people often appear to be inferior to
young adults in performance on some tasks, including those carried over from
experimental psychology. It may well be these contextual factors rather than a
deteriorating biological ontogeny with increasing age that account for many of
the performance losses commonly reported for elderly people. If this is the
case, then there is the hope of reversing such losses or perhaps minimizing the
importance of their decrement in the first place. Contextualism, as a byproduct
of the dialectical approach, will be discussed more thoroughly in Chapter 3.

The second indirect effect is the current willingness by many gerontological psychologists, including a number of experimental aging psychologists, to consider both generational membership and the historical time in which behavior is being measured as developmentally relevant variables that join age variation as potential causative factor for age differences in behavior. These nonage variables have been incorporated into methodological designs that are applicable to the kinds of research conducted by experimental aging psychologists. The nature of these designs and their implications for the experimental psychology of aging in general will be explored fully in Chapter 4. Finally, we should note that these indirect effects are represented in Figure 1.5 by the broken arrow.

Defining Old Age

An ingredient common to all components of gerontology is the study of older people. Also shared by all components is the problem of defining what is meant by the term older people. Phrased somewhat differently, the question becomes: "What defines the onset of old age?" This question is of more than theoretical concern to experimental psychologists. Their research studies commonly call for comparisons in performance on some task between a group of young adults and a group of old adults (i.e., as a minimal condition—sometimes other age levels in between these extremes are also included). At what point in the adult lifespan does a person qualify as a potential subject in the old group?

Variability in Aging and the Signs of Aging. A rigorous definition of old age would enable investigators to assign individuals unerringly to their elderly groups of subjects. However, such a definition is virtually impossible to attain. Much of the difficulty rests in the fact that old age is a relative concept. Use of the concept to classify people is contingent on what behavioral or biological process, function, or ability is being considered. For example, an Olympic-class gymnast is old at age 25, whereas a professional baseball player is old at age 35. By contrast, an Olympic-class yachting participant is young at age 45 (e.g., Sir Eyre Massey Shaw won a gold medal in the 1900 games at the age of 70) as is a candidate for the presidency of the United States. Clearly, aging affects various functions and abilities at vastly different rates. Moreover, there is a wide range of points along the lifespan at which the onset of aging for specific functions and abilities becomes apparent.

To illustrate the wide variation in aging for psychological processes and abilities, we will examine first two motor-skill tasks, each having proficiency measured by a time score. One is the time taken to write words (Birren & Botwinick, 1951), the other the time taken in tapping alternately on two side-by-side targets (Welford, Norris, & Shock, 1969). To give these tasks a common denominator, we have plotted scores for each task in Figure 1.6 so that a score of 0% is assigned to the age group (defined chronologically) earning the optimal score on the task in question. The mean score earned by each of the other age

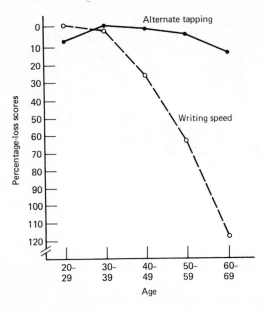

Figure 1.6. Loss with increasing age in proficiency on two motor-skill tasks expressed with respect to optimal performance—age 20 to 29 for writing speed and age 30 to 39 for tapping alternate targets. (Adapted from data in Birren & Botwinick, 1951; Welford, Norris, & Shock, 1969.)

groups is then expressed as a percentage loss relative to the performance of the optimal age group. It may be seen that, whereas the loss for the word-writing task is substantial with increasing chronological age, it is slight for the tapping task. Suppose we were to define old age as beginning at the age level that first shows some predetermined amount of performance loss, such as more than 10%. People in their 40s would then be identified as old on the basis of their writing speed, whereas even people in their 60s would not qualify on the basis of their tapping speed.

As a second illustration, we will examine losses in proficiency on two different recognition-memory tasks administered to the same subjects by Botwinick and Storandt (1974b). One task called for the visual presentation of words, the other for aural presentation. The results for the two tasks, again expressed in terms of percentage-loss scores, are shown in Figure 1.7. It can be seen that the loss in proficiency with increasing chronological age was moderate for the visual task and virtually nonexistent for the aural task. The memory-list words were presented slowly and clearly—consequently, sensory-perceptual problems associated with aging, of the kind noted earlier, were likely to have been a negligible factor. Application of the amount-of-loss criterion would again identify people in their 40s as being old on the basis of one task, whereas even people in their 60s would be excluded on the basis of the other task. Once more, the concept of functional age is more meaningful than the concept of chronological age, at least with respect to the memory abilities being evaluated on these tasks.

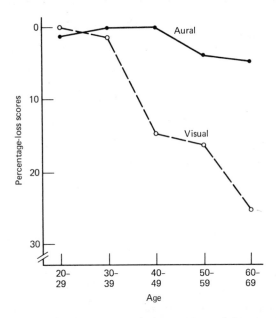

Figure 1.7. Loss with increasing age in proficiency on two recognition-memory tasks expressed with respect to optimal performance—age 20 to 29 for visual presentation of material and age 40 to 49 for aural presentation. (Adapted from data in Botwinick & Storandt, 1974b.)

Comparable variability exists in the aging of biological structures and functions. The existence of pronounced disparities in both rate of aging and the age of onset of aging were made quite explicit by Timiras, a prominent gerontological biologist:

> In certain functions, for example, regulatory mechanisms remain quite efficient until the age of 80 or 90; in others, decrements become apparent at an early age or remain hidden until they have progressed sufficiently to induce alterations that can be validated by tests. An example is atherosclerosis, the consequences of which become manifest in middle and old age even though the vascular lesions may have started in infancy. (1978, p. 607)

One's biological age, expressed with respect to the level of functioning in an average adult of, say, 30 years of age, clearly depends on what function it is that is being considered. If it is a function that remains quite efficient until age 80 or 90, then an average person of that age is relatively young, at least in terms of that particular function. However, if it is a function that decreases markedly in its proficiency beyond age 30, then even the average person of age 50 is relatively old. Some idea of the variation in the extent of loss for different physiological functions may be gathered by examining Figure 1.8. For each function, loss is expressed at age 75 relative to the proficiency manifested by the average adult of age 30.

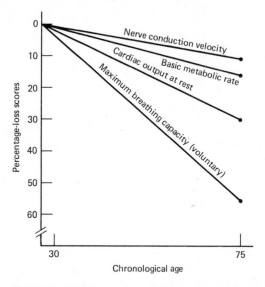

Figure 1.8. Relative loss by age 75 of various biological functions expressed with respect to normal functioning at age 30. (Adapted from data in Shock, 1962.)

Nor is sensory functioning immune to intercomponent variability in aging. Visual proficiency, for example, generally diminishes considerably with advancing chronological age. About half the men and women in the United States who are over age 65 have visual acuity that is poorer than 20/70, in contrast to the less than 10% with this same poor visual acuity who are under age 45 (National Center for Health Statistics, 1964). In addition, accommodation of the eye's lens to focus on near objects is generally much poorer at age 60 and beyond than at younger ages chronologically. This accounts for the large number of people older than 60 who need reading glasses or bifocals. Dark adaptation (i.e., the ability to see clearly in low illumination) also becomes poorer with advancing chronological age, as does color vision (blue and violet sensitivities tend to decrease, whereas yellow, orange, and red sensitivities remain largely unaffected). Many of these visual decrements are the result of changes in the ancillary equipment of the eye (e.g., the lens becomes thicker, less elastic, and more opaque with increasing age), although changes in the metabolism of the retina itself may also be involved (Fozard, Wolf, Bell, McFarland, & Podolsky, 1977). By contrast, changes in taste and smell with advancing age appear to be much less pronounced than those that occur in vision (Engen, 1977), seemingly because there is relatively little loss of taste and smell receptors with aging. Nevertheless, the decrease in proficiency that does take place, particularly for smell, is probably great enough to account for a common complaint expressed by many elderly people, namely, that food has lost its taste or that all food tastes alike. There is, indeed, evidence indicating that older people are less capable of identifying food substances than are younger people. Schiffman (1977) tested both college students and adults in their 70s for their ability to identify, while blindfolded, a number of blended food substances (blending was necessary to prevent identifications by means of texture). For the most part, college students were far more accurate. For example, the percentages of those identifying apple, strawberry, and fish were 81%, 78%, and 78% respectively for the young adults and 55%, 33%, and 59% respectively for the elderly adults. However, there were some reversals, specifically for tomato (69% for the elderly subjects versus 52% for the young subjects) and potato (38% for the elderly subjects versus 19% for the young subjects). Elderly people have also been found to be less able than young adults to identify common odors (e.g., vanilla extract) (Schemper, Voss & Gain, 1981).

A different, and especially effective, way of demonstrating the variability among the many biological and psychological functional components that are adversely affected by aging is through a correlational analysis. Proficiency scores may be obtained on each component for a large cross-sectional sample that bridges the adult lifespan. The correlation coefficient *(r)* between chronological age and score may then be calculated separately for each component. A value of 1.00 (+1.00 if scores increase in magnitude as proficiency decreases, as they do when errors serve as scores; −1.00 if scores increase in magnitude as proficiency increases, as they do when correct responses serve as scores) indicates a perfect covariation between chronological age and proficiency. On the other hand, a value of 0 indicates the absence of any systematic covariation between chronological age and proficiency. A value significantly greater than 0 reveals the presence of some effect of aging on proficiency, with the magnitude per se providing an estimate of the extent of that effect.

This approach was taken in an impressive study by Borkan and Norris (1980). Their total sample consisted of 1086 men ranging in age from 17 to 102 years (they were all participants in the Baltimore Longitudinal Study, a study described in Chapter 3). Each subject received a lengthy battery of tests; each test measured a functional component commonly believed to be affected adversely by aging. The results, expressed in terms of the observed correlation coefficients, are given in Table 1.1 for a representative set of components. The coefficient is significantly greater than 0 for each component (and for all of the

Table 1.1 Correlation Coefficients Expressing Covariations Between Chronological Age and Scores for Representative Biological and Psychological Functions

Functional Component	Sample Size	Coefficient (r)
Forced expiratory volume	969	−.70
Vital capacity	971	−.61
Systolic blood pressure	1077	.54
Diastolic blood pressure	1077	.37
Basal metabolic rate	1035	−.34
Hemoglobin	1071	−.22
Hand-grip strength	943	−.50
Reaction time (simple)	687	.29
Reaction time (choice)	701	.22
Visual memory (errors)	905	.50

Source: Adapted from data in Borkan & Norris, 1980, Table 1.

other components included in the battery as well). However, it may be seen that there is considerable variability in the degree of age-proficiency covariation among both biological and psychological components.

Another complicating factor in identifying who among us should be classified as old is the existence of considerable interindividual variability in the rate of aging for most biological and psychological functions. We discovered this earlier in our discussion of the basic skills relevant to driving competence. Such variability is equally present in biological functions. Consider, for example, the deterioration that occurs with aging in visual acuity. Although it does affect many elderly people, the fact remains that a number of them maintain remarkably proficient acuity. As another example, consider the loss of teeth with advancing age. It is true that about half the people in the United States who are age 65 and beyond are indeed "sans teeth." But what about the other half of the post-65 population? Are they still young by virtue of possession of their teeth? Conversely, we cannot ignore those people who are in, say, the 45 to 54 age range. A sizable number of them, over 15%, have lost their teeth (U.S. Department of Health, Education, and Welfare, 1975). Should they be admitted to an old-age group simply because they show a so-called sign of old age?

Interindividual variability is affected further by the presence or absence of various diseases. Chronic illnesses, such as arthritis and cardiovascular disease, increase steadily in their incidence with advancing chronological age (Figure 1.9). It is estimated that about 86% of the people in the United States who are age 65 and over have one or more chronic illnesses, compared to 72% of the people in the 45 to 65 age range and, of course, there is a much smaller percentage for still younger people (Harris, 1978). The presence of cardiovascular disease in particular can force people to perform on some psychological tasks at a level well below the one they would manifest in the absense of the disease (see Chapter 3). Similarly, people with cataracts (another illness that increases steadily in incidence with advancing age) suffer considerably more visual im-

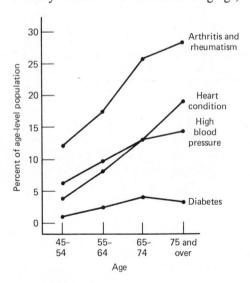

Figure **1.9.** Incidence of certain chronic illnesses from age 45 on. (Adapted from data in U.S. Health Survey, 1960.)

pairment than do other people of the same chronological age who are free of the illness. Interestingly, the incidence of acute illnesses (e.g., influenza and the common cold) actually decreases with advancing age (Wilder, 1974). However, the impact of an acute illness on various psychological and biological functions is far more debilitating when it occurs for people over age 65 than when it occurs in younger people.

Interindividual variability in aging obviously makes the signs of old age we use in our everyday classification of people highly unreliable. These signs often provide us with the means of either denying membership in old age for someone (e.g., "Martha sure shows no sign of aging") or admitting someone into membership (e.g., "Old Smitty sure shows signs of aging"). The signs are usually those pertaining to changes in physical appearance, such as the thinning and graying of hair that signifies to many people the onset of old age. It is true that aging often produces loss of hair through such factors as the gradual decline in the secretion of the adrenal glands and the involution of hair follicles, and the graying of the hair through the loss of pigmentation. However, we do encounter people of an advanced chronological age whose full head of black hair seems to deny their age, just as we encounter relatively young people chronologically who are prematurely bald or gray. Similarly, there is a trend with increasing age toward altered facial features. Many people who are beyond age 65 do have a wrinkled, dry, sagging, and pale facial appearance, presumably the result of such physical changes as the atrophy of sweat glands, the loss of facial skin cells, and a decrease in fatty deposits below the facial skin. But again, some people show these signs by the time they are 60 years old, whereas others are relatively free of them well into their 70s.

Finally, there is the intriguing possibility of using a combination of biological and behavioral signs that permit the construction of a person's profile with respect to others of the same chronological age. This procedure was followed, in fact, in the previously cited study by Borkan and Norris (1980). For each of their biological and psychological components (24 in all), the mean score obtained by all subjects at a given chronological age was determined. A profile may then be constructed for any subject of that same age by plotting that subject's standing (in standard deviation units relative to the age-level mean) on each component. The profiles for three hypothetical subjects, each 65 years old, were constructed in Figure 1.10 for the components listed in Table 1.1. The nature of the profile gives us a fairly good picture of a subject's overall functional age. Subject A may be seen to have a functional age that is somewhat younger than that subject's actual chronological age, whereas subjects B and C have functional ages that are either slightly (Subject B) or considerably (Subject C) older than their actual chronological ages. Based on these profiles, we may decide to include Subjects B and C as members of an old-age group in an experimental study of aging but exclude Subject A from the old-age group.

Although highly promising, the profile method has many practical problems in its implementation. For example, the method can be used only to the extent that there are extensive normative data for a wide range of biological and psychological functions. Such normative data are clearly quite sparse (the

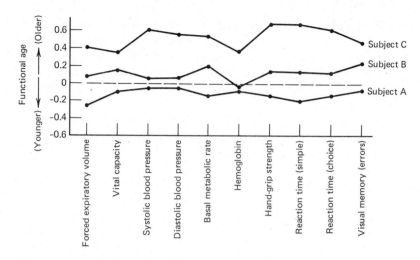

Figure 1.10. Profiles on the components, or signs, listed in Table 1.1 for three hypothetical 65-year-old subjects. Zero represents mean score on each component obtained by a sample of 65-year-old subjects. Values on the ordinate are deviations from the mean expressed in standard deviation units.

highly selective sample of subjects employed by Borkan and Norris, 1980, makes their data of limited normative use). Moreover, even if such normative data were available, they would probably be of little use in most experimental aging studies. It is highly unlikely that many potential subjects for these studies would volunteer to take the large battery of tests required to construct their profiles.

Chronological Age as an Arbitrary Criterion. In the absence of a viable alternative criterion for defining the onset of old age in the human organism, most laypeople and many gerontologists as well have turned to an arbitrary criterion. That criterion is the setting of a specific chronological age, in recent years 65, at which point an individual automatically crosses the gerontological border. But why 65 years of age? The obvious answer is that, until 1979, attainment of this age signaled forced vocational retirement for most people. Actually, retirement at age 65 is itself of relatively recent vintage. Apparently, it originated in Germany in 1889. Otto von Bismarck's statisticians determined, on an actuarial basis, that 65 was the ideal age for establishing a not-too-costly retirement-pension program. Retirement at age 65 eventually reached the United States and became the standard practice in 1935.

Now that the retirement age has been advanced by an amendment to the Age Discrimination in Employment Act to 70 years for many people (with certain classes of employees excluded), an interesting possibility is that old age will eventually be redefined as having its onset at age 70. In practice, however, many researchers in the psychology of aging set their own age criteria for selecting samples of elderly subjects in their investigations. It is not unusual to discover studies in which membership in an elderly group is set at age 60 or even in the 50s. Alternatively, other researchers prefer to set the minimal age

**Table 1.2   Characteristics of the Elderly Group of Subjects
Entering into Some Recent Aging Studies**

Investigator	Topic	Description of Elderly Group
Attig & Hasher (1980)	Age differences in frequency-of-occurrence judgments	Community residents, paid for their services; age range = 60–77 years, mean age = 68 years
Powell, Milligan, & Furchtgott (1980)	Relating age differences in autonomic nervous functions to learning and reaction time	Hospitalized patients; age range = 55–70 years, mean age = 63.2 years
Herzog (1979)	Age differences in attitude change	Residents of a retirement housing project; mean age = 77.5 years
Jacewicz & Hartley (1979)	Age differences in "mental rotation"	Volunteer college students over age 52; age range = 53–62, mean age = 55.9 years
Kleinman & Brodzinsky (1978)	Age differences in the strategy employed for making haptic (touch) discriminations	Community residents, paid for their services; mean age = 76 years
Salthouse (1978)	Age differences in performance on the digit-symbol test	Volunteers from senior-citizens' groups and retirement organizations; age range = 62–80 years, mean age = 71 years
Till (1978)	Age differences in visual backward masking	Unpaid volunteers from the community and staff personnel; age range = 54–56 years

for inclusion in their elderly groups at some age level beyond age 65. Examples of the composition of the elderly groups entering into recent studies in the experimental psychology of aging are given in Table 1.2. It can be seen that the concept of old means different things to different investigators.

To complicate matters further, some gerontologists prefer distinguishing between early old age (65 to 74) and advanced old age (75 on) (e.g., Butler & Lewis, 1973). Other classification systems are also in use, for example, Barrett (1972) identifies three periods of aging—later maturity (58 to 67), early longevous (68 to 77), and later longevous (78 on).

Demography of Elderly People

The importance of understanding and attempting to countermand the effects of aging on human behavior is perhaps best appreciated in light of the gerontological population explosion that is presently being experienced by our society and that is projected to continue well into the next century. In 1900, there were slightly more than 3 million people in the United States who were 65 years of age and older; today, that number is over 25 million. In relative terms, the proportion of people 65 years of age and older in this country's population has increased from a little over 4% in 1900 to over 11% today. Viewed from a slightly different perspective, our elderly population has increased by over 35% since 1960 whereas our total population has increased by only 19% (Myers & Soldo, 1977). It is not surprising that the proportion of people age 65 and over in a total population varies considerably from country to country, for example, in 1970 it was 3.1% in Japan, 3.6% in Kenya, 8.1% in Canada, 11.8% in the U.S.S.R., 13.1% in the United Kingdom, and 14.2% in Australia (Cutler & Harootyan, 1975). That same year, it was estimated to be 9.9% in the United States. In 1979, the world population of people age 65 and over was estimated to be about 200 million, that is, about 5% of the world's population (United Nations, 1972).

The nature of this country's gerontological boom together with its probable causes was described by Robert Butler, the first director of the National Institute on Aging:

> Every day 1000 people reach 65; each year 365,000. More than 70 per cent of the 65 and over age group in 1970 entered that category after 1959. With new medical discoveries, an improved health care delivery system and the presently declining birth rate, it is possible that the elderly will make up one quarter of the total population by the year 2000. Major medical advances in the control of cancer or heart and vascular diseases could increase the average life expectancy by 10 or even 15 years. Discovery of deterrents to the basic causes of aging would cause even more profound repercussions. The presence of so many elderly, and the potential of so many more, has been a puzzlement to gerontologists, public health experts and demographers, who don't know whether to regard it as the "aging problem" or a triumph over disease. What is clear is that it will result in numerous changes in every part of our society. (1975, pp. 16–17)

We should note that life expectancy at birth in the United States is presently more than 70 years of age for the sexes combined (approximately 69 for men alone and 76 for women alone). In 1900, it was about 49 years for the sexes combined. Life expectancy also varies greatly from country to country, being much lower than that of the United States in countries like Bolivia, Egypt, and Vietnam and slightly higher than that of the United States in countries like Denmark, Israel, and Sweden.

Other interesting demographic data have been reported in various places (e.g., Myers & Soldo, 1977). Four aspects of these data are aspects that should be of concern in experimental aging studies that attempt either to employ samples of elderly people that are representative of the total population of elderly people or to employ samples of elderly people that are matched on critical attributes with contrasting samples of young adults.

The first pertains to the composition of the 65-and-over population of the United States with respect to specific age ranges. Table 1.3 gives a breakdown

Table 1.3 U.S. Population by Age Ranges for People 65 Years of Age
and Older in 1960 and 1975

	Population		Percent Change	Proportion of Aged Population	
Age Range	1960	1975	1960–1975	1960	1975
65–69	6,257,910	8,099,000	29.4%	37.8%	36.2%
70–74	4,738,932	5,775,000	21.9	28.6	25.8
75–79	3,053,559	4,001,000	31.0	18.4	17.9
80–84	1,579,927	2,649,000	67.7	9.5	11.8
85+	929,252	1,877,000	102.0	5.6	8.4

Source: Adapted from Myers & Soldo, 1977, Table 2.

of this composition in 5-year ranges for 1960 and 1975 in terms of both absolute numbers and proportions of the total 65-and-over population. It can be
seen that age groups over 80 years increased to a much greater extent than did
age group below 80 years, with the greatest relative growth being experienced
by individuals 85 years of age and older. Interestingly, the composition by age
levels is rarely specified. Usually, only the range of ages in the sample and the
mean, or median, age of the sample are specified (e.g., see Table 1.2). The
generalization of an investigator's results to all people 65 and over must often
be tempered by the glaring absence of subjects from the now sizable population
of people who are 80 years of age and older.

The second aspect pertains to the sex composition of our elderly population. Myers and Soldo (1977) reported that the population of women age 65
and over increased by 46.1% between 1960 and 1975, whereas the population of
men age 65 and over increased by only 22.2%. Table 1.4 gives the sex ratio
(number of men per women) for age ranges in the 65-and-over population for
1960 and 1975. Note that this ratio decreases dramatically as age increases and
that the greater number of women to men was larger in 1975 than in 1960 at
each age range. The disparity in numbers between the sexes is another demographic fact that should not be ignored in the composition of samples entering
into experimental aging studies. This is especially the case when the behavior
being investigated is itself susceptible to pronounced sex differences.

Table 1.4 Sex Ratio (United States) by Age Ranges for People 65 Years
of Age and Older in 1960 and 1975

	Males per 100 Females	
Age Range	1960	1975
65–69	88.1	79.4
70–74	85.6	73.3
75–79	80.2	64.7
80–84	72.7	56.9
85+	63.9	48.5

Source: Adapted from Myers and Soldo, 1977, Table 3.

Table 1.5   Years of School Completed (Expressed in Percent of Population in 1974) by Age and Sex

	Less Than High School	High School	College: 1–3 years	College: 4 Years or More	Median Years Completed
Men					
25–34	18.9%	38.6%	18.8%	23.7%	12.8
35–64	38.9	33.7	11.3	16.0	12.3
65+	68.8	16.4	6.2	8.6	8.7
Women					
25–34	20.9%	46.6%	16.2%	16.4%	12.7
35–64	37.6	42.9	10.5	9.0	12.3
65+	65.4	20.9	7.8	5.9	9.0

Source: Adapted from data provided by the U.S. Bureau of the Census, 1975.

The third aspect concerns years of formal education for adults of varying ages. Table 1.5 gives the percentage per age level of both men and women completing various amounts of formal education. It can be seen that the median number of years of education completed shows a pronounced age difference favoring younger adults for both sexes. The disparity in educational backgrounds presents a serious obstacle when it is necessary to equate young and elderly groups of subjects in terms of educational levels (to be discussed more completely in Chapter 2). Often the young adults entering into a specific study are college students. Consequently, the elderly adults entering into the same study should also have had some degree of college training. As is evident in Table 1.5, the percentage of the current population of elderly people meeting this criterion is fairly small.

The final aspect concerns the residency of elderly people. In the vast majority of experimental aging studies, it is highly desirable to have active subjects (to be discussed more completely in Chapter 3). An important step in satisfying this criterion of subject selection is to recruit only subjects who are living in their own community, that is, subjects who have not been institutionalized. The breakdown of elderly people according to their living arrangement is given in Table 1.6. It can be seen that the proportion residing in an institution is actu-

Table 1.6   Living Arrangement in 1975 of People Age 65 and Over (Expressed in Percent of Population by Sex)

	Men	Women
In families	79.8%	56.1%
Head of family	76.1	8.5
Wife	—	35.0
Living alone	14.8	37.3
Living with a nonrelative	1.2	1.2
In an institution	4.2	5.3

Source: Adapted from data provided by the U.S. Bureau of the Census, 1976.

ally quite small. The belief held by many that virtually all elderly people eventually require institutionalization is obviously another myth about human aging. However, we should note that the percentage does increase with advancing age within the total population of elderly people. For example, when all people over 65 are included in the analysis, the percentage is less than 5%; when only people over 75 are included, the percentage is closer to 10%. In addition, it is estimated that over 20% of *all* elderly people spend some part of their lives in a nursing home (Crandall, 1980).

Overview and General Comments

A major objective in this book is to acquaint you with the contributions made by experimental psychologists to our knowlege about the effects of aging on human skills and behaviors. We will attempt to accomplish this objective in Chapters 7 through 10, where we will survey the main content areas of experimental psychology in terms of what is known about their extensions into age differences and age changes. Chapter 7 will cover research on sensory processes, perception, and attention; Chapter 8, research on learning, transfer, and retention; Chapter 9, research on memory; and Chapter 10, research on higher mental processes. There will be no chapter devoted exclusively to the extensions of physiological psychology into aging. Instead, physiological research will be reviewed at various places in conjuncton with its relevance to a specific psychological process, such as attention. Similarly, there will be no chapter devoted exclusively to extensions of motivational research into aging. This topic will be reviewed in Chapter 3 in conjunction with our discussion on the distinction between age differences in competence and age differences in performance. In line with our previously stated commitment, Chapter 11 will survey research in various nonexperimental content areas that qualifies as experimental aging research through its use of experimental methodology. This survey will be expanded to include other topics concerned with age differences and changes in intelligence, personality, and social behavior.

Throughout our survey you should keep in mind the following questions. Do all psychological functions show deterioration with increasing chronological age over the adult segment of the lifespan? If not, which processes and behaviors show progressive deterioration with age and which ones maintain a steady state beyond early adulthood? Does the deterioration of a given behavior and its underlying process occur at roughly the same rate for all people or are there pronounced individual differences in the rate of decline? Are there some behaviors that actually show continous increments over the full lifespan, at least well into old age? Given an apparent age deficit in behavior, is it permanent and irreversible? If some degree of reversibility is possible, how may it be brought about? Finally, and perhaps most important, what are the causes of age differences and age changes in a specific behavior, and what specific process mediating that behavior is affected by aging?

Despite the recent flurry of activity in the experimental psychology of aging, answers to the previous questions are only partially available for all of our content areas, and our knowledge about adult age differences and changes in perception, memory, and so on, has many gaps. One of the features of our surveys in Chapters 7 to 10 will consist of attempts to point out especially significant gaps in each content area and to indicate the kinds of research needed to fill the voids. We should not be unduly pessimistic however. Much is already known about age differences and changes in the various content areas of experimental psychology. It will be our job to make this information available to you. In so doing, we will be somewhat selective rather than exhaustive in our review of the studies in each content area.

You should finish this book with a far better understanding of human aging than you have at present. This is less immodesty on our part than it is faith in our conviction that your present knowledge about human aging is probably sparse and that it consists largely of the kinds of myths discussed earlier. Introductory psychology textbooks usually touch on human aging only in the context of adult-age differences in intelligence as measured by such tests as the WAIS. Even then, the issues and controversies involved in evaluating the evidence about true age changes in intelligence, as opposed to adult-age differences in intelligence test scores (to be considered more thoroughly in Chapters 2 and 3), are usually discussed superficially if they are discussed at all. Textbooks in specific content areas, such as perception and learning, have generally done little to fill the voids in your knowledge about the effects of aging on human behaviors. The standard approach in most of these textbooks is to concentrate on research findings obtained with young-adult subjects (human and animal). Extensions of these findings to adult-age differences and changes are rarely, if ever, considered.

Age differences and changes within the content areas of experimental psychology can not be fully comprehended, however, unless you have a prior understanding of the research requirements that must be satisfied before the effects of aging on human behavior can be reliably assessed and before the causative factors underlying these effects can be validly identified. Accordingly, as an indispensable step toward this understanding, we will discuss in considerable detail the methodologies of experimental aging research in Chapters 2 through 5. Chapters 2 and 3 will deal with the methodologies involved and the problems encountered in traditional cross-sectional (Chapter 2) and longitudinal (Chapter 3) research studies, which typically employ chronological age as the only independent variable. Along the way we will also examine a number of important issues that have considerable bearing on the interpretation given to the outcomes of cross-sectional and longitudinal studies. For example, one of these issues concerns the distinction between an age deficit because of a true loss of competence, or ability, on the task in question and an age deficit because of a performance factor, such as lower motivation for elderly subjects than for young-adult subjects. Chapter 4 will deal with the newer sequential methodologies that accomodate generational, or cohort, membership and time of measurement as well as chronological age as developmentally relevant independent variables that are in agreement with the emphasis given these variables by a dialectical approach to lifespan development. We will be especially concerned with the advantages, if any, to be gained by the application of these sequential methodologies to research in the content areas of experimental psychology relative to what is to be gained by the use of the more traditional cross-sectional and longitudinal methodologies. At stake is the identification of the true causative factor that produces observable age differences in performance on a given task. These differences could be due to age variation per se and, therefore, reflect a true age change. Alternatively, the age differences could result from variation in the generations to which adults of different age levels belong or from a cultural change that may have occurred during the time interval separating two or more measurements of performance on the task in question. This analysis will be followed in Chapter 5 by a discussion and analysis of the methodologies employed in experimental aging research when experimentally manipulable independent variables (e.g., instructions related to the use of imagery in paired-associate learning) are added to developmental research designs. Here our emphasis will be on the use of these methodologies to identify age-sensitive and age-insensitive psychological processes that mediate performances on various tasks.

Research in aging demands careful planning and equally careful conducting if it is to yield reliable and valid answers to important questions about aging effects. Without reliability and validity, a research study contributes nothing to further our knowledge about the effects of aging on human behavior. Consequently, various issues pertaining to the reliability and validity of aging research will be examined at various places in Chapters 2 through 5. Many of these issues as well as many other issues encountered in this segment of the book are not unique to aging research. That is, they are shared by other components of developmental psychology, such as child psychology. Hopefully, you will finish this portion of the book with a firm grasp of how much of the overall research in developmental psychology is conducted and why it is conducted in this manner.

Rarely does an experimental aging psychologist tackle a research problem just because it is there. Instead, the problems and hypotheses investigated in experimental aging research are likely to have their origins in psychological theories of varying degrees of scope and complexity, theories that, if supported, offer viable explanations of age differences in behaviors. It is, therefore, important that you acquire some familiarity with the nature of theory as it enters into the experimental psychology of aging. This acquisition will begin in Chapter 6. Here we will be concerned with the general characteristics of associationism and information processing, the two major approaches to conceptualizing psychological phenomena. We will attempt to demonstrate how the broad theoretical approach taken by an investigator shapes the nature of the processes hypothesized to be age sensitive as well as the research strategy taken to test this age sensitivity. Discussion of the details involving theories and theoretical issues will be reserved for later chapters, where they will be discussed in conjunction with their correlated content areas and the specific research studies relevant to those areas. In Chapter 6, we will also examine the concept of a developmental model and its role in conceptualizing and explaining age changes in performances on various tasks. Specifically, two such models will be considered, the mechanistic and the organismic. The content of Chapter 6, like that of Chapters 2 to 5, has important implications for all of developmental psychology, not just the experimental psychology of aging. Again, it is our hope that you finish Chapter 6 with a better grasp of all of developmental psychology. Many of the concepts discussed in this chapter enter into explanations of age-related changes in behavior that occur at all points along the human lifespan.

Summary

What many young adults know about human aging is based more on myth than on reality. These myths include the beliefs that elderly people become sexless, that people grow more conservative politically and socially as they grow older, and that a total de-differentiation sets in during old age as people deteriorate toward a common low level of overall competence. The de-differentiation myth is especially damaging in that it leads to a negative stereotype of old age commonly referred to as ageism. To believers in that stereotype, elderly people are perceived and evaluated in terms of the stereotype instead of in terms of their actual competencies and skills. The stereotype is acquired largely through frequent exposure to the negative view of old age and elderly people perpetuated in folklore, literature, the movies, and on television.

Through the scientific study of human aging, our knowledge of true age changes in behavior during the course of the adult lifespan can transcend the level of myths and stereotypes. Experimental psychology of aging has been importantly involved in this study. We have learned a great deal from experimental aging research about age differences and age changes in sensation, perception, learning, and so on. Illustrative of the potential value of experimental aging research for improving the welfare of elderly people is contemporary research on imaginal mnemonics in paired-associate learning. Elderly adults are less likely than young adults to employ spontaneously interacting images to relate stimulus and responses together, thus accounting for much of the age deficit commonly found in the proficiency of paired-associate learning. However, recent evidence indicates that elderly people may be trained to increase their use of an imaginal mnemonic, thereby improving considerably their proficiency in paired-associate learning and reducing, if not eliminating, the age deficit in learning proficiency. This research has important implications for foreign language learning by elderly adults who seek language training prior to visiting a foreign country as well as for learning other kinds of tasks mediated by the use of imaginal mnemonics. Intervention programs for the remediation of age-related learning-memory disabilities and other age-related disabilities are likely in the near future.

The experimental psychology of aging is part of a broader psychology of aging, or gerontological psychology, that includes psychometric and clinical-counseling approaches as well as the experimental approach to the study of age differences and age changes in behaviors and to the treatment of the elderly with respect to their unique problems. The psychology of aging, in turn, is part of the still broader discipline of gerontology that includes biological and sociological aspects of aging as well as psychological aspects. The psychology of aging is also part of the broader discipline of developmental psychology. This discipline traditionally treats development (defined as the study of age-related, or ontogenetic, behavioral changes) in terms of separate age ranges, thus yielding child psychology, adolescent psychology, and the psychology of aging. In addition, there is another broad discipline called lifespan developmental psychology that is characterized by its dialectical approach to developmental phenomena. Lifespan developmental psychology has had an indirect impact on the experimental psychology of aging by drawing attention to contextual factors in influencing behavior at various ages and by emphasizing the importance of generational membership and the historical time of measurement as potentially relevant developmental variables.

A common concern for all components of gerontology is the study of elderly people. In the experimental psychology of aging, the study of elderly people and the processes affected by aging usually requires the assignment of people to old age groups of subjects that are then contrasted with groups of young subjects. Such assignment is complicated, however, by the difficulty encountered in defining old age. One difficulty is created by the large variability found among psychological and biological functions in terms of both their onsets of aging and their rates of aging. A further problem arises through the large interindividual variability found for the effects of aging on many functions. In the absence of firm criteria for determining the onset of old age, the arbitrary criterion of reaching the chronological age of 65 is commonly set as marking the onset of old age. However, the minimal chronological age for defining membership in an elderly group of subjects varies greatly in the studies conducted by experimental aging psychologists.

The large number of elderly people (there are presently about 23 million people age 65 and older in the United States alone) readily justifies the considerable effort presently expended in all areas of gerontological research. The number of elderly people, expressed both absolutely and relatively, has increased dramatically in recent years, and further increments are projected well into the future. These increments have been especially pronounced for people age 80 and older and for women in all age ranges from 65 on. Other demographic data of interest to experimental aging psychologists concern the educational background of elderly people relative to young adults and the residential distribution of elderly people. Contrary to popular belief, relatively few elderly people reside in institutions.

Familiarity with the experimental psychology of aging requires an initial familiarity with the methodologies of experimental aging research and with the issues and problems that arise in the applications of these methodologies. Also important is a preliminary familiarity with the general nature of psychological theory as the usual source of hypotheses for research in the experimental psychology of aging and with the nature of developmental models that are coordinated with a theoretical model in the explanation of age changes in behavior. Chapters 2 through 6 will attempt to provide this familiarity. Chapters 7 through 10 will survey the results of experimental aging research in the various content areas of traditional experimental psychology; Chapter 11 will survey the results of studies using the experimental method, and other methods as well, in other content areas (intelligence, personality, and so on).

2

Cross-sectional Methodological Designs: Evaluating Age Differences and Age Changes

Age Differences Versus Age Changes

It does not take an especially astute observer to notice that today's young adults appear to be taller, on the average, than today's older adults. Not fully trusting our powers of observation, however, we decide to test the validity of what our eyes seem to tell us. Yardstick in hand, we are eager to begin. All we need to do now is recruit adult subjects of different ages. We begin the recruiting process by visiting psychology classes and asking men students to volunteer to have their heights measured. A number do, giving us a fairly large group of young-adult subjects. To recruit older adults, we hit on the bright idea of contacting the fathers of our young-adult subjects. So, we invite them to visit our laboratory and have their heights measured in the interest of science. Amazingly, our trust in the appeal of scientific contribution actually works, and all of our potential middle-age subjects contribute their services. We also decide that we have pushed our luck far enough. An attempt to extend our recruitment to still older men by seeking out the grandfathers of our student subjects may not be very successful. Besides, we already have two age levels (young adulthood and middle age) that are sufficiently separated to permit at least a gross test of our belief that adult-age differences in height do exist.

Does our study support our belief? To answer this question, we simply contrast the mean, or average, height of our young-adult group with the mean height of our middle-age group. These means are shown in Figure 2.1 as solid circles. Note that our middle-age subjects average about 1½ inches shorter than our young-adult subjects. A difference of this magnitude would surely turn out to be statistically significant (i.e., the observed difference in means is highly

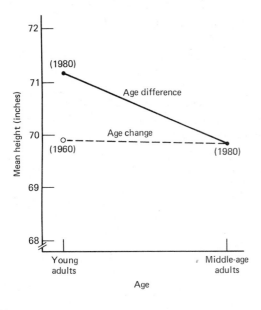

Figure 2.1. Mean heights for groups of young and middle-age adults measured in 1980 (solid circles). The solid line indicates the nature of the age difference in height. The open circle represents the mean height of the middle-age subjects in 1960 when they were young adults; the dashed line indicates the extent of the age change in height for these subjects from young adulthood to middle age.

unlikely to be a chance occurrence). Although our study is fictitious, our projected outcome probably comes close to what would have been found if this study had been done. A recent study at Harvard University compared the heights of current men students with the heights of their fathers when they were college students (at Harvard, of course). Even as young adults, the fathers averaged 1½ inches shorter than their sons (Youmans, 1975).

Our study may not qualify us for a Nobel Prize, nevertheless, two of its characteristics serve our purpose nicely. That purpose is to introduce you to some important terms, procedures, and concepts that have considerable relevance for experimental aging research.

First, our study is representative of what is called *descriptive research.* As the name implies, the objective of such research is merely the description of age differences in average performance scores on a task of interest to an investigator (and, presumably, to many others as well). Performance scores may seem like a strange concept to apply when the task consists only of having your height measured, but, in principle, inches tall is a score earned by performing on a stand-straight task. An important first step in describing age differences for this, and any other task, is the one we have already taken, that is, demonstrating the statistical significance of our observed age differences in average performance scores. Once statistical significance is established, an important second step must be taken. Specifically, we now need to describe how performance varies as chronological age increases. In our fictitious study, there is an obvious negative covariation between performance scores and increments in age, that is, the average performance scores decrease as age increases. The nature of this negative covariation may be readily seen in Figure 2.1 by the solid line connecting our age-group means. An *age-performance relationship* of this kind is an example of what psychologists call, more generally, a functional relationship. Any functional relationship describes the nature of the variation in a dependent variable (i.e., performance score) that accompanies transitions in an independent variable (i.e., the antecedent condition introduced by the investigator) from Level 1 to Level 2, from Level 3 to Level 4, and so on. In a purely descriptive aging study, the only independent variable is that of the different chronological ages selected by the investigator.

Second, our fictitious study employed the methodological design used in most descriptive aging studies. It is the traditional *cross-sectional design.* Methodological design in this context refers to the procedure used to introduce variation in chronological age and, therefore, variation in our sole independent variable. All that is needed to implement this design is to use a separate group of subjects for each level of age qua independent variable. The members of each group have in common one critical attribute—they are all of the age range specified by the level of the independent variable (e.g., they are all young adults in the sense that they all meet our criterion for defining this level of our independent variable).

Despite its merits, our height study does have one serious limitation. It offers no insight as to why there are age differences in height. At stake is the basic question of whether or not age differences in average performance on any given task occur because individual subjects manifest *age changes* in their performance on that task. Stated somewhat differently: Are observed differences in performance the consequence of the human organism's *ontogeny* (i.e., the individual course of development beyond young adulthood)? In terms of height differences, an ontogenetic explanation of those differences takes the position that middle-age men were once as tall as contemporary young men, with their present performance deficit resulting from a shrinking that is part of their overall ontogenies. For our study to support this explanation, however, we would have to be certain that our two age groups are alike with respect to all conditions that might affect height, except for chronological age per se. If we had assurance of such equality, then we would be in the reasonable position of concluding that the observed age difference was the consequence solely of a true age change. But therein lies the limitation of cross-sectional studies. By necessity, separate age groups come from different generations, as defined by the large differences in their birth years. With respect to our height interest, members of a later generation (such as our present group of young adults) encountered, during their childhoods, health-care and diet conditions that were more favorable to physical growth than the comparable conditions encountered by the members of an earlier generation (such as our present group of middle-age adults). In fact, the generational trend apparent in our study is part of the trend toward increasing height over the centuries. Consider, for example, the average height of young men who lived many generations ago, say in the Middle Ages. Many people are shocked when they visit a museum and see for the first time a suit of armor worn by a knight of that era. Most of today's fifth-grade boys would, indeed, find the suit to be a tight fit. Returning to our own study, there is no magic wand we can wave and make the contribution of generational differences to age differences in height disappear. Fortunately, however, the confounding between age and generation is of no consequence as long as we are content with merely describing age differences, whatever the reason for those differences.

It is also fortunate that for many of experimental psychology's tasks (e.g., paired-associate learning), unlike tasks involving height and other physical attributes, the cross-sectional method can be adapted for use in *explanatory research.* Explanatory research in the present context means research testing of the hypothesis that an age change *causes* the age differences in the performance found on a given task. How these tests are conducted will be discussed in detail later in this chapter.

Of more immediate concern to us is the demonstration of how explanatory research of a different kind could be conducted with our height task. This demonstration will serve to introduce further important terms, procedures, and concepts that have great relevance for experimental aging research. Our explanatory objective can be approached through the use of the traditional *longitudinal methodological design.* Design in this context again refers to the procedure used to introduce variation in chronological age. In this method, the same subjects, all of whom are from the same generation, represent each chronological age level by having their task performance evaluated as they grow older and reach each of the designated age levels. Because each age group now has the same generational background, there no longer is a confounding of an age change by a generational change. In principle, the age differences observed in performance are accepted as being caused by a true age change, to the extent that other potential confounding factors are eliminated (to be discussed further in Chapter 3).

Two options are available to us for converting our examination of age differences in height into a longitudinal study. The first calls for working forwards with our current group of young adults. We could wait 20 or more years (i.e., until the subjects reach middle age) and seek them out for a second measurement of height. Alternatively, we could work backwards with our current group of middle-age adults, that is, we could seek out objective records of measurements taken of our subjects' heights when they themselves were young adults. Being impatient for immediate results, we quickly choose the second option. The mean height for this "second group" of young adults, (measured in 1960) is shown by the open circle in Figure 2.1. Most important, the dashed line in this figure indicates the age change in height from young adulthood to middle age. It can be seen that the age change is slight and not nearly large enough to account for our present 1½-inch age difference. The age change in height, however, would have been more pronounced if we had a group of current elderly men and tracked down their heights as young adults. Shrinking does occur after young adulthood is attained, but the amount of shrinking does not ordinarily become appreciable until old age. The main shrinking process is the thinning of the cartilage that is found between the bones of the vertebral column.

The relationship between age differences and age changes is a complex one. For some tasks, age differences in performance appear to be attributable entirely to age changes; for other tasks, age differences in performance appear

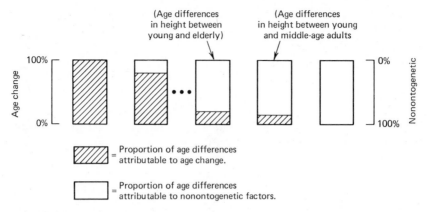

Figure 2.2. The range of relative contributions of true age changes and nonontogenetic factors in relation to the emergence of adult-age differences in performance on various kinds of tasks.

to be attributable entirely to such nonontogenetic factors as variation in generational membership. Between these extremes, there are many other tasks, such as our height task, for which part, but not all, of the age differences in performance is attributable to an age change. The proportion that is attributable to age change may, of course, vary greatly among tasks. The full range of possibilities is illustrated in Figure 2.2.

Our concern in the remainder of this chapter will be with the application of the first of the two traditional designs, the cross-sectional method, to both descriptive and explanatory research in the experimental psychology of aging. Of particular concern will be the difficult transition from descriptive to explanatory research through the use of the cross-sectional method. We will then examine (in Chapter 3) comparable applications of the second traditional design, the longitudinal method. We will discover at that time that the longitudinal method may be used in descriptive research as well as in explanatory research. A full understanding of the means by which these methods work in experimental settings, the kinds of research issues they address, and the problems arising in their applications is an essential first step to an understanding and appreciation of the experimental psychology of aging.

Frankly, as we will see, both of these traditional methodologies encounter interpretative problems when they are applied in explanatory research. Consequently, several modifications of these methodologies have been proposed in recent years. The modifications call for sequential designs. These designs combine the features of the traditional cross-sectional and longitudinal methods together with the features of yet another method, the time-lag method. Moreover, sequential designs are always bifactor rather than unifactor. That is, they employ two developmentally relevant independent variables simultaneously rather than one variable (chronological age), which is characteristic of the traditional cross-sectional and longitudinal designs. Interestingly, chronological age need not be one of the independent variables entering into a sequential design. We will discuss the nature of these modified designs and their implications for the experimental psychology of aging in Chapter 4.

Even sequentially designed research is limited at the explanatory level to the identification of gross molar factors (e.g., age per se or, alternatively, generational membership), which are responsible for observable age differences in human behaviors. For most of the tasks employed in the experimental psychology of aging, the investigator is interested in a more molecular explanation in which the specific process undergoing a change with increasing age (or, alternatively, undergoing a modification with changing cohort, or generational, membership) is identified. Explanation at this level requires a research design in which chronological age is joined as an independent variable by at least one other independent variable that stems from the investigator's own manipulations (e.g., rate of presenting material in a learning study). The nature of the interaction between chronological age and the experimental independent variable offers confirming or disconfirming evidence for some hypothesis the investigator has about the nature of the underlying process. Consequently, research of this kind makes use of what we call an interaction methodological design. We will consider the general characteristics of this design in Chapter 5. Interaction research may also be directed at determining the effectiveness of some manipulated independent variable (e.g., a specific training program) for modifying the efficiency of a process that seemingly demonstrates an age change. The intent here is to discover conditions that alleviate, at least partially, age related decrements in performance of a given task.

Cross-sectional Methodology: Application to Descriptive Research

General Characteristics of Descriptive Experimental Aging Research. Our interest in descriptive research rests, of course, in age differences on those tasks that are relevant to the content areas of experimental psychology. Suppose, for example, we want to examine the extent of adult-age differences in paired-associate learning for certain kinds of words (e.g., familiar abstract nouns). Our objectives are identical to the ones we had when we began our fictitious height study: (1) testing the statistical significance found for age differences in performance scores on our task and (2) determining the nature of the age-performance relationship for this task. Moreover, we plan to use the cross-sectional method, as in our earlier descriptive study. There is, however, a fundamental difference between the earlier study and our current hypothetical paired-associate study. In the earlier one, we had a clearly defined task and a standard procedure for measuring proficiency on that task. Anyone else doing that study would have used the same stand-straight task and the same dependent variable score (inches or meters tall). This is not the case for paired-associate learning. That is, there is no standard task format that sets the number of pairs, the rate of exposing those pairs, and so on; nor is there a standard dependent variable, or performance, score. Usually, the investigator is forced both to construct the task and to establish a scoring procedure for evaluating proficiency in performing that task.

Accordingly, our first step is to make up a list of, say, 10 stimulus and response pairs that meet our specified criterion (i.e., each member of a pair is a familiar abstract word as defined in some reference source). We decide that each subject in our study will receive four trials on this list and that a subject's performance score will be the total number of correct responses (i.e., correct anticipations of response words to their stimulus words exposed alone and summated over the four trials).

We are now ready to assess performance proficiency at two or more points on the adult-lifespan continuum. Given our limited time and resources, we decide to restrict our cross-sectional evaluation to just two age levels—early adulthood and late adulthood. These are the extremes of usual interest in the experimental psychology of aging. Of course, we need to establish firm criteria for identifying membership in our two age groups. This should not delay us very long. Reasonable criteria are those in their 20s and those 60 or beyond (for early and late adulthood, respectively). Now, we are confronted by the critical next step—recruiting a sample, or group, of subjects for each of our two age levels. Students in psychology classes no longer appeal to us—too few of them are in their 20s. So, to recruit our young-adult subjectss, we decide to go where people in their 20s congregate, namely the most popular local disco. On a lively Saturday night, we circulate among the crowd, seeking out potential subjects who satisfy our age criterion. Dozens of people of the right age are approached, but only 20 of them agree to participate in our study and then only after much cajoling on our part and much suspicion of our weirdness on their part. To our good fortune, all 20 volunteers show up in our laboratory the following week and receive our learning task under controlled laboratory conditions. The mean age of these volunteers turns out to be 24 years. To recruit our elderly subjects, we decide to go where they congregate, namely the most popular senior-citizens' club. We attend the next meeting of the club and apply the same strategy we used in recruiting young-adult subjects. Thus, we approach, cajole, and tolerate suspicions of our weirdness. Again, out of dozens of contacts, 20, with a mean age of 70 years, agree to be participants in our study, and, once more, all of them show up the following week to have their learning proficiency assessed under the same controlled laboratory conditions encountered by our young-adult subjects.

We now appear to have the requisite data for examining age differences in the proficiency of paired-associate learning. All that remains is to determine the mean number of correct responses for each of our two age groups. Once this is completed, we discover that the mean for our elderly group is somewhat less than the mean for our young-adult group and that the difference between means is statistically significant. To finish the descriptive job, we plot these two means in a graph that relates age level to mean performance proficiency and then we connect the two points by a straight line, as shown in Figure 2.3 (filled circles and unbroken line), just as we did in our height study. A glance at this figure reveals that we have uncovered an age difference—elderly adults are less proficient than young adults in learning the specific list we prepared. Moreover, the magnitude of the difference in means provides us with an estimate of the extent of the age difference in learning proficiency. In addition, our figure implies an age-performance relationship in which the decrease in proficiency

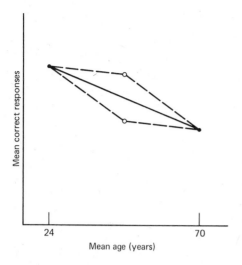

Mean correct responses

24   70
Mean age (years)

Figure 2.3. Solid line shows a hypothetical age difference in mean performance scores for paired-associate learning scores between a group of young adults and a group of elderly adults. Broken lines show alternative courses of the age-performance relationship that might have been found if a middle-age group has been included in the study.

from early to late adulthood occurs at a linear rate. Consequently, we are led to believe that, if middle-age adults were to have their proficiency evaluated on the same task, they would manifest a level of proficiency that falls about halfway between that of our young and elderly subjects.

Evaluating Descriptive Research. Our hypothetical paired-associate study was intended to illustrate the general nature of descriptive experimental aging research. As in any descriptive study, our objective was only to describe the nature of age differences in performance, not to explain why these differences occur. How well our study fulfilled this limited but, nonetheless, important objective rests ultimately on the soundness of the study itself. Not immediately apparent is the fact that, in planning this study, we faced a number of choice-points, each demanding a decision on some methodological issue. The overall soundness of our study clearly depends on the collective wisdom of these various decisions.

The nature of our decision-making demands is summarized in the form of a hierarchical flowchart in Figure 2.4. Many of these decisions were general ones in the sense that they must enter into *any* study involving paired-associate learning. Some dealt with routine task conditions, such as how many pairs to have in the list, how rapidly should the pairs be exposed, and so on. Our decisions here were likely to have been based on pilot research that preceded our formal study. Pilot research consists of small-scale projects of an exploratory nature. Thus, small groups of both young-adult and elderly subjects, comparable to the groups we expect to run in our main study, may have received six pair lists, more small groups may have received eight pair lists, and so on. From the results of this pilot research we were able to zero in on task conditions that are neither too easy for young-adult subjects nor too difficult for elderly subjects. The remaining general methodological decisions were directed at avoiding the confounding of our study. This would occur if our two age groups differed in any fundamental way (other than their age levels and also, of course,

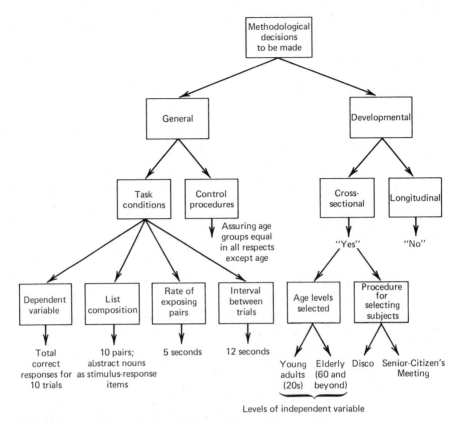

Figure 2.4. Hierarchical flowchart of the decisions to be made by an investigator in planning an experimental aging study.

their generations) that might affect proficiency in paired-associate learning. These decisions follow the logic of sound experimental design, a logic surely known to the investigator. Finally, decisions had to be made that were specific to the developmental content of our study. Our initial decision was the choice of the cross-sectional method over the longitudinal method. There is no reason to dispute this decision, given our reluctance to engage in time-consuming longitudinal research. Our remaining decisions concerned the means of implementing the cross-sectional method, that is, decisions regarding the number of age levels, the size and composition of our age groups, and where to find appropriate subjects.

To our credit, components of our paired-associate study were conducted the way they should be in a good descriptive study. For one thing, our only variable was chronological age (and its correlate, generational membership). Other potential variables that might affect proficiency in paired-associate learning were held constant in the sense of being made equal between our age groups. For example, the same pairs of words were learned by both groups. If we had used easier pairs or, alternatively, fewer pairs for the elderly group, then

we would not know the degree to which our observed age difference was mitigated by the inequality in task difficulty. Similarly, the pairs were practiced
under the same laboratory conditions (e.g., the same rate of exposing word
pairs—5 seconds per pair) for both age groups, again eliminating from consideration a non-age factor that might influence the observed age difference. Our
use of a number of subjects at each age level was certainly appropriate. Paired-
associate learning, in common with most of the other tasks employed in experimental psychology, reveals considerable interindividual variability in performance scores. This is true for every age level we might include in our study.
Consequently, we expect to find a fairly large range of scores within both our
young-adult group and our elderly group. In fact, it should not surprise us to
discover that several of our elderly subjects score higher than a number of our
young-adult subjects. Conversely, we may discover that several of our young-
adult subjects have scores that are nearly as low as the poorest of our elderly
subjects. The subjects tested at a given age level should reflect the variablility in
performance proficiency that exists within the population of people of that age.
Ordinarily, this requires testing a number of people at each of the age levels
included in a study. Given the variability between like-age subjects, no one
subject can be viewed as possessing a performance score that represents his or
her age level. Instead, an average score, usually the mean, is abstracted from
the set of scores obtained at each age level. These averages serve as the representative values for comparisons between age levels and for evaluations of the
extent of age differences. This general procedure was, of course, followed in our
hypothetical study.

On the other hand, our study has two problems that greatly limit the
generalizability and utility of the information derived from it. The first is created by the absence of data for one or more age groups between young and late
adulthood. Although we have a general picture of a performance deficit that
occurs over the adult lifespan, we really do not know the actual course of that
deficit. Our assumption that proficiency decreases linearly from early to late
adulthood is likely to be wrong. If a middle-age group had been included, its
mean may have been found to differ only slightly, if at all, from the mean of
our young-adult group. Alternatively, it may have been found to be only
slightly greater than the mean of our elderly group. In either event, the course
of the performance change over the adult lifespan would be decidedly nonlinear (illustrated by the broken line functions in Figure 2.3).

The second problem rests in the extent to which our average score at each
age level is truly representative of the performance of all adults at that age
level. At stake here is the adequacy of our sampling procedure in selecting a
representative group of subjects at a given age level, that is, a group that
displays a distribution of performance scores that would be found in the total
population of adults at that age level (i.e., if *all* members of the population
could be evaluated). If a sample's distribution of scores approximates that of its
underlying population, then the mean score for that sample approximates the
true, or parametric, mean that is characteristic of the entire population. However, if the sample's distribution departs markedly from that of the population,

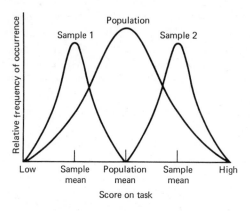

Figure 2.5. Hypothetical distribution of performance scores for a population of adults at some specified age level together with the distributions of scores for two nonrepresentative samples selected from that population.

then the sample's mean is likely to underestimate or overestimate the parametric mean, contingent on the direction of the disparity in distributions. These possibilities are illustrated in Figure 2.5. Scores on the task in question are assumed to be normally distributed for all adults of a given chronological age, with a parametric mean value that is indicated in Figure 2.5. However, the distribution of scores for each of two samples selected from that population in Figure 2.5 departs considerably from the distribution of scores for the population, resulting in an underestimation of the parametric mean for sample 1 and and an overestimation of the parametric mean for sample 2.

Returning to our hypothetical study, it is unlikely that the relative distribution of paired-associate learning scores for young adults recruited at a local disco matches that of all people in their 20s. Moreover, the representativeness of our particular sample is questioned even more by the fact that we have not even recruited a representative sample of disco-attending young adults. Remember that we had to rely on young adults who volunteered their services as subjects. It is conceivable that the nonvolunteers in the audience would have given us a different mean score to serve as our estimate of the parametric mean if we had somehow been able to entrap them as subjects. A similar problem occurs for our elderly subjects. The distribution of paired-associate learning scores for elderly adults attending a senior-citizens' meeting is unlikely to match the distribution of all people of age 60 and beyond. The restriction of involving only volunteer subjects again presents its own unique problems. The point is, with other samples of subjects selected from the same age levels, we would probably have obtained age-level means that differed somewhat from the means actually observed.

Several such possibilities are illustrated in Figure 2.6. Points a and b (filled circles) show the means actually obtained in our study (shown earlier in Figure 2.3). Points a' and a" depict means that might have been found with other samples of young adults. In one case (a'), the mean is above that found in our study; in the other case (a"), the mean is below that found in our study. Similarly, points b' and b" depict means that might have been obtained with other samples of elderly adults. Our estimate of the magnitude of age differences in the proficiency of paired-associate learning is obviously dependent on the spe-

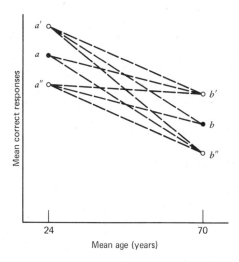

Figure 2.6. Alternative means for the hypothetical study illustrated in Figure 2.3. Points *a* and *b* are the means obtained for the original samples of young and elderly adults respectively. Points *a′*, *a″*, *b′*, and *b″*, are means obtained for different samples at each age level. Broken lines indicate the various estimates of age differences in performance that would be observed contingent on the specific samples selected at each age level.

cific samples of subjects that entered into our study. If the samples yielding the a′ and b″ means had been selected, the estimate of age differences would have been inflated relative to the estimate that emerged from our study. By contrast, if the samples yielding the a″ and b′ means had been selected, the estimate would be far less than that actually observed.

Our observed difference in group means (Figure 2.3) was sufficiently large that it seems unlikely to have resulted only from sampling artifacts. That is, it is highly likely that we are dealing with parametric means that do show some degree of decrease from early to late adulthood when these means are estimated cross-sectionally. However, we must realize that our quantification of this change in performance is probably, at best, a crude approximation of the true change in performance.

Parametric Descriptive Research and External Validity. There are occasions when it is important to estimate mean values for different age levels as closely as possible. This is most likely to occur when a cross-sectional descriptive study has as its objective the establishment of norms for evaluating the performance proficiency of the individuals of varying ages as well as the determination of the true course of the age-performance relationship. As noted earlier, the sample at each age level in such a study must be representative of the population from which that sample is selected. Once reliable estimates of parametric means have been obtained, the observed age differences among these means estimate closely the age differences in performance proficiency for the given task that exist within adults of all age levels. The results from such a study permit us to generalize from age differences between samples of subjects to inferred age differences between entire populations. The extent to which the results of a study generalize beyond the limited samples employed in a study is part of what is called the *external validity* of that study (Campbell & Stanley, 1966).

Phrased somewhat differently, high external validity means a high degree of consistency of results across replications of the same basic study on different cross-sectional samples of subjects. Thus, if we were to repeat a particular study with different representative samples from the same populations, we would expect the means for our new age groups and the differences among these means to agree closely with the means and differences found in the original study. Most important, the means obtained from a study with high external validity offer stable normative values for evaluating individual performance scores. Other components of external validity will be encountered later in this chapter and in subsequent chapters.

Conducting Parametric Descriptive Research. We need to elaborate a bit about parametric descriptive research in terms of how it should be done. We will do this with the aid of another hypothetical study. The task involved in this study is immaterial for our purposes and it will simply be called Task X. Our concern about age differences in Task X is with what these differences are like within the populations of individuals who collectively compose the adult-lifespan continuum. Because we obviously cannot measure all adults in Task X, we need to adopt a reasonable alternative procedure. One option is to select cross-sectional samples of subjects falling at various, moderately separated points on the adult-lifespan continuum. Thus, we might want samples of 20-year-old adults, 40-year-old adults, 60-year-old adults, and 80-year-old adults. To have a high degree of external validity for our study, each of the four samples must be representative of all people who are members of the population for the age level sampled. In effect, we are using the principle of cross-sectioning twice. Our various samples considered together give us a cross-section of all adults, and each sample, in turn, is a cross-section of the population it represents. We could make each sample a cross-section by drawing a number of people (e.g., 50) randomly from the underlying population. Ideally, the random drawings would be from a list (e.g., census data) of all people currently of the age in question. The next steps are to administer Task X to all subjects under standard laboratory conditions and then determine the mean score for each age group, just as in our hypothetical paired-associate study. These means and the differences among them should be reasonably good approximations of the means and differences among means we would have found if we had been able to evaluate the entire populations of 20-year-old people, 40-year-old people, and so on.

A plausible outcome of this hypothetical study is shown in Figure 2.7. Note the presence of a positively accelerated negative relationship between age level and performance level on Task X, that is, there is little change in means from age 20 to age 40, a larger change in means from 40 to age 60, and a still larger change in means from age 60 to age 80. In other words, chronological age and performance proficiency covary negatively and the rate of decline in performance increases as age level increases. We are assuming, quite reasonably, that the means for other age levels not specifically included in our study would fall close to the line connecting the observed means in Figure 2.7. With four points firmly anchored in our age-performance relationship by soundly conducted data, the intervening points are likely to fit the empirically plotted function.

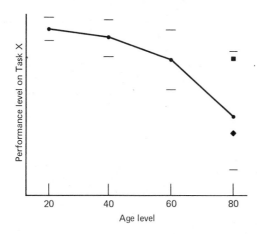

Figure 2.7. Hypothetical outcome for a descriptive aging study on Task X. The study employed a representative age group at each of four age levels. The mean and spread of scores around that mean are shown for each age level. Means for other age levels are estimated as falling along the line connecting the empirically observed means. The square and diamond represent scores earned by two 80-year-old subjects who were not part of the original study but who may now be evaluated normatively.

Also included in Figure 2.7 is an estimate of the spread of scores, both above and below the mean, for each age group. Note that variability about the mean is depicted as increasing progressively as chronological age increases. This, too, is a plausible outcome of our hypothetical study. Increasing variability (as indexed by the standard deviation) with increasing age is commonly found for the tasks employed in experimental aging research.

In addition to charting the course of age differences in performance on Task X, we now have the basis for evaluating the skills of individuals who are part of the total population but who were not included in the investigator's samples. In effect, the mean and standard deviation for each age sample provide norms for that age level if the sample is, indeed, representative of the population it came from. These norms serve to interpret the competence of individuals with respect to the competence of people their own age. For example, consider Mr. High, an octogenarian whose score on Task X is indicated by a square in Figure 2.7. He is clearly superior on this task to others his own age; his score falls well above the mean of his normative 80-year-old group (and also above the mean for the normative 60-year-old group and within the distribution of scores for the 40-year-old group). He would probably earn a standard score of around 70 (i.e., 2 *SDs* above a mean set at 50, with an *SD* of 10, for his own age group; alternatively, his score would be about 700 if the mean and standard deviation in standard score form are set at 500 and 100 respectively). By contrast, Mr. Lowe, another octogenarian, has a score (indicated by a diamond in Figure 2.7) that is somewhat below the mean of his age level. He would probably have a standard score of around 40 (i.e., 1 *SD* below the mean of 50 for his own age group; alternatively, his score would be about 400 if the mean and standard deviation for the standard scores had been set at 500 and 100 respectively, instead of at 50 and 10 respectively).

The usefulness of our norms, of course, would be much greater if our original study had included additional age levels (e.g., a 30-year-old group, a 50-year-old group, and so on). For each additional age level we would have the necessary information (mean and standard deviation) to serve as the norm for evaluating new individuals of that same age. In practice, however, it is unusual to select subjects at discrete chronological ages along the adult continuum when the establishment of age-group norms is the primary objective of a parametric descriptive study. Rather than representative samples of, say, 60- and 70-year-old adults, we are more likely to seek representative samples for ranges of chronological age (e.g., 60 to 64 years of age, 65 to 69 years of age, and so on). For each range, a representative sample of all people within that range is selected and evaluated on the given task. The mean and standard deviation for a particular range provide norms for all other people falling within the specified range. Our assumption is that the range is small enough so that there will be little performance change from one discrete age level to the next level within that range (e.g., from 60 to 61 years of age in the 60-to-64 age range), especially relative to performance changes from the mean of that range to the means of the ranges preceding and following it. This, too, is a reasonable assumption for most descriptive aging studies.

There is considerable similarity between normative descriptive research in the experimental psychology of aging and normative research in the standardization of various tests (e.g., intelligence tests). Both involve individual differences, norms, and the interpretation of individual scores with respect to these norms. Moreover, both approaches are interested in the correlated problem of determining the true course of age differences in performance over the adult lifespan. The differences between the approaches rest in the tasks employed (the laboratory tasks of experimental psychology versus intelligence tests, personality tests, and so on) and in the greater control over extraneous sources of confounding (i.e., factors that might inflate or deflate sample means that serve as estimates of population means) in experimental aging research than in traditional psychometric research. The greater control factor is evident even when there is considerable overlap in task content. For example, memory span for a series of digits is often studied by experimental psychologists, but it is also included as a subtest on the Wechsler Adult Intelligence Scale (WAIS). However, control over potentially confounding extraneous factors, such as the rate of reading the digits (which should be held constant for all subjects), is likely to be greater in the laboratory than in a clinician's office.

Finally, there is an unfortunate commonality between normative-parametric experimental research and normative-parametric test-oriented, or psychometric research. That is, they both suffer from the difficulty encountered in selecting truly representative samples across the lifespan. Random selection of subjects from a census list is a utopian dream that is all but impossible to achieve in a real-life descriptive study. Compromise procedures for selecting representative samples are the general rule. The usual procedure is to rely on nonrandom quota sampling. The procedure requires duplicating in a sample the distribution known to exist in the population for a critical non-age attribute (i.e., one believed to correlate highly with performance proficiency on the task in question). For example, if 20% of the 40-to-44-year-old population consists of people scoring at Level 1 of the critical attribute, then 20% of the 40-to-44-year-old sample should also consist of people scoring at Level 1. In principle, the population proportion at each level of the critical attribute determines a quota of subjects to be filled in the sample. This is the procedure followed by Wechsler (1944) in the monumental standardization of the initial form of his adult intelligence test and by many other descriptive psychometric researchers as well. In Wechsler's case, the critical attribute was occupational level (an attribute known to correlate highly with intelligence test scores). From a large pool of potential subjects, members were nonrandomly selected on the basis of their occupational level. Selection of subjects continued until the resulting sample had an occupational distribution approximating that of its parent population. The samples generated by this procedure are surely more representative of their populations than are the samples generated by recruiting volunteers at the local disco or the local senior-citizens' club. This is true even though the quota-based samples may not be representative of their populations with respect to other non-age attributes (e.g., Wechsler's subjects were all Caucasians from New York State).

Parametric descriptive research can be laborious, time consuming, and unromantic. For these reasons, experimental psychologists are reluctant to engage in it. Consequently, there is a paucity of parametric descriptive research for the kinds of tasks indigenous to experimental psychology. This is a pity. Normative data for these tasks would provide useful information in counseling elderly people. By contrast, much of psychometric aging research is parametric and normative in its intent and content.

Cross Sectional Descriptive Research: Age-Performance Relationships

Potential Outcomes. Cross-sectional studies with less than completely representative samples abound in the experimental psychology of aging. Many of these studies have included several age levels between young and late adulthood and have examined the course of performance changes over the adult lifespan. Of course, in each study, the accuracy with which each age group's mean estimates the mean for the underlying population is unknown. Nevertheless, the general nature of the relationship, or covariation, between chronological age and performance proficiency in many of these studies is probably not far removed from the relationship that would be found in the total population of adults.

For most of the tasks employed by experimental psychologists, cross-sectional descriptive research reveals some degree of decline in performance proficiency from early to late adulthood. Such declines are shown abstractly in Figure 2.8 for several additional hypothetical tasks (each graph is presumed to be based on a number of age groups, with a smooth, best fitting line, connecting the means of these groups). It can be seen that for some tasks the decline begins relatively early in adulthood (e.g., Tasks D, E, and F), whereas, for other tasks, the decline does not begin until late in adulthood (e.g., Task C). Similarly, the rate of decline beyond its onset may vary greatly. In some cases, the decline may be slow and linearly accelerated (Task D). In other cases, the decline may be more rapid, and it may be either positively accelerated (Task E; also Task X in Figure 2.7) or negatively accelerated (Task F). However, not all

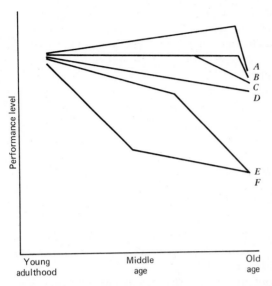

Figure 2.8. Hypothetical performance changes over the adult lifespan for a range of tasks. Onset of decline and rate of decline in performance varies over Tasks C, D, E, and F. Task A shows progressive increments over most of the lifespan, followed by a decline in advanced old age. Task B shows a steady state over most of the lifespan, followed by an eventual decline in advanced old age.

tasks show an appreciable decline with increasing chronological age. In fact, it is conceivable that performance on some tasks may increase steadily at a slow rate of change over the adult lifespan, at least until advanced old age is reached, at which point some deficit might set in (Task A). These tasks are likely to be ones that measure directly cumulative experiences with increasing age or measure aspects of behavior that are indirectly influenced by cumulative experience. For other tasks, performance may maintain a steady state, that is, remain roughly constant throughout the adult lifespan (again, perhaps, showing some decline with advanced old age as in Task B).

Examples of Age-Performance Relationships. Clearly, there is no single functional relationship, or law, that describes *all* performance changes with increasing age over the adult lifespan. To demonstrate the fact that actual laboratory studies yield the variety of relationships shown abstractly in Figure 2.8, we will draw on the results of studies recently completed in our laboratory. One of these studies (Kausler & Puckett, 1980a), contrasted young and elderly adults on each of two different learning or memory tasks. Our primary objective was to compare the change in performance with age that takes place for a task requiring the expenditure of considerable cognitive effort with the change that takes place for a task requiring little expenditure of such effort.

Our choice of an effortful task was that of paired-associate learning. Proficiency in learning paired associates increases to the extent that a subject applies such effortful strategies as the use of an imaginal mnemonic to relate stimulus and response elements. Our choice of a relatively effortless task was that of making frequency judgments. This task is analogous to what you would be doing if you served as an observer watching, say for an hour, people strolling past you as you leaned against a streetlight at a moderately busy streetcorner. Suppose at the end of that hour you were unexpectedly asked to make frequency-of-occurrence judgments. The judgments might include: "Did you see more men or women pass by during that hour?" "More men with beards or without beards?" "More toddlers or more adolescents?" Surprisingly, you would find that your judgments are fairly accurate. (We are assuming, of course, that someone kept an accurate count of the number of bearded men, toddlers, and so on.) You are likely to find also that you are fairly accurate on the laboratory counterpart of this task. For the laboratory task, words instead of people are exposed in a lengthy series, with some of the words being seen once, some three times, some five times, and so on. Subjects are told in advance that they will receive a memory test when the series of words is completed, but they may not be informed as to the precise nature of the memory test. For that test, a subject sees pairs of words for which one member of each pair had been exposed more frequently than the other member in the prior study list (e.g., a once exposed word paired with a thrice exposed word) and is asked to select the more frequent member of each pair. Considerable evidence has indicated that frequency judgments of this kind are based on relatively effortless, or automatic, memory processes. (We will examine this point more thoroughly in Chapter 9.)

Our paired-associate task closely resembled the one described earlier in connection with our hypothetical disco versus senior citizens study. That is, there were 10 pairs to be learned, 4 trials (making the maximum score equal 40 correct responses), and a 5-second rate of exposure per pair. The mean scores earned by our two age groups may be seen in the top panel of Figure 2.9. Also plotted in this figure is the mean score earned by a group of middle-age subjects on the same task. These subjects were run in a follow-up study in our laboratory under the same conditions our other subjects received. The age-performance relationship is clearly one of a decline in proficiency as age increases, with the rate of decline being positively accelerated (as for Task E in Figure 2.8). The decline, however, reflects only the slower rate of learning by our older subjects, not the absence of learning. In fact, all of our elderly subjects manifested increments in the number of correct responses over the four trials. There is every reason to believe that, with further practice, all of these subjects would have mastered the complete list.

Our frequency-judgment task was also given to our middle-age subjects as well as to our young-adult and elderly subjects. The mean scores for the number of correct judgments out of 18 test pairs are plotted in the bottom panel of Figure 2.9 for all three age groups. The age-performance relationship differs greatly from that found for the same subjects on paired-associate learning— note the absence of any age-related decline in performance. In fact, the means for the three age groups are nearly identical. The lack of an age effect on frequency judgment has also been found by others (e.g., Attig & Hasher, 1980), thus lending considerable reliability to our conclusion that performance on this task is insensitive to age-related changes.

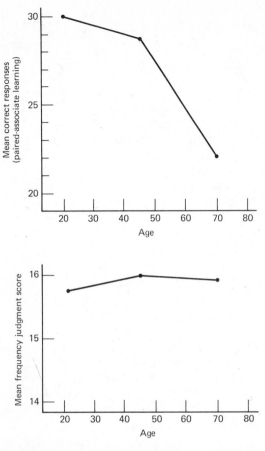

Figure 2.9. Top panel: Mean scores on a paired-associate learning task for groups of young, middle-age, and elderly subjects. Bottom panel: Mean scores on a frequency-judgment task that were earned by the same groups of subjects. (Adapted from data in Kausler & Puckett, 1980a.)

Our intention is to demonstrate that not all human behaviors decline in proficiency with increasing age over the adult lifespan. In fact, to complete the picture, we will report the results for an additional task, a nonexperimental one, namely a vocabulary test, that was given to all our subjects. The results, plotted as mean test scores (maximum score equals 40), are shown in Figure 2.10. Scores on this task reveal progressive increments with increasing age, much like the scores for Task A in Figure 2.8 (but negatively accelerated increments rather than linear). Vocabulary is the kind of skill that, as we noted earlier, might be expected to benefit from accumulated experiences over the lifespan.

Despite these exceptions, (and others like them), the occurrence of some degree of performance deficit with increasing chronological age is, nevertheless, the general rule in cross-sectional research, at least for the kinds of tasks carried over from experimental psychology. Consequently, we will use deficit as the prototypal case for age differences in our subsequent analysis of research directed at explanation of these differences.

Selection of Subjects. Our final comment on cross-sectional descriptive research concerns the selection of subjects at each age level for a given study. Specifically, our concern is with the vast majority of descriptive studies, those directed at a general understanding of an age-performance relationship rather than at a parametric assessment of age differences. From the examples we have encountered thus far, a general rule should be apparent. The investigator goes to places where people of a given age are likely to be found. For young-adult subjects, the favorite hunting ground is the college classroom (and then, usually, the general psychology classroom) rather than the more romantic, but less accessible, watering holes, like the local disco. This was the rule followed in our composite paired-associate/frequency-judgment study. The young adults were general psychology students, both men and women, who volunteered their services to fulfill a course requirement. Their average age was slightly more than 21 years; their average educational level was about 14 years (educational level is defined as years of formal education, with 12 years signifying completion of high school, 16 years completion of college, and so on). Both our middle-age and elderly subjects, again men and women, were recruited from the community, meaning, in this case, Columbia, Missouri, by means of membership in various social and religious organizations. All of these subjects were paid for their participation, a fairly standard practice with nonstudent subjects. Our middle-age subjects averaged about 45 years of age and had about 16 years of formal education; our elderly subjects averaged slightly more than 70 years of age and also had about 16 years of formal education. Our intention was to have older groups of subjects at least equal to our young-adult group in regard to educational level. The reason for this decision will become apparent later when we examine the results of such studies in terms of what they tell us about true age changes in learning and memory proficiency. For the time being, we need

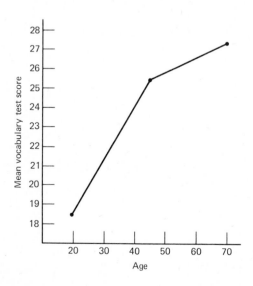

Figure 2.10. Mean scores on a vocabulary test for groups of young, middle-age, and elderly subjects. (Adapted from data in Kausler & Puckett, 1980a.)

to note that our selection procedure undoubtedly gave us samples of middle-age and elderly adults that were superior to their underlying populations. Consequently, the observed decrement in paired-associate learning proficiency with increasing age most likely underestimates what would be found for the broader populations of people at these age levels.

Cross-Sectional Methodology: Application to Explanatory Research

Beyond Age Difference: Inferring and Interpreting Ontogenetic Changes in Primary Factors. Suppose a cross-sectional descriptive study is extended to include preadulthood age variation as well as postadulthood age variation. Unfortunately, studies spanning virtually the entire lifespan are quite rare. Nevertheless, those that have been done usually reveal an interesting overall age-performance relationship. Our representative study is one by Laurence (1966) on age differences in free-recall learning. For this task, subjects receive a series of discrete items during one or more study trials. After each study trial, they recall as many items as they can in whatever order they wish (thus, the term, free recall). Six age levels entered into Laurence's study. In ascending order, the mean ages for these groups were: 5 years, 8 months; 6 years, 9 months; 8 years, one month; 10 years, 6 months; about 21 years (all college students); and 73 years (all college graduates). Given the tender age of her youngest subjects, items had to be presented in pictorial form (e.g., the picture of an apple) during the study trials. The names of the objects depicted in 16 such pictures were recalled in spoken form during test trials.

Mean recall scores for the six age groups are charted as an age-performance relationship in Figure 2.11. Each mean shown in this figure is for the number of names recalled per trial over the first four test trials. The interesting

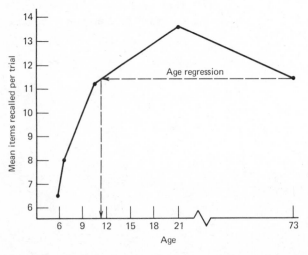

Figure 2.11. Mean scores on a free-recall learning task earned by groups of children of various ages and by groups of young and elderly adults. Age regression in performance for elderly adults is indicated by the correspondence of their mean score with the mean score earned by 10-to-11-year old children. (Adapted from Laurence, 1966, Table 1.)

phenomenon demonstrated in Laurence's study is the regression of her elderly subjects to a performance level characteristic of 10-to-11-year-old children. It is tempting to attribute such behavioral regression to deterioration with age in the proficiency of the task-specific process or processes postulated (usually by some prevailing theory) to determine performance proficiency on the task in question. For convenience, we will refer to these tasks-specific processes as primary ability factors (later we will encounter other factors—so-called secondary factors—that are also relevent to age changes in performance). In the case of free-recall learning, a probable primary factor is the process, or internal activity, of rehearsing the to-be-learned items (i.e., covertly verbalizing each item as it is studied). In general, the recallability of items is expected to increase as the number of rehearsals increases. The rehearsal rate of elderly adults seemingly corresponds to the rehearsal rate of children 10 to 11 years old. Both of these age groups, in turn, have rehearsal rates below the level of young adults, thus accounting for their performance levels relative to young adults.

By succumbing to our temptation, we have inferred that age plays a causative role in producing both the progression in performance from early childhood (see Figure 2.11) and the regression in performance that occurs in late adulthood. That is, the age-performance relationship manifested for free-recall learning reflects a continuous ontogenetic change in an underlying primary factor. From birth (and even before) through early adulthood, the maturational level of the human organisms increases progressively. From early adulthood through late adulthood, the sequence presumably is reversed and the maturational level decreases slowly but steadily, regressing eventually to a preadulthood level. It is this regression that defines aging as the term is commonly used.

Progression and regression over the full course of ontogeny is commonly viewed as involving a quantitative change in a primary factor. From this perspective, performance scores on a task change quantitatively in accordance with quantative changes in the proficiency of the primary factor regulating performance on that task. The nature of this cause-effect sequence over the entire lifespan is summarized in the top panel of Figure 2.12. This quantitative conceptualization of age changes is part of a mechanistic model of development, a model we will examine more completely in Chapter 6.

Some behavioral changes may be conceptualized as involving qualitative changes in a primary factor rather than mere quantitative changes in proficiency (i.e., an increase or a decrease in the magnitude of proficiency). This is, for example, the perspective of Jean Piaget's theory of cognitive development. The cognitive structures that form the basis for conducting logical thinking are different ones in late childhood than the ones in, say, middle childhood. Consequently, the older child is capable of qualitatively different forms of thinking (e.g., concrete operational) than is the younger child. Regression in these terms could involve a return in late adulthood to the more primitive cognitive structures of, say, middle childhood. The net effect would be the loss of the ability to perform concrete operations in thinking. The nature of this cause-effect sequence over the entire over the entire lifespan is summarized in the bottom panel of Figure 2.12. The concept of qualitative change is part of the organismic model of development that will also be examined in detail in Chapter 6.

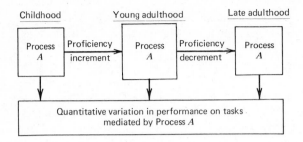

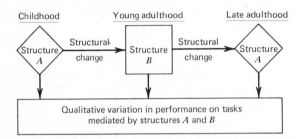

Figure 2.12. Top panel: Conceptualization of an age change over the lifespan in terms of a perspective that emphasizes quantitative changes in processes and the behaviors they mediate. Bottom panel: Conceptualization of an age change over the lifespan in terms of a perspective that emphasizes qualitative changes in cognitive structures and the behaviors they mediate.

The quantitative versus qualitative distinction does not concern us further at this point. Both concepts deal with an ontogenetic change in a primary factor. It is the problems encountered in establishing the presence of any ontogenetic change through cross-sectional research that does concern us for now.

Problems Inherent in Inferring Ontogenetic Change from Age Differences: Effects of Confounding on Internal Validity. As discussed early in this chapter, the transition from merely describing age differences in performance to attributing these differences to an ontogenetic change in a primary factor is not an easy one. The problems rest in the fact that variation in chronological age is not a true independent variable in the classic sense that an independent variable is employed in the traditional research of experimental psychology. A true independent variable is introduced into an experiment by means of the operations and manipulations of the investigator. It is the only condition, other than the dependent variable, that is allowed to vary across the groups of the experiment. All other conditions, or extraneous variables, that could effect performance on the experimental task, expressed as the score on the dependent variable, are controlled in terms of equating them for the groups receiving different levels of the independent variable. With only one antecedent condition that varies across groups, whatever differences are observed in performance between those groups must be caused by the changes in that condition (i.e., the independent variable itself).

How does a psychologist decide that a change in an independent variable *caused* a change in scores on a particular dependent variable? Decisions of this kind are complicated by the fact that performance on most dependent variables is governed by one or more primary processes (or factors). The level of proficiency of these processes determines the level of overt performance manifested on the dependent variable. Let us consider the simplest possible experiment, one in which there are only two levels of a single independent variable (Levels 1 and 2). For convenience, we will call the underlying primary process manipulated by this independent variable Process *A*. All other processes that might affect performance on the task in question will be grouped together and will be referred to as Process *B*. For example, if our task were paired-associate learning, Process *A* might be associating response words to stimulus words by means of a mnemonic. Process *B* would then include other primary processes entering into paired-associate learning (e.g., learning the response words independently of their associations with stimulus words).

Suppose, as shown in Figure 2.13, that greater proficiency of Process *A* occurs under Level 1 of the independent variable (e.g., giving subjects special instructions about the use of imaginal mnemonics) than under Level 2 (e.g., no special instructions are given). That is, the proficiency under Level 1 comes closer to the maximum proficiency possible with the organism's present maturational level than does proficiency under Level 2. We would then expect performance scores on the task to be greater under Level 1 than under Level 2. However, if the subjects receiving Levels 1 and 2 differed in their proficiency on Process *B*, then their differential performances could be due to this difference rather than to a difference in Process *A*.

Differential degrees of proficiency on Process *B* could result from a number of extraneous conditions. If these conditions are allowed to vary between

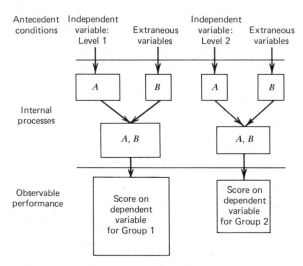

Figure 2.13. Postulated relationship between a manipulated antecedent condition (a traditional independent variable of experimental psychology) and observable performance (dependent variable), with potentially confounding extraneous variables equated across levels of the independent variable.

the groups of subjects receiving Levels 1 and 2, then our study would be confounded in that we do not know for certain if it is Process A or Process B that underlies our observed differences in performance. To avoid this confounding, the experimenter controls these extraneous conditions of variables by making them equal across Levels 1 and 2 of our independent variable.

The control procedure makes Process B equal for subjects receiving Level 1 (Group 1) and subjects receiving Level 2 (Group 2) of our independent variable (see Figure 2.13). Even with the control of these extraneous variables, the proficiency of the combined A and B processes should be greater for Level 1 than for Level 2. Because task performance is isomorphic with these combined causative factors, performance proficiency should also be greater for Group 1 than for Group 2 (see Figure 2.13). Most important, if we have good reason to believe that our independent variable is related to variation in Process A (as we would have for the variation in instruction given prior to paired-associate learning), then we now have good reason to believe that Process A is indeed a causative factor for performance variation on the task in question. The causative factor has been demonstrated without contamination by other processes (i.e., Process $B)$ that might play a comparable causative role. The extent to which a study identifies the true causative factor responsible for between-group differences on a dependent variable defines the *internal validity* of that study (Campbell & Stanley, 1963). Because our present study has correctly identified variation in Process A as the cause for variation on our dependent variable, it has a high degree of internal validity.

Alternatively, an extraneous variable could confound an experiment by directly affecting Process $A,$ that is, the process tied directly to the independent variable. A given process is quite likely to be related to more than one potential independent variable. For example, the nature of the words employed as stimulus and response items would certainly affect the use of an imaginal mnemonic in paired-associate learning. Imagery is more likely to be involved when the words are concrete nouns (i.e., have a readily imagined referent, such as apple) than when they are abstract nouns (i.e., do not have a readily imagined referent, such as idealism). Suppose our previous Group 1 differs from Group 2 with respect to one or more of these additional variables. Suppose further that the levels of these extraneous variables favor Group 2 over Group 1, in the sense of making the proficiency of Process A greater for Group 2 than for Group 1. This would be the case if Group 2 received a paired-associate list made up of concrete nouns, whereas Group 1 received a list made up of abstract nouns. The net effect could be the balancing of the advantage owing Group 1 through its receipt of Level 1 of the true independent variable. A null effect, or absence of a statistically significant difference between Groups 1 and 2 in their mean performance scores, is the likely consequence. In this event, we would be forced to make one or the other of two equally false conclusions. The first is that the independent variable selected for our experiment is not related to Process $A;$ the second is that Process A is not a causative factor for variation in performance on the given task. The second conclusion would be especially damaging in that it falsely rejects a true causative factor that may then be overlooked by future investigators. In either case, the study itself would clearly have low internal validity. Again, however, the risk of making these extraneous conclusions is largely eliminated by the experimenter's careful control procedures, whereby the extraneous variables are equated for Groups 1 and 2.

This kind of precision is not the case in a descriptive aging study. The variation in age level that generates our independent variable is created by selecting subjects of different chronological ages rather than by producing age variations directly in the laboratory. Strictly speaking, the research design of a cross-sectional descriptive aging study is correlational rather than experimental. That is, chronological age is correlated with performance scores rather than being manipulated and then related to variation in performance scores (as in a true experiment). For this reason the design of a cross-sectional descriptive aging study is an example of what is commonly termed a quasi-experimental design (Campbell & Stanley, 1966).

Most important, there is the definite possibility that the older subjects selected for participation in a cross-sectional study differ from the younger subjects in one or more attributes beside their chronological age levels. If these non-age attributes happen to covary with performance on the task in question, then variation in these other attributes rather than variation in chronological age per se could be the causative factor underlying the observed differences between age groups in their performance levels. Our aging study would be confounded in that we could not tease apart which of several possible variables is the actual causative variable. Ordinarily, confoundings are avoided in traditional experimental research by the control procedures of the investigator. As noted earlier, these procedures assure the equality of nonindependent variable attributes across the levels of the independent variable, thereby assuring that the groups receiving the various levels of the independent variable are not differentially affected by these other potentially confounding attributes. However, confoundings are difficult to avoid in cross-sectional descriptive research unless the attributes that covary with chronological age also happen *not* to covary with performance on the task in question.

Confounding of Age Changes by Non-age Attributes. Some of the possibilities alluded to above are illustrated in Figures 2.14 and 2.15. In both of these illustrations, two age levels are contrasted—Level 1 representing young-adult subjects and Level 2 representing elderly subjects. The only process determining proficiency on the task in question for both illustrations is presumed to be our previously designated Process *A*. For our purposes, we will assume further that Process *A* is insensitive to direct change with variation in chronological age. That is, the process does not regress with increasing age and its proficiency should, therefore, in theory, be the same for elderly adults, on the average, as it is for young adults. Consequently, performance level on the task should not show an age difference, provided the assessment of the age difference is not confounded by variation in some other attribute.

In both illustrations, we will also assume that chronological age is correlated with some non-age attribute (e.g., educational level), which is indicated by the horizontal lines in both figures. Looking at the situation illustrated in Figure 2.14, we see that variation in the non-age attribute is accompanied by a corresponding variation in the proficiency of Process *A,* the same process linked erroneously to variation in chronological age. Consequently, the young adult subjects (Level 1) in general have a greater proficiency on Process *A* and, therefore, greater scores on the dependent variable, than do the elderly adult subjects (Level 2) in general. The net effect is an observable age difference in performance for the samples of young and elderly subjects in the particular study being examined. If the samples, in turn, are representative of the entire populations of young and elderly adults, then the observed age difference in performance should estimate closely the age differences in performances that exists for these populations. Because our results permit us to generalize from an age difference between samples of subjects to an age difference between populations, our study has high external validity. However, even with this high degree of external validity, we would be wrong if we concluded that age qua age caused the age difference observed for our samples and inferred for our populations. That is, the true causative factor is variation in the non-age attribute that correlates with chronological age. If aging as an ontogenetic change is erroneously accepted as the causative factor, then our study would have no internal validity. These conditions are largely the ones that existed in our earlier hypothetical study on age differences in height. Remember that we concluded that most of these differences were caused by a non-age attribute, generational membership, that does correlate with chronological age. If we had concluded that shrinking with age per se is the primary process responsible for the smaller scores earned by our middle-age subjects, then our study would obviously have lacked internal validity.

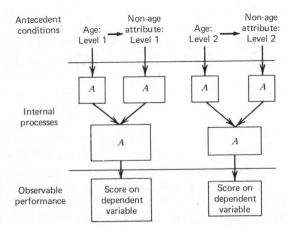

Figure 2.14. Postulated relationship between variation in chronological age (independent variable) and observable performance (dependent variable) in which a non-age attribute that correlates with both age and performance scores functions as a confounding variable. Although the process mediating performance is insensitive to direct change with increasing age, a difference in the process occurs nevertheless by means of the operation of the confounding non-age variable.

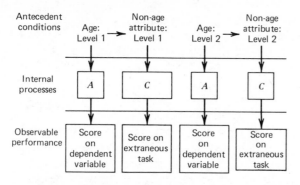

Figure 2.15. Postulated relationship between variation in chronological age (independent variable) and observable performance (dependent variable) in which a non-age attribute correlates with age but not with performance scores on the particular task. The non-age attribute is, therefore, not a confounding variable. No age difference in performance occurs because the process mediating performance is insensitive to increasing age.

The circumstances are quite different for the situation illustrated in Figure 2.15. Here the non-age attribute that correlates with chronological age influences only Process *C*, a process that does not bear a causal relationship to the task being investigated. The net effect would be the absence of an age difference in scores on our dependent variable. If our samples are again representative of their underlying populations, we would then infer the absence of an age difference in these populations. Of course, if our task happened to be one that is affected by Process *C*, then the outcome would have been very different. That is, an age difference would have emerged (see Figure 2.15), a difference we would have again erroneously attributed to an ontogenetic age change.

Origins of Confoundings from Non-age Attributes. The very merit of a cross-sectional descriptive study that gives it high external validity often disqualifies it as a means of identifying a true ontogenetic change in behavior. Because the samples selected are representative of their respective populations, the samples show the same disparities, other than chronological age (sex composition, educational level, IQ scores, and so on), as do the populations themselves. For example, years of formal education covary negatively with chronological age over the adult lifespan. This is true for presently existing populations of differential age levels, and it is likely to continue this way for some time to come. For current octogenarians, graduation from grade school was commonly considered sufficient formal education, and few members of this population graduated from high school, much less from college. By contrast, many members of the current population of 20-year-old adults, at least in the United States, are presently attending college; many of those who are not attending college, at least, graduated from high school. Thus, the means for years of formal education are quite disparate between the populations of, say, 20-year-old people and 80-year-old people. The educational levels for the populations intervening between 20 and 80 should fall between these two extremes, and they should show progressive decrements from 20 to 80. This progressive decline in years of formal education with increasing chronological age should be apparent for the representative samples. Consequently, the negative covariation between chronological age and educational opportunity during the intellectual growth years of preadulthood parallels the negative covariation between chronological age and health-dietary conditions during the physical growth years reported in our earlier height study. In both cases, we are dealing with differences among age groups that are attributable to their generational membership.

The systematic variation with age in educational level or, for that matter, any other non-age attribute showing a similar trend is a potentially confounding factor. Much of the progressive decline in a task, such as our prior hypothetical Task X (Figure 2.7), with increasing chronological age could be due to the lower educational levels of the older groups rather than to their greater age per se. If present, the confounding would take the form illustrated in Figure 2.14. At this time, we need to examine the conditions that could make educational level rather than chronological age the true causative factor for age differences on a given task.

To do this, we will refer again to Process A. This time we will identify it as the primary factor, or process, governing performance on our prior Task X. A feasible hypothesis is that the peak level of proficiency for this process (i.e., during early adulthood) is determined by an interaction between a subject's hereditary predisposition for the development of that process and the amount of environmental stimulation the subject receives during infancy, childhood, and adolescence. Thus, the final level of Process A attained in early adulthood reflects the nature of the familiar heredity potential $\times$ enviroment interaction stressed by developmental psychologists. If either of these terms is held constant, then the final proficiency of Process A would gain or lose in accordance with the contribution from the other term. A reasonable assumption is that inheritance as it is related to the development of Process A has differed little, if any, for people born during the past 100 years. Therefore, the average person born, say, in 1910 should differ little in heredity potential for Process A from the average person born, say, in 1950. On the other hand, a person born in 1950 may have more stimulation from educational experiences during the preadulthood period than a person born in 1910. Given equal heredity potential, but differential amounts of environmental stimulation, the conditions are present that would enable the average person born in 1950 to attain a higher peak level of proficiency on Process A than the average person born in 1910.

These conditions and their consequences for Process A (and, therefore, for performance on Task X as well) are summarized in Figure 2.16. Observe that the proficiency of Process A was greater in 1970 for an average 20-year-old subject who was born in 1950 than it was in 1930 for an average 20-year-old subject who was born in 1910. To illustrate the point we wish to make about these two individuals, we need to postulate again the unlikely—but, essential for our purposes,—hypothesis that Process A undergoes no change with increasing chronological age beyond age 20 (i.e., it is insensitive to an age change). Now, suppose our study on Task X took place in 1970. At that time, our average subject born in 1910 was 60 years old and our average subject born

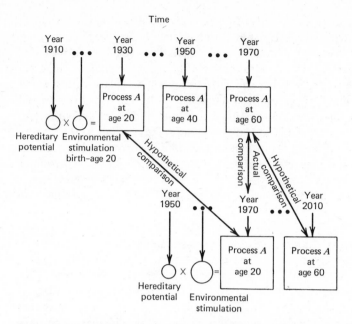

Figure 2.16. Comparisons for proficiency of a hypothetical process (Process *A*) between two average persons—one born in 1910 and the other born in 1950—who are equal in hereditary potential but differ in amount of environmental stimulation.

in 1950 was 20 years old. From Figure 2.16 we see that Process *A* and, therefore, performance on Task X were clearly more proficient for the average 20-year-old subject than for the average 60-year-old subject. Thus, we would have found a clearcut age difference in performance on Task X. However, we would have found the same difference if our 60-year-old subject had been evaluated in 1930 when that subject was only 20 years old. Similarly, we would have found the same difference in performance levels if we waited until 2010 and evaluated the subject born in 1950 at age 60 years. In the former case, we would be comparing two 20-year-old subjects; in the latter case, we would be comparing two 60-year-old subjects—and yet the comparisons would not differ from the comparison yielded in 1970 for two widely differing age levels! Our comparisons between two average persons may be extended to the two groups of people whose average proficiencies on Process *A* our two subjects represent (i.e., groups of 20- and 60-year-old subjects evaluated in 1970). Given these conditions and their consequences, we could easily fall into the trap of falsely concluding that the age difference revealed cross-sectionally in 1970 demonstrates an ontogenetic change from age 20 to age 60. Our study and our conclusion would obviously be void of internal validity.

How serious are potential confoundings of the kind illustrated above? As we have hinted earlier, not at all—provided our interest is purely descriptive. The lack of internal validity does not necessarily mean that a study is devoid of external validity. In fact, there is no reason to suspect that the means of our 20-

and 60-year-old groups depart markedly from the population means extant in 1970. However, when our interest shifts to an explanation of what caused our 1970 age differences in competence on Task X, we do have a serious problem. To resolve this problem, we must disentangle the *potential* confoundings between chronological age and other subject attributes that covary with chronological age. Note our emphasis on the word *potential*. In our prior hypothetical example, we knew for a fact that a non-age attribute both covaried with chronological age *and* affected our critical process. In practice, however, we have no mystical power of knowing a priori that such conditions exist. All we can do is to test empirically for the presence of a confounding factor and then introduce empirical means of controlling for this source of confounding. A brief overview of how psychologists attempt such debuggings will be given in the following section.

Detecting Ontogenetic Change with the Cross-sectional Method. Answers to questions about what causes age differences must be sought at several levels. At the grossest level, the question to be answered is simply whether or not an ontogenetic change underlies the age difference observed for a given behavior, such as performance on Task X. That is, does human aging as a maturational phenomenon cause the increasing performance deficits with increasing chronological age? If the answer to this question is yes, then a second question naturally follows, namely, "What process is altered by the maturational change?" Whatever that process is, it must be one that regulates behavior on the task in question (see Chapter 5). If the answer to our first question, however, is no, then it means that we have identified a behavior that is resistant to ontogenetic decline. For example, if the negative covariation between chronological age and performance on Task X disappears after the confounding effects of education are removed, then variation in educational level would appear to be the causative factor underlying the variation in scores on Task X. The reason for its causative role is likely to be the one we met earlier.

Our present concern is with the research strategies experimental psychologists of aging use to gain answers to the first question asked above. One way of determining if ontogeny plays a causative role in age differences is to modify the cross-sectional methodology as it is ordinarily employed in descriptive research. The modification is designed to disentangle whatever confoundings exist between chronological age and other attributes that happen to covary with age. Our strategy is to discover initially which of these other non-age attributes represent actual sources of confounding and then repeat our study with these sources of confounding controlled or equalized across our various chronological age levels. Not all of the attributes that covary with chronological age function are potentially confounding variables. Consider the by now well-known presence of age differences in height. There is no reason to suspect that height covaries with, say, learning proficiency. Consequently, we would be perfectly justified in ignoring the height variations that are certain to mark most cross-sectional samples in studies dealing with learning proficiency.

On the other hand, consider the case for age-related variations in educational level. Here our intuition tells us to proceed cautiously before dismissing this source of age-related variation. Amount of formal education could well affect the processes underlying our basic learning and memory skills, even for elderly adults years removed from their cherished school days. Our intuition may be abetted by recalling that other investigators have previously demonstrated substantial effects for variation in educational level on other kinds of learning-memory tasks. Knowing that neither our intuition nor our colleagues' contributions are completely trustworthy, we might test the validity of the educational-level/performance-level covariation as it applies specifically to our own Task X. To do this, we determine the magnitude of the correlation coefficient *(r)* between years of formal education and scores on Task X for each of our age groups. If these coefficients are near zero, and are obviously statistically nonsignificant, the education-level/performance-level covariation found for other learning-memory tasks does not seem to generalize to our own Task X. We would then drop the educational variable from further consideration. However, if the coefficients are positive, large, and statistically significant, then it is back to the drawing board because a new study is required—one in which educationally balanced groups (i.e., groups that are comparable in means and standard deviations for years of formal education, but that continue to differ, of course, in their chronological ages) are contrasted on Task X. The contrasts between these new groups give a truer picture of ontogenetic change than our previous contrasts between educationally imbalanced age groups that were, nevertheless, representative of their respective populations.

In actual practice, investigators testing for the presence of age changes on learning, memory, and other cognitive tasks usually short-circuit the trial-and-error procedure outlined above. They take for granted the probable correlation between educational level and task proficiency as it exists within the total population of all adults. Their age groups are, therefore, balanced with respect to this highly important non-age attribute. In addition, the sex composition of age groups is usually carefully balanced with respect to this equally important attribute on the general principle of why be half safe. Women tend to score higher on verbal tasks, men higher on quantitative tasks. Imbalanced age groups (e.g., predominantly men in a young-adult group and predominantly women in an elderly group) could either inflate or deflate age differences attributable to age changes, contingent on the kinds of processes mediating particular tasks. Incidentally, it is the potential correlation between education and learning proficiency that influenced our selection of older subjects in our composite paired-associate/frequency-judgment study. Our objective was to avoid having groups of older subjects that were inferior educationally to our group of young adults. As it turned out, our two older groups were actually superior to our young group. An imbalance in this direction is scarcely as serious as an imbalance in the opposite direction would be. The deficit found in paired-associate learning for our older groups, despite their superior educational backgrounds, argues strongly for a true age change in proficiency of paired-associate learning. Moreover, the absence of an age deficit for our frequency-judgment task (despite the presence of one for our other kind of learning-memory task) argues quite strongly that the memory process mediating this task is truly resistant to an age change. The fact that our subjects were somewhat imbalanced educationally does not really affect this argument. In addition, we should note that our study employed age groups that were carefully balanced with respect to sex composition.

The shift from representative to balanced age groups could have a drastic effect on the nature of the covariation between chronological age and task performance. One possibility is that the covariation may vanish, thus leaving us with the conclusion that performance on that task is immune to a true age change over the adult lifespan. A more likely possibility, however, is that the balanced groups will continue to show age differences in performance but that the nature of these differences departs somewhat from the difference found with more representative groups. That is, the magnitude of the adjusted age differences is likely to be less than the magnitude of the unadjusted age differences. In this case, it is conceivable that some moderate degree of ontogenetic deterioration does take place in the relevant primary process. However, there are two other possibilities as well. One is that the balancing of our age groups was incomplete, that is, the age groups remained unmatched on some yet un-identified non-age attribute that covaries with performance. The assumption here is that the age difference would have disappeared if balancing had been complete. The second is that age differences in a secondary process or factor (e.g., motivation) accounts for the remaining age differences in performance. Briefly, a secondary factor is unrelated to basic competence or ability on the specific task being evaluated. Instead, it influences the extent to which ability is manifested in momentary performance on that task. Performance differences attributable to age differences in a secondary factor could easily be mistaken for performance differences produced by an ontogenetic change in a primary factor. Again, the assumption is that the primary factor has been largely unaffected ontogenetically. If the age groups had been equated on the secondary factor, then the age differences in performance would have been negligible. We will return to a further discussion of secondary factors in Chapter 3.

One issue remains to be resolved. Among the many non-age attributes that exist among people, which ones are capable of being balanced across age groups? As a general rule, balancing is possible only if the distribution of scores on the non-age attribute for the total population of elderly adults overlaps, at least partially, with the distribution of scores on the same attribute for the total population of young adults. As illustrated in Figure 2.17 for years-of-education scores, the mean score for young adults exceeds the mean score for elderly adults. (The disparity in means reflects the fact that well over 50% of today's adults age 25 and over have had at least four years of high school; by contrast, the comparable percentage in 1930 was 20%.) Nevertheless, the overlap between the two distributions assures a sizable proportion of elderly adults from their total population who meet whatever criterion is established for construct-

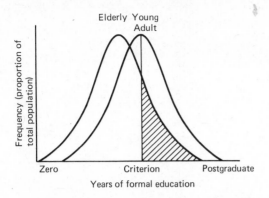

Figure 2.17. Overlapping distributions of years-of-formal-education scores for young-adult and elderly populations. The criterion represents the minimal years of education required for the inclusion of subjects. The cross-hatched area is the proportion of elderly adults qualifying for inclusion in the study.

ing balanced groups with respect to education (e.g., at least two years of high school education). Although the proportion of the elderly population meeting this criterion is less than the proportion of the young-adult population meeting the same criterion (see Figure 2.17), there nevertheless should be an ample supply of elderly people for entry into a particular study.

There are, of course, non-age attributes for which the population distributions of scores show virtually no overlap. In these cases, balancing across age groups is impossible in the sense that few, if any, elderly adults would satisfy any criterion that would in any way be representative of young adults. If the non-age attribute is suspected of correlating substantially with scores on the task being investigated, then there is no alternative to the use of the longitudinal method for a test of an age change in that task's proficiency of performance. Health and dietary conditions present during the growth years seem to be such attributes in testing for an age change in height. We indicated early the appropriateness of the longitudinal method for making this test. As another example, consider hours of watching television violence during childhood. This attribute might be of considerable importance when the possibility of an age change in the propensity toward aggressive behavior following frustration is under investigation. Current young adults are likely to show considerable variability in such television scores. Nevertheless, as illustrated in Figure 2.18, there would be virtually no overlap in these scores with the distribution of scores for current elderly adults, all of whom necessarily score zero hours, in that they had the good fortune of growing up in the pretelevision era. Consequently, balancing young and elderly age groups on this attribute is impossible (assuming that all current young adults have had at least some degree of exposure to television violence while growing up). Once more, only the longitudinal method seems appropriate for testing the presence of a true age change in the behavior of interest.

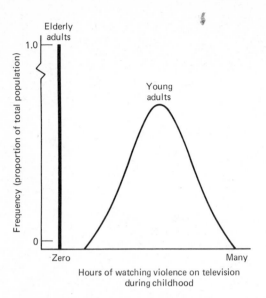

Figure 2.18. Nonoverlapping distributions of years-of-childhood-exposure-to-television-violence scores for young-adult and elderly populations. Balancing age groups for this non-age attribute is made impossible by the absence of any segment of the elderly population overlapping with any segment of the young-adult population.

Illustration of Cross-sectional Ontogenetic Research. At this point, we will drop our hypothetical study with Task X and turn instead to a real study that illustrates dramatically what a shift from representative to balanced age groups might yield. The task involved in this particular study by Green (1969) is performance on the WAIS. An intelligence test, of course, is not an experimental aging task. However, the principles involved in Green's study generalize to all tasks that differentiate between adult-age levels. Here is the rationale for Green's research:

> Wechsler [1958] pointed out that studies of the age-intelligence relationship had shown adult performance reaching a peak in the early 20s and then progressively declining. In answer to an objection that test scores may depend primarily on the acquired and stored knowledge of the individual, Wechsler agreed that evidence indicated that level of education is correlated with performance on intelligence tests. He went on to say that the age and education variables are confounded and that to examine the effect of age alone on adult test performance education must be held relatively constant. Studies of this nature have been lacking. Investigators of the age-intelligence relationship [Birren & Morrison, 1961] to date have given only inadequate consideration to what is undoubtedly a most important variable—this variable is formal education. (Green 1969, pp. 618–619).

Wechsler's standardization of the WAIS (conducted with representative lifespan samples of adults—up to about 65 years of age) revealed a progressive decline in mean scores between the age of 25 and 65 for both the verbal and performance components of the test (with the steepness of the decline being much greater for the performance component). His study is undoubtedly a classic piece of descriptive research, one that provides still useful norms for evaluating intellectual performance by adults of varying chronological ages. The trouble rests in the ease with which Wechsler's results may be taken as evidence for ontogenetic changes in intellectual abilities with increasing chronological age. Wechsler himself fell into this trap by stating ". . .the abilities by which intelligence is measured do in fact decline with age . . . and . . . this decline is systematic and after age 30 more or less linear" (1958, p. 142). The trap is set by the fact that educational level in Wechsler's study met both of the criteria necessary to fulfill its villainous role as a confounding variable. First, Wechsler's representative age groups did differ in their educational levels. For example, 72.8% of the subjects ranging in age from 25 to 34 years had nine or more years of formal education, in contrast to the 55.4% of the subjects ranging in age from 55 to 64 years. Second, for each representative age group, the number of years of formal education correlated positively and significantly with scores on the various subtests of the WAIS [rs ranging from .40 to .66 (Birren & Morrison, 1961)].

Green's research attempted to remove the confounding effects of educational level, thereby offering a truer picture of ontogenetic change in intelligence, at least as measured by the WAIS, than is possible with representative age groups. His effort began by standardizing a Spanish language version of the WAIS with representative adult-age groups residing in Puerto Rico. The results of this descriptive phase of Green's study are shown in the left panel of Figure 2.19. Note that mean scores on the verbal component (expressed in units other than IQ points) remain fairly invariant, or constant, with increasing chronological age until the early 60s, at which point a decline becomes noticeable, whereas mean scores on the performance component show a progressive decline over the entire adult lifespan once its peak is reached early in adulthood. These descriptive results are in general agreement with those of Wechsler's earlier study (1958). Also shown in Figure 2.19 are the progressive decreases in

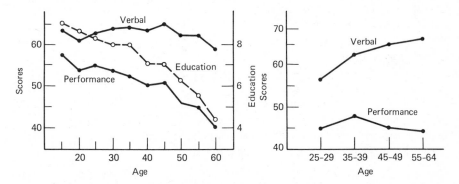

Figure 2.19. Left panel: Age differences in verbal and performance intelligence test scores for representative samples of Puerto Ricans. Also shown are age differences in educational level. Right panel: Age differences in test scores for samples matched, or balanced, in educational level. (Adapted from Green, 1969, Figures 1 and 3.)

mean years of formal education for Green's representative Puerto Rican age groups (the pattern parallels that found for Wechsler's original representative age groups).

In the second phase of Green's research, educationally balanced age groups were constructed by removing some subjects at one educational level and replacing them with other, randomly selected, equal-age subjects at a different educational level. This procedure continued until the age groups were equated educationally in terms of both means and standard deviations. The age contrasts for these newly constructed balanced groups are shown in the right panel of Figure 2.19. Note that verbal scores now show a progressive *increase* with increasing age and that performance scores now show a greatly reduced rate of decline, relative to the rate found with the original representative groups. The increment with age in verbal scores resembles the increment with age in vocabulary scores reported earlier in this chapter. This should not be too surprising in that the vocabulary test used in our own study is actually one of the tests that make up the verbal component of the WAIS. Among the other tests included in the verbal component of the WAIS is one of general information, a skill, like vocabulary, that might be expected to benefit from the increase in experience and knowledge accompanying the increase in chronological age over the adult segment of the lifespan. Conceivably, the trend toward improvement in verbal test scores would be reversed for age increments beyond the oldest level included by Green (see Figure 2.8). At any rate, we will have occasion to consider further age changes in intelligence in later chapters, especially in connection with our examination of sequential designs.

There are several additional observations worth making. These observations pertain not only to Green's study but also to any other study directed at explaining age differences and determining the part played by true age changes. Green's study with balanced age groups would appear to have considerable internal validity in the sense of identifying actual causative factors for age differences in intelligence. In this case, the differences take the form of progressive decrements in both veral and performance test scores as chronological age increases. Green's carefully conducted analysis reveals that variation in educational level is the dominant causative factor for these differences as they appear in verbal scores and that educational level *and* age per se are both causative factors for these differences as they appear in performance scores. High internal validity of any study, in turn, means high generalizability of the causative factors identified in that study, that is, the causative role played by these factors is not restricted to the specific samples studied nor is it restricted to the specific populations sampled in that study. The implication is that it applies to all populations of people that exhibit variation in these causative factors. Phrased in the language of statistics, a causative factor is assumed to represent a main effect rather than an interaction effect. That is, the factor's influence is not dependent on other conditions present so that its effect is manifested only under certain levels of these other conditions. This is especially true when aging qua aging is identified as a causative factor. Returning to Green's study, the principles of internal validity suggest a further interesting generalization, namely, age differences in verbal test scores for representative samples should disappear at some future time when variation in educational level among populations of different ages ceases to exist. Finally, we must observe that Green's study necessarily has poor external validity in that the age differences found for his balanced groups no longer estimate accurately the age differences extant for the entire population of adults living in Puerto Rico. By now we should realize that this is often true for studies with high internal validity—their very nature precludes the possibility of having external validity as well. "You can't have your cake and eat it too" applies as much to psychologists in the field of aging as it does to children suffering culinary conflict.

Implementing Cross-sectional Ontogenetic Research. Our intention in describing the Green study (and some other studies earlier in this chapter) has been to illustrate the potentially risky nature of a cross-sectional study for the detection and analysis of ontogenetic change rather than to condemn educational variation as the ubiquitous evil of aging research. In fact, just as age variation in height is often irrelevant with regard to performance variation on a cognitive task, so, too, is age variation in education with regard to performance variation on other kinds of tasks. It is not unusual to discover that an investigator working in the area of age changes in sensory discrimination does not even bother to report information about the educational backgrounds of the subjects entering the study. Far more important in this case is information pertaining to the current health status of the participants at each age level. For many tasks of a perceptual-motor nature, age variation in educational level is to be equally unlikely as a confounding factor. This may be seen in a study by Botwinick, Robbin, and Brinley (1960). Young-adult subjects (noncollege students; median age, 24.5 years) and elderly subjects (median age, 71 years) performed a sorting task in which selected members of an ordinary deck of playing cards were placed in serially ordered slots (e.g., the four of diamonds in the first slot, the ten of spades in the second slot, and so on). Time to sort the entire deck served as the performance score or dependent variable. As might be expected, there was a large age difference, favoring the young adults, in sorting time. However, education level showed no systematic relationship to performance scores at either age level. On the other hand, health status for elderly subjects does seem to be highly related to sorting time. That is, elderly people with disease are considerably slower than people of a comparable age who are seemingly free of disease (Botwinick & Birren, 1963). Consequently, cross-sectional comparisons of young and elderly adults on a sorting task (or, for that matter, on any other task yielding speed scores) calls for a careful selection of elderly subjects to match the likely healthy status of the young subjects. Our point is simply that ontogenetic changes in performance *can be* distorted by variation in *some* non-age attribute. For some tasks, that attribute may be education level, but, for other tasks, it may well be some other attribute, such as health status.

As observed early in this chapter, the opportunity for distortion by non-age attributes is created largely by the variation in generational membership that necessarily accompanies wide variation in the age levels of potential subject populations. Again, concern with generational variation has led to the emergence of the sequential designs that will be described in Chapter 4. For the time being, we will merely note that thus far these designs have had little direct impact on experimental aging research. Moreover, we will discover in Chapter 4 that there may actually be little need for these designs in many of the component areas of experimental aging psychology. The fact is, most research directed at age changes in behavior conducted by experimental aging psychologists continues to use traditional cross-sectional groups but groups that are appropriately balanced with respect to the major non-age attributes, such as sex, educational level, and current health status. If the non-age attribute used for matching groups is measured on a continuous dimension (e.g., educational level), then the balancing is done by selecting subjects who will insure that the resulting age groups have comparable means for that attribute. This, of course, was the procedure followed to the letter by Green (1969) and approximated by Kausler and Puckett (1980a) in their paired-associate/frequency-judgment study.

Alternatives to the Use of Balanced Age Groups. There are four other procedures for dealing with the potential biases created by non-age attributes in research directed at age changes. Three of these procedures continue to use the basic cross-sectional method. However, they employ representative age groups (e.g., randomly selected subjects) rather than balanced age groups, and they then rely on statistical manipulations to correct for biases from a non-age variable. In one of these procedures, an analysis of covariance is applied to scores on the task in question. Age level remains the independent variable, whereas score on the non-age attribute serves as an adjusting variable that corrects for disparities between the age groups on that attribute. Storandt and Hudson (1975) skillfully analyzed the problems inherent in this covariance procedure and recommended that it be used cautiously, if at all, in explanatory research. In the second cross-sectional procedure, the non-age attribute is treated as being equivalent to an independent variable, and it enters the investigator's overall analysis of variance for scores on the task in question. Storandt and Hudson (1975) pointed out, with reference to educational level as the non-age attribute, that this procedure ". . .generally produces a nonorthogonal design with unequal and disproportionate numbers of persons in the subclasses, since. . . fewer older subjects than young subjects will fall into the higher education" (p. 123). There are statistical means of adjusting the outcome of the analysis of variance to yield a fairly unbiased estimate of the non-age attribute's effect on performance scores (Storandt & Hudson, 1975). The third cross-sectional procedure involves a rather complex correlational and statistical regression analysis, the details of which will not concern us here (Humphreys, 1978; Storandt & Hudson, 1975). None of the three cross-sectional procedures have found wide application in experimental aging research, and the balancing procedure continues to provide the major format for extending the cross-sectional method into explanatory research. The fourth procedure, the traditional longitudinal method, abandons the cross-sectional approach entirely. We will turn to this method in Chapter 3.

This ends our formal coverage of the traditional cross-sectional methodological design. However, we have not finished our discussion of two of the issues raised in this chapter. The first deals with the role played by secondary factors in determining age differences in performance and, perhaps, in confounding the effect of a true age change in a primary factor. The second deals with external validity, specifically the fact that it involves generalizability of results from the laboratory to the real world outside the laboratory, in addition to the generalizability of results from samples to populations. Both issues enter as much into the research conducted by means of the longitudinal method as they do into the research conducted by means of the cross-sectional method. For this reason, we will delay further consideration until after we have examined the basic characteristics of, and the problems associated with, the longitudinal method.

Summary

Adult-age differences in performance are apparent for most of the tasks employed in experimental psychology. These differences are usually in the direction of decrements in performance as chronological age increases over the adult segment of the lifespan. That is, chronological age and performance generally covary negatively beyond early adulthood. However, the age of onset for a performance deficit varies greatly from task to task, as does the rate of decline beyond that onset. Moreover, there are exceptions in which performance maintains a steady state over most of the adult lifespan, and in some instances, performance may even show progressive increments over most of the adult lifespan.

Descriptive aging research attempts to assess mean performance scores at various adult chronological age levels and to test differences among these means for statistical significance. Of particular concern is the course of the age-performance relationship yielded by a particular task, that is, the rate of decreases (or increases) in mean performance scores over increasing age levels. In most descriptive research studies, the assessments are made for groups, or samples, of subjects, with each group representing a population at a specific age level. If the groups are truly representative of the populations from which they were selected, then the differences among these groups approximate the differences in performance that exist among the populations of people at the various age levels sampled in the study. The extent to which the results of a descriptive study generalize to the underlying populations determines, in part, that study's external validity.

In addition to providing estimates of population parameters (i.e., means for populations of various chronological ages and the course of differences among these means as age increases), descriptive research studies may provide norms for interpreting the performance scores of individual subjects. That is, a subject's performance score may be interpreted with respect to the mean and standard deviation for the representative group of subjects of the same age as that subject.

Most descriptive research is conducted by the application of the traditional cross-sectional method. In this method, different groups of subjects, each from a different age level, are evaluated at approximately the same time. The results from a cross-sectional study may have considerable external validity in the sense of indicating the general nature of the age-performance relationship present in total populations of adults, but, at the same time, these results have doubtful internal validity. Internal validity refers to the extent to which a study identifies the true causative factor responsible for observed age differences in performance. On the surface, age differences may appear to be caused by an age change in the primary factor that mediates performance on the task in question. However, representative groups of subjects differing in chronological age are also likely to differ in non-age attributes, such as educational level, that covary with chronological age and also covary with performance on the task in question. Consequently, chrono-logical age and a non-age attribute may vary simultaneously in a pure descriptive aging study. If they do, then the study is likely to be confounded in the sense of our inability to identify which variable (age per se or the non-age attribute) plays the causative role. Thus, the uncertain internal validity of many descriptive aging studies.

Explanatory research attempts to disentangle the confoundings between age and other factors that covary with age. At stake is the question of whether or not aging, as part of the organism's ontogeny (i.e., individual course of development), causes the observed pattern of age differences in task performance. Thus, explanatory research at this level is concerned with the explanation of age differences at the level of gross maturational changes that take place as the organism grows older. Further explication in terms of which specific psychological process is affected by the maturational change requires interaction research in which chronological age as an independent variable is joined by one or more traditional independent variables manipulated directly by the investigator.

The cross-sectional method is often used in modified form for explanatory research at the gross level. Rather than representative groups of subjects, balanced groups are employed at each age level evaluated. That is, the groups are balanced, or matched, with respect to critical non-age attributes known empirically to covary both with age and with performance scores on the task in question. The intent is to make chronological age the only causative factor permitted to vary across the groups employed in the study. If balancing is satisfactory, then whatever age differences occur in performance may be attributed to a true age change in performance. However, some non-age attributes that differ between generations or cohorts (and widely separated age groups necessarily differ in their generational memberships) may continue to resist an effective balancing, partic-ularly between groups of young and elderly adults. In such cases, the longitudinal methodological design offers a viable approach for conducting explanatory research. Another alternative is the use of the sequential designs that have appeared in recent years.

CHAPTER 3

Longitudinal Methodological Designs; Further Issues in Evaluating Age Differences and Changes

Longitudinal Research

Detecting Ontogenetic Change by the Longitudinal Method. Given the problems encountered in conducting impeccable cross-sectional explanatory research, some investigators prefer an alternative methodology for detecting the presence of, and the course of, ontogenetic age changes in performance. The standard alternative for many years has been the longitudinal method. From the brief introduction given in Chapter 2, we know that in a longitudinal study the same individuals are evaluated at least twice (preferably more often than that) in their performance on a particular task. The rationale for this methodological design is that each subject provides his or her perfectly matched counterpart at every contrasted age level. The subject's sex does not change (at least, it did not in the past), nor does educational level (this, too, is rapidly being altered— witness the growing popularity of adult-education programs), ethnic origin, and so on. Moreover, no age differences are possible from subtle cohort effects because all age groups in a given comparison are from the same cohort.

Consider, for example, a study initiated in 1930 with a group of 100 college students whose average age at that time is 20 years. All members of this group perform on our hypothetical Task X. Their mean score is found to be, say, 35. In 1955 we are able to reconvene the entire group for a second administration of Task X when the average age of the group has reached 45 years. Our good luck holds out, and a second reunion of the entire group, with a third administration of Task X, is held in 1980 when the group's average age has reached 70 years. On the second and third administrations of Task X the mean scores were found to be, say, 32 and 25. The age differences clearly apparent in the means

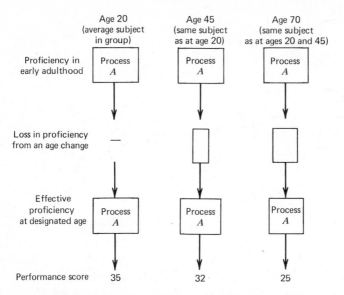

Figure 3.1. Schematic representation of the longitudinal change in process proficiency and the resulting change in performance score from age 20 to age 70 for the same average subject at each age level.

of 35, 32, and 25 seemingly are the result of an adverse ontogenetic change in Process *A*, the process presumed to mediate performance on Task X. Our conclusion is predicated on the reasonable assumptions that optimal proficiency of Process *A* is attained by age 20 and that this optimal proficiency determined the performance scores of our subjects in 1930 when they were young adults. The level of that proficiency for the average young adult in our study is illustrated in Figure 3.1. As indicated in this figure, the loss in proficiency owing to ontogenetic change is, of course, zero at this age level. Moreover, because this same subject serves again at ages 45 and 70, the optimal proficiency at these older age levels remains what it had been at age 20. It is this level of proficiency that would continue to be operative if there were no age change in Process *A*. However, there is indeed an age change in the form of a moderate loss of proficiency by age 45 and a more pronounced loss by age 70. These losses have reduced the net proficiency to the levels shown in Figure 3.1, and they have produced observable age differences in performance for our average subject. The same principle would apply to any one of our 100 subjects. That is, a given subject's proficiency for Process *A* at, say, age 70 is simply the difference between the proficiency of that process at age 20 and the loss in proficiency produced by ontogenetic change in the intervening 50 years. It is this straightforward logic that makes longitudinal assessment of the same individuals, in theory, an ideal means of evaluating the nature and extent of age changes in human behavior.

Problems Inherent in Longitudinal Research: Selective Attrition of Subjects.
Alas, longitudinal studies of the kind described above represent more the fan-

tasies of confounded investigators than they do unconfounded solutions of real-life research problems. To begin with, there is the obvious impracticality of conducting a study that covers a 50-year period. The odds, of course, are against the investigator being around that long and becoming an aging psychologist in both senses of the word. Even if the investigator makes it, his or her patience and enthusiasm for continuing the project would probably disappear long before the subjects themselves reached age 70. These problems may be abated by conducting a less ambitious project. That is, instead of trying to span 50 years, a more modest span of years might be studied. For example, Task X could be administered to a group of 65-year-old subjects and then readministered to the same subjects 5 years later. This would no longer be an adult lifespan study, but it would provide information about a potential age change over an especially critical period of the lifespan. It would, however, still demand considerable patience on the part of the investigator as well as the willingness to delay the gratification that comes from seeing a study completed and published.

Such practical problems represent only a segment of the total problems encountered by users of the longitudinal method in aging research. Far more important problems are those created by an investigator's likely failure to fulfill three basic assumptions that are implicit in the ideal longitudinal study of the kind described above. Violations of these assumptions seriously threaten the internal validity of a typical longitudinal study. Consequently, one of our main concerns at the moment is the consideration of the means of compensating, at least partially, for these violations.

The first assumption is that all members of the original group, that is, the group receiving the first assessment on Task X, serve as subjects on all follow-up evaluations. This was the case in our hypothetical study—all 100 of the original subjects were reassessed at both age 45 and age 70. In truth it is highly unlikely that all of the subjects evaluated initially will be available for even a second performance on Task X, much less for a third or fourth performance. Death will take its toll during the years intervening between evaluations. Moreover, not all of the survivors will be willing to reappear in the laboratory for a later reevaluation of their competence. The attrition rate will increase even more if we require additional reappearances. If death and willingness to continue in the project covary with level of performance on the initial administration of the task, then they would represent potent sources of confounding. For example, poor initial performers on the task may, on the average, die earlier than good initial performers. Similarly, surviving poor initial performers may be more reluctant to be reevaluated than good initial performers. We would then have a higher percentage of good performers represented in the second evaluation than in the first. If an ontogenetic deficit did occur for every subject over the intervening years, then the extent of that deficit would be underestimated by simply contrasting mean scores for the two performance sessions (Baltes, 1968; Baltes & Labouvie, 1973). In theory, it is also possible for the circumstances to be reversed. That is, the eventual dropouts may be subjects who scored higher on the initial evaluation than did the nondropouts. If true,

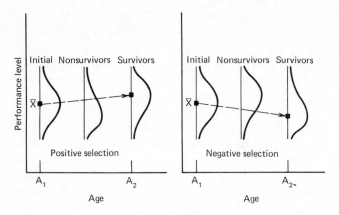

Figure 3.2. The effect of selective attrition and survival of subjects on mean values for performance scores. Left panel: Conditions resulting in overestimating the mean value at the older age level (A_2). Right panel: Conditions resulting in underestimating the mean value at the older age level. (From Baltes & Labouvie, 1973, Figure 4.)

then the amount of ontogenetic deficit would be overestimated by contrasting mean scores for the two sessions. The conditions producing these strikingly different outcomes have been summarized by Baltes and Labouvie (1973) and are reproduced in Figure 3.2.

Further understanding of the potential confounding that results from subject attrition may be gained by reconsidering our original longitudinal study with Task X in the light of the biases produced by subject attrition. We will continue to assume that an ontogenetic change reduces performance level by 10 points from age 20 to age 70 and that every individual suffers the same loss, regardless of that individual's initial score on Task X at age 20. Thus, subjects scoring 40, 35, and 30 on the initial administration of our task in 1930 are expected to score 30, 25, and 20 respectively in 1980—provided ontogenetic change is the only factor that reduces task proficiency below the optimal level manifested in young adulthood. Suppose further that only half of our original 100 subjects both survive and agree to be reevaluated in 1980 at age 70. To take one extreme case, suppose all 50 of the nondropouts scored above average at age 20, whereas all 50 of the dropouts scored below average at age 20. As a reasonable approximation, we will estimate the mean score of the nondropouts on Task X to have been 40 at age 20 and the corresponding mean of the dropouts to have been 30 (remember the mean for all 100 subjects at age 20 was 35). Given the 10 point loss owing to ontogenetic change over the intervening years, our nondropouts should have a mean score of 30 at age 70. Thus, the age change in performance on Task X is underestimated when this mean is compared with the mean of 35 recorded in 1930 for all 100 subjects when they were 20 years of age. That is, the performance deficit is estimated to be 5 points rather than the 10 points actually occurring ontogenetically. The reason for this underestimation is illustrated in Figure 3.3. Note that the average optimal proficiency attained by our nondropouts in young adulthood exceeds the aver-

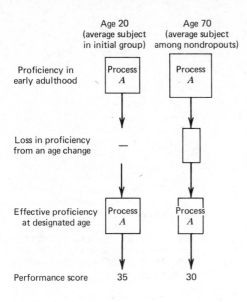

Age 20
(average subject
in initial group)

Age 70
(average subject
among nondropouts)

Proficiency in
early adulthood

Process
A

Process
A

Loss in proficiency
from an age change

Effective proficiency
at designated age

Process
A

Process
A

Performance score   35   30

Figure 3.3. Schematic representation of the longitudinal change in process proficiency and the resulting change in performance scores from age 20 to age 70 when the average subject at age 70 was initially superior to the average subject at age 20 (owing to positive selective attrition). Note that the degree of process change is underestimated relative to the change illustrated in Figure 3.1 under the condition of no subject attrition.

age optimal proficiency attained by our entire group of initially tested subjects. Consequently, even with an ontogenetic deficit, Process A's level of proficiency remains at a level well above the level that would have been found if all 100 of the original subjects had been reevaluated at age 70 (contrast with Figure 3.1).

To take the opposite extreme case, suppose we reverse who are the nondropouts and who are the dropouts. This time the nondropouts are those who score below the mean at age 20, whereas the dropouts are those who score above the mean. Consequently, the mean performance score at age 70 for those subjects who are retested should be 20 (30 − 10—their mean score at age 20—less the loss because of ontogenetic change). Now, the age change in performance on Task X is overestimated when the mean score for the nondropouts is compared with the mean of 35 for all 100 subjects at age 20. In other words, the loss is estimated to be 15 points rather than the 10 points actually occurring ontogenetically. The reason for this overestimation is illustrated in Figure 3.4. Note that the average optimal proficiency of Process A attained in young adulthood by our nondropouts is well below the average optimal proficiency attained by our entire group of initially tested subjects. The reduction in Process A's proficiency produced by ontogenetic change results in an effective level of proficiency that is well below the level that would have been found if all 100 of the original subjects had been reevaluated at age 70 (again contrast with Figure 3.1).

The solution to the attrition problem that is preferred by most investigators is a simple one, namely, restricting analyses to the scores earned throughout the study by the nondropouts. In effect, the end of the study determines the nature of the beginning. Those subjects remaining at the end of the study—who have, therefore, been evaluated at every age level included in the study—com-

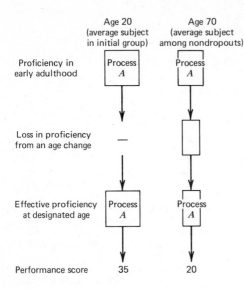

Figure 3.4. Schematic representation of the longitudinal change in process proficiency and the resulting change in performance scores from age 20 to age 70 when the average subject at age 70 was initially inferior to the average subject at age 20 (owing to negative selective attrition). Note that the degree of process change is overestimated relative to the change illustrated in Figure 3.1 under the condition of no subject attrition.

pose the only group of subjects for whom a mean score is determined at *each* age level. Ontogenetic change on the task in question is then defined in terms of the differences among the age-level means found only for this segment of the much larger group tested at the beginning of the study.

Illustrations of Interpretative Problems. To demonstrate the interpretative problems arising in this solution, we will rely on a famous longitudinal study by Owens (1966). Appropriately, our description of this study begins with its ending, namely, the testing of 96 men in 1961 when their mean age was 61 years. The test they received was the Army Alpha, a popular group test of intelligence. The subjects were the nondropouts following an earlier assessment in 1950 on the same test when the subjects averaged 50 years of age. At that time, 127 men were actually tested, 31 of whom became dropouts by 1961 (13 by death, 5 by physical disabilities, 5 by the fact they could not be located, and 8 by their stubborn refusal to continue participation). But 1950 was only an intermediate point in the full scope of Owen's study. The study actually began in 1919 with the testing of 363 freshmen male students at Iowa State University (average age 19 years) on the Army Alpha test. Thus, from 1919 to 1961, 267 out of the original 363 subjects, or 74%, became dropouts. Age changes in intelligence, at least as measured by performance on the Army Alpha test, were analyzed for the 96 hardy survivors of all three assessments (1919, 1950, and 1961). In this analysis, four scores were determined for each subject, the first being an overall, or total, score for all eight subtests of the Army Alpha (e.g, arithmetic, analogies, and synonyms-antonyms). The remaining scores were based on groupings of the subtests into factor components, specifically those of verbal, reasoning, and numerical abilities. Mean scores earned by the critical 96 subjects at each assessment are plotted in Figure 3.5. The values shown are in standard score form, that is, they are expressed relative to the mean scored by subjects in the original standardization on the Army Alpha test (the mean score here is set at a value of 5 with an SD of 1, instead of a mean of 50 and SD of 10 or a mean of 500 and SD of 100 as described in Chapter 2). Thus, the mean total score of 5.7 earned by the 96 subjects at age 19 indicates that they averaged 0.7 SD above the mean of the standardization sample.

How much faith can we place in what this longitudinal analysis of age differences in intelligence tells us about true age changes in intelligence? In its favor is the rather high degree of agreement with the basic results obtained cross-sectionally by Green (1969) that were described in Chapter 2. As in Green's study, some components of intelligence (here both verbal ability and reasoning ability) were found to increase with advancing age, whereas another component (here numerical ability) was found to decrease with increasing age. Nevertheless, there are good reasons for questioning what Owen's longitudinal analysis reveals about the nature of true age change in intelligence.

To begin with, we have to consider the consequences of the possible selective attrition of subjects created by Owen's procedure. How selective was this attrition? Some hint is provided by Owen's own analysis. For example, of the 201 potential subjects who could be located in 1950, 63 were classified as being noncooperating and 138 as being cooperating (of these, 127 were successfully retested in 1950 and 96 in both 1950 and 1961). The mean total score earned in 1919 by the noncooperating men was 5.20, as compared to the mean score of 5.63 earned by the cooperating men (a statistically significant difference). Note further that the mean score in 1919 for the end group of 96 men, who survived additional attrition, was even greater (5.7; see Figure 3.5). Clearly, selective attrition occurred in this study—in the direction shown in the left panel of Figure 3.2 and through the general principle illustrated in Figure 3.3. The 96 "real" subjects of this study were generally the superior members of the large (363) group of potential subjects tested initially as young adults. As a general rule, the selection bias introduced into a longitudinal study is likely to be

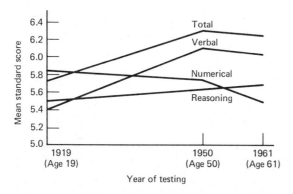

Figure 3.5. Longitudinally assessed intelligence test scores (Army Alpha) for a group of college students evaluated initially in 1919 and again in 1950 and 1961. Mean standard scores are shown separately for verbal, numerical, and reasoning components as well as for total scores. (Adapted from Owens, 1966, Figure 1.)

positive whenever the task being evaluated is a fairly demanding one. Many of the familiar tasks of experimental psychology are likely to join the intelligence test task in this category.

The consequences of the positive selection process are dramatically portrayed in a later study by Siegler and Botwinick (1979). Included in their study were 130 subjects who were tested on the Wechsler Adult Intelligence Scale (WAIS) for the first time when they were 65 to 74 years of age. Each subject had the opportunity to be retested 10 additional times over the next 10 or so years. Only 8 of these subjects, identified here as the 11 group, participated in all 11 testing sessions. Additional groups were identified on the basis of the number of successive tests for which they were participants. Thus, the 1 group consisted of those subjects who received only the first administration of the WAIS and then dropped out of the study, the 2 group consisted of those who received only the first two administrations and then dropped out, and so on, through the 11 group. Of interest are the mean scores earned on the first administration of the WAIS by these various groups (plotted in Figure 3.6 for full-scale scores). Note that the selection process operated positively and progressively in terms of its magnitude. Stated somewhat differently, the earlier subjects drop out of a longitudinal study the lower their scores are likely to have been at the start of the study, at least when the task itself is a demanding one. Again, the result is an end group that is clearly superior in its initial ability level. If the Siegler and Botwinick (1979) study were to be examined for age differences in intelligence in the manner employed by Owens, then the end group would be what we earlier identified as the 11 group.

Effects of Subject Attrition on Internal and External Validity. We now need to consider the challenges confronting both the internal validity and the external validity of a longitudinal study whenever a positive selection bias occurs. Concerning internal validity, the challenge rests in the degree to which the age-

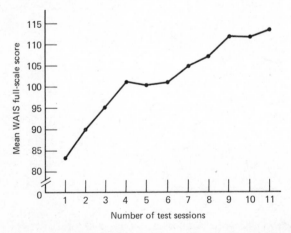

Figure 3.6. Mean WAIS scores—at the time of initial assessment—shown as a function of the number of subsequent longitudinal assessments (sessions) in which subjects (elderly adults) participated. (Adapted from Siegler & Botwinick, 1979, Figure 1.)

performance relationship demonstrated in a particular study (e.g., that found for reasoning in Owen's study) represents a true ontogenetic change. If we could be assured that the study is otherwise free of confounding, then we would have no reason to doubt that the relationship found in the study charts an ontogenetic change in performance, but only for individuals who are superior in ability on that task. Unfortunately, sources of potential confounding exist even in well-executed studies, like that of Owens (1966), as we will see shortly. These sources force us to question seriously how much of the age differences revealed longitudinally actually resulted from a true age change, even when our analysis is restricted to only the end group of subjects.

Even if these sources of confounding could be eliminated, there remains the challenge to a longitudinal study's external validity posed by the positive selection bias. Are we able to generalize the age differences manifested longitudinally on a given task by superior individuals to individuals of average and below ability? For example, would the slight gain in reasoning scores from age 19 to age 61 (Figure 3.5) also be found for individuals who scored well below 5 (i.e., the mean of the standardization sample) at age 19? Here, we find no ready answer. Moreover, the research bearing on the very important underlying issue is both sparse and conflicting. The issue is that of the interaction between level of ability as a young adult on a given task and the rate of change in performance on that task with increasing age beyond early adulthood. The absence of an interaction would indicate that the rate of change is independent of initial ability level. An interaction, in turn, could mean that the rate of change in performance for superior individuals is greater or less than the rate of change for less superior individuals.

The limited evidence that is available is what has been gathered in studies on intelligence. Owens (1959) examined the interaction between initial ability level and rate of change in performance in his own longitudinal study and found none. The implication is that the age-performance relationships present in his study apply to a much broader population of subjects than those of superior ability. However, it seems likely that even his less superior subjects were actually relatively superior to the average young adults of 1919 by virtue of being college students in the first place.

In fairness to Owens, we should note that other investigators have also found an absence of an interaction between initial ability level and rate of decline in intelligence test scores (Birren & Morrison, 1961; Eichorn 1973; Eisdorfer, 1962; Troll, Saltz, & Dunin-Markiewicz, 1976). However, still other investigators have reported the presence of an interaction. This was the case, for example, in Siegler and Botwinick's study. Representative of the outcome of their analysis are the results shown in Figure 3.7 for the subjects in their 3 group and in their 11 group. Progressive decrements in the mean score may be seen for subjects of initially lower ability (i.e., members of the 3 group) from age 68 (first testing) to age 72 (second testing) to age 76 (third testing). The pattern of age change was somewhat different, however, for subjects of initially higher ability (i.e., members of the 11 group). The decrement from age 68 to 72 was even more precipitous than it was for subjects of lower initial ability, but,

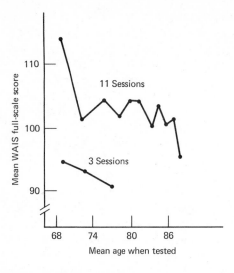

Figure 3.7. Longitudinal changes in mean WAIS scores for elderly subjects participating in either 11 or 3 longitudinal testing sessions (see Figures 3.6). (Adapted from Siegler & Botwinick, 1979, Figure 2.)

beyond that age, performance remained fairly stable, at least until the subjects reached their late 80s. To complete this puzzling area of investigation, Baltes, Nesselroade, Schaie, and Labouvie (1972) also found a decline in test scores for their initially superior subjects, but, if anything, their initially less superior subjects showed increments in test scores with increasing age. A different kind of interaction was found by Bayley and Oden (1955), Blum and Jarvik (1974), Raven (1948), and Riegel, Riegel, and Meyer (1967). In each case, declines in test scores with increasing age were found for both superior and less superior individuals, as defined by initial test score, but the rate of decline was less for the initially superior individuals. Conceivably, some intellectual abilities show one form of differential decline, whereas other abilities show a different form. This possibility is suggested by the results obtained by Foulds and Raven (1948) and Riegel and Riegel (1972). For an ability measuring fluid intelligence, the rate of decline in both studies was less for the initially superior individuals; however, for an ability measuring crystallized intelligence (see Chapter 11), the rate of decline was actually greater for the initially superior individuals in Riegel and Riegel's study (1972), whereas a decline was found only for the initially inferior subjects in Foulds and Raven's study (1948).

The ability level/rate-of-change issue deserves more attention that it has received thus far. Especially needed are longitudinal studies that compare age changes in performance at different levels of initial ability on tasks carried over from traditional experimental psychology. For example, are individuals with superior memory proficiency during early adulthood likely to experience less change in proficiency with increasing age than individuals with average or below-average memory proficiency during early adulthood? Unfortunately, there are a number of methodological problems that make the initial ability level/rate-of-change area of investigation a difficult one in which to work (see Baltes et al., 1972).

Problems Inherent in Longitudinal Research: Progressive Error. The second implicit assumption in the ideal longitudinal study is that a subject's second (and third, fourth, and so on) performance on a given task is unaffected by having performed on that task before. We may believe (as we did in the hypothetical ideal study described early in this chapter) that an age change is the only force operating to produce age differences in performance when, in actuality, another force, commonly called *progressive error* by experimental psychologists, may play an equally important role. Progressive error is basically a confounding that results from the repeated use of the same subjects on the same task. In most basic research studies with young-adult subjects, the repetitions are usually separated by fairly short intervals, thus, making the potential confounding by progressive error a major obstacle to avoid. However, the interval need not be brief nor do the subjects need to be young adults. For example, we will consider the implications of progressive error for a longitudinal study of paired-associate learning in which the subjects are evaluated for the first time when they are 65 years of age and then reevaluated 5 years later.

At the beginning of our study, all of our subjects would learn a paired-associate list, and they would be evaluated for their proficiency in mastering the list. We would then need to have the same subjects learn another list 5 years later when they are all 70 (to simplify matters, we will assume that no attrition occurs over the interval) and again are scored for their learning proficiency. What kind of list should these subjects receive on the second evaluation? One possibility is to give them the same list they had learned 5 years earlier. In doing this, we are really studying relearning rather than learning per se in the second session. That is, there may be some degree of retention of the list's content by our subjects, even after the hiatus of 5 years. The amount retained may, in fact, be sufficient to assure a savings for many subjects relative to the number of errors they made in learning that list for the first time 5 years earlier. The overall effect would be to underestimate the extent of the dificit in learning produced by whatever age change occurs from age 65 to age 70.

In lieu of relearning the same list, we could use alternate forms of the list that differ in specific item content but appear to be equal in difficulty, as determined by extensive pretesting of the lists with other groups of subjects. This presents no particular problem, given the existence of the many English words that could function as components of a paired-associate list. Of course, half of our subjects would receive Form I of our list age at 65 and Form II at age 70, whereas the other half would have the order reversed, with subjects being assigned randomly to the two different order conditions. This counterbalancing of forms over the temporal sequence should suffice to eliminate any remaining possibility that our estimate of an age change is confounded by the list content at one age level being more difficult that the list content learned at the other age level. Nevertheless, even with alternate forms, we are almost certain to have some degree of progressive error remaining. The error in this case comes from what psychologists call general, or nonspecific, transfer (see Chapter 8). For our present purposes, our only concern is with the fact that this

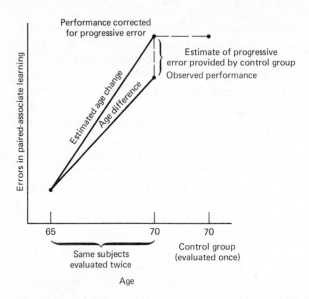

Figure 3.8. The effect of progressive error on evaluating an age change in proficiency in paired-associate learning with the longitudinal method. The age difference from age 65 to age 70 is corrected for the presence of progressive error by the use of a separate control group (age 70), thus yielding an estimated true age change in learning proficiency.

source of progressive error would also produce an underestimation of the true age change (assuming that the change is downward in learning proficiency) in proficiency in paired-associate learning from age 65 to age 70, as is indicated in Figure 3.8.

An effective way of determining the extent of progressive error is to run an additional 70-year-old group that is comparable in non-age attributes (and, of course, comes from the same generation) to the 70-year-old group being tested for a second time. This additional group receives a paired-associate list for the first time when the members are all 70 years old (half of the group would receive Form I of our list, whereas the other half would receive Form II). The difference between this control group's performance and the longitudinal group's performance at age 70 estimates the amount of progressive error in our main study (Baltes, 1968) (which is graphically demonstrated in Figure 3.8). Incidentally, if we examine further the contrast between the original group at age 65 and the control group at age 70, then we are employing an intracohort cross-sectional design, one we will encounter a bit later in this chapter in the context of a specific study.

Although our emphasis has been on progressive error as it enters into longitudinal studies of performance on learning tasks, there is no reason to believe that other kinds of tasks, including those involved in intelligence testing, are exempt from the effects of progressive error. Unlike paired-associate lists, alternate forms of intelligence tests that are equal in difficulty are rarely available for use with adult subjects in longitudinal studies. Retention of some item content is a distinct possibility, although its contribution to the confounding of age changes in performance is likely to be slight when a lengthy interval separates the test sessions. A more important source of progressive error rests in the general familiarity with the type of material that is gained by subjects during their first exposure to the test. This familiarity is almost certain to lead to increased test sophistication and an improvement in performance scores on subsequent administrations. This form of progressive error is much like that occurring through nonspecific transfer in the longitudinal research of paired-associate learning and it would be present even if different forms of an intelligence test (i.e., forms varying in the specifics of their item contents) were used in successive administrations. At any rate, it is impossible to tell how much effect progressive error had on the age-performance relationships demonstrated in either Owen's (1966) study or Siegler and Botwinick's study (1979). Neither study included the basic control necessary to estimate the distortion produced by progressive error. To make this estimate, for example, in Owen's study, a group comparable to his end group (i.e., a mean age of 61, all men, all equal in educational level, general health, and so on) would have had to be evaluated for the first time on the Army Alpha Test in 1961.

Problems Inherent in Longitudinal Research: Time-of-Measurement Effects. The third implicit assumption in the ideal longitudinal study is that the age change it purports to demonstrate is free of confounding from *time-of-measurement effects*. These effects are associated with the temporal separation of repeated measurements on the same subjects (Schaie, 1965). Most longitudinal studies require at least two widely separated evaluations on the same task, say at Time 1 for the first evaluation (e.g., in 1919) and Time 2 for the second evaluation (e.g., in 1950). This temporal separation permits the operation of at least three independent sources of potential confounding.

First, the experimental, or laboratory, environment (or the testing environment in psychometric studies) could be quite different at Time 2 than at Time 1. Examples might include a different data collector at Time 2 than at Time 1, different laboratory equipment at Time 2 than at Time 1, and so on. Overall, environmental alterations could produce either a positive or a negative performance change from Time 1 to Time 2, contingent on the weighting of the separate positive and negative changes that affect performance on the task in question. Some conditions present at Time 2, but not at Time 1, may facilitate performance scores relative to scores made earlier, whereas other such conditions may lower scores, quite independently of the age levels of the subjects at Times 1 and 2. Whatever the origin and the direction of these environmentally linked performance changes, their presence would serve to distort the nature of the true age change, defined in terms of the primary factor underlying performance on the particular task. The avoidance of confoundings by environmental shifts can be assured only to the extent that the environmental context of a study is kept constant from Time 1 to Time 2. Fortunately, major confoundings can often be avoided by an investigator who is well aware of the interpretative advantage gained by maintaining a constant environmental context and, therefore, makes every effort to duplicate at Time 2 the laboratory conditions extant at Time 1. Interestingly, environmental confoundings of this kind are unlikely to be a problem in cross-sectional research. The subjects at each age level are evaluated at approximately the same time and, therefore, with the same data collector, equipment, and so on.

There are occasions, however, when control over the laboratory context from Time 1 to Time 2 may be impossible to achieve. A cautious interpretation of whatever age-performance relationship was found in that study is certainly required. This is the case for a study by Botwinick and Birren (1965), a study that actually was a follow-up of the cross-sectional study on speed of card sorting that was described briefly in Chapter 2. Of the original 27 elderly subjects, 17 were reevaluated on speed of sorting approximately 5 years later. They averaged about 70 and 75 years of age at Time 1 and Time 2 respectively. The 17 end-group members were selected both on the basis of their good health status and their willingness to participate in the second session. Although the age span covered by this study is relatively short, it does represent a segment of the adult lifespan in which ontogenetic deterioration on many kinds of tasks may become especially apparent. The results for these subjects at both times of measurement are plotted in Figure 3.9 as mean sorting-time scores for each of four trials received in experimental session. Overall, performance averaged 8.65 seconds slower at Time 2 that at Time 1. The large amount of slowing down occurring over the critical 5-year span may best be appreciated by the fact that the cross-sectional difference in speed of sorting at Time 1 between these same elderly subjects and the young-adult subjects (average age, 24.5 years) was only 28.47 seconds. Thus, on the surface, it would appear that the ontogenetic change in performance over the critical 5-year span was nearly one third of what it was over the prior 45 years (as estimated cross-sectionally, of course). However, it is difficult to interpret these comparisons unambiguously. As noted by the authors, "The absolute values of the changes in performance times may

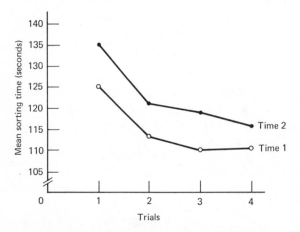

Figure 3.9. Mean sorting times for elderly subjects tested at age 70 (Time 1) and again at age 75 (Time 2). (Adapted from Botwinick & Birren, 1965, Table 1.)

be subject to error because of the differences in the conditions of measurement between initial and follow-up testing" (Botwinick & Birren, 1965, p. 209). These differences included different administrators of the task, different additional tasks that were given along with the card-sorting task, and so on. Botwinick and Birren concluded that ". . . it is possible that the experimental context of the two testing periods was so different that the difference in sorting time was more reflection of this fact than the aging of the Ss" (p. 209). Although it is highly unlikely to be true for an age difference of the magnitude reported by these investigators, it is, nevertheless, true in principle that *all* of that age difference could have been due to the change in laboratory environment. We have ignored the probable presence of progressive error in this study (no control group of 75-year-old-subjects tested for the first time on card sorting at Time 2 was included to provide an estimate of its magnitude). Of course, progressive error simply would have produced an underestimation of the true age change in performance.

Second, changes in the external environment are defined, by some psychologists, more broadly to include changes in the setting outside of the laboratory per se. Here the shifts from Time 1 to Time 2 are those of considerable interest to aging psychologists working from the dialectical perspective. The shifts are those that involve a nation's economy, moral climate, political atmosphere, and so on. Maintaining an invariant environment, as defined in this broader sense, is, of course, beyond the capability of any investigator. Consequently, environmental shifts of this nature have to be tolerated by an experimental aging psychologist. Fortunately, they should become a source of confounding only if they produce significant changes in subjects' attitudes or motivation, which, in turn, influence performance on any given laboratory task. For example, stressful international conditions at Time 2 relative to Time 1 could affect subjects to the point where even their performance on simple laboratory tasks suffer. Because Time 2 coincides with an older age level than Time 1, the adverse effect on performance may lead to an overestimation of the extent of a true age change in performance. Conversely, suppose the unfavorable environmental condition coincides with the onset of a longitudinal study (i.e., with Time 1) when the subjects are young adults. In this case, more favorable performance conditions are likely to exist at Time 2, thereby coinciding with an older age level of the same subjects. Here, the effect could be an underestimation of the extent of a true age change in performance. In these cases, we are clearly dealing with the potential confounding of an age change in the primary factor governing a task by an age difference in a secondary performance factor. Thus, variation in environmental conditions represent one way in which age variation in a secondary performance factor may originate, a way that is unique to studies employing the longitudinal method. A more detailed analysis of secondary performance factors will follow later in this chapter.

The third potential source of confounding through time-of-measurement effects is through what is called a cultural change during the interval between

Times 1 and 2 (Cunningham & Birren, 1976; Owens, 1966). Basically, this source of confounding, like the previous two sources, operates by altering secondary performance factors in a way that may mask the extent of the age change in performance attributable solely to an ontogenetic change in a primary factor. The argument is that individuals may gain experiences during the Time 1/Time 2 interval that increases their sophistication in performing on the task administered at both evaluation sessions. This argument enters into a component of Owen's study (1966) that we have not touched on before. Owens was well aware of the fact that adults of all ages living in 1919 were unfamiliar with intelligence tests in general and with subtests involving analogies in particular. By contrast, adults of all ages living in 1961 had become considerably familiar with intelligence tests and their various components through college psychology courses, popular magazines, and even by taking facsimiles of those tests in the Sunday newspaper supplements. To demonstrate his point, Owens included an additional group in his study, namely, a randomly selected group of male freshmen at Iowa State University that was tested for the first time on the Army Alpha Test in 1961. These freshmen scored higher on the test than did the freshmen evaluated in 1919 (an example of what is called a time-lag comparison). The gain through cultural change (i.e., mean for 1961 freshmen minus the mean for 1919 freshmen) was especially pronounced for the reasoning factor, owing primarily to the large gain in scores on the analogies-subtest-component of that factor. Owens assumed that this gain entered into the scores earned by his critical group of 61-year-old men evaluated for the third time in 1961. To provide what he considered to be a more accurate estimate of the true age change in these scores, Owens subtracted the gain constant identified above from the mean score obtained by his older subjects, thus yielding a value adjusted for cultural change. The net effect, as shown in Figure 3.10, is a revised

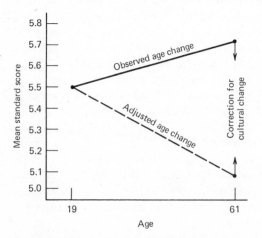

Figure 3.10. Longitudinally assessed age changes in reasoning scores (Army Alpha test) as adjusted for cultural change during the intertest interval (compare with Figure 3.5). (Adapted from data in Owens, 1966.)

description of the age-performance relationship from age 19 through age 61 as it involves the reasoning factor of the Army Alpha test. It may be seen that the revision indicates a performance decrement with increasing age rather that a slight increment, as is the case when cultural change is left uncorrected.

The concept of a cultural change makes sense in interpreting longitudinal studies examining adult-age differences in performance scores on intelligence tests. We cannot ignore the fact that intelligence tests were virtually unheard of when current elderly people were young adults, nor can we ignore the fact that intelligence tests have become widely publicized over the past 40 or so years. However, we also cannot ignore the fact that a cultural change could also be considered as contributing to a cohort effect rather than a time-of-measurement effect. In this view, an adjustment of the mean scores earned by elderly subjects would not be appropriate. This point is especially relevent to the application of sequential designs to the study of adult-age differences, and, accordingly, it will be discussed in detail in Chapter 4. We will also discuss at that time the implications of cultural changes for interpreting adult-age differences in performance on the standard laboratory tasks of experimental psychology.

Longitudinal Explanatory Research: A Summing Up. The lesson learned in our critical examination of the longitudinal method should be obvious. The method offers no panacea for the ills of explanatory aging research. Our examples illustrating the problems associated with the method have focused largely on research dealing with age changes in intelligence. This was forced on us by the paucity of longitudinal studies on learning tasks, memory tasks, and so on. (There are several important longitudinal studies in areas of experimental aging research that we have reserved for discussion in the next section.) Nevertheless, the problems inherent in the longitudinal method are largely free of content prejudice—they apply indiscriminantly to virtually all tasks.

Outlawing cross-sectional research and permitting investigators to employ nothing but longitudinal research for all aspects of the psychology of aging would simply mean substituting one set of methodological problems for another. The difficulty confronting both traditional methods is the fact that we cannot directly measure ontogenetic change in a primary factor. With both methods, we can only infer the existence and the extent of ontogenetic change from an observed change in performance scores over increasing age levels. We, therefore, run the risk, regardless of the method used, of inferring specific characteristics of an ontogenetic change that do not reflect the true nature of that change. That is, an observed performance change with increasing age could be the consequence of one or more factors other than ontogenetic change in a primary factor per se (or in addition to an ontogenetic change in that factor). This risk does not disappear when the longitudinal method replaces the cross-sectional method. However, the existence of its unique problems does not require abandoning the longitudinal method any more than the existence of a different set of problems requires abandoning the cross-sectional method. Instead, the longitudinal researcher needs to face these problems realistically, resolve them as adequately as possible, and then interpret the study's outcome cautiously in the light of those problems that remain unresolved. We are in basic agreement with the conclusion arrived at by Botwinick and Birren:

> Actually, to determine when in the life span functions change rapidly or are maintained, both cross-sectional and longitudinal studies of Ss of more than two age groups are needed. Both types of studies help determine the relative contribution of the immediate testing conditions and the more long-term effects of cultural and physiological changes to the age differences observed in the investigation. (1965, p. 210)

We should note that especially bothersome to some critics of the longitudinal method is the potential confounding by time-of-measurement effects (e.g., Schaie, 1965). It is this concern, combined with the concern for cohort effects that persist in cross-sectional research, that has stimulated the development of the sequential methodological designs that will be examined in the next chapter.

Application to Parametric Descriptive Research. Although longitudinal research ordinarily concentrates on age changes in behavior, the longitudinal method itself could, in principle, be adapted for use in parametric descriptive research. As with cross-sectional parametric research, the objective would be to assess parametric means (and variances) at different age levels or age ranges (concomitantly to establish norms for each level or range evaluated) and to determine the true course of performance changes with increasing age as it occurs in the entire population of adults (regardless of the reason for these changes in performance—whether ontogenetic or nonontogenetic in origin). At stake, therefore, is the external validity of a longitudinal study, that is, how accurately can an age difference found in such a study be generalized to populations of adults of varying ages.

Basically, the problems described earlier that challenge a longitudinal study's internal validity may also challenge that study's external validity. The sample selected initially for longitudinal follow-up may indeed be representative of the population for that initially selected age level, thus assuring a high degree of external validity for the youngest age level being evaluated. However, selective attrition of subjects from Time 1 to Time 2 and beyond is almost certain to mean that the sample available for the second, and all other later assessments, is no longer representative of the population for that now older age level. Interestingly, dropping out by dying would probably not present a problem. Because our initial sample of young adult was representative of the underlying population of young adults, there is no reason to suspect that the causes of dying differ in our sample from the causes found in the entire population as its members grow older. The problem, instead, rests squarely in those members of the original sample who do survive. From our earlier discussion, we surely realize by now that volunteers (i.e., nondropouts) for further evaluation may no longer possess performance skills that are representative of the age levels they represent. Similarly, progressive error, if present, means that the subjects who are available at later sessions exhibit distortions in performance that would not occur for a representative sample of that same age whose members are tested for the first time. Finally, the possibility of time-of-measurement effects must be considered, especially in terms of possible cultural changes. The possibility of such changes raises an issue concerning another aspect of external validity, namely, the generalizability of adult-age differences found longitudinally in one historical time period to the adult-age differences that would be found in a different historical time period. For example, would the increase in reasoning scores found on the Army Alpha test for adults growing older in the period from 1919 to 1961 generalize to adults growing older in, say, the period from 1961 to 2003? Not if we accept Owen's (1966) interpretation of his own results. The latter individuals would not experience the cultural change relevant to intelligence test performance experienced by the former individuals. Consequently, the decrement in their scores from 1961 to 2003 owing to an age change would not be compensated by a gain owing to cultural change.

Thus, the same precautions needed in interpreting the internal validity of a longitudinal study with respect to identifying age changes in a primary factor as the cause of age differences in task performance are needed in interpreting that study's external validity with respect to generalizability to populations and to other historical time periods. We should note that generalizability is further limited in a traditional longitudinal study by the use of subjects from a single cohort. For example, an investigator may determine mean digit-span scores for a group of 40-year-old people born in 1920. Ten years later, the investigator may reassess the same subjects at age 50. The extent of the age deficit found, whether that deficit results from ontogenetic change in a primary factor or a change in some secondary factor, need not be characteristic of members of other cohorts. Thus, a comparable evaluation of subjects from the 1930 cohort may reveal more or less of a deficit than the one found with subjects from the 1920 cohort. We are implying, of course, that digit span may be susceptible to a cohort effect (we will discover in Chapter 4 that it probably is not). That possibility necessarily restricts the external validity of the longitudinal study in the sense that its results cannot be generalized beyond the single generation included in that study. Generalizing the results of a longitudinal study to multiple generations requires the inclusion of more than one cohort in the design of that study. This design would then be sequential in nature (specifically, a cohort-sequential design of the kind to be examined in Chapter 4).

Comparison of Cross-sectional and Longitudinal Methods

Convergent Validity. The cross-sectional and longitudinal methods offer alternative routes to the common goal of detecting and charting an age change in behavior, a change presumably owing to a change in whatever primary factor underlies the behavior being studied. In theory, the two methods should yield the same picture of a performance change qua age change when applied to the same behavior on the identical task. This is true, however, only to the extent that both methods reflect age changes that are not markedly distorted by confoundings from nonaging sources. Close agreement between the results for soundly conducted cross-sectional and longitudinal studies offers convincing evidence for true age changes being the common causative factor producing the age differences observed with each method.

By definition, longitudinal data reflect a direct age change in performance and indirectly an age change in the process, or primary factor, mediating that performance. The problem, however, is that the age change assessed by our longitudinal data may distort the underlying true age change. In fact, what appears to be a true age change may actually be an artifact brought about by the confoundings inherent in our longitudinally collected data (e.g., the effects of subject attrition). The nature of the confoundings inherent in our cross-sectionally collected data on the same task is likely to be quite different (e.g., the effects of cohort differences among our various age groups). If the age differences revealed by the two sets of data are nevertheless comparable, then these differences imply the presence of age changes in performance that transcend the confoundings independently affecting the separate methods.

The use of two methods as independent tests of the operation of the same mechanism is an example of establishing what is called *convergent validity* (Campbell & Fiske, 1959). In aging research, the two methods are the cross-sectional and the longitudinal, and the mechanism of usual concern is that of ontogenetic change. Demonstration of convergent validity requires the inclusion in the same study of both cross-sectional and longitudinal sequences over the same age ranges. The appropriate strategy is illustrated in Figure 3.11. Note that groups of 40-, 50-, and 60-year-old subjects are evaluated at the same time (1970) on a given task. Differences in performance means between, say, the 40- and 50-year-old groups and the 50- and 60-year-old groups represent traditional cross-sectional assessments of age differences. Longitudinal assessments of age differences over the same 10-year span can then be obtained by evaluating again the original 40-year-old subjects in 1980 when they are 50 years old (i.e., those who are available for reevaluation) and the original 50-year-old subjects when they are 60 (again, those who are available). Of concern are the cross-sectional/longitudinal comparisons for the age difference between both age 40 and age 50 and age 50 and age 60. If both methods indicate a decrement in performance from, say, age 50 to age 60, and the magnitude of the decrement is about the same for both methods, then the investigator has a rather convincing argument that the decrement results from a true age change over that segment of the adult lifespan. The question arises, of course, as to the interpretation to be given to discrepant results yielded by the two methods. If the pattern found over one of the 10-year spans consists of a negligible age difference longitudinally and a pronounced age decrement cross-sectionally, then the implication is that the cross-sectional decrement stems from cohort differences between the age-level groups. Note that a cross-sectional comparison in Figure 3.11 does force the use of age groups from different cohorts, or birth years (e.g., 1930 versus 1920), which is a potential confounding factor that is absent in the parallel longitudinal comparison. The opposite pattern, namely, a negligible age difference found cross-sectionally and a pronounced age decrement found

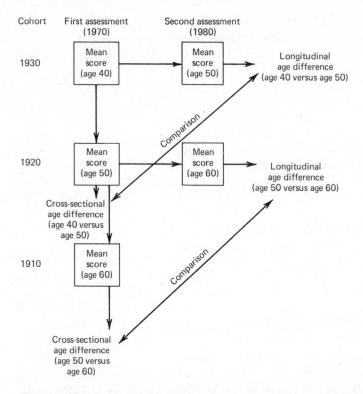

Figure 3.11. Basic strategy for testing convergent validity by comparing the age difference obtained independently on the same task with the traditional cross-sectional and longitudinal methods.

longitudinally, is considerably more ambiguous. It is conceivable that the longitudinal decrement reflects a true age change, a change that is compensated for cross-sectionally by a negative cohort effect, that is, one in which later born cohorts are at a disadvantage on the task in question relative to earlier born cohorts. On the other hand, the longitudinal decrement may imply an adverse time-of-measurement effect that enters into the longitudinal sequence (1970 versus 1980) but not into the cross-sectional sequence (1970 assessment only). Finally, the disparity may merely be the consequence of subject attrition in the longitudinal sequence, with the loss of subjects being concentrated largely in the better initial performers on the task.

Illustrative Research. Direct comparisons in the same study between cross-sectionally and longitudinally observed age differences on the same task and over the same age range have been rare in all areas of the psychology of aging. In principle, sequentially designed studies of the kind described in Chapter 4 offer the opportunity to make such comparisons. As we will see later, a sequential study calls for the simultaneous use of cross-sections and longitudinal sequences. However, the usual interest in these studies is with the statistical analysis that compares the effects on task performance of two different developmentally relevant independent variables (e.g., chronological age and cohort membership) rather that with the comparison between methods per se. Although between-methods comparisons are sometimes included in these studies as ancillary analyses, they involve the use of projected data points that may well obscure the true nature of equalities or disparities in the age differences observed cross-sectionally and longitudinally.

There are, however, studies by Douglas and Arenberg (1978) and Arenberg (1974) that serve as prototypes for soundly conducted research directed at a test of convergent validity. Douglas and Arenberg's study was concerned with age differences and age changes in personality. Sequential analyses were also incorporated into their study. These analyses generally supported those found for comparisons between cross-sectional and longitudinal age differences. Arenberg's study is especially important to us in that it examined age differences and age changes on a task carried over from experimental psychology, namely, a problem-solving task.

Douglas and Arenberg's task consisted of the 10 scales making up the Guilford-Zimmerman Temperament Survey (a widely used personality test). The subjects entering into the first assessment were 915 men ranging in age from 18 to 98 years. The first assessment on the scales was followed by a second from 5.6 to 9.9 years later. From these two assessments, a number of cross-sectional versus longitudinal comparisons of age differences were possible for each scale. For several of these scales (e.g., masculinity—a high score characterizing a person who does not cry easily, is comfortable with guns and hunting, and so on), the pattern was that of age differences (decrements with increasing age) both cross-sectionally and longitudinally, thus implying a true age change as the underlying causative factor. For several other scales (e.g., ascendance—a high score characterizing a person who stands up for individual rights, does not avoid verbal confrontation, and so on), the pattern was that of age differences found cross-sectionally but not longitudinally, thus implying cohort differences as the underlying causative factor for the cross-sectional behavioral differences. For still other scales (e.g., thoughtfulness—a high score characterizing an introspective, meditative person), the pattern was that of age differences found longitudinally but not cross-sectionally, thus implying time-of-measurement differences as a possible causative factor for the longitudinal behavioral differences.

Arenberg's task (1974) required subjects to solve a logical relationship among 10 lights that went on and off in a complex pattern. To solve the problem (i.e., discover the underlying pattern), subjects could seek out inputs of varying degrees of relevance to the solution. The main dependent variable was the number of informational inputs needed before arriving at the correct solution—thus, the larger the score, the less proficient the performance. A total of 263 men, ranging in age from their early 20s to their late 70's, successfully solved the problem on its first administration. Of these subjects, 193 successfully solved a similar problem when they returned to the laboratory 6 to 7 years later. Mean scores for these 193 subjects, grouped by age levels at the time of receiving the first problem, are given in Table 3.1 for both of the temporally

Table 3.1   Mean Number of Inputs in Problem Solving (Increasing Score Indicates Decreasing Proficiency) for Adults of Varying Ages. First and Second Sessions Were Separated by Nearly 7 Years.

	Age Level				
	Under 40	*40s*	*50s*	*60s*	*70s*
1st session	5.28	6.71	7.07	6.96	6.62
2nd session	4.00	3.90	5.39	5.08	11.37
Change	− 1.28	− 2.81	− 1.68	− 1.87	4.75

Source: Adapted from Arenberg, 1974, Table 3.

separated sessions. Arenberg's cross-sectional analysis of age differences was made by comparing first-session means over the various age levels. These comparisons generally indicated decreasing problem-solving proficiency with increasing age through the 50s, followed by a general leveling off of further change. Arenberg's longitudinal analysis consisted of comparing first- and second-session means at each age level. Thus, each age group yielded a longitudinal change score (second-session mean minus first-session mean) over a span of approximately 7 years. These change values are included in Table 3.1 (a minus value indicates an *increase* in proficiency longitudinally). It can be seen that only subjects who were initially in their 70s were characterized by a decrement in performance over the 7 year span. As pointed out by Arenberg, the longitudinal evaluations of age differences were affected by a positive selection bias in which the nondropouts were superior in first-session performance relative to the dropouts. Moreover, nonspecific transfer through increased familiarity with that kind of task probably served to improve performance scores on the second session relative to their values on the first session. These positive biases seemingly influenced age differences assessed longitudinally but not cross-sectionally. The finding of a pronounced longitudinal decrement for the oldest subjects is, therefore, especially significant in that an adverse age change was apparently severe enough to offset, and then some, the effects of these positive biasing factors. It is also conceivable that the cross-sectional age differences observed in this study reflect mainly cohort differences in problem-solving ability so that members of earlier cohorts (i.e., the older subjects) are less proficient than members of later cohorts (i.e., the younger subjects). The possibility of cohort variation in problem-solving ability seems less likely, however, than the possibility of cohort variation in different aspects of personality (a point to be explored further in Chapter 4).

There is another strategy for demonstrating the convergence of results found for age differences as evaluated by two different methods. The logic of this alternative strategy is illustrated in Figure 3.12. It can be seen that one of the methods is that of a conventional longitudinal evaluation. The other method is an intracohort analysis of two independent groups representing the same age range as that found in the longitudinal evaluation. The first is the same group that enters into the initial point of the longitudinal sequence; the second is another group from the same cohort as the first group that is assessed

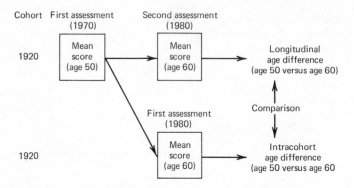

Figure 3.12. Modified strategy for yielding convergent validity by substituting intracohort age differences for cross-sectional age differences (compare with Figure 3.11).

for the first time at the time the second assessment in the longitudinal sequence is conducted. (An intracohort analysis may also be used in sequential research, as we will discover in Chapter 4). Comparable age decrements found by two methods imply a true age change over the age range studied. Moreover, the possibility of a confounding by cohort variation in performance on the task in question is eliminated through the use of age groups from the same cohort in both comparisons.

An excellent demonstration of the contribution made by the effective use of this strategy may be found in a study by Arenberg and Robertson-Tchabo (1977). For the time being, we will consider only the paired-associate component of their study (it also included serial learning). Subjects from a specific generation, defined by a small range of birth years, were assigned to different groups that were evaluated some years apart on the paired-associate task. For example, one group from that generation was evaluated when the members were around 40 years of age, and another group from the same generation was evaluated when the members were around 50 years of age. Subjects from a different generation were similarly divided, one group was evaluated when the members were around 55 years of age, the other group when the members were around 65 years of age, and so on. The results from this intracohort phase of Arenberg and Robertson-Tchabo's research with the specific age levels described previously are shown in Figure 3.13. Note the upward trend in mean errors from 40 to 50 years of age and the even greater increment in errors from 55 to 65 years of age.

The longitudinal phase of their study consisted of selecting members of each generation and reevaluating them on the paired-associate task (but with an alternate form to reduce the magnitude of progressive error) at least 6 years later. Thus, for one group of subjects, the first evaluation occurred when the members were around 40 years of age and the second when they neared 50 years of age. For another group, the first evaluation came when the members were around 55 years of age and the second when they were in their early 60s. This procedure was repeated for a number of other age contrasts. The longitudinal changes in mean errors are also shown in Figure 3.13. Note the commonality with the intracohort pattern. Again, mean errors increased somewhat from age 40 to age 50 and increased more substantially from age 55 to the early 60s. The overall course of an age change in paired-associate learning seems clear. The decrement in performance is relatively slight until the 50s are reached, at which age level the decrement increases progressively and substantially. Other age levels employed in this study confirm this analysis. For example, the decrement from age 65 to age 75, as revealed by both methods, far exceeded the decrement from age 55 to age 65.

In commenting on the use of two disparate methods to study the same phenomenon, Arenberg and Robertson-Tchabo stated: "It is argued here that if the repeated-measures (i.e., longitudinal) data indicate performance change over time, and the intra-cohort differences are similar to repeated-measures change, then the evidence for age changes is compelling" (1977, p. 422). Our confidence in knowing the true pattern of these age changes in paired-associate learning over the adult lifespan is, indeed, greatly strengthened by the congruity (i.e., convergent validity) between independently gathered intracohort and longitudinal data.

Finally, we should note that all three of the Arenberg studies reported in this section (Arenberg, 1974; Arenberg & Robertson-Tchabo, 1977; Douglas & Arenberg, 1978) were part of a large scale project that began over 20 years ago and is still continuing. The project is known as the Baltimore Longitudinal Study. The participants in this project are 463 men, most of them from the Washington, D.C., area who ranged in age at the start of the study from 20 through 99 (151 of them being beyond 60 years of age). The participants volunteered for a 3 day visit to the Baltimore City Hospitals every 18 months to

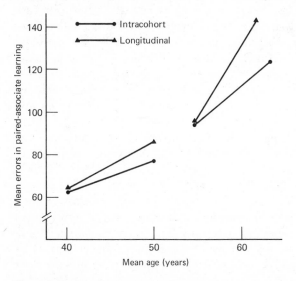

Figure 3.13. Age differences in paired-associate learning as assessed by two methods (intracohort cross-sectional and longitudinal). (Adapted from Arenberg & Robertson-Tchabo, 1977, Figure 1.)

receive a battery of physiological, biochemical, and psychological tests and tasks. The psychological tests have obviously included personality, learning, and problem-solving evaluations. A wealth of information regarding age difference and age changes that are of interest to the psychology of aging has already been produced in this project, and, surely, considerable more such information is yet to come. The unique opportunity to compare cross-sectional and longitudinal evaluations of age differences on the same tasks has made the project especially valuable. Another important component of the overall project rests in the generally superior nature of the initial subjects at all age levels with respect to such attributes as educational level and occupational level (see Stone & Norris, 1966, for a complete description of these subject attributes). Consequently, age differences reported in this project, particularly those found both cross-sectionally and longitudinally, are unlikely to be the consequence of confounding by age-level disparities in the major non-age attributes. At the same time, the contribution of the project to parametric assessments of age-level means (and variances) and differences between age-level means is necessarily restricted by the selective nature of the initial samples at each age level.

Secondary Factors and Age Differences in Performance

Effect of a Secondary Factor on the Functional Level of a Primary Factor (Process).

By this time, we should realize that performance on most psychological tasks is multiply determined. The score manifested on a given task by a specific subject is determined in part by the subject's primary factor level for that task and in part by any number of secondary factors. Again, a primary factor represents a subject's competence as determined by proficiency on the processes that govern performance on the task in question (e.g., Process A for our prior Task X). A primary factor is involved only in performance on that task and, perhaps, on other tasks that overlap that task somewhat. For example, the processes engaged in learning paired associates constitute a primary factor. This factor, however, may be partially engaged in other learning tasks (e.g., free recall) as well. Unlike primary factors, secondary factors are not restricted to any one task or group of related tasks. Instead, they consist of general processes that may affect performance level on a wide range of tasks varying greatly in their underlying primary factors or processes. Common secondary factors are those related to a subject's motivation, general health, and degree of recent practice of skills relevant to the kinds of tasks encountered in the laboratory. Thus, a subject's motivational level affects performance on many kinds of laboratory tasks, especially those involving learning, memory, and other cognitive activities. Similarly, a subject's general health may affect virtually every kind of performance by producing variations in sensory functioning, attention, stamina, and so on, and a subject's lack of recent engagement in cognitive activities may make it difficult to activate processes that, in effect, have become rusty during the lay off.

In general, primary and secondary factors interact together to determine a subject's performance level. Whether or not a subject's performance reaches its

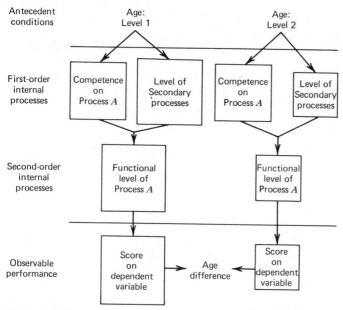

Figure 3.14. The effect of age variation in a secondary performance process, or factor, that interacts with a primary (competence) process to determine performance proficiency level. Two age levels are assumed to be equal in the absolute level of the primary process (first-order internal process) but differ in the functional level of the primary process (second-order internal process) because of a difference in their levels of a secondary process. Thus, an observable age difference in scores on the dependent variable is the consequence.

full potential as set by the competence (maximum proficiency) of the underlying primary processes depends on the nature of the secondary factors present at the time of performance on a specified task. If competence is unaltered from Age Level 1 to Age Level 2 but the overall weighting of the secondary factors shifts negatively with increasing age, then performance on the task will also shift negatively in accordance with the drift of these secondary factors. As illustrated in Figure 3.14, the resultant would be an age difference in performance favoring the younger age level. This would probably lead to the erroneous conclusion that competence per se decreases with increasing age for the task at hand. Even when there is an actual decrement in competence from Age Level 1 to Age Level 2, a concomitant negative shift in secondary factors is likely to result in a serious overestimation of the magnitude of that decline in competence.

The potential confoundings produced by age differences in secondary factors know no methodological boundaries. If elderly adults, for example, are less involved in a task than are young adults, then that difference in involvement should affect performance on that task regardless of the format of the comparison between age levels (i.e., cross-sectional or longitudinal). Moreover, an overestimation of a decrement in competence from Age Level 1 to Age Level 2 would occur regardless of the cause for the age difference in competence (i.e., whether it results from a true age change in a primary process or from a nonontogenetic source).

Investigators testing for the presence of a true age change in competence surely should use procedures designed to eliminate (or, at least, minimize as much as possible), confoundings from secondary factors. Every effort should be made to equate motivational levels for subjects of different ages, to select older subjects without health problems that could inhibit the expression of true competence on a task, and to give older subjects ample preliminary practice on a task before formal assessment of task competence begins. Similarly, whatever difference in rapport (as a possible contributor to motivation) that might exist between a comparatively young investigator and an older subject relative to the rapport established by the same investigator with a young-adult subject should be overcome by the patience and understanding of the investigator.

Critics of aging psychological research often express the view that the so-called age changes in competence demonstrated in this research stem largely from the failure of investigators to take into account the existence of pronounced age differences in secondary factors, especially motivation. A representative, and highly influential, critic is Comfort (1976). For example, in reference to the evidence of an age change in learning competence from early to late adulthood, he had this to say:

> Although perfectly able to learn, in a learning situation older people get upset and anxious because of fear of failure. They may in fact appear not to learn because they would rather risk not answering than to give a wrong answer which confirms their own fears and other people's prejudices. They are in the position of the only black pupil in a class of hostile whites where the teacher prefaces a test by expressing the view that black people are naturally stupid (p. 120).

There can be no denial of the potential importance of secondary performance factors for many aspects of the experimental psychology of aging. Again, the belief held by many nonpsychologists (and some psychologists as well) is that the elimination of age differences on these factors would all but make age differences on many tasks, especially those mediated by cognitive processes, disappear. Our need at this point is to examine the empirical evidence regarding secondary factors and to determine how justified this belief is.

Age Differences in Motivation and Their Effects on Age Differences in Performance. Why put out on a task when, in the eyes of your younger beholders, you are doomed in advance to failure? This is the situation confronting the elderly performer on learning tasks and many other psychological tasks (including intelligence tests) as viewed by Comfort (1976) and other critics. The situation is somewhat paradoxical however. On the one hand, the elderly are believed to be over motivated by their fear of failure and resulting heightened emotionality when faced with evaluation on a psychological task. On the other hand, the elderly are believed to be under motivated by their negative attitude toward participation on a trivial (in their eyes) task that has little relevance to everyday activities. The paradox vanishes, however, when motivation is appropriately viewed in the light of its complexities. Motivational increments can have either debilitating or facilitating effects on task performance, contingent on what component of motivation we are dealing with and what the intensity of that component is. Debilitating effects are associated primarily with an emotional component variously identified as arousal, fear, or anxiety. Moderate amounts of emotion may actually facilitate performance on many tasks both by contributing to the alertness and by energizing the participants. However, excessive emotionality is likely to be debilitating through its elicitation of responses that are incompatible with effective performance on the task at hand. These responses, in effect, freeze the participant by inhibiting appropriate task-relevant behavior and by allowing the participant to wallow in thoughts of impending failure. Facilitating effects are associated primarily with a task-involvement component defined in terms of the intrinsic appeal of the task at hand to subjects and the concentration of effort directed by subjects at engaging in the activities essential for successful performance on that task (e.g., rehearsing the items of a learning task). As task involvement increases, performance is expected to increase in proficiency to the extent permitted by a subject's competence on that task. However, even for this component of motivation, there is likely to be a point of motivational intensity that defeats the purpose of increasing motivation. That is, a subject may be trying too hard and become too easily discouraged and ineffective as a result.

The presumed relationship between age increments and motivational effects on performance for each component fits nicely into the inverted-U phenomenon long known to psychologists working in the area of motivation (Duffy, 1962). The phenomenon, as adapted for a motivational explanation of age differences in performance, is illustrated in the top panel of Figure 3.15 for the emotional component of motivation and in the bottom panel for the task-involvement component. For the first component, performance peaks at the moderate intensity of emotion presumed to be characteristic of young adults when they are subjects in psychological experiments. Beyond that optimal intensity, further increments in emotionality lead only to decrements in performance. These are the levels of intensity commonly believed to be characteristic of elderly adults. Note that the inverted-U phenomenon predicts age deficits in performance on a task even when competence on that task is unaltered by age. For the second component, performance peaks at a fairly high intensity of motivation, an intensity presumed to be characteristic of young-adult subjects. For intensities below that level, performance is less proficient. These are the intensities commonly believed to be characteristic of elderly subjects. Again, the inverted-U phenomenon predicts age deficits in performance in the absence of age deficits in competence.

Age differences in motivation do offer an intriguing way of explaining age differences in performance without having to postulate age changes in competence. Our concern is first with the evidence indicating that there are indeed pronounced adult-age differences in motivation and second with the evidence indicating that motivational differences, in turn, account for many observable age differences in performance.

Our review will begin with the emotional component of motivation. One way of conceptualizing this component is in terms of a psychological concept,

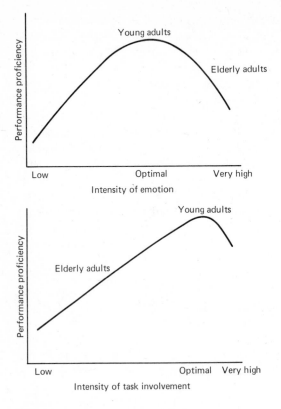

Figure 3.15. Inverted-U relationship between level of motivation and level of performance proficiency for emotional components of motivation (top panel) and task-involvement components of motivation (bottom panel).

anxiety, that has been the subject of numerous studies with both children and young adults. Individual differences in the intensity of anxiety are commonly assessed by means of a self-report in which subjects answer, with a simple yes or no such questions as, "The more important the testing situation, the less well I seem to do." The number of yes answers given to such questions determines a subject's test-anxiety score. Despite the flood of studies on test anxiety in young adults, there have been only a few studies in which young adults were contrasted with elderly adults on the level of self-reported anxiety. One of these studies (Whitbourne, 1976) did find a clear-cut age difference on a six-item test (one of the items being our previously cited question). The test-anxiety questions were administered to both young-adult and elderly subjects shortly after performing for two trials on a memory task involving recall of sentences. On the basis of their scores on this memory task, subjects at both age levels were split at the median recall score for their age level into high- and low-recall groups. Means on the anxiety test were then determined separately for the recall groups. As can be seen in Figure 3.16, elderly subjects, overall, appear to be more anxious than the young subjects, at least to the extent that self-reports of this kind are reliable indicants of actual anxiety level. In addition, the highest level of anxiety was manifested by the elderly group that had scored below the median on the memory task. It should be noted further that memory-task performance for the elderly subjects was well below the level found for the young-adult subjects. Unfortunately, however, there is no causal evidence in these results that permits the conclusion that the greater anxiety reported by Whitbourne's elderly subjects was responsible for their poorer memory performance. Remember that anxiety level was not manipulated directly in this study—it was merely assessed after the memory task had been completed. It would make as much sense to conclude that poor memory-task performance caused a high level of self-reported anxiety as it does to conclude that a high level of anxiety causes poor memory performance. It would require evidence demonstrating that the elimination of the age difference in anxiety is accompanied by an elimination of the age difference in memory before we could conclude that heightened anxiety rather than age deficit in task competence causes observed age differences in memory-task performance.

A further complication in interpreting Whitbourne's results is the fact that other investigators have either failed to find pronounced age differences in test-anxiety scores (e.g., Monge & Gardner, 1972; Mueller, Kausler, & Faherty, 1980) or they have found lower scores by elderly subjects than by young-adult subjects (Hutto & Smith, 1980). Interestingly, Mueller et al. administered the same anxiety test to their subjects as Whitbourne gave to her subjects. In their study, the test was given after performance on a speeded-judgment task in which subjects had to decide if paired words were either unrelated to one another or were related in some specified manner (e.g., they are homonyms of one another). Although a large age difference was found for each kind of judgment, with decision-time scores being much faster for young adults, the age difference in self-report anxiety scores was slight and clearly not statistically significant.

An alternative way of conceptualizing the emotional component of motivation is in terms of the physiological concept of arousal. Arousal refers to the degree of activation of the autonomic nervous system, with high arousal being

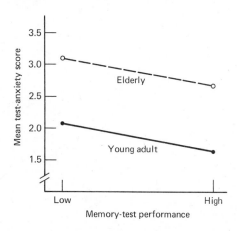

Figure 3.16. Relationship between memory-test performance (young and elderly groups divided at the median test score) and test-anxiety scores. (Adapted from Whitbourne, 1976, Table 2.)

characterized by accelerated heart rate, respiration, and so on. Like high levels of anxiety, high levels of arousal are viewed as being debilitating to performance on many kinds of tasks. Most important, elderly people in general, are regarded as being overaroused when they are performing on stressful tasks relative to young adults (Eisdorfer, 1967). Standard laboratory tasks of experimental psychology apparently qualify as such stressful tasks. Given the debilitating effects of overarousal, any means of reducing it is expected to improve performance. This hypothesis was tested in a widely cited study by Eisdorfer, Nowlin, and Wilkie (1970). Elderly subjects who were members of their experimental group were injected with propranolol, a drug known to mitigate the aversive physiological concomitants of autonomic-nervous-system activation. Other elderly subjects who were members of a control group were injected with a placebo (a substance that has no effect on autonomic-nervous-system activity but that is used as a control for the effects of suggestibility on performance). Following the injections, all subjects received 15 trials on an eight-item serial-learning task. In serial learning, a subject learns words in a specified order. On each trial, the subject anticipates with each word exposed what word appears next in the order. Errors of two kinds are possible: (1) errors of omission, in which there is a failure to say anything when responses of anticipation are owing, and (2) errors of commission, in which responses occur, but they are for words that are given in the wrong serial order. Eisdorfer et al. compared their two groups of elderly subjects on both types of errors as well as on total errors. Their results, expressed as mean errors made over 15 trials, are shown in Figure 3.17. It may be seen that the reduction in physiological arousal produced by the injection of propranolol (and not by the injection of the placebo) was accompanied by a reduction in error rate, both overall and for the separate kinds of errors. However, the error reduction was statistically significant only for total errors. The failure to find the reduction concentrated primarily in errors of omission runs contrary to Comfort's argument that elderly individuals "appear not to learn because they would rather risk not answering than to give a wrong answer which confirms their own fears and other people's prejudices" (1976, p. 120).

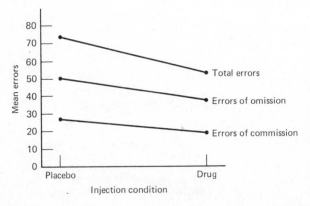

Figure 3.17. Mean errors (total errors and separate kinds of errors) made by groups of elderly subjects given either a placebo (control) injection or an arousal-reducing drug injection. (Adapted from Eisdorfer, Nowlin, & Wilkie, 1970, Figure 1.)

There is, however, a more important problem existing in the study of Eisdorfer et al. (1970). Strangely missing were experimental and control groups of young-adult subjects. Ideally, a factorial study was called for, one in which age variation was combined with variation in an experimentally manipulable independent variable, namely, the type of injection preceding the learning trials. Factorial studies of this nature will be discussed in detail in Chapter 5. For now, we merely need to observe that, in the absence of young-adult groups, it is impossible to determine the effect that arousal reduction has on age differences in learning performance. It is conceivable that a propranolol injection would have yielded a reduction in errors for a young-adult experimental group relative to a young-adult control group. In fact, there is a good probability that the difference in error rates between young and elderly subjects, favoring the young adults, would have been even greater under the experimental condition than under the control condition. If true, then arousal reduction would be regarded as increasing age differences in task performance rather than decreasing those differences. In all likelihood, neither elderly adults *nor* young adults fulfill their optimal competence under standard task conditions. The reduction of arousal is likely to permit both age levels to approximate more closely that optimal competence in performance. Nevertheless, that optimal level is likely to remain higher for young adults than for elderly adults. The role played by age differences in arousal is complicated considerably by the fact that not all specialists working in this area believe the elderly to be overaroused under stress. In fact, some contributors to this area of research (e.g., Botwinick & Kornetsky, 1960) have found evidence indicating *underarousal* on the part of the elderly relative to young adults. The apparent paradox may be resolved by the realization that arousal involves a number of physiological components, some of which appear to be overaroused in the elderly, whereas others appear to be underaroused (Powell, Milligan, & Furchtgott, 1980). At any rate, the concept of arousal seems too unreliable to place much faith in it as an alternative to competence in explaining most age differences in performance.

The issue of age differences in task involvement as a component of motivation has received considerable attention in recent years. Part of this attention has been directed at the intrinsic interest a task has for subjects of different ages. Many of the tasks employed by experimental psychologists undoubtedly have an air of artificiality about them. Tasks are intended primarily to permit identification and manipulation of psychological processes under controlled conditions. To accomplish this objective, a psychologist may find it necessary to use materials in a task that have little apparent ecological relevance, in the sense of pertinence, to the everyday activities of subjects (Bronfenbrenner, 1977). For example, learning a list of unrelated words in a specified order enables a psychologist to investigate basic serial-learning processes and, hopefully, to investigate adult-age differences in the proficiency of each process. Nevertheless, the standard serial-learning task of the laboratory, such as the kind employed by Eisdorfer et al. (1970) departs considerably from the kinds of serial-learning tasks encountered away from the laboratory. Here, serial learning consists of learning the letters and digits of a new automobile license plate, learning the symbols of a complex chemical formula, and so on. Most important, it may be argued that elderly people feel more negatively toward the artificiality of laboratory tasks than do young adults. The age disparity in attitude may be especially pronounced when college students serve as the young adults in a study examining age differences in performance. Most college students are accustomed to being exposed to abstract materials in many of their courses, and they are unlikely to find laboratory materials terribly unusual. The net effect may be less task involvement by elderly subjects than by young-adult subjects and, therefore, less effort directed at task performance by the former than by the latter.

The implication of the task-relevance issue in its extreme form is straightforward: equality of intrinsic interest in a task across age levels should result in equality of performance on a task across age levels (or, at least, a pronounced reduction in the magnitude of the age difference in performance). The issue needs to be raised for any task in which the degree of effort exerted by subjects is an important factor in determining performance level on that task. Learning, memory, concept-identification, problem-solving, and reasoning tasks, for the most part, belong in this category. The range of tasks to which the effort variable applies, however, should not be underestimated. Even many sensory and perceptual tasks demand high degrees of vigilance and attention to perform them proficiently.

There have been a scattering of studies that relate in some way to the issue of an age disparity in intrinsic task interest. One strategy in these studies is to administer tasks that the investigator believes will have comparable high interest to subjects of all ages. If an age disparity in task interest and its correlated age disparity in task effort are the only contributors to age differences in performance, then these age differences in performance should be greatly minimized and perhaps eliminated completely. This strategy entered into two studies by Hulicka. In the first (Hulicka, 1967a), adult subjects of various ages received several successive tasks. One of these tasks required recognition memory for faces, a task Hulicka believed would be just as appealing to elderly subjects as to young-adult subjects. Pictures of 10 faces were exposed one at a time for 5 seconds each. Recognition memory was then tested by presenting each study-list face with two distractors (i.e., two faces that were not part of the study list) and having the subjects select the previously seen face from within each triad. In agreement with the principle that equal task interest means equal task performance, the effect of age variation on recognition test scores was not statistically significant. Unfortunately, however, others (e.g., Smith & Winograd, 1978) who have made use of a memory-for-faces task have found a statistically significant age difference that favors young adults. It is conceivable that the short study list employed by Hulicka may have introduced a ceiling effect that masked potential age differences in memory scores (the concept of a ceiling effect will be explained in Chapter 5). A second task required paired-associate learning of a list in which the stimulus elements consisted of the pictures of eight men and the response elements consisted of common first names, another task suspected of being as interesting to elderly subjects as to young-adult subjects. The effect of age variation was again not statistically significant. However, the picture-name pairs were exposed for study at a very slow rate (8 seconds per pair). A ceiling effect for young adults is quite conceivable with this slow rate and with this kind of material, again making it possible that potential age differences were masked.

In the second study by Hulicka (1967b), a paired-associate list assumed to be of comparable interest to subjects of all ages was again employed. This time the stimulus elements were occupational titles (e.g., *teacher* and *doctor*), and the response elements were one-syllable surnames (e.g., *Wood* and *Bates*). As a further boost to ecological relevance, the subjects were asked to imagine that they had just moved to a new town and that they were trying to learn who does what in that town (just as people of all ages would do on moving in real life to a new town). This time no support was found for the task-interest explanatory principle—the elderly subjects required significantly more trials to learn the list to a criterion of mastery than did the young subjects (in this case, teenagers).

Perhaps the best known study using the "let's make the task intrinsically interesting" strategy is an intriguing one by Arenberg (1968a) that could almost have been coauthored by Agatha Christie. The task was that of concept learning, or, more appropriately, concept identification. In concept-learning research with young adult subjects (e.g., Bruner, Goodnow, & Austin, 1956), the materials are presented in abstract form, a simplified example of which is given in Table 3.2. The subject's task is to identify which one of a set of geometric forms (e.g., a triangle, a circle, and so on) is the concept designated in advance by the investigator (e.g., a square in the example given in Table 3.2). Arrays of items are presented along with feedback informing the subject whether that array is positive (i.e., contains the concept) or negative (i.e., does not contain the concept). Successive arrays are presented that provide sufficient positive and negative information to narrow the choice down to the designated concept (see Table 3.2). Arenberg (1968a) argued reasonably that elderly adults would find such abstract material uninteresting and difficult with which to work. He then proceeded to find an effective way of maintaining the basic nature of the concept-learning task, at the same time substituting materials of considerably

Table 3.2 Representative Concept-learning Problems that Use Either Abstract Materials or Real-life Materials as in Arenberg's (1968a) Study

Information Presented	Feedback	Possible Positive Instances
Abstract Materials		
1. Triangle, circle, square	Positive	Triangle, circle, square
2. Triangle, diamond, square	Positive	Triangle, square
3. Triangle, circle, cross	Negative	Square
Real-Life Materials		
1. Coffee, lamb, peas	Died (positive)	Coffee, lamb, peas
2. Coffee, veal, peas	Died (positive)	Coffee, peas
3. Coffee, lamb, corn	Lived (negative)	Peas

greater interest value to elderly adults (and, undoubtedly, to younger subjects as well). An example of such real-life materials is given in Table 3.2. The problem is basically the same as the previous one, except for the substitution of foods for geometric forms. The subjects' task was to find the poisoned food, and informational feedback consisted of knowing whether or not the consumer of those foods died or lived (equivalent to positive and negative feedback respectively). Despite the intuitively appealing nature of the modified concept-learning task, Arenberg found a large age difference favoring young adults for the number of poisoned-food problems actually solved.

A somewhat different strategy was followed by Wittels (1972). Her concern was more with the appropriateness of task materials for subjects of a given generation than with the intrinsic interest generated by those materials. Her belief in the unfairness of many aging studies in their evaluations of elderly people rested in the assumption "that the stimuli typically used in laboratory studies are generation-bound, i.e., they are less meaningful or appropriate for old subjects than they are for young subjects" (p. 372). Given more meaningful and generationally more appropriate materials, elderly subjects were expected to reduce considerably their age deficit in paired-associate learning.

To construct lists of varying degrees of generation (and age) appropriateness, Wittels had both young-adult and elderly subjects perform a preliminary task in which they gave 10 different word associations to each of 15 stimulus words (words like *anger* and *carpet*). The fifth association to every word then became the response element of a paired associate in which the original stimulus word of the word-association task served as the stimulus element. For example, if an elderly subject gave "vacuum" as the fifth association to *carpet,* then *carpet-vacuum* was one of the 15 pairs that subject received as a paired-associate learning task. This procedure created young and elderly groups who learned under what Wittels called a personal-list condition. Other subjects of both age levels also gave associations to the same stimulus words in the preliminary task. However, their associations did not enter into the selection of response elements for the paired-associate lists these subjects learned. Each member of one group of young adults received instead a list identical to the list learned by one of the young adults in the personal-list condition. Similarly, each member of a comparable group of elderly adults received a list corresponding to one learned by an elderly subject in the personal-list condition. Together, these groups learned under what Wittels called a generational-list condition. Finally, there was a crossgenerational-list condition in which each young subject received a list identical to one learned by an elderly subject in the personal-list condition and each elderly subject received a list identical to one learned by a young subject in the personal-list condition. Subjects in all conditions practiced the learning list to a criterion of mastery. Mean errors in reaching this criterion are plotted in Figure 3.18 for both age levels under all three list conditions. It can be seen that young adults were clearly superior to elderly adults in all three conditions. Most important the magnitude of the age difference was not affected by list condition, as indicated by the absence of a statistically significant interaction between age level and list condition (this study is another factorial study of the kind to be examined in Chapter 5). If

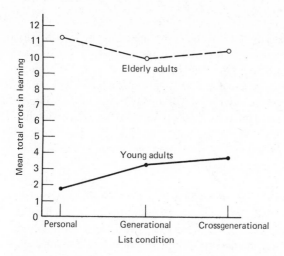

Figure 3.18. Mean errors on a paired-associate learning task made by young and elderly groups of subjects receiving different kinds of lists constructed from word associations. (Adapted from Wittels, 1972, Table 1.)

anything, the magnitude of the age difference was slightly greater in the personal-list condition than in the crossgenerational-list condition. Thus, no evidence was found to support the hypothesis that age differences in learning are largely mitigated by the use of generationally appropriate materials.

Overall, the evidence favoring the notion that increased intrinsic motivation for elderly subjects will erase their performance deficits is not very convincing. Nevertheless, this is an area of sufficient importance to justify continuing investigation. There is, however, an alternative approach to trying to make task involvement equal for adult subjects of all ages. This approach attempts to increase involvement by means of extrinsic motivation. The idea is to reward proficient task performance in some way, thereby encouraging elderly subjects, in particular, that it is worth their while to try harder. Here, too, we find a scattering of studies that have attempted to vary degree of task involvement, studies covering a wide range of tasks and kinds of rewards. Several of these studies (e.g., Hoyer, Labouvie, & Baltes, 1973; Leech & Witte, 1971) found rewards for proficient performance to improve the level of performance by elderly subjects. However, in the absence of young adults receiving comparable variation in extrinsic motivation (i.e., reward versus no reward), it is impossible to determine from these studies what effect rewards have on minimizing age differences in performance. As with arousal reduction, it is conceivable that rewards may actually improve performance proficiency more for young adults than for elderly adults, thereby increasing rather than decreasing the magnitude of age differences in performance. Our coverage will be only for studies in which variation in reward occurred for young-adult subjects as well as for elderly subjects.

In one of these studies (Grant, Storandt, & Botwinick, 1978), the task was the digit symbol subtest of the WAIS. This task requires substituting abstract symbols for numbers (e.g., writing in ">" every time the number "9" is encountered on an answer sheet). A subject's score is the number of substitutions completed in a limited time period. Of all of the components of the WAIS, this is the one that shows, under standard conditions (i.e., no extrinsic reward), the largest age difference in performance (Botwinick, 1967). Grant et al. argued that,"perhaps the combination of practice and motivation is what is lacking in the Digit Symbol performance of the elderly" (1978, p. 413). A practice component entered their study by their administration of twenty 30-second trials to all of their subjects, instead of the single 90-second trial given when the task is part of the WAIS. Motivation joined age level as an independent variable, thus making this another factorially designed study because no reward or reward conditions were included. One group of young adults and one group of elderly adults performed under a standard, or no extrinsic reward, condition, whereas comparable age groups performed under a reward condition. On each trial after the first, rewarded subjects received 20¢ for each substitution completed beyond the number completed on the first trial, but they also lost 20¢ for each substitution below the number completed on the first trial. The results are shown in Figure 3.19 for all four groups in terms of the mean number of substitutions completed per trial (with trials grouped for convenience into blocks of four trials each). There was obviously a whopping age difference in performance favoring young adults. Most important, the age difference was not really affected by giving a reward, that is, it was as great with reward as without reward (in statistical terms, the interaction between age and incentive condition was not statistically significant).

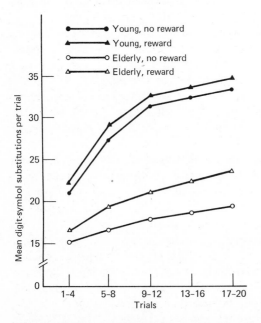

Figure 3.19. Mean number of digit-symbol substitutions completed per trial for groups of young and elderly subjects receiving either no monetary reward or a monetary reward. (Adapted from Grant, Storandt, and Botwinick 1978, Table 1.)

Similar outcomes were reported in studies by Hartley and Walsh (1980) and Hoyer, Hoyer, Treat, and Baltes (1978). In the study by Hartley and Walsh, the task was free-recall learning, and the reward condition consisted of offering money for each word recalled. In the study by Hoyer et al., tasks, such as letter cancellation, were employed, and rewards consisted of the innovative use of S&H green stamps (yes, the subjects were women). Both studies failed to find a reduction in the performance advantage of young adults over elderly adults because of the operation of an extrinsic reward. In fact, in Hartley and Walsh's study, there was a trend toward increasing the advantage in the reward condition.

Extrinsic motivation need not be induced by means of monetary incentives or their equivalent. An alternative means may be social incentives in the form of praise for a good performance and reproof for a bad performance. Verbal feedback is given after each trial on a task. This feedback, in effect, informs the subject of the investigator's evaluation of performance on that trial. Praise, or positive feedback, is offered through such statements as "That was a very good score," reproof, or negative feedback, through such statements as "You're not doing very well." Of interest are the contrasts in performance levels among subjects receiving praise and reproof and control subjects receiving no kind of verbal feedback. To some psychologists, both praise and reproof are viewed as conditions that should yield superior performance relative to the neutral condition, presumably because the former conditions increase task involvement and effort expenditure. To other psychologists, both incentive conditions are viewed as conditions that should yield inferior performance relative to the control condition, presumably because the former conditions arouse anxiety and the debilitating activities associated with anxiety. These opposing positions lead quite naturally to contrasting predictions regarding the effects of social incentives on adult-age differences in performance. The first offers the possibility of a reduction in these age differences, whereas the second seemingly implies that social incentives should only lead to increases in the magnitudes of age differences.

In common with research on test anxiety, there has been considerable research on social incentives, but nearly all of it has been with children or young adults as subjects. The picture emerging from these studies has been somewhat muddled (see Ferguson, 1976, for a review). The effectiveness of social incentives appears to depend on a number of other conditions, such as the degree of self-esteem possessed by the recipients of differential feedbacks. What little research has been done with elderly subjects has only added to the muddle. Lair and Moon (1972) varied social-incentive conditions for elderly subjects performing on a digit-symbol task. Both praise and reproof conditions yielded inferior performance levels relative to their control condition, although the differences in performance were not statistically significant. The trend, nevertheless, supports the position that the addition of social incentives to the overall performance conditions extant for elderly subjects serves only to evoke anxiety and its debilitating effects on performance. Although Lair and Moon did not vary incentive conditions for young adults, they did so for groups of middle-age subjects. Neither praise nor reproof were of any help in enabling their elderly subjects catch up with the performance levels of their middle-age subjects. To complicate matters further, Levendusky (1978) conducted a follow-up study in which letter cancellation replaced the digit-symbol task. This time, elderly subjects performed significantly better with reproof than with no verbal feedback, whereas praise remained no better than no feedback at all. The positive value of reproof was attributed either to its aversive value—making elderly subjects work faster to escape its unpleasantness—or to its challenging value—forcing its recipients to try harder. Unfortunately, no contrasting younger age groups entered into this study, again making it impossible to determine whatever benefit might have been gained from reproof in reducing age differences in performance. At any rate, social-incentive conditions seem to join other motivating conditions in offering little hope of leading to the promised land of pronounced reductions in age-related performance deficits.

Age Differences in Health and Their Effects on Age Differences in Performance. Age variation in health seems so obvious a possible source of confounding with age variation in competence that it scarcely needs calling to attention. Every investigator examining the effects of "normal" aging on some aspect of human behavior is surely aware of the fact that the incidence of such illnesses as cardiovascular disease is much greater in elderly adults that it is in young adults (Abrahams, 1976). There is considerable evidence indicating that abnormal cardiovascular functioning, as manifested, for example, in high blood pressure, is accompanied in elderly people by performance decrements on intelligence tests (e.g., Hertzog, Schaie, & Gribbin, 1978) and on tasks requiring rapid responding to sensory signals (e.g., Birren, 1965). But there is also some conflicting evidence (see Schultz, Dineen, Elias, Pentz, & Wood, 1979). Comparable decrements on learning, memory, and other kinds of cognitive tasks would not be surprising. Accordingly, screening subjects of all ages in terms of current health status should be an essential part of virtually every experimental aging study.

Of course, knowing all of this and doing something about it are two different matters. Not being physicians, psychologists are unable to give qualifying physical examinations, and they, therefore, have to get by with their own ersatz health-screening devices. The procedure usually followed is apparent from the following descriptions given in two representative studies: "All elderly subjects were active community residents and reported having fairly good health" (Wright & Elias, 1979, p. 705), and "All subjects were community residents reporting themselves to be in good health" (Salthouse, Wright, & Ellis, 1979, p. 55). The assumptions are that community residency demands reasonably good health and that global self-reports of good health may be accepted at face value. Neither assumption is necessarily true however. People can survive in a community without having good health, and people are not always aware of their own failing health, nor are they necessarily truthful in reporting it when they are aware of it. One way of improving the health-screening procedure is to elaborate on the nature of the self-report. This may be done by having potential subjects complete a checklist of symptoms indicative of a particular disease.

There is evidence (Botwinick & Storandt, 1974a) revealing a correlation between scores on one such checklist for cardiovascular symptoms and speed of responding to sensory stimuli. Another way is more indirect. It requires demonstrating that young and elderly groups are comparable in performance on some task other than the experimental task per se that is likely to be sensitive to at least pronounced variations in health status. This procedure was followed in a study by Smith (1979b). His elderly group was inferior to younger age groups in performance on a free recall learning task despite the fact that his age groups were comparable in performance on a digit-span task, a task likely to be affected adversely by failing health. Consequently, our conviction that the age deficit in free-recall learning reflects a true age change in learning-memory competence rather than an artifact produced by age-group differences in health status is strengthened greatly.

Included under health problems are the more insidious ones created by age differences in sensory functioning. Psychological tasks demand communication of information to subjects. For example, the items of a learning task have to be presented either visually or aurally. Subjects with uncorrected sensory deficits may fail to perceive many of the items as they are presented, leading, quite naturally, to an underestimation of their learning proficiency. This is especially a potential problem in aging research when items are presented aurally. Hearing deficits in elderly people are more likely to remain uncorrected than are visual deficits, and they could add substantially to the magnitude of age differences in performance on tasks requiring oral comprehension. The seriousness of this problem is indicated in an important study by Granick, Kleban, and Weiss (1976). They reported that even mild hearing losses by the elderly are accompanied by the gross lowering of scores earned on intelligence tests. Their observation of the possibility that "much of what has been reported in the past about cognitive decline in the aged may, in some measure, actually be a function of mild losses in auditory acuity rather than an outgrowth of the aging process *per se*" (p. 439) should forewarn investigators to make certain their elderly subjects are not suffering from auditory handicaps that may adversely affect their performance on a variety of laboratory tasks. Ordinarily, this objective may be accomplished by employing either a formal hearing test as a preliminary task or a preliminary task that requires a subject to shadow (i.e., listen to and then repeat verbatim) a string of aurally presented items. In either case, subjects with hearing deficiencies may be eliminated from further participation in the study. Finally, we should note that screening subjects in terms of sensory acuity has, quite appropriately, long been a standard practice in experimental aging studies dealing directly with perceptual phenomena. For example, in their study on adult-age differences in the magnitude of visual illusory phenomena, Lorden, Atkeson, and Pollack (1979) retained only subjects who scored at least 20/30 (corrected or uncorrected) in visual acuity as measured by an orthorater.

Another insidious problem associated with the decreased health status of even normally aging individuals is their presumed susceptibility to fatigue as a deterrent to proficient performance. Investigators are usually well aware of the potential confounding of an age differential in amount of fatigue accumulating during performance on a task. Fortunately, most laboratory tasks are fairly brief in duration and not unduly strenuous. Consequently, fatigue is unlikely to be a determining factor in producing age differences in performances on those tasks. Those tasks that are of a longer duration or that are more strenuous can often be divided into segments, with a rest break intervening between segments. Similarly, when multiple tasks are given, they may be separated by sufficient time to allow dissipation of whatever fatigue accrued on prior tasks. This was the procedure followed by Kausler and Puckett (1980a) in a study discussed earlier. Their subjects received both frequency judgment and paired-associate learning-memory tasks as well as several psychometric tests. To minimize fatigue effects, the learning-memory tasks were given on one day and the psychometric tests several days later. In addition, the tasks or tests given on the same day were separated by several minutes of a rest break filled with informal conversation. Thus, it seems highly unlikely that differential fatigue between young and elderly subjects influenced the outcome of their study.

Moreover, there is considerable evidence to indicate that elderly subjects are not nearly as susceptible to fatigue during laboratory performances as some people suspect. Various investigators (e.g., Cunningham, Sepkoski, & Opel, 1978; Furry & Schaie, 1979; Kamin, 1957) have preceded performance on intelligence test components with performance on a prior task involving moderately strenuous activity. Their results have revealed that these elderly subjects show no deleterious effect on intelligence test performance relative to other elderly subjects who did not perform on the prior task. Nor is the intelligence test performance of younger subjects affected by prior performance on a moderately strenuous task. Consequently, the magnitude of the age difference in intelligence test performance is about the same with or without participation in the prior activity. Illustrative of these results are those of Furry and Schaie. One group of experimental subjects at each of two age levels (middle age and elderly) participated in a prior task demanding physical activity (copying sentences), whereas a second group of experimental subjects at each age level had a mental activity added to the physical activity (transcribing upper to lower case letters and vice versa as they copied the sentences). Mean scores on the reasoning component of the Primary Mental Abilities Test earned by all six groups in their study are plotted in Figure 3.20. It can be seen that subjects at both age levels were unaffected by the nature of the activity preceding the reasoning test. In addition, the large age difference favoring the middle-age subjects was no greater under the experimental conditions than it was under the control condition. Furry and Schaie (1979) found almost identical patterns for the other components of the Primary Mental Abilities Test. On the other hand, Furry and Baltes (1973) did find that a highly strenuous prior task (in their case, a lengthy letter-cancellation task) can lower subsequent performance levels (on the components of the Primary Mental Abilities Test too) for both young and elderly subjects, with the decrement being especially large for the elderly (therefore, magnifying the magnitude of the age difference in test performance relative to the control condition). It seems unlikely, however, that the amount of activity required in the vast majority of experimental aging studies comes close to matching that entering in the prior task by Furry and Baltes.

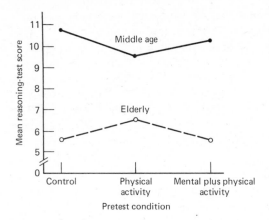

Figure 3.20. Mean reasoning scores (Primary Mental Abilities Test) made by groups of middle-age and elderly subjects receiving different kinds of prior tasks. (Adapted from Furry & Schaie, 1979, Table 1.)

Age Differences in Disuse and Their Effects on Age Differences in Performance. The argument that the skills needed to perform proficiently on a task will suffer from their disuse over a long period of time is an old one (e.g., Thorndike, Bregman, Tilton, & Woodyard, 1928). It carries with it the correlated argument that extensive practice on the task in question should bring proficiency back to where it was before the long layoff. If it is years of disuse rather than some decrement in competence that underlies a performance deficit on a task, then there is the hope that the magnitude of the deficit will diminish as practice continues and perhaps may eventually disappear completely. What little evidence there is, however, on the effects of practice on age differences in performance is not very encouraging. One direction taken in practice research is to give multiple trials on the same task, such as the digit-symbol task, and evaluate whatever changes occur for age differences in speed of performance as practice progresses. This procedure was followed in the study by Grant et al. (1978) discussed earlier. From Figure 3.19, it can be seen that elderly subjects did indeed improve in speed of responding as measured by the number of substitutions completed over successive trials. However, so did their young-adult subjects. In fact, the rate of improvement was greater for young adults than for elderly adults, with the net effect being the accentuation rather than the attenuation of age differences in performance proficiency as practice progressed, a finding replicating that reported earlier by Erber (1976) on the same task. The identical pattern of results was found for the letter-cancellation task by Hoyer, Hoyer, Treat, and Baltes (1978) in another study discussed earlier. That is, both age groups improved in proficiency with practice, but the amount of improvement was greater for young adults that for elderly adults. At any rate, studies such as these do suggest that elderly people often perform below the level of their competence and that it takes considerable warming up on a task before they begin to approximate the level of proficiency permitted by their competence. But, of course, the same may be said for young adults—only more so.

It can be argued that giving only 20 or so trials on a speeded task simply does not offer sufficient opportunity for elderly subjects to catch up with young adults. The only evidence in support of this extreme position comes from a widely cited study by Murrell (1970). After thousands of trials spread over several months, a single middle-age subject (a 57-year-old woman) caught up with, and even surpassed, two young subjects (a 17-year-old woman and an 18-year-old woman) in speed of responding on a choice reaction-time task. How generalizable this outcome is, especially with regard to elderly people versus young adults, remains untested, except in a study by Salthouse and Somberg (in press, b). Salthouse and Somberg found age deficits in several tasks to persist even after nearly 100 trials.

A second direction taken in extended practice research is the administration of a series of lists for a learning or memory task. Elderly subjects are expected to show pronounced increments in proficiency over successive lists as their long dormant, but essentially intact, learning-memory skills gain momentum and eventually become fully operative. However, the question remains as to whether or not these increments in proficiency would be sufficient to attenuate age differences in learning or memory. A study by Taub (1973) suggests that with respect to at least one important memory task, digit span, extended practice sessions serve only to increase the magnitude of age differences. Young and elderly subjects participated in four sessions on the digit-span task, one per week. Mean span scores (i.e., the longest series of digits repeated without error) for both age groups over the four sessions are plotted in Figure 3.21. As with the digit-symbol task, elderly subjects did improve as familiarity with the task increased. However, the gain was again greater for young adults, with the net effect once more being the accentuation of the age difference. Other investiga-

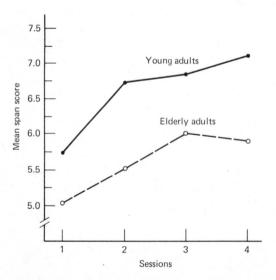

Figure 3.21. Mean digit-span scores earned by young and elderly subjects over four sessions (one per week). (Adapted from Taub, 1973, Table 1.)

tors have looked at the variation in the age difference found for both paired-associate learning (Freund & Witte, 1979; Monge, 1969) and free-recall learning (Hultsch, 1974) when both young and elderly subjects receive successive lists. In general, these studies have not found any systematic trend toward the attenuation of an age difference as subjects become increasingly familiar with the task in question.

Ecological Components Of External Validity

Earlier we raised the question of how a laboratory task's ecological relevance might contribute to age differences in motivation for performance on that task. Our concern at that time was with the potential confounding such age differences would have on estimates of age changes in competence. In this section, we will elaborate somewhat on the general issues raised by ecological relevance.

In effect, the absence of ecological relevance threatens the generalizability of age differences in performance that are observed in the laboratory. That is, valid age differences should be capable of being generalized to other settings, namely, those of real life as well as to other samples of subjects. Generalizability beyond the laboratory setting is, therefore, clearly another part of a study's overall external validity. This point has been made very effectively by Baltes, Reese, and Nesselroade:

> In many situations, conditions such as the physical surroundings in which the experiment is conducted may produce effects that will not be separable from the intended effect of the treatment. In such a case one may form an erroneous picture of the effect of the treatment. One does not know what outcome may occur if the treatment, per se, is applied in a somewhat different context or setting.
>
> For example, just knowing that an experiment of some type is taking place may cause the subjects to react differently to the treatment. If a treatment of some kind is tested in an experimental context and a given effect is observed, does this mean that a similar effect will be observed in a real-life kind of setting? "Deep Dimple" toothpaste may prove to be very effective in reducing cavities in a controlled experiment, but when it goes on the market and is purchased by the average person the user may not brush so strenuously as the subjects in the experiment did and thus the apparent effect of "Deep Dimple" toothpaste will be lost.
>
> It is easy to think of many situations in which the effect of some treatment ascertained under somewhat contrived conditions is unlikely to be repeated outside the experimental context. When an effect is observed in a highly controlled setting, it is at best risky to generalize from that observation to what one might observe in a real-life context. Such reactive arrangements may very seriously hamper our ability to generalize and thus may jeapordize the external validity of a design. (1977, pp. 54–55).

The degree to which task materials simulate those of real life is, therefore, only part of the challenge presented by ecological relevance to external validity. Equally important is the degree to which the restricted environment of the laboratory simulates real-life environments. Does the age deficit found for per-

formance in a laboratory setting generalize to more natural environmental settings even when the materials encountered in the laboratory are themselves a
reasonable facsimile of real-life materials? As observed by Baltes et al., the
answer is, not necessarily. Real-life settings may offer support systems for proficient performance that have no counterparts in laboratory settings. This is
especially likely to be true for elderly people. At home, for example, they can
turn up the volume of a radio to hear an aural message without appearing
decrepit in the eyes of a young investigator. Or they can learn new material in
accordance with their own practice schedules instead of those imposed on them
by an investigator. The need for broadening the settings as well as the materials
used in aging studies has been stressed by a number of contemporary gerontological psychologists (e.g., Labouvie-Vief & Chandler, 1978). Thus far, serious
attempts to initiate such broadening have been limited to research in intelligence (Scheidt & Schaie, 1978). These attempts are of considerable importance.
Schaie (1978) has observed that the age deficits in intelligence commonly reported by investigators appear on tests that were constructed originally for the
purpose of measuring abilities believed essential for successful performance in
academic settings. Such tests are likely to have high external validity in the
ecological sense when they are used with people currently performing in an
academic setting. Low scores on a test are expected to be related to deficits in
academic problem-solving proficiency. But academic settings are certainly not
where most elderly people are to be found. Of far greater significance is the
question of an age deficit in those intellectual abilities called for in the problem-solving settings actually confronting elderly people, namely, those indigenous to their own environments (to be discussed further in Chapter 11).

This further aspect of ecological relevance and external validity has become one of great concern to contemporary gerontological psychologists who
stress a particular perspective for psychological research that is called contextualism (Labouvie-Vief & Chandler, 1978). Among other things, contextualism
calls for "the careful naturalistic and ethological mapping of cognitive skills in
a life-span context" (Labouvie-Vief & Chandler, 1978, p. 203). Some areas of
contemporary experimental aging research, such as those dealing with age deficits in memory, could benefit from greater concern with the issues raised by
contextualism. We will discover in Chapter 9 that some of the current laboratory research on age differences in memory does not seem to have much relevance for the kinds of memory problems elderly people actually experience in
their natural environments.

Summary

The longitudinal method is the standard alternative to the cross-sectional method for
conducting explanatory research. In a longitudinal study, the same subjects are evaluated at different ages for their performance on the same task. Thus, each subject provides a perfectly matched counterpart (himself or herself) with regard to non-age
attributes at every contrasted age level. In the ideal longitudinal study, that is, one that
is not confounded by various factors, observed age differences in performance are the

result of an age change in the proficiency of the process governing performance on the task in question.

Unfortunately, however, longitudinal studies are unlikely to be free of confounding factors. The most serious source of confounding is through the selective attrition of subjects over the course of successive evaluations at different ages. Usually, the selection bias is positive in the sense that the nondropouts from the study (i.e., those subjects who remained to the end and were evaluated at every age level) were superior initally (i.e., at the youngest age level included in the study) to the dropouts (i.e., subjects who died or otherwise withdrew from the study before its completion). The net effect in this case is to underestimate the extent of a true age decrement in proficiency. When these conditions are reversed, with the nondropouts being those subjects who scored lower initially, the net effect is an overestimation of the age decrement in proficiency.

Further confoundings in longitudinal research may be contributed by progressive error effects and by time of measurement effects. Progressive error is the consequence of repeated performances on the same task or on alternate forms of a task. It may occur either through the direct retention of task content or through the operation of general, or nonspecific, transfer. When present, progressive error leads to underestimating the extent of an age deficit in proficiency. Its effect, however, may be corrected by the use of an appropriate control condition. Time of measurement effects may originate in three different ways: (1) by a change in the experimental, or laboratory, environment form Time 1 to Time 2 (i.e., the times of the first and second evaluations of the same subjects); (2) by a major shift in the extralaboratory environment (e.g., as produced by a major change in a nation's economy) that may affect a subject's motivational level; and (3) by the occurrence of a cultural change from Time 1 Time 2 (e.g., in increased test-taking sophistication by subjects). A time-of-measurement effect could lead to either an underestimation or an overestimation of an age change in proficiency, contingent on the nature of the time-related change.

An especially effective means of conducting explanatory research is to combine the cross-sectional and the longitudinal method in the same study and, therefore, with the same task. If the two methods demonstrate comparable age differences in performance (i.e., demonstrate convergent validity), despite their different kinds of potential confoundings, then the existence of a true age change in performance is fairly well established. On the other hand, an age difference in performance found cross-sectionally, but not longitudinally, is likely to be the product of variation in cohort membership. Similarly, an age difference found longitudinally, but not cross-sectionally, is likely to be the product of a time-of-measurement effect.

There are further complications in determining whether or not age differences in task performance result from a change in competence produced by the deterioration of the primary factor, or process, mediating performance on that task. Even when competence on a task remains unaffected ontogenetically (i.e., proficiency of the primary factor is unaltered by increasing age), age-related performance decrements may occur anyway through age-differences in secondary performance factors. These factors are broad in scope and enter into performance on many kinds of tasks. Confoundings owing to secondary performance factors know no methodological boundaries, that is, they are as likely to be present in longitudinal research as they are in cross-sectional research (or in sequential research). Age differences in secondary performance factors may be grouped into three broad categories: (1) differences between young and elderly adults in motivational level, (2) differences between young and elderly adults in current health status, and (3) differences between young and elderly adults in recency of practice for the kinds of skills entering into laboratory tasks (i.e., a disuse principle).

Age differences in motivation may be viewed in terms of emotional and task-involvement components. In the former case, elderly adults are commonly regarded as being overaroused relative to young adults; in the latter case, elderly adults are regarded as being less task involved than young adults. In neither case, however, does it seem likely that age differences in motivational level account for a great deal of the age differences in performance found on a wide range of psychological tasks. Health status is of direct concern because increasing age is accompanied by an increasing incidence of such illnesses as cardiovascular disease, a disease likely to lower performance proficiency on many kinds of tasks. Consequently, careful screening of subjects, especially elderly ones, with regard to current health status is an important preliminary step for most aging studies, but it is a step that is, nevertheless, difficult to accomplish. Health status may also enter into an aging study through the diminished sensory functioning of many elderly subjects and through the potentially greater susceptibility of elderly subjects relative to young subjects to performance-debilitating fatigue effects. However, screening of subjects with uncorrected sensory problems may be accomplished readily, and there is evidence to indicate that elderly adults are unlikely to experience debilitating fatigue while performing on most psychological tasks. Other evidence also reveals that elderly subjects do improve progressively with extended practice on many kinds of tasks, in agreement with the principle that task competence remains largely intact during long periods of disuse of the skills related to that competence. However, young adults also show increments with practice on a task and at a greater rate than do elderly adults. The net effect is that age differences are likely to become accentuated rather than attenuated by extended practice on many kinds of tasks.

Finally, an important component of external validity is the degree of generalizability of age differences in performance across various ecological settings. Of particular concern is the question of whether or not an age deficit in performance found in a laboratory setting will also be found in a more natural setting where various support systems are available to enable elderly people to maintain proficient performance. Unfortunately, there is little evidence to date bearing on this question, especially with regard to the kinds of tasks employed in the experimental psychology of aging.

4

Sequential Analyses of Age Differences: Modified Methodological Designs and Related Issues

From our discussion in Chapters 2 and 3, it is obvious that age variation per se is not the only reason why age differences might exist in primary-ability factors, that is, in competencies for various tasks. These other gross causative variables can be grouped into two broad categories, those associated with cohort membership and those associated with time of measurement, How to deal with multiple causation in explanatory research is a question of great importance to developmental psychologists working at all levels of the lifespan. To users of the traditional cross-sectional and longitudinal methods, the answer is a simple one—vary age while avoiding confoundings from the other potential sources of causation. Causation, in effect, is viewed in terms of a major causative variable, age, and other, less important, variables that irritatingly get in the way of testing the effects of age variation on task performances. The obstacles are sufficient, however, to force the users to make painstaking attempts to control or to adjust for the effects of these other variables. Only with such control or adjustment may a decision be justified that age differences in performance resulted solely from age variation.

The inability of this single independent variable (age) and the control-adjustment-for-other-variables strategy to give definitive answers to questions about the origins of age differences in human behaviors has long been recognized by both child development psychologists (e.g., Kessen, 1960) and adult development psychologists (e.g., Kuhlen, 1940). Like the weather, however, everyone talked about it but no one did anything about it. That is, no one until K. Warner Schaie appeared on the scene in the mid 1960s. Schaie's contributions began with a seminal methodological article that was published in 1965. In that article, Schaie proffered an alternative strategy to that shared by the two traditional methods. Rather than controlling or adjusting for cohort and time-of-measurement effects, he proposed treating the underlying variables in the same manner that age itself is treated, that is, as independent variables. To accommodate all three developmentally relevant independent variables, Schaie introduced the concept of *sequential analysis* of behavior as the foundation for extending the traditional methodologies. The extensions took the form of three new methodological designs that collectively seem to tease apart the separate roles of ontogenetic effects, cohort effects, and time-of-measurement effects in determining age differences in performance on a given task. Regardless of its specific format, each design calls for multiple evaluative sessions that are usually spread across a number of years.

To illustrate the basic logic of sequential analysis, we will return briefly to two studies described in Chapter 3. The first is that of Owens (1966). It will be recalled that Owens assessed intelligence in both 1919 and 1961 for subjects who were age 19 and age 61 at the time of the two assessments. In addition, a separate group of 19-year-old subjects was evaluated in 1961 for purposes of providing an adjustment for a time-of-measurement effect (i.e., cultural change over the 1919–1961 interval). In this design, age was really the only true independent variable, and time-of-measurement variation was treated as a confounding factor requiring an adjustment to obtain a pure picture of the effects of age variation on intelligence test performance. The possibility that members of the two cohorts involved in the study (those born around 1900 and those born around 1942) may have differed in the kind of intellectual stimulation received during childhood was ignored. Suppose, however, that Owens plans to continue his study. Specifically, suppose Owen plans to extend the study by retesting in the year 2003 the subjects who were age 19 in the year 1961. As is shown in the top segment of Table 4.1, a four-group design will emerge at the end of the study. The design permits the treatment of both age *and* cohort membership as bilevel independent variables (age 19 versus age 61; 1900 cohort versus 1942 cohort).

With this modified design, tests of statistical significance become possible for both age variation and cohort variation along with a test of the significance of the interaction between the two variables. Thus, the effect of variation in cohort membership (an effect ignored in the original study) would be separated from the age effect. Of course, as should be apparent in Table 4.1, the modified study will be confounded, at least potentially, by disparities in time of measurement for the four groups in the total design. Note that the 61-year-old subjects were tested overall in later years (1961 for Group 4 and 2003 for Group 2) than the 19-year-old subjects (1919 for Group 3 and 1961 Group 1). Similarly, the members of the 1942 generation were tested overall in later years (1961 and 2003) than the members of the 1900 generation (1919 and 1961). This disparity is a fact of life faced by any user of a sequential design. The design permits systematic variation of only two of the developmentally relevant independent variables, leaving the third variable uncontrolled.

Our modification of Owens's study produced what Schaie calls a *cohort-sequential design*. Again, cohort variation joined age variation as developmental

Table 4.1   Redesigns of Owens's (1966) Study.[a]

Cohort-Sequential Study

Cohort	Time of Measurement			
	1919	*1961*	*2003*	
1942		Group 1: 19-year-old subjects born in 1942 and tested in 1961 (a condition included in the original study)	Group 2: the subjects in Group 1 who are retested in 2003 at age 61 (a condition *not* included in the original study)	1942 cohort versus 1900 cohort
1900	Group 3: 19-year-old subjects born in 1900 and tested in 1919 (a condition included in the original study)	Group 4: the subjects in Group 3 who are retested in 1961 at age 61 (a condition included in the original study)		
	Age 19 ↙ versus	Age 61 ↙		

Time-Sequential Study

Age	Time of Measurement		
	1919	*1961*	
19	Group 1: 19-year-old subjects born in 1900 and tested in 1919 (a condition included in the original study)	Group 2: 19-year-old subjects born in 1942 and tested in 1961 (a condition included in the original study)	Age 19 versus Age 61
61	Group 3: 61-year-old subjects born in 1858 and tested in 1919 (a condition *not* included in the original study)	Group 4: the subjects in Group 1 who were retested in 1961 at age 61 (a condition included in the original study)	
	1919 time of measurement versus	1961 time of measurement	

[a]The new designs accommodate either Age and Cohort as independent variables, thus making the modified design conform to a cohort-sequential study (top segment), or Age and Time of Measurement as independent variables, thus making the modified design conform to a time-sequential study (bottom segment).

independent variables. Alternatively, Owens's study could have been converted into a *time-sequential design* in which time of measurement, rather than cohort, joined age as the independent variables. This design would have emerged if Owens had been blessed with the same degree of foresight we now possess as hindsight. Specifically, suppose he had included another group of subjects in his study, namely a group of 61-year-old men who were administered the Army Alpha test for the first and only time in 1919 (i.e., at the same time the original group of college students was evaluated). As is shown in the bottom segment of Table 4.1, a four-group design is again apparent. This time the bilevel independent variables are time of measurement (year 1919 versus year 1961) and age (age 19 versus age 61). Tests of statistical significance would now be possible for both time of measurement and age along with a test of the significance of the interaction between these two variables. However, the revised study continues to remain potentially confounded, this time by disparities in cohort memberships for the four groups of the overall design. Note that the 19-year-old subjects were born in later years overall (1900 for Group 1 and 1942 for Group 2) than the 61-year-old subjects (1858 for Group 3 and 1900 for Group 4). Similarly, the subjects tested in 1961 were born in later years (1900 and 1942) than the subjects tested in 1919 (1858 and 1900).

Our second study from Chapter 3 is one that, on reconsideration, fits what Schaie calls a *cross-sequential design*. It is the hypothetical study illustrated in Figure 3.11. This study served earlier to demonstrate how simultaneous cross-sectional and longitudinal analyses provide convergent evidence for the true effects of age variation. We can alter this study considerably by examining only the four conditions formed by the combinations of 1920 and 1930 cohorts with the two times of measurement (1970 and 1980). Our revised treatment is summarized in Table 4.2. Note that we have now identified two bilevel independent variables, cohort variation (1920 versus 1930) and time-of-measurement variation (1970 versus 1980). Thus, we would be able to determine separately the effects of each variable on performance as well as the effect of the interaction between the two variables. However, in the process of doing this, we are again confronted by an ugly fact of life, potential confounding by the third developmentally relevant variable. In this case, it is age variation that remains uncontrolled. The members of our later cohort are younger overall (40 and 50) than the members of our earlier cohort (50 and 60). Similarly, the members entering into our earlier time of measurement are younger overall (40 and 50) than the members entering the our later time of measurement (50 and 60).

Despite its obvious imperfections, sequential analysis has already had a considerable impact on the psychology of aging. The impact has been a direct one for research dealing with age differences in intelligence and personality in the sense that a number of sequentially conducted studies have been completed and published in these areas. By contrast, it has thus far been largely indirect for research dealing with age differences in the content areas of experimental psychology. One consequence has been the growing cautiousness of investigators in planning their cross-sectional studies to minimize potential confound-

Table 4.2   Redesign of a Study Comparing Cross-sectional and Longitudinal Analyses of Age Differences (See Figure 3.11) to Make It Conform to a Cross-sequential Study

Cohort Variable: Levels	Time-of-Measurement Variable: Levels	
	1970	*1980*
1930	Group 1: 40-year-old subjects born in 1930 and tested in 1970 (a condition included in the original analysis)	Group 2: the subjects born in 1930 and retested at age 50 in 1980 (a condition included in the original analysis)
		1930 cohort
		versus
1920	Group 3: 50-year-old subjects born in 1920 and tested in 1970 (a condition included in the original analysis)	Group 4: the subjects born in 1920 and retested at age 60 in 1980 (a condition *not* included in the original analysis)
		1920 cohort
	1970 time of → versus ← 1980 time of measurement	

ings from cohort effects and in interpreting the results obtained in their conventional studies. Another consequence has been the occurrence of confessions motivated by the sin of omission, that is, the sin of *not* conforming to the guidelines of sequential methodology. Comments by two investigators illustrate nicely what we mean here. In his review of research on the effects of aging on memory, Hultsch (1971a) remarked," While I have consistently referred to age differences in this paper, the possibility of cohort differences should not be overlooked. . . . Different cohorts of individuals may use different organizational strategies on memory tasks because of shifts in educational training practices, for example" (p. 26). In other words, prior research on the effects of aging on memory had failed to employ designs that separated cohort effects from age effects. In a study examining age differences in categorizing behavior (see Chapter 10), Cicirelli (1976) warned that, "While the findings would be consistent with a hypothesis of regressive age changes in certain categorization behaviors, it is not possible to determine whether observed cross-sectional age differences represent true age differences rather than generational without undertaking some kind of sequential design" (p. 679). Interestingly, Cicirelli went on to add, "However, the finding that differences in occupational or educational level between the elderly subjects did not account for age differences where they were observed lends support to the hypothesis of regressive age changes" (p. 679).

It may be only a matter of time before the spreading concern about traditional cross-sectional research leads to its virtual abandonment in favor of one or more sequential designs. Such action would, of course, greatly alter the nature of future experimental aging studies. We obviously need to take a critical look at sequential designs, especially in terms of their relevance for research in most content areas of the experimental psychology of aging. The remainder of this chapter will be devoted to these objectives.

Sequential Analysis and Sequential Designs

Trifactor Model and Confoundings in Traditional Designs. Schaie's (1965) formulation of new methodological designs was greatly influenced by his own trifactor model of developmental changes. Consequently, we need to examine this model and its implications for research conducted with the traditional methodologies before we turn to the new methodologies themselves. According to Schaie, the factors represent the three independent means by which differences in behavior or performance may emerge between two or more groups of subjects in a developmentally oriented study. The first means is through chronological age differences, the second through cohort differences, and the third through time-of-measurement differences. Briefly, age-differences result from differential age levels of contrasted groups, cohort differences from differential generational memberships of contrasted groups, and time-of-measurement differences from differential time periods in which the contrasted groups are evaluated. In other words, the model formalizes the roles played by all three developmentally relevant variables of concern to developmental psychologists.

To illustrate the implications of these three factors for research conducted by means of a traditional methodological design, we will make use of the 12 groups identified in the cells of Table 4.3. The cells are formed by intersecting selected points along two independent dimensions. The first dimension is year of birth. A given year defines the generation, or cohort, of all subjects born in that year. Four generations are represented in this table, corresponding to the birth years of 1930, 1920, 1910, and 1900. The second dimension is the year in which subjects are evaluated. The points selected on this dimension are the years 1960, 1970, and 1980. The intersections, therefore, determine the chronological ages of the various groups at the time of their evaluations on a particular task. For example, Group A, whose members were born in 1930 and evaluated in 1960, consisted of 30-year-old subjects at the time of evaluation.

Our 12 groups could enter into four different cross-sectional studies (identified by vertical arrows in Table 4.3), with each study contrasting four groups varying in chronological age by successive increments of 10 years. Thus, one of these studies would have been done in 1960 with Groups A, D, G, and J. These groups would have had chronological ages of 30, 40, 50, and 60 years respectively. However, the four age groups would also have varied in their cohort membership, having been born in 1930, 1920, 1910, and 1900 respectively. Our observed cross-sectional differences in task performances among these groups could, therefore, be due either to the age-difference factor or to the cohort-difference factor of the trifactor model. Or cross-sectional differences could be

Table 4.3 Groups Formed by Variation in Cohort (Birth Year) Membership, and Time of Measurement (Year Evaluated).

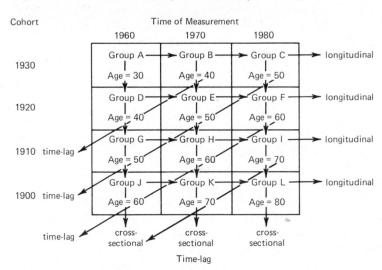

Age in years is that of subjects at the time they are evaluated. Arrows indicate the various cross-sectional, longitudinal, and time-lag comparisons among groups that could be made with these groups.

due to some combination of the two factors. However, cross-sectional differences could not be due to time of measurement differences in that all of the subjects were evaluated in the same year (1960). Thus,

$$CS\,d = Ag\,d + Co\,d$$

where $CS\,d$ = cross-sectional differences
$Ag\,d$ = age differences
$Co\,d$ = cohort differences

Time-of-measurement differences are controlled and the relative contributions of age differences and cohort differences to the overall magnitude of cross-sectional differences remain unknown. In other words, we have the by now familiar confounding between age and non-age attributes.

Similarly, our groups could enter into four longitudinal studies (indicated by horizontal arrows in Table 4.3), with each study contrasting three evaluations of the same subjects. For example, one such study would have begun in 1960 with a 30-year-old group (Group A). Reevaluation of these subjects would have been done in 1970 (Group B) and again in 1980 (Group C). Thus, groups A, B, and C would have chronological ages of 30, 40, and 50 respectively. However, our three groups also varied in their time of measurement. Observed longitudinal differences in task performance could, therefore, be due to either the age-variation factor or the time-of-measurement-variation factor. Or they could be due to some combination of the two. However, the longitudinal differences could not be due to cohort variation in that all subjects were from the same cohort (1930). Thus,

$$Lo\ d = Ag\ d + Tm\ d$$

where $Lo\ d$ = longitudinal differences
$Ag\ d$ = age differences
$Tm\ d$ = time-of-measurement differences

Cohort differences are controlled and the relative contributions of age differences and time-of-measurement differences remain unknown. Once more, we return to a familiar confounding, this one between age and time effects.

The trifactor model has ramifications for still another hoary methodological design, the *time-lag design*. In a time-lag study, chronological age is kept constant while both cohort and time of measurement vary. The usual intent is to determine the extent of cultural change, or "secular trend" (Schaie, 1977), in behavior at any given chronological age level. We touched on a time-lag study in our earlier discussion of Owens's research (1966). Of concern were mean scores on the Army Alpha test earned by 19-year-old men in 1919 and again in 1961. The difference between these means allowed Owens to estimate the extent of a cultural change from 1919 to 1961 through increased test sophistication. A similar upward trend in scores on the Army Alpha test was reported by Tuddenham (1948). Military personnel in World War II were found to score considerably higher than military personnel in World War I. The problem in a pure time-lag study, as we noted in Chapter 3, is the inability to separate cohort variation from time-of-measurement variation as the source of like-age differences in scores. That is, the like-age difference could be due to differential cohort memberships rather than to a cultural change over the interval separating evaluations. In principle, a time-lag study may be used to estimate the magnitude of a cohort effect, just as it is used to estimate the magnitude of a cultural change. The validity of either use depends on the validity of one's assumption that the alternative source exerted a negligible effect.

There are four potential time-lag studies represented in the cells of Table 4.3 (indicated by diagonal arrows), the first involving two groups of 40-year-old subjects (groups D and B), the second involving three groups of 50-year-old subjects (groups G, E, and C), the third involving three groups of 60-year-old subjects (groups J, H, and F), and the fourth involving two groups of 70-year-old subjects (groups K and I). We will consider only the study with 60-year-old subjects. For this study, a group of 1900 cohorts was evaluated in 1960, a group of 1910 cohorts in 1970, and a group of 1920 cohorts in 1980. Observed time-lag differences between these groups could be due to either the cohort-variation factor or the time-of-measurement-variation factor or to some combination of the two. Thus

$$TL\,d = Tm\,d + Co\,d$$

where $TL\,d$ = time-lag differences
$Tm\,d$ = time-of-measurement differences
$Co\,d$ = cohort differences

Age differences are controlled and the relative contributions of time of measurement differences and cohort differences remain unknown. As with the other traditional designs, confounding appears to be unavoidable in a pure time-lag study.

How does one go about unconfounding studies conducted under the auspices of the traditional methodologies? The solutions we offered in Chapters 2 and 3, although straightforward and relatively uncomplicated, were unable to give any guaranty of accomplishing their mission. These solutions rely on research designs in which chronological age is the only independent variable and potentially confounding variables are equated as much as possible across levels of that single independent variable. Schaie's (1965) solutions to the same problems are quite innovative, but they are also considerably more complex than our earlier solutions. The solutions are embedded in three new methodological designs that expand on the three traditional designs by (1) including two independent variables rather than one and (2) by analyzing simultaneously two or more behavior sequences. The new designs differ among themselves in terms of the two independent variables they accommodate and in terms of the nature of the behavior sequences they examine. Although the players change across the designs, the rules by which the methodological game is played are basically the same for all three designs. In each case, two of Schaie's trifactors are selected to serve as the source of independent variables and the third factor contributes uncontrolled and, therefore, potentially confounding variation.

The use of three separate bifactor designs (i.e., two independent variables) raises an interesting question, namely: Why not a single trifactor design that incorporates age, cohort, and time of measurement as independent variables? The answer, unfortunately, is quite simple. The three components of Schaie's model are not independent factors, each of which may be varied independently of variation in the other factors—as they must be to be considered true independent variables. Two factors may be selected as independent variables, and they are both free to be set at whatever levels the investigator chooses. However, once these levels are set, the third factor becomes fixed at those levels necessary to provide the selected levels of the other two factors. For example, suppose we want age and cohort to serve as independent variables, with age levels set at 40 and 50 years and cohort levels at 1920 and 1930. Referring to Table 4.3, it may be seen that we have no choice in our selection of levels for time of measurement. Measurement must occur in 1960, 1970, and 1980 to give us the required levels of our other variables. Similarly, if we want cohort and time of measurement to serve as independent variables, with cohort set at 1900 and 1910 and time of measurement at 1960 and 1970, then we again have no choice regarding the third factor. Again, referring to Table 4.3, it may be seen that we would have to employ 50-, 60-, and 70-year-old subjects. To resolve the problem created by lack of independence and still hold on to all three factors as potential independent variables, Schaie resorted to these three separate bifactor designs, thereby providing the opportunity for each factor to serve as an independent variable in combination with each of the other factors. By necessity, however, the third factor in each design is reduced to the role of an uncontrolled variable.

Collectively, sequential designs appear to offer ingenious solutions to methodological problems in research on aging and in research on child development as well (Houston-Stein & Baltes, 1976). However, completing an experimental aging study that adheres fully to the requirements of any one of these designs is not easy to accomplish. It requires the wisdom of a Solomon, the longevity of a Methuselah, the patience of a Job, and the backing of a Rockefeller. Moreover, as we will see later, the solutions arrived at through the use of a sequential design may be more illusory than real.

Cohort-Sequential Design. Schaie described his first sequential design as follows:

> Whenever the subset of samples to be examined contains measures for all cohorts measured at all ages, it may be concluded that it is the investigator's intention to generalize over cohort differences. Such a design samples cohort differences at many times within the life span of the cohorts. This design will be referred to as the cohort-sequential method since longitudinal sequences for two or more cohorts are examined simultaneously. The cohort-sequential method permits inferences as to age changes at all points of the age range covered and, also, inferences about cohort differences at all ages. (1965, p. 97)

The simplest study that may be conducted within a cohort-sequential design employs the four groups formed by a 2 × 2 factorial (an elaboration of this factorial design in general will be given in Chapter 5) in which age and cohort membership are bilevel independent variables. The cohort-sequential design of a study permits inferences about independent age differences and cohort differences as they pertain to performance on the task in question. It would also permit an inference about the interaction between chronological age and cohort membership in determining performance scores. However, a study conducted within this design would by necessity be confounded by uncontrolled variation in time of measurement. Consequently, the previously mentioned inferences would be valid only to the extent that the variation in time of measurement has negligible effects on performance. If this is not the case, then the internal validity of the study may be seriously questioned.

One of the four-group cohort-sequential studies that could be conducted with the groups shown in Table 4.3 is summarized in the top panel of Figure 4.1. The particular groups selected are B, C, D, and E. Other cohort-sequential studies could be conducted with Groups, E, F, G, and H or Groups H, I, J, and

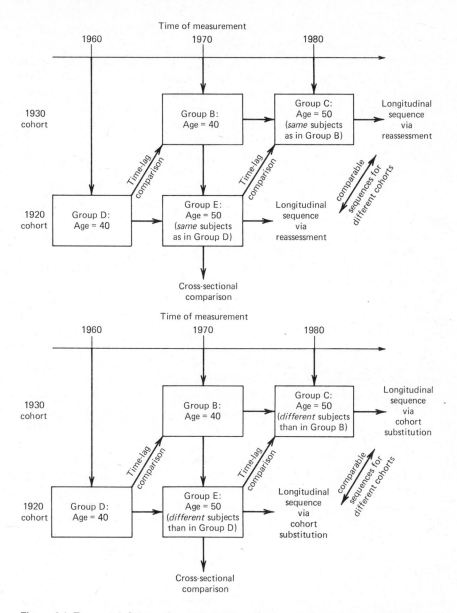

Figure 4.1. Top panel: Schematic representation of a four-group cohort-sequential study in which age (40 versus 50) and cohort (1920 versus 1930) are the independent variables; B, C, D, and E refer to groups identified in Table 4.3; and longitudinal sequences are established by means of reassessments of subjects tested earlier. Bottom panel: An alternative procedure in which longitudinal sequences are established by means of the use of "new" subjects from the cohorts tested earlier.

K. For our specific study, age is varied at 40 versus 50 years and cohort membership is varied at 1930 versus 1920. From Figure 4.1, we discover that Groups B, C, D, and E, when considered together, combine the features of conventional cross-sectional designs (Group B versus Group E), longitudinal designs

(Group B versus Group C), and time-lag designs (Group D versus Group B). This is true of any cohort-sequential study following the original guidelines established by Schaie. Within the design of that study, the defining feature that makes it cohort sequential is the evaluation of a longitudinal sequence of performance changes for all cohort levels involved in the study, so that the sequential evaluations occur at the same chronological ages for each cohort. In the present case, the cohorts are 1930 and 1920, and the sequential evaluations occur at ages 40 and 50 for each cohort (see the top panel of Figure 4.1).

The principle of evaluating a longitudinal sequence for each cohort need not be taken literally to mean longitudinal reassessments of the same subjects in each cohort at the different times of measurement. An alternative strategy to reassessment, and one with certain advantages, is to assess subjects only once and then replace those subjects at the later time of measurement with a new group of subjects from the same cohort. This, of course, corresponds to the intracohort manipulation we described in Chapter 3. When applied to our present study, Group E would consist of a "new" group of subjects from the 1920 cohort who were tested for the first time in 1970 (bottom panel of Figure 4.1). Similarly, Group C would consist of a "new" group of subjects from the 1930 cohort who were tested for the first time in 1980. The substitution of an intracohort manipulation for a subject reassessment does not violate the basic principle of evaluating a longitudinal sequence within the same generation of subjects. Nor are the basic components of the subsequent statistical analysis altered, although some of the technical details of that analysis are contingent on the choice made between subject reassessment and intracohort manipulation. The intracohort-manipulation strategy has the definite advantage of avoiding some of the major pitfalls associated with traditional longitudinal reassessments, namely, selective subject attrition and progressive error. As a general rule, reassessment of the same subjects encounters these pitfalls whenever it is applied, whether it be in a traditional longitudinal study or in a sequential study.

Performance scores collected for Groups B, C, D, and E are subjected to an analysis of variance that yields an age main effect, a cohort main effect, and an age × cohort interaction effect. The age main effect is derived by comparing the combined scores for Groups B and D (i.e., the 40-year-old subjects) with the combined scores for Groups C and E (i.e., the 50-year old subjects). The age groups are not confounded by variation in cohort membership in that the two overall age groups have balanced cohort representations. That is, for each age group, half of the subjects are 1920 cohorts (Group D for 40-year-old subjects and Group E for 50-year-old subjects) and half are 1930 cohorts (Group B for 40-year-old subjects and Group C for 50-year-old subjects). The cohort main effect is derived by comparing the combined scores for Groups B and C (i.e., the 1930 cohort subjects) with the combined scores for Groups D and E (i.e., the 1920 cohort subjects). The cohort groups are not confounded by variation in chronological age in that they have balanced age representations. That is, for each cohort group, half of the subjects are 40 years old (Group B for 1930 cohorts and Group D for 1920 cohorts) and half are 50 years old

Table 4.4   Comparisons Entering into the Analysis of Scores Obtained in a Cohort-Sequential Study

Age main effect: Age 40   versus   Age 50

Group B + Group D   Group C + Group E

1930 cohort   1920 cohort   1930 cohort   1920 cohort

(balanced)

Cohort main effect: Cohort 1930   versus   Cohort 1920

Group B + Group C   Group D + Group E

Age 40   Age 50   Age 40   Age 50

(balanced)

Age $\times$ cohort interaction effect: $(\text{Age } 40 - \text{Age } 50)_{1930} - (\text{Age } 40 - \text{Age } 50)_{1920}$

$(\text{Group B} - \text{Group C}) - (\text{Group D} - \text{Group E})$

(Group C for 1930 cohorts and Group E for 1920 cohorts). The age $\times$ cohort interaction effect represents the difference in performance between Groups B and C relative to the difference in performance between groups D and E. It contrasts the age difference in performance (i.e., 40 years old versus 50 years old) found for 1930 cohorts with the age difference found for 1920 cohorts. The comparisons entering into the statistical analysis are summarized in Table 4.4.

If the age main effect from this statistical analysis is significant but the cohort main effect is not, then the inference is that age variation per se rather than its correlated cohort variation accounts for performance changes on the given task. Conversely, if the cohort main effect is significant but the age main effect is not, then the inference is that cohort variation alone accounts for the observed performance changes. If both main effects are statistically significant, then both age variation and cohort variation appear to enter into performance changes. Moreover, the magnitudes of the two main effects—the magnitude of an effect may be estimated by such statistics as omega squared (ω^2) (Hays, 1963)—allow an inference about the relative importance of age variation versus cohort variation in evincing performance changes. However, the presence of two significant main effects carries with it a certain degree of ambiguity. It is conceivable that neither independent variable, given this outcome, bears a causative relationship with the dependent variable. That is, the observed age and cohort main effects may be spurious ones resulting from the confounding by the uncontrolled time-of-measurement variable. Note from Figure 4.1 that 50-year-old subjects overall have later times of measurement (1970 and 1980; average, 1975) than do 40-year-old subjects (1960 and 1970; average, 1965). If later measurements yield superior performance scores than earlier measurements, independently of the age and cohort membership of the subjects being evaluated, then the disparity in performance among the times of measurement should reduce the amount of the observed age effect. That is, the disparity favors older subjects, thereby reducing somewhat whatever disadvantage in performance they might have relative to the younger subjects. As we will see shortly, the artifact resulting from uncontrolled time-of-measurement variation is especially intriguing when age variation per se has no real effect on performance. On the other hand, the confounding from uncontrolled time of measurement would favor the later cohort (1970 and 1980; average, 1975) over the earlier cohort (1960 and 1970; average, 1965).

A nonsignificant interaction effect signifies that whatever age effect is observed generalizes across different cohorts and whatever cohort effect is observed generalizes across different chronological ages. A significant interaction effect, in turn, means that whatever main effects are present must be interpreted in light of this interaction. For example, the interaction might indicate that the age effect is considerably greater for one cohort than for the other cohort included in the study. The presence of a significant interaction effect in a study of any kind has important interpretative implications that will be discussed in Chapter 5.

Several hypothetical examples of outcomes from cohort-sequential studies should help us to understand the nature of main effects and confounding effects. Each example represents the fictitious outcome of a study on visual memory. The same task is administered in each study. It consists of 20 geometric designs. Subjects study each design for 10 seconds and then attempt to reproduce it from memory. Each reproduction is scored on a 0-to-10-point scale, with the points assigned to a given reproduction being contingent on the quality of the reproduction (maximum score on the entire test therefore equals 200). Four such examples are given in Table 4.5, in each case for our previously selected groups.

In example (a), cohort variation and age variation have independent causative effects on the dependent variable and, therefore, both seem to affect visual-memory proficiency. The best performance is for 40-year-old subjects from the 1930 cohort. We have arbitrarily set the mean for these subjects (Group B) at 100 points. The 10-year increment in age results in a 10-point decrement in scores. Thus, visual-memory proficiency appears to decrease with increasing age. Similarly, the use of subjects from the earlier cohort (1920) results in a 10-point decrement in scores. Thus, members of a later cohort appear to have better visual-memory proficiency than members of an earlier cohort. Consequently, the means for Groups C, D, and E are 90, 90, and 80 points respectively. The overall means become 95 and 85 points for 40-year-old and 50-year-old subjects respectively; the overall means become 95 and 85 points for 1930 and 1920 cohorts respectively. Presumably, both disparities in overall means are large enough to yield significant main effects in our analysis of variance. In example (b), cohort variation affects performance on the visual-memory task but age variation does not. Therefore, the means for both Groups B and C (the

Table 4.5 Four Hypothetical Outcomes of a Cohort-Sequential Study on a Visual Memory Task[a]

(a)

Cohort	Age 40	Age 50	Cohort Mean
1930	Group B: 100	Group C: 90	95
1920	Group D: 90	Group E: 80	85
Age mean	95	85	

(b)

Cohort	Age 40	Age 50	Cohort Mean
1930	Group B: 100	Group C: 100	100
1920	Group D: 90	Group E: 90	90
Age mean	95	95	

(c)

Cohort	Age 40	Age 50	Cohort Mean
1930	Group B: 100	Group C: 90	95
1920	Group D: 100	Group E: 90	95
Age mean	100	90	

(d)

Cohort	Age 40	Age 50	Cohort Mean
1930	Group B: 90	Group C: 100	95
1920	Group D: 80	Group E: 90	85
Age mean	85	95	

[a] Groups correspond to those identified in Figure 4.1; numbers represent mean scores on the particular task employed in that study: (a) both cohort variation and age variation have causative effects and time-of-measurement variation is not a confounding factor; (b) cohort variation but not age variation has a causative effect and time-of-measurement variation is not a confounding factor; (c) age variation but not cohort variation has a causative effect and time-of-measurement variation is not a confounding factor; and (d) neither cohort variation nor age variation have causative effects but confounding by variation in time of measurement yields spurious age and cohort effects.

1930 cohort groups) are set at 100 points; the means for both Groups D and E (the 1920 cohort groups) are set at 90 points. The overall means become 100 and 90 points for 1930 and 1920 cohorts respectively; the overall means are invariant at 95 points for the two age levels. Presumably, the disparity in means is large enough to yield a significant main effect for cohort but certainly not for age. In example (c), age variation affects performance on the visual memory task but cohort variation does not. Thus, the means for both Groups B and D (the 40-year-old groups) are set at 100 points; the means for Group C and E (the 50-year-old groups) are set at 90 points. The overall means become 100 and 90 for 40- and 50-year-old subjects respectively; the overall means are invariant at 95 for the two cohort levels. This time the disparity in means should be large enough to yield a significant main effect for age but not for cohort.

In each of the preceding examples, either one or both independent variables exerted causative effects on visual-memory proficiency, whereas the uncontrolled variable, time of measurement, did not. In example (d), however, neither independent variable exerts a causative effect, whereas time of measurement does. Mean performance is set at 100 points for measurement in 1980. Each 10-year-testing interval results in a decrement of 10 points, making mean scores equal 90 and 80 points in 1970 and 1960 respectively. Thus, later assessment of visual-memory proficiency appears to yield higher scores than earlier assessment. Consequently, the mean for Group C (1980 measurement) is 100 points, the means for Groups B and E (1970 measurements) are 90 points and the mean for Group D (1960 measurement) is 80 points. The resulting confounding makes the overall means for 50- and 40-year-old subjects equal 95 and 85 points respectively; the overall means for 1930 and 1920 cohorts equal 95 and 85 points respectively. As a result, we would expect to obtain spurious significant effects in our analysis of variance for both age and cohort. They are spurious in the sense that they are due entirely to the uncontrolled variation in time of measurement.

Note that the outcome of example (d) is identical to the outcome of example (a) in one critical respect—the presence of significant main effects for both independent variables. Of course, in example (d) the effect of age is in the direction of increasing performance on the visual-memory task with increasing age rather than in the opposite direction as in example (a). It is not inconceivable to find a performance increment with increasing age, at least for some tasks. Consequently, how can we tell whether an outcome of the kind shown in example (d) demonstrates the correct identification of two true causative factors or the misidentification of two innocent factors as being causative? We have no problem in our hypothetical example because we knew in advance that the effects were spuriously induced by uncontrolled variation in time of measurement. In actual research studies, however, we do not *know* in advance what the true causative factors are. We can only *infer* what they are from the presence of statistically significant effects. Given significant main effects for age and cohort variation in a real study, the question is: Are they valid or are they spurious? This is why it is extremely important in a cohort-sequential study to have very good reasons for assuming in advance that the uncontrolled variable, time of measurement, truly has negligible effects on performance.

Time-Sequential Design. Schaie described his second sequential design as follows:

> The first alternative procedure to be advocated is called the *time-sequential* method and applies whenever the subset of samples under examination contains measures of all ages at all times of measurement. The time-sequential method permits inferences as to age differences at all points of the age range covered, as well as inferences about time differences (or cultural shifts) at all ages. (1965, p. 98)

The simplest study within the constraints of a time-sequential design would again be a 2×2 factorial, this time with age and time of measurement as the bilevel independent variables and cohort the potentially confounding variable. Of particular concern in this design are sequential changes in behavior over a time interval in which age levels are held constant for both ends of the time interval. For example, the time interval may be from 1960 to 1970 and the age levels may be 40 and 50 years of age. We would, therefore, compare groups of 40- and 50-year-old subjects in both 1960 and 1970. We would, in effect, be conducting successive cross-sectional studies of 40- and 50-year-old subjects, once in 1960 and once in 1970. By necessity, however, the cross-sections in one year would have to involve different cohorts than the cross-sections in the other year.

As with the cohort-sequential design, several four-group time-sequential studies may be conducted with the groups represented in Table 4.3. Of these studies, the one that corresponds with the conditions described above is summarized in Figure 4.2. It involves Groups B, D, E, and G from our earlier matrix. Similar studies could be conducted with Groups G, E, J, and H, Groups E, C, H, and F, or Groups H, F, K, and L (see Table 4.3). From Figure 4.2 we discover that Groups B, D, E, and G considered together again combine the features of conventional cross-sectional, longitudinal, and time-lag analyses. Moreover, the longitudinal sequence being examined may be introduced through either reassessment or cohort manipulation, as in the cohort-sequential design.

In common with our prior cohort-sequential study, our present time-sequential study (see Table 4.6) yields a main effect for age (40 versus 50 years, with time of measurement balanced across age variations). However, the other main effect is now that of time of measurement (1960 versus 1970, with age balanced across time variations); the interaction effect is that of age with time of measurement. The comparisons entering into the overall analysis of variance are summarized in Table 4.6. Confounding from the uncontrolled variation in cohorts could result from the fact that 40-year-old subjects overall come from later cohorts (1920 and 1930; average, 1925) than 50-year-old subjects (1920 and 1910; average, 1915). If later cohorts have superior performance scores relative to earlier cohorts, then the resulting disparity in performance would inflate the advantage of the 40-year-old subjects over the 50-year-old subjects.

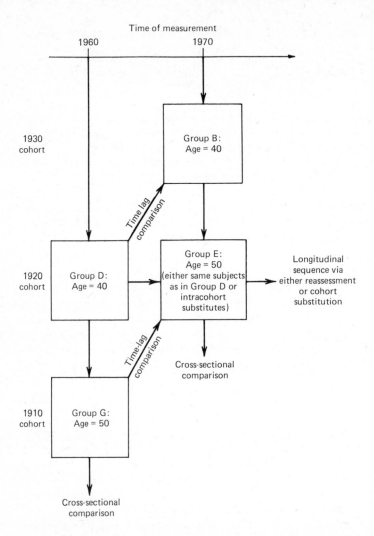

Figure 4.2. Schematic representation of a four-group time-sequential study in which age (40 versus 50) and time of measurement (1960 versus 1970) are the independent variables; B, D, E, and G refer to groups identified in Table 4.3.

Similarly, the cohort confounding would favor the 1970 measurement (1920 and 1930 cohorts; average, 1925) over the 1960 measurement (1920 and 1910 cohorts; average, 1915).

The interpretations given to significant main and interaction effects would be much like those given for a cohort-sequential study. Most important, if both the age and time of measurement main effects are statistically significant, then the relative contributions of each independent variable to performance changes would be reflected by the relative magnitudes of the two effects (as evaluated again by ω^2). However, roughly equal magnitudes could mean that both effects

Table 4.6 Comparisons entering into the Analysis of Scores Obtained in a Time-Sequential Study

Age main effect:

Age 40		versus	Age 50
Group B + Group D			Group E + Group G
1970 measurement	1960 measurement	1970 measurement	1960 measurement

(balanced)

Time-of-measurement main effect:

1960		versus	1970
Group D + Group G		Group B + Group E	
Age 40	Age 50	Age 40	Age 50

(balanced)

Age $\times$ time-of-measurement interaction effect: $(\text{Age } 40 - \text{Age } 50)_{1970} - (\text{Age } 40 - \text{Age } 50)_{1960}$

(Group B − Group E) − (Group D − Group G)

are spurious outcomes, resulting from confounding by the uncontrolled cohort variations that are comparable to those demonstrated in example (d) of Table 4.5. Because the time-sequential design has not entered into many aging studies, we will not bother to give hypothetical examples of the various outcomes that could occur in such studies.

Cross-Sequential Design. The cross-sequential design completes the picture. The two independent variables are now cohort and time of measurement. Surprisingly, age variation is uncontrolled, and $Ag\ d$ in performance represent the potentially confounding member of the trifactor family. Accordingly, studies with this design should be conducted only when performance is expected to maintain a steady state over the segment of the lifespan entering into a given study.

A cross-sequential study with Groups A, B, D, and E from Table 4.3 is summarized in Figure 4.3. Comparable studies could be conducted with other groups from that table (e.g., Groups B, C, E, and F). The groups entering our study collectively combine cross-sectional, longitudinal, and time-lag analyses; the longitudinal sequences being examined may again be introduced through either reassessment or cohort manipulation. The defining feature of our cross-sequential study is the evaluation of a cross-sectional sequence of performance

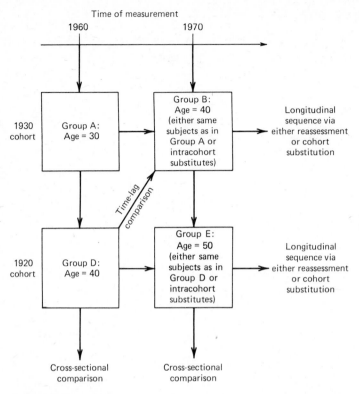

Figure 4.3. Schematic representation of a four-group cross-sequential study in which cohort (1920 versus 1930) and time of measurement (1960 versus 1970) are the independent variables; A, B, D, and E refer to groups identified in Table 4.3.

changes for the same cohorts over a fixed time period. In the present case, the cross-sectional comparisons are made at 10-year intervals between groups selected from 1920 and 1930 cohorts.

A summary of the analysis emerging from our study is given in Table 4.7. Interpretations of cohort and time-of-measurement main effects are likely to be quite intriguing. If both main effects are statistically significant and are roughly equal in magnitude, then the sequential analyst is confronted by considerable ambiguity, much like that found under comparable conditions in a cohort-sequential study. Remember that age variation is a potentially confounding factor in a cross-sequential study. If this factor is, in fact, actually confounding the study, then it should influence the effects presumed attributable to both cohort variation and time-of-measurement variation, and to about the same degree for each independent variable. Thus, equal main effects could actually mean that neither effect is due to its assumed underlying factor. Rather, both effects may be the consequence of uncontrolled age changes in performance on the task in question. The confounding with age is likely to favor both the later cohort (1930) and the earlier time of measurement (1960), assuming that younger subjects would perform more proficiently than older subjects. The 1930

Table 4.7 Comparisons Entering into the Analysis of Scores Obtained in a Cross-Sequential Study

Cohort main effect:

1930	versus	1920
Group A + Group B		Group D + Group E
1960 measurement 1970 measurement		1960 measurement 1970 measurement
(balanced)		

Time-of-measurement main effect:

1960	versus	1970
Group A + Group D		Group B + Group E
1930 cohort 1920 cohort		1930 cohort 1920 cohort
(balanced)		

Cohort $\times$ time-of-measurement interaction effect: $(1930 - 1920)_{1970} - (1930 - 1920)_{1960}$

(Group B $-$ Group E) $-$ (Group A $-$ Group D)

cohorts would have an average age of 35, whereas the 1920 cohorts would have an average age of 45. Similarly, subjects evaluated in 1960 would have an average age of 35, whereas subjects evaluated in 1970 would have an average age of 45.

If one main effect is pronounced and statistically significant, whereas the other is negligible and nonsignificant, then the analyst is faced with less ambiguity. Presumably, the significant factor (either cohort variation or time-of-measurement variation) is responsible for performance variation that cannot be accounted for by uncontrolled age variation (otherwise the second independent variable would also have a significant main effect). However, even here, as we will discover later, there is room for ambiguity when one of the independent variables has little separation among its levels.

To enhance understanding of cross-sequential research, examples of four hypothetical studies, similar to the examples given earlier for cohort-sequential research (Table 4.5), are summarized in Table 4.8. This time the task used in each study requires solving anagrams of fairly familiar five-letter words (e.g., MHANU as an anagram of *human*). There are 60 anagrams in the task, and each subject has 10 minutes to solve as many anagrams as possible (maximum score, 60).

Table 4.8 Four Hypothetical Outcomes of a Cross-Sequential Study on an Anagram-Solution Task[a]

(a)

Cohort	Time		Cohort Mean
	1960	1970	
1930	Group A: 40	Group B: 50	45
1920	Group D: 30	Group E: 40	35
Time mean	35	45	

(b)

Cohort	Time		Cohort Mean
	1960	1970	
1930	Group A: 50	Group B: 50	50
1920	Group D: 40	Group E: 40	40
Time mean	45	45	

(c)

Cohort	Time		Cohort Mean
	1960	1970	
1930	Group A: 40	Group B: 50	45
1920	Group D: 40	Group E: 50	45
Time mean	40	50	

(d)

Cohort	Time		Cohort Mean
	1960	1970	
1930	Group A: 50	Group B: 40	45
1920	Group D: 40	Group E: 30	35
Time mean	45	35	

[a] Groups correspond to those identified in Figure 4.3; numbers represent mean scores on the particular task employed in that study: (a) both cohort variation and time-of-measurement variation have causative effects and age variation is not a confounding factor; (b) cohort variation but not time-of-measurement variation has a causative effect and age variation is not a confounding factor; (c) time-of-measurement variation but not cohort variation has a causative effect and age variation is not a confounding factor; and (d) neither cohort variation nor time-of-measurement variation have causative effects but confounding by age variation yields spurious cohort and time-of-measurement effects.

For examples (a), (b), and (c), the mean score at the later cohort (1930) and later time of measurement confluence (1970) (i.e., for Group B) is set at 50 points and 10-point decrements in performance accompany 10-year variations in cohort membership and time of measurement when these factors are present as main effects. Our main interest, however, is in example (d), where neither cohort variation nor time-of-measurement variation exert causative effects. Instead, variation in age, the uncontrolled factor, affects performance. Mean performance is set at 50 points for 30-year-old subjects; each 10-year increment in age is assumed to result in a performance decrement of 10 points, making scores equal 40 and 30 points for 40- and 50-year-old subjects respectively (see Figure 4.3). Therefore, the mean for Group A (30-year-old subjects) is 50 points, the means for Groups B and D (40-year-old subjects) are 40 points, and the mean for Group E (50-year-old subjects) is 30 points. The resulting confounding makes the overall means for 1930 and 1920 cohorts equal to 45 and 35 points respectively; the overall means for 1970 and 1960 times of measurement equal 45 and 35 points respectively. Therefore, we would expect to find spuriously significant main effects in our analysis of variance for both independent variables. They are again spurious in that they are due entirely to the uncontrolled variation in age across levels of these independent variables. We would have difficulty inferring the presence of true causative effects for cohort membership and time of measurement in real cross-sequential studies unless we were certain that the uncontrolled variation in age does, indeed, have negligible effects on performance for the task in question.

Enhancing Sequential Research with Multiple Designs. The problems inherent in sequential research did not escape Schaie (1965). To circumvent many of the problems found in any study with a single sequential design, he recommended the use of combinational designs. Carried to its extreme, an expanded study would combine all three sequential strategies in a simultaneous attack on the causative factors underlying a particular behavioral phenomenon. Schaie (1977) himself feels that combining the time-sequential and cross-sequential designs in a single study is sufficient to enhance the internal validity of that study. But why be two-thirds safe? Our analysis will focus on the full scope of the use of multiple designs, that is, on the use of all three designs in a single study.

The investigator who uses this full-scale combination design would, in effect, be conducting three studies at the same time but with the same dependent variable in each study. For simplicity's sake, suppose the three studies are the ones described in the preceding sections of this chapter. The resulting 12 groups entering into this expanded, or multiple-component, study are shown in Table 4.9.

There is an important advantage to conducting a full-scale study that encompasses all three sequential designs. The pattern of results provided by the three studies offers valuable information that could make internal validity considerably greater than it would have been if only a single study with one sequential design had been employed. Consider, for example, a task in which

Table 4.9 Minimal Groups and Conditions Required for a Full-Scale Multiple Design That Combines All Three Sequential Designs Schematized in Figures 4.1, 4.2, and 4.3[a]

Cohort	Group	Age	Time of Measurement	Design Component
1930	A_1	30	1960	Cross-sequential
	B_1	40	1970	Cohort-sequential
	B_2	40	1970	Time-sequential
	B_3	40	1970	Cross-sequential
	C_1	50	1980	Cohort-sequential
1920	D_1	40	1960	Cohort-sequential
	D_2	40	1960	Time-sequential
	D_3	40	1960	Cross-sequential
	E_1	50	1970	Cohort-sequential
	E_2	50	1970	Time-sequential
	E_3	50	1970	Cross-sequential
1910	G_1	50	1960	Time-sequential

[a] Group letters refer to the groups identified in Figures 4.1, 4.2, and 4.3.

both age variation and cohort variation are known to cause differences in performance. If the investigator had conducted a single study with the cohort-sequential design, then the results would have implied causative roles for both of the true factors. However, the investigator could not be certain what part, if any, was played by uncontrolled variation in time of measurement in producing the observed effects. Unfortunately, the investigator does not *know,* as we do, that age and cohort are true causative factors—their causative roles can only be inferred from the outcome of the investigator's study. Suppose further that the investigator had elected instead to employ either the time-sequential design or the cross-sequential design. For both studies, there is a good chance that time of measurement would have erroneously appeared to be a causative factor owing to the confounding by cohort variation (which we know plays a causative role for the task in question) in the time-sequential study and to the confounding by age variation (which we know also plays a causative role) in the cross-sequential study.

Such misinterpretations are improbable, however, if the investigator invests in a full-scale multiple-design study. That is, the pattern of results should leave little room for doubt as to the causative roles played by both age variation and cohort variation. As part of this pattern, there should be a significant main effect for age in the analysis of variance for scores obtained by the four groups entering into the cohort-sequential component of the total study and also in the analysis of variance for the four groups entering into the time-sequential component (see Table 4.9). Most important, the age effect (as measured by ω^2) in the time-sequential study should be significantly larger than the age effect in the cohort-sequential study. Uncontrolled cohort variation (a true causative factor) in the time-sequential study would inflate the differences in means attributed to age variation. By contrast, uncontrolled variation in time of measurement would not affect differences between means in the cohort-sequential component because time of measurement is not a confounding factor. The net effect is to make the observed age effect larger for the time-sequential component than for the cohort-sequential study.

A comparable pattern should exist for cohort effects. That is, there should be a significant cohort effect for the groups entering into both the cohort-sequential component of the total study and the four groups entering into the cross-sequential component. The cohort effect in the cross-sequential component should be significantly larger than the cohort effect in the cohort-sequential component. The reason parallels that given above for the disparity in the main effects for age. In the present case, the confounding effect of age should inflate the differences in means attributed to cohort variation in the cross-sequential component, whereas the trivial effect of time-of-measurement variation should leave unaltered the differences in means attributed to cohort variation in the cohort-sequential component. Given both patterns, the investigator would be reasonably confident in concluding that both age and cohort variation are causative factors for the task in question. The conditions and comparisons for both age and cohort main effects in our total study are summarized in Figure 4.4.

The rationale for comparing the results obtained in independently, but simultaneously, conducted sequential studies seems sound enough. Nevertheless, serious questions have been raised regarding the legitimacy of the overall statistical analysis required in a multiple component study (Adam, 1978). Nor are these statistical problems eliminated when only two designs rather than all three designs are combined in a single study. In addition, whatever gain in

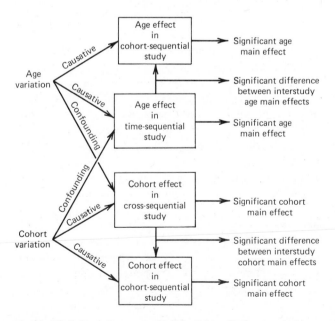

Figure 4.4. Schematic representation of the effects expected in a multiple sequential-design study in which both age and cohort variation are known to cause performance differences.

internal validity occurs from the use of a multiple design must be weighed against the impracticality of tracking multiple groups over a lengthy time period.

Justification of the Use of a Multiple Design. However, the investment in a multiple design may be worthwhile (even in light of the forementioned statistical and practical problems) for important areas of research where conventional methodological studies have yielded inconclusive results about true age changes in performance over the adult lifespan. It is conceivable that these studies may have failed to give proper consideration to nonontogenetic causative factors and that extensive sequential research offers the only means of giving final answers to questions about the origins of adult-age differences in performance.

There are also likely to be other important areas of research in which persistently found age differences are automatically assumed to be due to ontogenetic changes. If social analysis or psychological theory strongly imply that cohort or time-of-measurement variation may cause all, or even just part, of these age differences, then the investment in multiple sequential studies may well be worthwhile. As an example, we will consider research on learned helplessness (Seligman, 1975). The concept refers to individuals who have been exposed to prolonged situations in which they have no control over the outcome. They discover that no matter how they behave or perform, the outcome is the same—unpleasant and aversive. They eventually learn a helplessness that extends to new situations in which they actually have control over the outcome. However, their feeling of helplessness leads them to give up before they ever discover the control they possess. We will discover in Chapter 11 that elderly adults do display more learned helplessness than do young adults. But, is this a true ontogenetic effect? A reasonable alternative is that it is a cohort effect. Current elderly people lived through an economic depression that could have made many of them prone to learned helplessness. This does not necessarily mean that future generations of the elderly will be equally so prone to learned helplessness. Similarly, many elderly people today are forced to live on substandard incomes, a condition that readily fosters helplessness. Hopefully, this situation will be greatly changed for future generations. This is an important issue, one that has clear implications, for example, for the approach taken in counseling elderly people experiencing adjustment problems. There is good reason for investing in multiple design research that provides definitive answers to questions about the true causative factors underlying age differences in learned helplessness.

Our interest, of course, is with the content areas of experimental psychology. How relevant are cohort variation and time-of-measurement variation to performance differences on the tasks carried over from experimental psychology? If they are relevant, then many cognitive skills once thought to suffer irreversible loss from "normal" aging should be reconsidered and appropriate remedial programs should be given serious consideration. We will return to this important question later in this chapter when we examine the need for sequential research in the experimental psychology of aging.

Illustrations of Sequential Research

In this section, we will depart from the use of abstract examples and attempt to further your understanding of sequential analysis by considering several illustrative studies that have made full use of sequential designs. Along the way, we will introduce an important byproduct of one of these studies, namely, a procedure for constructing cross-sectional and longitudinal gradients for charting age differences in performance. As we will see, these gradients have become a major tool for the sequential analyst's evaluation of the causative role played by age per se in determining performance differences on the task in question.

The primary consumers of sequential designs have been psychologists engaged in research on age changes in intellectual abilities and in personality traits. A number of these psychometric studies have been published during the last 15 years, many of them by Schaie. By contrast, there appears to be only one published study that is truly part of the experimental psychology of aging, one by Eisner and Schaie (1971) that deals with visual illusions. The reason for the differential impact of sequential analysis on psychometric versus experimentally based research seems obvious. Massive evaluative programs with paper-and-pencil tests of the kind employed by psychometricians are economically and pragmatically feasible. A given testing program may capture simultaneously the performances of a wide range of ages and generations at a given time. Moreover, the program may readily be repeated several times with the replications separated by a number of years, again without undue economic and pragmatic constraints. The data inputs provided by massive testing programs offer appropriate grist for Schaie's design mill. In addition, the time commitment on the part of an investigator is often shortened greatly by the fact that the earlier testing sessions (e.g., at Time 1 and, perhaps, at Time 2 as well) may have been completed while the study was only a gleam in the investigator's eye. That is, the early evaluations may have been conducted years before as part of an agency's (e.g., a Veterans' Administration Hospital) routine testing program, and the resulting data protocols were filed away awaiting some enterprising sequential researcher to dig them out and put them to use. The situation is quite different for experimental aging research. Massive laboratory-based evaluations cutting across a wide range of ages and cohorts are unheard of (except for the Baltimore Longitudinal Study cited in Chapter 3). Nor is an experimental psychologist likely to find files of data protocols from earlier administrations of a task to subjects who are now available for reassessment on that task.

Three of our illustrative studies will be psychometric in content, two on intelligence and one on personality. The remaining illustration will be the highly influential experimental content study by Eisner and Schaie (1971).

Psychometric-Sequential Research: Intelligence. The main recipient of sequential research has been performance on the Primary Mental Abilities Test (PMA). The PMA is composed of five subtests, each measuring a separate intellectual ability identified years ago by means of factor analysis. These subtests are: Verbal Meaning, Space, Reasoning, Number, and Word Fluency. We have good reason for examining sequential research on this task. This research has provided many psychologists with a model for conducting sequential research in other content areas, including those of experimental psychology. For the two studies we have selected, one employed the cohort-sequential design and the other the cross-sequential design. These two designs have been, by far, the favored ones in sequential research to date.

The cohort-sequential study was done by Schaie and Parham (1977). Their subjects covered a wide range of ages and cohorts. The reassessment form of the longitudinal sequence was employed, with those subjects available for a second assessment being tested 7 years after the initial assessment. The use of the cohort-sequential design permitted a comparison between performance changes attributable to age variation and performance changes attributable to cohort variation. The results of Schaie and Parham's study revealed that, overall for the various subtests considered together, cohort variation yielded greater performance changes than did age variation. Cohort variation was generally more important than age variation for performance changes of subjects until they reached their late 60s. Beyond that age, further age variation was more important than cohort variation.

The cross-sequential study is the frequently cited one by Schaie and Strother (1968). As in Schaie and Parham's (1977) later study, this study included a wide range of ages and cohorts, and it also made use of the reassessment form of evaluating longitudinal sequences (a 7-year interval again separated the first and second testing sessions). The main effect for cohort was statistically significant for all five subtests of the PMA, whereas the main effect for time of measurement was statistically significant for only one subtest, Reasoning (implying a cultural change affecting performance, which is in agreement with Owens's earlier conclusion regarding the reasoning component of the Army Alpha test). The overall pattern of a significant main effect for cohort but not for time of measurement assumes special importance to a sequential analyst. The inference is twofold: (1) the cohort effect itself is a true consequence of cohort variation rather than being a product of uncontrolled age variation and (2) ontogenetic change plays little, if any, part in producing performance differences on at least four of the subtests (i.e., if it did, a time of measurement effect should also have emerged in the statistical analysis).

The results of Schaie and Strother's (1968) study, when considered together with those of Schaie and Parham (1977), suggest that cohort effects are, indeed, potent ones, potent enough to distort estimates of age changes in intellectual abilities when cohort membership is allowed to covary freely with chronological age. Such rampant covariation is the case, of course, for a number of studies that have examined the effects of aging on intelligence by means of the conventional cross-sectional method.

Schaie and Strother (1968) also introduced a new methodological gimmick to aging research. The gimmick consists of constructing longitudinal and cross-sectional age gradients from data collected in a cross-sequential study. Each gradient estimates the course of performance changes on a given task as chronological age increases. It is whatever deviation emerges between the separately charted courses that interested Schaie and Strother:

> Here we compare the age gradients obtained on the basis of current performance of individuals at different ages who are members of different cohorts (i.e., the cross-sectional) with the estimated longitudinal age gradient for a *single* cohort. If the cross-sectional age differences for a given variable are a function solely of maturational change, then we would expect the two gradients to coincide. If, on the other hand, cross-sectional differences include the effects of differential environmental opportunity and/or genetic changes in the species, then one would expect discrepancies between the two gradients. Whenever cohort differences are in the positive direction (i.e., improvement of the species with respect to a given variable), the cross-sectional gradient will have to drop below the longitudinal, since in such cases the performance of an older cohort will be below that of a younger one even if there is no maturational age change whatever. Conversely, the longitudinal gradient will fall below the cross-sectional for those variables where there is decrement in ability over generations for the population samples. (1968, p. 674)

Schaie and Strother (1968) were not very explicit about the procedures they used to construct their cross-sectional and longitudinal gradients. Consequently, we will rely on Botwinick's (1973) interpretation of these procedures in our illustration of the apparent operations. We will use Groups A, B, D, and E of Figure 4.3 in this illustration. Suppose the mean scores on a given task are 100, 90, 60, and 50 for Groups A, B, D, and E respectively. To construct the cross-sectional gradient, we begin with the mean performance score of our youngest group in the earliest cross-sectional component of our study (i.e., the cross-section represented at the 1960 time of measurement). This mean is 100 at age 30 years (i.e., the mean for Group A). Included in this original cross-sectional component is Group D (see Figure 4.3). Thus, 60, the mean score for Group D, is plotted on the gradient as the cross-sectionally appropriate value at age 40 years (the age of Group D's members). Thus far, the means entering into the gradient reveal an age difference in performance as assessed by the traditional cross-sectional method. Our problem, however, is to determine the appropriate mean score to assign at age 50 years. To maintain cross-sectional consistency, we need to know what that value would have been for a 50-year-old group included in the original 1960 cross-section. The problem occurs because Group E, our true 50-year-old group, was not part of this original cross-section (in fact, it consists of the members of Group D reassessed 10 years later). Cross-sectional consistency is obtained, however, if we now examine the other cross-sectional component of our overall study, namely, the groups entering at the 1970 time of measurement and involving ages of 40 years (Group B) and 50 years (Group E). The performance difference found cross-sectionally between these age levels is 40 points (i.e., $90 - 50$). We then simply assume that the cross-sectional difference between the same age levels in 1960 would also have been 40 points. Therefore, our estimated mean score at age 50 for

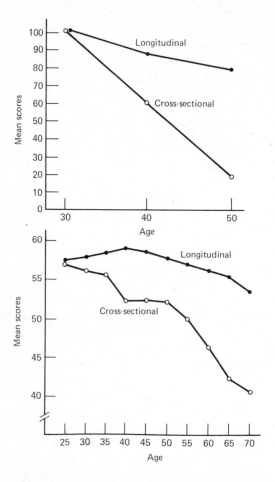

Figure 4.5. Top panel: Cross-sectional and longitudinal gradients constructed from hypothetical sequential data for the groups shown in Figure 4.3. Bottom panel: Cross-sectional and longitudinal gradients constructed from sequential data on the reasoning component of the Primary Mental Abilities Test (PMA). (Adapted from Schaie & Strother, 1968, Figure 3.)

gradient purposes is 20 (40 points below Group D's mean of 60). The resulting gradient in its entirety is plotted in the top panel of Figure 4.5.

Turning to the longitudinal analysis of the same four groups, the first point on the gradient is the mean of 100 earned by Group A, the 30-year-old group; the second point is the mean of 90 earned by Group B, the 40-year-old group formed by the reassessment of the members of Group A. These two points on the gradient chart an age difference (or change) in performance as revealed by the traditional longitudinal method. The next point on the gradient should be the mean score earned 10 years later by the same subjects at age 50. However, our only 50-year-old group (Group E) comes from an earlier cohort (1920) than our already-plotted 30- and 40-year old groups (1930 cohort). According to

Schaie and Strother (1968), adding Group E's mean to the gradient would be like adding oranges to apples—you would still have fruit, but it is now in a mixed salad. To maintain longitudinal consistency (or to add more apples to a prior collection of apples), we estimate a mean score that represents a projection of the expected mean score at age 50 for our *1930 cohorts*. To make this projection, the estimated decrement in means from age 40 to age 50 for 1930 cohorts is equated with the actually observed decrement from age 40 to age 50 for 1920 cohorts. This decrement is known to be 10 points, 60 (mean for Group D) − 50 (mean for Group E). Thus, 10 points is subtracted from the mean of Group B to give a projected mean of 80 as our presumably best estimate of the mean that would be earned by 1930 cohorts in 1980 when they reach the age of 50. Our resulting longitudinal gradient would, therefore, show means of 100, 90, and 80 at ages 30, 40, and 50 respectively for a single cohort in a partially simulated longitudinal analysis, as illustrated in the top panel of Figure 4.5. Note that this gradient clearly falls above our previously constructed cross-sectional gradient, with the divergence between gradients increasing as chronological age increases. According to Schaie and Strother's interpretation, such divergence supports the contention that most of the age differences for the task in question are attributable to cohort differences in the positive direction (i.e., later born cohorts have a performance advantage over earlier born cohorts). Nevertheless, a nagging question persists: Instead of oranges, have we not now added artificial apples (the simulated segment of each gradient) to our stock of real apples (the empirically observed segment of each gradient)? We will have more to say about the artificiality of these gradients later in this chapter.

When cross-sectional and longitudinal gradients were plotted for the sequential data obtained by Schaie and Strother on the PMA subtests, they revealed divergencies for four of the subtests that are strikingly similar to the divergence displayed in our hypothetical illustration. For example, the gradients found for the Reasoning subtest are shown in the bottom panel of Figure 4.5. From Schaie and Strother's perspective, age differences on the Reasoning subtest are attributable mainly to cohort differences in the positive direction. Fairly comparable divergencies were found for the Verbal Meaning, Space, and Number subtests, again implying cohort differences in the positive direction. An exception of a kind occurred for the Word Fluency subtest. There was again increasing divergence between the two gradients with increasing age, but this time the longitudinal gradient fell below the cross-sectional gradient. Undismayed by this reversal, Schaie and Strother stood their ground and simply concluded that the reversal resulted from cohort differences in the negative direction (i.e., there is a decrement in ability from early to later generations). Their post hoc explanation stressed the highly speeded nature of the word fluency task and the resulting physical demand it places on subjects: "Just as an enriched environment leads to higher ability levels, so does it obviate the necessity for physical exertion. The present findings certainly suggest decrement in the fluency and response latency of successive generations" (Schaie & Strother, 1968, p. 677). The flexibility offered by negative as well as positive directions for cohort differences makes it possible to explain, post hoc, virtually any divergence between cross-sectional and longitudinal gradients in terms of cohort effects.

Psychometric-Sequential Research: Personality. Our personality study is the one by Douglas and Arenberg (1978) that we touched on in Chapter 3. We noted at the time that the investigators included sequential analyses along with traditional cross-sectional and longitudinal analyses in their study. In fact, they employed a combinational sequential design involving both the time-sequential and the cross-sequential methods. For illustrative purposes, we will consider only the results found for the personal relations trait of the Guilford-Zimmerman Temperament Survey. A high score on this trait characterizes a trustful person who is not given to fault-finding or self-pity. The standard cross-sectional analysis for scores on this trait revealed no age differences, whereas the standard longitudinal analysis revealed a decline in scores from the first to second assessment for subjects *at each age level* included in the total sample. This pattern suggests a cultural change in the trait over the years intervening between the first and second assessments (5.6 to 9.9 years), a change that affected equally *all adults,* regardless of age level. The results of the sequential analyses were supportive of this interpretation. Specifically, the time-of-measurement main effect, as an index of a cultural change, was significant in both the time-sequential analysis and the cross-sequential analysis. The conclusion reached by Douglas and Arenberg, therefore, seems perfectly justified:

> The finding of declines in time-sequential analyses and the absence of cross-sectional differences suggested cultural change during the measurement period as an explanation. Therefore, men became less . . . tolerant and cooperative during the time frame of the current study. (1978, p. 745)

Experimental-Sequential Research. Age gradients played an important role in our final illustration of sequential research. The study is the previously mentioned one by Eisner and Schaie (1971). Again, this appears to be the only study in which traditional tasks of experimental psychology were examined from the perspective of a sequentially designed methodology. The results of the study were of a nature that could convince some experimental psychologists of the need to abandon cross-sectional research and become sequential converts. The tasks were those customarily employed to measure the extent of two familiar visual illusions, the Müller-Lyer illusion and the Titchener circles illusion. We will consider only that phase of their study dealing with the Müller-Lyer illusion. It is the illusion in which a horizontal line with diverging diagonal lines at each end (⤨) appears longer than an equal-length horizontal line with converging diagonal lines at each end (↔). Adult-age differences in the magnitude of the illusory effect have long been known to exist, at least as these differences are evaluated cross-sectionally (e.g., Wapner, Werner, & Comalli, 1960). Specifically, cross-sectional evidence indicates that the magnitude of the illusion increases fairly progressively from early adulthood to old age. But, could not these age differences be due to a cohort effect rather than to a true age change? This is the question Eisner and Schaie (1971) attempted to answer through sequential analysis.

Interestingly, Eisner and Schaie selected the cross-sequential method as the means of identifying the causative factors of age differences on this task. The cohort main effect was significant, but neither the time-of-measurement main effect nor the cohort × time-of-measurement interaction effect approached statistical significance. Given a significant main effect for cohort variation but not for time-of-measurement variation, the inferences are that cohort variation is a major determiner of age differences in the magnitude of the illusion and that maturational factors have little, if any, effect on the illusory phenomenon during adulthood.

These inferences gained further support from the diverging cross-sectional and longitudinal gradients constructed by Eisner and Schaie from their data points. These gradients are reproduced in Figure 4.6. It may be seen that the cross-sectional gradient falls above the longitudinal gradient for most of the lifespan covered in this study. Because increasing scores indicate decreasing performance proficiency for this particular task, the nature of this divergence actually corresponds to that found with the PMA subtests. The interpretation is, therefore, much the same as that given in PMA studies—cohort differences are viewed as accounting for much, if not all, of the age differences observed on this basic perceptual task. In effect, ontogenetic change is relegated to the explanatory boondocks. More generally, the implication is that sequential research, particularly that conducted through the use of the cross-sequential method, will eventually indicate that many of the basic skills investigated in the experimental laboratory are, in common with intellectual skills, relatively in-

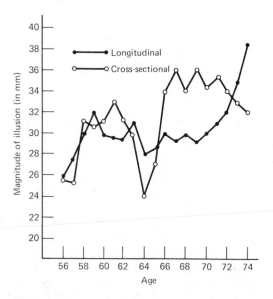

Figure 4.6. Cross-sectional and longitudinal gradients constructed from sequential data on the Müller-Lyer illusion task. (Adapted from Eisner & Schaie, 1971, Figure 3.)

sensitive to ontogenetic change. The lesson supposedly to be learned from Eisner and Schaie's study has, in fact, not escaped the attention of some experimental aging psychologists. For example, Michael Eysenck (1977), a prominent researcher in the area of adult-age differences in memory, remarked, "Until experimenters regularly use the cross-sequential method, conclusions about age differences must be tentative" (p. 245). Given this intended lesson and its potential uncritical acceptance by well-intended researchers, we need to examine carefully some hidden dangers inherent in the use of the cross-sequential method.

Evaluation of Cross-Sequential Research

The choice of a cross-sequential design as the panacea for the ills of experimental aging research is a strange one. By its very choice, the researcher has accepted as a fait accompli that ontogenetic change is a trivial factor in causing age differences on the task in question. Despite its peculiar nature, the strategy of employing a design for the purpose of demonstrating the absence of an effect for a factor that is not deemed worthy enough to be included as an independent variable in the first place seems defensible, in principle, when the outcome is like that obtained by Eisner and Schaie (1971). Their outcome of a main effect for cohort variation, but not for time-of-measurement variation, parallels that found for example (b) in Table 4.8 in our earlier hypothetical cross-sequential study. We noted at the time that this pattern indicates both an effect for cohort variation, a true independent variable, *and* the absence of an effect for age variation, a nonindependent variable. However, the unequivocal acceptance of the validity of these conclusions is possible only when a critical condition has been satisfied in the study. The condition is that the time span covered between levels of the cohort independent variable approximates the time span between levels of the time-of-measurement independent variable. In our prior hypothetical example, the time span was 10 years between the two levels of each independent variable (1920 to 1930 for the cohort variable and 1960 to 1970 for the time-of-measurement variable). Given this equality in time spans, the combination of a pronounced cohort main effect and a negligible time-of-measurement main effect does provide unambiguous support for our causative conclusions. At the same time, a significant departure from this condition of time-span equality could well mean that the investigator is arranging a stacked deck. That is, the situation is structured so that, even when there are actual age changes in performance on the task in question, the outcome of the study is paradoxically likely to indicate the absence of those changes.

The reasons for this paradox were described in an excellent article by Botwinick and Arenberg (1976). Their description makes use of a hypothetical example in which (1) age differences are entirely caused by age changes, (2) the age changes produce a linear decrement in performance with increasing age, and (3) cohort variation spans a much wider range of years than does time-of-measurement variation. It is their third stipulation that represents a significant departure from the condition extant in our own earlier hypothetical example.

The logic of Botwinick and Arenberg's argument is not an easy one to follow, and it does require some degree of familiarity with statistical concepts to follow it precisely. However, even without that familiarity, the gist of their argument can be understood with some effort. Here is their account of the conditions present in their hypothetical study and the consequences of these conditions:

> The following example was conducted to illustrate the point quantitatively. This example demonstrates that, even when cohort differences are entirely attributable to ontogenetic change, when the cohort variable spans a time range greater than the time range of the time-of-measurement variable, F values are higher and F tests are more likely to be statistically significant for the cohort variable.
>
> In this example, the only factor operating to produce age differences in time-of-measurement effects is maturational change. Individuals decline, and the mean decline is linear; therefore, neither null hypothesis is true. In this example, there are two independent samples from each of six cohorts, and all intervals between contiguous cohorts and between times of measurement are equal. (The independent-samples design (N.B. the reference is to what we have been calling the intra-cohort manipulation or substitution in a longitudinal sequence) was chosen because it is advocated by Schaie and his colleagues, and because it requires no assumption about the correlation between repeated measurements). The mean age decline is a constant (K); i.e., the mean performance measure for each age group is K less than the mean for the next younger group. (1976, pp. 56–57)

The means for the various groups in Botwinick and Arenberg's hypothetical example are shown in Table 4.10. The values for the six cohorts are given in the column on the right, and the values for the two times of measurement are given in the bottom row. It may be seen from this table that the variability between cohort means is much larger than the variability between time of measurement means. As proven by Botwinick and Arenberg, this difference in variabilities would produce an F value (the statistic yielded in an analysis of

Table 4.10   A Constructed Example of an Outcome from a Cross-Sequential Study in which Cohort Variation Spans a Much Wider Range of Years Than Does Time-of-Measurement Variation[a]

Cohort	Time 1 (1960)	Time 2 (1970)	Mean
1890	$G - 5K$	$G - 6K$	$G - 5.5K$
1900	$G - 4K$	$G - 5K$	$G - 4.5K$
1910	$G - 3K$	$G - 4K$	$G - 3.5K$
1920	$G - 2K$	$G - 3K$	$G - 2.5K$
1930	$G - K$	$G - 2K$	$G - 1.5K$
1940	G	$G - K$	$G - 0.5K$
Mean	$G - 2.5K$	$G - 3.5K$	$G - 3.0K$

[a] Mean differences are based entirely on a linear age change; G = mean of 20-year-old subjects, K = mean decline per decade.
Source: Adapted from Botwinick and Arenberg, 1976, Table 1.

variance) for the cohort main effect that would be $2\frac{1}{3}$ times the F value for the time-of-measurement main effect (see Adam, 1977, for further mathematical verification). Given this ratio of F values, a sequential researcher is almost certain to conclude that, because the cohort effect is pronounced and the time-of-measurement effect is relatively negligible, age changes are indeed a trivial causative factor for the task in question. This conclusion would, of course, be wrong. We know that the performance differences among the groups in this hypothetical example are entirely due to age changes! In effect, the disparity in time spans for the two independent variables alters the outcome otherwise expected [i.e., the one shown in example (d) of Table 4.8] when the uncontrolled factor of age exerts a pronounced effect and the varied factors of cohort membership and time of measurement exert trivial effects. The result is to distort the outcome and to make it spuriously equivalent to the kind of outcome shown in example (a) of Table 4.8.

Botwinick and Arenberg's (1976) example is not nearly as hypothetical as it might appear to be. The disparity in levels for the two independent variables is actually not far removed from that found in some cross-sequential studies. For example, in Eisner and Schaie's (1971) study, there were 10 cohort levels and only 2 time-of-measurement levels. Most important, the measurement levels were separated by only 6 months, whereas the cohort levels were separated by 2 years.

There is another problem linked to a disparity in interlevel time spans for the independent variables of a cross-sequential study. With only 2 time-of-measurement levels and many cohort levels, the investigator is comparing what amounts to "a 40- or 50-year difference in cross-sectional research with a briefer time difference in longitudinal research (e.g., 7 years, as in the study of Schaie & Strother, 1968, or 14 years, as in the study of Schaie & Labouvie [-Vief], 1974)" (Botwinick & Siegler, 1980, p. 49). The examples selected by Botwinick and Siegler are cross-sequential studies of performance on intelligence tests. We may add that the time differential is equally true of Eisner and Schaie's (1971) perceptual study. Here the total cross-sectional time span was 20 years, whereas the total longitudinal span was only 6 months. Botwinick and Siegler (1980) noted that a pronounced temporal inequality between cross-sectional and longitudinal comparisons of age differences "does not permit statements regarding whether one or the other design reflects greater change" (1980, p. 49). Their point is that diverging cross-sectional and longitudinal gradients of the kind illustrated in Figures 4.5 and 4.6 are basically uninterpretable when the total time lapsing in cross-sectional comparisons is much greater than the total time lapsing in longitudinal comparisons. In their study, Botwinick and Siegler made a careful effort to equate the total time entering into each kind of age gradient. Their results for scores obtained in full-scale performance on the Wechsler Adult Intelligence Scale (WAIS) are shown in Figure 4.7. It may be seen that their age gradients differed considerably from those obtained by Schaie and Strother (1968)—with unequal time spans—for scores obtained on the PMA (bottom panel, Figure 4.5). For Botwinick and Siegler's (1980) age gradients, statistically significant age differences were found longitu-

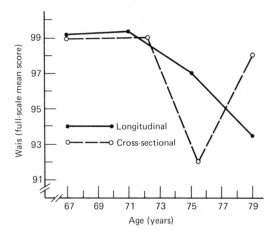

Figure 4.7. Empirically determined cross-sectional and longitudinal gradients for full-scale scores on the WAIS. (Adapted from Botwinick & Siegler, 1980, Figure 1.)

dinally (but the absolute change with age was slight) but not cross-sectionally rather than vice versa as found in Schaie and Strother's (1968) age gradients.

The problem detected by Botwinick and Siegler (1980) adds to the other major problem associated with the age gradients reported in cross-sequential studies, namely, their constructive nature. As constructions rather than observed phenomena, these gradients may be manipulated in various ways that are, in principle, mathematically acceptable. Nevertheless, the construction of a gradient, the longitudinal one in particular, may not conform to reality because the gradient would not be manifested through long-term longitudinal observations of a single cohort. In fact, different gradients may be constructed from the same sets of scores, with the variants depending on specific data points selected and the specific procedure used for making age projections. This point was nicely demonstrated by Botwinick (1977) with data taken from Schaie's own prior studies on PMA performance (e.g., Schaie & Strother, 1968). The longitudinal gradients plotted by Botwinick showed quantitative variation from their contrasted cross-sectional gradients, but they clearly did not show any major qualitative variation.

The artificiality of cross-sequentially generated age gradients must be taken seriously in evaluating Schaie's (1970; Schaie & Strother, 1968) position that the qualitative difference between longitudinal and cross-sectional gradients has great theoretical and practical significance. To Schaie (1970), these qualitative differences, which reveal considerably less decline longitudinally than cross-sectionally, indicate the importance of nonmaturational factors, and abrogate the importance of maturational factors in producing adult-age differences in intelligence and, presumably, many other cognitive activities as well. Schaie's position has led to the speculation that the so-called decline of intelligence with human aging is more a myth than it is a reality (Baltes & Schaie, 1976; Schaie & Baltes, 1977), a speculation that has not gone unchallenged

(Horn & Donaldson, 1976, 1977). We will return to this important issue in Chapter 11 in the context of laboratory studies concerned with the modification of adult-age deficits in intelligence test performance.

Implications of the Trifactor Model and Sequential Analysis for Experimental Aging Research

Rationale for Including Developmental Independent Variables in Experimental Aging Research. We have tried to present a critical, but realistic, description of Schaie's (1965) trifactor model and the model's translation into sequential research. The model and the methodological designs that follow from it undoubtedly represent significant contributions to the overall psychology of aging. Most important, the model has forced gerontological psychologists to accept cohort variation and time-of-measurement variation as potentially causative factors for adult age differences in some human behaviors. But, does this mean they are potentially causative factors for adult-age differences in *all* human behaviors? This seems highly unlikely, yet the indiscriminate use of sequential designs appears to accept this radical position. Unfortunately, such indiscriminate use of sequential designs in experimental aging research is more likely to impede than to advance progress. Why should a cross-sequential design be forced on a researcher when it seems quite unlikely that either cohort variation or time-of-measurement variation exert causative effects on the behavior being investigated? The consequences of unnecessary use could be devastating, in terms of wasted time and expenditures as well as in terms of distorted conceptions of the true causative factor determining age differences in performance on a given task.

An experimental aging researcher has the responsibility of justifying the inclusion of each developmental independent variable, whether it be age per se, cohort membership, or time of measurement, in the study conducted by that researcher. If there is a sound rationale for expecting cohort effects in performance on a task, for example, then there is a good reason for the researcher to include cohort variation in the planned study. Unfortunately, this rational approach need not guide aging research. In fact, it did not in our prototypal study by Eisner and Schaie (1971). Interestingly, there would have been ample justification in this study for including age variation as a true independent variable (which, of course, the investigators did not do). The perceptual processes accounting for the Müller-Lyer illusion have not been fully identified (see Hochberg, 1978). Whatever these processes are, however, they are likely to be sensitive to maturational changes in the visual system with increasing age (Atkeson, 1978). But, what about cohort variation? Why should the magnitude of the illusion be affected by a subject's generational membership? Eisner and Schaie offered no justification for making cohort variation an independent variable other than to state vaguely that age differences "could be due to differences in experiential factors (cohort differences)" (1971, p. 147). It does seem to be true that very different qualitative experiences among members of Western and primitive cultures can affect the magnitude of the illusion (Segall, Campbell, & Herskovits, 1966). But, how do these different experiences apply to not very widely separated generations from the same Western culture?

Aging research appears to be reaching the point where a blanket endorsement of the inclusion of cohort variation in studies is replacing rational judgments as to the need of its inclusion in these studies. As hinted at earlier in this chapter through remarks made by prominent researchers, experimental aging research is no exception to this movement toward a blanket endorsement. After all, if cohort effects are responsible for adult-age differences on a simple perceptual task, as is indicated by an uncritical acceptance of Eisner and Schaie's (1971) results, then why should they not also be responsible for at least a large proportion of the age differences found in learning and memory tasks, for example?

Attribution of large and far-ranging causative effects to cohort variation seems to have had its origin in the belief held by some psychologists that major environmental changes have occurred over successive generations in the United States and that these changes resulted in cognitively more stimulating environments during childhood for members of later generations than for members of earlier generations. The possible consequences of this hypothesized positive-cohort effect were initially identified with age differences in performance on intelligence tests. As described by Baltes (1968), these consequences are indeed striking:

> [In Figure 4.8] the broken lines represent the hypothetical average developmental gradients for the generations 1900–1950 for the age range from 10–60 years. These developmental gradients are based on two assumptions concerning the dependent variable: (a) age development as a linear progression, and (b) an acceleration from generation to generation. In a cross-sectional study conducted in 1960 there is available only one observation per cohort at a specific age level. The cohort of 1900 is observed at the age of 60, the cohort of 1910 at the age of 50, the cohort of 1920 at the age of 40, etc. The resulting age curve (solid line) corresponds neither to any

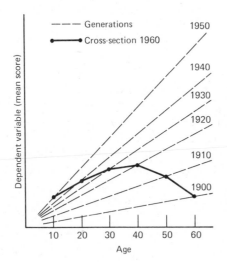

Figure 4.8. Differential performance curves (broken lines) for cohorts showing acceleration in growth from generation to generation. Also shown is the expected outcome (solid line) of a cross-sectional study conducted in 1960. (Adapted from Baltes, 1968, Figure 1.)

of the single developmental gradients nor to the average of all of them. Therefore, if generation effects are present, the results of a cross-sectional study can not be interpreted as pure age effects. In the obtained sample differences . . . , age effects and generation effects are confounded. This confounding might take various forms. The example in [Figure 4.8] was chosen since it explains the well-known textbook curves of intelligence as a function of the interaction between age and generation effects, whereas usually this curve is interpreted as a function of age alone. (pp. 152–153)

From expounding on the dangers of cohort confounding in intelligence to expounding on the dangers of cohort confounding in virtually every aspect of human behavior is a short step to take, as may be seen in Botwinick's influential remarks:

The confounding of cohort and age is most apparent in cross-sectional studies, i.e., studies in which two or more age (cohort) groups are compared during the single period of the examination. The age groups are compared in intelligence and other test performances, with the knowledge that the quality and quantity of formal education has been different for old and young. Age groups are compared although researchers know that so many of today's sources of cognitive stimulation were unknown generations ago. Social patterns, values, and attitudes were different when grandmother was a girl—how can people of different ages be compared? (1973)

Taken literally, Botwinick is arguing for the abandonment of traditional cross-sectional research in virtually all areas of the psychology of aging. Clearly, any effort directed at correcting for cohort differences between Botwinick's grandmother and a contemporary young adult is, a priori, doomed to failure. No matter how well two age groups are matched on such important non-age attributes as years of formal education, they could be criticized for differing on such subtle attributes as quality of education. This criticism makes it all but impossible to discount on rational grounds the potential role played by cohort differences on any task. There is, however, an empirical means of testing for the probable involvement of a positive cohort effect on a given task. The test consists of multiple time-lag comparisons in performance between like-age groups. To show how this test works, we must modify somewhat Baltes's (1968) account of how cohort variation produces age differences in performance. In Baltes's account, performance is hypothesized to increase linearly with increasing age throughout the lifespan. A more reasonable assumption for most tasks, and one that does not violate the spirit of Baltes's position, is that performance increases progressively until early adulthood and then remains constant over the rest of the lifespan. Predictions for time-lag comparisons may then be made for a given task by restructuring Figure 4.8 in the form shown in Figure 4.9. It is a restructuring that is consistent with our earlier analysis of cohort effects in Chapter 2.

Our revised figure accounts for cross-sectional differences among groups of 20-, 40-, 60-, and 80-year-old subjects, all of whom were evaluated in the

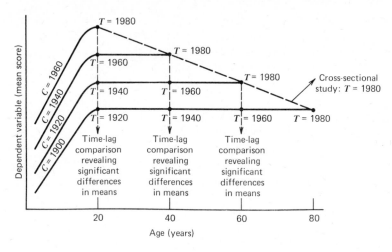

Figure 4.9. Maximum levels of performance for various cohorts (*C* indicates year of birth). The level increases progressively from early to late cohorts and is assumed to be unchanged throughout adulthood. Expected results of time-lag comparisons for mean performance scores obtained at various times of measurement (*T*) with subjects of the same age are indicated by vertical arrows, and expected results of a cross-sectional study conducted in 1980 are indicated by the broken diagonal line.

same year (1980), as indicated by the broken line in Figure 4.9. As in Figure 4.8, the cross-sectional differences appear in the absence of any sign of decrement in performance beyond young adulthood for the members of any generation. Most important, the figure reveals the outcomes of a number of time-lag comparisons, beginning with 20-year-old subjects from various cohorts who were evaluated on the same task at different times. From the 1960 cohort, 20-year-old subjects may be seen to excel 20-year-old subjects from the 1940 cohort who, in turn, excel 20-year-old subjects from the 1920 cohort, and so on. When the task in question is an intelligence test, such gains in score have indeed been found in time-lag comparisons that have been limited to a single age level. In some of these comparisons, the age level involved has been that of adolescence (Wheeler, 1942); in other comparisons, it has been that of young adulthood (Owens, 1966; Tuddenham, 1948). To some psychologists (e.g., Baltes, Reese, & Nesselroade, 1977), the gain in scores represents a positive cohort effect. However, to other psychologists (e.g., Owens, 1966), the gain represents a positive time of measurement effect. Consider again the details of Owens's study. Subjects who were 19 years old when tested in 1961 on the Army Alpha test scored higher than 19-year-old subjects tested in 1919 on the same test, a gain attributed by Owens to a positive cultural change (by means of increased test sophistication) over the years 1919 to 1961. Note, nevertheless, that the time-lag difference could just as easily be considered a positive cohort effect, which results from the cognitively more stimulating environment experienced during childhood by subjects born in 1942 (i.e., the subjects tested at age 19 in 1961), relative to subjects born in 1900 (i.e., the subjects tested at age 19 in 1919). The distinction between age differences because of a cohort effect and age differences due to a time of measurement effect is obviously a nebulous one. To eliminate the confusion between cohort and time-of-measurement effects, some psychologists (e.g., Buss, 1973) have proposed reducing Schaie's (1965) trifactor model to a bifactor model in which age and cohort variations are the only nontrivial causative factors for producing age differences in human behaviors.

Abandoning time of measurement as a potential causative factor is a drastic step to take, especially when there are aspects of human behavior, namely, those related to certain personality traits, that appear to be sensitive to cultural change. Fortunately, there is an empirical procedure that offers a means of reducing, and perhaps even eliminating, the confusion created between a cohort effect and a time-of-measurement effect when only one age level enters into a time-lag comparison. Although the procedure is a simple one, it does require considerable data. From Figure 4.9, it can be seen that the positive cohort effect responsible for cross-sectional age differences in the absence of age changes in performance extends to every time-lag comparison that could be made. Thus, as indicated in Figure 4.9, the progressive increment in means from early to late generations should be about the same for both 40- and 60-year-old groups as it is for 20-year-old groups. Such comparability would not be the case if the time-lag difference in means for 20-year-old groups is solely the result of a time of measurement effect. The underlying cultural change should affect adults of *all* ages living during the period of change. Consider, for example, the situation illustrated in Figure 4.10 in which a positive cultural change is assumed to have occurred between the years 1920 and 1940. There should be a significant time-lag difference between 20-year-old subjects born in 1900 and 20-year-old subjects born in 1920 (and tested in 1920 and 1940 respectively) that favors the subjects born in the later cohort. That is, the cultural change would have occurred in time to affect the performance of 1920 cohorts

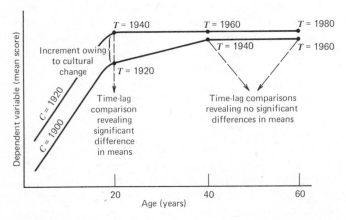

Figure 4.10. Intercohort differences (*C* indicates year of birth) expected between like-age groups when there are no postmaturity age changes in performance and when there is a positive time-of-measurement effect from 1920 to 1940. Expected results of time-lag comparisons for means obtained at various times of measurement (*T*) are indicated by vertical and diagonal arrows.

but not the performance of 1900 cohorts. But, this difference would also be predicted on the basis of a positive cohort effect in the progression from 1900-to-1920 birth years. On the other hand, the cohort difference, as reflected by a time-lag comparison, should have disappeared by the time the 1900 cohort subjects attained the age of 40 (see Figure 4.10). In other words, they should have increased their scores from age 20 to age 40 by an amount roughly equal to the disparity in means between the two groups of 20-year-old subjects. The absence of time-lag differences between older subjects from different cohorts would surely not be predicted on the principle that cohort variation underlies the emergence of age differences on the task in question. Only a time-of-measurement effect would account for this particular pattern of time-lag comparisons.

As we discovered earlier in this chapter, negative cohort effects may be expected for some tasks. Given such a task, the conditions depicted in Figure 4.9 would simply be reversed. That is, for each age level, mean scores should decrease progressively as we move from the earliest cohort evaluated to the latest cohort evaluated. For example, at age 20, the highest level of performance for the groups included in Figure 4.9 would be that of the 1900 cohorts evaluated in 1920 and the lowest level that of the 1960 cohorts evaluated in 1980.

Finally, we should note that the locus of a cohort effect may be in the postmaturity environment instead of the prematurity environment. One possible hypothesis stipulates that an optimal amount of environmental stimulation is required to maintain competencies at the levels reached in early adulthood. The level reached in early adulthood may vary from task to task, but, most importantly, it does not, according to this hypothesis, vary from generation to generation. Earlier generations are then viewed as having fallen farther below this optimal amount of stimulation than have later generations. In principle, a future generation will eventually attain this optimal stimulation, thereby maintaining steady states in performances throughout adulthood. The net outcome is, therefore, a positive cohort effect. Another feasible hypothesis is that the postmaturity competencies of later generations are maintained at higher levels than those of earlier generations owing to the better health care received by later generations. Better health care could mean less pronounced ontogenetic deterioration of primary processes for members of later generations than for members of earlier generations. In principle, members of some future generation may receive such beneficial health care that their primary processes will show virtually no ontogenetic change. In addition, disparities in general health represent potential disparities in secondary performance factors as well as potential disparities in primary processes. Members of later generations may be less adversely affected by these secondary factors than were members of earlier generations, and members of these later generations should, therefore, maintain performance levels closer to their true competence levels than did members of earlier generations. The outcome would again be a positive cohort effect.

The net result for either of the previous hypotheses is the situation outlined in Figure 4.11 for three widely separated generations, each evaluated on

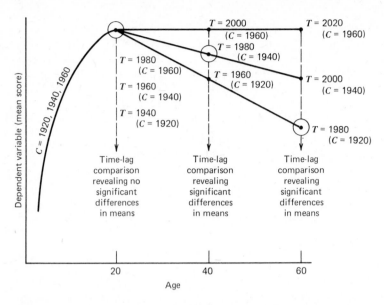

Figure 4.11. Differential rates of deterioration in performance for various cohorts (*C* indicates year of birth) that attain the same maximum level in early adulthood. Rate is assumed to decrease progressively from early to late cohorts. Expected results of time-lag comparisons for means obtained at various times of measurement (*T*) with like-age subjects are indicated by vertical arrows, and expected results of a cross-sectional study conducted in 1980 are indicated by the circled means.

the same task. It can be seen that the present hypotheses lead to three different predictions. The first is the emergence of age differences as they appear in a standard cross-sectional study conducted, for example, in 1980 (indicated by the circled means in Figure 4.11). The second prediction is a more unusual one, namely, the absence of any pronounced cohort differences among young adult groups evaluated at different times (indicated by the time-lag analysis for 20-year-old groups in Figure 4.11). The final prediction is that of cohort differences for like-age groups beyond early adulthood. Moreover, the extent of these cohort differences, all of which favor later born cohorts, should increase progressively from middle age to old age. The present hypotheses are considerably more optimistic than the earlier one that placed the locus of cohort effects in environmental stimulation during childhood. That is, the present hypotheses offer greater hope as to the possibility of reducing performance disadvantages of current and future older adults. Because these disadvantages are not viewed as resulting from initially lower levels of optimal competence in young adulthood, they are open to possible remediation. This would not be the case if the current disadvantages resulted from reduced levels of competence that existed from early childhood on for the present generation of elderly people.

We should note at this point that there could be some tasks for which postmaturity-induced cohort effects are in the negative direction, just as there could be for prematurity induced cohort effects. On such tasks, earlier generations of elderly adults would be expected to perform at higher levels than later generations of elderly adults. One important factor that could produce this reversal is the presence of more debilitating postmaturity environmental conditions for later than for earlier generations with respect to the maintenance of competence on some task that is sensitive to variation in environmental conditions. For example, noise pollution in the environment has been increasing regularly since the turn of the century (Corso, 1977). Because environmental noise may decrease competence levels on various auditory tasks, we might expect to find decreasing performance proficiency on these tasks for successive generations, with age level per se held constant.

How Extensive Are Cohort Effects in the Experimental Psychology of Aging?
Time-lag analyses of the kinds described in the preceding section can be used to provide empirical justification for the widespread concern about either cohort effects or time-of-measurement effects in any given area of the psychology of aging. Our interest, of course, is in the experimental psychology of aging. Because the concern expressed by experimental aging psychologists has been largely with suspected cohort effects, our consideration of time-lag analyses in experimental aging reseach will be limited to what they seem to reveal about cohort effects.

Unfortunately, there has been little effort expended by experimental aging psychologists on the kinds of time-lag analyses proposed in the preceding section. One reason for this lack of interest in time-lag comparisons has been the general lack of concern in the past about the contributions of cohort effects to age differences on the tasks carried over from experimental psychology. This lack of interest should dissipate in the near future in light of the impact sequential analysis seems to be making on many experimental aging psychologists. Another, and more important, reason is that time-lag analyses are, in fact, difficult to accomplish for many of the frequently used tasks in experimental psychology. The paired-associate learning task demonstrates nicely why this is true. The task has been a staple of experimental psychology for nearly 90 years. During that time, it has been administered to numerous groups of young adults (usually college students from many different cohorts), and it has also been administered to a number of older adults (again from many different cohorts). Consequently, we do have mean performance scores to compare for young adults from such widely scattered cohorts as 1910, 1930, and 1950 as well as for older adults from such cohorts as 1870, 1890, and 1910. These means should offer ideal sets of scores for testing the rise in values from early to late generations for both young and older adults predicted on the basis of a suspected positive cohort effect. The difficulty in making valid comparisons between these scores stems from the fact that paired-associate learning proficiency is extremely sensitive to many other conditions beside variation in the competence levels of the subjects mastering the task. These conditions include the nature of the linguistic elements composing the task's stimulus-response pairs (their pre-experimental familiarity to subjects, the ease with which they elicit an image, and so on), the number of pairs in the task (the more pairs, the harder the task), and the rate of exposing the elements of the task (the faster the rate, the more trials needed to learn the pairs). Meaningful comparisons between like-age groups from different cohorts demand that these non-age conditions be the same for the contrasted groups. For most of the studies on paired-associate learning reported in psychological journals, there has been considerable cross-study variability in these non-age conditions, thus making like-age contrasts between cohorts uninterpretable. That is, these contrasts are highly likely to be confounded by variation in these extraneous conditions. By contrast, time-lag comparisons are readily accomplished in the areas of intelligence and personality testing. Here, the same materials (e.g., the Army Alpha test or the Guilford-Zimmerman Temperament Survey) are received by every group, and they are received under the same standardized conditions.

Nevertheless, there have been occasional temporally separated paired-associate learning studies in which the same task elements were employed under almost identical practice conditions. Two such studies are those of Gladis and Braun (1958) and Arenberg (1967b). In each study, the task was administered to both a group of young adults and a group of elderly adults. The mean score did not change greatly from 1958 to 1967 for either age group. Consequently, the difference in means between age levels, favoring the young adults, was about the same in 1967 as it was in 1958. The fact that like-age groups did not show improved performance from an earlier cohort (i.e., the group tested in 1958) to a later cohort (i.e., the group tested in 1967) implies that the age difference found in these studies, and probably in many other similar studies that do not permit a time-lag analysis, is unrelated to cohort differences originating from differential amounts of early environmental stimulation. That is, the equality in like-age group means departs markedly from what is expected on the basis of a positive cohort effect (see Figure 4.9). The fact that an age difference is unrelated to cohort differences represents another facet of external validity. In the present context, a study's external validity refers to the extent to which the age differences found in that study are replicable with comparable age levels coming from different cohorts than those entering into the original study. In this sense of the concept, the studies by Gladis and Braun (1958) and Arenberg (1967b) have high external validity. Low external validity implies that the age differences reported in the study in question were probably strongly influenced by the specific cohort composition of that study's age groups. Consequently, subsequent replication of that study is unlikely to yield comparable age differences in that the cohorts involved in the new study have been changed. A study with external validity, as presently defined, should also have high internal validity. That is, the causal factor underlying the reported age differences may seemingly be truly identified with age variation rather than with cohort variation.

There are two reasons, however, why we must be cautious in ruling out the causative role played by cohort differences in the previously described time-lag studies. First, the separation between cohorts for the like-age groups (approximately 9 years) may not have been great enough to reflect significant changes in childhood environments. On the other hand, this degree of separation has been large enough to yield performance differences on intelligence and personality tests between like-age groups. Second, we have no assurance that sampling differences between the two studies did not result in a larger proportion of superior learners within the 1958 groups than within the 1967 groups. If this were the case, then the sampling artifact might have obscured the overall superiority of the later cohort at both age levels, while maintaining a nearly invariant performance difference between young and elderly groups from 1958 to 1967. Our best answer to this objection is the reminder that age differences in paired-associate learning are not restricted to cross-sectional studies, such as those of Gladis and Braun (1958) and Arenberg (1967b). They appear both in longitudinal comparisons of the same individuals at different ages and in comparisons of different subjects from the same cohort evaluated at different ages (remember the study by Arenberg & Robertson-Tchabo, 1977; described in Chapter 3). Because the younger and older subjects entering into these comparisons come from the same cohort, the difference in their learning proficiency cannot be due to a cohort effect.

Paired-associate learning is not the only traditional verbal-learning task that seems immune to a pronounced cohort effect. Eisdorfer (Eisdorfer & Service, 1967; Troyer, Eisdorfer, Bogdonoff, & Wilkie, 1967; Wilkie & Eisdorfer, 1977) employed the same serial-learning list in several studies separated by 10 years. Studies dealing with age differences in serial-learning proficiency will be reviewed in detail in Chapter 8. For the moment, we will merely note that collectively these studies also argue against the existence of any sizeable effect of cohort variation on verbal-learning tasks. That is, both young adults and elderly adults from earlier cohorts are about as proficient as young adults and elderly adults from later cohorts, with the magnitude of the age difference favoring young adults being about the same for later cohorts as it is for earlier cohorts. In addition, Arenberg and Robertson-Tchabo (1977) included a serial-learning task in their study. They again found age differences in learning proficiency in the absence of cohort variation (i.e., different age groups were from the same cohort).

An even more impressive argument against age differences resulting from cohort differences in early environmental stimulation may be made for the familiar digit-span task, a task that has been in use even longer than the paired-associate and serial-learning tasks. The very nature of this task assures its administration with the same content and under virtually the same conditions every time it is given to groups of subjects. Contrary to the hypothesis that members of later cohorts are cognitively superior to members of earlier cohorts, the mean digit span for young adults has remained about the same over the years. In his review of early digit-span studies (beginning in the 1880s), Woodworth (1938) concluded that "the average span for college students without preliminary practice is not over 8" (p. 18). Years later, Craik (1977) reviewed more recent studies and concluded that the average digit span for young adults is about seven items. There have been fewer studies with elderly adults than with young adults. Nevertheless, the studies that have been conducted reveal an unaltered mean digit span for elderly people from different cohorts, again contrary to the hypothesis that later cohorts excel earlier cohorts.

For illustrative purposes, we will consider only two temporally separated studies, each employing both young adults (people in their 20s) and elderly adults (people in their 60s). Moreover, digit span in both studies was measured separately for visually and aurally presented items. In the earlier study, Gilbert (1941) reported mean spans of 8.21 and 6.87 for young adults and 7.51 and 6.06 for elderly adults with visual and aural presentations respectively. In the later study, Botwinick and Storandt (1974b) reported mean spans of 7.76 and 7.08 for young adults and 7.45 and 6.10 for elderly adults again with visual and aural presentations respectively. At both age levels there is obviously little variation in mean span length between two widely separated cohorts. Moreover, there does appear to be a slight age deficit in span that generalizes across cohorts (0.70 and 0.81 in 1941 and 0.31 and 0.98 in 1974 for visual and aural presentations respectively).

As with paired-associate and serial learning, the age difference in span performance is difficult to explain in terms of a cohort effect when like-age groups from different cohorts do not differ greatly in performance. This is by no means a trivial implication. Measurement of digit span has long been part of tests purporting to measure intelligence (e.g., the WAIS). Moreover, digit-span scores have been found to correlate positively and moderately with other components of intelligence at all age levels and also with years of formal education (Birren & Morrison, 1961). Given the seemingly cognitive nature of the digit-span task, we might have expected it to be especially sensitive to cohort disparities in early environmental stimulation. This, of course, does not appear to be true.

A similar picture emerges for many of the tasks that are popular with information-processing psychologists. They are tasks that had been fairly widely used in psychological or physiological research during the late 1800s. For various reasons, interest in those tasks all but disappeared for many years, only to be rekindled in the 1960s. One of these is the perceptual-span or span-of-apprehension task. In one variation of this task, letters are flashed briefly (e.g., 50 milliseconds). Following this brief exposure, subjects report as many of the letters as they can. Young adults average about four letters in their span. This was discovered initially by J. McK. Cattell (1886) and later rediscovered by Sperling in 1960 (and subsequently replicated by many others). A second task also requires a display of letters. This time the display is left on for a varying number of milliseconds. After each interval, a second stimulus, called a masking stimulus (e.g., a flash of light), is presented. Its function is to terminate the processing of the letters in the first stimulus. Following the masking stimulus, subjects report as many of the letters from the display as they can. Through the use of this procedure, Baxt (1871) was able to determine the average rate of processing individual letters for young adults. When the interval between stimuli was 40 milliseconds, subjects were able to report about four letters. When the interval was 60 milliseconds, they were able to report about six letters. This indicates that the rate of processing is about 10 milliseconds per letter. A nearly identical rate of processing was found for young adults many years later by Sperling (1969). Like-age groups from widely separated cohorts obviously do not differ greatly in their performances on these tasks. Whatever differences exist among generations in either quantity or quality of environmental stimulation seem to have remarkably little effect on either the spanning or the scanning of visual information.

Generalizing from verbal-learning, memory-span, and perceptual-span tasks to other tasks of experimental psychology is undoubtedly a risky proposition. Nevertheless, there just does not seem to be good reason for holding on to the belief that there are widespread cohort effects in the experimental psychology of aging. It is hard to believe that cohort effects would be rampant in these other tasks when they are absent for a set of tasks cutting across a wide range of cognitive processes. Whatever effects there are from generational differences in environmental experience may well be limited to tasks tapping habits or knowledge unique to a specific environment rather than to tasks tapping more general processes of the kind mediating learning, memory, and basic perceptual phenomena. Included here would be general information tests and vocabulary tests, especially those tests that contain items that are likely to be more familiar to members of one generation than to members of other generations. For example, Butterfield and Butterfield (1977) presented pictures of objects that have been in use only recently, such as a felt-tip marking pen. Only one of their elderly subjects used the word, marker, to label the object, whereas nearly all of their young subjects assigned the correct name to the object. By contrast, we would expect many elderly adults, but few young adults, to apply the label, churn, to a picture of one. In addition, elderly adults respond faster to pictures of objects familiar to their generation than do young adults, whereas the opposite is true for pictures of objects of a more recent vintage (Poon & Fozard, 1978). Assessment of general knowledge and vocabulary are, like digit-span assessment, part of many intelligence tests. If there are indeed pronounced cohort effects in performance on intelligence tests, then the presence of experientially oriented tasks on these tests probably account for most of them.

We have focused on cohort effects that are derived from generational differences in prematurity environmental experiences. Our belief that such effects are unlikely to be widespread is based on a number of time-lag comparisons revealing the absence of cohort differences in mean scores for either young adults or elderly adults. The absence of cohort differences for elderly adults is of further importance in that it seems to rule out widespread cohort effects that are derived from generational differences in postmaturity rather than prematurity, environmental experiences. As indicated in Figure 4.11, postmaturity cohort effects may not be manifested in time-lag differences for intercohort groups of young adults, but they should be in intercohort differences for groups of elderly adults. Again, evidence from paired-associate learning, serial learning, and digit-span studies indicates the existence of neither positive nor negative postmaturity cohort effects.

Final Comments. We have attempted to demonstrate in the preceding section that there is little reason to believe in the existence of far-reaching cohort effects in the experimental psychology of aging. That is, the cross-sectional age differences in performance reported in most experimental aging studies are unlikely to be the products of cohort confoundings. Our conclusion admittedly is based on limited evidence from only a few tasks. Nevertheless, they are tasks that surely would be affected by cohort variation if, indeed, such variation is a major factor in accounting for age differences. There are other cohort comparisons that may be made for young adults only. These are for tasks that have long been employed in basic research on young adults but without long-term application to research on elderly adults. These comparisons strengthen our conclusion by revealing little, if any, differences in performance between contemporary subjects and subjects from an earlier generation of young adults. For example, performance on the frequency-judgment task described in Chapter 2 by contemporary college students (Attig & Hasher, 1980; Kausler & Puckett, 1980a) is strikingly similar to that of college students from the late 1960s (e.g., Hintzman, 1969). As another example, imagery ratings given to words by contemporary college students (Emmerich, 1979; Kausler, 1980) correlate very highly with the ratings given by students of the late 1960s (Paivio, Yuille, & Madigan, 1968).

Our argument is that neither prematurity nor postmaturity environmental changes over the past 80 or more years have been sufficient to produce substantial intercohort differences in most primary processes for like-age individuals. In other words, intercohort commonalities in the environment have been more prevalent than intercohort differences. We should note further that intercohort consistencies in performance on various tasks argue against another potential factor that could contribute to intercohort differences in performance on learning, memory, and other cognitive tasks, namely, major changes in the total population's genetic composition over the past 80 or more years (Buss, 1973). For most experimental aging studies, the careful use of the traditional cross-sectional method seems readily justified. Of course, for those behaviors, such as aggression and altruism, that rational judgment indicates the strong possibility of variation owing to intercohort variation in experiences, the value of applying a sequential method in aging research remains unchallenged.

At the same time, we do not want to convey the impression that the primary processes of interest to experimental psychologists are necessarily immune to cohort effects. Future environmental changes could very well be large enough to make consideration of cohort variation a requirement in experimental aging research of the future. This seems especially possible with regard to postmaturity environmental changes. The increased concern about the welfare of older people that has been expressed in recent years, combined with our continuously increasing understanding of human aging, could lead to markedly superior postmaturity environments by the time current generations of children and adolescents attain adulthood. The effects these environmental changes might have on adult-age differences in learning, memory, and so on, are, of course, unknown. To detect these effects and assess their magnitudes, future experimental aging psychologists would provide a valuable service by including in their studies replications of earlier studies in terms of task contents, task conditions, and subject-sampling procedures. Independent variables other than age that are of particular interest to these investigators could still be incorporated in their studies without diminishing their value as replications of earlier studies. Tests of cohort effects can be made only indirectly through time-lag analyses of data collected under comparable conditions on members of different generations. More such comparative data points are badly needed in the experimental psychology of aging. Such data obviously cannot be provided directly in that cohort variation, like age variation per se, cannot be harnessed and brought into the laboratory as a manipulable independent variable.

Summary

Dissatisfaction with the traditional cross-sectional and longitudinal methods as means of identifying causative factors for age differences in performance has led to the development of alternative methods. These alternative methods were introduced by K. Warner Schaie in the 1960s. They call for sequential designs that combine the features of the cross-sectional, longitudinal, and time-lag methods. Sequential designs have been employed to date largely in psychometric research. However, experimental psychologists of aging are beginning to express concern about causative interpretations that have been given to research conducted without the use of a sequential design.

Sequential designs were greatly influenced by Schaie's trifactor model of development. According to this model, the three factors represent independent means by which differences in performance may emerge between two or more groups in a developmental study. These means are through age variation, cohort variation, and time-of-measurement variation. When translated into the independent variables of specific studies, the three factors are not truly independent of one another. That is, variation in two factors automatically determines the levels of the remaining factor. Consequently, only two factors may serve as actual independent variables in any one study. The third factor necessarily becomes a potentially confounding factor. Thus, a sequentially designed study always has two independent variables, in contrast to a traditional cross-sectional study or a traditional longitudinal study in which age is the only independent variable.

Three different sequential designs are needed to assure that each trifactor serves as an independent variable with each of the other trifactors as the second independent variable. In the cohort-sequential design, age and cohort are the independent variables, and time of measurement is the uncontrolled, or potentially confounding, variable. Age and time of measurement are the independent variables in the time-sequential design, with cohort the uncontrolled variable. Similarly, cohort and time of measurement are the independent variables in the cross-sequential design, with age the uncontrolled variable. In principle, choice of a design in a particular study is determined by which factor is believed to have a negligible effect on performance for the task to be investigated. That is, that design in which this variable remains the uncontrolled one should be the selected design. If the excluded variable has, in fact, pronounced effects on performance, then the independent variables of a given study may be falsely interpreted as bearing causative relationships with performance on that task.

Researchers may attempt to enhance the internal validity of a sequential study by employing two, or even all three, designs simultaneously on the same task. The pattern of main effects and interaction effects emerging from the multiple design components should provide important information for identifying true causative factors. Although serious questions remain concerning the statistical validity of comparing cross-study outcomes, multiple designs may produce sufficient gains in internal validity for some content areas to justify their use. However, whatever gain does occur in internal validity must be weighed against the substantial increase in time commitment and cost of the investigation.

The cohort-sequential and cross-sequential designs have been preferred by sequentially oriented researchers. Applications of these designs in research on the PMA have revealed potent effects attributable to cohort variation. Other applications have revealed potent effects attributable to time-of-measurement variation, particularly in the area of personality assessment. The cross-sequential design has also been applied to the study of performance differences in magnitude of the Müller-Lyer illusion. Cohort variation was found to exert a significant effect on performance scores. This research has been especially influential in that it implies the necessity of utilizing sequential designs in identifying causative factors underlying developmental performance differences on the common tasks of experimental psychology.

Sequential studies are not without their serious problems however. Procedural flaws, such as those created by the selective attrition of subjects in longitudinal reassessments, are no more unlikely to occur in sequentially designed studies than they are in studies employing traditional methods. More important, sequential studies have their own unique methodological problems. These problems are especially apparent in cross-sequential studies. Because age is an uncontrolled variable in these studies, the effects of age variation per se can be evaluated only indirectly through the construction of cross-sectional and longitudinal age gradients. An age effect is identified only when the gradients show highly similar declines with increasing age. A large disparity between the two gradients is viewed by sequential analysts as providing strong support for the major role played by cohort effects in causing observed age differences in performance. However, the artificial nature of these gradients, especially the longitudinal one, makes interpretation of such disparities difficult. This is particularly true when the time spanned longitudinally in a study is considerably less than the time spanned cross-sectionally. In addition, a short separation between levels of the time-of-measurement variable relative to longer separations between levels of the cohort variable creates a situation in which a true age change may be artifactually identified as a cohort effect.

The methodological problems associated with sequential designs combined with the considerable expense and time involvement encountered in the implementation of sequential studies force us to question their widespread use in the experimental psychology of aging unless there is a sound rationale for suspecting nontrivial contributions to age differences on a task from either cohort or time-of-measurement variation. Moreover, time-lag comparisons between like-age groups from different generations on the same tasks fail to reveal any major cohort differences in performance. The judicious use of the traditional cross-sectional and longitudinal methods seems appropriate for much of the research that has been conducted in the past by experimental aging psychologists. There is, however, the possibility of much greater changes in the postmaturity environment of the future. The effects of these changes on task performances may be detected by frequent replications of past studies that may be incorporated into future experimental studies.

CHAPTER 5

Factorial Designs with Experimental Independent Variables: Process-Oriented Research

Familiar examples of what generations of introductory psychology students have, hopefully, learned to recognize as experimental, or manipulable, independent variables are such situations as (1) requiring some hapless men students to perform a difficult task before the eyes of the experimenter's attractive woman assistant, while more fortunate performers are spared this embarrassment or (2) forcing some innocent freshmen to identify briefly exposed obscene words, while their equally innocent classmates are identifying words like mother and flag. These independent variables are manipulated in the sense that the investigator has full control over their variation. A given subject is assigned, usually randomly, to a specific level, or condition, of a particular manipulable independent variable. Once the assignment is made, the subject receives the treatment defining that specific condition (e.g., having to perform with an attractive woman accomplice present). With a few exceptions, the kinds of research we encountered in Chapters, 2, 3, and 4 did not involve manipulable independent variables. Instead, our interest was in research originating from methodological designs that involve only developmentally relevant, and nonmanipulable, independent variables. Strangely missing in these designs are experimental independent variables that represent variations in task content or variations in the procedural conditions under which a task is administered. In fact, when studies derived from these designs were analyzed, task content and procedural conditions for administering the task were usually described as being invariant across the various groups representing the levels of the developmentally relevant independent variables. For example, in the hypothetical paired-associate learning study described in Chapter 2, the task consisted of abstract word pairs presented at a 5-second rate. These conditions applied to all subjects participating in that study. Similarly, the studies on visual illusion and digit span described in Chapter 4 required the same content and procedural conditions for all subjects.

In practice, most experimental aging studies are not nearly this barren. The typical study includes one or more independent variables of a traditional experimental nature as well as a developmentally relevant independent variable. The experimental variables usually relate either to changes in task content or to changes in task procedures. Thus, we may discover a study in which young and elderly adults are contrasted in their learning proficiencies for both abstract word pairs and for concrete word pairs (see Chapter 8). In this case, chronological age as an independent variable is joined by word type (a task-content manipulation) as another independent variable in the same study. Or we may discover a study in which chronological age is joined by rate-of-exposing word pairs (e.g., 2 seconds versus 5 seconds—a procedural manipulation) as an additional independent variable, with task content remaining invariant across age levels and exposure rates. We may even discover a more complex study in which both of the previously described manipulations are included. Here, either abstract word pairs or concrete word pairs are practiced with either a 2-second rate of presentation or a 5-second rate at all age levels represented in that study.

Experimental independent variables, such as word variation along the abstract-concrete dimension, are included in most experimental aging studies for two sound reasons. The first is that their inclusion increases our knowledge about the generality of an age deficit or, alternatively, about the generality of an absence of an age deficit. Having discovered that older adults are less proficient than young adults in learning lists containing abstract words, we would quite naturally wonder if the deficit is also apparent for other kinds of words. If we had included two classes of words rather than only one in our original study, we would have been in the position of knowing if the age deficit in learning is limited to only abstract words. We are likely to discover that the deficit is not so limited, thus indicating that the age deficit has some degree of generality over different task contents. A similar void is created when we discover that older adults are much less proficient than young adults in learning a fast-paced task. We would be a strange breed of psychologists if we did not wonder what the deficit would be like when the items are presented at a much slower pace. Again, if we had included at least two rates of presentation, one fast and one slow, in our original study, we would have been in the position of knowing if the deficit generalizes over a wide range of presentation rates.

In effect, we are describing here another important component of a study's external validity. Our previous discussion of external validity focused largely on the generalizability of adult-age differences in performance from observed samples of subjects to the populations underlying those samples. Equally important is the generalizability of these age differences across content or procedural variations. Incorporating experimental independent variables into a given study provides an investigator with a means of testing this aspect of external validity.

The second reason for including experimental independent variables is their analytical power in identifying specific processes (e.g., rehearsing items by either rote repetition or by forming images of them) that are affected either directly by aging or indirectly by age-correlated factors. Our assumption is that these processes are responsible for the adult-age differences that appear on those tasks regulated by the processes in question. Analytical research of this kind is usually conducted as a test of some hypothesis regarding the identity of the specific age-sensitive process underlying either a known or a suspected age deficit in performance. An experimental variable is selected for inclusion in a particular study because that variable is known from previous research (usually with young-adult subjects only) to yield changes in the process suspected of being age sensitive. The investigator's hypothesis is likely to be stated in this general form: "If Process X is the causative factor for adult-age differences in the present task, then the extent of these age differences should be greater for subjects receiving Level 1 of my independent variable than for subjects receiving Level 2 of that same variable." Differences in performance that are in the predicted direction support the investigator's contention that Process X is a causative factor for age differences on the task in question. We are assuming, of course, that other potentially confounding factors have been carefully equated over the levels of the experimental independent variable.

The inclusion of experimental independent variables in human aging studies often contributes to their internal validity as well as their external validity. Our previous interest in internal validity largely concerned the extent to which either ontogenetic or nonontogenetic effects could be assigned a true causative role for producing adult-age differences in performance. In the present context, the internal validity of a study takes a different form, namely, the extent to which a specific process can be assigned a causative role for producing adult-age differences in performance. Even though a specific process may be so identified, the reason for its age sensitivity may remain unknown. That is, age differences in the proficiency of that process could result from a true ontogenetic change with increasing age or they could result from nonontogenetic factors, such as the variation in cohort membership of the age groups entering into the analytical study.

Our objective in Chapter 5 is to enhance your understanding of truly experimental aging research—research that accomodates both experimental manipulations and age (or some other developmentally relevant condition) as independent variables. We will discuss in the first section the general characteristics of the research designs and methodologies that guide the planning, conducting, and interpretation of most experimental aging studies. Our belief is that you cannot follow the game without knowing the rules by which it is played. Hopefully, you will be encouraged to read journal articles dealing with experimental aging research. Comprehension of many of these articles demands the kind of methodological sophistication we hope to give you in this chapter. Our interest in interpretation in this initial section will focus on the implications studies have for the generalizability of age differences across variations in task content and procedural conditions. We will then examine in the following section how these designs and methodologies permit, through inference, the identification of age-sensitive processes and the identification of age-insensitive processes as well. Along the way we will encounter several issues and problems that may make process identification sometimes difficult and somewhat ambiguous. Eventually, we will discover that there are alternative strategies and methods for identifying age-sensitive processes.

The processes tested for age sensitivity are rarely treated as isolated entities by psychologists. As we will see, they are likely to be components of a multiple process theory or model that has been constructed to explain overall variation in performance on the kind of task of interest to an investigator. Specific theories that explain relatively circumscribed behavioral phenomena are not constructed within a vacuum. They are built on a foundation laid down by a broad theoretical perspective, such as that offered by behaviorism or stimulus-response (S-R) psychology, regarding the fundamental nature of human behavior, including its ontogeny. The processes entering into a behavioristically oriented theory may differ considerably from the processes entering into a theory with the same explanatory objective but built on a quite different theoretical foundation, such as that offered by information-processing psychology. The choice of an experimental independent variable to include in a process-oriented aging study is often influenced by this underlying theoretical foundation. Moreover, the results of the study engaging that variable are likely to be interpreted in the light of that same theoretical foundation. Chapter 6 will conclude our methodological review with the consideration of several general characteristics of psychological theory and with a discussion of how these characteristics influence the flow of experimental aging research.

General Characteristics of Heterogeneous Factorial Designs in Experimental Aging Research

Combining a developmentally relevant independent variable and one or more manipulable independent variables into the same study requires the use of a factorial design. The concept of a factorial design is no stranger to us. We encountered it most explicitly in our analysis of sequential research. Two independent variables are included in each sequential design, thus always making it a factorial design. However, both independent variables are always nonmanipulable. They are nonmanipulable in the sense that the investigator does not control their variation. The investigator can only select levels of a given variable, whether it be age, cohort, or time of measurement. Nor can the investigator assign subjects randomly to levels of an independent variable. Historical fact, such as birth year, defines the level to which a given subject belongs. The term, *homogeneous factorial design,* will be used here to refer to one in which the relevant independent variables all come from the same class, whether that class consists of nonmanipulable or manipulable variables. Thus, sequential designs correspond to homogeneous factorial designs. By contrast, our present interest is in what we will call the *heterogeneous factorial design.* It is heterogeneous in the sense that it includes two different classes of independent variables, nonmanipulable (usually choronological age) and manipulable (usually a task-content or procedural variable).

As indicated earlier most experimental aging studies do employ a heterogeneous factorial design. Much of the interest in these studies rests in the nature of the interaction between age variation and variation in the manipulable variable. The presence or absence of an interaction effect often provides a valuable insight into the extent of an age difference and the identification of an age-sensitive process. Our main intention in this chapter is to enhance your understanding of how the introduction of a manipulable independent variable permits such insight. However, for background purposes, we must first be certain that you are familiar with the basic characteristics of heterogeneous factorial designs.

Before beginning this overview, we should point out that a number of studies employing a heterogeneous factorial design were discussed briefly at various places in the earlier chapters. They were included for purposes of elaborating on a particular issue, such as the relevance of aging research to the real world in Chapter 1 and the competence-performance distinction in Chapter 3. At this time, we will return to one of these studies cited earlier. It should help to clarify exactly what is meant by the presence or absence of an interaction effect in a heterogeneous factorial study. Such clarification is needed in that we largely ignored interaction effects in our discussion of sequentially designed studies. Here, the major emphasis is on main effects of the independent variables rather than on their interaction effect.

The study selected is that of G. Cohen (1979). A brief review of the study will reveal that it included a manipulable independent variable (the type of question asked following aural presentation of discourse) as well as age variation. G. Cohen discovered that the age difference in performance favoring young adults was greater at one level of her manipulable variable (inference questions) than at the other level of the same variable (verbatim questions). It is precisely this disparity in age differences for different levels of a manipulable independent variable that defines the presence of an interaction effect in a heterogeneous factorial study. To expand further on this point, suppose G. Cohen had found instead that the age difference favoring young adults had been about the same for verbatim questions as for inference questions. In that case, there would be no interaction between age and type of question asked. This alternative fictitious outcome is illustrated in Figure 5.1. Note that, as in the original study, an overall age difference exists—young adults make fewer errors than elderly adults, regardless of the type of question asked. That is, there remains an age main effect. Similarly, verbatim questions overall continue to be easier than inference questions, regardless of age level. That is, there remains a main effect for type of question. What has changed is the now-apparent equality of the age difference in errors for the two types of questions. In other words, there is now the absence of an interaction between age and type of question (cf. Figure 5.1 with Figure 1.3). The altered outcome would change greatly the interpretation given to the study, a point we will return to later.

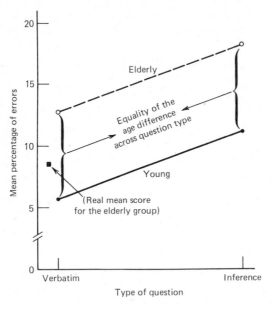

Figure 5.1. A fictitious outcome for the study by G. Cohen (1979) in which an interaction effect between age variation and variation in type of question asked following aural discourse was actually found (see Figure 1.3). In the altered outcome, there is an absence of an interaction effect.

Basic Structure of a Heterogeneous Factorial Design. In its simplest form, a heterogeneous factorial design calls for only two independent variables, one of each class, with each variable existing at only two levels. This alignment of conditions defines the 2 × 2 factorial design we met in Chapter 4. At this time we will expand on the terminology commonly applied to factorial designs in general. We will then show how the 2 × 2 design and its simplest extensions are utilized with heterogeneous classes of independent variables.

Each number in the symbolization of a factorial design represents a specific independent variable entering into a given study, and the value of each number, in turn, represents the number of levels of the designated independent variable. Thus, there are two independent variables, each existing at two levels, in any study initiated by a 2 × 2 design. Upper case letters, starting with A, are often used to represent abstractly the independent variables entering into a factorially designed study; these letters are given subscripts to represent the levels of the abstracted variables. Accordingly, a 2 × 2 design translates into an A × B design, with Level A_1 and Level A_2 for the A independent variable (which we will make the nonmanipulable one) and Level B_1 and Level B_2 for the B independent variable (i.e., the manipulable one). For a human aging study employing this minimal design, A_1 and A_2 refer to young adulthood and late adulthood respectively (or some other contrasting age levels, such as young adulthood and middle age), whereas B_1 and B_2 refer to the two levels of whatever experimental variable enters into the study (e.g., verbatim questions as B_1

and inference questions as B_2). The design translates into an experiment requiring four groups of subjects: a young-adult group receiving the B_1 level of the experimental independent variable (Group A_1B_1), a young-adult group receiving the B_2 level (Group A_1B_2), an elderly group receiving the B_1 level (Group A_2B_1), and an elderly group receiving the B_2 level (Group A_2B_2).

The minimal 2×2 design is outlined in Table 5.1 for a hypothetical study with 30 young-adult subjects and 30 elderly subjects. The manipulable independent variable is the age of the experimenter administering a learning task (maximum score equals 12) to our subjects. For Level B_1, the experimenter is a graduate student who appears to be about 25 years of age; for Level B_2, the experimenter is a person who appears to be at least 70 years of age. The investigator in this study is curious to see if the learning deficit commonly found for elderly subjects with a young experimenter is as pronounced when the experimenter is more nearly the same age as the elderly subjects. In other words: Does the age deficit generalize to a variation in the age of the experimenter (a procedural variation)? The investigator probably suspects that the large performance deficit commonly found for elderly subjects on most learning tasks (typically administered by a young experimenter) will be less pronounced when the experimenter's age is much closer to the subjects' age.

The 30 subjects at each age level are assigned randomly to two groups, one performing under Level B_1 (Groups A_1B_1 and A_2B_1) and the other under Level B_2 (Groups A_1B_2 and A_2B_2) ($n = 15$ in each group). Once the study is completed, scores on the learning task are analyzed by means of an analysis of variance (mean scores for the four groups are given in Table 5.1). This analysis enables us to test the null hypothesis as it applies separately to the A main effect [A_1 (young subjects) versus A_2 (elderly subjects) combined over the two levels of the B variable]; the B main effect [B_1 (young experimenter) versus B_2 (old experimenter) combined over the two age levels of subjects]; and the A $\times$ B interaction effect (age deficit for elderly subjects found with a young experimenter versus age deficit for elderly subjects found with an old experimenter).

The A main effect tests the statistical significance of the difference between the overall mean for young adult subjects (7.5) and the overall mean for elderly subjects (5.5). For our purposes, we will assume that this test is significant and that we are able to reject the null hypothesis of no difference in performance on our learning task between populations of young adults and elderly adults. Our conclusion, therefore, is that there is an overall age deficit on our learning task. The B main effect tests the statistical significance of the difference between the overall mean found for subjects performing with a young experimenter (8) and the overall mean for subjects performing with an old experimenter (5). Once more we will assume that this test is statistically significant, permitting us to reject the hypothesis that performance on our learning task is unaffected by an experimenter's age. Our conclusion is that performance on this particular task is more proficient with a young experimenter than with an old experimenter, regardless of a subject's age level.

Faith in our conclusions about main effects is contingent on how well the investigator avoided confounding by extraneous factors. Surely the investigator

Table 5.1 Design for a Hypothetical 2 × 2 Heterogeneous Factorial Study and the Comparisons Entering into the Analysis of Scores[a]

	B Independent variable (age of experimenter)		
A independent variable (age of subjects)	B_1 (young)	B_2 (old)	Overall mean
A_1 (young)	Group A_1B_1 $n = 15$; mean $= 9$	Group A_1B_2 $n = 15$; mean $= 6$	7.5
A_2 (elderly)	Group A_2B_1 $n = 15$; mean $= 7$	Group A_2B_2 $n = 15$; mean $= 4$	5.5
Overall mean	8	5	

A (age of subjects) main effect:

A_1 (young) versus A_2 (elderly)

$$\underset{B_1\ \text{Level}}{\text{Group } A_1B_1 + \text{Group } A_1B_2} \qquad \underset{B_2\ \text{Level}}{\text{Group } A_2B_1 + \text{Group } A_2B_2}$$

(balanced)

B (age of experimenter) main effect:

$$B_1\ \text{(young)} \qquad \text{versus} \qquad B_2\ \text{(old)}$$

$$\underset{A_1\ \text{Level}}{\text{Group } A_1B_1 + \text{Group } A_2B_1} \qquad \underset{A_2\ \text{Level}}{\text{Group } A_1B_2 + \text{Group } A_2B_2}$$

(balanced)

$A \times B$ interaction effect: $(A_1 - A_2)_{B_1\ \text{Level}} - (A_1 - A_2)_{B_2\ \text{Level}}$

$(\text{Group } A_1B_1 - \text{Group } A_2B_1) - (\text{Group } A_1B_2 - \text{Group } A_2B_2)$

[a] Both main effects are significant; the interaction effect is not significant.

matched the young and elderly groups of subjects on important nonontogenetic attributes (e.g., educational level) and made certain that all subjects received the same task content under the same pacing conditions. A more subtle factor to have controlled is the sex of the experimenter. Failure to do so would have been a monumental goof. Given a young experimenter of one sex and an old experimenter of the opposite sex, the causative factor for the B main effect would be hopelessly confounded. Is it the age or the sex of the experimenter? In addition, it is likely that the investigator employed more than one experimenter at each age level. A reasonable number would be three different young experimenters and three different old experimenters. Group A_1B_1 would then have consisted of three subgroups, each formed by the random assignment of five young-adult subjects. Subgroup I would be assigned to Young Experimenter I, Subgroup II to Young Experimenter II, and Subgroup III to Young Experimenter III. A similar procedure would be followed for each of the other main groups in the study. By so doing, the investigator has increased considerably the generalizability of the age-of-the-experimenter effect. That is, it is not limited to any one pairing of a young versus old experimenter.

The absence of an A $\times$ B interaction effect is obvious from the means reported in Table 5.1. Note that the difference in means between young and elderly subjects at Level B_1 ($9 - 7 = 2$) equals the difference at Level B_2 ($6 - 4 = 2$). Our statistical analysis will reveal that we have no basis for rejecting the relevant null hypothesis, which in this case states that the age difference in performance for populations of young and elderly adults is independent of the experimenter's age. Our failure to reject the interaction null hypothesis, therefore, adds to the generalizability of the age deficit typically found on this learning task with a young experimenter, contrary to the investigator's expectation.

We selected identical age differences at B_1 and B_2 for illustrative purposes only. In practice, it is extremely unlikely that these differences will be exactly equal. Instead, some degree of disparity is almost certain to be observed, so that the difference at B_1 will depart somewhat from the difference at B_2. If that disparity is not large enough to permit rejection of the interaction null hypothesis, then our conclusion is unaltered—namely, we have no reason for inferring that the age difference in performance for our underlying populations varies in magnitude with the specific B treatment received.

The outcome of a factorial study is often presented in graphical form. In fact, a number of these graphic representations appeared in our analyses of factorial studies in earlier studies (e.g., Figures 1.2 and 1.3). To complete the analysis of our present hypothetical learning study, we will add the graphic representation of its outcome to our collection. One form of this representation is shown in the top panel of Figure 5.2. We simply plotted the means of our four groups in a graph having the level of the B variable (i.e., age of experimenter) along the abscissa and then connected by a straight line the means for the two groups created by variation of the A variable (i.e., age of subjects). Especially apparent in this figure is the absence of an interaction effect. As a general rule, the extent of an interaction is reflected by the degree to which the two lines in the graphic representation of a 2 $\times$ 2 study deviate from being

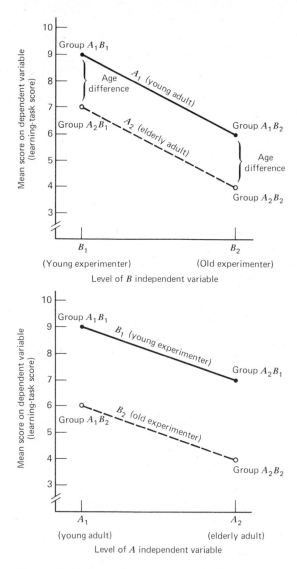

Figure 5.2. Means plotted for the hypothetical study outlined in Table 5.1. Top panel: Results indicate main effects for the A (age of subjects) and B (age of experimenter) variables, but there is no interaction effect. Bottom panel: Means replotted with age of subject levels on the abscissa.

parallel. In our present study the lines are obviously perfectly parallel, and the absence of an interaction glares at us.

Also apparent in the bottom panel of Figure 5.2 is another important principle of 2 × 2 studies—the fact that an interaction effect traverses two different paths. The effect may be viewed in terms of the differential between Mean B_1 − Mean B_2 at Level A_1 (i.e., Mean for Group A_1B_1 − Mean for Group A_1B_2) and Mean B_1 − Mean B_2 at Level A_2 (i.e., Mean for Group A_2B_1

— Mean for Group A_2B_2) as well as in terms of the differential between Mean A_1 — Mean A_2 at Level B_1 (i.e., Mean for Group A_1B_1 — Mean for Group A_2B_1) and Mean A_1 — Mean A_2 at Level B_2 (i.e., Mean for Group A_1B_2 — Mean for Group A_2B_2). We are now considering the interaction in terms of the performance difference between B_1 and B_2 for young adults relative to the performance difference between B_1 and B_2 for elderly subjects. From this perspective, our graphic representation is altered so that levels of the A variable replace levels of the B variable along the abscissa and our two straight lines now connect the means for Groups A_1B_1 and A_2B_1 and Groups A_1B_2 and A_2B_2, as shown in the bottom panel of Figure 5.2. Restructuring our interaction effect does not change our statistical outcome however. Note that Mean B_1 — Mean B_2 at Level A_1 yields 3 (9 — 6) and that Mean B_1 — Mean B_2 at Level A_2 also yields 3 (8 — 5). Thus, the differential in our differences between means remains 0, signifying again the complete absence of an interaction between our A and B independent variables. Moreover, the restructuring does not alter the fact that our interaction continues to deal with variation in the amount of an age difference in performance. Nevertheless, the preferred way of depicting an A × B interaction in most aging studies is with variation in the manipulable (B) variable chartered along the abscissa, as in the top panel of Figure 5.2.

Another hypothetical study should aid considerably in your understanding of 2 × 2 heterogeneous factorial studies. This time our study is one in which both main effects and an interaction effect are present. The investigator in this study believes that elderly adults are less likely than young adults to take risks in situations where success is uncertain. However, the investigator also suspects that the age difference in risk-taking is likely to be influenced by the actual probability of succeeding on the task at hand. Risk-taking is to be assessed by the amount of money a subject is willing to bet on his or her successful completion of a problem-solving task devised by the investigator. With a moderate probability of success, such as 0.50, no subject, young or elderly, is expected to bet much money on future success. However, the greater cautiousness of the elderly should make them especially chicken in terms of the amount of money they are willing to risk losing. That is, the age difference in amount of money bet should be quite large at this level of risk-taking. With a high probability of success, such as 0.90, all subjects, regardless of age, are expected to increase considerably the amount of money they are willing to bet. The greater cautiousness of the elderly should now be less of a factor than it is when the probability of succeeding is moderate. Nevertheless, it should continue to exert some influence on betting behavior. Thus, there should continue to be an age difference in the amount of money bet—but the magnitude of the difference should be much less than it is when there is only a moderate probability of succeeding. The research hypothesis of primary concern in this study, therefore, consists of a predicted age by probability of success interaction effect.

To test this hypothesis, 30 young-adult and 30 elderly subjects are assigned randomly to two levels of the B independent variable. Level B_1 is set at a moderate probability of success, defined by the investigator as being 0.50, and Level B_2 at a high probability of success, defined as being 0.90. Prior to beginning work on a problem-solving task, each subject is given \$20 and is told that any amount of that money may be bet on the successful completion of the task. Whatever amount of money the subject bets becomes the subject's—provided the subject wins on the subsequent task. On the other hand, the amount of money bet is deducted from the $20 the subject already has if the subject loses on the subsequent task. Level B_1 subjects are informed further that the task has been given to a number of subjects in the past and about 50% of them have solved the problem. For Level B_2 subjects, the percentage of past subjects solving the problem changes to 90%. The dependent variable, of course, is simply the amount of money a subject bets, with possible scores ranging from 0 to $20.

The outcome of our study is shown graphically in Figure 5.3. It is structured with levels of the B variable (probability of success) along the abscissa in the top panel and levels of the A variable (age) along the abscissa in the bottom

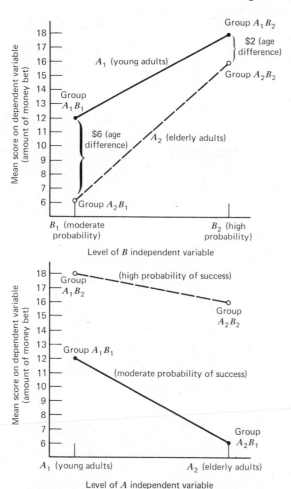

Figure 5.3. Top panel: Means for a hypothetical study in which the A (age of subjects) × B (probability of success on a task) interaction effect is significant. Bottom panel: Means replotted with age levels on the abscissa.

panel. In both panels, the deviation of the straight lines from being parallel is striking. Note in the top panel that an age difference in the mean amount bet is obvious for subjects receiving Level B_1 of the manipulable independent variable, with the difference in means between Groups A_1B_1 and A_2B_1 equaling \$6 (\$12 − \$6). However, the age difference diminishes greatly at Level B_2, with the difference in means between Groups A_1B_2 and A_2B_2 equaling only \$2 (\$18 − \$16). Consequently, the differential in the two differences equals \$4 (\$6 − \$2), a disparity probably large enough to permit rejection of the interaction null hypothesis. If so, we conclude, with a stated risk of being wrong (i.e., the significance, or alpha, level established by the investigator in advance of collecting the data), that the age difference in risk-taking between young and elderly populations of subjects is greater at Level B_1 than at Level B_2. In other words, the investigator's interaction hypothesis has been confirmed.

Given a statistically significant interaction effect, our next step is to analyze what are called *simple effects*. Two simple effects need to be examined in a 2×2 study whenever the overall interaction effect is significant. For the format shown in the top panel of Figure 5.3., our simple effects consist of (1) the age difference present at B_1 and (2) the age difference present at B_2. Our procedure calls for testing separately the significance of the difference in means between Groups A_1B_1 and A_2B_1 and Groups A_1B_2 and A_2B_2, employing either additional analyses of variance or some other appropriate statistical test (e.g., a t test). The simple effect is likely to be significant at both B_1, where the age difference is \$6, and B_2, where the age difference is \$2. Further statistical analysis, however, is likely to indicate that the magnitude of the effect of age variation is greater at B_1 than at B_2. This analysis requires computing omega squared (ω^2) for each simple effect [ω^2 (as noted in Chapter 4) indicates the proportion of total variance behavior that is attributable to variation of the independent variable in question (in this case, age)]. We would expect ω^2 to be greater for the simple effect at B_1 than for the simple effect at B_2.

The pattern of simple effects found in a study markedly affects the interpretation of a significant main effect for age variation obtained in that study. It does seem likely that the main effect for age in our betting study is statistically significant—the overall mean amount of money bet is \$15 for young adults (i.e., the average of \$12 and \$18) and only \$11 for elderly adults (i.e., the average of \$6 and \$16). However, we know at this point that the effect for age variation resulted largely from the whopping age difference found at Level B_1. The age difference at Level B_2 is considerably smaller (but still statistically significant as a simple effect). Consequently, we must qualify the generalizability of an age difference in risk-taking behavior, at least as far as it is assessed by the task employed in our hypothetical study. Clearly, the magnitude of the age difference depends on what other conditions are present at the time risk-taking behavior is being evaluated.

Our hypothetical examples represent only two possible outcomes of a 2×2 heterogeneous factorial study. There are numerous other possibilities, four of which are shown in Figure 5.4. In the first (top-left panel) there is an apparent main effect for age, shown as an overall age deficit in performance, but not for

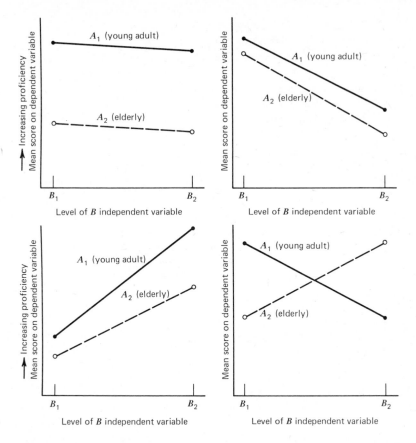

Figure 5.4. Sample of possible outcomes for 2 × 2 heterogeneous factorial studies. Top-left panel: Age main effect significant; no main effect for the manipulable variable; no interaction effect. Top-right panel: Main effect significant for the manipulable variable; no main effect for age; no interaction effect. Bottom-left panel: Significant interaction effect with an age deficit at both levels of the manipulable variable but greater at Level B_2 than at Level B_1. Bottom-right panel: Significant interaction effect showing a crossover in which the direction of the age difference at Level B_1 is reversed at Level B_2.

the manipulable independent variable (the slight superiority of performance under Level B_1 is assumed to be so small that it does not permit rejection of the B main effect null hypothesis). Given the nearly parallel straight lines, it is also unlikely that the interaction null hypothesis can be rejected. In the second (top-right panel) the age main effect is slight and nonsignificant, whereas the B main effect is large enough to be significant (with B_1 superior to B_2). The interaction effect is again slight and most likely nonsignificant. The third possible outcome (bottom-left panel) reveals an interaction effect but of a different kind than that found in our betting study. As in that study, the magnitude of the age difference in performance differs at the two levels of the B variable. However, in our prior study, the age difference was greater at the level of the B variable where overall performance, combining age levels, was lower (i.e., at Level B_1; see

Figure 5.3). By contrast, in the present example, the age difference is greater at the level of the B variable where overall performance, again combining age levels, is greater (i.e., at Level B_2; see Figure 5.4).

The fourth outcome (bottom-right panel) is an especially intriguing one. It shows a complete crossover in terms of directionality of age differences. That is, young adults excel in performance at Level B_1, whereas elderly adults excel at Level B_2. Although this is an unusual outcome, it is far from being impossible. Our final hypothetical study, in fact, is one in which a crossover effect is a reasonable expectation. Our investigators are baseball fanatics who decide to combine their devotion to the game with a nearly equal devotion to aging research. Accordingly, the B independent variable for this aging study consists of the time period in which historically significant baseball events took place. Specifically, Level B_1 becomes the 1970s and Level B_2 the 1930s (strictly speaking, the variable is not a truly experimental variable—its variation is not controlled by the investigators). Ten questions are made up for each decade. Included are questions like, "Who is the only pitcher to pitch two consecutive no hit games?" for the 1930s and "How many bases did Lou Brock steal in setting a new major league record?" for the 1970s. The test is then given to 20 young-adult and 20 elderly baseball fans (identified, perhaps, by their presence in the bleachers at Wrigley Field, Chicago). Each subject receives two dependent variable scores, one for the number of correct answers given to the 1970's questions, the other for the number of correct answers given to 1930's questions. The young adults will probably have a higher mean score than the elderly adults on the 1970's test (Level B_1), whereas the reverse will probably occur on the 1930's test (Level B_2). Our expectation is based on the popular notion that older adults recall old memories better than they recall more recent memories, whereas young adults remember best events that actually happened during their lifetimes. We will discover in Chapter 8 that there is limited support for this notion.

Extensions and Modifications of A × B Designs. Three additional points need to be made about the basic A × B heterogeneous factorial design. The first is that research employing this design is in no way limited to bilevel independent variables. The most obvious extension is to have more than two levels of the nonmanipulable independent variable. Thus, we might add a middle-age level to the A variable while maintaining two levels of the B variable. In this event, the basic A × B structure translates into a 3 × 2 design. Similarly, we might add a third level to our B variable (e.g., a middle-aged investigator in addition to young and old investigators) in combinaton with, say, two age levels of subjects (a 2 × 3 design) or three age levels of subjects (a 3 × 3 design). Nor are we limited to three levels of each independent variable. For example, in some aging studies five age levels are employed, each corresponding to a decade in chronological age from the 20s through the 60s. In combination with bilevel and trilevel manipulable independent variables, the design becomes a 5 × 2 and a 5 × 3 factorial respectively. The interpretation of the results obtained in a multiple level A × B study does not differ greatly from the interpretation of results obtained in a purely bilevel study. Again we are testing for the presence of statistically significant main effects for age and the manipulable independent variable and for the presence of a significant A × B interaction effect. The statistical analysis continues to be conducted through the use of analysis of variance (Winer, 1971), and a graphic representation of a study's outcome continues to be a useful communicative device. We will limit our discussion to one example, the outcome of which is illustrated in Figure 5.5.

This study followed the guidelines of a 3 × 3 factorial design. There were, therefore, 9 groups of subjects, 3 at each age level, with one receiving Level B_1, the second Level B_2, and the third Level B_3. Note that we now have three straight lines, one for each age level, and each line connects three mean scores. The existence of an interaction between age and the manipulable independent variable is again indicated by the extent to which our lines deviate from being parallel. There seems to be sufficient deviation in this case to suspect that the interaction is statistically significant. The nature of this interaction can be seen from an inspection of Figure 5.5. At each level of the B variable, there are pronounced age differences in mean scores on the dependent variable. However, the pattern of these age differences changes across the levels of B. At B_1 a large deficit is manifested for both middle-age and elderly subjects relative to young-adult subjects. At the same time, there is little difference between middle-age and elderly adults. An analysis of the simple effect at B_1 (i.e., analyzing age differences at the B_1 level only) is likely to reveal that the young-adult group is significantly superior to the combined older groups (or to either older group considered alone) and that the two older groups do not differ significantly from one another. The same pattern holds at Level B_2, but the overall magnitude of the age differences is diminished. In fact, a statistical comparison is likely to show that the magnitude of age differences at B_1 significantly exceeds the magnitude at B_2. The pattern is quite different at Level B_3. Here, there is little difference in performance between the young and middle-age groups, both of which are now clearly superior to the elderly group. Thus, variation in the B variable proved to be an effective means of altering age differences in

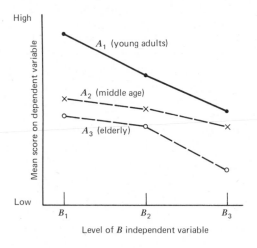

Figure 5.5. Means for a hypothetical 3 × 3 heterogeneous factorial study in which the age × manipulable variable interaction effect is significant.

performance on the task in question. We are likely to find the main effect for both age and the B variable to be statistically significant. Of course, the main effect for age must be interpreted in light of the significant interaction and the pattern of simple effects that yielded the interaction. That is, generalizability of the extent of age differences on the task can be made only in reference to the specific level of the B variable in operation.

The second point is that, in principle, the nonmanipulable independent variable in a heterogeneous factorial study may consist of variation in either cohort membership or time of measurement rather than variation in chronological age. With this altered design, chronological age would remain invariant for all groups. The use of a non-age variable would necessarily mean that years would be required to complete the study, with complications of the kind described in Chapters 2, 3, and 4 being the consequence. If a heterogeneous factorial study were to be conducted in which, say, cohort variation served as the nonmanipulable independent variable, then we would be dealing with cohort differences rather than age differences at each level of the manipulable independent variable. For example, we might contrast 60-year-old subjects born in 1910 with 60-year-old subjects born in 1920. The task might consist of learning lists composed of either abstract nouns or concrete nouns, thus making the design a 2 × 2 factorial. One group of 1910 cohorts would receive an abstract-noun list and the other a concrete-noun list—with both groups entering the laboratory in 1970. Comparable groups of 1920 cohorts would, in turn, be run in 1980. Although this design is perfectly feasible, it does not seem to have been applied to date in a human experimental aging study.

The third point is that a heterogeneous factorial study may involve either a *between-subject* or a *within-subject* treatment of the manipulable independent variable. A between-subject treatment simply means that each level of the variable is administered to a separate group of subjects. Consequently, each subject at each age level serves only once in the study, namely, under the level of the B variable to which the subject has been assigned. Because variation in the A variable (i.e., age level of subjects) is also a between-subject treatment, the design is called a *pure between-subject factorial*. The design of our hypothetical study with age of subjects and age of the experimenter as the A and B variables is an example of a between-subject factorial. A within-subject treatment means that each subject at each age level serves under each level of the manipulable variable. As a result, each subject earns as many dependent variable scores as there are levels of the B variable. Because variation in the A variable is a between-subject treatment, the design is called a *mixed factorial* (i.e., it mixes together between-subject and within-subject treatments in the same study). The design of our hypothetical study on knowledge of baseball trivia is an example of a mixed factorial. Remember each subject in that study was evaluated twice, once at Level B_1 and again at Level B_2. The mixed factorial design has the advantage of requiring fewer subjects than does the between-subject factorial design. Consider a 2 × 2 study calling for 10 subjects in each of the four groups or conditions. Only 10 young and 10 elderly subjects would be required if the study were conducted as a mixed factorial, whereas 20 young and 20 elderly subjects would be required in the between-subject counterpart. In many cases, however, the use of a subject more than once may be impossible. For example, in a study calling for deception at Level B_2 but not at Level B_1, it would make no sense to have a subject perform under Level B_2 after having already performed under Level B_1. In such cases, the investigator has no option other than the use of a pure between-subject design.

It is also possible to combine a within-subject manipulable independent variable with age as a within-subject independent variable. This would be the case for a longitudinal study in which the contrasting age levels are provided by testing the same subjects at different chronological ages, with each subject being tested at each age under all levels of the manipulable independent variable. This variation is called a *pure within-subject factorial design.*

Inclusion of One or More Additional Independent Variables: A × B × C Designs.
Unlike the sequential studies considered in Chapter 4, heterogeneous factorial studies are not limited to bifactor manifestations. That is, a study may have two, three or even more independent variables. Usually, however, only one additional independent variable is added to the basic A × B structure, making the overall design trifactor in nature. Labeling the three factors as A, B, and C, the resulting design is symbolized as A × B × C. The specific form of the design is then contingent on the levels planned for each of the independent variables. The simplest form is a 2 × 2 × 2 design in which each independent variable is bilevel. We could, of course, have a 3 × 2 × 2 design, a 2 × 3 × 3 design, and so on, with each number again identifying the number of levels planned for the designated independent variable.

The structure of a trifactor design is flexible in the sense that the added independent variable may be either manipulable or nonmanipulable. The study cited early in this chapter in which task content (concrete versus abstract words) and exposure rate (2 seconds versus 5 seconds) are combined with variation in age level (young adult versus elderly adult) flows from a 2 × 2 × 2 factorial in which one independent variable is nonmanipulable (A: age) and two are manipulable (B: word type; C: rate of exposure). Alternatively, a study may be planned in which both the A and B variables are nonmanipulable (incidentally, nonmanipulable variables like age and sex are often called *organismic variables* in the parlance of experimental psychology) and only the C variable is truly manipulable. For example, in a 2 × 2 × 2 study, the A and B variables may be age and sex (obviously, man versus woman) and the C variable rate of exposure. Factorial designs of this kind are fairly common in experimental aging studies.

The interpretation of a trifactor study's results has much in common with the interpretation of a bifactor study's results. We continue to test the statistical significance of the main effects for the A and B variables, and we add to these tests one for the significance of the C variable. Moreover, we continue to test the significance of the A × B interaction, that is, age with first of the other two independent variables (e.g., word type). This interaction is interpreted just like the A × B interaction in a bifactor study. That is, the magnitude of the effect determines whether or not the extent of an age difference varies across the levels of the B variable. For this analysis we ignore the segregation of subjects into groups based on their assignments to levels of the remaining C variable (e.g., rate of exposure). Because there is another independent variable to be considered, namely C, there are two other *first-order interactions* (i.e., interactions involving only two independent variables) to be examined as well. They are the A $\times$ C and B $\times$ C interactions. The A $\times$ C interaction is of special importance in that it, like the A $\times$ B interaction, involves variation in age level. This interaction enables us to determine whether or not the extent of age differences varies across levels of the C variable. To test the statistical significance of the A $\times$ C interaction, we ignore the segregation of subjects into groups based on their assignments to levels of the B variable. A significant A $\times$ C interaction is interpreted in the same manner as a significant A $\times$ B interaction with respect to generalizability of age differences on the task in question.

The real uniqueness of a trifactor study occurs through the emergence of a *second-order interaction,* that is, an interaction involving all three independent variables (A $\times$ B $\times$ C). A statistically significant A $\times$ B $\times$ C interaction effect means that both the main effect of age and first-order interaction effects involving age must be interpreted in light of the complexities introduced by the nature of this higher order interaction effect.

A hypothetical study should clarify both the operations of a 2 $\times$ 2 $\times$ 2 design and the meaning of a second-order interaction. The study is both a replication and an extension of our earlier study with age of subjects as the A variable and age of experimenter as the B variable (and a learning-task score as the dependent variable). Our present investigator includes both prior independent variables in a new study (the replication part of the study) along with a new independent variable (the extension part). The new manipulable variable, C, consists of the attitude expressed toward the subjects by the experimenter. For Level C_1, the experimenter, regardless of age (experimenter's or subject's), is friendly and supportive; for Level C_2 the experimenter, again regardless of age, is hostile and critical of a subject's performance. Eighty subjects, 40 young adult and 40 elderly, are assigned randomly to the eight groups needed in this study. The groups are identified as Group $A_1B_1C_1$ (young-adult subjects, young experimenter, friendly attitude), Group $A_1B_1C_2$ (young-adult subjects, young experimenter, hostile attitude), and so on, up to Group $A_2B_2C_2$ (elderly subjects, old experimenter, hostile attitude).

The design, analysis, and results of this study are summarized in Table 5.2. The summary indicates that (1) young-adult subjects performed more proficiently than elderly subjects (significant A main effect), (2) subjects performed more proficiently with a young experimenter than with an old experimenter (significant B main effect), and (3) subjects performed more proficiently with a friendly experimenter than with a hostile experimenter (significant C main effect). The main effects for the A and B variables replicate the findings of our earlier study. Note further that the A $\times$ B (age of subjects $\times$ age of experimenter) and B $\times$ C (age of experimenter $\times$ attitude of experimenter) first-order interaction effects were slight and probably did not permit rejections of their relevant null hypotheses. The absence of a significant A × B interaction effect also replicates the findings of the earlier study. On the other hand, the A × C (age of subjects × attitude of the experimenter) first-order interaction effect was somewhat larger and most likely permitted rejection of the relevant null hypothesis. This interaction resulted from the greater age difference (favoring young-adult subjects) found when an experimenter (regardless of age) expresses a friendly attitude (Level C_1) than when the experimenter expresses a hostile attitude (Level C_2). This outcome modifies the generalization we can make about the magnitude of an age deficit on our learning task. That is, the magnitude of the deficit seems to be a function of the performance conditions existing with respect to our C variable, being greater under C_1 than under C_2. By contrast, in agreement with the earlier study, the magnitude of the age deficit in performance on the learning task is unaffected by the conditions existing with respect to the B variable (i.e., age of experimenter), at least as indicated by the trivial A × B first-order interaction effect.

This latter conclusion must be interpreted cautiously, however, in light of the significant second-order A × B × C interaction effect. As indicated in Table 5.2, this interaction may be analyzed from each of three different approaches, all of which yield the same magnitude. The first views the higher order interaction in terms of the disparity between the A × B interaction found only at Level C_1 (i.e., a friendly experimenter) and the A × B interaction found only at Level C_2 (i.e., a hostile experimenter). The second does the same thing with respect to differential A × C interaction effects at Levels B_1 (young experimenter) and B_2 (old experimenter) and the third with respect to differential B × C interaction effects at Levels A_1 (young subjects) and A_2 (elderly subjects). From any approach taken, we discover that the magnitude of the second-order interaction effect is moderately large (see Table 5.2). Assuming it is statistically significant, we need to restrict still further our generalization about age deficits in performance on our learning task.

This further restriction may best be seen in terms of the A × C interaction, the only first-order interaction effect attaining significance in our study. With this particular first-order interaction in mind, our interpretation of the second-order interaction effect centers on the second approach described above. The graphic representation of the second-order interaction that is yielded by this approach is shown in Figure 5.6. Actually, two graphic representations are needed to convey the nature of the interaction. The first (top panel of Figure 5.6) is a graph of the means entering into an A × C interaction for half of the subjects, namely, those in the four groups receiving Level B_1 of the B variable; the second (bottom panel of Figure 5.6) is a graph of the means entering into an A × C interaction for the other half of the subjects, namely, those in the four groups receiving Level B_2 of the same variable. It should be noted that the age deficit in performance is less pronounced at Level C_2 (hostile experimenter) than at Level C_1 in both panels (i.e., for both levels of B). It is this differential in the magnitude of the age deficit with variation in the C condition that accounts for the overall (i.e., ignoring B variable condition) significant A × C interaction effect described earlier. However, it is also appar-

Table 5.2　Design for a 2 × 2 × 2 Heterogeneous Factorial Study and the Results for a Hypothetical Study Employing That Design[a]

	C_1		C_2	
	B_1	B_2	B_1	B_2
A_1	Group $A_1B_1C_1$ 10	Group $A_1B_2C_1$ 8	Group $A_1B_1C_2$ 6	Group $A_1B_2C_2$ 4
A_2	Group $A_2B_1C_1$ 6	Group $A_2B_2C_1$ 4	Group $A_2B_1C_2$ 6	Group $A_2B_2C_2$ 2

Overall means for main effects:

Mean A_1 ($\bar{A}_1$) = 7; Mean A_2 ($\bar{A}_2$) = 4.5
Mean B_1 ($\bar{B}_1$) = 7; Mean B_2 ($\bar{B}_2$) = 4.5
Mean C_1 ($\bar{C}_1$) = 7; Mean C_2 ($\bar{C}_2$) = 4.5

First-order interaction effects:

$A \times B = (\bar{A}_1 - \bar{A}_2)_{B_1} - (\bar{A}_1 - \bar{A}_2)_{B_2} = (8 - 6) - (6 - 3) = 2 - 3 = -1$
$A \times C = (\bar{A}_1 - \bar{A}_2)_{C_1} - (\bar{A}_1 - \bar{A}_2)_{C_2} = (9 - 5) - (5 - 4) = 4 - 1 = 3$
$B \times C = (\bar{B}_1 - \bar{B}_2)_{C_1} - (\bar{B}_1 - \bar{B}_2)_{C_2} = (8 - 6) - (6 - 3) = 2 - 3 = -1$

Second-order interaction effects:

First approach

$A \times B \times C = (A \times B)_{C_1} - (A \times B)_{C_2} = [(10 - 6) - (8 - 4)] - [(6 - 6) - (4 - 2)] = 2$
$(4 - 4) - (0 - 2) = 2$

Second approach

$A \times B \times C = (A \times C)_{B_1} - (A \times C)_{B_2} = [(10 - 6) - (6 - 6)] - [(8 - 4) - (4 - 2)] = 2$
$(4 - 0) - (4 - 2) = 2$

Third approach

$A \times B \times C = (B \times C)_{A_1} - (B \times C)_{A_2} = [(10 - 8) - (6 - 4)] - [(6 - 4) - (6 - 2)] = 2$
$(2 - 2) - (2 - 4) = 2$

[a]There are 10 subjects ($n = 10$) in each group or cell (e.g., Group $A_1B_1C_1$) of the design. The number given for each group is the mean performance score for that group.

A = age of subjects; A_1 = young adult; A_2 = elderly adult.
B = age of experimenter; B_1 = young; B_2 = old.
C = attitude of experimenter; C_1 = friendly; C_2 = hostile.

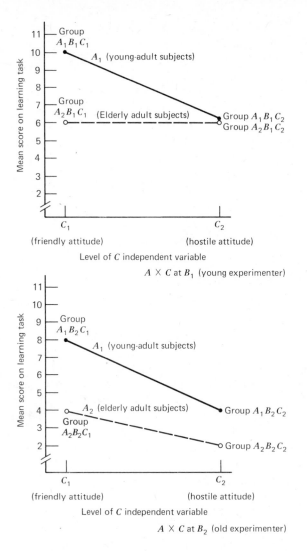

Figure 5.6. Means for the hypothetical study outlined in Table 5.2. Top panel: Means plotted to show the A × C (age of subjects × attitude of experimenter) first-order interaction present at Level B_1 only. Bottom panel: Means plotted to show the A × C first-order interaction at Level B_2 only. Considered together, the panels reveal the presence of a significant second-order (A × B × C) interaction effect.

ent from Figure 5.6 that the variation in the age deficit from a friendly to a hostile experimenter (i.e., from Level C_1 to Level C_2) is greater for subjects having a young experimenter (Level B_1) than for subjects having an old experimenter (Level B_2). In fact, the deficit disappears at Level C_2 under the B_1 condition but not under the B_2 condition. The significant second-order interaction effect simply reflects the disparity in the age of subjects by attitude of experimenter interaction produced by accompanying variation in the age of the experimenter. Thus, generalization about an age deficit on the learning task should take into account the likelihood that the deficit is negligible under certain performance conditions, namely, those formed by the combination of a young *and* hostile experimenter. With other combinations of experimenter's age and attitude, the magnitude of the age deficit in performance on the learning task is considerably greater.

Finally, we should make it clear that trifactor heterogeneous designs may enter into the same between-subject versus within-subject variations as do bifactor designs. Usually, A, B, and C are all between-subject independent variables, thus making the trifactor design pure between-subject in format. However, there are occasions in which one or more of the independent variables is within-subject, thus making the trifactor design a mixed factorial or even a pure within-subject factorial.

Identifying Age-Sensitive/and Age-Insensitive Processes Through Interaction Effects

Soundly conducted ontogenetic research of the kind reported in Chapter 2 may convince us that a gross behavioral phenomenon, such as performance on a paired-associate learning task, undergoes a maturational change during adulthood. However, as noted earlier, that research leaves us with an unanswered question: What structure or process is altered by the maturational change? At stake is the identification of a specific primary process that is affected by human aging. Once that process is identified, there is always the possibility of finding ways of retarding its deterioration or finding ways of reversing, at least partially, its loss. A potent means of gaining insight into what processes are age sensitive and what processes are age insensitive is through the presence or absence of interaction effects in heterogeneous factorial studies. Thus, interactions assume much more importance than merely modifying the extent of generalization permitted about the nature and extent of age deficits. The rationale underlying process identification through interaction effects will now be described.

Multiple Components of Behavioral Phenomena. Identification of a primary process that is age sensitive is made difficult by the fact that many gross behavioral phenomena, for example, paired-associate learning, are governed by multiple structures and processes. Which one (ones) is age sensitive can be determined only by carefully conducted analytical research. Appropriate analytical research must be preceded, however, by the theoretical analysis of the behavioral phenomenon into its component parts together with the subsequent validation of this analysis in the laboratory. This preliminary stage is the province of basic researchers in the relevant content area of experimental psychology rather than being the responsibility of researchers in the experimental psychology of aging.

For example, experimental psychologists working in the area of verbal learning have given us a fairly complete picture of what a subject must do to learn a paired-associate list [see Kausler (1974) for a more complete description]. These implicit activities of a subject during the learning of a paired-associate list constitute the processes of paired-associate learning. One such process is to make the response elements (the second element of each pair—see Chapter 1) available for recall or retrieval by themselves, that is, independent of their connections with their paired-stimulus elements (the first item of each pair). These response elements must be available to the subject before they can enter fully into associations with their related stimulus elements (Underwood & Schulz, 1960). Another critical process is associative learning. It requires hooking up each available response element with its related stimulus element. This process may take the form of generating images that depict the S-R elements of the separate pairs interacting with one another (see Chapter 1). This associative process, or mnemonic, enables a subject to relate S-R elements together quickly and efficaciously.

There are additional processes that enter into the overall learning of a paired-associate list, processes that will not concern us at this time (see Chapter 8). Our present point is simply that not all of the processes involved in a gross phenomenon need be susceptible to change with increasing age. The age change in paired-associate learning, as reflected by total errors in learning a list, is merely a change in a gross phenomenon. It tells us nothing about which process or processes are affected by aging and are, therefore, responsible for the age change in paired-associate learning. Conceivably, associative learning through an imaginal mnemonic may be sensitive to an aging effect, whereas response availability may not, or vice versa. Alternatively, both processes or neither process might experience a decline in proficiency with increasing age. In the latter event, the culprit responsible for the age change in the gross phenomenon would have to be one of the other processes entering into paired-associate learning. A major challenge for experimental aging psychologists is to isolate these processes and then determine which one (ones) contributes to the increasing difficulty of paired-associate learning as chronological age increases.

Similar component analyses may be made for many other gross phenomena yielded by the tasks employed in the experimental psychology laboratory. We will have frequent occasions to conduct such analyses when we review specific content areas in later chapters and attempt to identify which components display age sensitivity. In advance of these reviews, you should know that some component analyses will involve structures as well as, or instead of, processes. A process, as we observed earlier, signifies an activity by a subject, an activity of which the subject may or may not be consciously aware. Retrieving available response elements and forming interacting images during paired-associate learning are previously given examples of psychological processes. Later on we will encounter a host of other processes, such as encoding information from stimulus inputs and attending selectively to portions of a total stimulus input. In contrast to a process, a structure signifies some static attribute of the subject that has its own relatively invariant properties. It often refers quite literally to a container or store that functions as a depository for the products of a subject's processes. For example, the images generated by a mnemonic process may be viewed as entering into a memory store from which they may later be recovered by a retrieval process. For some tasks the effects of human aging may be viewed as resulting from a change in the structural properties of a memory store rather than from a change in the processes that affect entry into, and departure from, that store. The property of a store that is most likely to be altered by aging is its capacity. In fact, diminishing capacity of a memory store with increasing age is a commonly held explanation of age decrements in tasks involving short-term memory.

Whether a component analysis deals with structures or processes or both, there are various means of determining which specific components are sensitive to age changes and which ones are insensitive. Several of the more important means will be described in the remainder of this section. All of them involve inferences derived from interaction effects or the absence of interaction effects in heterogeneous factorial studies.

Multiplicative Versus Additive Relationships. One important means of demonstrating the age sensitivity or insensitivity of processes is through the nature of interactions in heterogeneous factorial studies. If an interaction effect implies a multiplicative relationship involving a single process, then there is good reason to believe that the process in question is sensitive to an age change. On the other hand, if the absence of an interaction effect implies an additive relationship between two processes, then there is good reason to believe that one of those processes is insensitive to an age change. Understanding the logic involved in such identifications demands prior understanding of the meanings of multiplicative and additive relationships in general. As a preliminary step, we will examine the meanings of these relationships as they exist in basic experimental psychology.

Our examination begins with still another hypothetical study—this time one that has nothing to do with aging per se. Consider a task for which the performance proficiency of young adults is affected by variation of two different manipulable independent variables, A and B. For each variable, performance at one level (A_2 for the A variable and B_1 for the B variable) is less proficient, say by 20% (on the average), than it is at a second level (A_1 for the A variable and B_2 for the B variable). What should happen if these two variables are combined in the same factorial study? Actually, two different outcomes are possible. Which outcome occurs depends on the nature of the process or processes mediating performance on the task in question and on the nature of the relationships between the A and B variables and those processes.

For our purposes we will assume that two separate processes, X and Y, are potentially involved in mediating performance on the task. The outcome resulting from combining the A and B variables depends on whether the two variables affect the same process, say Process X, or different processes, that is, Process X by one variable and Process Y by the other. In the first condition, the proficiency of Process X is 20% less proficient at Level A_2 than at Level A_1, and 20% less proficient at Level B_1 than at Level B_2. The proficiency of Process Y, however, is unaffected by variation of either variable. Combining these two

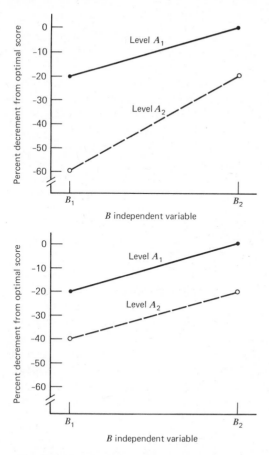

Figure 5.7. Decrements in dependent variable scores expected on the basis of a multiplicative relationship (top panel) and an additive relationship (bottom panel) for two manipulable independent variables that are combined in a factorial study.

variables is expected to result in a multiplicative relationship of the kind illustrated in the top panel of Figure 5.7. Optimal performance (at least for the conditions prevailing in this study) occurs for the group receiving Levels A_1 and B_2 (i.e., Group A_1B_2). The group receiving Levels A_1 and B_1 (Group $A_1 B_1$) suffers a performance loss of 20% relative to Group A_1B_2, as does the group receiving Levels A_2 and B_2 (Group A_2B_2). In both cases, the loss results from the diminished proficiency produced by one of the two variables. That is, the proficiency of Process X is decreased by 20% relative to the optimal level, which, in turn, yields a performance decrement of 20%. The group receiving Levels A_2 and B_1 (Group A_2B_1) is the intriguing one. Both variables should, in principle, produce a 20% loss, thus making the combined loss 40%. However, the actual loss is substantially greater than that expected on the basis of simply adding together the adverse contributions of the two variables. In effect, the joint operation of two adverse conditions serves to compound, or multiply, the total decrement in proficiency for Process X (and, therefore, in performance proficiency as well) (Massaro, 1975; Sternberg, 1969 a,b). It is this compounding that constitutes a multiplicative relationship. A multiplicative relationship obviously results in an interaction effect that is much like the one we observed in our hypothetical study on risk-taking behavior (see Figure 5.3, top panel).

In the second condition, Variable A alters performance proficiency by affecting the proficiency of Process X (20% loss from A_1 to A_2), whereas Variable B alters performance proficiency by affecting Process Y (20% loss from B_2 to B_1). Combining these two variables is expected to result in an additive relationship of the kind illustrated in the bottom panel of Figure 5.7. Note that, except for Group A_2B_1, the outcome is identical to that found with a multiplicative relationship. For Group A_2B_1 the performance loss is the amount expected by the addition of the separate losses contributed by Levels A_2 and B_1 of the two independent variables (i.e., 40%). An additive relationship is obviously characterized by the absence of an interaction effect (compare the bottom panel of Figure 5.7 with the top panel of Figure 5.2).

Identifying Age-Sensitive/Age-Insensitive Processes Through Multiplicative and Additive Relationships. The role played by multiplicative and additive relationships in process-oriented aging research becomes clear when we shift gears somewhat and return to our practice of making variation in chronological age our A independent variable. That is, Levels A_1 and A_2 once more consist of young adulthood and late adulthood respectively. B then becomes a manipulable independent variable known from prior basic research (usually with young-adult subjects) to alter the proficiency of a specific process mediating performance on a given task. If that process is age sensitive in the sense of being less proficient late in adulthood than early adulthood, then the factorial combination of variation in age and variation in the critical B variable should yield a multiplicative relationship. The relationship should be apparent from an interaction effect resembling that shown in the top panel of Figure 5.7. Both variables are presumed to affect the same Process X, the nature of which is specified by a theoretical analysis of the component processes regulating performance on the task in question. By contrast, a different outcome is expected if the process altered by B variation is age insensitive. Now the factorial combination of A and B variation should yield an additive relationship—and, therefore, the absence of an interaction effect. Our inference is that age variation affects Process X, whereas B variation affects Process Y. The age insensitivity of Process Y follows from the fact that the performance decrement from Level B_2 to Level B_1 is no greater for elderly adults than it is for young adults (as in the bottom panel of Figure 5.7). The nature of Process Y, like that of Process X in a multiplicative relationship, is specified in a preexisting component analysis of the processes regulating performance on our task.

Our hypothetical study on age differences in risk-taking behavior demonstrates nicely how an age-sensitive process may be inferred through the presence of a multiplicative relationship. A reasonable hypothesis is that adults of any age will be more cautious in their risk-taking when the probability of success is moderate than when it is high. The question of primary concern, however, is whether or not cautiousness changes with increasing age. If elderly adults are, indeed, more cautious than young adults, then variation in age affects the same underlying process as does variation in probability of success. Both variables would, therefore, relate to the same Process X, namely cautiousness in taking risks. The age sensitivity of this process is attested by the presence of an interaction effect (Figure 5.3) matching that expected with a multiplicative relationship.

We have also encountered in earlier chapters real studies that have reported interaction effects conforming to those expected with multiplicative relationships. One such study was by Hulicka and Grossman (1967). The process suspected of being age sensitive in their study is that of imaginal mediation in paired-associate learning. To test the age sensitivity of their Process X, Hulicka and Grossman combined age variation with variation in a B variable expected to alter the likelihood of imaginal mediation independently of age variation. Their choice was variation in instructions. Level B_1 subjects received no special instructions about the use of imagery (i.e., a control condition), whereas Level B_2 subjects received instructions about the advantages of using imagery in learning paired items (i.e., an experimental condition). A reexamination of Figure 1.2 reveals that an interaction effect conforming to a multiplicative relationship was indeed found in their study. That is, the age difference favoring young adults was greater at Level B_1 than at Level B_2. In our current terminology, a compounding of adverse effects occurred for Group A_2B_1 (i.e., elderly subjects receiving control instructions), a compounding that permits us to infer the age sensitivity of the imaginal process.

Our faith in the age sensitivity of imaginal mediation should grow if a similar multiplicative relationship emerges when another manipulable independent variable replaces the instructional variable. The substitute variable, of course, must be one that has been demonstrated in earlier basic research to alter the likelihood of imaginal mediation during paired-associate learning. A good choice would be variation in item content—abstract nouns at Level B_1 and concrete nouns at Level B_2. Considerable basic research over the years has indicated the greater involvement of imaginal mediation with concrete nouns as items than with abstract nouns as items (see Kausler, 1974). Further support for the age sensitivity of imaginal mediation requires that the age difference favoring young adults be greater for abstract nouns than for concrete nouns. Exactly this pattern was found in a study by Rowe and Schnore (1971). As illustrated in Figure 5.8, pairs of concrete nouns were easier to learn than pairs of abstract nouns for both young-adult and elderly subjects. More important, the age deficit in learning proficiency increased as proficiency decreased overall. Again, this is the pattern we would expect to find if imaginal mediation is an age-sensitive process.

Our final example of inferring the existence of an age-sensitive process from a multiplicative relationship also comes from learning research. The process at stake is the rehearsal of items during practice on a serial-learning task. Learning a serial list obviously requires some kind of rehearsal of each item in

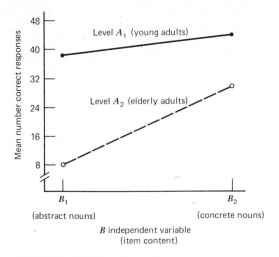

Figure 5.8. Multiplicative relationship for paired-associate learning yielded by the interaction between age variation and variation of items along the abstract-concrete dimension. (Adapted from Rowe & Schnore, 1971, Figure 1.)

that list as it is presented for study. A reasonable hypothesisis is that the rate of rehearsal slows down as people grow older (to be elaborated on later). Elderly adults are, therefore, expected to emit fewer rehearsal responses per unit of study time than are young adults, thus accounting for the less proficient serial learning commonly found for elderly adults (see Chapter 8). To test the age sensitivity of the rehearsal process requires a factorial study in which age variation is combined with variation in some manipulable variable that is also expected to alter rate of rehearsal. A logical choice is variation in the rate of exposing items. With a relatively fast rate (Level B_1) (e.g., 4 seconds per item), fewer rehearsal responses are possible than with a slow rate (Level B_2) (e.g., 10 seconds per item), regardless of a subject's age. This design was employed in a study by Eisdorfer and Service (1967). Their results, expressed in mean errors made in learning the eight-item list, are summarized in Figure 5.9. Note that the age deficit in learning scores is considerably larger at Level B_1 than at Level B_2, thus enabling us to infer the age sensitivity of rate-of-rehearsal activity (there are problems, however, in accepting this inference, as we will see in Chapter 8).

Although multiplicative relationships offer valuable insights into age-sensitive processes, they are not without their limitations and interpretative problems. We will examine some of these limitations and problems before turning to examples of studies that make use of additive relationships to infer the age insensitivity of processes [see Baron & Treiman (1980) for a discussion of other problems and possible solutions to those problems].

An obvious limitation of a multiplicative relationship is its inability to identify the reason why a process *appears to be* age sensitive. Its apparent age sensitivity could be the consequence of a true ontogenetic change—but it could

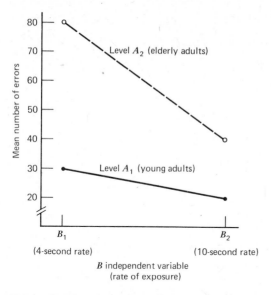

Figure 5.9. Multiplicative relationship for serial learning yielded by the interaction between age variation and variation in rate of exposing the to-be-learned items. (Adapted from Eisdorfer & Service, 1967, Figure 1.)

also result from nonontogenetic factors. Identification at this more fundamental level can be made only through the kind of ontogenetic research described in Chapter 2. Of course, there is no earthly reason why researchers conducting factorial studies cannot simultaneously satisfy the criteria of sound ontogenetic research. Especially important is an investigator's ability to avoid the pitfalls of employing young-adult subjects who are superior to their elderly counterparts on critical non-age attributes. Another limitation centers on the possible confusion encountered in distinguishing between primary ability and secondary performance factors as the source of a process's apparent age sensitivity. Again, there is no reason why the conditions of a heterogeneous factorial study could not be combined with the conditions described in Chapter 3 for testing the competence-performance distinction.

A major interpretative problem exists when a significant interaction effect results from a ceiling effect rather than from a true multiplicative relationship. A *ceiling effect* occurs when the scores on a given task have a maximum value that cannot be exceeded (e.g., 100% of the items recalled correctly on a learning-memory task) no matter how large an increment is added to the process mediating performance on that task. Performance for many young-adult subjects may level off at this value even though their performance could show further increments with the use of a more sensitive measure. As illustrated in Figure 5.10, the net effect would be the understimation of the true age deficit at Level B_2, thereby making the deficit observed at this level much less than the deficit observed at Level B_1 (and, thus, giving the appearance of a multiplicative relationship). Confounding by a ceiling effect can usually be avoided by

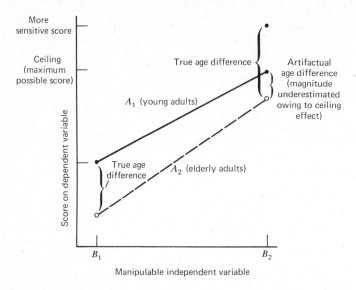

Figure 5.10. Means for a hypothetical 2 × 2 heterogeneous factorial study in which the absence of a significant interaction effect is an artifact resulting from a ceiling effect for young adults at Level B₂ of the manipulable variable.

pilot research. If a pilot study suggests the possibility of a ceiling effect, the investigator should take heed of the warning and increase the overall difficulty of the task for the main study.

Another major problem arises whenever an assumption implicit in the interpretation of a multiplicative relationship is violated. The critical assumption is that a linear relationship exists between the degree of proficiency on Process X and the degree of proficiency on the task governed by that process. In actuality, there may be process-to-task translations that are decidedly non-linear in form. For example, large increments in process proficiency could be accompanied by relatively small increments in task proficiency. If this were the case, an observed interaction between age and a manipulable independent variable would not be interpretable in terms of identifying an age-sensitive process. The issues at stake and the solutions to such cases of nonlinear relationships are subtle and complex, and they fall beyond the scope of our coverage (see G. R. Loftus, 1978, for further discussion). It seems likely, however, that most process-to-behavior relationships encountered in research on human aging are linear in form. Nevertheless, it remains true that the form of most of these relationships is assumed to be linear rather than demonstrated to be linear.

As initial examples of additive relationships, we will return briefly to two hypothetical studies mentioned earlier in this chapter. The first one resulted from our shameless tampering with the outcome of G. Cohen's (1979) study. The actual outcome of that study, as shown in Figure 1.3, indicated a multiplicative relationship—the magnitude of an age deficit in performance increased as overall performance proficiency on the task decreased. Suppose, however, that the fictitious outcome summarized in Figure 5.1 had actually been found. The decrement in performance for inference questions relative to verbatim questions would then have been no greater for elderly subjects than for young subjects. We would, therefore, have been forced to conclude that variation in the type of question asked alters a process that is basically age insensitive. The other hypothetical example is the study in which both age of subjects and age of experimenter were varied. The absence of an interaction effect in this study (see Figure 5.2) implies that the process affected by variation in the experimenter's age is age insensitive. That is, the adverse effect created by the use of an old experimenter relative to the effect created by the use of a young experimenter is no greater for elderly subjects than it is for young-adult subjects.

Our remaining example will be considered in greater detail. It is an actual study by Taub (1975) dealing with age differences in memory for the content of paragraphs. Taub employed three age levels, including a group of middle-age adults (Level A_2) as well as groups of young-adults (Level A_1) and elderly (Level A_3) adults. His bilevel manipulable independent variable was the modality of presenting the to-be-memorized paragraph. Level B_1, received by half of the subjects at each age level, consisted of having the paragraph read to the subjects by the experimenter. Level B_2, received by the remaining subjects at each age level, consisted of having the subjects read the paragraph themselves at their own rates. Taub referred to these two levels as auditory (B_1) versus visual (B_2) modalities of presenting materials. It should be noted that the rate of reading paragraphs to subjects at Level B_1 approximated the rate subjects at each age level, on the average, read to themselves.

The outcome of Taub's 3×2 factorial study is shown in Figure 5.11 in terms of mean number of ideas recalled from the paragraph. It may be seen that there were pronounced main effects for age (young > middle-age > elderly) and modality of presentation (visual > auditory). However, the age $\times$ modality interaction was slight, falling far short of statistical significance. The

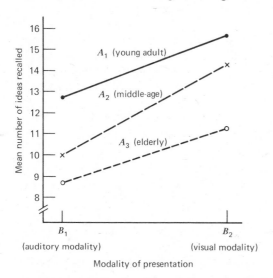

Figure 5.11. Means for retention of a paragraph's content as affected by simultaneous variation of age and modality of presentation. The absence of an interaction indicates an additive relationship. (Adapted from Taub, 1975, Table 1.)

logic of an additive relationship leads us to conclude that the memory process altered by variation of modality is basically insensitive to age decrements. Taub viewed this process to be one of reviewing previously presented material as new material is encountered. The proficiency of this process should clearly be greater for visually presented material than for aurally presented material. Only in the former case are subjects able to return directly to prior material for review purposes. The absence of an interaction implies that the loss in proficiency for this process in the shift to aural presentation is no greater for elderly adults than it is for younger adults (a further implication, of course, is the generalizability of the age deficit in recall over variation in modality of presentation.) On the other hand, the overall age deficit for recalling ideas embedded within a paragraph does implicate some process as being age sensitive. One possibility is that the encoding of paragraph information (i.e., during reading or listening and reviewing) into a format appropriate for transmission and storage in long-term memory (see Chapter 9) decreases in proficiency with increasing age. This age deficit in a memory process (Process X in our analysis of additive relationships) appears to occur quite independently of modality of presentation, which affects only an age-insensitive process (reviewing prior material—Process Y in the language of additive relationships).

As with multiplicative relationships, we should be aware of the interpretative problems inherent in the use of additive relationships to infer age-insensitive processes. An obvious problem is set by the method's necessary reliance on accepting a null effect (i.e., for the interaction) as being truly null. Psychologists have a general reluctance to accept a null hypothesis, whether it be for an interaction effect or a main effect. The feeling is that the failure to reject a null hypothesis statistically may be an artifact attributable to the specific samples included in a study and may, therefore, not be generalizable to the total populations underlying those samples. However, confidence in the true absence of an interaction may be established through multiple replications of a study involving independently selected samples of subjects at each age level. Our confidence should grow with each empirical demonstration of a statistically nonsignificant interaction effect. In addition, valid conclusions about additive relationships draw on the same implicit assumption as do valid conclusions about multiplicative relationships. Again, the assumption is that of a linear relationship between, in this case, composite process strength (i.e., Process X + Process Y) and degree of performance proficiency on the given task. Violation of this assumption may result in the absence of an observed interaction, despite the existence of a latent multiplicative relationship between variation in age and variation in the manipulable variable. Our earlier remarks about violation of this assumption continue to apply.

Identifying Age-Sensitive Processes Through Divergent Relationships. We discovered earlier in this chapter that not all interactions between age and a manipulable variable follow the course predicted by a multiplicative relationship. A different, and fairly common, course is the one charted in the bottom left panel of Figure 5.4. Note that the age deficit in performance is greater at

Level B_2 than at Level B_1—that is, as overall performance proficiency increases, the age deficit in proficiency also increases. Viewed graphically, our two straight lines show a trend toward divergence with increasing scores on the dependent variable. This pattern, of course, is just the opposite of the one found with a multiplicative relationship. Here the two straight lines show a trend toward convergence with increasing scores on the dependent variable (e.g., Figure 5.8).

Divergent relationships seemingly occur when two processes mediate performance on a task. Only one of the processes, say Process Y, is activated at Level B_1 of the manipulable variable, whereas both processes, X and Y, are activated at Level B_2. Most important, the added involvement of Process X leads to enhanced performance on the task regardless of age level. Thus, both young and elderly subjects are expected to have greater dependent variable scores at Level B_2 than at Level B_1. Given this assumption, divergence in mean dependent variable scores implies that Process X is age sensitive to a much greater extent than Process Y. That is, the loss in competence from early to late adulthood affects primarily Process X, leaving Process Y largely unaffected. These underlying relationships are summarized schematically in Figure 5.12.

The processes entering into a divergent relationship, like those entering into other kinds of relationships, have their roots in a theoretical analysis of a particular task. For example, a currently popular memory theory, one that will

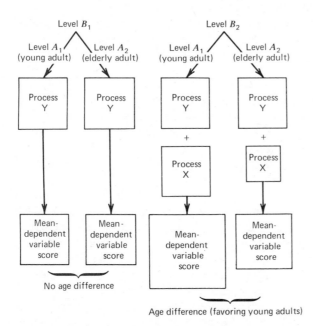

Figure 5.12. Schematic representation of the events postulated to yield a divergent relationship between variation in age (A) and variation in a manipulable variable (B). Only Process Y, an age-insensitive process, is activated at Level B_1, whereas both Process Y and Process X, an age-sensitive process, are activated at Level B_2.

be examined more completely in Chapter 9, argues that the number of words recalled from a list of words depends on the depth of processing the individual words receive. Sensory, or shallow, processing is expected to result in poor recall relative to semantic, or deep, processing. To induce processing at any level, subjects are given an orienting task to perform as each word in a list is exposed, a task that assures attention is directed to each word. Following the last word, subjects are given an unexpected recall test. That is, they are asked to recall as many of the words as they can, even though they had not been informed in advance that they would be so tested (an example of incidental learning).

Variation in depth of processing may be accomplished by varying the kind of orienting task subjects are required to perform. Suppose at Level B_1 they are asked simply to decide for each word as it is exposed whether or not it contains either the letter E or the letter G. Only sensory features of a word need to be examined, namely, those involving a word's orthography. Because analysis of a word's meaning is not demanded by this orienting task, processing should terminate at a sensory level. At Level B_2, subjects are asked to decide whether an exposed word is pleasant or unpleasant in the emotional tone it conveys. Now, both sensory *and* semantic features of a word must be examined before a decision can be made. Sensory processing is necessary to assure recognition of a word and semantic processing is necessary to evaluate its connotative meaning. Memory theory clearly predicts that the number of incidentally learned words should be much greater at Level B_2 than at Level B_1.

If we now add age variation to variation in an orienting task, we have a situation likely to produce a divergent relationship. Process Y becomes the sensory processing engaged in at both Level B_1 and Level B_2, and Process X becomes the semantic processing engaged in only at Level B_2. A popular notion among experimental aging psychologists is that the proficiency of semantic processing is highly age sensitive, whereas the proficiency of sensory processing is largely unaffected by aging. A test of this notion, such as one conducted by Erber (1979), leads us to expect a significant age deficit in number of words recalled at Level B_2 (pleasant/unpleasant decisions) but not at Level B_1 (presence/absence of an E or a G). Her results, expressed as the mean number of words recalled out of the 28 words exposed, are shown in Figure 5.13. Note that both age groups recalled considerably more words at B_2 than at B_1, as predicted by the guiding-memory theory. More important for our purposes, the age deficit attained significance only at Level B_2, yielding the divergent relationship clearly apparent in Figure 5.13. Not surprisingly, Erber inferred that semantic processing is age sensitive and that sensory processing is not.

For a second example of inferring an age-sensitive process from a divergent relationship we will return briefly to research on memory span. Only now our interest is in length of span for words rather than digits. With words as the to-be-spanned items, the extent of the age deficit in span length depends on the frequency of occurrence of the words in printed material (e.g., magazines, books). Variation in frequency yields a divergent relationship, as may be seen in the results obtained by Kausler and Puckett (1979) (see Figure 5.14). Span

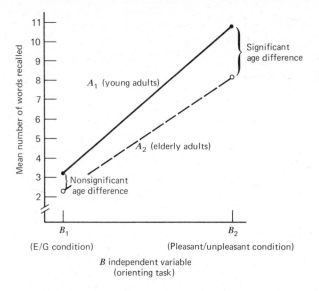

Figure 5.13. Divergent relationship for recall of items yielded by the interaction between variation in age and variation in an orienting task. (Adapted from Erber, 1979, Table 1.)

length increases as frequency increases from low (Level B_1) to high (Level B_2) for both young and elderly subjects—but the increment is greater for young adults. With low-frequency words, span length is limited largely by the capacity of a subject's short-term memory store, and this decreases only slightly over the adult lifespan. Thus, Process Y is a structural attribute, one that is modestly age sensitive. With high-frequency words, an additional process is activated, but to a lesser extent for elderly subjects than for young-adult subjects. Our Process X consists of organizing words into larger units, or chunks, which enable two or more words to be squeezed into a single bin of the short-term store. The net effect is to increase span length for high-frequency words relative to low-frequency words. The fact that the increment is less for elderly subjects than for young subjects (see Figure 5.14) permits us to infer that the underlying organizational process is highly age sensitive. We will discover in Chapter 9 that there is considerable evidence from other sources indicating the age sensitivity of this process.

One final interpretative problem needs to be faced. An inference drawn from a divergent relationship can be distorted by the presence of a *floor effect*. A floor effect occurs when a task is extremely difficult at Level B_1 for all subjects. Consequently, scores at this level of the manipulable variable approach a zero value regardless of age level. Obviously, no age difference in performance could be detected under these conditions. For example, suppose the orienting task at Level B_1 in Erber's (1979) study simply required subjects to decide for each word whether it is exposed in uppercase letters or lowercase letters. This decision can be made with little attention being directed at the actual letter content of a word. Consequently, there would be so little process-

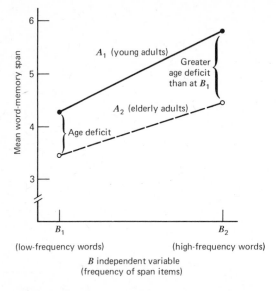

Figure 5.14. Divergent relationship for word span yielded by the interaction between variation in age and variation in preexperimental frequency of the span items. (Adapted from Kausler & Puckett, 1979, Table 1.)

ing, even at a sensory level, of each word that later recall of that word would be virtually impossible. The mean score for both age groups would, therefore, have to be close to zero. Even a modest age difference in mean scores at Level B_2 would then assure the presence of a significant interaction effect. This interaction could be artifactual, as illustrated in Figure 5.15, in the sense that a less constraining condition at Level B_1 may have yielded an age difference close to the magnitude of the difference found at Level B_2. (This is not the case in Erber's study however. The mean number of words recalled for both age groups at Level B_1 was sufficiently greater than zero to rule out the possibility that the absence of an age difference is an artifact produced by a floor effect.) As with a ceiling effect, the threat of confounding by a floor effect can be avoided by effective pilot research. The objective of this research is to find an appropriate condition at Level B_1 that makes performance difficult but without being overly constraining for young adults as well as for elderly adults.

Identifying an Age-Sensitive Process by the Deletion Method. The last method we will consider bears some resemblance to the multiplicative method. As in that method, an age-sensitive process is inferred from the presence of convergence of age groups from Level B_1 to Level B_2 of the manipulable variable. The methods differ primarily in the kind of manipulable variable needed to produce the convergence.

We will begin our description of the method with the assumption that a theoretical analysis of performance on a particular task has implicated the involvement of at least two mediating processes, our familiar Process X and

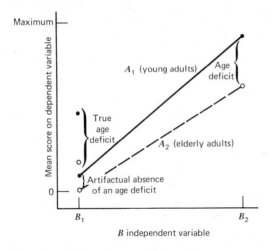

Figure 5.15. Means for a hypothetical 2 × 2 heterogeneous factorial study in which the significant interaction effect is an artifact resulting from a floor effect for both age groups at Level B₁ of the manipulable variable.

Process Y. Our strategy then calls for the inclusion of a manipulable independent variable that at one level, B_2, eliminates the involvement of one of these components, say Process X, and at another level, B_1, continues to require that component. By eliminating Process X, we should, in effect, make performance easier (i.e., greater dependent variable scores) at Level B_2 than at Level B_1, regardless of age level. Having found a manipulable variable that accomplishes this objective, we are now in position to test the age sensitivity of Process X. We would simply make that variable our B term in an age × B heterogeneous factorial study. Suppose further that the remaining component, Process Y, is believed to be resistant to an aging decrement. Because only Process Y enters into performance at Level B_2, there should be no age deficit at this level. On the other hand, there should be a pronounced age deficit at Level B_1 where the age-sensitive process continues to be required in working on the particular task. These hypothesized variations in processes and the resulting effects on dependent variable scores and schematized in Figure 5.16.

Of course, there is the strong possibility that the process remaining after the deletion of Process X is also age sensitive. If this is the case, then an age deficit should be present at Level B_2 as well as at Level B_1, but the magnitude of the deficit should be considerably less at Level B_2 than at Level B_1. These possible outcomes are illustrated in Figure 5.17. The top panel shows the expected outcome when all age-sensitive processes have been deleted; the bottom panel shows the expected outcome when an age-sensitive process continues to influence performance on the given task. In either event, our predicted outcome—based on the hypothesis that Process X is age sensitive and on the assumption that this process is effectively eliminated at Level B_2—includes a statistically significant interaction effect. Most importantly, the interaction ef-

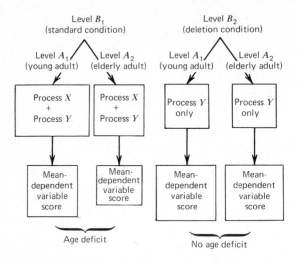

Figure 5.16. Schematic representation of the events postulated to identify an age-sensitive process (Process X) by the deletion method. The process is eliminated at Level B_2 of the manipulable variable but not at Level B_1.

fect must reflect the fact that the age deficit *decreases* as the overall level of performance on the task increases, as indicated in both panels of Figure 5.17. Evidence in agreement with this predicted outcome enables us to infer that Process X is indeed age sensitive.

The success of the deletion method rests in finding an effective eliminator of a process. One research area in which a fairly good means of deleting a component process exists (which may then be tested for its age sensitivity) is that of paired-associate learning. Consequently, we will use research on this task to provide an example of the deletion method in actual practice.

We will focus on the response-availability process, and we will examine how an investigator may apply the deletion strategy to test the age sensitivity of this process. Our manipulable independent variable should be a procedural one that requires the learning of response elements (to make them available for recall) at Level B_1 and that eliminates the necessity of learning these elements at Level B_2. This may be accomplished by varying the procedure by which subjects are tested during practice on the paired-associate list. At Level B_1, subjects are tested by the standard recall method. This is the method commonly employed in research on paired-associate learning. Subjects receive alternating study and test phases on each trial. On each study phase, subjects study the entire list, one pair at a time, with the S-R elements of each pair in juxtaposition. On each test phase, subjects receive only the stimulus element of each pair, and they attempt to recall the response element that belongs with each stimulus. A subject's dependent variable score on a given trial is the number of response elements correctly recalled *and* paired with the appropriate stimulus. The subject's performance level is clearly dependent on the proficiency of both the response-availability process and the associate-learning process. At Level B_2, subjects are tested by a modification of the standard method, one that is called the associative-matching method. Study and test phases again alternate, and the study phases are identical in their format to that of the recall method. The test phases, however, differ considerably. Now, the subject is given two columns of words, one containing the stimulus elements arranged in a random order and the other the response elements also arranged in a random order. All the subject has to do is match each stimulus element with its associated response element. A subject's dependent variable is the number of correctly matched elements. Note that performance level for this method is still contingent on the proficiency of the associative-learning process. However, it is no longer contingent on the proficiency of the response-availability process. In fact, the response elements do not have to be retrieved and recalled at all—they

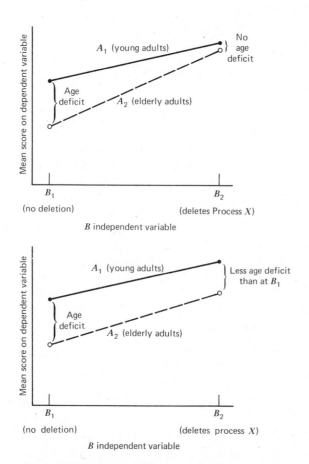

Figure 5.17. Expected outcomes for studies employing the deletion method. Top panel: Remaining processes are age insensitive, thus eliminating the age deficit after the deletion of the age-sensitive process. Bottom panel: Remaining processes are also age sensitive, thus decreasing but not eliminating the age deficit after the deletion of an age-sensitive process.

are given to the subject. Consequently, we would expect performance to be better for both young-adult and elderly subjects with the associative-matching method (Level B_2) than with the recall method (Level B_1). This is not our main concern however. That concern is with whether or not the disparity in mean-dependent variable scores between age groups is less at Level B_2 than at Level B_1. If it is, then we have reason to believe that the response-availability process undergoes a decrement from early to late adulthood.

Exactly such a test of the response-availability process's age sensitivity was made by Witte and Freund (1976) as part of a more comprehensive experiment. We will consider only a segment of their results. These results are expressed as the percentage of list pairs answered correctly by subjects on their third study-test trial. For young adults, these values were approximately 93% under the matching method (Group A_1B_2) and approximately 80% under the recall method (Group A_1B_1); for elderly adults the comparable values were approximately 63% (Group A_2B_2) and 30% (Group A_2B_1). Thus, the age deficit was less at Level B_2 (30%) than at Level B_1 (50%), leading to Witte and Freund's tentative conclusion that response availability is an age-sensitive process. On the other hand, it does not appear to be the only age-sensitive process mediating paired-associate learning. If it were, then the age deficit should have been eliminated under the matching condition. We know, of course, from our earlier discussion about imaginal mnemonics that associative learning is certainly included among these other age-sensitive processes.

Any conclusion regarding age sensitivity that emerges through the use of the deletion method is necessarily tentative. One reason for this cautiousness is that the method encounters the same problems and limitations that are imposed on other methods, such as those presented by ceiling effects and nonlinear process-to-task translations. In other words, the reduced disparity in the age deficit at Level B_2 relative to the deficit at Level B_1 may be more artifactual than real.

There is another reason for being cautious in interpreting the results obtained with the deletion method, one that may easily be overlooked. It is conceivable that the means of deleting a process at Level B_2 has an ancillary adverse effect on the performance of elderly adults but not on the performance of young adults. The addition of a negative performance, or secondary, factor may reduce, or even eliminate, the gain expected by means of the deletion of a primary factor or process. For example, elderly subjects may find the matching procedure employed by Witte and Freund to be somewhat confusing in the early stages of its implementation, thereby interfering with its efficient use. Such confusion would probably be the result of the considerable change in context from that in which pairs are studied to that in which they are tested. Young adults are unlikely to experience similar confusion and, therefore, are unlikely to suffer diminished savings from the deletion of the response-availability process. The net effect would be an underestimation of the reduction in the age deficit at Level B_2 that is attributable to the deletion of the critical process. In fact, in some instances, the adverse performance factor may be sufficient to make the overall age deficit found at Level B_2 comparable to that found at Level B_1. The investigator is likely to conclude, erroneously, that the primary process in question is age insensitive. Fortunately, there are alternative strategies for deleting a given process's involvement on many of the tasks employed in experimental psychology. With regard to the response-availability process in paired-associate learning, the matching procedure of Witte and Freund is only one of several possible methods (see Kausler, 1974; pp. 130–134). An investigator should conduct extensive pilot research with the various methods relevant to the task and process in question to determine which one is relatively free of confounding by secondary performance factors.

A remaining issue concerns the generalizability of an age-sensitive process identified by the deletion method. Our focus has been on a particular process that is only one of two or more processes that collectively mediate performance on a task. If that process were, in fact, the only process mediating performance on the task, then there would be no need to employ any of our inferential methods. Performance on the task per se would operationally define proficiency on the underlying process, and an observed age difference in performance on the task would identify the process itself as being age sensitive. Of course, most of the tasks employed in experimental psychology are multiply determined, as we have often noted. If they were not, then there would be no reason to apply the deletion method or any other inferential method. Most important, although the deletion method identifies a process as being age sensitive, it does so in the context of the multiply-determined task in which the process is embedded. Within that task-bound context, the operation of Process X must be coordinated with the operation of Process Y. For some tasks, Processes X and Y may operate simultaneously or, phrased somewhat differently, *in parallel.* For other tasks, Processes X and Y may have to operate sequentially or, in other words, *serially.* Assuming that Process X is age sensitive in the overall task context, does it necessarily mean that it is also age sensitive when the task constraint of engaging Process Y, either in parallel or serially, is removed?

An answer to the above question is possible, of course, only through the use of another task in which Process X is the sole mediating process. Unfortunately, such tasks are hard to come by (to be discussed further shortly). Nevertheless, it is reasonable to assume that the total resources for cognitive activity are more limited for elderly adults than for young adults. Consequently, the strain on the limited resources of elderly people proffered by activating Process Y is likely to reduce Process X's proficiency well below the level it would be in the absence of Process Y. In fact, the proficiency level of Process X functioning alone may actually be comparable to that of young adults. The net effect would be to make Process X age sensitive but only when it is but one of several processes entering into a task, as illustrated in Figure 5.18.

Alternative Methods of Identifying Age-Sensitive Processes

There are other methods of identifying age-sensitive structures and processes, methods that do not depend on inferences derived from predicted interaction effects between age and some manipulable independent variable. Applications of these methods are occasionally found in experimental aging research.

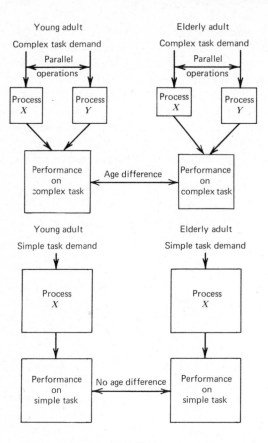

Figure 5.18. Top panel: Age sensitive process (Process X) yielding an age difference on a complex task when engaged in parallel (simultaneously) with an age insensitive process. Bottom panel: Process X is no longer age sensitive when it is the only process mediating performance on a modified, single-process task.

Age Simulation. The most fascinating of these alternative methods involves *age simulation.* The idea behind this method is to produce a time compressed, or accelerated, change in a structure or process that approximates the change hypothesized to take place ontogentically over the adult lifespan (Baltes & Goulet, 1971). The recipients of the accelerated change are usually young adults. Their performance under the accelerated condition is contrasted with the performance of comparable young adults who do not experience the induced change. If progressive error presents no problem, then the same subjects may serve in both the changed condition and the standard condition. Suppose that a performance difference is found between these conditions and that this difference closely resembles the performance difference commonly found between young adults and elderly adults on the same task. By inference, the structure or process that is aged artificially in the simulation condition is the one that accounts for the age deficit found au naturel. Conversely, failure to find an induced performance difference resembling that found for contrasting age groups implies that the structure or process in question is relatively age insensitive. However, this conclusion does not occur without considerable ambiguity. It is conceivable that the procedure used to induce the time-compressed change simply failed to accomplish its objective. Other means of inducing the change could yield evidence in support of the age sensitivity of the underlying structure or process.

The brilliance of the simulation method rests in its ability to minimize confoundings produced by age-group disparities in non-age attributes. Obviously, if the same subjects enter into the young and old groups of a simulation study, then the groups must be perfectly matched with respect to such attributes as intelligence and educational level. Even when different groups of young adults must serve in the young-and-old conditions of a simulation study, the ease of matching groups on non-age attributes is much greater than in traditional cross-sectional studies. This is particularly true for matching groups on cohort membership.

Unfortunately, the brilliance of the method is dimmed considerably by the difficulty of inducing realistic simulation of true age changes in structures and processes. Perhaps the closest to simulating a true age change in young adults is in research on certain visual illusions, namely, those that decrease in the magnitude of the illusory experience from early to late adulthood. A contributing causative factor to this perceptual age change is believed to be the decreased amount of illumination that reaches the retina of the aging eye. The decrease results from the yellowing of the lens and the diminished size of the pupils found in elderly people. The effects of these structural changes can be simulated by having young adults view illusory stimulus materials through a light filter. That is, the filter produces a reduction in illumination reaching the retina, much like the reduction produced by the yellowing of the lens with aging. Young adults performing under this condition do show a decrease in illusory magnitude relative to young adults performing under unrestricted illumination (Sjostrom & Pollack, 1971), thus supporting the causative role played by structural changes in the visual system.

Use of Supplementary Performance Measures. It is not unusual for a task employed by experimental psychologists to have performance dimensions that, although secondary to the major dimension serving as the dependent variable, are, nevertheless, quite informative as to the processes regulating that task. Assessing one of these dimensions during the course of a study often yields scores that may be meaningfully correlated with dependent variable scores per se. The direction and amount of this correlation may provide valuable information about the process governing overall proficiency on that task. These supplementary scores range from self-reports given by subjects about their performance on a task, such as their attempts to use imagery in hooking up the S-R items of a paired-associate list, to highly sophisticated scores derived from a subject's performance protocol, such as measures of organization in free-recall learning.

Our interest, of course, is in the utility of a supplementary measure for identifying an age-sensitive process. This utility is contingent on satisfying two criteria. The first is an obvious one—the supplementary performance dimension must be logically relevant to the process hypothesized to mediate task performance and believed to be age sensitive. The second is more or less an empirical expression of the first criterion—there should be convincing evidence from prior research, usually with young adults, to indicate at least a moderate positive correlation between scores on the supplementary performance dimension and dependent variable scores. Because the same process presumably enters into both sets of scores, a positive correlation is to be expected.

Having satisfied these criteria, the method may then be applied in an experimental aging study. Two outcomes are needed in the study to support the hypothesis that the process evaluated by the supplementary measure is age sensitive; (1) the previously described positive correlation should be at least moderate for the investigator's elderly group as well as for the young adult group because the same process regulates performance at both age levels and (2) there must be an age deficit for the supplementary performance dimension as well as for the primary dependent variable. It is the former deficit that seemingly explains the latter deficit.

The problem with the present correlational method is the very fact that it is correlational in nature. Correlation, of course, does not necessarily mean causation. Conceivably, the observed correlation between supplementary scores and dependent variable scores could be due entirely to the covariation both scores share with another unidentified attribute of the subjects. The true age sensitive process could, therefore, be linked to this unidentified attribute. Because this confounding attribute correlates highly with supplementary performance scores, an age deficit in it would covary with an age deficit in the supplementary performance dimension. Consequently, the real source of the age deficit may remain undetected and unsuspected. Fortunately, experimental aging researchers are well aware of the dangers and limitations of correlational evidence, regardless of the source of that evidence.

In practice, a supplementary performance measure is likely to be used in lieu of a manipulable independent variable. That is, it substitutes for the inclusion of an independent variable that could be hypothesized to enter, for example, into a multiplicative relationhip with variation in age level. Thus, the only real independent variable in the study is likely to be variation in age level. Research on multiple trial free-recall learning illustrates effectively how this substitution works. Before we consider this illustration, however, we need to give some background information about the particular task in question.

This variant of free-recall learning was described briefly in Chapter 2. Subjects are given a list of unrelated words that may be recalled in any order after the last item is presented. A series of alternating study-recall trials is given, with the items being assigned randomly to serial positions on each study, or presentation, component of a trial. The total number of items recalled over the series of trials may serve as the primary dependent variable in a study employing this task. The number of items recalled may be seen to increase progressively as learning occurs with practice on the task. The questions we ask are: What process governs learning the list of items? and Is that process age sensitive? An important hypothesis in basic memory theory maintains that the critical process is that of organizing the unrelated words of the list into subjective units so that the unitized items are recalled together (Tulving, 1964). Evidence in support of this hypothesis comes from the use of a supplementary performance measure, called a subjective organization (SO) score. This score consists of the repetitions across trials of recalling two list items together, even though the items may have been widely separated during presentation sequences. Presumably, such pairs had been subjectively organized into units by the subject whose recall protocol is being examined. Research with young adults has revealed a moderate positive correlation between SO scores and item-recall scores (i.e., the primary dependent variable; see Kausler, 1974, for a review of these studies). Thus, the measurement of our supplementary performance dimension satisfies the criteria needed before it can be considered useful as a means of testing some hypothesis about age sensitivity.

A number of studies have found an age deficit for the primary dependent variable of multiple trial free-recall learning (e.g., the study by Laurence, 1966, cited in Chapter 2). A reasonable hypothesis is that the age-sensitive process accounting for the deficit in free-recall learning is the ability to organize seemingly unrelated items into units (a process we met earlier in connection with research on word memory span). One approach to testing this hypothesis would be to conduct a factorial study in which the manipulable independent variable leads to variation in organization. This variable would be predicted to interact with variation in age level, in accordance with the multiplicative principle (studies of this kind will be described in Chapter 9). However, an alternative strategy, summarized schematically in Figure 5.19, would be to rely solely on our supplementary measure of subjective organization. The age sensitivity of the organizational process would be supported nicely if an age deficit is found for SO scores as well as for item-recall scores. In the original study employing this strategy, Laurence (1966) failed to find a significant difference in SO scores between young-adult and elderly subjects, even though she did find a significant difference in mean item-recall scores. We should note, however, that more recent studies, to be reviewed in Chapter 9, using the same basic strategy but with a superior measure of subjective organization have supported the hypothesis of an age-sensitive organizational process.

Multiple Dependent Variables. This method is one that is rarely used in experimental aging research, even though it has considerable potential for the detection of age-sensitive processes. Its application to date has been primarily in research dealing with the effects of aging on intelligence.

The method requires administering a number of tasks, each yielding a separate dependent variable score, to the same subjects. For example, subjects may perform on a memory-span task, a paired-associate learning task, and a free-recall learning task. A composite weighted score is then found for each subject. The weight assigned to each of the dependent variables is based on the

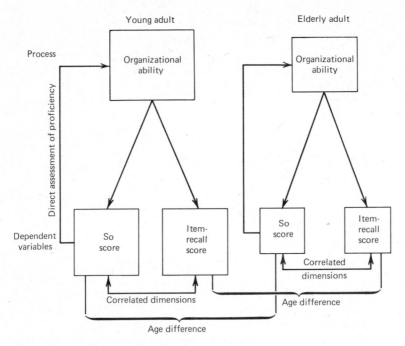

Figure 5.19. Schematic representation of identifying organizational ability as an age-sensitive process affecting item-recall scores through the use of a supplementary dependent variable [subjective organization (SO) scores] known to correlate with recall scores.

correlations between the sets of separate scores. The effects of variation in age together with the effects of variation in one or more manipulable independent variables on this composite score may be determined by what is called a *multivariate analysis of variance*. The implications of this analysis for identifying age-sensitive processes are contingent on the correlational pattern existing among the separate dependent variable scores. Further discussion of this method would demand considerable coverage of statistical concepts, a coverage that is beyond the scope of our review.

Psychological Reductionism. In some instances, a single structure or process may be defined operationally, or behaviorally, just as a gross phenomenon (e.g., paired-associate learning proficiency) is defined operationally. In Chapter 2, we defined this concept as the number of correct responses made in 10 practice trials on specific list content administered under specified procedural conditions. This definition is somewhat arbitrary—it could, for example, just as easily be defined as the number of trials needed to learn the same list to some criterion of mastery. The point is, the definiton given at that time is fully operational in the sense of giving us a measurement procedure that may be applied objectively and invariably to each subject. By contrast, we might have defined the same concept nonoperationally in terms of the investigator's subjective impression of a subject's progress in mastering the task, with highly unreliable assessments of learning proficiency being the likely outcome. We know by now, however, that such gross phenomena as learning proficiency are usually mediated by two or more irreducible structures or processes of a more fundamental psychological nature. It is in those primary factors that can be operationalized and measured directly that our present interest lies.

The trick, as hinted at earlier, is to find a task in which a suspected age-sensitive process is the only mediating primary process. Given a task of this nature, a subject's score would operationally define his or her proficiency on its underlying process. The extent of the age difference on the task would, in turn, assess the extent of the age difference for the process in question, assuming that the age difference is not confounded by secondary performance factors. This rationale is deceptively simple however. Where do we find such a task?

In effect, our objective becomes that of *psychological reductionism.* A complex, multiply-mediated task is to be reduced to subtasks, each mediated by a single process. There is no assurance, however, that our objective will be accomplished. It is very likely that a reductionist task will involve processes that did not enter into the complex task in the first place. If one or more of these processes is age sensitive, then the fulfillment of our objective has surely met a formidable obstacle.

Consider, for example, an attempt to reduce the paired-associate task into separate tasks, X and Y, so that Task X involves only Process X and Task Y only Process Y. If Process X is that of response availability, then Task X is to be structured so that subjects learn discrete items as responses independently of one another, independently of associations with stimulus elements that restrict the appropriateness of emitting the critical items, and independently of the serial order in which the items are presented. Superficially, the free-recall learning task appears to meet these requirements. Discrete items, as free-floating response elements, are presented, and they may be recalled in any order. To maintain consistency with the study by Witte and Freund (1976), an investigator might want to employ the same 10 words (all concrete nouns) used as the response elements in the earlier study. These words would simply function as the items of a free-recall task serving to test the age sensitivity of the response-availability process. The simplest procedure would be to present the list of nouns for a single study period, followed by a test trial in which the subject attempts to recall the previously studied words.

In all probability, a young-adult group would average a higher recall score than an elderly group, seemingly in agreement with the hypothesis that response availability is an age-sensitive process. However, it is conceivable that the age difference in recall scores reflected an age difference in memory span for familiar words instead of, or in addition to, an age difference in the availability of discrete items. A further complication is the probable involvement of subjective organization as a determiner of the number of words recalled on a free-recall task. That is, subjects are likely to show organization of the words in our surrogate availability task, just as they do any other free-recall task. Because subjective organization itself may be an age-sensitive process, it may be the primary source, if not the only one, of whatever age difference occurs on our so-called pure test of response-availability's age sensitivity. The seemingly hopeless plight of the investigator should be abated by the reminder that our interest rests mainly in the age sensitivity of response availability as it enters into paired-associate learning and not as it exists in isolated form. In this context, the use of the deletion method seems adequate to demonstrate the process's age sensitivity.

Psychological reductionism is most commonly associated with the area of sensory psychology. Here, a major concern is with sensitivity, or the organism's responsiveness, to stimuli impinging on sensory receptors. Age changes in sensitivity are assumed to result from structural deterioration with increasing age either in receptor cells, the ancillary biological structures coordinated with those cells, or higher order brain areas receiving neural transmissions from the receptor cells. As a primary factor, sensitivity is a component of the multiple determiners mediating performance on various complex perceptual tasks. Consequently, age changes in sensitivity should account, at least partially, for age changes on those tasks. Direct assessment of the degree of biological deterioration for an entire sensory system is ordinarily impossible. Instead, indirect assessment is conducted by means of psychological reductionism. As with response availability, the trick is to find an appropriate Task X that reflects only age changes in Process X, which, in this case, is sensory sensitivity.

Traditionally, this task has consisted of the psychophysical asssessment of threshold values (to be described in Chapter 7). For some years, age differences in threshold values were believed to measure age differences in sensitivity and in sensitivity alone. The fact that age differences, in the form of increasing threshold values with increasing age, exist for the various sensory modalities will become readily apparent in Chapter 7. In recent years, however, it has been discovered that age deficits in threshold values are determined by age variation in a decision-making process (with elderly adults being more cautious, or conservative, than young adults) as well as by age variation in sensitivity per se. Thus, the problem in selecting a pure task to measure age differences in sensitivity alone is comparable to the problem encountered in selecting a pure task to measure age differences in response availability alone. Fortunately, recent developments in sensory psychology have now made it possible to assess separately age differences in the two components (i.e., sensitivity and degree of cautiousness). These developments will be discussed in Chapter 7.

Biological Reductionism. A structure or process may be defined biologically rather than psychologically. Here, explanation of a behavioral phenomenon is sought at the level of mediating anatomical structures and physiological processes. It is an approach to explanation that we will call *biological reductionism.* This approach, when applied to adult-age differences in a behavioral phenomenon, looks for an age-related change in the biological mechanism presumed to mediate that phenomenon. For example, the slower reaction time of elderly adults relative to young adults has been explained by the slowing down of a critical brain process, referred to as cortical arousal or excitability, that occurs with brain deterioration over the adult lifespan (Woodruff, 1975a). Age differences in this critical brain process may be operationally defined and measured in terms of age differences in the frequency of the electroencephalogram's (EEG's) alpha wave component (Surwillo, 1963). We will discuss further the utilization of this biological concept when we discuss the mechanistic model of development in Chapter 6. For the moment, we will merely note that, although a biological process such as that of cortical arousal may be readily operationalized (i.e., made directly observable and measured), its role in mediating reaction time and in determining age differences in reaction time is not directly observable and must be inferred from experimental evidence.

In addition, there are times when a gerontological psychologist will make use of a biological concept that is not operationally defined. The reason is that the psychologist is not content with an explanation of age differences at the level of psychological processes. In other words, the psychologist insists on a more basic explanation at the level of a biological structure or function—even if that explanation must be fully inferential. For example, we have discovered that at least part of the difficulty encountered by elderly subjects in learning paired associates is explained in terms of decreased proficiency in the psychological process of imaginal mediation. But, why this age deficit in mediation? By going beyond the psychological explanation, we are, in effect, asking what biological age change accounts for the psychological age change.

A biological explanation of the imaginal age deficit might begin with the common assumption that the locus of imaginal activity is in the nondominant cerebral hemisphere (the right hemisphere for most people, see Paivio, 1971). An age-related increase in lateral asymmetry of the hemispheres may then be postulated to underlie the age deficit in imaginal activity. The problem, however, is that in the absence of an operationally defined measure of lateral asymmetry, our explanation remains speculative and untestable. Direct biological assessment of the extent of lateral asymmetry found among a group of elderly subjects is highly unlikely. However, various behavioral procedures may be used to provide an indirect assessment of the degree of asymmetry. One of these procedures requires measuring the magnitude of what is called the right-ear advantage on the dichotic listening task (to be discussed in Chapter 7). Scores on this behavioral measure could then be related to paired-associate learning scores earned by the same elderly subjects. A negative correlation (the greater the asymmetry score, the poorer the learning score) would support our reductionist explanation of the imaginal age deficit. Nevertheless, our evidence would be only correlational—some unknown factor could be causing both the variation in our asymmetry scores and our paired-associate learning scores. A definitive answer to the causative role played by variation in lateral asymmetry could be obtained only by some yet unknown experimental procedure that would permit an investigator to manipulate directly asymmetry in the laboratory.

Finally, operationally defined biological concepts, such as EEG frequency, are of value in some areas of descriptive aging research. For example, a question of interest to most people is whether or not the sleeping behavior of elderly adults differs from that of young adults. An answer to this question requires, of course, reliable indices of the stages of sleep. These indices have been provided

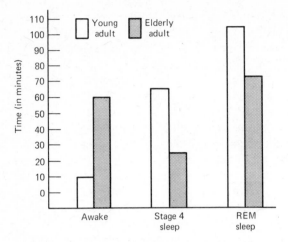

Figure 5.20. Adult-age differences in sleeping behavior. Scores are expressed in mean time per night spent in various stages of sleep. (Adapted from Prinz, 1977, Table 2.)

by the use of biological measures, specifically those of brain-wave frequencies (recorded on EEG's) and eye movements [recorded on electro-oculograms (EOG's)] of sleeping subjects. Through these measures it is possible to assess the amount of time a given subject spends awake, in rapid eye-movement (REM) sleep, Stage 4 (deep) sleep, and so on. A study by Prinz (1977), making full use of these measures, revealed that there clearly are pronounced adult-age differences in sleeping behavior. Her major results are summarized in Figure 5.20. It may be seen that elderly subjects (average age, 82 years) spend many more minutes per night awake than do young adults. By contrast, young adults spend many more minutes in both the REM stage of sleep and Stage 4 sleep. The decrease in REM sleep over the adult lifespan may have important implications for decreasing cognitive competence with aging.

Final Comments. This ends our formal coverage of the methodological designs and strategies that guide the conductance of experimental aging research. However, we have not finished our confrontations with methodological issues and problems. Some of these issues and problems will be faced in the next chapter during our discussion of the interface between theory and experimental aging research. Others will be faced in later chapters at points where a specific content area poses special difficulties in its extensions to experimental aging research. For example, as we have already discovered, research in verbal learning (e.g., paired-associate learning) often introduces variation in such item attributes as meaningfulness and imagery-provoking potential. Levels of meaningfulness and imagery are based on ratings of words that were made by normative samples of young adults, usually college students. Comparable ratings made by normative samples of elderly adults are generally not available. Consequently, extensions of this type of investigation into aging research are more arcane than would appear to be the case at first glance. An investigator wanting to determine the interaction between age and, say, meaningfulness is forced to vary meaningfulness on the basis of norms obtained only on young adults. Highly meaningful words at one age level are not necessarily of equal meaningfulness at a widely separated age level. This issue will be discussed more thoroughly in Chapter 8.

Summary

Most experimental aging studies include variation in one or more experimental, or manipulable, independent variables as well as variation in a nonmanipulable, developmentally relevant, independent variable (usually chronological age). The manipulable variables usually consist of variation either in task content or the procedure of administering a task. Interactions between age and manipulable variables enable us to determine the generalizability of age differences over varying task and procedural conditions. They also offer potent means of identifying inferentially those processes that are age sensitive, (i.e., those that undergo decrements in proficiency with increasing age), and those processes that are age insensitive, (i.e., those that are resistant to decrements in proficiency with increasing age).

Research designs accommodating both nonmanipulable and manipulable independent variables are called heterogeneous factorial designs. The simplest such design, a 2 × 2, employs only two bilevel independent variables, one of each class. This basic A × B structure, in which A symbolizes the age independent variable and B the manipulable independent variable, may be expanded by including additional levels of one or both variables. For example, a 3 × 3 variation of the A × B structure translates into a study involving three age levels and three levels of the manipulable independent variable. The basic structure may also be expanded by including an additional independent variable (or more) that may be either non-manipulable (e.g., sex) or manipulable (e.g., a second traditional experimental variable) in format. This expansion yields an A × B × C heterogeneous factorial design with many variations, contingent on the number of levels employed for each independent variable (e.g., a 2 × 2 × 2 variant, with each variable being bilevel).

An age × manipulable variable interaction effect that is slight and statistically nonsignificant implies that the age difference found for the task in question generalizes over variation in the conditions defined by the manipulable variable. That is, the simple effect for age (the extent of the age difference) found at one level of the manipulable variable is equivalent to the simple effect for age (again, the extent of the age difference) found at the other level (or levels) of the same variable. On the other hand, a significant interaction effect implies that generalizability of the extent of an age difference must take into account the specific condition of the manipulable variable under which the task is performed. In this case, the simple effect for age variation at one level of the manipulable variable is more pronounced than the simple effect for age variation found at another level (or levels) of the same variable.

Interaction effects emerging from heterogeneous factorial studies are also critical components of three main methods employed to identify age-sensitive processes. The multiplicative method requires the inclusion of a manipulable variable whose variation is believed (based on prior research with young adults) to alter the proficiency of the hypothesized age-sensitive process (Process X). If Process X is truly age sensitive, then the low proficiency manifested by elderly adults for this process should be compounded, or multiplied, by the low proficiency expected for all subjects, regardless of age, at Level B_1 (the less favorable level) of the manipulable variable. A significant interaction should be the consequence, with the age deficit in performance decreasing as the overall level of performance proficiency increases. That is, the age deficit must be greater at Level B_1 of the manipulable variable, where performance is relatively low for all age levels, than at Level B_2 (the more favorable condition), where performance is relatively high for all age levels, before we can infer that Process X is really age sensitive.

The divergence method employs a manipulable independent variable believed (again based on prior research with young adults) to activate only one process (Process Y) at Level B_1 and two processes (Process X as well as Process Y) at Level B_2. Moreover, the activation of Process X leads to enhanced performance, regardless of age level. If Process X is age sensitive and Process Y is not, then the age deficit in performance should increase as the overall level of performance proficiency increases from Level B_1 to Level B_2 of the manipulable variable. A significant interaction effect should again be the consequence. This time, however, the age deficit must be greater at Level B_2, where performance is relatively high for all age levels, than at Level B_1, where performance is relatively low for all age levels, before we can infer that Process Y is age sensitive. The multiplicative and divergence methods must be interpreted cautiously in light of several limitations and problems associated with their applications. These include the possible presence of a ceiling effect (multiplicative method) or floor effect (divergence method) that would produce an artifactual interaction effect and the possibility of a nonlinear relationship between process proficiency and performance proficiency.

The deletion method requires the inclusion of a manipulable variable whose variation includes a condition in which a postulated age-senstive process, again Process X, is no longer required for performance on the task in question. Deletion of Process X, in turn, leads to improved performance on the task (i.e., increased dependent variable scores) at all age levels. If Process X is truly age sensitive, then a significant interaction effect should be observed. Support for its sensitivity demands that the age deficit in scores be greater at Level B_1 (no deletion of the process) than at Level B_2 (deletion).

There is an important restriction on the generalizability of an age-sensitive process identified in the usual context of a complex task (e.g., paired-associate learning) in which that process is but one of the multiple determiners of performance proficiency. The fact that a process is age sensitive when constrained by the engagement of one or more other processes, either in parallel or serially, does not necessarily mean that the process in question is age sensitive when it is the only process entering into a task. Unfortunately, testing the age sensitivity of a process in the absence of the involvement of other processes is a difficult objective to accomplish.

The absence of an age $\times$ manipulable variable interaction effect, when combined with a significant main effect for each variable, may be taken as evidence for the age insensitivity of the process (Process Y) altered by variation of the manipulable variable. The absence of an interaction under these conditions implies that Process Y and Process X (the process altered by variation in age) combine in an additive manner. Additive relationships, as indices of age-insensitive processes, are interpreted cautiously in light of the usual reluctance by psychologists to accept null hypotheses.

In addition, several alternative methods that are sometimes used to identify age sensitive processes were described. That is, they are alternatives to the use of methods that draw on inferences based on the nature of the interaction effect obtained in a heterogeneous factorial study. Included among these alternatives are the simulation method, the multiple dependent variable method and the multiple task, or multivariate, method. Most important, it was noted that operationally defined processes and structures may enter into experimental aging research as alternatives to inferred psychological concepts. They may be the products of either psychological reductionism or biological reductionism. In psychological reductionism, the objective is to find a task that is mediated by only one process. Age differences on this task should, therefore, define operationally age differences in the underlying process, a principle that is straightforward in its rationale but difficult in its implementation. In biological reductionism, structures and processes are defined operationally by biological assessment procedures (e.g., EEG recordings). Age differences in these structures and processes are then related to age differences in behavior. Despite its operationalization, the role played by a biological process in determining age differences in behavior often has to be inferred from behavioral evidence.

6

Theory and Its Interface with Experimental Aging Research

A process tested for age sensitivity in an experimental aging study is usually part of a theory constructed to explain a specific behavioral phenomenon (e.g., the learning of a free-recall list). Once more, the validity of that process's role in mediating a behavioral phenomenon has usually received substantial empirical support before the age sensitivity of that process is ever tested in the laboratory. The theory itself is likely to be one of a fairly narrow scope, dealing, for example, only with performance on a free-recall task. However, a theory of this kind most likely is only one of a number of such miniature theories derived from a more general theoretical approach that provides a broad conceptualization of a much wider range of behavioral phenomena. Both the levels of processing theory and the organizational theory of free-recall phenomena we encountered briefly in Chapter 5 involve structures and processes that are indigenous to an *information-processing approach* to human learning and memory. This approach offers a model for conceptualizing (details of which will be examined later in this chapter and in Chapter 9) many learning and memory phenomena beside those of free recall. By contrast, the theory of paired-associate learning that postulates the learning of responses and the hooking up of those responses with their paired-stimulus items is derived from an associative approach to human learning and memory. This approach also offers a general model for conceptualizing a wide range of other learning and memory phenomena. Not surprisingly, an information-processing approach may be used as the base for constructing a theory of paired-associate learning, just as an associative approach may be used for constructing a theory of free-recall learning (see Kausler, 1974, pp. 189–197, 391–410).

From the preceding comments, it should be obvious that explanations of psychological phenomena occur hierarchically. At one level of the hierarchy is a broad conceptual model, such as associationism or information processing, that offers a set of principles, rules, and generic concepts for theorizing about any number of specific phenomena, such as those found for paired-associate or free-recall learning. Below that level, a particular theory derived from the conceptual model postulates the processes relevant to a given phenomenon (e.g., paired-associate learning), whereas another theory postulates the processes relevant to a different phenomenon (e.g., free-recall learning). Thus, the separate theories flow from the basic principles and language system of a shared broader conceptual model. The course of theory construction is, therefore, from the conceptual model to the processes needed to explain a specific phenomenon.

The theories originating from a particular psychological/conceptual model are by no means limited to learning and memory activities. Theories dealing with higher mental activities, including concept learning and problem solving, are just as likely to have their origins in the basic tenets of associationism (or, alternatively, in the basic tenets of information processing). Similarly, theories dealing with simpler sensory and perceptual phenomena have their origins in a given conceptual approach, whether it be associationism or information processing.

The hierarchy for each conceptual approach does not end here however. There are additional levels culminating at the top in what is variously called a metamodel (Reese & Overton, 1970), paradigm (Kuhn, 1962), world view (Seeger, 1954), or world hypothesis (Pepper, 1942). A metamodel is of such generality that it incorporates all natural phenomena, including human behavior. Psychological theories are commonly viewed as stemming from either a mechanistic or an organismic metamodel (Reese & Overton, 1970). Mechanistic and organismic world views have dominated thinking about the fundamental nature of human behavior throughout psychology's history. As metamodels they offer contrasting perspectives regarding the essential characteristics of the human being. These perspectives are that of a reactive organism in the mechanistic world view and an active organism in the organismic world view. The hierarchy for either metamodel then moves downward to the conceptual approach, or model, for theory construction that is relevant to the hierarchy's perspective of human behavior, and from there to the processes of specific theories.

The conceptual model most clearly consonant with the mechanistic metamodel is that of associationism. Associationism's role as the base for constructing theories about the behavior of a reactive organism is acknowledged as much by today's psychologists as it had been by past generations of psychologists. Our comments in earlier chapters about associationism concentrated on theories emanating from it that explain verbal learning and memory phenomena. However, as noted above, associationism is by no means limited to explanations of these phenomena. Other classes of behavioral phenomena are handled just as readily.

The hierarchical organization inherent in explanations by means of associ-

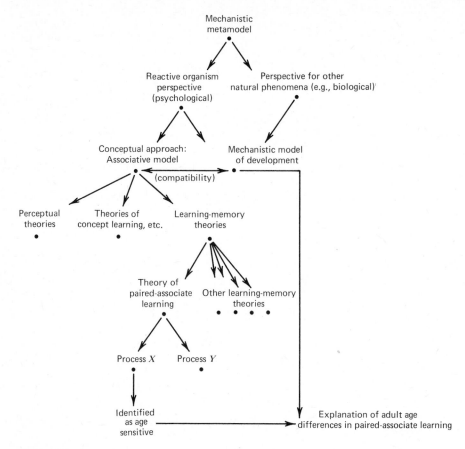

Figure 6.1. Explanation of adult-age differences in a given phenomenon, in this case, paired-associate learning, as derived from a mechanistic metamodel that subsumes both an associative conceptual model for psychological theories and a mechanistic model of development.

ative theories is illustrated in Figure 6.1. The hierarchy is completed in this figure for a theory of paired-associate learning. The final product consists of the component processes, symbolized here abstractly as Process X and Process Y, postulated to mediate paired-associate learning in a manner consistent with the basic concepts of the overall associative model and its governing mechanistic metamodel. It is these processes that would then be tested for their age sensitivities through the methods described in Chapter 5. We have assumed that these tests have revealed Process X, but not Process Y, to be age sensitive. Similarly, the final products for other theories derived from the associative model would be processes capable of being tested for their age sensitivity.

The picture is a bit more equivocal for a conceptual approach that is fully consonant with the organismic metamodel. An appropriate model should surely be one that falls within the domain of cognitive psychology, long viewed by psychologists as offering an antithetical conceptual framework to that of associationism. However, for many years, cognitive psychology existed largely as a diffused conglomeration of attitudes and vague speculations rather than as a systematic model precise enough to generate specific theories covering a wide range of behavioral phenomena. A partial exception was the emergence of Gestalt psychology during the pre-World War I era. The emphasis in Gestalt psychology was on perception as determined by inborn organizational principles rather than on perception as determined by acquired associations (see Dunham, 1977, for elaboration of the nativism versus empiricism issue). In addition, memory as a byproduct of perception was stressed instead of learning existing independently of perception. The basic continuity between perception and memory is one of the cornerstones of contemporary cognitive psychology as it is represented by information processing. However, memory was described in passive terms by Gestalt psychologists. Memory traces were seen as progressing rotely toward good forms, without intervention by an active organism. The result was a rather sterile conceptual model that failed to capture the active nature of human cognition that is consonant with the organismic metamodel.

Information-processing psychology, a far more formidable challenger to associationism than Gestalt psychology, had diverse origins, such as attempts during the 1950s to apply the principles of communication theory to human behavior (see Lachman, Lachman, & Butterfield, 1979, for a fascinating account of the historical development of information-processing psychology). Eventually, information processing became widely accepted as offering an appropriate psychological representation of the organismic metamodel, even though, as we will see, the match-up between information processing and organicism is often ill fitting (Hultsch, 1977; Reese, 1973b). At any rate, information-processing psychology, like associationism, does offer an effective conceptual base for constructing specific theories that range over a broad spectrum of behavioral phenomena. The spectrum includes phenomena of perception and higher mental activities as well as phenomena of learning and memory. Most important, information-processing analyses of behavioral phenomena, unlike those of Gestalt psychology, have been major factors in stimulating experimental aging research.

The hierarchical organization inherent in explanations by means of information-processing theories is illustrated in Figure 6.2. The hierarchy is again completed for a theory of paired-associate learning. In this case, the component processes of the theory are symbolized as Process A and Process B. The implication is that these processes differ considerably from those of the associative theory directed at an analysis of the same task. This difference is to be expected in that the present processes are intended to be consistent with the concepts of an information-processing model rather than an associative model. Our further assumption is that Process A, but not Process B, has been identified by experimental aging research as being age sensitive.

Shown in Figures 6.1 and 6.2 are two other important aspects of the metamodel-to-age-sensitive-process sequence that we have largely ignored thus far. First, the metamodel in each hierarchy is so universal that it applies to phenomena other than those of a psychological nature, such as biological phenom-

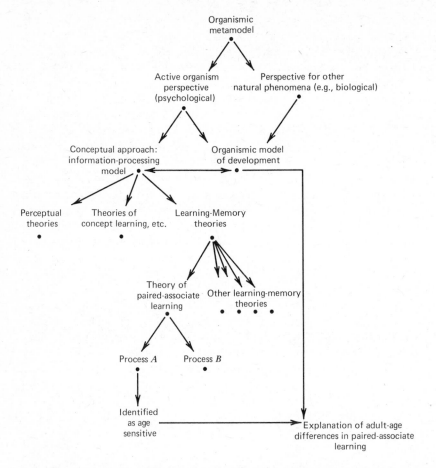

Figure 6.2. Explanation of adult-age differences in a given phenomenon (paired-associate learning) as derived from an organismic metamodel that subsumes both an information-processing conceptual model for psychological theories and an organismic model of development.

ena. This may be seen in the bifurcation occurring near the top of each hierarchy. Second, coordinated with the psychological/conceptual model in each hierarchy is a corresponding developmental model. Gerontological psychologists are not content simply to identify *what* processes are age sensitive. Of further concern is the reason *why* processes undergo changes with human aging. Explanation of a change over any segment of the lifespan, whether it be prematurity or postmaturity, is usually conducted from the perspective of a broad developmental model that, in turn, is coordinated with the psychological model serving as the framework for postulating potentially age-sensitive processes.

Like a model for psychological theory construction, a developmental model offers a set of principles, rules, and generic concepts. Only this time the components of the model provide guidelines for interpreting age-related changes in behavior independently of the specific tasks being examined with respect to those changes. The guidelines become operative whenever a task-specific theory is extended to include an explanation of age differences on the task in question.

In summary, a task-specific theory merely identifies the processes presumed to mediate performance on that task, whereas experimental aging research identifies which, if any, of these processes are age sensitive. The question remains, however, as to why a particular process should be age sensitive. It is at this level of explanation that the developmental model becomes involved.

As indicated in Figure 6.1, the mechanistic metamodel subsumes a mechanistic model of development that is consonant with that metamodel's perspective of a reactive organism. In general, the mechanistic model of development is compatible with its coordinated associative model for constructing psychological theories. Consequently, age changes in whatever processes are identified as being age sensitive are usually explainable through the principles of the developmental model. As indicated in Figure 6.2, the organismic metamodel subsumes an organismic model of development that is consonant with that metamodel's perspective of an active organism. In principle, the organismic model of development is also expected to be compatible with its coordinated organismic model for constructing psychological theories. However, this compatibility is strained somewhat when information processing serves as the base for theory construction. It is this strain that accounts for much of the misfit noted earlier (to be discussed further later in this chapter).

Familiarity with the theoretical backgrounds of aging studies is indispensable for full comprehension of the contributions these studies make to our knowledge about age differences and changes in behavior. Eventually, this familiarity will have to be with the specific processes entering into the miniature theories accounting for performances on many kinds of tasks. Our immediate objective, however, is to increase your familiarity with the broader psychological/conceptual and developmental models that both guide experimental aging research and serve as the foundation for explaining age changes in various psychological phenomena. Our initial concern will be with associationism. We will examine the transition from metamodel to psychological model and from psychological model to the kinds of associative theories that have entered into experimental aging research. We will then examine the developmental model with which these transitions must be coordinated. A similar analysis will follow for information processing and its coordinated developmental model.

Associationism and Experimental Aging Research

Mechanistic Metamodel. Our comments earlier in this chapter established the fact that in the mechanistic metamodel the basic model for all natural phenomena is the machine. Expressed somewhat differently, the Newtonian concept of a machine proffers a broad metaphor for viewing all phenomena of the universe, including human behavior (see Reese & Overton, 1970, and Overton & Reese, 1973, for more detailed descriptions of the mechanistic metamodel).

Our interest rests in the reasons for a machine's activity. In a fundamental sense, a machine reacts only to external forces that are applied to it. That is, it does not act spontaneously in the sense of generating its own internal forces. Given an appropriate external force, the machine reacts. Without that force, the machine remains inactive. In some instances, an external, or environmental, force is sufficient to elicit a reaction from the machine throughout the machine's history or period of existence. Observation of that specific force's application to the machine, therefore, explains completely the machine's observed reactivity. In other words, there is a perfect correlation between the force's application and the machine's reactivity. Given that perfect correlation, the force may be said to have *caused* the reaction. Stated somewhat differently, observation of the force's application, for all practical purposes, *explains* the machine's behavior. The innate, or natural, substance of the machine assures its reactivity to the force in question. In effect, the mechanism for mediating the reactivity is built into the machine at the time of its construction. In other instances, however, a particular external force elicits a reaction only after new pieces have been added to the machine's original substance. That is, modification of the machine's natural substance must be accomplished before the particular external force can assume its causative role. In such instances, we clearly must have knowledge about the machine's altered substance as well as knowledge about an external force to predict and explain the machine's behavior.

Whatever the nature of an instance of reactivity, the external force need not be an immediate causative factor. That is, the force may merely initiate a chain-like sequence of events in which internal components of the machine react successively until, at the end of the chain, an observable component of the machine reacts. The immediate causative factor is, therefore, the force applied by the terminal internal component. However, because the application of this internal component is completely dependent on the prior application of the external force, the latter may be conveniently referred to as *the* causative factor.

Most important, the deletion of a critical component from the machine's substance disrupts a prior chain of events and, therefore, eliminates what had previously been a causative chain. Such deletion may occur as the machine grows old and component parts wear out. Predicting and explaining the absence of a reaction that had at one time occurred reliably to an initiating external force again requires knowledge of the machine's history and knowledge of the machine's current substance. In this case, however, such knowledge pertains to the machine's *deterioration* rather than to its growth defined in terms of additions of components to the machine's substance.

Translation of the Machine Metaphor to Psychological Concepts. A metaphor is a representation of reality—it assumes that the events being represented *act* in the manner prescribed by the metaphor. Our current assumption is that behavioral phenomena act as if they are produced by a machine. If they are, then what attributes should these phenomena possess? They are, of course, those attributes that are inherent in the products of a machine: reaction to external forces rather than spontaneous activation; additions in behavior because of additions of new pieces to the machine's substance, additions that permit reactions to novel external forces (thus expanding the range of external causative factors that make the machine behave); and decrements in behavior because of the wearing out of component pieces so that previously effective external forces no longer serve as causative agents. The adequacy of the metaphor for psychology depends on how well the conceptual system derived from it generates theories about human behavior that are empirically supported. However, even if these theories prove to be highly effective, we have only demonstrated that the human organism acts like a machine—not necessarily that it *is* a machine.

Associationism—as the machine metaphor's application to psychology—translates force, reaction, and substance into psychologically relevant concepts. The nature of the translation varies somewhat in accordance with the class of behavioral phenomena being analyzed (sensory, perceptual, and so on). The product of each translation is an associative theory dealing with the processes and structures entering into a particular content area (e.g., sensory, perceptual, and so on). We will attempt to demonstrate how associative analyses lead to hypotheses about age-sensitive processes that may then be tested through the methods described in Chapter 5. Further explanation as to why these processes are age sensitive in the first place usually relies on biological concepts that are consonant with the mechanistic model of development.

What we are calling associationism is a distillation of a number of associative concepts. Our coverage of these concepts will begin with a description of the innate components of the organism/machine and the means by which these components interact with the environment. We will then examine in some detail how associationism treats learning phenomena and how this treatment leads to explanations of age deficits in those phenomena. It is through learning that new components are added to the organism's substance. Through these additions there is a substantial increase in the number and variety of environmental forces that are capable of eliciting reactions from the organism. Learning plays an especially important role in associationism's conceptualization of most psychological phenomena. For example, perception of objects in our environment is determined by the associations we have acquired to those objects. As another example, purposiveness of behavior is viewed in terms of learned associations that incorporate responses made in the presence of goal objects. If current stimuli are similar to the original stimuli entering into these associations, then they are likely to elicit, in reduced form, the responses directed at the goal object, even though the goal object is absent. It is these anticipatory goal responses that define purposiveness to an associationist (Hull, 1930, 1931). Similarly, other complex cognitive phenomena, such as concept learning, can be explained in terms of simple learning concepts. In effect, all behavioral phenomena, except those determined by reflexive reactions and inborn associations, are reducible to learning processes and the products of those processes.

Our analysis of learning will concentrate on basic principles that cut across most of the specific associative theories of learning that have appeared over the years. In so doing, we will ignore some of the prominent issues that created diversification among specific theories. One of these issues concerns the necessity of having some form of reward, or effect, follow a response to promote learning an association involving that response. Some associative theories (e.g., Hull, 1943; Thorndike, 1931) stress that all learning requires effects (or reinforcement), whereas other theories (e.g., Guthrie, 1935) argue that effects play only an indirect role in learning and, therefore, are not essential for learning per se to take place. This issue has not entered into aging research on learning. The emphasis has been mainly on age differences in learning associations between verbal elements. Here, the role played by reinforcement is vague and poorly defined.

Our analysis will also ignore the radical form of associationism espoused by operant psychologists, such as Skinner (1938). Here, the focus is decidedly on reinforcers that serve to maintain the occurrence of responses in the presence of certain stimuli rather than on the acquisition of associations. Operant psychology has actually had little impact on the experimental psychology of aging—and with good reason. Age is treated by operant psychologists (e.g., Baer, 1970) as being simply an uninteresting parameter that determines rate of responding by an organism, and it is reduced to the status of a secondary variable relative to such primary variables as the schedule of reinforcement.

Basic Concepts and Principles; Innate Associations. Reactions of the human organism consist of responses (R's), or behaviors, that are elicited by stimuli (S's) originating in either the organism's external environment or the organism's internal environment. The causative role of a particular stimulus as the force for eliciting a particular response is symbolized as S→R (the arrow is read as elicits). This causative role is fulfilled, however, only if an association, or connection, exists between the S and R elements (the association is symbolized as S-R) in the organism's substance at the time the S element impinges on the organism. Thus, an association's presence as part of the organism's substance must be considered along with the immediate cause (the S's actual impingement on the organism) to predict and explain the occurrence of a given R element.

Some S-R associations are innately built into the organism. The R elements of these associations are automatically, or reflexively, activated whenever their S elements make contact with the organism. For example, a light (S) directed at the eye elicits a detection response (R) (i.e., you see the light), and a puff of air (S) directed at the same eye elicits a reflexive blinking response (R). In both cases, the association necessary for the S→R sequence to unfold is part of the organism's species inheritance and is, therefore, inborn. Although the S and R elements are overt events, open to direct observation by others, the S-R associations themselves are inferred to exist within the organism. The relationship between the observable S and R elements and the inferred innate association between these elements is illustrated in Figure 6.3. It may be seen that the S element is assumed to trigger an internal series of events, just as an external force triggers a chain of events within a machine. The chain begins with the organism's sensory-perceptual responses (r) to the external stimulus. This internal, and inferred, behavior is also known as a representational response. A

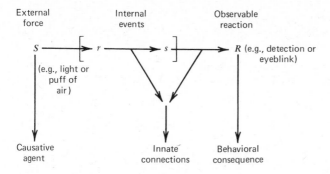

Figure 6.3. The chain of events postulated to underlie the activation of an innate association between S and R elements.

representational response produces its own internal stimulus (s). This stimulus may be viewed in terms of neural impulses originating in an afferent system and ending in the brain, where a connection is made with an efferent pathway leading to the given behavior (R). Reference to an S-R association is merely a convenient way of summarizing the connections intervening between the overt S and R elements (i.e., S→r, r→s, and s→R). Thus, even the simplest reactions of the human organism, such as detecting a light or blinking an eye, involve chain-like sequences.

Despite their apparent automaticity, inborn associations are not necessarily activated by the presence of their initiating S elements. A critical contingency rests in the intensity, or energy level, of the S element. Thus, a faint light source may not be detected, whereas a more intense one is readily noticed. The probability of detection of a sensory stimulus for a given individual is contingent on the extent to which the intensity of that stimulus exceeds the individual's threshold value. Most importantly, threshold values for the various sensory modalities are likely to increase as the underlying sensory structures deteriorate through biological aging (i.e., the wearing out of the machine). Consequently, weak-sensory stimuli that once elicited detection responses lose their causative power. Age differences and changes in sensory thresholds represent associationism's main contact with the experimental psychology of aging. Further analysis of these changes will be reserved for Chapter 7. Also reserved for Chapter 7 is our full discussion of age changes in various perceptual phenomena as viewed associatively. We will discover then that these age changes are explained in terms of age differences in the duration of the internal stimulus (s) depicted in Figure 6.3. The internal stimulus is hypothesized to persist longer for elderly adults than for young adults. As we will see, the hypothesized difference in stimulus persistence leads quite naturally to certain kinds of independent variable manipulations that permit tests of the validity of the hypothesis.

Classical Associationism and Rote Associative Learning. Most S-R associations are not innately present in the human organism. Instead, they must be added to the organism's substance. These acquisitions take place through the processes of learning. Given the importance of learning to the vast array of human behaviors, it is little wonder that the main focus of associationism is on the understanding and explanation of learning per se.

Early learning theorists—who collectively represent what we will call *classical associationism* (e.g., Guthrie, 1935; Hull, 1943; Thorndike, 1931)—viewed learning solely in terms of acquiring S-R associations. Because S-R associations are the only products of learning, the processes yielding these associations are the only ones to be considered in analyses of learning phenomena, including the phenomenon of adult-age differences in performance on many kinds of learning tasks.

Classical associationism's account of learning is quite consistent with the mechanistic perspective of the human organism. Learning is assumed to occur rotely through the contiguous occurrences of previously unrelated stimuli and responses. Each elicitation of a response in the presence of an initially neutral stimulus element yields an increment in the S-R association now serving to connect these previously disparate events. These increments continue until some maximum, or asymptotic, level of strength is reached for the S-R association. Alternatively, some associative learning theories (e.g., Guthrie, 1935) assume an all-or-none principle with regard to gains in associative strength. That is, the strength of an association remains zero until learning occurs—at which point the strength reaches its maximum value. The issue of incremental gains in associative strength versus none-to-all leaps has had no real impact on experimental aging research. The incremental notion has been the more popular one in associative learning theories, and it is, therefore, the one followed here.

What we have described is what is labeled rote learning by psychologists. It calls to mind the repetitive rehearsal, or vocalization (whether overt or covert), of the to-be-learned elements many of us experienced in learning multiplication tables, spellings of words, and so on. Rote learning is commonly studied in the laboratory by giving subjects a paired-associate list to master. Suppose one pair in a list consists of *apple* as the S element and *table* as the R element. Our assumption is that there is no direct connection between these words prior to encountering their pairing in the learning list. Rehearsing *table* in the presence of *apple* leads to the association symbolized in Figure 6.4. The association relates the representational response, r_S, elicited by the S element to the internal stimulus, s_R, that elicits the vocalization of the R element. Eventu-

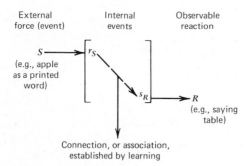

Figure 6.4. The chain of events postulated to underlie the activation of a learned association between S and R elements.

ally, presentation of S alone leads to the evocation of R by means of the $r_s{\rightarrow}s_R$ mediating association. However, the mere existence of associative strength is not sufficient to assure the elicitation of R by its appropriate S element. An added concept is that of an association's threshold value, a concept similar to that of a threshold for eliciting a detection response to a sensory stimulus. The threshold represents the minimal degree of strength that must be exceeded before the association is manifested in observable performance (i.e., for R to occur overtly in the presence of S). Thus, an association may be latent within an organism without ever actually becoming part of that organism's behavioral repertoire. In general, the probability of an association entering into observable performance is contingent on the extent to which its strength exceeds the threshold value.

The basic role played by rote rehearsal in associative learning makes it a prime candidate as an age-sensitive process responsible for age deficits found on learning tasks. Older adults are hypothesized to rehearse R elements fewer times during a fixed study interval than do young adults. With fewer rehearsals, there should be fewer contiguous occurrences of S and R elements on a given trial and, therefore, less gain in associative strength per trial for elderly adults than for young adults. The net effect should be more trials required for elderly adults than for young adults before a given association exceeds its threshold value, as indicated in Figure 6.5. Tests of the rehearsal process's age sensitivity call for variation in the duration of study intervals as a critical manipulable independent variable. We have already discovered a study employing this means of testing the age sensitivity of rehearsal rate. It is the study by Eisdorfer and Service (1967) reviewed briefly in Chapter 5. The task they employed was that of serial learning. We will see in Chapter 8 that the same strategy has been employed in several paired-associate learning studies—and with outcomes that are not fully supportive of rehearsal rate as the *only* age-sensitive learning process.

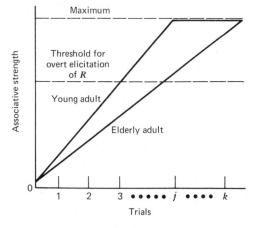

Figure 6.5. Schematic representation of the gain in strength of a specific S-R association with practice over trials. Given less rote rehearsal per trial for an elderly subject than for a young adult subject, the rate of growth in strength is slower for the elderly subject. Regardless of a subject's age level, an association is not manifested in performance unless its strength exceeds a threshold value.

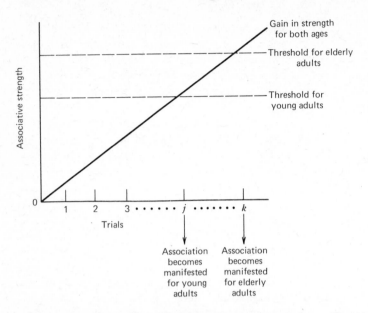

Figure 6.6. Explanation of an age deficit in learning expressed in terms of a postulated age differences in threshold values (an association must exceed threshold to be manifested in performance for each age level), with elderly adults having a higher threshold value than young adults.

What other options are there in classical associationism, other than the rehearsal deficit principle (Kausler, 1978), for explaining age deficits in performance on learning tasks? Actually, there are several options available to classical associationists, only two of which will be mentioned here. One option is to postulate an age change in an association's threshold value, a change much like that found for a sensory threshold. That is, the rate of gaining strength may be the same for elderly adults as for young adults, but the threshold value that must be exceeded may be greater for the elderly adult (as illustrated in Figure 6.6). If true, elderly adults would suffer a performance decrement but not a true learning deficit. Apparently, this hypothesis has not been seriously entertained by experimental aging psychologists. At least, there appear to be no studies testing the validity of this alternative explanation of age deficits in performance on learning tasks.

The other option we will consider also places the responsibility on a performance factor rather than on a learning factor per se. In this case, it is the familiar notion that elderly adults are less motivated than young adults, and they may, therefore, perform at a lower level even though they may have learned as much. The separation between learning and performance is an important one in classical associationism (e.g., Hull, 1943). The key determiner of performance level is the drive (or motivational) level of the organism. Like all machines, the human organism requires a power source to energize its operations. Drive level determines the amount of energization, and it, therefore, influences the proficiency of the machine's operations. The difficulty encountered in a motivational explanation, as we discovered in Chapter 3, is that there is little evidence to indicate that motivational factors influence greatly age differences in performance on many kinds of tasks.

Stage Analysis: Mediated Associative Learning and Multiple Learning Processes. For the past 25 or so years, there have been few experimental aging psychologists who adhere rigidly to classical associationism as their conceptual model. However, associationism has not been abandoned completely. A number of contemporary researchers have gravitated toward modified forms of associationism, such as *stage analysis* (Underwood & Schulz, 1960). In stage analysis, S-R associative learning is only one, albeit an important one, of the stages, or processes, involved in acquisition of new material. Moreover, S-R associative learning is itself treated more liberally than it is by classical associationists. In agreement with classical associationists, stage analysts recognize that S-R associations may be acquired by rote rehearsal activity. However, stage analysts also believe that S-R associations may be the product of mediation by an active subject who constructs interacting images between S and R elements or sentences incorporating both S and R elements.

The concept of an active subject, at first blush, smacks of incompatibility with the tenets of the mechanistic metamodel. However, activity is used here in a way that differs from the use derived from the organismic metamodel (see Spiker, 1977, for a detailed discussion). It is in reference to some response, or behavior, by the subject, but it is a more general response, one that transcends the specific responses entering into associations on the learning task in question. Specifically, it is a generalized habit of a strategic nature that has been learned at some time in the subject's past history. It was learned because its use was found to facilitate learning of some specific task or tasks. Once learned, the habit, or generalized response, transfers to a new learning situation, and, once activated in the new situation, it is likely to be applied to all of the S-R components of the novel material.

The use of such mediators as imagery is assumed by stage analysts to be governed by a generalized response of the kind described above. Mediation consists of forming an interacting image that incorporates both the S element and the R element of a given pair (remember the example given in Chapter 1 of a king chomping away at a juicy red apple). This mediational process would be extended to every pair of S and R elements in a given list. (Contrast this form of constructive mediation with the rote chained-response form of mediation found in classical associationism.) Adult subjects are assumed to have learned the advantages of employing imagery to mediate associative learning long before they appear in the laboratory to master a list of paired associates. In effect, the skill of evoking images to represent linguistic events may be considered an R element that is associated with learning task as a broad, generic S element. Because even a novel learning task bears some degree of similarity to the many previous learning tasks encountered by a subject, it serves as an exemplar of the generic S element. Consequently, the very fact that a subject is confronted by that task serves to activate the use of imagery for mediating the specific S-R

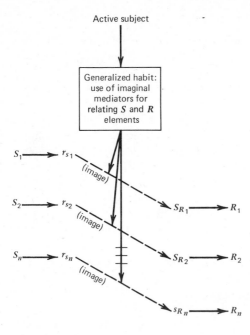

Figure 6.7. Conceptualization of the manner by which the generalized habit of using an imaginal mediator affects the learning of multiple S-R pairs in a learning list.

associations of the new task (Kausler, 1970). The nature of this exchange between the relevant generalized habit and the to-be-acquired novel associations is illustrated in Figure 6.7.

The shift in perspective from that of classical associationism to that of stage analysis has important implications for the experimental psychology of aging. From the perspective of stage analysis, it is conceivable that age deficits occur in paired-associate learning because of the elderly individual's failure to use imagery for mediating S-to-R connections, in addition to, or instead of, the elderly individual's diminished amount of rote rehearsal activity. In other words, it may be a *qualitative change* in the nature of rehearsal activity (i.e., from mediated to rote) from early to late adulthood rather than a mere *quantitative change* in the amount of rote rehearsal (a change that may readily be compensated by allowing elderly adults additional rehearsal time), that accounts for the age deficits found on many learning tasks. The shift in emphasis from rote contiguity learning to mediated learning is an especially important one. It is conceivable that rote rehearsal alone is not sufficient to promote increments in the strengths of S-R associations. That is, additional activity by a learner, such as mediation, may be necessary to promote associative learning. The evidence from basic learning studies is surprisingly meager on this point. There is some evidence (Spear, Ekstrand, & Underwood, 1964) indicating that rote rehearsal is sufficient to promote associative learning, but there is also evidence (Glenberg & Bradley, 1979) indicating that it is not.

Our preceding analysis suggests two possible reasons for a qualitative change in rehearsal activity with aging. One possibility is simply the failure of the generalized habit (Figure 6.7) to be activated by many elderly adults when

they encounter novel learning tasks, such as a laboratory-based paired-associate task. The assumption, here, is that the basic ability to employ imagery and
other forms of mediation is unaffected by aging—only the spontaneous activation of that ability is affected. In this case, the elderly adult would be regarded
as experiencing a production deficit. The other possibility is the actual loss of
the ability to employ mediation. In this case, elderly adults would be regarded
as experiencing a true mediational deficit.

Tests of the qualitative change hypothesis require different kinds of manipulable independent variables than do tests of the quantitative change hypothesis. Variation in the instructions subjects receive (i.e., those stressing the
use of mediators versus those that do not) and in the attributes of S and R
elements (i.e., high- versus low-imagery value) now assume critical importance.
We touched on studies employing these kinds of variables in earlier chapters. A
more thorough review of these studies and other related studies will be given in
Chapter 8.

The other major innovation of stage analysis is its identification of learning processes other than S-R associative learning. One of these processes, response learning, was discussed briefly earlier. The other processes identified by
stage analysis are those of stimulus learning and backward (R-S) associative
learning. We will reserve further discussion of these processes until our review
of aging studies on paired-associate learning proficiency in Chapter 8.

Beyond the Prototype. The paired-associate task is a prototypal one for examining classical associationism's approach to learning phenomena in that both the
S elements and the R elements are clearly identifiable to the investigator and
may be objectively defined. There are other learning tasks, of course, in which
the S and R elements are equally identifiable and objectively defineable. For
example, in classical conditioning, the S element is the conditioned, or neutral,
stimulus, and the R element is the response elicited originally only by the
unconditioned stimulus. However, the classical conditioning task departs from
the paired-associate task in two important respects. The first is in the involvement of only one S element and one R element. Thus, only a single association
is learned rather than a number of associations, as in the paired-associate task.
The second, and more critical, departure is in the absence of a variable rehearsal activity. On each conditioning trial, the unconditioned stimulus automatically elicits its relevant unconditioned response. Thus, the response is not
rehearsed in the same way responses are rehearsed in practice on a paired-
associate list. And yet, as we shall discover in Chapter 8, age deficits in the rate
of learning are clearly manifested for classical conditioning tasks. Obviously,
there must be reasons for age deficits in classical conditioning as a form of
learning other than the existence of age differences in rate of rehearsal. Some
possible explanations of these deficits in conditioning will be examined in
Chapter 8.

There is another important way in which a learning task may depart from
the prototypal paired-associate task. There are learning tasks in which the S
elements are far from being objectively defined. The dilemma confronting the

associationist, or S-R psychologist, in dealing with these tasks was described by Kausler:

> S-R psychologists take very seriously the notion that learning is the formation of associations between S and R units. Thus, to have learning, we must have discrete S units as well as discrete R units. . . .this notion readily adapts to the paired-associate task. But what about other verbal learning tasks, such as serial learning and free recall? Here the tasks themselves do not include intrinsic, experimenter-defined S units. For example, in free recall learning the subject may be asked to learn a lengthy set of words: *table, lion, street, apple,* etc. Most importantly, the words are presented for study in a different order on each trial, and the subject is free to recall the words in whatever order they come to mind. The list words themselves may be viewed as R units, but where are the S units? (Kausler, 1974, p. 3)

The associationist's answer to the above question is simply, "The S elements are embedded in the task somewhere and somehow." If the S elements cannot be defined objectively, then they must be inferred to exist in some component of the task itself or in some component of the environment in which the task is practiced. In effect, S elements for such tasks are constructs rather than operationally defined entities. The validity of the inference is contingent on the support obtained by testing hypotheses derived from the inferred nature of the stimulus element.

The missing-stimulus dilemma appears in an associative analysis of serial learning, a task which, like paired-associate learning, has long been a favorite of associationists. For this task, a series of words must be learned in the precise order they are studied (real-life counterparts are learning the months of the year in order and the names of U.S. presidents in order). Identification of the R elements for this kind of learning presents no problem. They are the specific words, or items, in the serial list. But what are the S elements? One possibility is that a given item's S element is the item in the list preceding that specific item. As illustrated in the top panel of Figure 6.8, Item A is viewed as being the S element for Item B, Item B as the S element for Item C, and so on. Another possibility is that an item's actual ordinal position in the list serves as its S element. As illustrated in the bottom panel of Figure 6.8, First is the S element for Item A, Second the S element for Item B, and so on. There is evidence to support the utilization of both sources of S elements (see Kausler, 1974, pp. 267–274). In fact, a subject may even make use of both preceding items and ordinal position as stimulus sources in mastering a serial list. For our purposes, the important point is that age deficits in serial-learning proficiency, like age deficits in paired-associate learning proficiency, may be interpreted as resulting from either a quantitative change in amount of rote rehearsal or a qualitative change in the kind of rehearsal activity.

Resolution of the missing-stimulus dilemma is even more innovative for free-recall learning. Contextual stimuli present in the laboratory setting (e.g., the apparatus used to present items at a controlled rate) function collectively as a broad S element that is shared associatively by all of the R elements (i.e., the

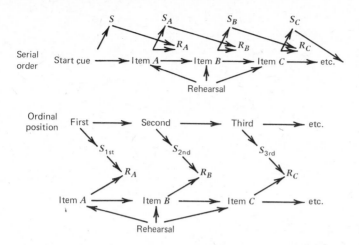

Figure 6.8. Top panel: Schematic representation of the hypothesis that the preceding item in a serial list serves as the stimulus for a given item in the formation of an S-R association involving that given item. Bottom panel: An alternative hypothesis in which the stimulus for a given item is its ordinal position in the serial list.

words in the list). The nature of this stimulus-sharing principle is illustrated in Figure 6.9. The hypotheses advanced to explain age deficits in paired-associate learning proficiency may then be applied to age deficits in free-recall learning. Other free-recall learning phenomena, such as the emergence of subjective organization over a number of trials, may also be explained by the creative application of associative concepts (see Kausler, 1974, pp. 403–410). This approach to subjective organization has not influenced experimental aging research. Nor, for that matter, has the overall associative conceptualization of free-recall learning. Most aging research on free-recall phenomena has been conducted from the perspective of information processing. Consequently, the associative conceptualization of free-recall learning will not be considered further.

Retention/Forgetting and Transfer. Associationism's account of learning phenomena is incomplete without an accompanying account of forgetting as well. Once acquired, does an association remain forever part of the organism's substance, so that it will always be reactivated whenever the S element of that association is reintroduced? The answer to this question is, "It depends." An association is postulated to be immune to spontaneous decay over the passage of time per se. Hence, the degree of retention, or maintenance, of an association is independent of the length of time lapsing before the S element is reintroduced to the organism. However, the degree of retention is dependent on the nature of the organism's further learning experiences during the intervening time period. If a new association is learned that bears an interference relationship with the previously learned association, then the older association may be unlearned (or extinguished) in the sense of losing some, if not all, of its original associative strength. In effect, the association has been forgotten to the extent that its strength has been weakened through the unlearning process. Of equal

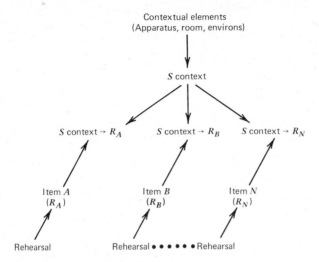

Figure 6.9. An associative explanation of free-recall learning. Contextual elements function as a broad stimulus for each item in a list in the formation of S-R associations involving each item.

concern is the fate of the new association over the course of the retention interval. To the extent that the old association is not unlearned during practice on the new association, it remains as a source of competition during later attempts to recall the new association. This competition may be sufficient to block the recall of the more recently learned association, in effect leading to the forgetting of that association.

The processes of unlearning and competition at the time of recall form the core of associationism's well-known interference theory of forgetting (McGeoch, 1933; Melton & Irwin, 1940). As indicated above, these processes become operative in the presence of an interference relationship between associations. An interference relationship is created whenever a new R element is to be connected with the S element of a previously learned association. Thus, having learned *apple-table* as an S-R association, a subject is likely to encounter interference while learning *apple-pencil* at a later time (note that two different R elements are being associated with the same S element). We can readily construct paired-associate lists in which interference relationships exist. Critics of interference theory, however, ask how often in real-life do we encounter situations in which we have to learn associations corresponding to the S_1-R_1, then S_1-R_2 sequence. Actually, there probably are a number of occasions in which we do learn successive lists of associations that conform to the interference relationship. Consider, for example, the learning required when a new president of the United States is elected and an entirely new cabinet is appointed. People who have already learned the associations *Secretary of State*→Jones, *Secretary of Defense*→Brown, and so on, must now learn the new associations *Secretary of State*→Smith, *Secretary of Defense*→Johnson, and so on. Titles of the cabinet positions function as the S elements shared by both lists (i.e., old and new cabinets), and the names of the holders of these positions function as old and new R elements. This analysis leads us to expect considerable forgetting of the old names and also difficulty in recalling the new names as well. Anecdotal reports from many people, including the present author, support the occurrence of both phenomena.

An understanding of the processes responsible for forgetting is especially important to the experimental psychology of aging. Elderly people commonly report memory loss as one of their major concerns (e.g., Lowenthal, Berkman, Beuhler, Pierce, Robinson, & Trier, 1967). To explain these seemingly pronounced deficits in retention with aging, associationists must work within the confines of interference theory. Accordingly, elderly people are simply defined as being more *interference prone* than are young adults (Kausler, 1970). The assumption is that the magnitude of both unlearning and competition at recall is greater for the elderly than for the young. Consequently, elderly people are expected to show deficits in the retention of both old associations (e.g., those involving prior cabinet members) and new associations (e.g., those involving current cabinet members). Laboratory tests of the interference-proneness principle call for comparisons in the amounts of retroactive and proactive inhibition found for young-adult versus elderly subjects. Retroactive inhibition provides an assessment of old-list forgetting and proactive inhibition of new-list forgetting. The results of these comparisons will be reviewed in Chapter 8. At that time, we will discover some serious complications in accepting increments in interference proneness as the causative factor for age deficits in retention.

The concept of increasing interference with increasing age has another important implication. Given lists having an interference relationship, acquisition of the second, or new, list is made difficult by the prior acquisition of the first, or old, list. Presumably, responses from the old list intrude as the subject practices the new responses now paired with the old S elements. This hindrance continues until the first-list associations are sufficiently weakened by unlearning to eliminate their elicitations. The effect of prior learning on new learning in general is called *transfer*. Transfer may be either positive (i.e., facilitating new learning) or negative (i.e., hindering new learning). In the present case, the transfer effect is decidedly negative. The amount of negative transfer is expected to be greater for elderly subjects than for young-adult subjects, again owing to the greater interference proneness of the former. The evidence relevant to this component of the interference-proneness concept will also be reviewed in Chapter 8. We will also reserve our discussion of positive transfer until Chapter 8. We will discover then that stage analysis has contributed substantially to our understanding of the conditions and mechanisms yielding positive transfer and also to our understanding of various conditions and mechanisms that may yield negative transfer.

Mechanistic Model of Development and Aging

Pre-maturity Phase of Development. There is no one mechanistic conceptualization of development that spans its full continuum. Instead, there appear to be clearly distinctive models for the prematurity and postmaturity phases of development. The prematurity model is more an extension of the behavioristic-associationistic approach to various behavioral phenomena, particularly those of learning, than it is a conceptualization of development per se. In this extension, variation in chronological age is not admitted as a causative factor for behavioral changes over the prematurity period. Age reduces to time; time per se causes nothing. Behavioral changes are produced by other variables that are correlated with age and, therefore, with time.

The other variables that correlate with age consist of a myriad of new environmental situations that confront the organism continuously as it progresses from infancy to adulthood. New learning opportunities are the result, thus providing the organism with an increasing repertory of learned behaviors as age increases (Reese & Overton, 1970). Quantitative rather than qualitative change is the rule. More associations are added to the organism's substance by learning—not by qualitative changes in the substance of the organism. Of course, changes do occur in the organism's substance through biological maturation. However, these changes are also merely quantitative. Through maturation, the growing organism becomes a more proficient learner—but not a different kind of learner.

Post Maturity Phase of Development: Implications for Human Aging. Changing environmental situations and new associations resulting from contacts with these new situations are likely to continue their contributions to behavioral changes over the adult phase of the lifespan. In some instances, new learning may produce increased behavioral competence as the organism grows older. This would be especially true for behaviors reflecting the acquisition of new knowledge through the learning of new associations and indexed by performance on such tests as that of vocabulary. That is, continuing additions to knowledge allow the older person to know more than the younger person. In other instances, new learning resulting from contacts with aversive environmental situations may yield decrements in behavioral competence as the organism grows older. For example, a newly acquired behavior by an elderly person may be that of excessive cautiousness when confronted by a novel task, thereby lowering performance on that task. However, there is an additional causative factor that assumes critical importance during adulthood, particularly during later adulthood. It is causation stemming from the biological degeneration of an aging organism (Hultsch, 1977).

Why biological degeneration occurs at all with increasing age remains largely unresolved. Answers to this fundamental question continue to be pursued by many contemporary biological theorists and researchers. The general tenor of one class of biological theories of aging has been captured nicely by Timiras:

> For some scientists engaged in the study of development and aging the pursuit of isolated areas of investigation has been superseded by a need to formulate a biologic "master plan" based on selected observations and hypotheses concerning the life cycle. This approach suggests that a program for aging in higher organisms may be genetically encoded in the brain and expressed in a precisely scheduled

timetable of growth, maturation, and aging. More specifically, controlling signals from discrete centers in the brain are thought to be relayed to peripheral tissues and organs by hormonal and neural (somatic and autonomic) stimulation or inhibition.

Evidence to support the concept that such a program exists is still tentative, although similar programs regulating other timed physiologic interactions—that is, biologic clocks—are well documented. Given the central role of the brain and endocrines in the control of all bodily functions, it appears reasonable to accept the hypothesis that a biologic clock for aging does exist, that it is located in a specific brain area(s) , and that it is influenced by environmental factors. Some of the data supporting the theory derive from observations of the aging nervous and endocrine systems and from experiments confirming that alterations in neuroendocrine interrelations seem to be capable of modifying the course of growth, maturation, and aging (see Everitt & Burgess, 1976; Finch & Hayflick, 1977). (Timiras, 1978, p. 609).

It is the nature of the biologic clock itself that remains hypothetical and subject to alternative theories. Timiras herself favors a brain-endocrine theory of genetically programmed aging. According to this theory, the pacemakers for regulating the biologic clock reside in neurons of higher brain centers. They stimulate or inhibit the neurosecretory cells of the hypothalamus and, through this activity, control anterior pituitary secretions of tropic hormones. The latter secretions serve either to regulate other endocrine systems or to act directly on the metabolic activity of various organs. Some of the many other hypotheses concerning the nature of aging's genetic program are summarized in Table 6.1.

A major alternative to biologic-clock theories of aging is that of running-out-of-a-program theories. Prematurity development is assumed to be programmed genetically, but the genetic regulation ends at maturity (Wilson, 1974). From that point on the organism is susceptible to the ravages of "wear

Table 6.1   Selected Sample of Programmed Theories of Biological Aging

Locus	Mechanism	Primary Reference
Cellular	Errors in the sequence of deoxyribonucleic acid (DNA) transmission of information necessary for the synthesis of proteins	Orgel (1963)
Cellular	Mutations of chromosomes resulting in abnormal functioning of cells	Curtis (1966)
Cellular	Limited number of cell divisions after which the cells age and die	Hayflick (1965)
Physiological System	Breakdown of endocrine regulatory control of body functions	Miller & Shock (1953)

Source: Adapted from information in Hayflick (1974) and Shock (1977).

and tear" (Sacher, 1966)—"from repeated use parts wear out, defects occur, and the machinery finally comes to a grinding halt"(Shock, 1977, p. 106). The obvious analogy to the wearing out of a machine with continuous use makes this alternative view of biological aging an especially appealing one for coordinating with classical associationism's view of psychological aging. However, as pointed out by Shock (1977), the analogy is far from being perfect. Biological systems, unlike true machines, have the capability of self-repair. For some systems (e.g., the skin), new cells form to replace old ones; for other systems (e.g., muscles), new cells are not formed but other self-repair mechanisms exist.

The reason why biological aging takes place at all is of less importance to us than the fact that, for whatever reason, cells, tissues, and organs obviously do undergo aging in the sense of manifesting some form of degeneration with advancing age. It is the aging of the central nervous system, however, that is commonly inferred to be the causative factor for many behavioral decrements with increasing age. Beginning at about age 35, the human brain, in particular, is often assumed to lose, through death, neurons at the rate of approximately 100,000 a day. At this rate, about 10% of the brain's 10 to 12 billion neuronal cells are presumed lost by age 65. This estimate is with normal aging—the estimate becomes considerably greater when the effect of normal aging is compounded by the effects of pronounced pathology and injury. The loss of neurons is viewed as being fairly diffuse rather than focal (i.e., spread widely rather than being concentrated in only a few brain centers), and it is spread over the various lobes of the cerebral cortex and cerebellum (but leaving relatively unaffected the lower brain centers that maintain the vital functions of life). The loss of many neurons by elderly people would seemingly identify a critical causative factor for many of their behavioral deficits.

However, the evidence regarding universal neuronal loss with increasing age is not conclusive (Diamond, 1978). Diamond's own animal research (summarized in her 1978 review) as well as the animal research by other investigators (see Woodruff, 1975a), indicates that, "In the absence of disease, impoverished environment, or poor nutrition, the nervous system apparently does have the potential to oppose marked deterioration with aging" (Diamond, 1978, p. 70). But, what about the human brain? For the human being, disease, an impoverished environment, and poor nutrition may not be unusual, even with so-called normal aging—at least, not as unusual as they are for pampered laboratory animals. The traditional method of determining the extent of neuronal loss in old age is through postmortem analyses of people who died at different ages. Here, there is evidence supportive of considerable neuronal loss with aging. For example, the results obtained by Devaney and Johnson (1980) indicate this to be true for at least one area of the cerebral cortex, that of the occipital lobe (or primary visual center). Their postmortem analysis revealed that neuron density decreased from about 46 million neurons per gram of brain tissue at age 20 to about 24 million per gram at age 80. However, a different pattern seems to be emerging through the application of an exciting new methodology, that of computerized tomographic brain scans of living people. Although the evidence accumulated thus far has been slight, what has been found is that the amount of neuronal loss in old age may not be very great (Jernigan, Zatz, Feinberg, & Fein 1980).

On the other hand, there is convincing evidence of structural changes in neurons with aging other than changes in their absolute numbers. For example, the loss of dendrites and, therefore, the loss of synaptic connections with aging, has been related to concomitant alterations in neurotransmission (Timiras, 1978). In addition to structural changes, there is good reason to believe that brain cells suffer metabolic interference with aging through their diminished oxygen supply (McFarland, 1968). The consequence is decreased cellular functioning with, once more, concomitant alterations in neurotransmission.

The occurrence of deterioration of the brain, regardless of its structural/-functional format, is certainly not antagonistic to the associationist's explanation of age deficits in behavior. In fact, given the critical importance of the nervous system in mediating the connections between S and R elements, such deterioration offers a reductionistic explanation of many behavioral age deficits. The problem, however, rests in identifying specific structural/functional changes in the nervous system that are fully correlated with specific behavioral changes. The psychology of aging and the biology of aging have simply not advanced together to the point where many precise biological/psychological covariations have been firmly established. One area where the biological changes underlying behavioral changes is often assumed to be well understood is that of sensory psychology. The assumption is that much of the decreased sensitivity to low-intensity sensory stimuli found in elderly people results from structural degeneration at the level of sensory receptors. It is here, of course, that the neural pathways leading to sensory experience originate. There is good reason to believe that such peripheral degeneration does indeed play a major role in decreased visual sensitivity in late adulthood. Moreover, as noted above, there is also reason to believe that central degeneration (i.e., at the level of visual brain centers) may account, at least in part, for this decreased visual sensitivity. However, for the other sensory modalities, the nature of the biological changes leading to reduced sensitivities over the adult lifespan is less than fully understood.

Biopsychological Theories: Implications for Age Deficits in Behavior. A well-established functional change in the central nervous system can serve, however, as the foundation for theorizing broadly about the biological causation of age-related behavioral deficits. One of these functional changes is the slowing of transmission within the nervous system. For some psychologists (Birren, 1964; Birren, Riegel, & Morrison, 1962; Salthouse, 1980a, 1980b), this slowing has, as we will soon see, assumed critical importance. A preliminary question, however, is why this slowing should occur in the first place. There is no certain answer to this question. One possibility, proposed by Salthouse (1980a), attributes the slowing of neural transmission to an increase in neural noise with increasing age (also see Crossman & Szafran, 1956; Gregory, 1957; Welford, 1958). The assumption is that the diminished functioning of aged brain cells either lowers the strength of neural signals or it increases the level of random background activity. In either case, the result is a decrease with aging in the signal-to-noise ratio as well as the slower transmission of neural messages. The implications of the presumed decrease in signal-to-noise ratio for sensory phenomena will be discussed in Chapter 7.

Salthouse (1980a, 1980b; Salthouse & Somberg, in press a) has argued for a universal decrement principle whereby slowing is the primary mechanism responsible for virtually all age differences in behavior. For many years, gerontological psychologists have known that elderly adults are slower than young adults on many kinds of tasks. For example, research on simple motor behaviors has revealed that the elderly are slower in simple movements of the hand toward a target (Hodgkins, 1962), in movements of a lever from side to side (Singleton, 1955), in tapping alternately between targets (Welford, Norris, & Shock, 1969), and in writing words and digits (Birren & Botwinick, 1951). The classic area of research serving to demonstrate the slowing down of behavior with aging is that on reaction time. The elderly are generally slower than the young (e.g., Botwinick, 1971) on simple reaction-time tasks in which a response (e.g., pressing a button) is made as quickly as possible to the onset of a single stimulus (e.g., a tone) and even slower on choice-reaction time tasks (e.g., Botwinick, Brinley, & Robbin, 1959; Goldfarb, 1941) in which Response A (e.g., pressing Button A) is made to Stimulus A (e.g., a tone of a given frequency) and Response B (pressing Button B) to Stimulus B (a tone having a different frequency). It is difficult, however, to accept these slower behaviors at face value as indicating a universal decrement. The difficulty rests in the fact that the magnitude of the deficit in response time varies greatly from task to task. If the decrement is universal, should it not affect all behaviors to the same extent?

Salthouse (1980b) has an interesting answer to this question. His answer may best be seen with respect to the results he obtained, shown in Figure 6.10, for a battery of tests administered to groups of young and elderly subjects, with time per item serving as the dependent variable for each test. Note that the absolute difference in time scores between the age groups varied greatly among the tasks, ranging from 0.16 seconds per item (color naming) to 0.71 seconds per item (digit symbol). Note further that the absolute age difference increased progressively as the time required by young adults increased. As a result, the proportional age difference, that is, the ratio of old to young mean scores, was roughly constant across tasks—ranging from 1.34 to 1.55. Thus, elderly adults average about 1.5 times slower than young adults, regardless of task complexity. With simple tasks, the absolute age difference is slight, but, with complex tasks, the absolute age difference becomes pronounced. It is this proportional constancy that Salthouse believes reflects a universal (generalized to all processes) decrement in the performance of elderly people (see Cerella, Poon, & Williams, 1980, for a similar analysis and rationale for a generalized decrement principle).

The universal decrement principle fits classical associationism's approach to aging deficits nicely. Learning deficits occur because the elderly are slower than the young in rate of rehearsal, and perceptual deficits occur because the neural traces of the elderly are slower than those of the young in clearing the

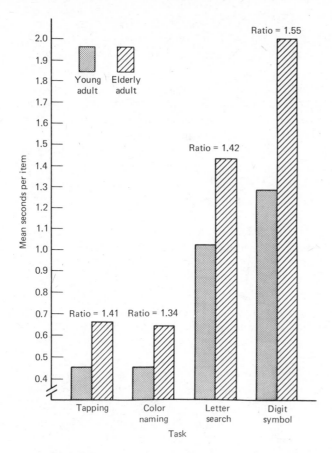

Figure 6.10. Mean time score for young and elderly subjects plotted separately for each of several tasks. The roughly equal ratio in mean scores across tasks supports the universal decrement theory. (Adapted from Salthouse, 1980b, Table 1.)

nervous system. In fact, the principle fits any approach to aging that stresses only temporal age changes in the processes mediating behavior. It conflicts, however, with any approach that stresses other kinds of age changes, as can be seen in the following remarks by Salthouse:

> In fact, if we accept the implication that the central nervous system is functioning at a slower rate in older adults, mental operation time may be the principal mechanism behind age differences in nearly all aspects of cognitive functioning. It certainly seems more reasonable and parsimonious to suggest that the elderly are doing the same things as the young but merely at a slower rate, than to suggest that for some unknown reason they have shifted to a strategy utilizing less imagery, less organization, or less depth of encoding. (1980a, p. 61)

The parsimony of the principle is challenged, however, by the question of just how universal is the slowing down in old age. If truly universal, there should be no exceptions—all behaviors should be affected by the slowing down. But this is clearly not true. For example, Waugh (1980) found no adult-age differences in the rate of reading words, and Nebes and Andrews-Kulis (1976) found no adult-age differences in the speed of forming sentences. In addition, Nebes (1978) found that the slower reaction time of elderly subjects appears only when the response required is a manual one (depressing a key in Nebes's study) and not when the response required is a vocal one (saying a designated word at stimulus onset in Nebes's study). Moreover, we discovered in Chapter 2 that there are certain memory experiences that are remarkably age insensitive. Why should they be immune to a universal decrement?

A somewhat related biopsychological theory is that of Surwillo (1963, 1968). The theory draws its empirical support from the correlation found between age differences in reaction time and age differences in the alpha rhythm of the electroencephalogram (EEG). The implication is that the level of cortical arousal, as assessed by frequencies of the alpha rhythm, is lower in elderly adults than in young adults. According to Surwillo, the EEG alpha rhythm is a master timing mechanism in behavior. Information processing in general is assumed to be controlled by the alpha rhythm. Thus, the alpha rhythm serves as a gating mechanism whereby information enters the central nervous system and is analyzed only when the EEG wave provides the appropriate signal. That signal is slower for elderly adults than for young adults, thus accounting for the slowing of many behaviors in elderly people.

An interesting implication of Surwillo's gating theory is that increases in alpha frequencies for elderly people should improve their proficiencies on many kinds of tasks. To test this notion, Woodruff (1975b) succeeded in increasing alpha frequencies somewhat through biofeedback training (i.e., signaling a subject whenever the frequency exceeded some predefined level). However, increments in the speed of responding on a simple reaction-time task were, at best, only modest. Although untested in her study, it seems highly unlikely that other, more complex, behavioral deficits would be alleviated at all by such biofeedback training. On the other hand, there are other kinds of evidence (e.g., Woodruff & Kramer, 1979) to support Surwillow's gating theory. A final decision on its validity must await many other kinds of empirical tests. In the meantime, evidence is accumulating (e.g., Michalewski, Thompson, Smith, Patterson, Bowman, Litzelman, & Brent, 1980; Smith, Thompson, & Michalewski, 1980) to indicate the value of assessing age-related changes in various components of the EEG as subjects perform on different kinds of tasks varying in their complexity and difficulty.

Information Processing and Experimental Aging Research

Organismic Metamodel. As observed by Reese and Overton, the organismic metamodel offers an *active organism metaphor* for psychological theories: "A primary characteristic of this model is its representation of the organism as inherently and spontaneously active, a view of the organism as the source of acts, rather than as the collection of acts initiated by external (peripheral) forces" (1970, p. 133).

Activity as an inherent, spontaneous attribute of the organism is the product of psychological structures (means), far more complex than simple associations, that function purposefully (ends). Thus, structures are not regarded as mere collections of associations derived from the organism's learning history. Instead, a structure is an organized pattern of a particular behavioral system (Piaget, 1970b) for which "purpose or form is primary and heavily determinative (Looft, 1973, p. 32)."

The contrast between mechanistic and organismic perspectives can be seen clearly in their respective approaches to imagery as a learning mnemonic. To the mechanistic psychologist, the use of imagery is a response to an appropriate external stimulus. Its use in learning situations has been shaped by the organism's learning history. To the organismic psychologist images are self-initiated constructions emanating from cognitive structures that are inherent components of the organism's form and that function purposefully in the sense of guiding the organism to some anticipated end state or objective.

Translation of the Active Organism Metaphor to Information-Processing Concepts. The human information processing system is postulated to possess inherent structures and processes that regulate the registration, transformation (or encoding), storage, and retrieval of information (i.e., knowledge) the organism receives from its external and internal environment. From this perspective, human behavior is viewed in terms of the mechanisms governing the flow of information through the organism.

In many respects, the flow of information through the human organism is like the flow of information through a computer. Like a computer, the human information processor has a central processor, various storage structures, an outputting component, and so on. The analogy with a computer creates an immediate paradox. Information processing presumably offers a conceptual model for psychological theorizing that is consonant with an organismic, or active organism, metamodel—and yet its conceptualization resembles that of still another machine, namely the computer (Reese, 1973a, 1973b)! There is, however, a key distinction between the processing system of a human being and that of a computer. This rests on the fact that the human processor participates actively in the construction of its own knowledge, or cognitive, content. The computer is limited to what it has been programmed to process. The human-processing system does not have a similar constraint. It may indeed be modeled in many respects by computer simulation. However, the human system itself remains organismic in that it possesses attributes (i.e., the capacity for constructing cognitive contents) that are not inherent in the otherwise close approximations offered by computer simulation.

We should note that not all psychologists agree in their acceptance of information processing as an exemplar of an active organism model. For example, Rychlak (1975) has argued that information-processing principles are basically mechanistic in their form. Such arguments take on special significance when age deficits are explained in terms of information-processing concepts. We will discover in the final section of this chapter that age deficits in information processing are usually accepted as being the consequence of biological deterioration with increasing age. Thus, the postmaturity developmental model coordinated with an information-processing conceptual model is surprisingly indistinguishable from the postmaturity developmental model coordinated with associationism.

Information Processing as a Conceptual Framework. Information processing, like associationism, is extremely broad in its application. Virtually all of the content areas of experimental psychology are amenable to analysis in terms of its concepts and models, thereby making virtually all of the experimental psychology of aging a potential target for study by information-processing psychologists. A full treatment of an information-processing approach to psychological theory and research is obviously beyond the scope of our coverage (see Lachman et al., 1979, and Solso, 1979, for extensive reviews of information-processing psychology). Instead, we will merely highlight in the remainder of this section some of the basic characteristics of this approach, particularly those characteristics that provide substance for the translation of an active organism into a conceptual framework for theories of human behavior.

These characteristics will be presented in the context of information-processing approaches to memory phenomena. Memory is the content area in which information processing to date has had its greatest impact on the experimental psychology of aging. Along the way we will attempt to demonstrate how these characteristics eventually guide thinking about age-related changes in behavior and lead to experimental procedures that offer the means of testing the age sensitivity of specific structures and processes. Details about relevant studies will be reserved for Chapter 9.

Memory Versus Learning. The concept of learning is largely missing from information-processing psychology (an important exception will soon be noted). Learning often connotes rote practice on a task in which proficiency of performance improves progressively with practice. This connotation fits nicely, for example, the events that took place when you *learned* to ride a bicycle—you had the intent to master the skill and you practiced long and hard. But it does not fit the *memory* you still have of the first bad spill you had while learning. The very act of perceiving that event resulted in a *memory trace* that remains highly *retrievable,* or accessible, after many years—and neither intent to learn nor practice were necessary for the trace's registration in memory. In effect, a memory trace of an event, or *episode,* in one's life is a residue of the perceptual analysis the event receives as input to the total processing system. Thus, *episodic memory,* or the memory of personally experienced events (e.g., the first bad spill off a bicycle), reflects a basic continuity between perception and cognition, or knowledge, and demonstrates the wholistic functioning of the human being stressed by the organismic metamodel. Moreover, how the organism perceives the event determines what components of the event will be *encoded* and retained as a memory trace and how well these components will be remembered. This analysis is in full agreement with the concept of an active subject. Not surprisingly, research on episodic memory is one of the major activities of information-processing psychologists, including those who are working in the experimental psychology of aging.

Craik (1977) has made a valiant effort to clarify the distinction between learning and memory. His effort is well worth repeating here:

> Running parallel to the change in emphasis from S-R to information-processing theories, there has been a change in emphasis from studies of learning to studies of memory. Within the general framework of S-R theories, human learning and retention have been described and analyzed in terms of interference theory (e.g., Postman, 1961; Postman & Underwood, 1973); this theory focuses attention on the hypothesized association between stimuli and responses (or, at least, between their internal representations). Thus, empirical work in this tradition has been directed toward elucidating the factors relevant to the acquisition and breakdown of the associative bond; "learning" is the formation of new associations and "forgetting" is their loss or inhibition. In human learning, much of the experimental work has used the paired-associate paradigm in which stimuli and responses are verbal units—numbers, letters, words, or nonsense syllables; short lists of such stimulus-response pairs are typically presented for several learning trials and this acquisition phase is then followed by a task to measure retention or transfer. By way of contrast, information-processing studies of memory have more often involved situations in which the material to be learned is presented for one trial only—the focus has thus been on factors which affect the subject's *memory* for once-presented events: factors concerned with registration, storage, and retrieval of the events (pp. 384–385).

We will follow Craik's distinction in the remainder of this book. Thus, aging studies dealing with paired-associate and serial learning (plus retention and transfer) will be reviewed in our learning chapter (Chapter 8), whereas studies dealing with free recall and several other tasks will be reviewed in our memory chapter (Chapter 9). In addition, aging research dealing with conditioning and motor skills will be reviewed as part of learning. These assignments seem appropriate. Conditioning has long been viewed as a kind of S-R learning, as has motor-skill acquisition.

Our distinction between learning and memory is obviously arbitrary and imperfect. Free recall may certainly be analyzed in terms of S-R associations, and the assignment of it to the class of memory phenomena becomes dubious when we deal with multiple trial free-recall learning (e.g., the study by Laurence, 1966, cited in Chapter 2) in which the material is certainly presented for more than one trial. Similarly, we will discover in Chapter 9 that paired-associate learning may be analyzed as an episodic memory phenomenon, and we will discover in Chapter 8 that classical conditioning need not be viewed in S-R, rote-learning terms. In fact, many of today's psychologists view it in terms of information-processing principles and concepts. Hopefully, you will be able to tolerate the imperfection of the way in which we will be handling the learning-memory distinction.

Structures and Processes: Theories and Models of a Memory System. One of the fundamental characteristics of any information-processing theory is the

postulation of both structures and processes as mediators for the flow of information. It is here that the analogy of the human-processing system to a computer is most striking. Structure conforms to the computer's hardware and
processes to the computer's software. The close interaction between structures
and processes in the flow of information is especially apparent for memory
phenomena. As illustrated in Figure 6.11, any model of the human memory
system requires the use of two kinds of structures, operative and storage. Specific models differ in terms of the number of storage structures they require and
in the attributes they assign to both kinds of structures.

An operative structure provides the space for conducting such processes as
the encoding of information in the form of a memory trace. Most models of
memory assume that there is only one such structure, that of a *central processor,*
or executive control unit, which is the site for the initiation and regulation of
most cognitive processes, including those of perception and memory. The central processor is generally assumed to have a limited capacity for conducting
effortful activities and that capacity is commonly assumed to diminish with
increasing age over the adult lifespan. Consequently, performance on tasks
calling for cognitive effort is likely to be adversely affected by increasing age.

A storage structure provides the space for holding on to, and gaining
access to, information that has been encoded as a memory trace. At least three
separate, but interacting, stores appear to be components of every memory
model invented by information processing psychologists (see Figure 6.11). The
first is a *sensory store* that is modality specific. That is, there is one store for
visual input, another for auditory input, and so on. It is in this store that
sensory stimuli are registered, retained briefly (often less than a second) in their
sensory format (e.g., as a pattern of retinal stimulation), and acted on by perceptual processes (the feature analysis and matching processes identified in
Figure 6.11; these processes will be discussed in Chapter 7). Questions arise
quite naturally both about the capacity of this store (i.e., how much sensory
information can it hold at any one time) and about the duration of information

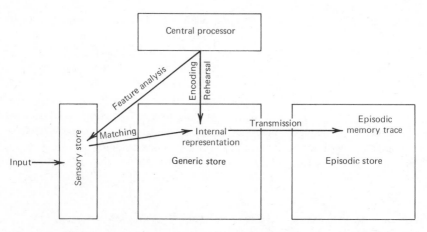

Figure 6.11. The interaction between operative and storage structures that are components
of any information-processing model of the human memory system.

retained in this sensory format. Answers to these questions are obtained through highly innovative and sophisticated procedures that will be described in Chapter 9. Not surprisingly, these procedures have been used with elderly subjects to determine the age sensitivity of sensory stores with respect to both their capacities and the durations of their contents. Unfortunately, the results have been somewhat ambiguous, as we will see in Chapter 9.

The second store is that of *generic memory* (Tulving, 1972). It is a storehouse of permanent knowledge about digits, letters, words, concepts, facts, and rules. Such knowledge is stored without an autobiographical record of when and where it was acquired. When and where, for example, did you learn the name of the line configuration making up the printed letter A, the meaning of the word *king*, the attributes of a bird that make both a robin and a penguin exemplars of that concept, the fact that St. Louis is the largest city in Missouri, and the rules for long division?

The huge amount of information held in the generic store presents a problem analogous to that of a library containing thousands of books. Access to any one book would be grossly inefficient if the books were stored randomly on shelves. To avoid such inefficiency, assignments to shelves follow an organizational plan whereby categories (e.g., Psychology) are created and exemplars (i.e., specific books) of each category are stored in close proximity to one another. A similar principle has been applied to the shelving of concepts (and the words that represent those concepts) in generic memory (Collins & Quillian, 1969). The organizational plan is assumed to be a hierarchical one in which concepts are arranged from the general to the less general and on down to highly specific exemplars of each concept (e.g., as illustrated for the concept of bird in Figure 6.12).

Two questions of special significance to the experimental psychology of aging may be raised about generic memory. The first concerns the means by

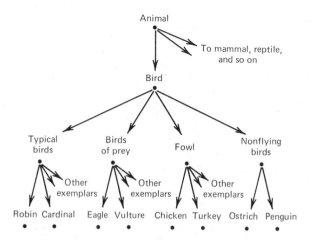

Figure 6.12. Hypothetical organizational plan for storing information in an individual's generic memory. The hierarchial nature of the plan (from superordinate to subordinates to exemplars) is illustrated for the superordinate concept of birds.

which generic information is acquired initially. Unfortunately, little is known about the underlying learning process. Incidentally, it is here that information-processing psychology does need to consider learning processes, whether or not the products are viewed in terms of associative bonds. Whatever the nature of this learning, its efficacy appears to be greatest during childhood. It is then that a large amount of generic information is acquired, much of it without intentionality and without having to be taught in any formal sense. Nevertheless, there is no doubt that accretions to the store can, and do, take place throughout the lifespan. The second question concerns the stability of knowledge within the store. Here both scientific evidence and everyday observation tell us that generic information is remarkably robust and resistant to forgetting over the entire lifespan. For example, once *king* is firmly established in generic form, there is little reason to doubt that it will persist through old age. This observation is consistent with the fact that performance on vocabulary components of intelligence tests show little, if any, deficit in old age. Memory problems of the elderly seldom refer to generic memory. Instead, the usual reference is to difficulties encountered in the third basic storage structure of all memory models.

This third structure is no stranger to us. It is that of *episodic memory* (Tulving, 1972). Unlike generic memory, episodic memory deals with autobiographical information: "The essence of an episodic memory is that it recaptures the temporal and spatial context of a person's past experience" (Lachman et al., 1979, p. 215). In other words, it retains information about personally experienced episodes. In a laboratory context, one such episode might be *king's* presence as a to-be-remembered item in a lengthy free-recall list. *King*, of course, is not learned in the laboratory—it was acquired years before and stored in generic memory forevermore. What is now acquired, or rather remembered, is the occurrence of that word in a particular temporal-spatial context (i.e., as part of a list practiced on a given day in a given laboratory). This occurrence is appropriately encoded and transmitted as a memory trace to the episodic store. Conversely, to forget *king's* episodic representation in no way means that *king's* generic representation has been forgotten.

The laboratory researcher's interest in list-inclusion episodes rests in the assumption that these episodes simulate those of real life—such episodes as remembering whether or not you took your prescribed medicine in the morning. These are the kinds of episodic events the elderly usually have in mind when they refer to their memory problems. Although the validity of this simulation can be questioned on ecological grounds, it can scarcely be denied that age deficits are found for list-inclusion episodes. Although laboratory studies may overestimate the magnitude of age deficits in episodic memory, they may, nevertheless, serve effectively to identify the reason why deficits of any magnitude occur in everyday episodic memory experiences.

Also shared by all memory models are the perceptual processes needed to transform physical sensory information into a psychological representation. (These perceptual processes will be discussed more fully in Chapter 7.) Thus, *king*, as a typical item in a free-recall list, begins its entry into the memory system as a visual pattern projected on the retina (assuming visual presentation of the list items). There, its physical features are analyzed and compared with the features of thousands of words stored in the subject's generic memory. A match is soon found between *king*'s physical features and the features of *king* stored permanently in memory. Some of these permanent features of *king* are then selected for encoding as the item's episodic memory trace, and the trace per se is transmitted to the episodic store.

Specific Models of Memory: Dual Store and Levels of Processing. The remaining issues confronting any memory model concern the durability, or permanence, of the episodic trace and the retrievability of that trace after it has been stored. Memories clearly differ in their durability and their accessibility. But, what accounts for such variability? It is at this point that specific models part company and take different routes in answering this question. Our interest is in two major models that have offered different answers. The first is the dual-store model advanced by Atkinson and Shiffrin (1968); the other is the levels-of-processing (or depth-of-processing) model (Craik & Lockhart, 1972) we met briefly in Chapter 5. Each of these models has greatly influenced experimental aging research. We will examine the main characteristic of each model in this section, and we will review aging studies pertinent to each model in Chapter 9.

The dual-store model postulates an additional episodic store, a *short-term store*. It serves as a buffer between the sensory store and the episodic store we identified earlier and called the *long-term store* in the dual-store model, as illustrated in Figure 6.13.

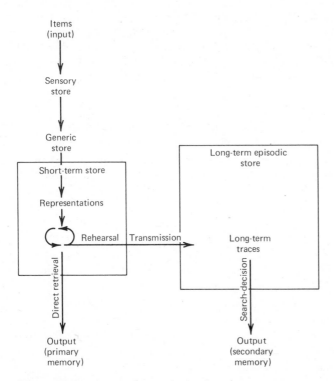

Figure 6.13. A dual-store model of episodic memory containing separate, but interacting, short-term (primary) and long-term (secondary) components.

According to the dual-store model, representations of items (usually in the form of sounds) (Conrad, 1964) are transmitted directly to the short-term store immediately after they have been perceived. Once in the store, the representations experience one of three possible outcomes. The first is simply that they may be forgotten without leaving a record of their entry into the memory system. The store itself is viewed by its proponents as having a limited capacity. New representations generated by ongoing perceptual activity may be entering the store. To make room for these new entries, something has to give. Prior entries may have to be displaced and, therefore, lost, or forgotten, from the store. The limited capacity of the short-term store may be contrasted with the virtually unlimited capacity of the long-term store. It may be argued that once information reaches the long-term store as an episodic memory trace, it is never lost in the sense of being booted out of the store. Forgetting, instead, is likely to occur for reasons of retrieval failure. That is, a search initiated by the active organism is unable to find the stored information. The second possible outcome is that the representations may be rehearsed. Rehearsal has two objectives: (1) it serves to block off the entry of further information into the short-term store, thereby maintaining the presence within the store of current representations, and (2) it also serves to encode these representations further (e.g., semantically) and to transmit the resulting traces to the long-term store where they become retrievable even after lengthy retention intervals. Finally, representations may be retrieved directly from the short-term store. Two kinds of retrieval operations are possible. The first is direct printout of the store's content, as in a test of memory span. The second is a scanning process in which the stored representations of prior inputs to the memory system are searched to determine the presence or absence of a particular representation. For example, suppose you hear a television sportscaster say, "Today's winners in the National League were the Dodgers, Padres, Reds, Cardinals, Pirates, and Cubs." Then someone in another room asks you, "Did the Braves win today?" Your no answer cannot be given until you have scanned the content of your store and discovered the absence of a Braves's representation.

Several of these outcomes are nicely illustrated in the familiar experience of looking up a telephone number for dialing purposes. You often discover that several digits of the number are forgotten (i.e., displaced from the short-term store) on the way from the telephone to the dial. To avoid such forgetting, you may find yourself repeating the digits as you bridge the gap between reading them and dialing them. That is, you maintain the information by rehearsing it. Finally, a printout occurs in the form of actually dialing the remembered sequence. For numbers that are called rarely, there is no need to rehearse them to the point that they become stored in long-term memory—it would only be unnecessary cognitive effort that would add to the clutter of information stored in that component. Of course, it is a different matter for the telephone number of a relative or close friend. Here the frequent dialing makes it worth the effort to rehearse the number sufficiently to assure its placement in the long-term store from where it may be retrieved on demand.

The combined operations of the short-term store make up what is commonly called *primary memory*, whereas the combined operations of the long-term store make up what is commonly called *secondary memory*. The distinction between primary and secondary memory preceded the advent of information-processing psychology by many years, having been introduced by William James (1890). However, the distinction had little impact on experimental psychology until it was reintroduced by Waugh and Norman (1965) and subsequently incorporated into the dual-store model of memory. Of great interest to gerontologists are the relative contributions of primary and secondary memory to the decreased memory proficiency of elderly people. A popular belief (Craik, 1977) is that primary memory is only slightly age sensitive, whereas secondary memory is highly age sensitive. This is indeed an intriguing proposition. However, it is also one that is very difficult to test. The difficulty rests in the fact that performance on most memory tasks reflects contributions from both primary and secondary memory. Consequently, an observed age deficit in overall performance could be due to either component alone or to both components. We discovered this difficulty earlier when we considered a study that examined age differences in span length for words of varying frequency. On the surface, length of memory span seems to measure the capacity of a subject's short-term store. Thus, the modest age deficits commonly observed in span lengths could be viewed as indicating a slight decrement with increasing age in the capacity of that store, deficits seemingly attributable to primary memory. However, this view ignores the possibility that some of the items in a memory span string are processed sufficiently, especially by young adults, to be transmitted to, and retrieved from, the long-term store (i.e., a secondary memory contribution to overall performance on a span task). This was our argument in interpreting the results of the study cited in Chapter 5. An age difference in organizing words into units larger than single items, a secondary memory phenomenon, was seen as contributing to the observed age deficit in span length.

To many psychologists who follow the dual-store model, the best available means of isolating the separate contributions of primary and secondary memory to overall performance is through the use of the free-recall task. The task, therefore, permits separate evaluations of age deficits for primary and secondary memory. The logic behind this procedure will be examined in Chapter 9 along with the results of aging studies making use of it.

The starting point for Craik and Lockhart's (1972) levels-of-processing model is the model's rejection of a separate short-term store. That is, the model assumes that there is only one episodic memory store. What is transmitted to that store is contingent on the depth of the perceptual processing, or analysis, conducted on to-be-remembered items, such as *king* as a component of a free-recall list. We discovered earlier that the depth of processing falls on a shallow to deep continuum. Shallow processing means that only *king*'s sensory features (i.e., its phonemic and orthographic components) stored in generic memory are perceived and encoded as the memory trace transmitted to the episodic store. A sensory-based memory trace is assumed to be fragile and susceptible to rapid forgetting. Deep processing means that *king* is perceived and encoded in terms of its meaning, or semantic features, that are stored in generic memory. A semantic-based memory trace is assumed to be robust and temporally durable.

Our interest in the levels-of-processing model rests largely in its ready application to explanations of age deficits in episodic memory. According to Craik (1977), elderly adults simply engage spontaneously in less deep processing than do young adults. Elderly adults, therefore, characteristically establish less durable memory traces, or records of events, than do young adults. Tests of Craik's hypothesis have employed various innovative procedures that deviate considerably from the standard trial-by-trial procedure employed in traditional learning studies. These tests, however, have failed to provide any firm evidence in support of Craik's hypothesis (to be reviewed in Chapter 9). Healthy, cognitively alert adults of *all* ages appear to process to-be-remembered words in terms of their semantic features.

There is another component of the levels-of-processing model that has considerably greater relevance for explanations of age deficits in episodic memory than does the shallow-to-deep component. This component stresses the existence of two different kinds of rehearsal activity that follow the initial processing of to-be-remembered words. The first is called *maintenance rehearsal*. In effect, it amounts to the rote repetition of a word's auditory representation. Such rehearsal is seen as perpetuating a word in consciousness (i.e., it is attended to), but, at the same time, as having little effect on increasing the eventual retrievability of that word's long-term trace. Maintenance rehearsal merely serves to keep a word available for immediate recall without increasing its availability for delayed recall. Thus, a used-only-once telephone number receives maintenance rehearsal while awaiting its dialing—without leaving a more durable memory trace. The functional equivalence of maintenance rehearsal to rote rehearsal, as that concept is employed by associationists, is obvious. However, the postulated absence of a direct relationship between the amount of rehearsal and delayed recall proficiency runs contrary to one of associationism's basic tenets, namely, that repetition per se leads to gains in associative strength. There is some evidence with young adults (e.g., Glenberg & Adams, 1978) to indicate that the retrievability of a memory trace does increase somewhat as the amount of maintenance rehearsal increases. Nevertheless, the gain is not nearly as pronounced as would be expected from the perspective of classical associationism. At any rate, age changes in the amount of maintenance rehearsal are unlikely to account for many of the age deficits in memory phenomena reported in the literature that will be surveyed in Chapter 9.

By contrast, the other kind of rehearsal activity, *elaboration*, is of considerable interest to experimental aging researchers. Elaboration is essentially a still deeper form of semantic analysis whereby the semantic features of a to-be-remembered word "trigger associations, images or stories on the basis of the subject's past experience with the word" (Craik & Lockhart, 1972, p. 675). In effect, elaboration is a further analysis of information that has already been analyzed deeply in the sense of identifying semantic features, as illustrated in Figure 6.14. Thus, elaboration is akin to what stage analysts call mediated rehearsal, only it is viewed as being regulated by a subject's own control processes rather than by the transfer of a generalized habit. Given the well-known existence of age differences in the use of imaginal mnemonics, the implication

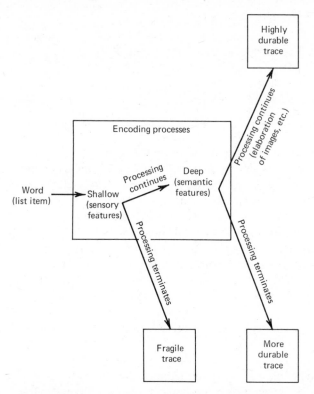

Figure 6.14. A levels-of-processing conceptualization of variations in the encoding of memory traces. Processing may be seen to vary along a shallow-to-deep (sensory-features-to-semantic-features) dimension. In addition, deep features may be further processed by elaboration. Durability of a memory trace is assumed to vary in accordance with the kind of processing entering into the formation of that trace.

is that age changes in the extent of elaborative rehearsal may account for much of the age deficit in human memory (in agreement, of course, with a similar implication in stage analysis with regard to mediated rehearsal). We will explore this line of reasoning and its supporting evidence more fully in Chapter 9. Interestingly, we will discover then that the shift in perspective from stage analysis to levels of processing has brought with it a shift in tasks. The age sensitivity of elaborative rehearsal is usually tested with free-recall and recognition-memory tasks rather than with the traditional paired-associate task favored by stage analysts in their study of mediated rehearsal. The use of different tasks, however, does not necessarily mean that the elaborative process itself is any different from what it is in traditional paired-associate learning.

Stages of Mental Operations. The breakdown of a processing system into component structures and processes provides a ready source of hypotheses about age sensitivity. In addition, there is another way of conceptualizing a processing system that is especially valuable in thinking about age differences in information processing. To processing psychologists, the total mental operations

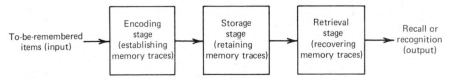

Figure 6.15. Sequence of processing stages intervening between input and output during performance on a memory task.

intervening between input into the system and output may be viewed in terms of a sequence of stages. The stages represent the separate mental operations performed on the input during its flow through the processing system. Now questions arise as to which stage, or stages, in the sequence is age sensitive.

Our present discussion of stages will be limited to those of the memory system. (The stages entering into perception will be examined in Chapter 7.) The major stages of memory (see Figure 6.15) are those of *encoding, storage,* and *retrieval.* For some years, a fairly convincing argument was made (e.g., Schonfield & Robertson, 1966) that retrieval is the major, it not the only, age-sensitive stage of memory. That is, elderly adults were assumed to establish and maintain memory traces adequately, but they suffered memory problems, nevertheless, because of their inability to recover those traces, at least at the level displayed by young adults.

This argument is intriguing in that it can be tested empirically. The test calls for the use of the deletion method described in Chapter 5. The rationale for applying this method demands two fundamental assumptions, both of which are commonly made by memory psychologists: (1) recall of an item requires an active search of the episodic store to locate its trace and (2) recognition of an item bypasses the need for an active search of the store's contents. It is this bypass that accounts for the usual superiority of recognition over recall in memory tests. [Incidentally, associationists account for the superiority by assuming that the threshold value for recognition of the R element of an association is lower than the threshold value for recall of the same R element (see Kausler, 1974)]. If retrieval is the only age-sensitive process, then an age deficit should be manifested in the recall of list items but not in the recognition of those same items. This suggests a simple means of applying the deletion method. All that is needed is to contrast the adult-age difference in the recall of items with the age difference in the recognition of those items. The search process present in the recall test should, in principle, be deleted in the recognition test. In our review of aging studies on recall and recognition (Chapter 9), we will discover that the age deficit is usually less for recognition than for recall, which is in agreement with the hypothesized age sensitivity of retrieval. However, the deficit does not disappear when memory is tested by recognition, thus implying the age sensitivity of one or more other stages besides retrieval.

Measurement of Mental Time. The final characteristic of information-processing psychology we will consider is derived from the concept of mental stages. The operation in a given stage is assumed to take real time to complete. If an experimental procedure permits the isolation of that stage from other stages, then the time lapsing between input and output on the task permitting isolation measures the mental time required to complete the operation indigenous to that stage. Thus, reaction time, the time intervening between the onset of stimulus input and the onset of behavioral output, assumes critical importance as a measurement of mental time. Two operations differing in their mental times presumably differ in their mental complexities. Similarly, if the same mental operation takes more time to complete for elderly subjects than for young subjects, then the operation (and stage of processing) may be regarded as slowing down with aging and is, therefore, age sensitive.

In some cases, the mental time for one stage in a sequence may be impossible to assess directly. That is, its operations cannot be isolated from the operations bound to the other stages in the processing sequence. However, if the other stages can be isolated, and their mental times measured, then the remaining stage may have its mental time measured indirectly. This indirect procedure for measuring reaction time is called the subtractive method. It is an old method, dating back to Donders (1868/1869), a Dutch physiologist. However, the method had been relegated to the methodological scrap heap for many years before it was resurrected by contemporary information-processing psychologists. The subtractive method works in the manner shown in Figure 6.16. In the example shown in this figure, the illusive stage is Stage 2. Input A of a particular task requires both Stage 1 and Stage 2 to be processed. Reaction time to Input A, therefore, measures the mental time for the combined stages. Input B of a modified task requires only Stage 1 to be processed. Reaction time to Input B, therefore, measures the mental time for Stage 1 alone. Accordingly, the difference in reaction times for the two inputs estimates the mental time for performing the operation at Stage 2.

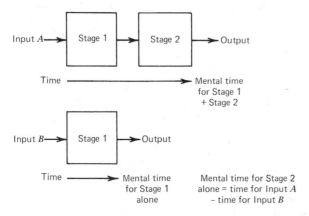

Figure 6.16. Schematic representation of the subtraction method's use in measuring indirectly the mental time for performing the mental operations in Stage 2 of a two-stage sequence. The time to perform the mental operations in Stage 1 is measured directly.

Both direct and indirect assessments of mental time have been valuable tools in information-processing research and in extensions of that research to age differences in processing. Some of the most effective applications of these assessments have been in research on age differences in pattern recognition, information-processing's perceptual component, as we will see in Chapter 7. Other important applications will be encountered in later chapters.

Organismic Model of Development

Prematurity Phase of Development. Piaget's theory of cognitive development (e.g., 1970a) is the generally accepted prototype for an organismic model of development, at least for development over the prematurity segment of the lifespan. According to this well-known theory, cognitive development progresses discontinuously from early childhood to early adulthood. The discontinuity is characterized by the appearance of a sequence of stages (e.g., preoperational and concrete operational), each of which is qualitatively distinctive from the stages preceding it. The order of stages is invariant (i.e., the same for all human beings) and irreversible (i.e., always unidirectionally in the same sequence). The invariance and unidirectionality are teleologically determined (i.e., development moves inexorably toward a final goal—the mature state of the organism). In Piagetian theory, the final cognitive state is one characterized by the presence of formal operations.

A given stage, say the concrete operational, differs qualitatively from the prior stage, say the preoperational, in a fundamental way. The cognitive structures, or schemes (as they are labeled in Piagetian theory), that emerge because of maturational-environmental interactions are qualitatively distinguishable in a later stage from the cognitive structures present in an earlier stage. Consequently, the cognitive operations, or mental surrogates of overt behaviors, emanating from the later structures are also qualitatively distinguishable from the cognitive operations emanating from the earlier structure. The older child is now capable of performing cognitive operations that were not possible, even in an inefficient way, at an earlier age. The contrast with a mechanistic model of development is striking. In the mechanistic model, growth consists only of quantitative increments in behavior that are brought about by age-related increases in the proficiency of associative processes and increases in experiential background. This basic distinction between qualitative and quantitative variation in development was touched on in Chapter 2 and illustrated schematically in Figure 2.12. Another look at that figure should help to clarify the qualitative versus quantitative change concept.

Our concern, of course, is with developmental changes in information processing over the course of the prematurity segment of the lifespan. Do these changes correspond to the kind of qualitative changes stressed in a Piagetian-like theory? Specifically, our interest is in operative structures, that is, structures from which cognitive processes, or operations, originate. (Storage structures by definition are expected to show only quantitative changes. Capacity for storage simply increases with increasing age.) Of particular interest is the central processor. Does it change qualitatively from early to late childhood so that the older child is capable of vastly different cognitive operations than the younger child? Alternatively, the change may be only a quantitative one. That is, the older child performs the same operations as the young child—but at a level of considerably greater proficiency.

In a careful evaluation of the evidence relevant to the qualitative versus quantitative distinction, Estes (1978), a prominent information-processing psychologist, reached the conclusion that a Piagetian-like model of development does not fit the development of information-processing capabilities. He noted that, although many investigators who deal with the development of information-processing abilities do make use of the results of research in the Piagetian tradition, they do so without adopting the formal theoretical framework of a progression of qualitatively different stages (see Farnham-Diggory, 1972, for a number of examples).

The problems encountered in fitting the stage model of development to information processing are especially apparent in the area of visual processing, an area of research we will survey in Chapter 7. Here, the evidence reveals that most of the differences between children and young adults rest at the level of rate of processing, a quantitative dimension, rather than at the level of qualitatively distinguishable processes that are regulated by sequentially ordered discrete structures (see reviews by Hoving, Spencer, Robb, & Schulte, 1978, and by Wickens, 1974).

One example should serve to illustrate the dilemma facing the qualitative-stage theorist. It comes from research on a visual-search task in which a subject is given a target letter to find within an array of letters (Neisser, 1963). The search continues until the target letter is located. The subject receives a score that expresses the average time, per letter in the array, to find the target letter. This score may then be compared with another score for the same subject, this time for a task in which there are two target letters, either one of which may be embedded in the array. Surprisingly, after extensive practice, young adults do not differ in their search rates for these two kinds of tasks. The implication is that the young adult conducts a parallel search for both target letters simultaneously rather than a considerably slower serial search in which the array is searched for one target letter and then for the other. Even more surprising, Gibson and Yonas (1966) found that children are equally characterized by a parallel search process, given multiple target letters. Thus, there is no reason to infer the occurrence of qualitative changes from childhood to young adulthood in the cognitive operations underlying this aspect of visual information processing. On the other hand, children are characterized by slower search rates than those of young adults, regardless of the nature of the target. This quantitative behavioral change, of course, is highly compatible with a mechanistic model of development.

Piagetian-like stage theory has obviously not fared well as information-processing's coordinated developmental model for the prematurity segment of the lifespan. Its failure has resulted in the consideration of several alternative nonmechanistic models of development by organismically oriented psychologists (e.g., Klahr & Wallace, 1976). It is too early to determine the success of these alternatives.

Postmaturity Phase of Development. Explanation of age deficits in terms of a teleological progression toward a final end-state requires "changing the time variable from a positive to a negative value" (Reese, 1973b, p. 474). The result is a mirror-image principle in which the organism's cognitive end-state regresses or returns to a prematurity stage of development. From the perspective of the organismic developmental model, the sequence of development over the entire lifespan is as represented schematically in the top panel of Figure 6.17. (This figure is an elaboration of the representation shown earlier in the bottom panel of Figure 2.12.) Note that the cognitive structure has regressed to what it was qualitatively in childhood. The consequence should, therefore, be a qualitative change by late adulthood in the cognitive operations regulating behavior, a change marked by a return to a more primitive form of functioning characteristic of childhood. This is indicated in Figure 6.17 by the regression from Stage

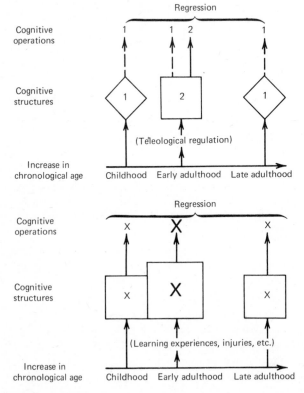

Figure 6.17. Regression in old age to an earlier stage of development as viewed from an organismic, Piagetian-like model (top panel) and from the mechanistic model (bottom panel).

2 to Stage 1 and the accompanying regression to the cognitive operations characteristic of Stage 1.

The organismic lifespan developmental model shown in Figure 6.17 has been accepted by some psychologists. Changes in various perceptual phenomena have been especially prone to stage regression explanations (Pollack & Atkeson, 1978; Werner, 1957). One example is for a class of illusions known as Type II illusions. They are illusions, such as the Usnadze illusion, that increase in magnitude from early childhood to early adulthood and then decrease in magnitude from early adulthood to late adulthood (Pollack & Atkeson, 1978). The increase during childhood is readily interpreted by means of sequential changes in cognitive structures (Piaget, 1969). Of greater importance to us is the fact that the decrease during adulthood is believed to be the consequence of stage regression [i.e., a return to the structure present in childhood (Pollack & Atkeson, 1978)]. Type I illusions show the opposite pattern—a decrease in magnitude from childhood to early adulthood followed by an increase from early to late adulthood (to be discussed more fully in Chapter 7). Interestingly, Pollack and Atkeson believe that increases in magnitude over the adult segment of the lifespan result from biological changes with aging, in agreement with the mechanistic model of aging.

There is an intriguing question that follows quite naturally from the cognitive regression principle. What is the course of adult development for logical thinking, the content area that has formed the core of Piagetian stage theory? Piagetian theorists have generally assumed that the development of logical thought ends before adulthood is reached (Flavell, 1970) and, until recently, have ignored the possibility that mirror-image development occurs over the course of the remainder of the lifespan. The possibility of a regression in logical thought has, in fact, become the subject of a number of recent aging studies. Is it possible that an adult once capable of functioning at the level of formal operations now finds it difficult to function at the level of concrete operations? As we will discover in Chapter 10, what age deficits there are in logical thought are more likely to be performance deficits than true deficits in competence.

Most psychologists feel that true stage regressions in late adulthood are highly unlikely. Various critics (e.g., Flavell, 1970) have pointed out that behavioral changes with aging do not conform to the changes expected on the basis of a Piagetian-like stage regression. They are: (1) not universal (i.e., there are many exceptions to age deficits); (2) not necessarily irreversible (i.e., many deficits may be alleviated by appropriate training); (3) not necessarily movements toward child-like operations (i.e., most deficits simply reflect less proficient manifestations of young-adult cognitive operations); and (4) subtle rather than dramatic (the latter would be the case if there were true stage regressions).

Overall, the full sweep of lifespan changes in structures and operations, at least as they are represented in information-processing psychology, seems to be explained better by the course of events illustrated schematically in the bottom panel of Figure 6.17. (This figure is an elaboration of the representation shown earlier in the top panel of Figure 2.12.) Our concern, of course, is really with postmaturity age changes in the concepts relevant to information-processing psychology. It is here that a continuity-based, quantitative-change-only, model of development seems unavoidable as the one to be coordinated with information-processing's approach to psychological theorizing (Reese, 1973b). Mental processes simply become quantitatively less proficient as the organism ages biologically.

We are, therefore, left with a mixed metaphor for information processing—an organismic one to represent the active organism's behaviors and a mechanistic one to represent the lifespan development of that organism, especially the postmaturity segment of the lifespan. Paradoxically, at the level of a coordinated developmental model, there seems to be little, if any, difference between associationism and information processing. Reliance on a mechanistic model of adult development is really nothing more than an expression of faith in biological reductionism. It is hard to deny that psychological concepts, regardless of their theoretical origins, must ultimately be reducible to underlying biological concepts.

Finally, we should note that there is one area of aging in which a stage theory of development departs considerably from the regressive model shown in the top panel of Figure 6.17. Our reference is to personality development. To some psychologists (e.g., Bühler, 1953; Erikson, 1959), personality changes in stages over the entire lifespan. However, the stage found in old age is as unique as is the stage found in any other segment of the lifespan. Thus, old age is not a regression to a second childhood, it is characterized by its own uniqueness of personality development. A current popular stage theory of personality development is that of Levinson (1977, 1978). The theory is decidedly Piagetian in its approach. Personality changes over the lifespan are due to changes in what Levinson calls a "life structure," a concept with attributes much like those of a Piagetian cognitive structure. Changes in this structure are viewed as being qualitative rather than quantitative and as being universal, thus conforming to the expectations of a true cognitive stage theory of development. Interestingly, Hultsch and Plemons (1979) have demonstrated that age changes in the "life structure" are interpretable from the perspective of associationism and the mechanistic model of development. Further discussion of Levinson's stage theory and its reinterpretation by Hultsch and Plemons is not germane to our focus on the experimental psychology of aging.

Summary

The identification and interpretation of age sensitive processes/structures usually involve a metamodel-to-specific-theory hierarchical sequence. A metamodel, or world view, offers a broad perspective for interpreting all natural phenomena, including those of human behavior. Subsumed under a metamodel are both a conceptual model and a developmental model. The conceptual model provides the guidelines for constructing specific psychological theories, regardless of the behavioral phenomenon to be explained. The processes and structures hypothesized by a theory to underlie a particular phenomenon (e.g., paired-associate learning) must be consistent with the concepts and principles of the broader components within which that theory is nested hierarchically, that is, the metamodel and the conceptual or psychological model. The developmental model, in turn, offers the means of conceptualizing the reasons why age changes occur in the processes/structures postulated by a given theory. That is, age sensitive processes/ structures are those components of a theory that undergo changes with age in a manner explainable by the developmental model coordinated with that theory.

Two kinds of conceptual models have competed for dominance in psychology's history—those derived from associationism and those derived from cognitive alternatives to associationism. Associationism is subsumed under a mechanistic metamodel of natural phenomena and coordinated with a mechanistic model of development. By contrast, information processing, the currently popular cognitive alternative to associationism, is subsumed under an organismic metamodel of natural phenomena. However, its coordination with an organismic model of development is questionable. Research directed at identifying age-sensitive processes/structures has been historically, and continues to be, guided by both associationism and information processing. The manipulable independent variables selected for the purpose of identifying age-sensitive processes often depend on the particular theoretical framework within which the phenomena in question are being interpreted (i.e., associationism or information processing).

The basic metaphor for the mechanistic metamodel is that of a Newtonian machine. The metaphor adopts a reactive, or passive, model of man. Classical associationism is the metaphor's transformation into a conceptual model, or framework, for constructing psychological theories. The conceptual model translates force, reaction, and causative factors into stimulus (S) and response (R) concepts.

The primary explanatory concept offered by classical associationism is that of S-R associations, or connections, between internal representations of stimulus and response elements. In many cases, S-R associations are innately established in the organism. Sensory phenomena are explained by the existence of such innate connections. However, a critical contingency in the activation of these connections rests in the intensity, or energy level, of a sensory stimulus. Detection (R element) of a sensory stimulus (S element) depends on the extent to which the stimulus's intensity exceeds the organism's threshold value. With regard to human aging, the emphasis is on decrements with increasing age in the ability to detect weak sensory stimuli. Whatever adult-age differences exist in perception are explained in terms of an age change in stimulus persistence. Neural traces of sensory stimuli are presumed to have longer durations for elderly adults than for young adults.

The main focus of associationism, however, is on learning. Many S-R associations are not innately present in the organism. Instead, they must be built into the machine by the process of learning. According to classical associationism, the learning of S-R associations occurs through repeated rote rehearsals of R elements that are contiguous with the presence of their related S elements. Rehearsal leads to progressive increments in the strength of a given S-R association. Eventually, the strength of that association sufficiently exceeds a threshold value to assure the automatic elicitation of the R element whenever its corresponding S element is presented. Age deficits in learning may be accounted for by the hypothesis that the rate of rehearsal slows down with increasing age, thus promoting slower rates of increments in associative strength.

However, most contemporary associationists have abandoned classical associationism for a more moderate position called stage analysis in which learning is viewed as being a multiple process phenomenon rather than one in which the acquisition of associations is the only process. Processes, such as making responses available for associative learning, are as much a part of learning as is S-R associative learning. Moreover, the acquisition of S-R associations is seen as being frequently accomplished by the use of mediators (e.g., images) that relate S and R elements to one another, thereby bypassing the necessity of rotely rehearsing those elements. The use of mediators reflects the transfer of a generalized habit that extends to all pairs of S-R elements in a task. From this perspective, age deficits in performance on a learning task may result from either the failure to activate the generalized habit (a production deficit) or the diminished ability in late adulthood to construct images and other kinds of mediators (a true mediational deficit).

The paired-associate learning task is a prototypal one for associationists in that it has clearly identified S and R elements. However, all learning tasks, including those of serial and free-recall learning, may be conceptualized in terms of S and R elements even though the S elements must be inferred to exist. The processes entering into the learning of these other tasks are the same as the processes entering into the learning of a paired-associate task. Consequently, the explanation given for age deficits in paired-associate learning applies equally well to age deficits found for these other tasks.

Of further concern in associationism is the retention (or, conversely, the forgetting) of associations once they are learned. In principle, associations are viewed as being retained at full strength over lengthy retention intervals unless the learner encounters new associations that bear an interference relationship with the originally learned associations (new responses paired with the original stimuli). Elderly adults are commonly viewed as being susceptible to greater forgetting of associations than are young adults, presumably owing to their greater interference proneness. The greater interference proneness is also expected to yield greater negative transfer for elderly adults than for young adults in learning the new associations. Both retention and transfer analyses have been greatly expanded by the advent of stage analysis. These expansions have considerable importance for the experimental psychology of aging.

A mechanistic model of development explains age changes in behavior in terms of causative variables that correlate with age. During the prematurity phase of development, the primary causative variable consists of the continuously new environmental situations that provide the growing organism with an increasing repertory of learned behaviors as age increases. During the postmaturity phase of development, the primary causative variable consists of the degeneration of biological structures, particularly those of the nervous system, as age increases. Why degeneration occurs at all is far from being understood. One popular notion is that an aging program is genetically encoded into the organism. However, the exact mechanism of this biological clock remains highly speculative. One biopsychological theory, the universal-decrement theory, stresses that neural degeneration produces a slowing down of all processes and behaviors of the organism.

The organismic metamodel translates into an active organism metaphor that stresses the human organism as a source of acts. Information processing, as the metaphor's conceptual framework for constructing psychological theories, specifies an active organism that selectively acts on the inputs into its total processing system.

Memory served to illustrate the basic characteristics of an information-processing system. Memory involves traces of initial perceptions that persist over time and become available for subsequent recall or recognition. An episodic memory trace, as an internal representation of a previously perceived event, is the product of an encoding process (or operation) performed on perceived information. Any model of a memory system is described in terms of component structures and processes. Two kinds of structures are required; operative and storage. The operative structure is the central processor. It is the locus for conducting such processes as encoding and retrieval as well as being the locus for perceptual processes and processes related to other cognitive activities. The central processor is assumed to have a limited capacity that is at its peak in early adulthood and diminishes by late adulthood. Three kinds of storage structures are part of any memory model. The first is a modality-specific sensory store in which sensory information is retained briefly in its physical format. The second is a generic store that contains knowledge about words, facts, and so on, without retaining an autobiographical record of that knowledge's acquisition. The large amount of generic information demands that it be stored in some efficient manner, such as in hierarchies that are organized from superordinate to subordinates. The third store is an episodic one that retains traces of personally experienced events. The memory problems encountered by elderly people usually refer to episodic memory rather than generic memory.

One specific model of the human memory system, called the dual-store model, distinguishes further between two episodic stores, one for short-term storage and one for long-term storage. The combined operations of the short-term store make up primary memory, whereas the combined operations of the long-term store make up secondary memory. Within this classification, primary memory is viewed as being largely age insensitive, whereas secondary memory is viewed as being highly age sensitive. Another specific model of memory, that of levels of processing, rejects the notion of separate primary and secondary components and stresses, instead, that encoding falls along a shallow-to-deep dimension. The memory trace yielded by shallow processing is composed of sensory features and is believed to be fragile and susceptible to rapid forgetting. The memory trace yielded by deep processing is composed of semantic features and is believed to be highly durable over time. From this perspective, age differences in memory may reflect a decrease with increasing age in the use of deep processing. Another aspect of the levels-of-processing model is the distinction between maintenance rehearsal and elaborative rehearsal. Maintenance rehearsal corresponds somewhat to classical associationism's concept of rote rehearsal and elaborative rehearsal to neoassociationism's concept of mediation through imagery. An elaborated trace is especially accessible to later recovery and utilization. Much of the age deficit in episodic memory seems attributable to the reduced use of elaboration by elderly adults relative to young adults.

A processing system may also be analyzed in terms of sequential stages of mental operations. For a memory system, these stages are those of encoding, storage, and retrieval. The retrieval stage is commonly hypothesized to be highly age sensitive. This hypothesis is tested by the deletion method. The test calls for a contrast between the recall and the recognition of prior-list items. A processing stage is assumed to take time to complete. Assessment of a given stage's time, either directly or indirectly, provides a means of comparing young and elderly subjects in their proficiencies for the operations confined to that stage.

There are difficulties in fitting information processing to a coordinated organismic model of development. This model stresses a teleological progression of cognitive stages in which each stage has its own qualitatively distinctive structures, operations (or processes), and behaviors. Research with children, however, indicates that prematurity age changes in information-processing attributes are more quantitative than they are qualitative. To explain aging deficits in information-processing attributes, an organismic model of development assumes regression in late adulthood to earlier (childhood) cognitive stages. This assumption is contradicted, however, by considerable evidence that indicates elderly adults differ mainly quantitatively from young adults. Consequently, adult-age deficits in information processing are usually explained reductionistically in terms of biological degeneration with increasing age, which is in agreement with the mechanistic model of development.

CHAPTER 7

Sensory Psychology, Perception, and Attention

Sensory psychology is the logical content area for beginning our review of experimental aging research. Experimental aging research began with a famous study dealing largely with age differences in sensory sensitivity, a concept of primary concern in sensory psychology (Scharf, 1975). The pioneering researcher, Sir Francis Galton, succeeded in attracting over 9000 visitors to the International Health Exhibition (London) in 1884 to his laboratory on the exhibition grounds. Amazingly, the visitors paid a slight fee, in contrast to the present practice of paying subjects to participate in a research project, for the privilege of being assessed on 17 different abilities. Included among these abilities were several of a sensory nature, such as the ability to hear tones of varying frequencies (see Birren & Clayton, 1975). Galton (1885) discovered that higher frequency tones became harder to hear as age increased over the adult segment of the lifespan, a finding that has since been replicated many times (Corso, 1971, 1977).

There is another reason for beginning our review with sensory psychology. It is through our senses that we initiate contact with stimulus events and objects in our environment. Age-related changes in sensory sensitivity have obvious implications for the overall adaptability and welfare of elderly people. For example, the inability to detect the presence of a faint odor could result in a disastrous outcome when the odor stems from smoke or a gas leak. A similar disastrous outcome could result from the failure to hear a distant siren warning citizens of a tornado in the vicinity. Given the increasing incidence of sensory defects with increasing age and the extent of degeneration of sense receptors with increasing age, it should not be surprising to discover substantial decrements in sensory sensitivity from early to late adulthood.

In our review, we will approach aging research on sensory sensitivity from two perspectives. The first is that of traditional psychophysics, with its emphasis on threshold values as general indices of sensory sensitivity. As we will discover, this perspective is highly consonant with classical associationism's conceptualization of human behavior and age changes in behavior. The second perspective is that of contemporary signal-detection theory. Here, the emphasis is on the involvement of higher order cognitive processes even in simple sensory behaviors. In this case, the higher order process is that of decision making. Detection of a weak sensory stimulus is viewed as being contingent on an individual's decision-making characteristics as well as on that individual's actual sensory sensitivity. Consequently, age differences in the detection of a stimulus may be due, at least partially, to age differences in that decision-making process.

The question of age changes in sensory sensitivity leads to the further question of age changes in perceptual sensitivity, that is, in the ability to integrate, organize, and interpret the stimuli registered by the senses. Accordingly, the second content area to be reviewed is that of perception. Age-related changes in perceptual sensitivity, like age-related changes in sensory sensitivity, have many implications for the adaptability and welfare of elderly people. For example, diminished proficiency in depth perception for elderly people leads to misjudgments of the nearness of obstacles in the environment, the distance of a step from the ground, and so on. It seems likely that such misperceptions are potent contributing factors to the high degree of accident proneness found for elderly adults. For example, elderly people are involved in nearly 25% of the accidental deaths occurring in the United States, a proportion well above the representation of the elderly in our total population, and their overall accident rate is nearly triple that of most other age-level groups (U.S. Bureau of the Census, 1978).

Our initial concern will be with age differences in classic perceptual phenomena, such as form perception, perceptual constancies, illusions, and so on. For many years experimental psychologists have been testing hypotheses regarding the processes accounting for these phenomena. Our concern will not be with these processes per se. Instead, our interest is in the existence of adult-age differences for many of these phenomena. Some of these age differences are readily explained in terms of age-related deficits in sensory stimulation that accompany age changes in sensory structures. However, age differences for many other phenomena are not so readily related to direct age changes in sensory structures. To explain these age differences, some experimental aging psychologists have relied heavily on a single principle, namely, that of increasing stimulus persistence with increasing age, which is highly consonant with associationism's analysis of perception. Consequently, this principle will be examined carefully in the present chapter, and it will provide the framework for explaining the presence of age differences on a number of specific perceptual phenomena.

Our focus will then shift to age differences in perception as viewed from the perspective of information processing. Here, the emphasis is on perception in terms of pattern-recognition principles and processes. A pattern refers to a collection of stimulus elements that is recognized, or perceived, with respect to its representation in a class of objects. Age differences are analyzed separately for a peripheral, or lower order, stage of pattern recognition in which features of a stimulus input are extracted and a central, or higher order, stage in which those extracted features are subsequently compared and matched with information stored permanently in memory. Biologically, the peripheral stage is assumed to involve lower centers, such as sensory receptors, whereas the central stage is assumed to involve higher stages at the level of association areas in the brain.

As an example of pattern recognition, consider your recognition of the pattern X. At the peripheral stage, you have extracted two intersecting diagonal lines as features. At the central stage, you have matched these features with information in your memory that tells you the pattern corresponds either to a letter of the alphabet, a multiplication sign in arithmetic, or an interaction sign in statistics. How you did perceive it probably depends on a number of factors, including your recent experiences with similar patterns (e.g., reading the content of Chapter 5).

Attention, the final content area to be reviewed in this chapter, bears a close relationship to perception. Our senses are constantly bombarded by many stimuli, only a limited segment of which are attended to and processed for subsequent perception. Most important, it may be argued that the human organism has a limited capacity for the amount of environmental stimulation it can process at any given moment. Attention serves to allocate this limited capacity among simultaneously present stimuli. That is, some stimuli are attended to selectively, whereas others are ignored. The possibility of age differences in selective attention has been of considerable interest to a number of experimental aging psychologists for many years. A popular hypothesis is that elderly adults are easily distracted by irrelevant stimuli at the expense of attention directed at relevant stimuli (i.e., stimuli conveying information essential for effective performance on a task at hand). If true, this would account for performance deficits by elderly adults on many kinds of tasks that require a discrimination between relevant and irrelevant stimuli. Other popular hypotheses are that elderly adults are less proficient than young adults in maintaining attention directed at a sequence of stimuli and in dividing attention between two sources of incoming stimuli. Our review will focus on studies testing these hypotheses, hypotheses that are obviously derived from an information-processing conceptualization of behavior.

Sensory Sensitivity and Psychophysical Research

Age Changes in Threshold Values. Despite their apparent automaticity, inborn associations are not necessarily activated by the presence of their initiating stimuli (or S elements). A critical contingency rests in the intensity, or energy level, of the S element. Thus, a very weak puff of air directed at the eye may not be sufficient to elicit an eyeblink. Similarly, a faint light may not be intense enough to elicit a detection response. Consequently, the physical presence of the light may not be known to a potential observer. Nor may the presence of a weak sound or a slight odor be detected unless they possess sufficient intensity. Just how intense a sensory stimulus must be to be detected provides a means of assessing an individual's sensitivity for the sensory modality in question. High sensitivity indicates that very weak stimuli are detectable, whereas low sensitivity means that considerably greater intensity of stimulation is required before detection is possible. Even among young adults, there is a large degree of variability in sensitivity for each sensory modality. Nevertheless, there is good reason to believe that, in general, young adults have greater sensitivity than do elderly adults. The most likely causative factor producing age-related changes in sensitivity is the overall degeneration of sense organs and their ancillary structures (e.g., the lens) with increasing age.

For many years, subjects' sensory sensitivities have been evaluated through the use of one of many available psychophysical methods (e.g., the method of limits—see Anderson and Borkowski, 1978, for a lucid description of it and several other methods). One of the indices of a subject's sensitivity yielded by a psychophysical evaluation is that subject's *absolute threshold value*. An absolute threshold is simply the minimal intensity of a particular stimulus (e.g., a light) required for the subject to detect its presence half of the time (i.e., the probability of detection is .5). Increasing threshold values are assumed to reflect decreasing sensory sensitivities and overall decreasing sensory proficiencies among subjects for that particular modality (e.g., vision) being evaluated.

Age changes in absolute threshold values are quite compatible with associationism's analysis of human behavior, as is illustrated in Figure 7.1 for hypothetical average young-adult and elderly adult subjects. Operationally, either subject's absolute threshold is defined, as indicated earlier, by the weakest intensity of the sensory stimulus that is reported with a probability of .5. Stimuli below threshold value are detected with a probability less than .5, with the

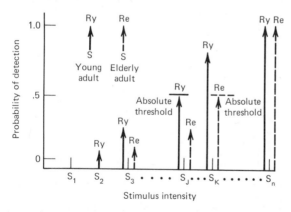

Figure 7.1. Associationism's conceptualization of absolute threshold values as extended to include age changes in sensory sensitivity. The intensity of stimulation needed to exceed the threshold value for an average elderly adult (S_k) is greater than the intensity needed for an average young adult (S_j).

probability eventually reaching 0 as the stimulus intensity decreases progressively. On the other hand, stimuli with intensities above the threshold value are reported with a probability greater than .5, with the probability eventually reaching 1.0 as the stimulus intensity increases progressively. Again, there is good reason (i.e., biological changes in sensory receptors) to expect the threshold intensity of the stimulus source to be lower for our average young-adult subject than for our average elderly adult subject (S_j and S_k respectively in Figure 7.1).

There is another kind of threshold that also serves as a general index of a subject's sensitivity for a particular modality—the *difference threshold.* Our concern now is with a just-noticeable difference between two stimuli. Consider, for example, two tones of equal intensity (or loudness) but different frequency (or pitch). The minimal difference in frequency that is detected half of the time by a subject defines that subject's difference threshold for pitch discrimination. A difference below this threshold value is detected with a probability less than .5, with the probability decreasing to 0 as the difference in frequency decreases progressively. Similarly, a difference above threshold value is detected with a probability greater than .5, with the probability increasing to 1.0 as the difference in frequency increases progressively.

Age changes in difference thresholds, like age changes in absolute thresholds, are quite compatible with associationism's analysis of human behavior, as is illustrated in Figure 7.2, again for average young and elderly adult subjects. Only now the detection response in question is one that occurs to a pair of stimuli. One member of each pair is a standard stimulus, such as a tone having a frequency of 1000 hertz and the other member is a comparison stimulus having a frequency different than that of the standard. The comparison stimuli may be ordered in terms of increasing frequency values relative to the standard, that is, as $S_1, S_2, \ldots, S_k$ (e.g., 1010 hertz, 1020 hertz, and so on). The stimulus actually evoking a detection response by a subject is the difference in pitch between the standard stimulus, S, and whatever comparison stimulus the stan-

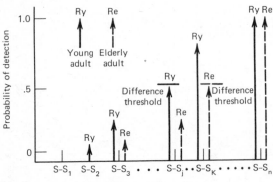

Figure 7.2. Associationism's conceptualization of difference threshold values as extended to include age changes in sensory sensitivity. A greater disparity between stimuli is needed for the average elderly adult than for the average young adult to be a just-noticeable difference.

dard is paired with, for example, S-S$_1$. Our assumption is that the threshold value for a just-noticeable difference in pitch is reached at a smaller disparity between paired stimuli for the average young-adult subject (S-S$_j$ in Figure 7.2) than for the average elderly adult (S-S$_k$ in Figure 7.2).

We should note that our associative interpretation of age changes in threshold values is for purposes of maintaining continuity with our later interpretation of age changes in perception. Actually, the concept of a threshold is operationally defined, and it, therefore, does not require treatment as an inferred process that is derived from any theoretical model, including that of associationism. By contrast, the concept of stimulus persistence is not operationally defined and its status is that of an inferred process. Consequently, the age sensitivity of the threshold process is operationally defined by the observation of age differences in threshold values, whereas the age sensitivity of stimulus persistence must be inferred indirectly from the outcomes of various experiments.

Representative Studies of Age Differences in Threshold Values. A good starting point for a review of studies that demonstrate age differences in sensory sensitivity is with studies assessing auditory thresholds. Galton's evidence of a decline in sensitivity for higher frequency tones (a condition called presbycusis) has since been replicated in a number of studies. The results obtained in a number of these studies were summarized by Spoor (1967) in the manner shown in Figure 7.3. Hearing loss in this summary is expressed with reference to the mean threshold values found for 25-year-old subjects. These results are for hearing loss of men only. Comparable studies with women (e.g., Corso, 1963) indicate that, with age held constant, their hearing loss is slightly greater than that of men for frequencies of 1000 hertz and below, whereas it is somewhat less than that of men for frequencies of 2000 hertz and above. These sex differences in hearing loss are probably due to sex differences in exposure to environmental noises rather than to innate sex differences in the biological components of hearing. The importance of prolonged exposure to environmental noise, in general, as a contributing factor to age changes in auditory sensitivity is apparent from studies examining age differences in auditory sensitivity

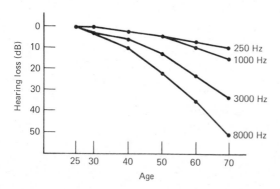

Figure 7.3. Decrements with increasing age in auditory sensitivity for tones of varying frequencies. (Adapted from data summarized by Botwinick 1978, from data in Spoor, 1967.)

for people living in isolated areas that are exceptionally free of noise (e.g., Rosen, Bergman, Plester, El-Mofty, & Sath, 1962; Rosen, Plester, El-Mofty, Rosen, 1964). For example, hearing loss for Sudanese men in their 70s was found to be about 15 decibels for a 3000-hertz-tone, a loss that is about half of that shown in Figure 7.3 for elderly American men.

From Figure 7.3, it may be seen that auditory sensitivity remains fairly stable with increasing age for tones of 1000 hertz and below. However, for higher frequency tones, age losses emerge by age 50 and increase progressively beyond that age. The practical significance is clear—sounds of higher frequency to be heard need to be louder than middle-frequency sounds. Without such amplification, the higher frequency notes played, for example, on a piano (up to 4000 hertz) may not be heard. There may be other less obvious adverse effects as well. In particular, perception of some spoken words, especially those involving high-frequency consonant sounds (e.g., the s in said) may be distorted. Having to speak louder to be understood is not an uncommon experience for those communicating orally with the elderly. The possibility of an even more subtle adverse consequence was discussed in Chapter 3. There, we discovered that lower auditory sensitivity may be a contributing factor to the lower intelligence test scores often earned by elderly adults relative to young adults.

Substantial age differences have also been found for the difference threshold in pitch discrimination. A representative study is that of König (1957). Separate thresholds were found for standard tones of various frequencies, all of which were 40 decibels in loudness. Age differences in the magnitudes of these thresholds are plotted in Figure 7.4. For each standard tone, the threshold value is the change in frequency required to produce a just-noticeable differ-

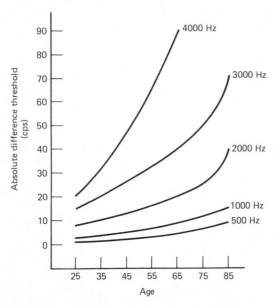

Figure 7.4. Age differences in difference threshold values for standard tones of various frequencies. (Adapted from data in König, 1957.)

ence in pitch between it and a comparison tone. Note that age differences in sensitivity to pitch variation are slight for standard tones less than 1000 hertz. However, for higher frequency standards, age differences are considerably larger, with increments in threshold values becoming especially pronounced beyond age 55. As observed by Corso (1977), age deficits in pitch discrimination are certain to lower the quality of music experienced by the elderly and are also likely to contribute to diminished speech perception by the elderly, again most likely for words involving high-frequency consonants.

Age differences in visual sensitivity have been examined mainly for dark-adapted vision. Dark adaptation occurs whenever there is a sudden change from high to low illumination—a phenomenon familiar to all of us when we enter a dark movie theater. At first, we can see little as we stumble around looking for an empty seat. Eventually, however, we can easily see who is sitting where. Our cones and rods have adapted to the lower illumination by increasing their sensitivities. That is, our absolute thresholds have been lowered so that less intense stimuli may now be seen. Studies by both Birren and Shock (1950) and McFarland and his associates (McFarland, Domey, Warren, & Ward, 1960; Domey, McFarland, & Chadwick, 1960) have revealed substantial age differences in dark adaptation. Their results indicate that maximum sensitivity under low illumination, which is attained after about 40 minutes in the dark for every age level, is more than 200 times greater for young adults than for elderly adults. In addition, the results obtained by McFarland, as shown in Figure 7.5, reveal another kind of age difference, namely, in the rate of attain-

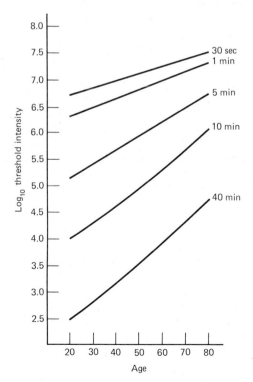

Figure 7.5. Age differences in dark-adaptation threshold values after 0.5 to 40 minutes in the dark. (Adapted from data in Domey, McFarland & Chadwick, 1960.)

ing maximum sensitivity. For elderly subjects, the rate of change in sensitivity is slower than for young adults. Consequently, the extent of age differences in sensitivity becomes increasingly greater as adaptation time increases, with the greatest magnitude of age differences occurring at the level of maximum sensitivity for each age level. However, Birren and Shock (1950) did not find comparable age differences in rate of adaptation. That is, their results indicated that the magnitude of age differences in sensitivity remained about the same throughout the period of adaptation.

The age deficit in dark adaptation is viewed as being an index of an overall decrement in visual sensitivity for elderly people. In addition, the diminished dark adaptation evident in elderly people has its own direct adverse effects, as noted by McFarland:

> Old and young alike undertake tasks that frequently require partial adaptation, for instance, the operation of motor vehicles at night under conditions of intermittent unpredictable changes of luminance. The range of luminance in night driving has been shown to be quite great, and high enough to involve both the rods and cone cells of the retina. Therefore, the continuous process of bleaching and adaptation of the retina means that crossing over from rod to cone vision and vice versa is a common event. Rate of adaptation then becomes exceedingly important, but it is precisely in this region that certain types of inefficiency arise. The terminal level of adaptation of the cone cells almost defines the moment when three-dimensional vision, acuity, and color vision become greatly limited, and the moment before the rod cells have generated any useful degree of sensitivity. Older persons are known to be greatly handicapped under such conditions of luminance. (1968, p. 18)

Age differences in difference thresholds under high illumination have received little investigation. What evidence there is (Gregory, 1957) indicates decreasing sensitivity with increasing age. Most important, the increment in difference threshold values appears to accelerate greatly beyond age 60.

The results of studies on age differences in threshold values for the other senses have been difficult to interpret. Problems arising from either faulty methodology or the use of very small samples of subjects have been the general rule. Fairly pronounced age changes in taste sensitivity were reported in a number of early studies (e.g., Cooper, Bilash, & Zubek, 1959). However, a more recent soundly conducted study by Grzegorczyk, Jones, and Mistretta (1979) indicates that the magnitude of age changes in taste sensitivity may have been overestimated. Unfortunately, only sensitivity to salt was tested in their study. Although the absolute threshold was found to increase progressively for age 23 to age 92, the amount of the increase was far less than that found in earlier studies. Generalizing to other tastes is risky of course. Clearly needed are similarly well-controlled studies of age differences in sweet, bitter, and sour sensitivity. Smell has not been a widely studied sense at any age level. The limited data available on adult-age differences in sensitivity suggest only a modest loss with increasing age over most of the adult lifespan (see Engen, 1977, and McFarland, 1968, for reviews). Nor has touch sensitivity been widely investigated. It seems likely, however, that the magnitudes of age changes vary for different parts of the body. The age decrement in sensitivity appears to be substantial for some parts of the body (e.g., the big toe), whereas it may be much smaller for other parts of the body. Of particular interest are age changes in the threshold value for the fingers, especially the index finger. Although early investigators (e.g., Cosh, 1953) found modest declines in sensitivity, more recent investigators (Thornbury & Mistretta, 1981) have found more substantial age decrements in sensitivity of the index finger. The decrement in sensitivity correlates with the decline with aging in the number of Meissner's corpuscles (one of the tactile receptors) in the skin of fingers (Bolton, Winkelmann, & Dyck, 1966; see Kenshalo, 1977). As observed by Thornbury and Mistretta, the decline in sensitivity for the fingers in general could have important adverse consequences for the adaptability of elderly people to their environments through their declining ability "to locate, manipulate, and identify objects in the environment" (1981, p. 39).

The last area of sensitivity we will consider, and one of the most intriguing, is that of pain. The intrigue arises from clinical evidence suggesting that elderly people do not feel pain as intensely as do younger people. In his review of age differences in pain sensitivity, Botwinick observed that "minor surgery can often be performed on old people without inflicting severe pain; coronary thrombosis occurs often without the agony found in young people. Paradoxically, however, subjective sensory complaints are very common in old age" (1978, p. 150). The implication is that the pain threshold increases with increasing age during adulthood, thus making older people less sensitive to pain than younger people. Several studies have supported this implication, but they disagree as to when age changes in pain sensitivity become apparent. Chapman and Jones (1944) found the pain threshold to increase fairly early in adulthood, whereas Schluderman and Zubek (1962) found no increase before the late 50s. On the other hand, Harkins and Chapman (1976, 1977) found no change at all in pain threshold from early to late adulthood.

In summary, psychophysical research has, in general, confirmed the expected decrease in sensory sensitivity, as measured by threshold values, during old age. However, the amount of the decrease varies greatly among the senses, being more pronounced for audition and vision than for the other senses (see Corso, 1981, for a further review).

Sensitivity Versus Decision-Making Processes

Signal-Detection Theory and Methodology. Reporting the presence (or absence) of a weak sensory stimulus is only partly dependent on a subject's biologically determined sensitivity. At least, that is the argument advanced by signal-detection theorists. With a low-intensity stimulus, a subject is confronted by a decision-making dilemma. The classic example is the dilemma facing a radar operator. How intense must a blip on the screen be before the operator sees it? The dilemma occurs because the blip is superimposed on the variable brightness, or noise, of the screen itself. Given an intense blip, there is no problem—the blip is clearly discernible from the background noise. But with a faint signal, the operator cannot be certain: Is it really a blip or is it only noise? The operator has to decide whether or not to report the approach of what could be an enemy aircraft. The decision is likely to be influenced strongly by the cost of certain kinds of errors. Failure to report what is really an enemy aircraft (a *miss*) could have a disastrous outcome. On the other hand, reporting noise to be an enemy aircraft (a *false alarm*) would make the operator appear foolish. The processes likely to determine the operator's ultimate decision were aptly summarized by Lachman, Lachman, and Butterfield:

> The intensity of blip necessary to get the operator to report that he has seen something depends on how he weighs the costs of false alarms and the cost of significant "misses." These relative weights determine the operator's decision criterion. A radar operator with a lenient criterion will report anything that might be a blip; he will turn in many false alarms but he will not miss an enemy aircraft. An operator with a strict criterion will report nothing unless he is sure; he will seldom turn in a false alarm, but enemy craft will be relatively close by the time he tells anyone about it. Signal detectability theory provides a mathematical way of describing separately the perceiver's sensitivity to the signal and his decision criterion; these analytic conventions have been subsequently used in information processing psychology to study perception and memory. (1979, p. 59)

We need not restrict our analysis to such esoteric tasks as spotting enemy aircraft on a radar scope. A combination of sensory and decision-making factors is involved whenever a subject performs a task in which there is uncertainty about the addition of a signal to a background of noise. Sensory tasks that call for the assessment of an absolute threshold meet this requirement. Here, the signal is a weak light, tone, odor, and so on. Noise, in turn, exists within the pertinent sensory system of the subject. Sensory neurons have a low rate of firing, or discharging, when they are at rest, that is, they are not being stimulated directly by any incoming stimulus. What an incoming stimulus, even a weak one, does is to increase the rate of firing above this resting level. The subject's task is, therefore, to discriminate between the spontaneous rate of firing (i.e., noise) and the slight increase in rate produced by weak stimulation (i.e., noise plus signal). The same combination of sensory and cognitive factors is involved on many tasks calling for the assessment of a difference threshold. But now noise is literally noise. For example, it may be the white noise (a random mixture of sound frequencies) produced by a random noise generator. The noise is present constantly at some specified level of loudness. On occasion, a signal, consisting of a pure tone, or single-frequency tone, is superimposed on the noise. The subject, on cuing, simply reports the presence or absence of the pure tone. In either condition, failure to report the addition of a signal to noise may be the consequence of either the subject's insensitivity to sensory inputs per se or to the subject's decision-making cautiousness (i.e., the criterion set for making signal/noise decisions) or to a combination of the two.

The signal-detection theory (Green & Swets, 1966) mentioned by Lachman, Lachman, and Butterfield (1979) views background noise, whatever its source, as having a variable intensity. In effect, its intensity may be considered to be distributed randomly in the form of a normal probability curve. Over the period of time a subject performs on a detection task, the average intensity of noise corresponds to the mean of this distribution. Suppose a subject's performance on a detection task is divided into a series of discrete trials. For half of the trials, a stimulus is added to the background noise, making the total intensity of stimulation equal to that of the specific stimulus plus whatever the intensity of noise happens to be at a given moment. For the other half of the trials, the stimulus is omitted, making the total stimulus intensity equal to that of the noise level alone. The two kinds of trials are presented in a random sequence with the subject being forewarned of a trial's onset but not forewarned as to the presence or absence of the specific stimulus or signal. The subject simply reports a yes or a no on each trial, thereby indicating the detection or nondetection of the signal.

Again, accuracy in discriminating between the presence/absence of a signal depends, in part, on a subject's sensitivity either to weak stimulus inputs or to slight differences between two stimuli (i.e., physical noise and a pure stimulus). The hypothetical distributions of stimulus intensities for noise alone and for noise plus a weak signal are shown in Figure 7.6. The top panel represents a subject who has a high level of sensitivity, the bottom panel one who has a low level of sensitivity. It may be seen that the two subjects differ with respect to the distance separating the means of their two distributions. This distance, labeled d' in signal detection theory, is measured by means of the mathematical procedure noted by Lachman et al., and expressed in standard deviation units.

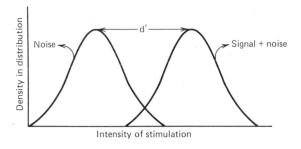

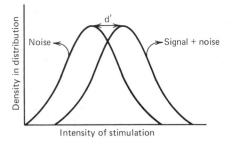

Figure 7.6. Hypothetical distributions of noise alone and noise plus a weak signal for a subject with a high level of sensitivity (d') (top panel) and a subject with a low level of sensitivity (bottom panel).

For a given subject, d' is computed through a comparison of that subject's hit rate (i.e., the proportion of signal-present trials in which the subject confirms the signal's presence) and false alarm rate (i.e., the proportion of noise-only trials in which the subject incorrectly reports the presence of a signal). Increasing d' values indicate increasing degrees of sensitivity. For a group of subjects, an average sensitivity score may be determined by computing the mean d' score of its members.

Between-subject differences in hit and false alarm rates need not be the consequence of differential sensitivities however. Subjects with equal sensitivities may differ in their performances on a detection task anyway, provided their approaches to making decisions about the presence/absence of a signal differ. Between-subject differences in the decision process become especially important when the signal plus noise distribution overlaps considerably with the noise-alone distribution, as it would when the signal's intensity is only slightly greater than the intensity of noise alone. A subject performing under these conditions must establish some intensity level of stimulation that functions as a criterion value (labeled β in signal-detection theory) for deciding yes or no on each trial. If the perceived intensity of stimulation equals or exceeds this value on a given trial, then that intensity will be followed by a yes decision. An intensity below the criterion value will be followed by a no decision. A liberal criterion (i.e., one set at a relatively low-intensity level) will yield more hits for true signals than will a conservative criterion (i.e., one set at a relatively high-intensity level), but it will also yield more false alarms for those trials in which a true signal is omitted. The contrast between a liberal (top panel) and conservative (bottom panel) decision maker is illustrated in Figure 7.7. In principle, β's value for a given subject is the ratio of the ordinates in the signal plus noise distribution and the noise-alone distribution found at the point where the criterion intensity is located on the abscissa (b and a respectively). For a conservative decision maker, the ratio, b/a, is much greater than 1 (see the bottom panel). With increasing liberalism, the ratio decreases in magnitude (e.g., it equals 1 in the top panel). The mathematical procedure for computing a subject's β value, like the procedure used to compute d', transforms hit and false alarm rates into the appropriate score (in this case, a ratio of ordinates), A group's average criterion value may then be determined by finding the mean β score of its members.

Implications for Experimental Aging Research. A signal-detection approach to age differences in sensory behavior implies that those differences could result from either an age change in sensitivity or an age change in conservative decision making, or to some combination of the two. If age changes in sensitivity are largely responsible for observed age differences in threshold values (as is assumed to be true in traditional psychophysical studies), then a group of elderly subjects should have a much smaller mean d' value than a group of young-adult subjects. In effect, the condition shown in the bottom panel of Figure 7.6 would correspond to that found for the averge elderly subject, whereas the condition shown in the top panel would correspond to that found

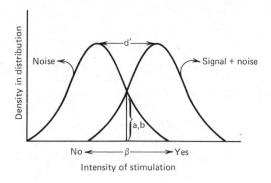

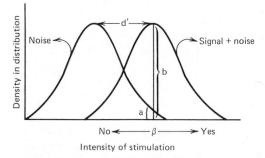

Figure 7.7. Criterion values (β) for a liberal decision maker (top panel) and a conservative decision maker (bottom panel).

for the average young-adult subject. The disparity seemingly results from increasing neural noise with increasing age.

There is good reason to believe, however, that age differences along the conservative-liberal decision-making dimension should also influence age differences in the proficiency of detecting sensory signals. One of the most persistent beliefs about human aging is that people tend to become more cautious when they reach late adulthood . If true (the available evidence will be reviewed in Chapter 11), then the greater cautiousness of elderly subjects could translate into a conservative decision-making strategy relative to the strategy employed by young adults on detection tasks. In effect, the condition shown in the bottom panel of Figure 7.7 would correspond to that found for the average elderly subject, whereas the condition shown in the top panel would correspnd to that found for the average young-adult subject. Note that the elderly subject is viewed as setting a more stringent criterion for responding yes to a possible signal than the young-adult subject. A greater intensity of a signal would, therefore, be needed to produce a yes response for older subjects than for younger subjects, even if sensitivity per se is equal at all age levels. Given a low-intensity stimulus, older subjects would have a lower hit rate than younger subjects when the stimulus is actually present. At the same time, older subjects would also have a lower false alarm rate than younger subjects when no stimulus is added to the background noise level. The increase in response bias with increasing age could easily be mistaken for a decrease in sensory sensitivity, especially in traditional threshold studies where age differences in sensitivity and age differences in response bias are confounded.

How valid are the pronounced losses in sensory sensitivity with aging that have been reported in psychophysical studies? It is conceivable that these losses have been grossly overestimated through the failure to separate sensory and decision-making factors. The development of signal-detection methodology has given experimental aging psychologists the opportunity to determine just how great these overestimations have been (see Danziger, 1980; Hertzog, 1980; Marks & Stevens, 1980; and Williams, 1980, for further discussion of the application of signal-detection methodology to age differences in sensory processes). Surprisingly, however, there have been only a scattering of aging studies that have made use of signal-detection methodology.

Studies Applying Signal-Detection Methodology. The first attempts to apply signal-detection methodology in aging research were by Craik (1966) and Rees and Botwinick (1971). In both studies, young and elderly adult subjects reported the presence/absence of a weak tone. The procedure and the results were both quite similar for the two studies. Our description will be limited to the study by Rees and Botwinick (1971).

Each subject's signal was set at the highest intensity of the tone that was reported 100% of the time by that subject. This resulted in an averge stimulus intensity that was somewhat lower for the young-adult group (college students) than for the elderly group (median age, 71 years)—2.9 versus 9.9 decibels respectively. Once a subject's signal-intensity level was determined, that signal was presented in a random order on half of the 200 trials. No tone at all, of course, was presented on the other half of the trials. The onset of a trial was indicated to the subjects by a cue, with the subjects responding yes or no (i.e., tone present or no tone present) following each cue. The age difference in d′ values was clearly not statistically significant. If anything, the elderly subjects displayed slightly greater sensitivity (median d′ = 1.44) than the young subjects (median d′ = 1.36). On the other hand, the median β value was much greater for the elderly subjects (2.41) than for the young subjects (1.21), indicating a more conservative decision-making strategy by the elderly. Rees and Botwinick concluded that the amount of loss in auditory sensitivity reported for elderly people in traditional psychophysical studies may be exaggerated. That is, much of that loss may actually reflect the conservative nature of elderly people rather than a true age change in auditory sensitivity.

Rees and Botwinick were well aware of a problem inherent in their study that seriously questions the validity of their conclusion. To demonstrate comparable sensitivity between age groups in terms of d′ values, the intensity of the signal source itself had to be considerably greater, on the average, for their elderly subjects than for their young subjects (i.e., 9.9 versus 2.9 decibels). A more adequate separation between age differences in sensitivity and age differences in response bias was accomplished in a later study by Potash and Jones (1977). Their task called for detecting the presence/absence of a signal against a random noise background set at 30 decibels. The signal was a 6000-hertz pure

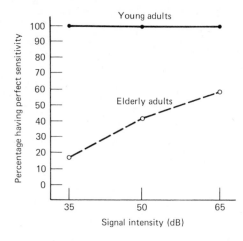

Figure 7.8. Age differences in sensitivity for tones (signals) of varying intensities that are embedded in noise. (Adapted from Potash & Jones, 1977, Table 1.)

tone presented at either 35, 50, or 65 decibels. A high-frequency tone was selected intentionally to demonstrate as effectively as possible what the investigators believed in advance to be an exaggeration of the hearing loss actually experienced by older people. Remember that it is for high-frequency sounds that hearing loss with aging is viewed as being especially pronounced. If little loss in sensitivity could be demonstrated for high-frequency tones, then there would be no reason to doubt that loss of sensitivity to lower frequency tones is a highly unlikely consequence of human aging.

Unfortunately, Potash and Jones discovered that this loss had not been exaggerated in earlier threshold studies. All of their young-adult subjects had perfect sensitivity, even for the 35-decibel tone. That is, the tone's presence or absence was correctly detected on every trial by each young subject. A very different pattern emerged for their elderly subjects, however, as may be seen in Figure 7.8. Even with a 65-decibel tone, less than 60% of the elderly subjects displayed perfect sensitivity. This percentage, of course, was reduced considerably through the use of less intense signal tones (see Figure 7.8). The investigators subsequently repeated their study with lower intensity tones (e.g., 20 decibels) and with young-adult subjects only. At these reduced levels of signal intensity, the young adults manifested about the same sensitivity found for the elderly subjects with louder tones. Despite the forced equality in sensitivity, their elderly subjects set more stringent criteria in their decisions than did their young subjects. Overall, the outcome of this study closely replicates the outcome of Rees and Botwinick's (1971) earlier study. There seems to be no reason to doubt that auditory sensitivity decreases considerably with advancing age. At the same time, even with sensitivity equated across age levels, older adults are likely to appear insensitive to auditory stimuli because of their stringent criterion values for making decisions about the presence or absence of an auditory stimulus.

The remaining applications of signal-detection methodology have been to the study of adult-age differences in pain detection, in discriminations between weights, and in contour sensitivity. In their pain research, Clark and Mehl

(1971) applied a radiant-heat stimulus to a subject's forearm as the pain signal. Young adults were found to be more sensitive (i.e., a larger mean d' score) than middle-age adults for both sexes. In addition, a more stringent criterion score was found for middle-age men than for young men, in agreement with the results obtained on age differences in auditory signal detection. Interestingly, a comparable age difference was not found for women. If anything, young women set a more stringent criterion than did middle-age women. Subsequent studies by Harkins and Chapman (1976, 1977) made use of a different stimulus for inducing pain, electrical stimulation of an unfilled tooth. In addition, elderly rather than middle-age adults were contrasted with young adults. This time, a more stringent criterion was found for older subjects of both sexes.

The studies on weight discriminations were conducted by Watson, Turpenoff, Kelly, and Botwinick (1979) and Danziger and Botwinick (1980). In both studies, young and elderly adults were required to detect a difference between weights lifted successively by the same hand. On half the trials, the two weights were equal (no difference being the correct response); on the other half of the trials, the two weights differed by a fixed amount (e.g., 210 grams for one weight, 225 grams for the other). No difference in response bias was found between the two age groups when they were equated in sensitivity. Watson et al. (1979) concluded that "caution on the part of older people may be specific to certain classes of tasks" (p. 551). Just how specific it is will remain unknown until age differences on a wider range of sensory tasks, especially visual ones, are analyzed by means of signal-detection methodology. Such studies are needed to test more systematically than in the past the generalizability of the age difference in response bias found primarily on auditory tasks. Especially useful would be studies in which detection tasks that involve various modalities are administered to the same subjects, both young and old. Of interest is the extent to which individual differences in response bias at both age levels persist across modalities. At any rate, the full potential of signal-detection applications to aging sensory phenomena has yet to be realized.

The studies on contour sensitivity (Hutman & Sekuler, 1980; Sekuler & Hutman, 1980; Sekuler, Hutman, & Owsley, 1980) did involve a component of vision, albeit a highly technical one. Specifically, the investigators compared young and elderly adults on their sensitivities to changes in contour. Elderly subjects were as sensitive as young-adult subjects to a target with a fine structure, that is, one having many contour changes over a limited space. However, the elderly subjects were less sensitive than the young subjects to a target with a coarse structure, that is, one having few contour changes over the same limited space. Their signal-detection analysis revealed that the age deficit in contour sensitivity was not attributable to criterion differences between age groups. Although the visual deficit observed in these studies is a subtle one, the investigators believe that it could have important ramifications. One possibility is that the deficit may impair recognition of critical features of the visual environment, resulting, perhaps, in the occasional failure to recognize faces and objects that have a coarse structure (i.e., few contour changes). Another possibility is that the deficit may affect adversely both locomotion and postural stabilization, behaviors that are guided in part by visual information. Conceivably, some of the locomotor problems afflicting some elderly people could be linked to the probable age change in contour sensitivity.

In summary, signal-detection research has supported the argument that age deficits in sensory behavior are only partly due to decrements in sensory sensitivity with increasing age. The contributions to overall sensory deficits by the conservative decision-making characteristics of elderly people relative to younger people can be substantial, at least for some forms of sensory behavior, such as the detection of weak auditory stimuli. However, little is known about the generalizability of this conservatism to many forms of sensory behavior.

Classical Perceptual Phenomena: Age Differences Attributable to Sensory Changes

Age differences in postsensory, or perceptual, sensitivity are well documented for a multitude of perceptual tasks and abilities. Some of these differences have been clearly linked to age changes in peripheral factors. That is, they are the consequence of the deterioration in sensory receptors and their ancillary structures that accompanies human aging. In some cases, the age deficit in a perceptual skill produced by peripheral factors has considerable practical importance. One such skill, as noted in Chapter 1, is the ability to discriminate between colors. There is evidence to indicate that accuracy in identifying the colors of objects is reduced by nearly 25% at age 70 and by nearly 50% at age 90 (Dalderup & Fredericks, 1969; Gilbert, 1957). A major factor producing this age deficit in color sensitivity is the yellowing of the lens and the resulting filtering of light reaching the retina. However, it may be argued that the magnitude of the loss in color sensitivity is too great to be explained solely in terms of changes in the lens. Specifically, changes at the level of the retina itself may become increasingly involved in diminished color sensitivity during the late stages of adulthood (Lakowski, 1962).

Another age deficit of practical significance occurs for the ability to perceive depth. A standard procedure for testing the proficiency of depth perception requires subjects to view three vertical bars projected on a transilluminated screen. Their task is to identify the spatial position of a single bar that is either in front or behind the plane of the other two bars (a modification of this task is commonly included as part of the visual test people take in qualifying for a driver's license). Using this procedure, Bell, Wolf, and Bernholz (1972) tested adults ranging in age from the 30s through the 70s. As may be seen in Figure 7.9, they found accuracy to drop precipitously from the 40s to the 50s, with smaller decrements occurring thereafter. There appear to be several peripheral factors responsible for the overall decline in depth perception. Some of these peripheral changes, such as the increased susceptibility to glare with increasing age, presumably distort monocular cues for depth perception, whereas other changes, such as the decrease in illumination reaching the retina, presumably distort binocular cues (Fozard, Wolf, Bell, McFarland, & Podolsky, 1977).

Not all of the perceptual skills that are adversely affected by sensory aging have everyday implications. Age differences are present for some perceptual phenomena that have little ecological relevance, but they are nevertheless of

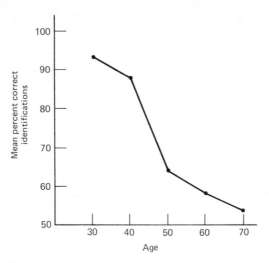

Figure 7.9. Age differences in depth perception. (Adapted from data in Bell, Wolf, & Bernholz, 1972.)

great interest to experimental aging psychologists. Included here are age differences found for Type I visual illusory phenomena. Remember that Type I illusions, such as the Delboeuf and Müller-Lyer illusions, are those whose illusory effects increase in magnitude from early to late adulthood. The increases are believed to result from various sensory changes over the adult lifespan, including decreasing illumination reaching the retina and decreasing inhibitory functioning of damping neurons in the retina (Atkeson, 1978). The Delboeuf illusion (see the top panel of Figure 7.10) is the one that entered into the simulation study described in Chapter 5. At that time, we discovered that young adults who were forced to view the stimulus materials through a filter, thereby simulating a sensory age change by reducing the amount of illumination at the retina, experienced a greater illusory effect than young adults who viewed the materials unimpeded. This increment in illusory magnitude corresponds to that found when adults of increasing age are tested on the same materials, as may be seen from the results obtained by Lorden, Atkeson, and Pollack (1979) (bottom panel of Figure 7.10). As we noted in Chapter 4, a similar age-related increment in the magnitude of the Müller-Lyer illusion has been found by a number of investigators. There is good reason for the importance attached to these illusory tasks by experimental aging psychologists. They provide general indices of changes in perceptual competence across the adult lifespan, at least as far as that competence is affected by peripheral factors.

Classical Perceptual Phenomena: Age Differences Attributable to Changes in Stimulus Persistence

A number of perceptual tasks and phenomena reveal substantial age differences over the adult lifespan that are not readily explained by means of biological reductionism. It is for these tasks and phenomena that the concept of an age

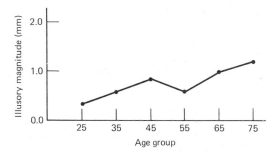

Figure 7.10. Top panel: Stimulus materials for tests of the Delboeuf illusion. The two circles on the left are the inducing circle (the larger one) and the standard circle (inside the inducing circle). The circle on the right is the comparison circle that is adjusted to make it appear equal in diameter to the standard circle whose diameter appears larger than it is (the illusory effect) due to the presence of the inducing circle. Bottom panel: Age differences in the magnitude of the Delboeuf illusion. (Adapted from Lorden, Atkeson, & Pollack, 1979, Figure 3.)

change in stimulus persistence has been widely applied as a unifying explanatory principle. Explanation of age differences is in terms of an inferred process, with the biological locus of the process remaining unspecified. In fact, for some phenomena the locus of the age change may be peripheral, whereas for other phenomena the locus may be central (Botwinick, 1978).

Our strategy calls for an initial analysis of the concept itself and for a review of the few studies that have provided a direct test of the concept's validity. We will then survey a number of perceptual phenomena for which adult-age differences have been explained by application of the stimulus-persistence concept. These applications have typically been made in a post hoc manner. Thus, we will be dealing largely with studies that were conducted simply to assess the extent of age differences for a given perceptual phenomenon—not to test a prediction derived from the persistence concept. The nature of many of these age differences, however, seems to fit what might be predicted on the basis of age changes in stimulus persistence. The persistence concept is an especially intriguing one in that it predicts reduced perceptual proficiency on some tasks with increasing age, but increased proficiency on other tasks.

The Stimulus-Persistence Concept and Direct Tests of Its Validity. The concept of age differences in stimulus persistence was advanced originally by Axelrod (1963). The stimulus whose persistence is in question is the s event shown in Figure 6.3. As noted earlier, this event refers to a neural activity initiated by an environmental stimulus. Continuation, or persistence, of this neural activity after the originating external stimulus ceases has long been postulated by associationists (e.g., Hull, 1943). The importance of persisting neural traces for perceptual phenomena has been described by Botwinick (1978):

> If a person responds to a stimulus and then responds to a second one shortly afterward, the second response is often different from the first one, even if the two stimuli are identical. One theory explaining this is that the first stimulus, in its neural representation, must be "cleared through the nervous system" before the second stimulus can be responded to as was the first one. Before the nerve impulses are so cleared through, before neural transmission is complete, the person is not optimally ready to process the input of the second stimulus. The trace of the first stimulus persists, so to speak, leaving the responder either relatively refractory to subsequent stimulation or, more often, responsive but in a different way. (p. 156)

The principle takes on meaning for interpreting the effects of aging on perceptual phenomena as follows:

> In the senescent nervous system, there may be an increased persistence of the activity evoked by a stimulus, i.e., . . . the rate of recovery from the short-term effects of stimulation may be slowed. On the assumption that perception of the second stimulus as a discrete event depends on the degree to which the neural effects of the first have subsided, the poorer temporal resolution in sensescence would then follow. (Axelrod, Thompson, & Cohen, 1968, p. 193)

The "poorer temporal resolution" of the elderly is in reference to perceptual phenomena that require the integration of responses to a series of sensory stimuli, $S_1, S_2, \ldots, S_n$. That is, S_1 is presented first, then S_2, and so on. For an elderly subject, the response, R_2, to S_2 is assumed to be fused upon s_1, the neural trace of S_1 that persists as S_2 comes into view. For some perceptual tasks, such fusion alters the nature of the response to S_2 and makes its meaningful integration with the response, R_1, to S_1 difficult. In Botwinick's (1978) words, "the person is not optimally ready to process the input of the second stimulus" (p. 156). By contrast, fusion may not occur with a young-adult subject in that the neural trace to S_1 is likely to cease prior to the onset of S_2. In other words, S_2 elicits $R_{1,2}$ (i.e., a fused response) for the elderly subject and R_2 (i.e., a discrete response) for the young-adult subject. Young adults are clearly expected to be superior to elderly adults in performance on these tasks, despite the fact that R_1 and R_2, considered only as discrete perceptual responses, are unlikely to differ between the two age levels. On the other hand, there are other perceptual tasks for which a fused response is a prerequisite for adequate performance. Most intriguing, the expected age differential in stimulus persistence leads to a reversal of the usual direction of age differences in performance. That is, elderly adults are expected to be superior to young adults.

For the principle of an age differential in stimulus persistence to exert a major influence on the experimental psychology of aging, it must be capable of predicting in advance the course of adult-age differences on any specified perceptual task. To the extent that this prediction is confirmed, stimulus persistence has been identified as an age-sensitive process for that task. What is needed is an experimental aging study employing a manipulable independent variable that may reasonably be expected to affect stimulus persistence. Variation in the interstimulus interval (ISI), the temporal gap between S_1 and S_2, should be especially effective as the B variable of an A $\times$ B study. The nature of this interpretation may best be understood with reference to the events schematized in Figure 7.11. Both s_1 and s_2, the neural traces to S_1 and S_2, are presumed to last longer (symbolized by longer arrows connecting s with r in Figure 7.11) for an average elderly subject than for an average young-adult subject. With a short ISI (Level B_1), there should be no age difference in the perceptual response to the S_1, S_2 sequence. That is, regardless of age level, s_2 should overlap with s_1, yielding a fused perceptual response ($R_{1,2}$) as indicated in the left half of Figure 7.11. By contrast, with a moderate ISI (Level B_2), there should be a clear age difference in perceptual responses to the S_1, S_2 sequence. At this interval, s_1 should have "cleared through the nervous system" for the young adult but not for the elderly adult before the onset of S_2. The net effect should be discrete R_1 and R_2 occurrences for the young adult but a continuing $R_{1,2}$ occurrence for the elderly adult. Of course, with still longer ISI's, even the elderly subject should display discrete R_1 and R_2 occurrences whenever the interval exceeds s_1's duration.

There has been a direct test of the concept's validity by Kline and Orme-Rogers (1978) that followed the general guidelines described above (i.e., variation in ISI served as the manipulable independent variable). In their test, a

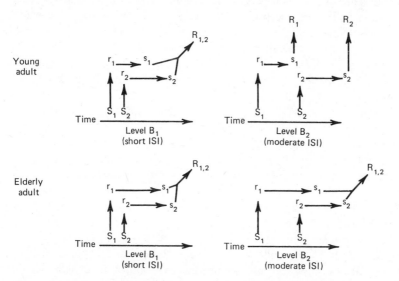

Figure 7.11. Schematic representation of the concept of age differences in stimulus persistence. S_1 and S_2 are successive external stimuli separated by either a short interstimulus interval (ISI) or a moderate interval; s_1 and s_2 are neural traces of S_1 and S_2 respectively; R_1 and R_2 are discrete perceptual responses to S_1 and S_2 respectively, whereas $R_{1,2}$ is a fused response to S_1 and S_2 that is attributable to the prolonged persistence of s_1.

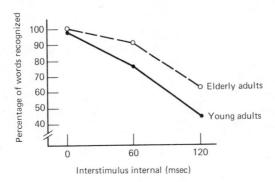

Figure 7.12. Percentages of young and elderly subjects recognizing words that are exposed in halves, with a varying interval separating the two exposures. (Adapted from Kline & Orme-Rogers, 1978, Figure 2.)

fused response was a prerequisite for proficient performance. Consequently, the persistence concept clearly predicts more proficient performance by elderly subjects than by young subjects.

Kline and Orme-Rogers employed a clever procedure in which S_1 and S_2 were sequentially exposed straight-line patterns, each pattern making up half of a printed three-letter word. For example, S_1 would be the pattern ⌐ ⊢ ⁻ whereas S_2 would be the pattern ⊔ ⌐ I . Superimposed upon one another (i.e., a 0 millisecond ISI), the two patterns combine to form the word 5 Ħ T. Of course, our concern is with a subject's ability to recognize the word when the two halves are exposed sequentially (i.e., with an ISI greater than 0) rather than simultaneously. The perceptual effect, however, should be the same as that found for simultaneous exposure if a trace of S_1 remains at the same S_2 is exposed. That is, the physically present second half of the word should be superimposed upon the remaining trace of the first half of that word, thus permitting recognition of the word. Suppose we now vary the length of the interval separating the exposures of S_1 and S_2 (i.e., the ISI). With longer separations, we would expect more words to be recognized by elderly subjects than by young subjects owing to the more persisting trace of S_1 that is available for the elderly subjects. By contrast, with a short temporal separation, a fused response should occur for young adults as well as elderly adults, resulting in a decrease in the extent of the age difference that favors elderly subjects in word-recognition proficiency. Exactly this outcome was obtained by Kline and Orme-Rogers. From Figure 7.12 it can be seen that the age difference in the percentage of words recognized out of 12 was pronounced with an ISI of 120 milliseconds, and it decreased progressively as the ISI decreased. The support given by this study to the validity of the persistence concept is substantial.

A different kind of direct test of the concept's validity involves a twist of the above procedure. In effect, the ISI now functions as a dependent variable rather than an independent variable. The modification yields a procedure much like that involved in threshold studies. S_1 and S_2 are now identical physical stimuli that are exposed sequentially. The temporal separation between their presentations begins at 0 milliseconds (i.e., only S_1 is, in effect, exposed) and is increased progressively until the subject reports no longer seeing a continuously present stimulus. That specific interval defines the subject's threshold value, a value that estimates the duration of S_1's persistence as a trace for that subject. Given greater persistence with increasing age, larger threshold values are expected for elderly subjects than for young subjects. This expectation was confirmed in a study by Amberson, Atkeson, Pollack, and Malatesta (1979). S_1 and S_2 were flashes of a light. The interval separating the two flashes was extended until a subject could discriminate darkness separating the flashes. The mean dark-interval threshold was found to be greater than 90 milliseconds for 70-year-old subjects and only about 65 milliseconds for 20-year-old subjects—an age difference in agreement with the persistence concept. A similar outcome has been reported in older studies using a variation of this basic procedure in which a light is flashed on and off. The critical-flicker-fusion threshold is defined in terms of the rate of alternating on and off states of the light before the light is seen as being on continuously (i.e., a fused response occurs). Elderly adults perceive such continuity at a slower rate of alternation than do young adults (Falk & Kline, 1978; Misiak, 1974), an age difference much like that found by Amberson et al. (1979) and one that is in agreement with predictions derived from the persistence principle. Unfortunately, another study (Walsh & Thompson, 1978) that made use of the threshold procedure was far less kind to the persistence concept. This time S_1 and S_2 were both the letter O. The interval separating the two letters was increased systematically until a subject reported no longer seeing a continuously present letter. Contrary to the persistence concept, the mean threshold value was significantly greater for young adults (289 milliseconds) than for elderly adults (248 milliseconds). There is a problem, however, in accepting this evidence as striking a decisive blow at the persistence concept. It is conceivable that a conservative response bias mitigated whatever effect greater persistence had for elderly subjects. They may simply have been less willing than the young subjects to accept a fading percept of a letter as being truly visible. But this resolution only creates another problem. Why should an age difference in response bias be a factor when the stimulus is a letter but not when it is a light? Moreover, a later study by Kline and Schieber (1981), closely patterned after that of Walsh and Thompson (1978), found the opposite outcome. That is, the mean threshold value for their elderly subjects was greater than that of their young subjects (in agreement with the stimulus-persistence concept). In general, direct tests of the persistence concept have been sufficiently supportive to maintain an active interest in the concept's value for explaining age differences over a wide range of perceptual phenomena.

Application to Various Perceptual Phenomena. The persistence concept is a strong contender for any prize to be awarded to experimental aging psychology's most versatile explanatory mechanism. The number of perceptual phenomena for which it serves as the only available means of explaining the existence of age differences is startling. Many of these phenomena deal with visual aftereffects, that is, a visual experience that continues after the physical

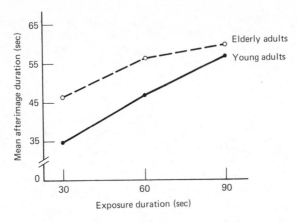

Figure 7.13. Age differences in the duration of a color afterimage following varying exposure durations. (Adapted from Kline & Nestor, 1977, Figure 1.)

stimulus itself terminates. Assuming greater persistence of the stimulus trace, elderly subjects are expected to have longer aftereffects than young subjects. For some aftereffects this does seem to be the case. This is especially true for complementary-color afterimages. The aftereffect here is the familiar one you have after staring for a period of time at, say, a green square on a red background and then fixating on a white square. An image of a red square surrounded by green (i.e., the complementary colors of the original materials) may clearly be seen for a number of seconds. Kline and Nestor (1977) demonstrated that the duration of the after effect, or afterimage, is significantly longer for elderly subjects than for young subjects. They included variation in the amount of initial stare time as a manipulable independent variable. As can be seen in Figure 7.13, there was a statistically significant longer aftereffect for the elderly subjects at each level of the manipulable variable.

The spiral aftereffect is another afterimage for which a longer duration is expected for elderly subjects than for young subjects. It is created by rotating a spiral on a disc at a fast speed for a number of seconds. The afterimage of the rotating spiral continues for some seconds after the physical rotation has ceased. Some investigators (Griew, Fellows, & Howes, 1963) have reported a longer afterimage for elderly subjects than for young subjects—but only when lengthy rotation periods are employed. However, other investigators (Coyne, Eiler, Vanderplas, & Botwinick, 1979) have failed to find an adult-age difference in duration of the afterimage even with lengthy rotation periods. The remaining aftereffect we will consider is the figural aftereffect. There are several ways by which it may be induced. One way is to have a subject fixate for a number of seconds on a dot that has a rectangle placed to its left. This rectangle is then removed and is replaced by another rectangle located to the left of where the original rectangle had been placed. An aftereffect occurs in which the second rectangle appears to be displaced farther to the left of the dot than it actually is. The magnitude of this aftereffect diminishes gradually over time. As it diminishes, it eventually shows a greater magnitude for elderly subjects than for young subjects (Eisdorfer & Axelrod, 1964). A similar age difference has been found for a quite different version of the stimulus materials used to induce a figural aftereffect (Cowart, Atkeson, & Pollack, 1979).

Aftereffects, like visual illusions, are of interest to psychologists mainly in terms of their value as general indices of perceptual competence. There are, however, perceptual phenomena of more ecological importance that are also capable of having their age differences accounted for by application of the persistence concept. One such phenomenon is that of speech perception. As indicated earlier, elderly people do have problems in speech perception when conditions for the intelligibility of words depart markedly from optimal conditions. To explain these problems, Botwinick (1978) reasoned that the prolonged trace of a speech sound (e.g., the phonemes making up a word) characteristic of elderly people interferes with the perception of subsequent sounds. In effect, elderly people may experience an inappropriately fused response to sequential speech components. Another problem in speech perception for elderly adults lies in their greater difficulty of integrating binaural cues (i.e., a sound reaches the two ears at slightly different times) to locate the source of a sound (Herman, Warren, & Wagener, 1977; Warren, Wagener, & Herman, 1978). Other applications of this kind have been made by Botwinick (1978). Although they are of potentially great significance, these applications are decidedly post hoc in nature, and they have yet to receive critical empirical tests.

Two final comments. First, there are classical perceptual phenomena for which adult-age differences are present, but they are not readily handled by the persistence concept. Specifically, we have in mind age differences on Type II illusions, that is, those illusions that show a decrease in magnitude from early to late adulthood. As far as we can tell, there has been no serious attempt to explain these decrements in terms of the persistence concept.

The second is a very important comment. There are classical perceptual phenomena for which there is no need to apply the persistence concept. That is, there are no adult-age differences that demand explanation. One such phenomenon appears to be size constancy (Leibowitz & Judisch, 1967). It seems likely that the other basic perceptual constancies, such as brightness constancy, are also resistant to age changes. Surprisingly little attention has been given to these constancies by experimental aging psychologists. Their usual approach is to accentuate the negative and to seek out those phenomena for which there are readily discernible age deficits. Null effects, meaning, in this case, the absence of adult-age differences, are all too often treated as being uninteresting and unworthy of reporting. In fact, as a general rule, much of human perception is unaltered by aging. Many perceptual activities are absolutely essential for maintaining fundamental interactions with the environment, and, as such, they seem to be protected from deterioration with aging by our species inheritance. Above all, perception of familiar objects and events, defined in terms of perceiving their meanings, continues unthwarted throughout the lifespan. From the perspective of associationism, these are highly overlearned perceptual responses—overlearned to the point that they have become automatic, routinized, and impregnable to the ravages of aging. The similarity to automatic memory activities is obvious.

At the same time, we cannot deny that there is some loss of perceptual sensitivity with aging, a loss sufficient to diminish overall adaptability to the environment. Over 90% of an ability may remain undisturbed by aging, but what is disturbed can have important practical consequences. An automobile continues to be perceived as an automobile by elderly adults, just as it is by young adults (however, some objects, such as faces, may become less readily recognized as people grow older). The meaning response attached to an automobile is highly overlearned to the point of being immune to age changes. Nevertheless, an automobile pulling suddenly out of a parking space into the way of an elderly driver may not be perceived quickly enough for the driver to respond appropriately. The stimulus-persistence concept explains this perceptual problem nicely: other stimuli perceived just prior to the unexpectedly moving automobile have not "cleared the nervous system," and a fused perceptual response and a confused individual may be the consequence.

Adult-Age Differences in Pattern Recognition

Our attention now shifts to age differences in perception as approached by information-processing psychologists. The transition means a shift from the phenomena of classical perception to the phenomena of pattern recognition. We will begin with a general discussion of the basic principles of pattern recognition and how these principles lead to questions concerning age sensitivity.

Pattern Recognition: Processes, Stages, and Age Sensitivity. Consider your response to the visual pattern A. Hopefully, you found yourself responding with "It's the letter *A.*" But why should you? To an associationist, the answer is that the present stimulus is a copy of some past stimulus element that is the initiating point of an already established $S \rightarrow s_R \rightarrow R$ chain, in which R consists of saying *A*. Or, alternatively, the present stimulus falls on the generalization gradient of some past stimulus, sufficiently so that it activates the associative chain linked to the past stimulus. But how closely does the present visual pattern copy previous instances of the letter *A* you have been exposed to and have had the opportunity to learn a naming response? The strain on an associative explanation becomes even greater when we make the pattern ⁀𝐼 or ⱴ or ⱴ, patterns that are even less likely to be copies, or near copies, of stimulus events entering into learned associations that terminate in the response of saying *A*. Yet, your perception of these patterns as the letter *A* remains unaltered.

A comparable strain does not exist for information processing's explanation of why you continue to perceive the same letter. For each pattern, the physical format of the representation existing in the retina must obviously be different. Nevertheless, each representation shares two common features, namely, the presence of two converging lines combined with the presence of a horizontal line intersecting each of the converging lines. It is this information that is assumed to be extracted from the physical pattern in the retina by means of a process known as *feature analysis*. The product of feature analysis is a transformed representation of the specific pattern registered on the retina itself. This transformed representation is shared by all patterns analyzable into the same basic set of featural components, regardless of their other differences in physical representations. Stored in your permanent memory is the long-established prototypal information that any pattern composed of the above features, and only those features, is an exemplar of a letter called *A*. Thus, you do not need an exact copy in memory of a present-stimulus pattern. The stored protypal information provides a rule for recognizing any specific exemplar of that prototype. All that is needed for our explanation of your ability to recognize *A*-ness are the further assumptions that the prototypal information is retrieved automatically (i.e., without conscious effort) from your memory system and then compared with the featural representation of the present input. The match between the featural representation and the prototypal knowledge assures your decision that, say $\vee$ is indeed the letter *A*, even though it is upside down. This decision results in the observable output, or behavior, in which you vocalize your decision.

This example illustrates information processing's general approach to perception, namely, its equating of perception with pattern recognition. Pattern recognition enters into virtually all aspects of our interactions with our environment, such as our understanding of sound patterns as spoken words and our reading of printed letter patterns as words. The importance of understanding the nature of pattern recognition has been nicely stated by Lachman et al.:

> Adults, children, and animals recognize common objects in their environment. You undoubtedly would recognize a picture of the Statue of Liberty: very young children recognize their parents' faces; and dogs can recognize such things as their food dishes. Objects are only one type of the many kinds of patterns in environmental stimulation that people recognize. For example, to understand speech we must recognize the auditory patterns that correspond to meaningful words. Reading similarly involves recognition of the arbitrary visual patterns used to represent letters of the alphabet. These examples illustrate that pattern recognition is essential to almost all our waking activities. In fact, every living thing must recognize patterns when it interacts meaningfully with its world. (1979, p. 492)

The feature-analysis/matching-decision approach to pattern recognition that we followed in our letter recognition example is a popular, but not the only, one taken by information-processing psychologists (Lachman et al., 1979; Solso, 1979). Its popularity owes a great deal to the fact that there is considerable biological evidence to support the existence of real feature-detecting structures in the sensory-perceptual systems of living organisms (e.g., Hubel & Wiesel, 1959). The approach leads to further important questions about the nature of the processes and structures entering into each of the three components, including eventually questions about their age sensitivities. In fact, nearly all of the effort directed by information-processing psychologists at ex-

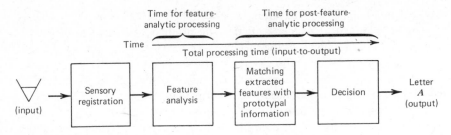

Figure 7.14. Stages of pattern recognition from input through output.

amining age changes in perception has been conducted within the feature-analysis-to-matching-decision framework.

Our theorizing about the nature of pattern recognition conforms to one of the basic characteristics of information processing, namely, its analysis of mental operations in terms of a sequence of stages intervening between the input of an environmental stimulus and output in the form of an overt response. For pattern recognition, the sequence outlined above is summarized in Figure 7.14. Most important, as indicated in Figure 7.14, the mental operations incorporated into each stage require time to complete. The fact that a given stage takes time to execute means that time itself provides an index of that stage's operating level of proficiency, assuming the time taken for that stage can be separated from the time taken for other stages. The time factor also suggests a plausible basis for expecting an age change in pattern recognition. Over the course of the adult lifespan, people may simply slow down in their rate of conducting the mental operations necessary for pattern recognition. That is, the operations per se may be essentially unaffected, only their quantitative attributes may change with increasing age. The overall effect would be a decrement in the proficiency of pattern recognition for older people, particularly with a rapid pacing of stimulus materials (e.g., as in accelerated speech).

A number of studies have revealed the age sensitivity of pattern recognition at a gross level. Older subjects, for example, are less proficient than young subjects at identifying complex patterns, whether they are printed words or pictures of objects, when segments (i.e., some featural components) are deleted from the pattern (Crook, Alexander, Anderson, Coules, Hanson, & Jeffries, 1958; Danziger & Salthouse, 1978; Kline, Culler, & Sucec, 1977; Kline, Hogan, & Stier, 1980). Older subjects are also less proficient at identifying geometric figures when they are embedded in more complex figures (Basowitz & Korchin, 1957); in identifying where a gap appears in a circular figure (Eriksen, Hamlin & Breitmeyer, 1970); in identifying briefly exposed forms, letters, and digits (W.R. Miles, 1942; Rajalakshmi & Jeeves, 1963); and in comprehending speech spoken at a rapid rate (Calearo & Lazzaroni, 1957). (Incidentally, some of these are phenomena for which age differences can be explained, with some effort, in terms of the persistence concept, see Botwinick, 1978). Unanswered by such studies is the important question of the locus of age sensitivity. Are age differences found only in a peripheral (feature-analytic) stage, only in a central (post-feature-analytic) stage, or in both stages? The separation into only two stages follows the practice commonly employed by psychologists working in the area of pattern recognition (e.g., Turvey, 1973). Feature analysis is assumed to be conducted at the level of biologically peripheral structures, and it is, therefore, identified as peripheral processing of information. In the case of visual-pattern recognition, peripheral processing occurs in the visual pathway running from the retina through the striate, or primary visual, area of the cortex. Identifying, or naming, patterns through comparisons with prototypal information is assumed to be conducted at the level of biologically central structures, and it is, therefore, identified as central processing of information. For visual-pattern recognition, central processing occurs in the secondary visual areas of the cortex. In general, peripheral processing is affected by physical attributes of stimuli (e.g., energy content), whereas central processing is affected by informational attributes (e.g., number of prototypes in a generic class, such as letters of the alphabet).

To test the age sensitivity of either peripheral processing or central processing requires some method of separating one stage from the other. Once a stage is isolated, processing proficiency may then be contrasted for adults of varying ages. Two of the methods developed by information-processing psychologists for accomplishing this objective have been fairly extensively applied in tests of age sensitivity. The first is the method of chronometric analysis introduced by Posner (Posner & Mitchell, 1967). It is basically an extension of Donders's (1969) subtractive method described in Chapter 6. The second is the method of backward masking introduced by Turvey (1973). Its effectiveness in separating stages of processing is derived from the disruptive effects a masking stimulus has on the processing of a prior stimulus (Kahneman, 1968).

Chronometric Analysis. Consider two different stimuli, one consisting of two uppercase forms of the same letter, for example, *AA,* the other of the uppercase and lowercase forms of the same letter, for example, *Aa.* Other stimuli of the form *AB* and *Ab* are also constructed. A subject's task is to decide, as rapidly as possible, whether the elements within a given stimulus have the same name, as in the first two examples, or a different name as in the second set of examples. The decision is indicated by moving a switch in one direction for same and in the opposite direction for different.

This simple task makes up the core of a chronometric analysis. All that is needed to complete the analysis is the measurement of reaction time for each class of stimulus elements. Our interest lies in the two classes for which same is the correct response. For one class, exemplified by *AA,* peripheral processing is sufficient to yield a same decision. Given identical physical features, the two elements of a given stimulus must have the same name. For the other class, exemplified by *Aa,* central processing is required before a sameness decision can be reached. The two elements of a given stimulus no longer have physical identity. However, both sets of features extracted from the stimulus match prototypal information in permanent memory signifying the same name of a letter. As shown schematically in Figure 7.15, our analysis of the processes governing pattern recognition predicts a longer reaction time for a match based only on name identity *Aa* than on a match based on physical identity *(AA).*

Given a number of stimuli having physically identical elements, a subject's mean reaction time for those stimuli evaluates that subject's proficiency of peripheral processing relative to other subjects. Similarly, means for these scores derived from groups of young and elderly subjects may be contrasted, thereby testing the age sensitivity of peripheral processing. Evaluation of a subject's central-processing proficiency can be made by subtracting that subject's mean reaction time for physical matches from the subject's mean reaction time for name matches (see Figure 7.15). The difference score estimates the time required to match the extracted features for each letter with information stored in memory and to discover that the two letters have the same name. Means for these difference scores derived from groups of young and elderly subjects may be tested, thereby testing the age sensitivity of central processing.

Age contrasts of this kind were first made by Hines and Posner (1976). Their results are plotted in Figure 7.16. Note first that their elderly subjects averaged over 200 milliseconds slower than their young subjects on physically identical stimuli. The implication is that peripheral processing slows down in old age. However, the magnitude of the age deficit is probably overestimated by the use of this method. Speed of executing the motor response required to

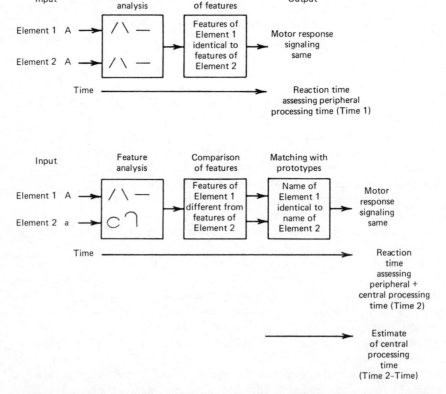

Figure 7.15. Schematic representation of the processing stages entering into chronometric analysis when the paired stimulus letters are physically identical (top panel) and when they are physically dissimilar but identical in name (bottom panel).

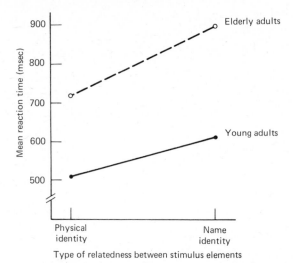

Figure 7.16. Age differences in reaction time in a chronometric analysis as a function of the type of relatedness (physical identity versus name identity) between paired stimulus letters. (Adapted from data in Hines & Posner, 1976).

signal sameness is likely to be slower for elderly subjects than for young-adult subjects, thus inflating the age difference somewhat. Nevertheless, the observed age difference in reaction time is too large to be explained solely in terms of the motor speed factor (e.g., compare this age difference with other age differences in reaction time reported in Chapter 6).

The next step is to estimate the rate of central processing for each age group. This estimate, as given by the difference in mean scores for physical identity and name identity, is 107 milliseconds for young subjects and 181 milliseconds for elderly subjects (values closely approximated in a later study by Parkinson, 1977). The implication is that central processing also slows down in old age. This is apparent from the fact that elderly subjects required, on the average, about 75 milliseconds more than young adults to complete the matching-decision process. The slowing down in central processing with advancing age becomes even more apparent as the processes themselves become more complex. This may be seen in a study by Poon, Fozard, Vierck, Dailey, Cerella, and Zeller (1976) in which the stimulus materials extended those of Hines and Posner (1976). Sameness was now contingent on a rule identity instead of a name identity. The two elements of a stimulus were to be judged as being the same if they were both vowels (e.g., *AE*) or if they were both consonants (e.g., *NR*), and they were to be judged as being different if one was a vowel and the other a consonant (e.g., *AR*). In some instances the two vowels or the two consonants in the same condition were the same letter (e.g., *AA* and *RR*), thus replicating the physical-identity condition present in Hines and Posner's (1976) study. Mean reaction times for young and elderly subjects on all three classes of same stimuli are plotted in Figure 7.17. The multiplicative relationship apparent in the interaction between age and type of stimulus adds to our conviction that rate of central processing is age sensitive. Note further that the age

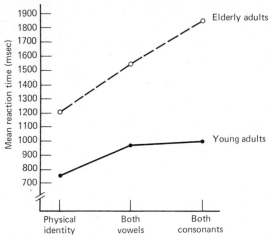

Figure 7.17. Age differences in reaction time in a chronometric analysis for paired stimulus letters varying in terms of physical versus rule (both vowels or both consonants) identity. (Adapted from data in Poon, Fozard, Vierck, Dailey, Cerella, & Zeller, 1976.)

deficit in processing time for nonidentical vowels exceeded the age deficit in processing time for nonidentical consonants. There are, of course, more consonants than vowels in our alphabet. Consequently, more prototypal information has to be searched to equate N and R with the same class name (i.e., consonant) than to match A and E with the same class name (i.e., vowel).

There is another interesting phenomenon to be observed in the results obtained by Poon et al. (1976). Note that the mean reaction time in the physical-identity condition is considerably greater for both young and elderly subjects (but especially so for the elderly) than in the physical-identity condition employed by Hines and Posner (1976). It is conceivable that increasing task complexity slows down the rate of peripheral processing at all age levels, with the adverse effect being particularly pronounced for older subjects.

The potential of the chronometric method for testing age sensitivity has barely been scratched. For example, we will discover in Chapter 9 that it has important implications for research on age differences in short-term memory phenomena. For the moment, however, our concern is with a further implication it has for research on age differences in visual-pattern recognition. Our reference is to the use of the method to distinguish between parallel and serial peripheral processing. There is evidence to indicate that young adults engage in parallel peripheral processing (e.g., Beller, 1970). Consider a physical-identity condition in which the stimulus contains either four identical elements (e.g., *AAAA*) or the standard two identical elements (e.g., *AA*). Young adults seem to make same decisions as rapidly with four elements, and even eight elements (Beller, 1970), as they do with only two elements. Such equality would not be possible if feature analysis had to proceed serially from element to element. That is, serial processing would have to progress from element to element, leading to increasing reaction time as the number of elements to be processed increases. Other evidence for parallel peripheral processing by young adults comes from research using a visual-search task (Neisser, 1964). Here, subjects are given a target letter (e.g., *Q*) to find in an array of letters arranged in rows. The target may be embedded in the first row on one trial, the second row on another trial, and so. Search time may be seen to increase linearly as the depth of the target in the rows increases. More important, however, search time is relatively unaffected by the breadth of the rows. That is, it is about the same for rows containing, say, six letters as it is for rows containing, say, only four letters. If in-row letters are processed serially for the presence/absence of the target letter's features, then search time should increase progressively as breadth increases. The implication again is that young adults engage in parallel peripheral processing. Would time scores for elderly adults remain similarly constant under these conditions? If not, we would have good reason to suspect that the slower peripheral-processing rate found for elderly adults is the consequence of their transition from a fast-paced parallel processing in early adulthood to a slower paced serial processing in later adulthood.

Backward Masking. The backward-masking method is considerably more complex than the chronometric method, as may be seen in the summary of its procedural operations given in Figure 7.18. These operations call for two tachistoscopically exposed stimuli (i.e., by means of a widely used apparatus called a tachistoscope) that are separated by a brief temporal interval (i.e., an interstimulus interval or ISI). The first, or target, stimulus, is typically a single letter, whereas the second is either a pattern mask (top panel of Figure 7.18) or a random-noise mask (bottom panel of Figure 7.18). The role of any masking stimulus is to disrupt the processing of the target stimulus. Processing of the target terminates with the arrival of the mask. Only if processing is sufficiently complete prior to the mask's onset will a subject be able to identify the target by name. The type of mask selected by an investigator depends on the level of processing being investigated. For central processing of a target, a pattern mask fulfills its disruptive role by having overlapping features with the target (i.e., line segments of the kind shown in Figure 7.18). For peripheral processing, a random-noise mask fulfills its role by having a greater energy content than the preceding target stimulus. One other procedural variable serves to separate central processing from peripheral processing. Disruption of central processing occurs even though the target stimulus is exposed to one eye (usually the right) and the masking stimulus to the other eye (usually the left). This disparity in eye stimulation defines what is called dichoptic vision (top panel of Figure 7.18). Masking is effective because the informational content from each eye eventually reaches the same secondary visual area of the cortex. Disruption of peripheral processing does not take place with dichoptic vision. Such disruption occurs only if the target stimulus and the masking stimulus initiate neural activity that traverses the same peripheral channel, beginning with stimulation of the same eye. This may be accomplished either by means of monoptic vision, in which both stimuli are exposed to the same single eye (usually the right), or by means of binocular vision, in which both stimuli are exposed to both eyes.

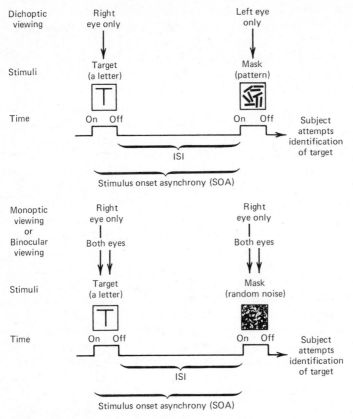

Figure 7.18. Schematic representation of the conditions and the sequence of events entering into a backward-masking analysis of either central processing (top panel) or peripheral processing (bottom panel).

Age differences in rate of central processing are examined with respect to the minimal ISI (i.e., the ISI separating the offset of the target and the onset of the mask, see Figure 7.18) required for a subject to identify a series of target letters without making an error. This interval, in turn, depends on how long the target itself had been physically exposed. The basic assumption underlying the use of the masking method is that processing of a target's informational content begins during the brief time the target is physically present (e.g., 20 milliseconds or 10 milliseconds) and continues during the ISI. This continued processing presumably operates on a trace, or image, of the target stimulus (we discovered earlier that a trace seems to persist for over 200 milliseconds). Consider a young-adult subject who needs at least 75 milliseconds of processing time to identify a target stimulus. If the target is exposed for 20 milliseconds, then the onset of the mask would have to be delayed at least 55 milliseconds to allow the full 75 milliseconds needed for target identification. If the duration of the target's exposure is decreased to 10 milliseconds, then the delay of the mask's onset would have to be increased to 65 milliseconds. In effect, there is a tradeoff between target exposure time and duration of the ISI—the longer the target's exposure, the briefer the ISI that may be tolerated without disruption of target identification. The nature of the tradeoff may be seen in the resulting constancy for the period termed *stimulus onset asynchrony* (SOA)—the time between the onset of the target stimulus and the onset of the masking stimulus (i.e., SOA = target duration + ISI). For our hypothetical young-adult subject, the value of this constant is 75 milliseconds.

Proficiency of any subject's central processing may be evaluated by determining that subject's critical ISI under conditions of dichoptic vision and the use of a pattern mask. All that is needed is the determination of the ISI needed to just-barely escape masking for each of a number of target durations. If our preceding analysis is valid, then that subject's SOA values should remain relatively constant throughout our variation in target duration. Our analysis may then be extended to age differences in rate of central processing by employing separate groups of young-adult and elderly subjects. Assuming slower processing by the elderly, we should find larger critical ISI values and larger constant SOA values for our elderly subjects than for our young subjects.

Several studies have made these important age comparisons. The results of one of these studies (Walsh, Williams, & Hertzog, 1979) are plotted in Figure 7.19. Note initally the presence of a tradeoff effect for both age levels, that is, a decreasing ISI value as target duration increases. The tradeoff, however, is more apparent for the young subjects than for the elderly. Nevertheless, SOA for various target durations remains relatively constant for both age levels, ranging from mean values of 76.6 to 79.9 milliseconds for young subjects and 103.0 to 130.5 milliseconds for elderly subjects. Our conclusion is that the elderly subjects averaged about 30 milliseconds longer than young adults to complete the central processing necessary to identify a single letter. Fairly comparable adult-age differences have been reported by Walsh (1976) and Walsh, Till, and Williams (1978).

A further question of considerable importance concerns the ability of elderly subjects to increase their rate of central processing with practice in target identification. Judging from the results obtained by Hertzog, Williams, and Walsh (1976), there is little reason to doubt this ability. Their elderly subjects

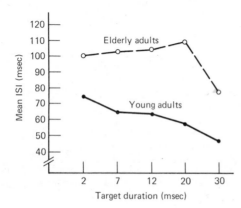

Figure 7.19. Age differences in time (ISI) needed to avoid central masking for target letters exposed at varying durations. (Adapted from Walsh, Williams, & Hertzog, 1979, Table 1.)

received many target identification trials on each of five different days. Throughout these sessions, the duration of target exposure was always set at 20 milliseconds. As can be seen in Figure 7.20, the mean ISI needed to escape disruption by the mask did decrease over the five practice sessions. In fact, the SOA on the fifth day was more than 25 milliseconds less than on the first day. As can also be seen in Figure 7.20, the young-adult subjects also benefited greatly from practice. The SOA value on the fifth day was nearly 30 milliseconds less than on the first day. Obviously, practice did not eliminate the age difference in processing proficiency, if anything, it increased the magnitude slightly. This is a familiar theme we encountered in Chapter 3. It seems highly unlikely that still more practice on the target-identification task would ever eliminate, or even markedly reduce, the age difference favoring young adults.

Proficiency of any subject's peripheral processing may also be evaluated by determining that subject's critical ISI needed to just-barely escape masking over various target exposure times, only now the determination is made with monoptic (or binocular) vision and a random-noise mask. The relationship between target duration and the critical ISI, however, departs greatly from the relationship found in central masking. Of interest is the product found by multiplying target duration and the critical ISI duration. This product is expected to remain constant over variation in target durations, just as the sum of the two durations remains constant in central masking. Adult-age differences in the magnitude of this constant have been found in several studies (Kline & Szafran, 1975; Till, 1978; Walsh, et al., 1978). Typical results are those obtained by Kline and Szafran and plotted in Figure 7.21. Note first that the course of the target duration/ISI relationship is curvilinear in contrast to the linear relationship found in central masking (see Figure 7.19). The curvilinearity reflects the multiplicative constant described above. For example, with a 4-millisecond-target duration, mean ISI's of 52 and 115 milliseconds were necessary to avoid masking for young and elderly subjects respectively. With an 8-millisecond-target duration, the mean ISI's shrink to 26 and 50 milliseconds, but the products remain about the same (208 and 400 for young and elderly subjects respectively). The age difference is a clear indication of a slower rate of

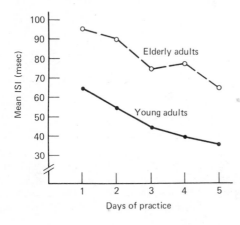

Figure 7.20. Effects of practice for both young and elderly subjects on central-processing time needed to avoid masking. (Adapted from Hertzog, Williams, & Walsh, 1976, Table 1.)

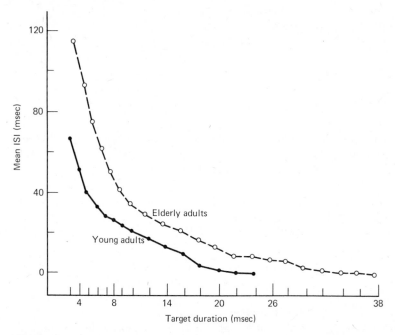

Figure 7.21. Age differences in time (ISI) needed to avoid peripheral backward masking for target letters exposed at varying durations. (Adapted from Kline & Szafran, 1975, Figure 1.)

peripheral processing by elderly adults than by young adults, although other evidence (Till & Franklin, 1981) indicates that the magnitude of the age deficit is less pronounced than the magnitude of the deficit occurring for central processing. Another indication of the slowing down in old age is the age difference in the target duration required to escape interference when the ISI is 0 (i.e., the mask follows immediately after the offset of the target). From Figure 7.21, it can be seen that elderly subjects required, on the average, 38 milliseconds of target exposure, whereas young adults required, on the average, only 24 milliseconds.

Adult-Age Differences in Auditory Processing. Our analysis of age differences in processing rates has concentrated on visual-pattern recognition—and with good reason. There has been relatively little research examining adult-age differences in processing rates for auditory stimuli. However, evidence provided by Elias and Elias (1976) suggests that auditory processing also slows down in old age. They employed an auditory form of chronometric analysis in which successive tones were judged to be the same or different. Mean reaction times averaged more than 160 milliseconds longer for elderly subjects than for young-adult subjects. The age deficit assessed in this study appears to be in peripheral processing. That is, recognition of tone identity should require no central processing in the sense of having to match extracted featural information with prototypal information. Age differences in auditory central processing are difficult to assess. Consider, for example, judgments involving successive words that are either the same or different. Elias and Elias found an age deficit in speed of detecting sameness that approximated the deficit they found for successive tones. This should not be surprising. Detecting identical speech sounds can be accomplished with little, if any, central processing involving name matches. All a subject needs to do is detect the identity of the physical features inherent in the successive sounds.

Implications for Age Differences in the Real World: Automatic Versus Controlled Processes in Pattern Recognition. The evidence we reviewed makes it hard to deny that a slower rate of processing information, both peripherally and centrally, is characteristic of old age. Of course, slower in this context is at the level of milliseconds. Nevertheless, with briefly exposed stimulus patterns, as in our standard laboratory tasks, the adverse effects of slowing down with aging can be readily demonstrated. But what about pattern recognition in the real world? Here, stimuli exposed for fractions of a second that demand immediate decisions are more the exception than the rule. Still, there are some real-life counterparts of our laboratory tasks that call on rapid processing of information. For example, traffic control operators at a large airport are confronted with constantly changing visual patterns on a radar scope. An operator's ability to process that information rapidly is essential for the avoidance of both accidents and traffic jams. The wisdom of employing elderly operators must be seriously questioned.

There is another reason for the nonspecialist to have an interest in aging research on pattern recognition. Both the chronometric task and the masking task have potential value as diagnostic tests of overall neurological functioning in old age. Someday routine physical examinations and checkups may well include these kinds of tasks. An elderly person with a considerably slower rate of processing than found at the time of that person's last physical examination may be showing an early sign of a neurological impairment that would otherwise be difficult to detect.

The fact remains, however, that most everyday pattern-recognition activities, such as those involved in reading, are largely unaffected by aging. The probable reason for these constancies over the adult lifespan is that many pattern-recognition activities become automatic through their frequent occurrences (Posner & Snyder, 1975; Shiffrin & Schneider, 1977). Automatic perceptual processes, like automatic memory processes, do not strain an individual's limited processing capacity. These processes should, therefore, be unaffected by any decrement in capacity with aging. The automaticity of reading for young adults is clearly demonstrated by what is called the Stroop color-word interference effect (Stroop, 1935). The demonstration requires two versions of a color-naming task. In the first, a subject sees a series of color patches and names the colors as rapidly as possible. In the second, a subject sees a series of colors, but this time each color is the ink of a printed word, specifically a word naming a color that differs from that of the ink (e.g., the word *blue* is printed in green ink, with green being the correct response). Young adults take nearly twice as much time to name all of the colors in the second version of the task than in the first version (Stroop, 1935). The automaticity of reading *blue* when that word is being viewed interferes dramatically with naming the color of ink in which the word is printed. That is, reading is so automatic that it cannot be inhibited to avoid interference on the Stroop task. Given the automaticity of reading, the fact that elderly adults do not differ from young adults in speed of reading individual words (e.g., Waugh, 1980) should not be surprising. The absence of an age deficit simply confirms the automaticity of reading.

Of great interest is the extent to which elderly people can acquire automaticity of processing on a novel task. The acquisition of automaticity should be apparent by the absence of an age deficit in performance on that task. One kind of task for which such acquisition may be possible is a task calling for consistent mapping (Shiffrin & Schneider, 1977). On a consistent-mapping task, a subject searches for the same targets over a number of practice sessions. For example, the letters *A* and *Y* are designated target letters printed on index cards. Each card in a stack for each practice session contains either an *A* or a *Y* along with several other distracting letters (which also stay the same in each practice session). If a card contains an *A* it is placed in one pile; if it contains a *Y*, it is placed in a different pile. Under these conditions, Plude and Hoyer (1979) demonstrated the absence of an age difference in total sorting time averaged over a number of practice sessions (see Figure 7.22). It should be noted that the investigators used an adjusted time score for their age comparison. The adjustment was made by subtracting from each subject's sorting-time score the time required by that subject to sort a stack of cards containing either a symbol (a horizontal arrow) without distractors or nothing at all. This adjustment corrects for the age difference in speed of executing the motor response demanded by the task (i.e., placement of a card in a pile). (We observed earlier

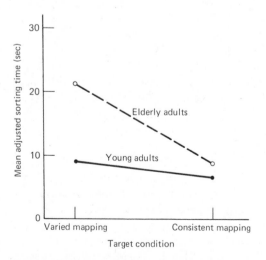

Figure 7.22. Age differences in sorting time under varied mapping (controlled processing) and consistent mapping (automatic processing). (Adapted from Plude & Hoyer, 1979, Figure 1.)

that the failure to make this kind of adjustment inflates the magnitude of age deficits in peripheral rate of processing found with chronometric analysis.)

Plude and Hoyer also demonstrated that an age deficit persists, again with adjusted sorting-time scores, when the task requires varied mapping (Shiffrin & Schneider, 1977) instead of consistent mapping (see Figure 7.22). In the varied-mapping form of their task, different target letters were used for each practice session (e.g., *A* and *Y* for the first session, *L* and *J* for the second session, and so on) along with differing distracting letters across sessions. The constantly changing targets and distractors places a memory load, or demand, on a subject from session to session. Under these conditions, controlled, or cognitively effortful, processing is needed to analyze each stimulus pattern. This kind of processing strains a subject's limited processing capacity. Consequently, an age deficit in performance is expected on the basis of the older subject's diminished processing capacity. A similar deficit occurs when subjects have to sort a number of stimuli into more than two categories or piles (Rabbitt, 1964). Age-sensitive controlled processing also appears to be needed for such tasks as identifying briefly exposed letters. We discovered earlier that the age deficit on this task does not disappear with extended practice (Figure 7.20). The conditions existing in that study approximate those defining varied mapping—a large number of target letters (eight, in fact) was employed and the specific targets were randomly presented over trials. Processing under these conditions does introduce a memory load and should, therefore, require cognitive effort.

Of interest would be a replication of the Hertzog el al. study (1976), but with a smaller number of target letters. With only a few target letters, randomly ordered, it is conceivable that automaticity would occur, as evidenced by the eventual disappearance of the age deficit. As a general rule, an age deficit in processing rate seems inevitable whenever a pattern-recognition task introduces a large number of stimuli presented in varying random orders over a number of trials. For example, Thomas, Fozard, and Waugh (1977) had their subjects name pictures of common objects (e.g., dice and a book). There were 16 pictures presented in different random orders over eight trials. Mean naming-time decreased considerably for both young and elderly subjects from the first to the last trial. However, a pronounced age deficit in time scores persisted throughout the trials—a finding much like that obtained by Hertzog et al. (1976) on their masking task. The implication is that age-sensitive controlled processing guided performance for picture naming as well as letter naming.

Stability over the Lifespan. To complete this section, we will examine how pattern-recognition theory explains the fact that most perceptual activities are really unaffected by human aging. We faced this happy dilemma earlier in our analysis of associationism's approach to age changes in perception—over 90% of perceptual activities may be unaltered by aging, and yet it is the segment that is affected that is the subject of experimental aging research.

The core component of pattern recognition is generic memory. It is in generic memory that the information giving meaning to stimulus patterns is stored—and generic memory itself is remarkably insensitive to age changes.

Consider an individual seeing a new make of automobile for the first time. The new model may have design changes that are strikingly innovative, and yet people, young and old alike, have no difficulty in *seeing* that it is an automobile. The reason, of course, is that the basic features of an automobile are still there. It has tires, headlights, a bumper, and so on. These are the features that provide the physical input to the retina. There, the physical pattern of stimulation is processed by feature analysis, and the component abstracted features are matched with information stored in generic memory. That information identifies tires, headlights, bumper, and so on, as signifying an automobile. (Incidentally, associationism must also struggle with the problem of how we perceive this unique model as being an automobile. As we indicated earlier, the new model must be considered a stimulus that falls along the generalization gradient of prior stimuli that are firmly attached to the response of automobile.) The basic operations of feature analysis and matching obviously remain intact over the adult lifespan. What elderly adult do you know who would fail to identify the new model as an automobile? Consequently, even fairly novel stimuli are perceived as accurately by elderly adults as by young adults. It is only the speed of conducting the basic operations that is known to be affected by aging. However, slowing down of these operations can, as we indicated earlier, have many important adverse effects.

Adult Age Differences in Attention

Some idea of the importance of attention in our everyday lives may be gleaned from the many statements we hear or read that refer to some aspect of attention: "Be alert!" "Watch for any sign of activity." "Get ready, get set, ..." "He's listening, but he's not hearing." "Probable cause of the accident—inattention of the driver in vehicle A." "He can't walk and chew gum at the same time!" The importance of attention has not escaped the notice of experimental psychologists. Beginning in the early 1950s, research on attentional phenomena has been very popular, as has theorizing about the processes mediating these phenomena. Nor have age differences in attentional phenomena escaped the attention of experimental aging psychologists. In fact, studies of age differences have been keeping pace with the rapid expansion of basic research on attention. Our objective in this section is to acquaint you with what these studies have revealed about age changes in attentional phenomena. To accomplish this objective, we will necessarily have to touch on some of the theories and models that have guided basic research on attention. Our treatment of these theories and models will be somewhat superficial. Fortunately, excellent overviews of attention are available (e.g., Lachman et al., 1979; Solso, 1979). They are well worth reading for extending your basic knowledge about attention.

As hinted at early in this chapter, there are actually three different attentional phenomena of interest to experimental aging psychologists: vigilance, selective attention, and divided attention. In each case, attention influences either the kind of information or the amount of information processed from a stimulus input or a series of inputs. Although age differences are commonly found for each phenomenon, explanations of these differences vary among the phenomena. We will review the phenomena separately, beginning with vigilance, the simplest of the three.

Vigilance. In its simplest form, vigilance refers to a person's readiness for detecting a stimulus change. The change occurs during exposure to an otherwise invariant sequence of stimuli. In the real world, readiness of this kind presents a potential problem for the automobile driver traveling a monotonous stretch of highway, a quality-control inspector examining a steady stream of objects and looking for those with a defect, and a machine operator keeping an eye on a dial for any deflection that signals a malfunction. In each, a letdown in vigilance could spell disaster. The cognitive demand for efficient performance on a simple-vigilance task is slight. Needed, instead, is a combination of sustained high arousal (see Solso, 1979) and resistance to fatigue. Given the common beliefs of age changes in both arousal and susceptibility to fatigue, there is ample reason for investigating age differences in performance on simple-vigilance tasks.

Our representative study is one by Surwillo and Quiller (1964). Their task required monitoring the movements of a pointer on a clock-like device. The pointer, like the second hand of a clock, moved in discrete steps of one per second. However, at irregular intervals the pointer made a double jump, that is, it traveled through twice the usual distance. Over the 1 hour a subject performed on this task, only 23 of the total 3600 movements of the pointer were double jumps. Thus, a stimulus change—defined here as a double jump amidst a long series of single jumps—was, indeed, a rare event, much like that found on real-life vigilance tasks. The subjects ranged in age over the entire adult lifespan, but, for purposes of analysis, they were grouped into two levels, one below age 60 and the other age 60 and beyond. A common argument in the aging literature is that vigilance holds up well before age 60 and deteriorates beyond that age (e.g., Talland, 1966). Age differences were examined with respect to the percentage of double jumps detected in each quarter-of-an-hour period. Any age difference in vigilance owing to an age difference in arousal level at the start of the monitoring would be expected to show up in performance during the first 15 minutes. No such difference in performance was found however. The younger subjects averaged a detection rate of 82.3%, whereas the older subjects averaged 78.3%, a nonsignificant difference. Any age difference in vigilance owing to an age difference in fatigue would be expected to show up in performance during the last 15 minutes. Here, there was a clearly significant age difference—71.1% and 58.0% for the younger and older subjects respectively. In a somewhat similar study, Talland (1966) found performance to deteriorate steadily and progressively beyond the 20s when the to-be-monitored stimuli were presented at a much faster rate than in Surwillo and Quiller's (1964) study. The vocational lession is obvious—the assignment of older workers to routine vigilance assignments could be a costly mistake.

Another kind of vigilance task calls for the short-term retention of stimulus information as well as keeping track of stimulus changes. The memory requirement adds greatly to age deficits in performance (Kirchner, 1958; Welford, 1962). The drastic effect produced by the addition of a memory requirement is especially visible in Kirchner's clever study. Young and elderly subjects were confronted by a panel of 12 lights and 12 keys, one key corresponding to each light. One light was on at a time, and it was followed 1.5 seconds later by a different light going on. This procedure continued through a sequence of 36 going-on lights. In the standard, or 0-back, condition, a subject pressed the key corresponding to the light presently on. Obviously, no memory requirement entered into this condition. In two experimental conditions, 1-back and 2-back, a subject pressed the key corresponding either to the light that had been on just prior to the presently on light (1-back) or to the light that had been on two steps prior to the presently on light (2-back). A memory load that increased in amount from 1-back to 2-back was clearly introduced in the experimental conditions. The results, expressed as percentage of correct responses for the 36 stimulus changes, are shown in Figure 7.23. Note that the monitoring performance of elderly adults deteriorated relative to the performance of young adults only when the task demanded the short-term retention of stimulus information. Note further that the extent of the deterioration increased greatly as the complexity of the memory requirement increased.

The addition of a memory requirement is not the only way a vigilance task may be modified to increase the involvement of cognitive activity. Specifically, a stimulus sequence may be structured so that the stimuli follow a nonrandom order of occurrence. Of concern is a subject's ability to discover the structure and to make effective use of it in monitoring the series of stimulus inputs. Consider, for example, a task in which a subject tracks a tone that is on and off on each of two auditory channels, one for each ear (Griew, 1968). The subject listens on earphones, but is allowed to listen to only one channel at any one time. Most important, the subject is free throughout the monitoring interval to choose channels by means of a selection lever. The subject's objective, of

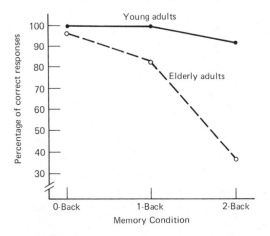

Figure 7.23. Age differences in monitoring flashing lights under varying memory-load conditions. (Adapted from Kirchner, 1958, Table 3.)

course, is to hear as many tones as possible over the duration of the experimental interval. What the subject does not know in advance is that 70% of the signals occur on one of the channels and only 30% on the other channel. Discovery of the input's statistical structure should lead eventually to a greater concentration on the experimenter-favored channel than on the less favored channel. Subjects who utilize the statistical structure are, therefore, certain to have higher hit rates than subjects who utilize some form of random shuffling back and forth between channels.

Interestingly, this kind of task is one for which some psychologists have argued that elderly adults should outperform young adults (Griew, 1962, 1968). The greater experience of elderly people in learning to anticipate future events (Welford, 1958) is expected to give them the advantage over young adults in detecting the statistical attributes of any novel situation that involves the anticipation of future events, including tones on selected channels. Support for this hypothesis was obtained by Griew (1968). During the final minutes of monitoring tones, Griew's elderly subjects were listening to the high-frequency-of-occurrence channel over 80% of the time, whereas his young-adult subjects were listening to that channel barely over 50% of the time. Consequently, the elderly subjects were experiencing more hits than the young subjects. However, as observed by Rabbitt and Rogers (1965), there is a basic flaw in the kind of procedure used by Griew. Suppose the left-ear channel is the one having the higher signal frequency. Having selected that channel at Time 1, it is to the subject's advantage to repeat that selection response at Time 2, again at Time 3, and so on. However, the repeated selection of the left-channel may be explained in simpler terms than the discovery of a stimulus sequence's statistical structure. Suppose a subject adopts either a simple-response-repetition (e.g., left-left-left-left) or response-alternation (e.g., left-right-left-right) strategy. Adoption of the response-repetition strategy would clearly result in a higher hit than adoption of the response-alternation strategy, quite independently of discovering the statistical structure. If older subjects are more likely, in general, than young adults to repeat prior responses, then their greater proficiency would be accounted for on a Griew-like task without having to postulate an age difference in a more complex, higher order cognitive activity. Rabbitt and Rogers (1965) failed to find an age difference in responding to a more predictable stimulus than to a less predictable stimulus when repetitions of response as a confounding factor were controlled. Other investigators (Fozard, Thomas, & Waugh, 1976; Waugh, Fozard, Talland, & Erwin, 1973) have also failed to find any pronounced age differences in expectancies acquired during performance on vigilance-like tasks. Moreoever, there is also evidence (Maule & Sanford, 1980; Rabbitt, 1965a; Rabbitt & Birren, 1967) to indicate that older adults may be less likely than young adults to adjust to the structure offered by stimulus probabilities. At any rate, our safest conclusion seems to be that age deficits in performance on vigilance tasks are limited largely to tasks requiring either sustained monitoring of generally invariant stimuli or a memory prerequisite for monitoring sequential stimuli.

Selective Attention. Our limited processing capacity does not permit us to analyze all of the stimuli impinging on us at any one time. Consequently, our
attention focuses on, or selects, some components of the complete array of
stimuli, whereas other components are presumably left unattended (i.e., not
subjected to pattern-recognition analysis). Selective attention is a common occurrence in our everyday living. As an example of real-life visual selective attention, consider the experience that most people have while watching a football
game in a crowded stadium. When the action heats up on the field, their attention turns to the players handling the ball after it is snapped by the center.
Tuned out from their perception are the violent collisions taking place among
the opposing linemen. To these spectators, the quarterback and the running
backs constitute *relevant stimuli,* whereas the remaining players constitute *irrelevant stimuli.* Relevant stimuli are the targets of selective attention; irrelevant
stimuli are potentially distracting elements that are present simultaneously. As
an example of real-life auditory selective attention, consider the familiar cocktail party phenomenon. The guests at the party find themselves confronted by
several simultaneous conversations. Usually, one conversation, the relevant
stimulus, is selected for polite, if not enthusiastic, listening, whereas the other
conversations, or irrelevant stimuli, are ignored to the point of becoming background noise.

It was actually a laboratory simulation of the cocktail party phenomenon
that initiated contemporary interest in selective attention. The simulation
(Cherry, 1953) made use of what is called dichotic listening. In dichotic listening, a subject receives, through earphones, two different messages simultaneously, one to each ear. To force selective attention, Cherry had subjects
shadow (i.e., repeat verbatim the message as it is heard) a story arriving at one
ear, while ignoring a different story arriving at the other ear. Cherry discovered
that the unattended message appears to be truly ignored. His subjects had
virtually no memory of its content. Moreover, they were unaware of the fact
that some of the irrelevant stories switched languages (English to German)
midway through the tape recording or that other irrelevant stories were played
backwards.

The results of Cherry's study and other similar studies conducted in England during the early 1950s led to the first formal model of selective attention.
Broadbent (1958) reasoned that the limited capacity of a person's perceptual
processing system is protected from being overloaded by means of a filter that
operates on information shortly after its entry into a sensory register. The
major components of Broadbent's model of selective attention are illustrated in
Figure 7.24. Stimuli, whether relevant or irrelevant, are assumed to receive
gross peripheral processing on their registration by a sense receptor. The informational products of this very preliminary analysis are transmitted to a short-
term store where they reside briefly. Information derived from relevant stimuli
is then passed through the filter to receive further peripheral and central processing. The final outcome is identification of the relevant stimulus components. By contrast, information derived from irrelevant stimuli is blocked from

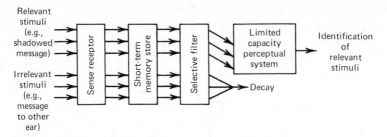

Figure 7.24. Schematic representation of Broadbent's (1958) filter model of selective attention.

further processing by the filter and soon decays. Broadbent's model has no difficulty explaining the results obtained by Cherry (1953). Eventually, however, experimental anomalies were discovered that could not be explained simply by an impermeable filter principle. For example, Moray (1959) found that subjects did recognize their own names when they were included as part of the irrelevant message directed to the presumably unattended ear. (The same thing happens at a real cocktail party—your name mentioned in the background is not likely to go unnoticed.) The implication is that all inputs, relevant *and* irrelevant, receive some degree of central processing. The concept of a filter that is impermeable to virtually all of the informational content of irrelevant stimuli is obviously untenable. Over the years, a number of different models of selective attention have appeared. One of the popular models (Treisman, 1960) stresses a peripherally located filter that functions as an attenuator of irrelevant stimulus information rather than as an impenetrable barrier for irrelevant information. Another popular model (Deutsch & Deutsch, 1963; Norman, 1968) places the filter-like function at a central level.

Our concern is with age changes in the efficacy of filtering information, regardless of the nature of the specific filtering mechanism. A popular notion is that the perceptual noise attributable to the failure to filter out, or at least to attenuate greatly, irrelevant stimuli increases over the adult lifespan (Layton, 1975). Stated somewhat differently, elderly adults are believed to be susceptible to greater distraction effects from irrelevant stimuli than are young adults. The increase in distractability by irrelevant stimuli should result in inferior performance by elderly adults on perceptual tasks demanding selective attention to simultaneously present stimuli. If true, elderly people are more likely than young adults to miss seeing the tricky handoff made by a quarterback to a tailback. More important, they are also more likely to experience mishaps crossing busy intersections, avoiding obstacles in their pathways, and so on. There is, in fact, evidence (Planek & Fowler, 1971) that indicates many automobile accidents involving elderly drivers are attributable to the inordinate attention they direct to irrelevant stimuli.

There is a great deal of laboratory evidence in support of the hypothesis that elderly people are distracted more by irrelevant stimuli than are younger people. One kind of evidence comes from studies using the Stroop task described earlier. Given the combination of the word *blue* printed in green ink, and the requirement to name the ink color, green functions as a relevant stimulus and the word *blue* as an irrelevant stimulus. We discovered that it is impossible to escape the interference produced by the irrelevant stimulus in this case. Nevertheless, as illustrated in Figure 7.25, the magnitude of the interference is far greater for elderly subjects than for young subjects. In this study (Comalli, Wapner, & Werner, 1962), subjects of varying ages were scored in terms of the total time it took them to go through a stack of cards and name the color ink on each card. For the sake of comparison, the results obtained by Comalli et al. for total time to go through another stack containing color patches (and no color words) are also included. Note that the age deficit in the absence of interfering irrelevant stimuli is fairly slight.

Studies by Rabbitt (1964, 1965b; Jordan & Rabbitt, 1977) have also been quite effective in demonstrating an apparent age change in susceptibility to interference from irrelevant stimuli. Our representative study (Rabbitt, 1965b) employed a card-sorting task like the one used in Plude and Hoyer's study (1979). There were two target letters, for example, *A* and *Y*, with one of these letters printed somewhere on each of the cards in a stack. The subject's task was simply to sort the cards into two piles—an *A* pile and a *Y* pile. The manipulable independent variable was the number of irrelevant letters, or distractors, printed on each card—0, 1, 4, or 8. The nature of these materials is illustrated in the top panel of Figure 7.26. Note that the target letter (*A* for two of the sample cards, *Y* for the other two) varies in its placement on the cards. In fact, a target letter could be at any one of the nine locations in the sample card with eight distractors. The results, expressed in mean seconds per age group to sort 48 cards, are plotted in the bottom panel of Figure 7.26. A progressive decrement in performance may be seen to occur for both age groups as the

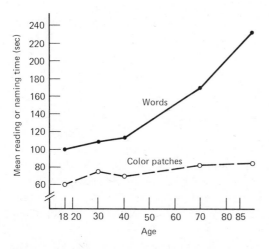

Figure 7.25. Age differences in time to name color inks of printed color words (Stroop effect) and time to name color patches. (Adapted from data in Comalli, Wapner, & Werner, 1962.)

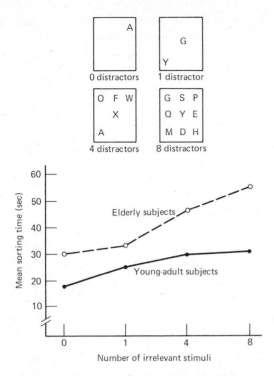

Figure 7.26. Top panel: Card-sorting task with two target letters (*A* and *Y*) and either 0, 1, 4, or 8 distracting letters or irrelevant stimuli. Bottom panel: Age differences in sorting time as a function of number of irrelevant stimuli. (Adapted from Rabbitt, 1965b, Table 1.)

number of irrelevant stimuli increased from 0 to 8. However, the magnitude of the deficit is clearly much greater for the elderly subjects than for the young subjects.

Rabbitt's results are readily interpretable in terms of the controlled (and, therefore, age-sensitive) versus automatic (and, therefore, age-insensitive) distinction made earlier. All of the letters of the alphabet, except, of course, the two target letters, served as the distractors or irrelevant stimuli. Consequently, a different set of distractors surrounded a target on virtually every card containing multiple distractors. Thus, the conditions were those of varied mapping, and they, therefore, required controlled processing. The interference produced by irrelevant stimuli on the proficiency of a controlled search for a target letter seems obviously to be much greater for elderly adults than for young adults.

Age deficits attributable to differential amounts of interference produced by visual irrelevant stimuli are by no means limited to simple perceptual tasks. Later we will discover that age differences in attention directed at irrelevant stimuli play an important part in determining age difference for certain memory, problem-solving, and concept-learning phenomena.

There have been, however, two studies that considered together raise serious doubts about the generalizability of age differences in interference from irrelevant stimuli. In the first study, Wright and Elias (1979) pointed out that tests of the interference effect from irrelevant stimuli have typically used tasks in which it is impossible to ignore the irrelevant stimuli while searching for relevant stimuli. This is certainly true of the sorting task used by Rabbitt (1965b). The distracting letters on each card cannot be fully ignored, they have to be scanned to some degree as the subject searches for a specific target letter. According to Wright and Elias (1979), "Such results support an age-related performance decrement in the ability to discriminate relevant from irrelevant items (Rabbitt, 1965b), but do not necessarily support the idea that there is an age-related decline in the ability to ignore irrelevant items" (p. 704).

Wright and Elias proceeded to test the interesting hypothesis that there may be no age-related decline at all when the task does not demand processing of any kind for irrelevant items while making decisions about relevant items. A visual search task was employed in which a target letter was exposed tachistoscopically in the middle of a subject's visual field. In their no-noise condition, the target appeared alone. For example, an *H* shown by itself signaled moving a switch to the right, whereas the other target letter, an *S*, signaled moving the switch to the left. In their noise condition, each target letter still appeared in the middle of a subject's visual field but now it was flanked by irrelevant letters (e.g., *JUSUJ*, with *S* the target signaling a left-movement response). Note that in the noise condition there is no need for a subject to glance at the irrelevant letters. A subject may ignore them and focus only on the center of the visual field where target letters appear consistently. Nevertheless, both young-adult and elderly subjects performed significantly slower (but only slightly so in the absolute sense) in the noise condition than in the no noise condition. Most important, however, there was clearly an absence of an age difference in the extent of the decrement produced by the presence of irrelevant letters. That is, the decrement from the noise to the no noise condition was about the same for their elderly subjects as for their young subjects.

In the second study, Ford, Hink, Hopkins, Roth, Pfefferbaum, & Kopell (1979) found an effect with auditory stimuli akin to the effect found by Wright and Elias (1979) with visual stimuli. Their subjects listened to tones of high and low frequencies presented to both ears. The higher frequency tone presented to one ear constituted the target stimulus, whereas the lower frequency tone to the same ear and both the higher and the lower frequency tones to the other ear constituted irrelevant stimuli. A physiological measure, the event-related potential, served as the means of contrasting young and elderly subjects in their degrees of attention to both target and irrelevant stimuli. These scores were larger (signifying greater attention) to tones in the attended ear (i.e., the ear carrying the target stimulus), and they were largest to the actual target tone in the attended ear. Young and elderly subjects appeared to be equally proficient in attenuating processing of irrelevant tones. When a task does not demand searching irrelevant stimuli to find a relevant stimulus, adult-age differences in the amount of attention directed at the irrelevant stimuli appear to be nonexistent. This is as true for auditory stimuli as it is for visual stimuli.

Thus, an age deficit in performance on selective attention tasks seemingly occurs only when irrelevant stimuli must be processed at least peripherally to be distinguished from relevant stimuli (as in Rabbitt's 1965b, sorting task). The slower rate of peripheral processing characteristic of older people would then account for their overall poorer performance relative to younger people as the number of to-be-processed irrelevant items increases. There is also the possibility that older adults engage in more thorough but redundant processing of irrelevant stimuli than do younger adults (Rabbitt, 1977). That is, elderly adults, but not young adults, may process irrelevant items centrally to the point of identifying (or naming) them. This, of course, is an unnecessary and time-consuming step. For example, Q as an irrelevant distracting item may be readily discriminated from A and Y as target items on the basis of physical features alone—its full identification as the letter Q only retards scanning for whatever specific target letter is present amidst the distractors.

This raises the interesting question of what should happen when a search among irrelevant stimuli is needed to locate a target but the irrelevant stimuli are all highly dissimilar from the targets. In effect, virtually no processing should be required of any irrelevant stimulus to detect the fact that it cannot possibly be a target stimulus. This condition was included in an intriguing study by Farkas and Hoyer (1980). The target stimuli were the letter T in two different degrees of rotation. For example, one target might be ⊣ and the other ⊢ . As illustrated in the top panel of Figure 7.27, a target was placed on a card along with three highly distinctive distractors (all of which were the same symbol). The targets appeared equally often in each of the four positions indi-

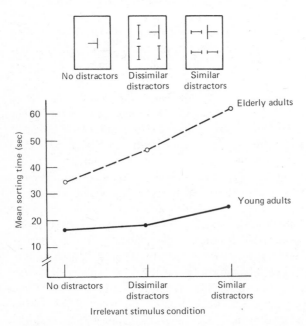

Figure 7.27. Top panel: Card-sorting task with two target stimuli (⊣ and ⊢) and either no distractors, dissimilar distractors, or similar distractors. Bottom panel: Age differences in sorting time as a function of target-distractor similarity. (Adapted from Farkas & Hoyer, 1980, Figure 2.)

cated on the sample card over a number of to-be-sorted cards, thus forcing a search as each card was presented. The task as usual was to sort the cards into two piles, one for each form of the target stimulus. Two other conditions were included in the study. The first was a 0 distractor condition like the one used by Rabbitt (1965b) (see top panel for Figure 7.27). The second employed irrelevant stimuli that were highly similar to the targets (see top panel of Figure 7.27). In effect, this condition exaggerates the kind of similarity involving overlapping physical features when letters serve as distractors as well as targets (e.g., Y as a target and X as distractor have obvious commonality in their line features). The results obtained for all three conditions are plotted in the bottom panel of Figure 7.27. Young adults were not affected at all by the presence of highly dissimilar stimuli. That is, their sorting time was about the same as it was in the no distraction condition. By contrast, elderly adults were adversely affected by the presence of even highly dissimilar irrelevant stimuli relative to the no distraction condition. When given a search task to perform, older people seem to find it impossible to ignore the presence of irrelevant stimuli, regardless of their attributes. Not surprisingly, the elderly subjects were also affected adversely to a much greater degree than the young subjects by the presence of highly similar irrelevant stimuli.

In addition, the conditionality of an age deficit in selective attention on the task demand (e.g., search versus no search) conforms to the general principle that the greater the demand, the greater the amount of a subject's limited processing capacity required to maintain attention (Kahneman, 1973). The kind of task used by Rabbitt (1965b) presumably requires more processing resources than the kinds of tasks used by Wright and Elias (1979) and Ford et al. (1979). Performance proficiency is, therefore, more sensitive for the former than for the latter to any decrement in processing capacity over the adult lifespan.

In summary, elderly people do appear to have greater difficulty than younger people in attending selectively to relevant stimuli in their environments. Much of this difficulty stems from an age difference in distractability produced by the presence of irrelevant stimuli. However, the age difference is largely restricted to situations demanding that irrelevant stimuli be searched to find relevant stimuli, even when the irrelevant stimuli are highly dissimilar to the relevant stimuli.

Divided Attention. In its simplest form, divided attention refers to the shared processing of multiple sensory stimuli, all of which are relevant to the ongoing activity of the organism. A familiar example is the automobile driver's division of attention between the visual stimuli inherent in the flow of traffic and the auditory stimuli provided by a passenger's conversation. As long as the traffic flow is slow and predictable, the driver manages to divide attention with little effort between the two inputs. However, as the traffic picks up in intensity, the driver is likely to tune out the incessant chattering of the passenger. Once again, the constraint placed on the human organism by its limited processing capacity is all too apparent. Routine sensory monitoring of the kind conducted when traffic is light uses little of this capacity, thus freeing the driver to attend simultaneously to an additional sensory input. The processing demand is much greater when traffic is heavy. Something has to give, namely, the segment of attention previously spent monitoring the auditory input.

Basic research on divided attention between two sensory inputs is essentially an extension of research using signal-detection methodology. Two weak stimuli, for example, a tone and a light, each embedded in noise, are presented simultaneously. Sensitivity to the tone in the multiple-input condition is compared with sensitivity to the tone when it is presented alone. Similarly, sensitivity to the light in the multiple-input condition is compared with sensitivity to the light when it is presented alone. For young adults, sensitivity for each stimulus in the multiple-input condition is just about as good as sensitivity in the single-input condition (e.g., Moore & Massaro, 1973). However, there is also evidence indicating that simultaneously occurring visual and auditory stimuli are not detected simultaneously—the visual stimulus is likely to be detected slightly before the auditory stimulus (e.g., Colavita, 1974; see Glass, Holyoak, & Santa, 1979, for further review). In addition, there is evidence indicating that divided attention is easier to accomplish for two inputs in different sensory modalities than for two inputs in the same modality (e.g., two tones in different spatial locations) (Treisman & Davis, 1973).

These studies imply that divided attention is relatively easy for young adults to accomplish when the stimuli themselves are simple and the operations performed on those stimuli are also simple (i.e., mere detection of their presence or absence). Is it equally easy for older adults? Unfortunately, there has been little effort directed at examining the sensitivity of elderly adults to simultaneous sensory stimuli relative to their sensitivity to either stimulus alone. A major exception is in a recent study by Somberg (1981). His study revealed that elderly subjects are as capable as young-adult subjects in dividing attention when the age groups are equated in sensitivity for each stimulus alone.

Somberg's subjects received two visual stimuli, A and B, for detection, with one of the stimuli being presented more foveally than the other. In one control condition, subjects detected the presence of Stimulus A under conditions approximating those of undivided attention. This was accomplished by paying them a fixed amount of money for each correctly detected Stimulus A, and no money for detecting the presence of simultaneously exposed Stimulus B. For each subject, duration of Stimulus A was set at a level that permitted a hit rate between 80% and 90%. This procedure resulted in durations that averaged over 200 milliseconds longer for Somberg's elderly subjects than for his young-adult subjects. Additional conditions were then introduced that required subjects to divide their attention between Stimulus A and Stimulus B. In one condition, 70% of attention was to be directed at Stimulus A and 30% at Stimulus B; in another condition, 50% of attention was to be directed at each stimulus. Variation in allocation of attention was achieved by varying the amount of money paid for correct detections. In the 70/30 condition, the payoff was according to that ratio, whereas in the 50/50 condition, the payoff was equal for each stimulus. In a second control condition, the roles of Stimuli A

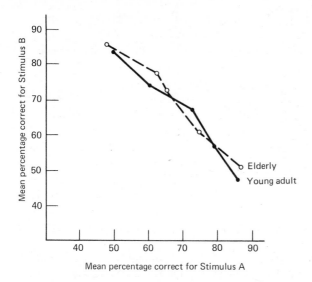

Figure 7.28. Accuracy of detecting one visual stimulus as affected by dividing attention with the detection of a second visual stimulus. (Adapted from Somberg, 1981, Figure 1.)

and B were reversed, as they continued to be in 70/30 and 50/50 variations of attention. Through this procedure, Somberg was able to determine the accuracy of detecting a target stimulus as it is affected by dividing attention with another stimulus. His results are plotted in Figure 7.28 in terms of mean accuracy (i.e., hit-rate score) for each age group. Note that accuracy of detecting either Stimulus A or Stimulus B decreased progressively as the amount of attention allocated to the other stimulus increased and eventually reached chance (50%) when attention was divided equally. Most important, there was no sign of an age difference in the effect of dividing attention on subsequent accuracy. Somberg argued effectively that the allocation of resources for dividing attention shows little, if any, change over the course of the adult lifespan. Of course, the absence of an age difference required an initial adjustment in target duration to assure equal detection of target stimuli for the two age groups under conditions of undivided attention. The extent to which this restriction affects generalizability of these results remains unknown.

There have been a number of aging studies in which divided attention to multiple inputs has been tested under more complex conditions, namely, the inclusion of a memory requirement. For example, Broadbent and Gregory (1965) examined the effect of divided attention on adult-age differences in memory for a series of six items, three digits and three letters. The items occurred as three successive pairs, with one member of each pair presented visually and the other aurally. An age deficit in amount recalled was found for this bisensory, divided-attention condition. By contrast, no age deficit in amount recalled was found in a control condition without divided attention. Here, all six items were presented to the same modality (visual), one item at a time. The absence of an age deficit should not be surprising here in that six digits or letters are within the memory span of most adults, regardless of age. An intriguing feature of Broadbent and Gregory's study is the manner in which it was conducted. The subjects were members of the audience watching television on the BBC in England. They were asked to view (and listen to) the items, record their responses on a form contained in a weekly television magazine, and then mail the form to the investigators. Over 1400 individuals, spanning the adult lifespan, volunteered their services, either for the advancement of science or for escape from television's usual boredom.

In a study (Craik, 1973) with an outcome much like that found in Broadbent and Gregory's study (but conducted in a more mundane laboratory setting), the multiple stimuli in the divided-attention condition were both auditory. One consisted of a tone-noise combination played over a speaker placed to the subject's right. The other consisted of a series of digit pairs played over a speaker placed to the subject's left. Two tasks had to be performed simultaneously: (1) detecting the tone's presence or absence against the noise background and (2) remembering the digit pairs. In addition, each subject performed on the tone-detection task in the absence of the digit-memory task and on the digit-memory task in the absence of the tone-detection task. No age deficit was found when either task was performed alone. When the tasks were performed simultaneously, however, elderly subjects scored more poorly than young-adult subjects, both for tone detection and digit memory. To explain this outcome and also that found by Broadbent and Gregory (1965), Craik (1973) suggested that elderly adults, unlike young adults, have to commit a large share of their processing resources to the chore of organizing, or programming, their division of attention for multiple inputs when those imputs involve complex tasks (e.g., memory tasks). Consequently, under conditions of divided attention and complex task demands, elderly subjects have relatively little residual processing capacity for performing the specific operations required by each task. Age deficits on these tasks are, therefore, expected, even though neither task shows a deficit when performed alone

The most active area of research on divided attention has involved dichotic memory. Simultaneous auditory stimuli, usually digits, are delivered in successive pairs, one member of each pair to the left ear and the other member to the right ear. For example, a representative sequence might be 3/6 (left ear/right ear), 7/2, and 1/8. Following the last pair, subjects attempt to recall the just-heard digits by ear, or channel, under the conditions specified by the investigator. The ear reported first is designated Channel 1, with the delayed ear being designated Channel 2. In one condition, subjects are given complete freedom to decide after each series of digit pairs which channel they wish to report first. With such freedom, there is little, if any, age deficit for Channel-1 recall but a pronounced deficit for Channel-2 recall (e.g., Inglis & Caird, 1963) (see the top panel of Figure 7.29.)

The pattern is quite different, however, when the order of channel recall is fixed, that is, subjects are cued as to which channel must be recalled first. One possibility is to delay the cue until just after the last pair of digits is heard. On half of the trials, left first is the cue; on the other half, right first is the cue.

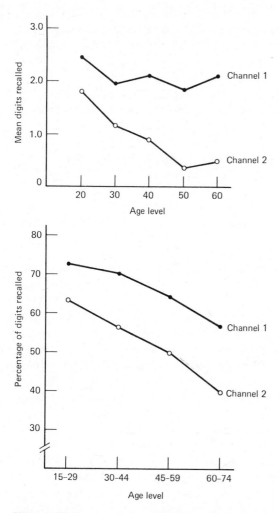

Figure 7.29. Top panel: Age differences in dichotic memory as a function of channel reported, given freedom of choosing which ear to report first. (Adapted from data in Inglis & Caird, 1963.) Bottom panel: Age differences in dichotic memory when order of ear recall is cued after the digits are heard. (Adapted from data in Clark & Knowles, 1973.)

Given this cuing condition, an age deficit in recall is apparent for *both* channels (e.g., Clark & Knowles, 1973) (see the bottom panel of Figure 7.29). Note that Channel-1 recall is superior to Channel-2 recall for all age levels and that the amount of the age deficit is about the same for both channels (i.e., there is no interaction between age and channel). Another possible condition is one in which subjects know in advance of hearing a series which channel must be recalled first. That is, the cue for order of recall is given just prior to the transmission of the series. The results have been somewhat conflicting under this cuing condition. Craik (1965) found an age deficit for both channels, but the extent of the deficit was greater for Channel 2 than for Channel 1. Schonfield, Trueman, and Kline (1972) also found an age deficit for both channels (with words rather than digits as the to-be-recalled items and recognition rather than recall as the test format), but the extent of the deficit was no greater for Channel 2 than for Channel 1. Finally, Parkinson, Lindholm, and Urell (1980) found an age deficit for Channel 2 but not for Channel 1.

Various explanations have been offered for the presence of age deficits in dichotic memory. Two of these explanations are derived from Broadbent's (1958) filter model of attention. Each places the locus of the age deficit in the short-term storage component of the flow of information (see Figure 7.24). Channel-2 information is forced to reside there while Channel-1 information is being processed for immediate recall. An age deficit for Channel 2 only (as found by Inglis & Caird, 1963, and Parkinson et al., 1980) implies that the stored information decays more rapidly for elderly adults than for young adults. On the other hand, Channel-1 information suffers no similar decay, and it is, therefore, immune to an age deficit.

The two explanations differ in terms of the short-term store presumed to be age sensitive. According to Inglis and Caird (1963), the store is a prelinguistic one in which the physical, or phonemic, features of the to-be-recalled items remain briefly available beyond the duration of the actual stimuli. That is, it is a sensory store of the kind described in Chapter 6. As argued by Craik (1977), there is actually little reason to hold on to this explanation. Several studies (e.g., Weiss, 1963) have indicated that the dichotic memory of elderly subjects is unaffected by the rate at which the paired digits are presented. With a slower rate of presentation, more time is allowed for the physical features of Channel-2 items to decay before attention can be shifted away from Channel 1 to their processing for recall. Consequently, Channel-2 performance should be poorer for a slow rate of presentation than for a fast rate, which clearly is not true. According to Parkinson et al. (1980), the store in question is linguistic, of the kind that mediates performance on standard memory-span tasks. That is, it is the standard short-term store of a multiple-store model of memory. Although the age deficit in memory span is relatively slight, it is considered large enough to suggest a smaller capacity for elderly adults than for young adults. It is this small capacity that adversely affects Channel-2 recall for elderly subjects. Parkinson et al. had an interesting way of testing their hypothesis. In one of their experiments, groups of young and elderly subjects were equated with respect to their scores on a preliminary digit-span task. Consequently, the two groups were assumed to be equated in the capacities of their short-term stores. These two groups were subsequently found to be comparable in their Channel-2 scores on a dichotic memory task, as expected if a linguistic short-term store is, indeed, the locus of the age deficit typically found for dichotic memory. The hypothesis of Parkinson et al. certainly remains a viable one.

Another explanation is derived from an interesting phenomenon known as the right ear advantage in dichotic memory. Young adults characteristically recall more digits delivered to the right ear than digits delivered to the left ear (e.g., Bryden, 1963). The advantage results from two factors: (1) the left cerebral hemisphere, for most people, is the dominant one for processing language inputs and (2) in the dichotic memory situation, messages from the right ear are transmitted directly to the left hemisphere, where, as language imputs, they may be processed immediately, whereas messages from the left ear are transmitted directly to the right hemisphere from where they must be relayed to the left hemisphere to be processed (Kimura, 1961). Thus, digits delivered to the right ear are processed more proficiently than digits delivered to the left ear. We encountered in Chapter 5 the argument that neural degeneration with aging may be more pronounced for the nondominant right hemisphere than for the dominant left hemisphere. If true, we would expect the age deficit in dichotic memory to be found largely for the left ear (and, therefore, the right hemisphere), whether it serves as Channel 1 or Channel 2. Of interest, therefore, is the pattern of age differences found in dichotic memory when the channels are separated on the basis of left-right laterality. This kind of analysis was conducted by Clark and Knowles (1973). As shown in the top panel of Figure 7.30, no age deficit appeared for Channel 1 when the right ear served as that channel. This pattern contrasts sharply with the one found for Channel 1 when no distinction is made on the basis of laterality (i.e., a pronounced age deficit occurred in their study) (see the bottom panel of Figure 7.27). On the other hand, an age deficit was apparent for Channel 1 when the left ear served as that channel (bottom panel Figure 7.30). Note also that elderly subjects recalled more digits presented to the right ear, even when it served as Channel 2 (bottom panel of Figure 7.30), which is in agreement with the laterality principle. Thus, the laterality hypothesis is a highly attractive one for explaining age deficits in dichotic memory.

The final explanation we will consider is one that is difficult to subject to an empirical test. It is an extension of Craik's (1973) argument that the programming of divided attention uses up an inordinate amount of elderly adults' processing resources. Applied to the dichotic memory task, the argument is that little processing capacity is left for Channel-2 items following the division of attention. The net effect is the shallow processing of these items relative to the deeper processing received for the same items by young adults who waste little of their resources in the programming of divided attention. Items processed at a shallow level are assumed to yield memory traces with less durability than items processed at a deeper level. By contrast, Channel-1 items are presumed to be processed at a deep level by elderly adults as well as by young adults. Consequently, little age deficit is expected for these items. The depth-of-processing notion is a popular one in contemporary memory theory. Nevertheless, tests of its validity in explaining age deficits in dichotic memory remain to be conducted.

Finally, there is another class of situations calling for a time sharing between simultaneous activities. Only now the sharing is between two skilled behaviors rather than between the processing of multiple sensory inputs. This is the kind of situation Lyndon Johnson had in mind when he said that Gerald Ford could not walk and chew gum at the same time. Walking and chewing

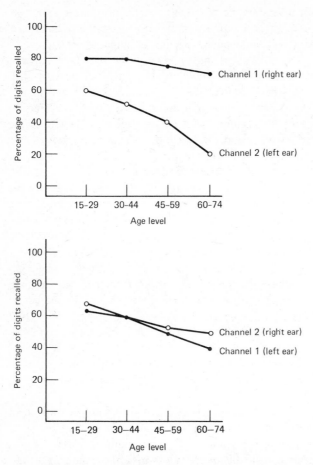

Figure 7.30. Age differences in dichotic memory when the right ear is cued to be reported first (top panel) and when the left ear is cued to be reported first (bottom panel). (Adapted from data in Clark & Knowles, 1973.)

gum obviously are behaviors we know people engage in simultaneously. The question arises: "Is gum chewing less proficient when combined with walking than when performed by an otherwise motionless organism?"

To the extent that a given behavior draws on a subject's limited processing capacity, its proficiency will be diminished by the simultaneous performance of another behavior that also draws on that limited capacity. The reduced processing capacity suspected of elderly people may make them especially prone to performance decrements under time-sharing conditions. Some support for this hypothesis comes from studies by Talland (1962) and Broadbent and Heron (1962). The dual tasks in Talland's study were manipulating a manual counter with one hand and picking up beads with tweezers held in the other hand. Speed of manipulating the counter in the dual task condition showed a greater age decrement than in a control condition in which the task was performed alone. Presumably, manipulating the tweezers was sufficiently demanding that it reduced the processing resources available for sustaining counter movements. A comparable age deficit under time sharing was found by Broadbent and Heron. A digit-cancellation task was performed either alone or in combination with an auditory-monitoring task. The decrement in cancellation performance under the dual-task requirement was greater for elderly subjects than for young subjects. More recent studies of time sharing have examined age differences in the ability to perform more complex cognitive behaviors simultaneously. We will review these studies in Chapter 10.

The research surveyed in this section provides a well-documented case for the existence of a decrement in information-processing resources during late adulthood. The decrement, although seemingly modest, is large enough to affect activities heavily involving divided attention and time sharing, such as piloting a 747, refereeing a basketball game, and crossing a street in midtown Manhattan. There is one further point regarding this decrement that we failed to make earlier: When in the adult lifespan does competence on divided-attention tasks begin its decline? A number of the studies we reviewed included middle-age subjects as well as young and elderly subjects. In some of these studies (Broadbent & Gregory, 1965; Craik, 1973), the middle-age subjects were virtually indistinguishable from the young-adult subjects, thus implying little loss of processing capacity by middle age. The picture is quite different, however, for studies on dichotic memory. From Figures 7.29 and 7.30, it can be seen that the decline in performance, particularly for Channel 2, occurs progressively beyond early adulthood, and a deficit is clearly manifested by middle age. Thus, there does seem to be at least a slight decrement in processing resources by middle age. Most likely, many divided-attention tasks do not tax processing resources sufficiently to affect adversely the performance of middle-age people. However, performance on more demanding tasks, like that of dichotic memory, is adversely affected even when the decline in resources is only slight.

The reduction in resources, or capacity, represents a third facet of the overall age changes that take place in the processing of information. The other facets, of course, are the slowing down in the rate of processing and the increased susceptibility to the interference produced by irrelevant stimuli in some kinds of selective attention tasks.

Methodological Comments

For the most part, the studies reviewed in this chapter have been impeccable from a methodological perspective. Typically, they made use of age groups that were carefully balanced (or overbalanced favoring the elderly) on important non-age attributes. Consider, for example, two of the studies on backward masking. In the study by Hertzog et al. (1976), the young-adult subjects (mean age, 18.8 years) averaged 13.8 years of formal education, whereas the elderly subjects (mean age, 66.5 years) averaged 14.6 years of formal education. In the study by Walsh, et al. (1979), the young-adult subjects (mean age, 19.6 years) averaged 13.5 years of formal education, whereas the elderly subjects (mean age, 68.5 years) averaged 13.8 years of formal education. The age deficits reported in these studies for speed of central processing can scarcely be attributed to the use of an inferior sample of elderly adults, unless we hold to the argument that subtle cohort differences may have produced the apparent age deficits. Nor can the age deficit in processing speed found in these and in the other studies on backward masking be attributed to gross visual defects among the elderly subjects. A careful selection procedure was employed in each study whereby all subjects were screened visually and had to have a minimal visual acuity of 20/30 in each eye (including vision corrected with glasses). Comparable control procedures entered into most of the other studies we touched on, including the careful selection of subjects without visual problems in research calling for visual stimuli (e.g., Kline & Orme-Rogers, 1978, and Walsh & Thompson, 1978, in their tests of the stimulus-persistence concept; and Lorden, Atkeson, & Pollack, 1979, in their illusion research) and subjects without hearing problems in research calling for auditory stimuli (e.g., Ford et al., 1979). Moreover, problems associated with either ceiling effects or floor effects are unlikely to occur in sensory-perceptual research.

Possible expectations to the use of carefully balanced age groups are the older studies cited that assessed sensory thresholds. In most of these studies, little detail is given about the non-age attributes of the subjects. It may be argued that such attributes as educational level are irrelevant with regard to level of sensory proficiency. There is a complicating factor in this argument however. As we have discovered, age differences in decision-making behavior are likely to affect somewhat age differences observed in threshold values. Consequently, balancing age groups educationally is probably a wise step to take in any research on sensory sensitivity. Fortunately, such balancing (or, again, overbalancing in favor of the elderly subjects) did occur in the signal-detection studies we reviewed. For example, the elderly subjects in Potash and Jones's (1977) study were all university professors!

Summary

This chapter examined adult-age differences in the related areas of sensory psychology, perception, and attention. Both associative and information-processing approaches to explanations of phenomena, including age differences/changes, were considered.

Adult-age differences in sensory sensitivity have traditionally been investigated through the use of psychophysical methods. Of interest have been age differences in both absolute-threshold values and difference-threshold values as indices of sensory sensitivity. From the perspective of associationism's analysis of sensory behavior, age deficits in sensitivity reflect the greater intensity of stimulation required by elderly adults relative to young adults to detect both the presence of a weak sensory stimulus and the presence of a difference between two similar stimuli. The deficits presumably result from the biological deterioration with aging of sensory receptors and their ancillary structures.

Psychophysical research in audition has revealed that auditory sensitivity remains fairly stable for detecting tones of 1000 hertz and below. However, for higher frequency tones, age deficits in sensitivity, as assessed by absolute-threshold values, appear by age

50 and increase progressively beyond that age. Substantial age deficits have also been found for the difference threshold in pitch discrimination. Visual sensitivity, as assessed particularly by absolute thresholds in dark adaptation, shows large age deficits. Age differences in the other senses have been more difficult to interpret. Limited data indicate that age deficits in both taste sensitivity and smell sensitivity are modest. The age deficit in touch sensitivity is substantial for some parts of the body and only slight for other parts. Pain sensitivity appears to decrease with aging. However, studies disagree as to the extent of the age change in pain sensitivity and the age of onset of that change.

The advent of signal-detection theory and methodology has provided a fresh perspective for understanding adult-age differences in sensory behavior. The theory stresses the fact that weak sensory stimuli, or signals, must be detected against a background of noise. Hits (detected signals that are truly present) and false alarms (erroneously identifying noise as a true signal) are affected by both the observer's sensitivity to weak stimuli and the observer's decision-making processes. Age deficits in hit rates could, therefore, be due either to the lower sensory sensitivity of elderly people or to the more conservative decision-making processes (i.e., setting a high criterion value that must be exceeded before the intensity of stimulation identifies the presence of a true signal)—or to a combination of the two factors.

Signal-detection methodology has been applied mainly to aging research in audition. Several signal-detection studies have confirmed the conclusion reached in earlier psychophysical research—auditory sensitivity decreases in old age. However, these studies have also revealed that part of the apparent loss in sensitivity is due to the more conservative response bias adapted by elderly subjects relative to young subjects in the signal-detection context. Detection research with pain stimuli has yielded a similar pattern. However, detection research with weights as signals has failed to find an age difference in response bias, thus questioning the generalizability of the more conservative decision-making process presumed characteristic of elderly people.

Age differences in perceptual sensitivity have been widely investigated for a number of the phenomena of classical perception. For some of these phenomena, such as color perception and depth perception, age deficits in performance are readily interpretable in terms of the biological deterioration occurring with aging in various sensory structures. However, the age deficits found for most of the phenomena studied in classical perception (e.g., flicker fusion, aftereffects) are not readily explained by biological reductionism. It is for these phenomena that the concept of age differences in stimulus persistence has been applied. The concept stresses that the neural trace of an environmental stimulus persists longer, following its physical termination, for elderly adults than for young adults. Given a brief interval between successive stimuli, the expected outcome is a fused perceptual response for the elderly and discrete perceptual responses for young adults. For some tasks, a fused perceptual response should enhance performance; for other tasks, it should hinder performance. Direct tests of age differences in the duration of stimulus persistence have generally been supportive of their existence.

An age change in stimulus persistence has been widely applied, in a post hoc manner, to explain the age differences found for a number of perceptual phenomena. Included are the age differences found for color afterimages, figural aftereffects, and speech perception. Considered together, age differences for these various phenomena indicate a general decline in perceptual competence during late adulthood. However, many basic perceptual phenomena, such as size constancy, appear to be immune to age changes.

In information-processing psychology, perception is viewed in terms of the processes regulating pattern recognition. Processing occurs in stages, beginning with a peripheral stage in which the physical features inherent in inputs to the senses are analyzed and ending with a central stage in which these extracted features are compared with prototypal information stored in permanent memory. Two standard laboratory methods have been used to evaluate the extent of age differences in the rates of peripheral and central processing. One method involves chronometrical analysis in which either physically identical or name identical letter pairs are judged for sameness. The other method involves the backward masking of briefly exposed target letters. Both methods have revealed a slowing of processing rate, both peripherally and centrally. Tasks, such as identifying target letters, appear to draw on age-sensitive controlled, or effortful, processes. There are, however, other forms of pattern recognition that are regulated by age-insensitive automatic, or routinized, processes.

Three different attentional phenomena have been studied by experimental aging psychologists. The first, vigilance, deals with sustained attention in monitoring a sequence of constant stimuli while awaiting the occurrence of a stimulus change. Elderly adults appear to be less likely than young adults to detect a stimulus change after prolonged monitoring. The age deficit in vigilance is especially pronounced when a memory requirement is added to the monitoring task.

The second phenomenon, selective attention, refers to the focusing of attention on relevant stimuli while attempting to ignore irrelevant, or distracting, stimuli. In some situations, irrelevant stimuli cannot be completely ignored while searching for a relevant stimulus. Elderly adults appear to be more susceptible than young adults to interference effects from the presence of irrelevant stimuli in these situations. On the other hand, elderly adults do not differ from young adults in the ability to ignore truly irrelevant stimuli, that is, extraneous stimuli that do not have to be processed while searching for a relevant stimulus.

The third phenomenon, divided attention, deals with the processing of simultaneous sensory inputs, each relevant to a task at hand. Experimental aging research has concentrated on divided attention in situations calling for a memory requirement in addition to attending to simultaneous inputs. The favorite task in aging research on divided attention has been that of dichotic memory. Members of digit pairs are delivered simultaneously and separately to the left and right ears, and subjects recall one channel (i.e., one ear) first and then the other channel (i.e., the other ear). Age deficits appear largely in the second channel recalled. Various explanations have been offered for these deficits, stressing such factors as age changes in memory storage, ease of programming divided attention, and cerebral hemisphere laterality.

8

Learning, Retention, and Transfer

Imagine what life would be like if all learning suddenly stopped at some point in late adulthood. Knowledge would, of course, be frozen. That is, there would be no further additions to knowledge—no updating of information concerning, for example, local, national, and international events. The names of a new mayor, a new senator, and a new prime minister for a foreign country would all be perceived, but they would be unfamiliar every time they were encountered. An elderly person planning a trip to a foreign country would find nothing but frustration in trying to acquire a working vocabulary for traveling in that country. Attendance at adult-education classes would be a wasted effort.

Knowledge is far from being the only aspect of human behavior to suffer if all learning suddenly ceased. There would be no hope of the elderly acquiring new recreational skills. Golf and bridge would be impossible, unless they had been mastered before the void in new learning (even if they had been learned before, there would be no hope of further improvement in skill). Suppose illness forced confinement to a wheelchair. There would be no chance of ever mastering the maneuverability of the wheelchair. Conditioning therapies of either physical or psychological illness could not possibly be successful. Movement to a new apartment in a new neighborhood would be chaotic and most likely disastrous. The operation of a tricky lock on the front door would have to be rediscovered by trial and error every time the lock were used. Each day's outing to a supermarket would be a brand new adventure, requiring assistance each time from some good Samaritan to find the way to and from home. A loose step would be a hazard every time the staircase were ascended or descended. New neighbors would stay strangers forever—there would be no way of associating their names with their faces.

There is a brighter side, however. Without new learning, attitudes would also remain frozen, as would fears and hates. There could be no additions to the prejudices and irrational fears people possess.

Learning is obviously critical for adaptation to our environments. It is little wonder that it has long been an area of great importance in psychology. From our analysis of a learningless world for elderly people, it should be apparent that learning is just as important for the elderly as it is for young adults. Fortunately, learning has no age barrier. Given normal aging, elderly people remain highly active learners. They acquire new information, they learn new recreational skills, they learn to operate new gadgets and devices, they learn their way around new neighborhoods, they learn to avoid hazardous obstacles, they learn to relate new names to new faces, and they also learn new prejudices and fears. Of course, to say that learning occurs in late adulthood is not to say that it occurs without losses in proficiency relative to the proficiency manifested earlier in the lifespan. The critical importance of learning to human adaptability makes it essential that we discover the extent to which learning proficiency is affected by human aging and that we understand the reasons why it is so affected. Without such knowledge and understanding, we can never hope to understand fully what it means to become old.

Adult-age differences/changes in learning are no strangers to us. A number of aging learning studies were discussed briefly in earlier chapters. Moreover, we discovered in Chapter 6 that age changes in learning are usually interpreted from the perspective of associationism, both in its classical form and in the form of stage analysis. In this chapter, our task is to review more systematically the many studies that have been concerned with adult-age differences/changes in learning. Our review will also cover the closely related areas of retention and transfer, phenomena for which age changes have also been interpreted largely from the perspective of classical associationism and stage analysis.

Our review of experimental aging studies on learning is complicated by the tremendous diversity of learning activities. This diversity should have been apparent in the sample of activities missing in a learningless life. Reflecting this diversity, the psychology of learning along with its extension into the experimental psychology of aging is commonly divided into four areas. The areas clearly differ in terms of the task structures and complexities they represent. But, do the areas differ in the nature of the processes postulated to mediate learning or in the products postulated to result from learning? To associationists, the answer is no—all learning involves contiguity between S and R elements, and the products of all learning are S-R associations. This monistic concept of learning (i.e., only one kind of learning), however, has been challenged by a number of learning psychologists who view learning pluralistically. That is, they believe that there are truly different kinds of learning, both in terms of mediating processes and in terms of what the products of learning are.

The four areas are conditioning, instrumental learning, motor-skill learning, and verbal learning. According to some psychologists, learning fears and prejudices are examples of conditioning. To these same psychologists, learning to avoid a hazardous situation is also an example of conditioning, but conditioning of a different kind than the conditioning entering into the acquisition of a fear or prejudice. Learning one's way around a neighborhood or apartment is an example of instrumental learning, whereas learning to maneuver a wheelchair and to play golf are examples of motor-skill learning. Learning title-name and face-name associations are examples of verbal learning. In verbal learning, linguistic elements (e.g., words or letters) always serve as sources of response elements, whereas either linguistic elements or pictorial/graphic elements (e.g., a picture of a face) serve as stimulus elements. Our review will touch on all four areas. However, it is verbal learning that has been the primary medium for research on age differences/changes in learning. The impact of associationism has been especially great on verbal-learning research, both basic research and experimental aging research, as we indicated in Chapter 6. Accordingly, associationism and its stage analytic modernization will be stressed heavily in most of this chapter. However, we will take a more flexible approach in covering aging research on conditioning, instrumental learning, and motor-skill learning. Surprisingly, it is in these areas that cognitive alternatives to associationism have often been proposed.

Adult-Age Differences in Conditioning

Conditioning is generally considered to be the simplest kind of learning. Simplicity in this context refers to the fact that single response elements are involved in learning—not to any allusion that the mechanisms underlying learning are simple and fully comprehended.

Actually, the existence of two kinds of conditioning has long been recognized by learning psychologists, *classical, or Pavlovian, conditioning* and *operant conditioning*. They differ procedurally in a fundamental way. In classical conditioning, a response—the unconditioned response (UCR)—is naturally (i.e., reflexively) elicited by a particular stimulus—the unconditioned stimulus (UCS). The objective of conditioning is to transfer control of the response's elicitation to another stimulus element—the conditioned stimulus (CS)—an element that at the start of conditioning bears no relationship to the response (i.e., it is neutral). To accomplish this objective, conditioning trials are initiated in which the CS just precedes (or overlaps) the UCS. Periodically, a test trial is given in which the CS is presented without the UCS. To the extent that the CS elicits the response in question—now called a conditioned response (CR)—learning, or conditioning, has taken place. A standard conditioning task with human subjects employs a puff of air to the eye (UCS) for eliciting an eyeblink (UCR). On study trials, the puff of air is preceded by some designated CS, usually a change in brightness of a glass disc facing the subjects. On test trials, the change in brightness occurs alone and the presence/absence of a blink is observed. This sequence of events, a sequence that defines the classical conditioning task, is summarized in the top panel of Figure 8.1. In operant conditioning, the to-be-modified response is emitted by the subject. Procedurally, the critical element is the stimulus event that follows emission of the response. In some

Classical Conditioning Training

Sequence

Study Trials · · ·

Trial 1
CS (e.g., brightness change in a glass disc) UCS → UCR (e.g., puff of air to eye) (eyeblink)

CS

Trial n
UCS → UCR

Extinction Trials

Trial 1
CS → CR (alone) (eyeblink)

Time ———→

Extinction Training

Sequence

Study Trials

Trial n (last one)
CS UCS→UCR

Extinction Trials

Trial 1
CS→CR

Trial 2
CS→CR

... Trial j
CS – – –→CR (weakening elicitation)

... Trial n
CS no CR (extinction reached)

Time ———→

346

Differentiation Training

Study Trials   Test Trials

	Trial 1	Trial 2	Trial n-1	Trial n	Trial 1
Sequence CS	UCS→UCR	CS' (no UCS)	CS UCS	CS' (no UCS)	CS→CR (alone) CS' no CR (alone)

Time

Figure 8.1. Procedures involved in classical conditioning. Top panel: Acquisition training. Middle panel: Extinction training. Bottom panel: Differentiation, or discrimination, training.

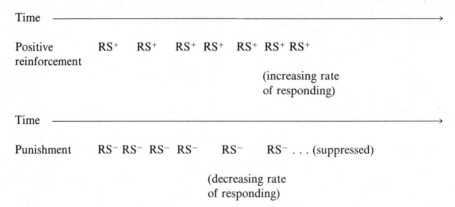

Figure 8.2. Procedures involved in operant conditioning. Top panel: Increasing rate of responding by following a response (R) with a positive reinforcer (S+). Bottom panel: Decreasing rate of responding by following a response with punishment (S−).

cases, the stimulus event is designed to increase the rate of emitting the response in question. That is, the event is something that is attractive to the subject (a positive reinforcer, such as, an M & M, beer, praise, or whatever else works with the subject at hand). In other cases, the stimulus event is designed to decrease the rate of emitting the response in question. Here, the stimulus event consists of a punishment (an electric shock, spinach, an insult, or whatever else works with the subject at hand). This sequence of events, a sequence that defines the operant conditioning task, at least in its simplest form, is summarized in Figure 8.2 for both positive reinforcement and punishment.

Classical Conditioning. To those of you who think of classical conditioning in terms of training a dog to salivate when a bell is sounded, the existence of an age deficit in classical conditioning is likely to be a stimulus for eliciting a yawn and a so what response. Actually, classical conditioning is a learning phenomenon of considerable practical importance. For example, the therapies mentioned earlier in this chapter are attempts to modify behavior by means of the application of classical conditioning training. Systolic blood pressure is an example of a behavior that seemingly can be so modified (Whitehead, Lurie, & Blackwell, 1976). The treatment calls for the establishment of a UCS that elicits a lowering of the blood pressure (the UCR). To produce this natural stimulus, the patient is tilted head down through an arc of 15°. As the body moves through the arc, a bell (the CS) is sounded. Amazingly, in some cases, the bell becomes associated with a lowering of blood pressure, and it, therefore, serves as a psychological control over heightened pressure. Alcoholism is another behavior that has been successfully treated, at least in some cases, by means of classical conditioning. The treatment, known as aversion therapy, will not be described in detail here (see Sherman, 1973, for elaboration). Briefly, it consists of pairing the taste of an alcoholic beverage as the CS with either electric shock or a nausea-producing drug as the UCS. The unpleasant biological state elicited by the UCS is the UCR, and a modified form of this state eventually becomes the CR elicited by the taste of the alcoholic beverage. If elderly people are indeed more difficult to condition than younger people, then there is good reason to question the effectiveness of these therapeutic methods beyond middle adulthood. This highly significant ecological issue has received surprisingly little attention in the gerontological literature.

The importance of classical conditioning goes well beyond its practical use in therapy. For many years, classical conditioning has served as a kind of minimodel for conceptualizing and, therefore, explaining how a number of specific human behaviors are acquired. Included are many fears, phobias, attitudes, and prejudices (Baron & Byrne, 1977; Staats & Staats, 1958). For example, a phobia is viewed in terms of the phobic object being a CS that is associated with fear (or conditioned pain) as the CR. Presumably, the conditioning occurred because the CS was innocently present at the time the victim experienced a painful, or noxious, stimulus (the UCS). Pain itself is, therefore, the UCR elicited by the UCS, that is, the noxious stimulus. Pain, however, is a complex physiological response that has many components, only some of which are conditionable in the sense of becoming part of the CR elicited by the CS. Those components make up the experience of fear or anxiety that is felt on subsequent encounters with the CS, or phobic object. Our awareness of adult-age deficits in classical conditioning should make us wonder about the extent of acquiring new phobias during late adulthood—or, for that matter, new prejudices, attitudes, and any other behavior presumed learned through classical conditioning. We may also wonder about the extent to which those new behaviors that are successfully learned through conditioning by elderly people can be eliminated through extinction training. Again, these important ecological issues have received little attention in the gerontological literature.

Our speculation that elderly people are less conditionable than younger people in the real world of therapy, phobias, and prejudices is based on laboratory studies of age differences in classical conditioning. Although adult-age differences in classical conditioning have been more widely studied than adult-age differences in operant conditioning, the amount of aging research on classical conditioning with human subjects has not been very large. The tasks employed in this research, on the surface, seem far removed from real-world examples of conditioning. Nevertheless, these tasks capture the essence of the procedures and processes of classical conditioning wherever they take place. Moreover, laboratory tasks permit the analysis of age differences in conditionability under carefully controlled conditions. Thus, confoundings of age differences by extraneous, nonconditioning factors are highly unlikely. As a result, there is good reason for our confidence in the generalizability of these laboratory-based results to age differences in real-world conditionability.

One of these laboratory tasks is that of eyeblink conditioning of the kind described earlier. This task was employed in two widely cited studies by Braun and Geiselhart (1959) and Kimble and Pennypacker (1963). Interestingly, Braun and Geiselhart found that children (average age, 9.4 years) conditioned more rapidly than young adults who, in turn, conditioned more rapidly than elderly adults (average age, 70.5 years). Their results are presented graphically

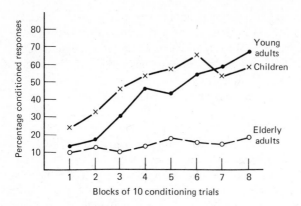

Figure 8.3. Age differences in rate of classical conditioning (eyeblink response). (Adapted from Braun & Geiselhart, 1959, Figure 1.)

in Figure 8.3. Note that their elderly subjects showed very little sign of conditioning (or learning). Kimble and Pennypacker also found considerably faster conditioning for young adults than for elderly adults, although the amount of conditioning manifested by their elderly subjects was somewhat greater than the amount manifested by Braun and Geiselhart's subjects. The age difference favoring young adults has also been found in several studies using other kinds of conditioning tasks. For one of these tasks (Botwinick & Kornetsky, 1960; Shmavonian, Miller, & Cohen, 1968, 1970), the UCR is a change in the galvanic skin response (GSR) produced by an electric shock as the UCS. The CS is a tone that precedes the shock and the CR is a change in the GSR elicited by the CS. For another task (Marinesco & Kreindler, 1934), the UCR is a reflexive retraction of the hand produced by an electric current as the UCS. The CS is a colored light, and the CR is a withdrawal of the hand as elicited by the CS.

The study by Marinesco and Kreindler is especially informative. Not only did their elderly subjects require more than twice as many trials as their young subjects, they also extinguished considerably more slowly once they were conditioned. Extinction means getting rid of the CS's control over the conditioned variation of the UCR after that control has been firmly established. It is accomplished by presenting the CS repeatedly without any additional occurrences of the UCS (see the middle panel of Figure 8.1). In effect, the CS eventually regains its earlier neutrality with respect to the to-be-learned response. Marinesco and Kreindler also discovered that their elderly subjects had considerably greater difficulty in establishing differentiation, or discrimination, than did their young subjects. Differentiation means distinguishing between the actual CS and other neutral stimuli (symbolized as CS') that bear some form of relatedness to the CS. In the laboratory, the CS may be a red light and the CS' a yellow light; in the real world, a phobic CS may be a horse and the CS' a pony. Differentiation in the laboratory is accomplished by having two kinds of study trials that are intermingled: (1) those in which the CS is presented and then followed by the UCS and (2) those in which the CS' is presented alone (see the bottom panel of Figure 8.1).

There is little reason to believe that these striking age differences in rate and amount of conditioning and its related phenomena are the consequences of cohort or time-of-measurement effects. But why an apparent age change in conditionability? Is it due to some kind of deterioration in a basic learning process? To attempt an answer to this question, we must first ask what subjects are learning during the course of classical conditioning.

To associationists, as we intimated in Chapter 6 and earlier in this chapter (i.e., the monistic position), classical conditioning is simply another form of learning in which an S-R association is acquired through contiguous occurrences of the association's S and R elements. This account of classical conditioning has met considerable opposition over the years for reasons that are beyond the scope of our review (see Anderson and Borkowski, 1978, for an excellent analysis of theoretical issues involving classical conditioning). Contemporary theorists have stressed, instead, the cognitive nature of classical conditioning. According to one view (e.g., Logan, 1977), subjects being conditioned learn an association between two stimulus elements (i.e., the CS and the UCS) rather than an association between stimulus and response elements. According to another view (e.g., Rescorla, 1972), one that is highly consonant with information-processing psychology, subjects being conditioned simply learn the informational value of the CS, namely, the fact that its onset reliably predicts the forthcoming occurrence of the UCS. The CR then serves to prepare the subject for the arrival of the UCS. For example, blinking to a CS protects the eye from the seemingly inevitable puff of air (UCS). Unfortunately, the age deficit in classical conditioning is difficult to explain from any of these theoretical perspectives. The to-be-learned response element is not rehearsed in the traditional sense of rote repetition. Consequently, less rehearsal per trial by elderly subjects than by young subjects, the standard associative explanation of a learning deficit, does not apply. Moreover, to hypothesize that healthy, cognitively active elderly people are less capable than young adults of learning the informational value of the CS and the nature of the CS-UCS contingency seems far fetched (although this hypothesis has been defended by some psychologists, e.g., Birren, 1964).

It seems far more reasonable to explain age differences in conditionability in terms of age differences in some nonlearning factor. One possibility (Elias & Elias, 1977) is to place the responsibility on the presumed omnipresent autonomic overarousal of the elderly. Overarousal is assumed to affect performance of the conditioned response and not learning per se. The problem with this explanation, however, is that learning psychologists (e.g., Spence, 1958) have found that on the eyeblink conditioning task, high arousal yields superior performance relative to low arousal, at least for young adult subjects. Thus, elderly subjects would be expected to excel young subjects in performance on this task, which, of course, is decidedly not true. There is an alternative explanation, however, one that is perfectly consonant with the mechanistic model of adult development. Braun and Geiselhart speculated that "in the course of many years of living, the eyelid response as well as probably other responses have been 'adapted out' and thus are less susceptible to subsequent conditioning" (1959, p. 388). Basically, this is a restatement of the wear-and-tear principle. A somewhat related explanation was offered by Kimble and Pennypacker (1963). It calls for greater habituation of the to-be-learned response by elderly adults than by young adults. Habituation is a familiar phenomenon in classical conditioning at all age levels. It refers to the fact that the repeated application of a stimulus (e.g., a UCS) results in a progressive decline of the response (i.e., the UCR) elicited by that stimulus.

Operant Conditioning. There is not much we can say about research on adult-age differences in operant conditioning. And with good reason—there just has not been much research. As we discovered in Chapter 6, operant psychologists themselves are not particularly enchanted by age variation as a condition in their studies. There is sufficient evidence, however, to indicate that operant conditioning with positive reinforcers is not nearly as sensitive to age differences as is classical conditioning. One shred of evidence comes from a study cited in Chapter 5. We discovered then that normally aging elderly adults are perfectly capable of increasing the probability of a response when a positive reinforcement follows each occurrence of that response. The response in question is the emission of high-frequency alpha waves of the electroencephalogram (EEG), and the positive reinforcer is biofeedback. Most important, there have also been a few studies indicating that elderly psychotic patients (Ayllon & Azrin, 1965), senile dementia patients (Ankus & Quarrington, 1972; Mueller & Atlas, 1972), and nursing home residents (Baltes & Zerbe, 1976) are amenable to behavior modification through the use of positive reinforcers. This is information of considerable ecological relevance.

We should note that there has been a scattering of studies contrasting young and old rats in their rates of operant conditioning (bar pressing) with a simple positive reinforcer (see Jakubczak, 1973, for a general review of these studies). The greater possibility of the involvement of higher order cognitive processes in even simple learning-memory activities by human subjects than by animal subjects makes generalizability from animal to human research uncertain. Nevertheless, there are areas of learning-memory research in which considerable commonality in outcomes has been found between studies with animal subjects and studies with human subjects. For example, the substantial age deficit in spatial memory found for rats (Wallace, Krauter, & Campbell, 1980) closely parallels the age deficit found for human subjects (Krauss & Quayhagen, 1977), and the slight age deficit found for rats (Wallace et al., 1980) on a task involving short-term memory parallels that found for human subjects on somewhat comparable tasks. There are important areas of learning in which virtually all that is known about the effects of aging on learning proficiency comes from studies comparing young and old rats. Our preference is to touch on this animal research, again with the realization that generalization to human aging must be viewed cautiously. Operant conditioning is one of these areas. Unfortunately, the aging animal studies in this area have yielded highly conflicting results. For example, Goodrick found greater responding for young rats than for old rats in one study (1965), greater responding for old rats than for young rats in a second study (1969), and no age difference at all in a third study (1970)!

Another variation of operant conditioning with a more complicated kind of reinforcement should be of great interest to gerontological psychologists, but, apparently, it has not been. It is avoidance learning. Here a response is emitted that enables the organism to avoid receipt of a noxious stimulus event. Learning to move cautiously around a loose step to avoid a painful fall is an example of such learning. Buying fire or automobile insurance to avoid the painful experience produced by loss or damage of property is another example. The processes of avoidance learning are complex and not fully comprehended. One popular conceptualization, but one with many opponents as well, is that of two-factor theory (see Bolles, 1979, for elaboration). The theory views the avoidance learner as progressing through two stages. The nature of this progression is illustrated in Figure 8.4 with respect to the loose-step situation. In the first stage, fear is learned by means of classical conditioning. Falling on the step is the UCS for producing pain as the UCR. Because falling is preceded by the sight of the step itself, such sight meets the criterion for serving as a CS, one that becomes associated with conditioned pain, or fear, as the CR. In the second stage, the response of circumventing the loose step (the avoidance behavior) is positively reinforced. The positive reinforcement results from the alleviation of the fear elicited by the sight of the step (out of sight, out of fear). An obvious reason for having a gerontological interest in avoidance learning is

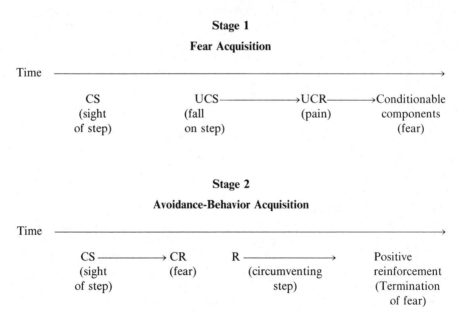

Figure 8.4. Schematic representation of the two-factor theory of avoidance learning as applied to learning to avoid a loose step.

the presumed involvement, at least according to two-factor theory, of age-sensitive classical conditioning in the total learning activity. If elderly adults are slower in fear acquisition, then they should also be slower in overall avoidance learning. The fact that elderly adults may differ from young adults in pain threshold adds further to our conjecture about possible age differences in avoidance learning as well as all other pain-derived fear acquisition.

What is actually known about age differences/changes in avoidance learning is, unfortunately, based solely on animal research. Most of these animal aging studies were conducted by Doty (1966a, 1966b; Doty & Doty, 1964; Doty & Johnston, 1966). In general, they indicate poorer avoidance learning by old rats than by young rats. However, the extent of the age deficit seems to depend on the complexity of the avoidance task—the greater the complexity, the greater the age deficit. Interestingly, Doty and Johnston (1966) also found that the avoidance-learning proficiency of old rats is greatly improved by the administration of certain drugs (e.g., eserine) that may affect fear acqustion. Generalization from the rat to the human avoidance learner is certainly tenuous. But there really is not much choice. Conducting avoidance-learning research with elderly human subjects may certainly be questioned on ethical grounds. At any rate, we will return to avoidance learning when we resume the analysis of learned helplessness intiated in Chapter 4.

Ethical issues also abound in the remaining component of operant conditioning we will touch on. That component is the suppression of behavior through the administration of an aversive stimulus after each occurrence of that behavior (S− in the bottom panel of Figure 8.2). In other words, punishment lowers the probability of an unwanted response's occurrence. Whatever adult-age differences exist in susceptibility of response suppression through the use of punishment appear to be unknown. Given the ethical problems in conducting research on punishment, they should remain unknown.

Adult-Age Differences in Instrumental Learning

The traditional apparatus for studying instrumental learning is the familiar multiple choice-point maze. The learner's task is to learn the correct path leading from a starting point to some goal at the end of the maze. (The learner's behavior is instrumental for reaching the goal, thus the name for this kind of learning.) For example, there might be five left-right choice-points, with the correct path being left-left-right-left-right-goal. Instrumental learning is obviously more complex than conditioning in the sense of dealing "with the arrangement of responses" (Anderson & Borkowski, 1978, p. 337) rather than with a single response. With human subjects, the maze is a paper one for which subjects see only one choice-point at a time, and they respond verbally by saying left or right at each choice-point. With animal subjects, the maze is a spatial one through which the subjects move their entire bodies.

Age Differences in Maze Learning: Human and Animal. There has been very little research on maze learning by noncollege-age subjects; what there has been has not examined maze learning by elderly subjects per se. An early study by Husband (1930) compared undergraduate students as subjects with older subjects. Although the older subjects averaged only 36.7 years of age, they were, nevertheless, poorer maze learners than the undergraduates. Their inferior performance, however, was relatively slight with respect to the number of trials needed to learn the maze (about 25% more trials) but quite large with respect to total time taken in learning the maze (about 80% more time). A later study by von Wright (1957) contrasted young adults with somewhat older adults (median age, 50 years). Older subjects were again less proficient than young adults, with the deficit in trials-to-learn being more pronounced than in Husband's (1930) study (nearly 50% more trials).

By contrast, aging research on maze learning by rats has been quite popular for many years, beginning with pioneering studies by Hubbert (1915) and Stone (1929). These earlier studies (see Jerome, 1959, for a detailed review) revealed little difference in maze-learning proficiency between young-mature and old rats. More recent studies (e.g., Goodrick, 1972; see Arenberg and Robertson-Tchabo, 1977, for a detailed review), however, have indicated that old rats are slower maze learners than young rats, but only when the task itself is a complex one. Complexity of a maze is defined in terms of the number of choice-points intervening between the start and goal components. With only 1 choice-point, age differences appear to be nonexistent. With 4 choice-points, age differences are modest, and, with 14 choice-points, they become pronounced. Interestingly, these studies also indicate that the age deficit largely disappears, even with a highly complex maze, when the old learner is guided through the maze. Guidance simply means that cul-de-sacs (blind alleys) are closed off during study trials, thus avoiding errors (i.e., wrong turns) while practicing the maze. The cul-de-sacs are open, of course, during the test trials to permit comparisons in learning scores (e.g., number of errors) between age groups.

Explanation of Age Differences in Maze Learning. Explanation of age differences in maze learning, whether for human or animal subjects, like explanation of age differences for any kind of learning, depends on one's broader perspective regarding what is being learned and how it is being learned during practice on the task at hand. To associationists (e.g., Hull, 1943), what is acquired during practice on a maze is a chain of S-R associations. Each link of the chain involves one of the choice-points. The R element of a given link is the correct turning response at that choice-point (i.e., either left or right), and the S element is some unspecified distinctive cue present at the choice-point. Age deficits in human maze learning are then accounted for in terms of the standard rehearsal-deficit principle. Rehearsal in this case refers to the verbal representation of a correct-turning response. Thus, if that turn is left, the subject is assumed to say left over and over—but to a smaller degree by older subjects.

For many years, cognitively oriented learning theorists have rebelled against this response-centered explanation of maze learning. The pioneer in this rebellion was Tolman (1932). Tolman argued that even rats (and certainly human beings) learn environmental information during their exposure to a maze. In effect, the learner acquires a cognitive map, a map that relates representations of stimuli in the maze to one another. Thus, a perception-centered explanation replaces the response-centered explanation of associationists. Turning responses at choice-points remain important in this cognitive explanation, but only for performance on the maze. Explanation of age deficits from this cognitive perspective follows an interesting course. Elderly learners may be assumed to be distracted by irrelevant stimuli in the maze environment, at least to a greater extent than young learners, thereby delaying their acquisition of truly relevant environmental information. This explanation is perfectly consonant with what we discovered earlier about age differences in selective attention. We now need to argue that elderly rats, like elderly human beings, are especially susceptible to distraction by irrelevant stimuli. Interestingly, we discovered earlier that the age deficit in animal maze learning disappears when subjects are guided through the maze. Such guidance should prohibit attention directed at irrelevant stimuli present in cul-de-sacs. Of course, guidance also prohibits making erroneous turning responses and its effects on age differences in learning could, therefore, be explained associatively.

Spatial Cognition. Knowing how people learn to navigate about a strange environment is undoubtedly an important objective of learning theory and research. The importance was stated quite clearly by Allen, Siegel, and Rosins*i:

> An important issue in the study of spatial cognition concerns the representation of spatial information in memory. Of particular interest is the representation of information from a geographic area that cannot be perceived simultaneously. A traveler in a large-scale environment, such as a city, typically cannot see his destination from his starting point. Thus, he must rely on his ability to interpret perceptual information accompanying his own movement in order to reach his destination successfully. Occlusion, parallax, expansion, and other perceptual cues indicating motion, orientation, and velocity form the visual context of the traveler's movement, and it is this context that is structured as spatial knowledge. Recognizing the contextual features (i.e., the unique perceptual characteristics) of a spatial event is the difference between finding one's way and getting lost. (1978, p. 617)

They are talking about the acquisition of a cognitive map that represents a novel environment, such as a strange city (or strange campus for beginning college students). But a novel environment may also be a new neighborhood in an already familiar city, a new apartment in an already familiar neighborhood, and, perhaps most important, a new institutional residence. The ability to acquire representations of these kinds of environments is essential for unrestrained mobility, which, in turn, is essential for the overall adaptability of the organism.

An awareness of the problems elderly people face in acquiring cognitive maps of their own physical environments is needed to be in the position to enhance their adaptability and to reduce the stress produced by getting lost. Planning environments that aid spatial cognition and accelerate the rate of acquiring cognitive maps of those environments is a likely consequence of this awareness. The fact that problems do exist in the spatial learning of elderly people is dramatically illustrated in a study by Weber, Brown, and Weldon (1978). Their primary subjects were residents, ranging in age from 72 to 93 years, of a nursing home, all of whom were ambulatory, had adequate vision, and were cognitively alert, as indicated by their highly effective communicative skills. Cognitive maps of their residential environment were evaluated by an intriguing procedure that was used originally to assess recognizability of locations in a city (Milgram, Greenwald, Kessler, McKenna, & Walters, 1972). The procedure consisted of showing slides of scenes from various areas of both the interior and the exterior of the nursing home. For each slide, a subject attempted to identify on a map of the total area where the depicted scene was located. The results, expressed in percentages of correct identifications, are shown in Table 8.1 for four different residential halls and several other areas. Note that the halls were especially poorly identified correctly and that even presumably distinctive areas, such as the dining room and the nursing station, were identified correctly by relatively small percentages of the residents. Weber et al. (1978) also found that accuracy in identification correlated negatively (and statistically significantly) with age (in general, the older the resident, the poorer the accuracy), but, surprisingly, they failed to find a significant correlation between accuracy and duration of residence in the home (a positive correlation was expected). For comparison's sake, the investigators included a small group of undergraduates as part of their study. As a course assignment, they toured the home, spending about 40 minutes spread equally over all of the areas. After the tour, they were tested unexpectedly in the same manner as the residents. Their strikingly superior identification scores are also given in Table 8.1. There is one obvious conclusion from these results—the design of a nursing home, in general, fails to provide distinctive and attractive stimuli that prod interest among the residents in exploring their environment and becoming comfortably familiar with that environment. Hopefully, designers of such homes will be more cognizant of these problems in the future.

Table 8.1 Accuracy of Identifying Scenes in a Nursing Home for Elderly Residents of That Home and Undergraduates Who Had Visited the Home

	Mean Percentage of Correct Identification	
Area	*Elderly Residents*	*Students*
Hall 1	12.7%	47.5%
Hall 2	5.0	27.8
Hall 3	3.9	19.8
Hall 4	13.2	33.3
Dining room/ living room	60.5	80.8
Nursing station/front lobby	51.7	85.2
Exterior	32.5	48.2

Source: Adapted from Weber, Brown, & Weldon, 1978, Table 2.

There is a direct connection between spatial cognition and maze learning. In principle, a maze simulates a novel spatial environment. Accordingly, maze learning should offer a means of evaluating age differences/changes in the acquisition of spatial cognitive maps. Frankly, however, we have serious reservations about the effectiveness of paper mazes in accomplishing this important kind of simulation. Fortunately, contemporary psychologists have introduced new, and highly innovative, procedures for studying the acquisition of spatial cognitive maps, procedures that appear to have considerably greater ecological validity than the older maze-learning procedure (see Anderson, 1980, for a review of spatial cognition). For example, Allen et al. (1978) had their young-adult subjects take a walk through a novel environment. The walk was simulated by means of a series of slides showing various scenes and locations in a community. The subjects were then tested for their ability to recognize not only previously exposed scenes but also other scenes that were not actually seen but could be inferred to be in the environment covered by the walk. This procedure is one that could be, and should be, extended to use with elderly subjects. In fact, we are likely to see considerable future use of this procedure and other similar procedures by experimental aging psychologists interested in age differences/changes in spatial cognition. Interestingly, aging studies of this kind are just beginning to attract attention (e.g., Walsh, Krauss, & Regnier, 1981; see Hartley, Harker, and Walsh, 1980, and Ohta, 1981, for further discussion).

Adult-Age Differences in Motor-Skill Learning

Motor-skill learning refers to any learning in which an individual must acquire a sequence of precise motor responses (i.e., bodily movements of some kind). Usually these responses must be closely coordinated with the perception of a sequence of stimuli (for this reason, this kind of learning is often referred to as perceptual-motor learning.) As stimuli change, the sequence of responses must change accordingly. In some instances, there is little, if any, stimulus change involved, and the underlying motor-skill learning is relatively easy. This is the case in learning to operate a lock or the ignition of a car. In other instances, there is a great deal of stimulus change involved and motor-skill learning increases greatly in complexity as a result. This is the case in learning to drive a car in traffic or to play tennis. Consider as an example the complexity involved in learning to hit a fast ball or a curve ball thrown by a major league pitcher. Here tracking the trajectory of the ball must be coordinated with a number of bodily movements. Programming a computer to accomplish this hitting task is at least as complicated as programming a computer to play chess (Fitts, 1964).

The importance of motor-skill learning to human adaptability is indicated in the following remarks by Fitts:

> "Living, moving, and behavior are almost synonymous terms. Thus the study of motor and perceptual-motor skill learning is in a very real sense the study of a large segment of the field of psychology" (1964, p. 243).

Attesting to the importance of motor-skill learning is the virtually endless list of everyday activities that are the products of our motor-skills learning: pouring a cup of coffee without spilling a drop, brushing our teeth in the precise way dentists recommend, tying our shoes, driving a car, starting a power mower, playing catch with someone, playing the piano, and so on. These are motor skills that once acquired in childhood or early adulthood become highly overlearned and largely automatized. As a result, they are usually maintained throughout the adult lifespan with considerable proficiency (although the speed of performance may slow down in late adulthood), unless, of course, they are decimated by a crippling illness or accident. Witness the many great performances by Pablo Casals and Arthur Rubinstein at very advanced ages. Claudio Arrau, the great Chilean pianist, celebrated his 75th birthday with a recital in which he played faultlessly the technically strenuous Sonata No. 3 in F Minor by Brahms. There is good reason to believe that Ted Williams, now in his 60s, can hit a major league fast ball at least as well as most current major league players. At age 40, Jack Nicklaus displayed the same great stroke he had years earlier as an amateur golfer—still great enough to continue winning major golf championships.

We do not have to turn to aging virtuosos or Hall of Famers to demonstrate the overall stability of many motor skills during middle and late adulthood. Birren (1964) reports, for example, that pilots between age 40 and age 60 have, if anything, fewer accidents than younger pilots. The absence of an age effect, at least through age 60, cannot be attributed solely to the greater experience of the older pilot. Even when years-of-experience is held constant for all ages, there is a slight decline in accident rate with increasing age (again through age 60). Analysis of industrial accidents also reveals an interesting pattern (McFarland & O'Doherty, 1959). The rate of accidents producing disabling injuries is actually lower for workers age 65 and over than it is for workers age 25 to 34 years. Of course, this does not mean that no changes occur in performance with increasing age. The primary change, not surprisingly, is in speed of response, an age change we discussed earlier. Slower performance can lead to an increased accident rate with increasing age, at least for certain kinds of accidents. This may be seen in analyses of agricultural accidents (King, 1955). Accidents that result from being hit by a falling or moving object (i.e., accidents produced often by failure to respond fast enough) increase slowly but progressively from early to late adulthood. On the other hand, agricultural accidents that are seemingly unaffected by speed, such as being injured by a frequently used tool, decrease slowly but progressively with increasing age.

Our main concern, however, is with adult-age differences/changes in new motor-skill learning. As with other kinds of learning, there are no age limits regarding the necessity of, or the desire for, participating in new motor-skill learning. Adults of all ages may have to learn to master a wheelchair, to drive a stick shift car after years of driving with automatic transmission, to eat with chopsticks, to play golf, to operate a complicated piece of machinery, and so on. What happens to proficiency in skill learning over the adult lifespan is obviously a question of great practical importance.

Laboratory Studies: Real-World Tasks. Research on adult-age differences in mo-tor-skill learning was off to a rousing start. Early studies employed a number of tasks carried over from the real world, including learning archery (Lashley, 1915), shooting a basketball (Noble, 1922), and learning to use chopsticks (Tachibana, 1927). Although these studies provided contrasts between young and older subjects, they also suffered from a number of methodological defi-ciencies (see Ruch, 1933, for a thorough analysis). In a number of them, the investigator was simply curious to see if learning continues beyond the teens and early 20s. Thus, Lashley's (1915) oldest archery subject was only 36 years of age, and Noble's (1922) oldest shooting subject only 32. This is not a prob-lem in Tachibana's (1927) chopsticks study. But there is a different kind of problem. Only two subjects were employed—a 21-year-old woman (who learned readily) and an 89-year-old woman (who did not learn at all). The sample size was not much larger in Noble's (1922) basketball study—there were only three 20-year-old and three 32-year-old shooters. There is another, more insidious, problem inherent in this type of study, namely, control over prior experience with the task at hand and other related tasks. The standard control, as applied by Lashley (1915) in the archery study, is to use only naive subjects, that is, subjects who report having had no formal contact with the particular task. However, an investigator cannot have complete faith in the reliability of a subject's self-reported past history. At any rate, Lashley found very little age decline in learning archery (again through age 36), and Noble (1922) found that his older subjects (again only age 32) learned basket shooting more readily than his younger subjects.

Many of these methodological problems even enter into what gerontologi-cal psychologists generally consider to be the best of these early real-world studies, those of Thorndike, Bregman, Tilton, & Woodyard (1928). In one of their studies, young subjects, 20 to 25 years of age, and old subjects, 35 to 57 years of age, were given 15 hours of practice writing left handed (all of the subjects, of course, were right handed). There was little effect of age variation on the degree to which the quality of writing improved over the lengthy, and surely tortuous, practice sessions. However, a pronounced age difference was found in the degree to which speed of writing increased with practice. Not surprisingly, the young subjects increased their speed considerably more than did the old subjects. In another of their studies, Thorndike, et al. had a group of five subjects, ranging in age from 23 to 38 years, practice typewriting. Al-though the subjects made considerable progress, it is difficult to determine with so few subjects and such a limited range of age what effect, if any, age variation had on mastering the typing skill.

Laboratory Studies: Controlled Tasks. Assurance of age equality in prior expe-rience and familarity can best be accomplished by the use of artificial labora-tory tasks, tasks that represent novel experiences for subjects of all ages. In using such tasks, investigators risk concerns about the degree of external valid-ity and ecological validity inherent in their results, as we discovered in Chapter 3. The hope, however, is that these tasks, like the laboratory tasks employed in other areas of learning, do gain access to the basic processes that enter into real-world activities. A number of these tasks have been introduced over the years into basic research on motor-skill learning, and many of them eventually entered into experimental aging research on motor-skill learning. The pioneers in this component of the experimental psychology of aging were Snoddy (1926) and Ruch (1934), Snoddy with research on mirror-vision tracing of a figure and Ruch with research on the pursuit-rotor task. A number of excellent aging studies on motor-skill learning have appeared since 1934. Our review will examine only a few representative studies (for more comprehensive reviews, see Welford, 1958, 1959, 1977). In our review we will be guided by the distinction made by researchers in motor-skill learning between tasks that involve *discrete response* and tasks that involve *continuous responses* (Ellis, 1978).

Among the real-world tasks involving a discrete response are kicking a football and turning the ignition of a car. A laboratory task that approximates these kinds of activities must require a movement of some specified distance, amplitude, or direction. The classic variant is to have subjects draw a line having a specified length, such as 6 in. (Thorndike et al., 1928). Subjects practice on this line-drawing task either with or without knowledge of results. Knowledge of results consists of feedback concerning the amount of error present in a just-drawn line (i.e., information regarding how far off it is from the specified distance). As you might expect, accuracy improves steadily with knowledge of results but not without it. A modification of the line-drawing task has been used in aging studies by Szafran (1953) and Anshel (1978). In Szafran's study, subjects in three age groups (18 to 29, 30 to 49, and 50 to 69) attempted to move a hand sideways a set distance with and without knowledge of results regarding accuracy. The results of this study, expressed as the mean error averaged over trials, are shown in Figure 8.5. It can be seen that age differences were not very pronounced in the absence of knowledge of results. With little learning occurring, there is no reason to expect age differences to

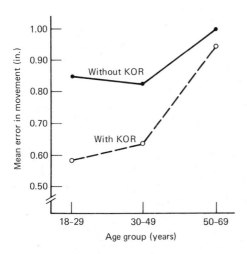

Figure 8.5. Age differences in accuracy of hand movement with and without knowledge of results (KOR) following movement. (Adapted from Szafran, 1953, as reported in Welford, 1959.)

appear. However, with knowledge of results, the oldest subjects were decidedly poorer in performance than the young and middle-age subjects (who did not differ from one another). Most important, both young and middle-age subjects benefited greatly from knowledge of results, whereas the oldest subjects benefited only slightly. As noted by Welford (1959), younger subjects seem to find the translation from vision to kinesthesis easier to accomplish than do older subjects. That is, for visual feedback to be effective in improving performance on this kind of task it has to be converted somehow into kinesthetic cues (i.e., stimuli produced by muscle movements) that signal when to stop movement.

The later study by Anshel (1978) employed only a knowledge-of-results condition. Young and elderly subjects were required to move a cylinder 80° from a resting point. Overall, the young subjects were superior to the elderly subjects in terms of the mean error averaged over 20 trials. However, the improvement in accuracy from the first to last trial was as great for the elderly as it was for the young. Thus, the poorer performance of the elderly resulted from their initially poor performance level rather than from their ability to utilize knowledge of results.

Driving a car through traffic and running with a football while dodging tacklers are examples of real-world tasks involving continuous responses. In each case, the proficiency of motor performance is greatly dependent on the ability to coordinate movements with rapidly changing visual-stimulus inputs. One of the standard laboratory tasks that simulates the kind of learning involved in such activities requires subjects to trace a figure while looking at the figure in a mirror. This is a difficult task at all ages, but it is especially difficult for the elderly. This differential difficulty was demonstrated in Snoddy's (1926) pioneering research. Young and elderly subjects received many trials tracing with a stylus a six-pointed star cut through a metal plate. The early stages of practice were particularly difficult for the elderly subjects. It is here that the novel input provided by a reverse, or mirror-image, display is highly disruptive. Eventually, even elderly subjects learn to adapt to this novel input, and they begin to improve both their accuracy and time scores in tracing this figure.

A similar result was obtained by Ruch (1934), this time with a pursuit-rotor task. For this task, subjects attempt to hold a stylus on a small button located on a disk that revolves rapidly. In one of Ruch's conditions, subjects were allowed to view the apparatus directly while holding the stylus; in a second condition, they could see the apparatus only in a mirror. The results for three age groups under both conditions are plotted in Figure 8.6. The scores are the mean number of revolutions produced over 25 trials of 30 seconds each (the disk revolved only when the stylus was on target, and the subject attempted to keep it revolving). It may be seen that an age deficit existed under each condition. However, expressed relatively, the deficit was especially pronounced in the mirror-vision condition (bottom panel of Figure 8.6), with elderly subjects averaging a score that was about 55% of that earned by middle-age subjects. By contrast, in the direct-vision condition (top panel of Figure 8.6), the elderly subjects earned a score that was about 82% of that earned by middle-age subjects. A number of other studies reviewed by Welford (1959) reveal further the

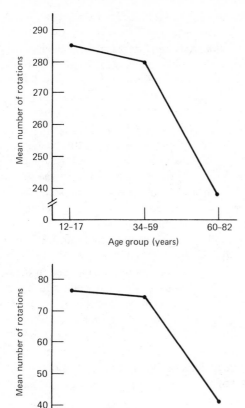

Figure 8.6. Age differences in pursuit-rotor performance under direct-vision (top panel) and mirror vision (bottom panel). (Adapted from data in Ruch, 1934.)

considerable difficulty encountered by elderly people in mastering a task with mirror-image visual inputs. The difficulty persists when the mirror-image is imaginary rather than real. That is, subjects are required to draw a figure the way it should look if seen in a mirror without actually seeing the mirror image. As noted by Welford:

> The subject is required in a mirror task to, as it were, turn the display round mentally or to employ some rule of procedure. The mirror does, in short, require that some additional stage or process be inserted in the translation from display to action, and the fundamental question would seem to be why such an extra stage causes difficulty for older people and whether some types of stage cause more difficulty than others. (1959, pp. 595–596)

We will discover in Chapter 10 that the question of age differences in the ability to rotate figures mentally has been an important one in recent years. It is a question that bears some relevance to the existence of age differences in the ability to translate mirror-image inputs into a format suitable for coordinating with movements.

More generally, the mirror-image research suggests that age deficits in motor-skill learning are likely to increase as the involvement of cognitive processes intervening between visual input and motor responding increases. The translation of mirror images is only one such intervening process. Problem solving is another potential intervening process for affecting age differences in motor-skill learning, as may be seen in studies by Kay (1954, 1955). Subjects of various ages performed on a task in which they pressed keys continuously as lights above the keys went on. There were 12 keys and 12 corresponding lights. In one condition, the keys corresponded directly to the lights. That is, the key on the far left was pressed when the light on the far left went on, and so on. In a second condition, a translation process was required to press the correct key. For example, the key on the far left might correspond to the fifth light from the left, and so on. The results for both conditions are plotted in Figure 8.7 in terms of the mean time to complete a run. It may be seen that age differences were slight in the direct-correspondence condition and quite pronounced in the translation, or problem-solving, condition. However, the age deficit in the translation condition need not be interpreted in terms of age differences in problem-solving ability. A simpler explanation stresses the greater interference proneness of elderly subjects relative to young subjects. The translation condition introduces obvious interference in that old ordinal habits (e.g., implicitly identifying the light on the far left as one instead of five) have to be suppressed. The elderly may simply be less capable of such suppression than young adults.

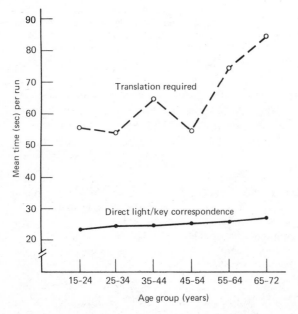

Figure 8.7. Age differences in responding to a pattern of lights both directly and with an intervening translation process. (Adapted by Welford, 1959, from data in Kay, 1954, 1955.)

Interestingly, Ruch (1934) gave a similar interpretation of the difficulty his elderly subjects had with mirror-vision operation of the pursuit rotor. Old habits associated with direct vision simply interfere more as age increases.

Finally, the pursuit-rotor task has figured in research on age differences in *reminiscence*. Reminiscence refers to an increment in performance on a motor task following a rest break. That is, performance, defined, for example, as contact time with the target area on the revolving disk, is greater following the rest than preceding the rest. Reminiscence obviously conflicts with forgetting (which predicts poorer performance following the rest than preceding it). Its presence is presumably due to the recovery during the rest break from various negative performance factors, such as fatigue. Thumin (1962) found that reminiscence did occur for elderly adults as well as for young adults. However, the amount of reminiscence (i.e., postrest gain in performance) was greater for the young adults than for the elderly adults (a finding later replicated by Gutman, 1965). This outcome is somewhat surprising in that fatigue, a likely major contributor (through its dissipation during the rest break), is expected to accumulate at a faster rate for elderly subjects than for young subjects.

Explanation of Age Differences in Motor-Skill Learning. To associationists, motor-skill learning has been traditionally viewed as being essentially equivalent to instrumental learning. As in maze learning, a subject needs to acquire a sequence of responses. It is the nature of the stimuli associated with these responses that offers the primary distinction between the two kinds of learning. For maze learning, the stimuli are largely external cues present in the maze environment. For motor-skill learning, the stimuli are proprioceptive, or kinesthetic, cues produced by the organism's own movements. A given response in a series of motor responses is presumed to be linked associatively to the stimuli generated by the prior response in the series. Age differences in motor-skill learning may be accounted for nicely from this perspective in terms of an old friend of ours, the stimulus-persistence concept. The trace of proprioceptive stimuli from any response in a chain of responses may be postulated to persist longer for elderly subjects than for young-adult subjects. These persisting stimuli should interfere with the elicitation of later responses in the chain that are temporally far removed from the source of the persisting stimuli. This conceptualization of motor-skill learning emphasizes the operation of what is commonly referred to as an *open-loop system*. An open-loop system has to rely on trial and error for the organism to hit upon, eventually, appropriate response elements in the chain.

In recent years, neoassociationists (e.g., J.A. Adams, 1971) have proposed a vastly different alternative to the open-loop view. The alternative emphasizes the operation of a *closed-loop system*. The basic component of this system is a feedback loop, much like that of a thermostat (Ellis, 1978). A thermostat is set at some specific temperature. When the actual temperature in a room dips below this set value, the disparity is detected and the heating unit is activated. Thus, the system allows for the detection *and* the correction of an error (i.e., disparity from a set value). In motor-skill learning, information provided by

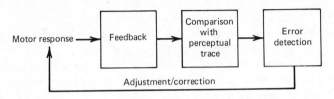

Figure 8.8. Model of a closed-loop system for motor responding.

feedback of some kind, such as knowledge of results, enables an individual to acquire gradually a perceptual trace, or image, of what task movements should be like. This trace functions like the standard temperature on a thermostat. If feedback for a given movement fails to match this standard, then an adjustment in movement toward the standard is made on the next trial. Thus, an attempt is made to correct an error, just as a heating system corrects an error (see Figure 8.8). From this perspective, motor-skill learning is largely a problem-solving task. That is, the organism attempts to solve the problem created by an error, defined, in this case, as a disparity from some standard value. Accordingly, we could argue that age deficits in motor-skill learning result from the less proficient problem-solving ability of elderly adults relative to young adults (see Chapter 10). Specifically, elderly adults are seen as having greater difficulty than young adults in abstracting perceptual traces to serve as standards for evaluating the accuracy of subsequent responses. This is an interesting way of conceptualizing age differences in motor-skill learning that apparently has not been tested in the laboratory. We should note, however, that this conceptualization is nicely consistent with the evidence indicating that elderly subjects have difficulty making use of knowledge of results on simple-movement tasks. From our present perspective, the implication is that they are largely unable to construct an image, or perceptual trace, of the feedback through proprioceptive stimuli, which should follow an accurate response.

Both open-loop and closed-loop theories of motor-skill learning have met serious opposition over the years, at least for explaining highly skilled motor operations, such as typing and playing the piano (e.g., Lashley, 1951). Responses in a complex chain are believed to unfold too rapidly to serve effectively as the source of proprioceptive stimuli for subsequent responses in the chain. That is, continuous interchanges between stimuli and responses would slow down performance to the point where highly skilled high-speed levels would be impossible. (This objection has been hotly debated in recent years, particulary at the physiological level; see Solso, 1979, pp. 340–343, for a review of these counter objections.) To explain rapid, errorless complex sequences of motor responses, many psychologists (e.g., Keele, 1968) have argued for the acquisition of a motor program with extensive practice on a task. Such a program is viewed as being a cognitive structure that, once acquired, may be subsequently activated and translated into a flow of movements that progress automatically and without interruption.

Consider, for example, the operations of skilled typists (Shaffer, 1973). Their typing, having become programmed and, therefore, automatic, makes virtually no demands on their processing capacities. Consequently, they are able to read ahead in approximately eight-letter chunks as they are typing. Thus, as they are typing one set of letters, they are reading ahead and preparing the program for the next set of letters. By contrast, beginning typists are occupied entirely with the letters they are presently typing.

Earlier in this section we argued that motor programs remain largely intact during late adulthood. Once established, adults maintain the ability to speak fluently (a programmed motor skill), ride a bicycle, play difficult compositions on the piano, and type skillfully. Our earlier comments were based on anecdotal evidence, such as that provided by Claudio Arrau. There is, however, one study (Hill, 1957) providing more objective confirmation of our point, even though the study is a real-world one and has many methodological complications (e.g., only one subject provided, in this case, longitudinal data). Hill, the single subject mastered typewriting at age 30. At the time of mastery, he typed the same 100 word-passage many times and had maintained records of his performance on this passage. At age 55 and again at age 80, Hill returned to the keyboard and again practiced typewriting. According to his own account, there had been very little practice during the many intervening years. At age 80, his first typing of the 100-word passage was at the level he had attained after 8 days of typing at age 30. After approximately 30 days, he attained the level that had taken 126 days of practice to reach at age 30. This is a truly remarkable savings, one indicating that the motor program for typing had suffered very little damage over 50 years, years filled with little additional practice.

We are talking, of course, about motor programs that were acquired during early stages of the lifespan. What we do not know is the effect of aging on the acquisition of new motor programs. Could, for example, Hill have mastered the program for typing if he had waited until age 80 to practice for the first time? It does seem unlikely that elderly adults could ever hope to acquire new programs of the kind they acquired during childhood and early adulthood.

Adult-age Differences in Verbal Learning: Paired Associates

The paired-associate learning task should need no introduction. Its basic characteristics and its importance as a prototypal task for investigating age differences/changes in associative learning were described in Chapter 6. Its importance is highlighted by the fact that much of real-life learning over the adult lifespan can be conceptualized in terms of learning associations between S and R elements. Included are associations between faces as S elements and names as R elements, foreign language words as S elements and their English translation as R elements, names of cities as S elements and names of athletic teams in those cities as R elements, and so on.

Historical Perspective: Early Studies. The broad scope of paired-associate learning is indicated further by the fact that many tasks, although not formally structured as paired associates (i.e., S and R elements are not identified as such to the learner), may, nevertheless, be conceptualized in terms of paired-associate learning. The digit-symbol test is such a task. Here, subjects are given a coding system in which the digits 1 through 9 are each equated with an abstract symbol (e.g., $9 = >$). The code itself is in full view as subjects substitute the symbols for the digits as they appear over and over in random order in a test booklet. In principle, each digit-symbol combination can be viewed as a paired associate (e.g., 9 as the S element for $>$ as the R element). Following performance on this task, subjects may be tested, unexpectedly, for the extent of paired-associate learning occurring during performance. This is accomplished by presenting the digits alone and asking subjects to reproduce for each one the symbol previously paired with it. It is exactly this procedure that provided the first evidence of adult-age differences in paired-associate learning (Willoughby, 1927, 1929). In general, Willoughby found a trend toward lower symbol-recall scores with increasing age over the adult lifespan. The fact that the subjects in this study were not informed in advance that their learning of digit-symbol pairs would eventually be assessed makes this a test of age differences in incidental learning. We will have more to say about age differences in incidental learning both later in this section and in Chapter 9.

The first study to examine adult-age differences in paired-associate learning with formally structured S and R paired elements and under intentional learning conditions was that of Ruch (1934). This is the same study that examined age differences in pursuit-rotor learning (the same subjects served in both phases of the study). Interestingly, Ruch broadened the generalizability of his results by having all of his subjects practice on three different kinds of lists (see Table 8.2 for examples of pairs in each list). One list consisted of word pairs in which the S and R elements were deliberately made to be logically related. In effect, the relationship was created by selecting R elements that were low-word associates of their paired S elements (e.g., white and pink). Ruch believed that age differences in learning would be relatively slight for this kind of familiar material. A second list consisted of false equations of the kind shown in Table 8.2. Ruch believed that age differences, favoring younger subjects, would be especially pronounced for this kind of material. The reasoning was much like that given earlier for mirror-vision performance on the pursuit rotor. He assumed that the list material generated interference from past habits (e.g., the habit of responding 9 to 3×3, instead of responding 4, the R element actually

Table 8.2 Sample Pairs Used in the Three Lists Employed by Ruch (1934) and by Korchin and Basowitz (1957)

		Type of List			
Word Pairs		False Equations		Nonsense Equations	
S Element	R Element	S Element	R Element	S Element	R Element
Soft	Chair	3×3	4	$B \times D$	M
Nest	Owl	3×1	3	$A \times M$	B
Room	Light	5×5	11	$S \times Q$	H
White	Pink	6×3	5	$L \times B$	D

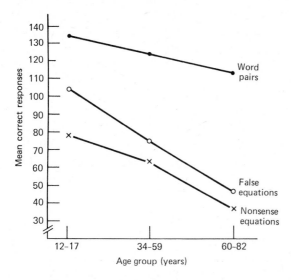

Figure 8.9. Age differences in paired-associate learning for three different kinds of material. (Adapted from data in Ruch, 1934.)

paired with 3 × 3; see Table 8.2) and that this interference increases with increasing age. The third list consisted of nonsense equations of the kind shown in Table 8.2. Age differences for this list were expected to fall in between those found for the other two lists. Ruch's predictions were fully confirmed, as can be seen in Figure 8.9 for the total number of correct responses (summed over the 15 trials given on each list; maximum score = 150 for each 10-pair list). From these results, Ruch concluded that there is an age deficit in paired-associate learning and that the magnitude of the deficit varies greatly with the attributes of the to-be-learned material.

Historical Perspective: Methodological Problems and Issues. Ruch was a pioneer, alas, in another way as well. His study was not only the first to report age deficits in formal paired-associate learning, it was also the first to suffer from many of the interpretative problems that long plagued aging research on verbal learning. The first problem in his study is the classic one of whether the reported age deficits resulted from a true ontogenetic change or from cohort differences. His description of his age groups sheds little light on this issue. No information is given about non-age attributes of his subjects other than the brief notation that all of his subjects appeared to have a high socioeconomic background. Fortunately, awareness of the importance of balancing age groups on critical non-age attributes had grown to the point that when Korchin and Basowitz (1957) replicated Ruch's (1934) study nearly 25 years later, they carefully matched their young (mean age, 26.8 years) and elderly (mean age, 78.1 years) age groups with respect to scores on the Wechsler vocabulary test. Even with this matching, elderly subjects continued to have lower learning scores than young adults on all three lists (now abbreviated to eight pairs and to six learning trials). As in Ruch's study, the age difference favoring young adults was least for word pairs. Unlike Ruch's study, however, age differences were about the same for the false-equations list as for the nonsense-equations list. These cross-sectional results, combined with those of later studies employing elderly subjects with superior educational levels and vocabulary scores (e.g., Kausler & Puckett, 1980a; see Figure 2.9), make it highly likely that the age deficits found in paired-associate learning are the products of ontogenetic change. This conclusion is strengthened, as noted in Chapter 3, by the longitudinal decrement in paired-associate learning scores reported by Arenberg and Robertson-Tchabo (1977) and by others as well (Gilbert, 1935, 1973).

A second problem inherent in Ruch's (1934) study is the difficulty of determining whether the age differences reported there represent true differences in learning ability or merely differences in performance. Ruch was well aware of the learning-performance distinction we discussed at length in Chapter 3. In fact, he was quite concerned about the possibility that his older subjects could be less motivated and less involved with the task than his younger subjects. To enhance motivation, he paid his subjects for their participation. (An interesting pay scale was devised. Subjects received 2¢ per year of age for a two-hour laboratory session. Thus, a 60-year-old subject earned the grand sum of $1.20!). Moreover, Ruch observed that his oldest subjects gave every indication of being highly involved with the tasks. It does seem unlikely that motivational factors alone could account for the pronounced age differences found in this study. A more serious problem, however, is the possibility that age differences in fatigue contributed substantially to the age differences in learning scores (Jerome, 1959). The verbal learning tasks were always given after the two practice sessions on the pursuit-rotor task (which can be a fatiguing experience). Of course, confounding by fatigue was not a problem in Korchin and Basowitz's (1957) study, and pronounced age differences on the same task remained.

The final problem is an important one that has received all too little attention by experimental aging psychologists. It concerns the nature of the dependent variable, or performance scores, employed by Ruch (1934), namely, total correct responses over a fixed number of trials. Do age differences on this overall score necessarily indicate age differences in learning when learning is defined in terms of the rate of acquiring new material (Jerome, 1959)? It is conceivable that elderly adults learn new material as rapidly as young adults—once the elderly get going on the task at hand. If true, the low overall score earned by the elderly would be attributable entirely to their slow start. Beyond the first few trials, learning proficiency may be as great for the elderly as it is for the young.

Answers to questions about age differences in rate of learning require a finer grained analysis than the kind used by Ruch. What is needed is a trial-by-trial analysis of increments in scores on the learning task. This analysis yields what is called a *learning curve*. Our interest rests in age differences in learning curves, differences that presumably reflect differences in rates. Unfortunately,

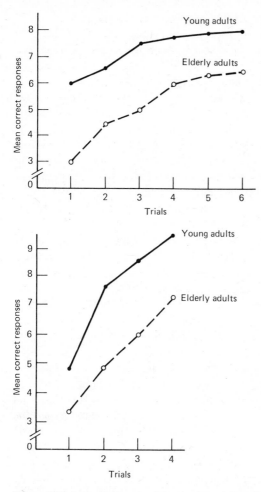

Figure 8.10. Learning curves for paired-associate learning by young and elderly subjects. (Top panel: Adapted from Korchin & Basowitz, 1957, Figure 1. Bottom panel: Adapted from data in Kausler & Puckett, 1980a.)

many of the aging studies on paired-associate learning that followed Ruch copied his mode of analysis and reported only total scores. There have been important exceptions, however. One of the first was in Korchin and Basowitz's (1957) replication study. They reported learning curves for both age groups on all three of their lists. The curves for the word-pair list are shown in the top panel of Figure 8.10. It may be seen that the age groups differed greatly in amount recalled after one study trial. Beyond that point, the two groups gained in amount recalled at approximately the same rate (by the fourth trial, age comparisons are complicated by an obvious ceiling effect for young adults that was not present for elderly adults). The learning curves for the other two lists revealed very similar patterns. From this evidence, it could be argued that the elderly do have trouble activating their learning processes (a point we will return to in our later discussion of nonspecific transfer), but, once these processes are activated, the elderly progress as well on a learning task as do the young.

Unfortunately, the results obtained by Korchin and Basowitz are more the exception than the rule. There have been several studies over the years for which trial-by-trial data are available. In general, these studies do indicate a slower rate of learning for elderly subjects than for young-adult subjects. As one example, we will reconsider the study by Kausler and Puckett (1980a) that was described in Chapter 2 (also see Figure 2.9). At that time, we discovered an age deficit in terms of total correct responses summed over four learning trials. When these scores are analyzed trial by trial, the learning curves shown in the bottom panel of Figure 8.10 emerge. Note the disparity on Trial 1 between age groups, but, more important, note the more rapid gain from Trial 1 to Trial 2 and from Trial 2 to Trial 3 for the young adults than for the elderly adults (by Trial 4 a ceiling effect is apparent for the young adults). Similar age differences in rate of learning are obvious in data reported by Monge (1971) and by Winn, Elias, and Marshall (1976). Their learning curves are expressed in a different format than that of a trial-by-trial analysis. The mean number of trials taken to reach successive criteria of mastery are determined for each age group. These successive criteria are one correct response, two correct responses, and so on, through N (the number of pairs in the list) correct responses. The list consisted of 10 word pairs in Monge's study and 7 nonsense-shape/nonsense-syllable (S element/R element) pairs in Winn et al.'s study. The curves found in Monge's study for subjects in their 20s and 50s are plotted in Figure 8.11. It can be seen that the older subjects manifested a slower rate of mastery of the pairs than the younger subjects. An even greater disparity in rate of learning between young (mean age, 20 years) and elderly (mean age, 65 years) is apparent in the results

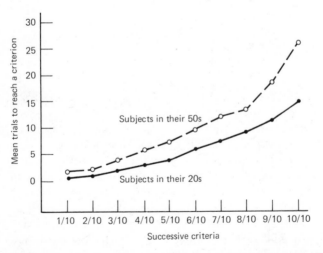

Figure 8.11. Learning curves for paired-associate learning by young and elderly subjects plotted as trials to attain successive criteria. (Adapted from data in Monge, 1971.)

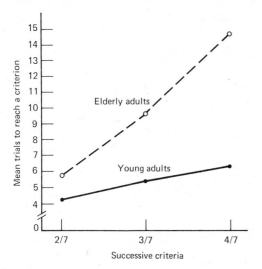

Figure 8.12. Learning curves for paired-associate learning by young and elderly subjects plotted as trials to attain successive criteria. (Adapted from Winn, Elias, & Marshall, 1976, Table 2.)

obtained by Winn el at. and plotted, in part, in Figure 8.12. The greater disparity in learning rates found by Winn et al. than by Monge is probably the consequence of the greater difficulty of the learning materials entering into the former study.

Theoretical Analysis of Age-Sensitive Processes. Although expressed only vaguely, Ruch's (1934) theoretical orientation in his pioneering study was decidedly that of classical associationism. Old habits, defined as associations learned prior to performance on the laboratory tasks, were expected to benefit elderly subjects in learning weakly related words pairs and to hinder them in learning false equations. Positive and negative effects were to be evaluated relative to the presumed neutral condition of learning nonsense equations. Here learning from scratch was demanded. That is, learning had to start from zero associative strength between S and R elements and build connections gradually by means of rehearsal responses. The age deficit manifested in this condition could, therefore, be viewed as evidence for decreasing associative learning proficiency with increasing age. Implicit in this view is the hypothesis that the adverse effect of increasing age results from decreasing rehearsal responses with increasing age. The adversity could be either diminished, as in the word-pairs condition, or increased, as in the false-equations condition, contingent on the kind and amount of transfer from past associative learning extant during practice on the task at hand.

This single-process view of age deficits in paired-associate learning remained dominant until the advent of stage analysis in the 1960s (Underwood & Schulz, 1960). There was, however, an interesting precursor to formal applications of stage analysis to age deficits in paired-associate learning. Korchin and

Basowitz (1957) had the foresight to observe that one of the probable factors contributing to age deficits in their study is the fact that "the older person requires more time for the integration of a response" (p. 68). As we have noted on several occasions, response learning is one of the stages of overall learning identified by stage analysts. Just how age differences in response learning may have contributed to the age differences in total learning scores (and rate of overall learning) found in Korchin and Basowitz's study is not very clear. It is possible that numbers, the R elements in their false-equations list (see Table 8.2), are easier to learn than are letters, the R elements in their nonsense-equations list. If true, the reduction in overall difficulty produced by easier response learning could compensate for the added difficulty produced by the interference present in the false-equations condition. The net effect would be lists that are roughly equal in the amount of age deficit they produce (as found in Korchin and Basowitz's study).

There is evidence of a more direct nature to support the hypothesis that response learning is indeed an age-sensitive process. Part of that evidence was given in Chapter 5 when we discussed the study by Witte and Freund (1976). Other direct evidence comes from a study by Canestrari (1964; see Botwinick, 1967) who employed a procedure quite different from that employed by Witte and Freund. His experimental subjects, both young and elderly, learned the R elements of a paired-associate list (i.e., as a separate free-recall learning list) prior to their practice on the actual paired-associate list. The paired-associate learning scores for these subjects were then compared with those obtained by control subjects, both young and elderly, who practiced on the same paired-associate list but without prior learning of the R elements. The magnitude of the age deficit in paired-associate learning scores was considerably less for experimental subjects than for control subjects. Thus, the savings produced by eliminating the age-sensitive response learning process for experimental subjects, or, at least, greatly reducing its involvement, was sufficient to reduce the handicap elderly subjects face in paired-associate learning.

Less direct support for response learning's age sensitivity comes from the finding that the age deficit in rate of learning is especially large when nonsense syllables serve as the R elements of a paired-associate list. This was the case in the study by Winn et al. (1976) cited earlier (see Figure 8.12). Nonsense syllables are elements for which response learning is especially important when those elements function as responses in a paired-associate list. Syllables, such as *QOJ,* are unfamiliar to subjects prior to being encountered as the R elements of a learning list. Consequently, letters have to be integrated into novel sequences to become available as R elements for entry into S-R associations. This integrative form of response learning is generally accepted as being a special case of associative learning in which subjects learn associations between individual letters (see Kausler, 1974, pp. 10–12). The importance of the probable age sensitivity of this form of response learning should not be taken lightly. In real-life learning situations, response elements composed of unfamiliar letter sequences, such as *Ayatollah Khomeini,* are fairly common. Elderly people are likely to experience greater difficulty than young adults in intergrating such sequences. Of course, the void in direct laboratory research on age differences in response integration as a form of response learning makes this conclusion quite tentative.

Another stage, or process, identified in stage analysis as being involved in paired-associate learning is that of R-S, or backward, associative learning. In effect, this process supplements, S-R, or forward, associative learning. The existence of R-S associative learning becomes apparent when subjects are given an unexpected test after they have completed practice on a paired-associate list. On this test, they receive the R elements from the list, one at a time, and they are asked to recall the S element that had been paired with each R element. This test reverses the usual procedure in which the S elements are presented and recall of the R elements is requested. It is not unusual to discover that a number of the S elements can be recalled when they are cued by their paired R elements. The process accounting for the learning of R-S associations offers no great mystery to stage analysts. They simply expand on the concept of rehearsal to include rehearsal responses directed at S elements as well as at R elements. Connections in the backward direction are especially likely for subjects whose rehearsal is characterized by repeating the names of both elements of a pair throughout the pair's exposure during a study trial. For example, during exposure of the pair *apple-table,* the subject is assumed to be saying, covertly, "apple table apple table . . ." for as long as the pair is shown. Note that *apple-table* are rehearsed contiguously but so are *table-apple,* thus promoting increments in the strength of both associations. Nevertheless, the flow of rehearsal is such that the two associations accrue strength asymmetrically, with the forward association gaining strength more rapidly than the backward association, as indicated in Figure 8.13. Consequently, more S-R associations than R-S associations

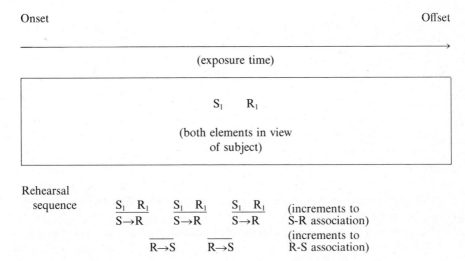

Figure 8.13. Schematic representation of rehearsal activity postulated to underlie the incidental learning of R-S, or backward, associations in addition to the intentional learning of S-R, or forward, associations.

should be recalled following a fixed number of trials on a paired-associate task. This expectancy has been confirmed in a number of studies with young-adult subjects (see Kausler, 1974, pp. 169–175).

The overall age deficit expected in rehearsal rates leads to the further expectancy of less recall of R-S associations by elderly subjects than by young-adult subjects. In agreement with this hypothesis, Kausler and Lair (1965) found that their older subjects had a level of R-S recall that was about 71% of the amount of their S-R recall, whereas their younger subjects had a level that was about 85% of their S-R recall. Similar results were obtained later by Winn and Elias (1978). The age deficit found for R-S learning qualifies as another example of an age deficit in incidental learning. R-S learning, like the associative learning that occurs during practice on the digit-symbol test, is incidental in the sense that it occurs in the absence of intentionality to learn. However, there is nothing mysterious about either incidental learning per se or the existence of age deficits in incidental learning. The processes promoting the intentional learning of S-R associations are the same processes promoting the incidental learning of R-S associations. Consequently, if these processes themselves are age sensitive, whatever kinds of learning they produce should reflect that age sensitivity.

The bidirectional nature of associative learning has its real-life implications. Consider, for example, the postelection rehearsal of the list of new cabinet appointments. As subjects rehearse the fact that the new Secretary of State is Fillmore Jones, they are also rehearsing the fact that Fillmore Jones is the new Secretary of State. Thus, some learning of the R-to-S (name-to-position) association accompanies learning of the S-to-R (position-to-name) associations. Our previous analysis suggests that elderly adults are less able than young adults to acquire the "Fillmore Jones is Secretary of State" association. This should be true even though the "Secretary of State is Fillmore Jones" association has been practiced enough at both age levels to reach a common criterion of mastery.

The final stage identified by stage analysts, that of *stimulus learning,* is a complex activity with several component processes. The only one we will consider, *stimulus selection,* is a further candidate for age sensitivity. Its operation forces the distinction between a nominal stimulus and a functional stimulus (Underwood, 1963). The distinction is probably uncalled for when a stimulus consists of a well-integrated element, such as a familiar word, as in our earlier *apple-table* example. It may be a different matter, however, when a stimulus consists of multiple components that are loosely related, if at all, to one another (e.g., the letters of a nonsense syllable, such as *JIX*). The separate components are likely to be redundant in the sense that any one alone would serve reliably as a cue for association with the response assigned to the total-stimulus element (i.e., the nominal, or experimenter-defined, stimulus). An active subject may resolve the dilemma by selecting consistently only one of the components to serve as an effective, or functional, stimulus. Selection itself is assumed to be a generalized habit that transfers from many past learning experiences. Like other generalized habits, its activation may decrease with increasing age, thus making stimulus selection an age-sensitive process. There are methods available for testing the operation of a selection habit (e.g., Postman & Greenbloom, 1967). Apparently, these methods have not been extended to use with elderly subjects. Consequently, nothing is known about age changes in the proficiency of this selection process.

There are many real-life situations in which opportunities for applying stimulus selection are rampant. For example, for many years Lincoln Continental automobiles contained two distinctive stimuli—a tire hump in the back and oval rear windows. These stimuli are redundant in the sense that either one alone may be noticed, or selected, and be associated reliably with the name of the car. Real-life exemplars of this kind offer intriguing possibilities for investigating age differences in stimulus selection under ecologically valid conditions.

Research with Manipulable Independent Variables: Preexperimental Associative Strength. In the remaining sections we will review some of the major paired-associate learning studies that have combined variation of a manipulable independent variable with variation of age level. From our discussion in Chapter 5, we realize that such research is essential for expanding our knowledge about the generalizability of age deficits in paired-associate learning across variations in task and procedural conditions. We also realize that such research serves to test the age sensitivity of processes that are components of associative theories of paired-associate learning. Our review will concentrate on three major areas of investigation: (1) studies that vary degree of preexperimental associative strength between S and R elements (2) studies that vary rate of presenting S and R elements, and (3) studies that vary instructions.

As we indicated earlier, associative strength need not be zero at the start of practice on a paired-associate task. Some degree of learning for S-R pairings may have already taken place through contiguous occurrences of elements in the subject's natural environment. Consequently, only a few rehearsal responses may be needed in the new (i.e., laboratory) context before their associative strengths reach above threshold values. In general, as the degree of preexperimental learning increases, the ease of learning on a laboratory task should increase accordingly. Tests of this hypothesis require S and R elements that clearly vary in the strength of their preexperimental associations. Fortunately, there is a ready source of these elements, namely word-association norms (e.g., Palermo & Jenkins, 1964). These norms permit selection of word pairs in which the R element is a strong associate of the S element (e.g., fast as an associate of *slow*) as well as pairs in which the R element is a weak associate of the S element (e.g., fly as an associate of *eagle*). When transferred to paired-associate lists, *slow* and *eagle* become S elements paired with *fast* and *fly* as R elements.

Given lists of high- and low-associative strengths, we would clearly expect subjects to acquire the high-strength list in fewer trials than the low-strength list. More important, we would also expect the difference in trials to learn between young and elderly subjects to be less for a high-strength list than for a low-strength list. In fact, there is good reason to believe that age differences would all but disappear with pairs of high preexperimental associative strength. At this level, there should be little need to engage in rote rehearsal of R elements. Consequently, the contribution of this suspected age-sensitive process should be miniscule. If associative learning is the only process mediating paired-associate learning, then its deletion, through the use of high-strength pairs, should yield comparable levels of performance for young and elderly subjects.

This predicted outcome has been found in a number of studies (Canestrari, 1966; Kausler & Lair, 1966; Zaretsky & Halberstam, 1968a, 1968b). The results of one of these studies (Zaretsky & Halberstam, 1968b) are plotted in Figure 8.14. Both young (an age range of 20 to 45 years) and elderly (an age range of 60 to 85 years) were hospital patients who received five pair lists containing pairs of either high, medium, or low preexperimental associative strength. Note that the age difference in trials to learn the list is virtually nonexistent with high-strength pairs (although it takes a surprisingly large number of trials for both age groups to learn the list), modest with medium-strength pairs, and quite pronounced with low-strength pairs. Interestingly, nearly identical results were obtained with separate groups of brain-damaged young and elderly subjects.

There is a methodological problem inherent in all of the studies that have combined age variation with variation in associative strength as defined by word-association norms. The available word-association norms have all been obtained with young adults (specifically, college students) as subjects. It is conceivable that strength-of-association values found with young adults do not generalize to elderly adults. This is the same problem we encountered earlier (Chapter 5) with respect to words that are rated for their ease of eliciting images. The solution of the imagery problem was the demonstration that mean

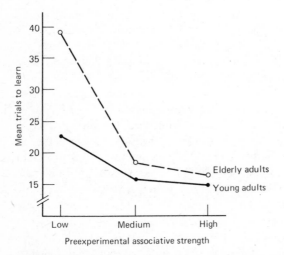

Figure 8.14. Age differences in paired-associate learning proficiency as affected by level of preexperimental associative strength. (Adapted from data in Zaretsky & Halberstam, 1968b.)

ratings obtained for a sample of elderly subjects on a sample of words correlate highly with mean ratings in the imagery norms. Similar studies have been conducted on word associations (Perlmutter, 1978a; Riegel & Birren, 1965). These studies do indicate some modest differences in the word associations given by young and elderly adults. However, the differences do not appear to be large enough to question seriously the generalizability of young-adult norms to elderly subjects. Nevertheless, it would be useful if some enterprising, and compulsive, researcher were to collect substantial word-association normative data for elderly (and middle-age, as well) adults.

Research with Manipulable Independent Variables: Rate-of-Item Presentation. Traditionally, basic research in paired-associate learning has been conducted with fairly rapid pacing conditions. That is, to-be-learned items are exposed, usually visually, at a rate varying across studies from 1 to 4 seconds per item. Extensions of this research to the study of adult-age differences in paired-associate learning proficiency have largely continued this tradition. For example, the age differences found by Korchin and Basowitz (1957) and Kausler and Lair (1965) were obtained with a 4-second rate, whereas those found by Kausler and Lair (1966) were obtained with a 3-sec rate. Of great concern is the generalizability of these age differences, and those found in other similar studies, to slower rates of presentation (and still faster rates as well). Much of this concern follows from the evidence that indicates a general slowing down of responding in later adulthood (see Chapter 6). Conceivably, 3 or 4 seconds may not be enough time for many elderly subjects to give responses to S elements, even when the underlying associations have been fully learned. If true, then many age deficits in paired-associate learning proficiency reported in the literature may represent performance decrements attributable to the slowness of responding by the elderly rather than decrements in learning ability per se. In support of a performance decrement is the fact that most errors made by the elderly during practice on a paired-associate list are errors of omission (i.e., failure to give any kind of response to S elements; Korchin & Basowitz, 1957).

Tests of the generalizability of age differences over varying rates-of-item presentation call for a heterogeneous factorial design in which the systematic variation of rate is combined with age variation. The earliest study to employ this design was by Canestrari (1963). Unfortunately, the results obtained are ambiguous (for further analysis of this and other studies that vary rate of presentation see Witte, 1975). The source of the ambiguity is linked to the method used to present list materials to subjects, namely, the anticipation method. This is a frequently used method in paired-associate learning research (e.g., it was used by Korchin and Basowitz, 1957, and Kausler and Lair, 1965, 1966), but, as we will soon see, it is not the only method available. The nature of the anticipation method is illustrated in Figure 8.15 with reference to the rate conditions employed in Canestrari's (1963) study. Specifically, there were three levels of the rate variable: 1.5 sec per item, 3 sec per item, and self-pacing (i.e., subjects progress through the list at their own rate). For each pacing condition, a trial consists of exposing first the S element of a pair followed by

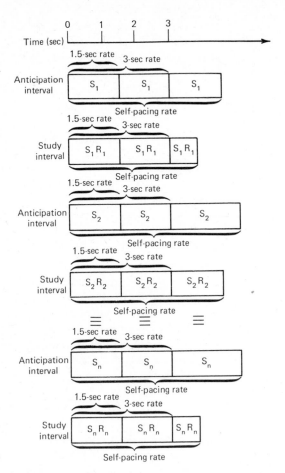

Figure 8.15. Schematic representation of the procedures used to vary duration of anticipation and study intervals in paired-associate learning. Durations are either 1.5 seconds, 3 seconds, or self-paced.

exposure of both the S element and the R element. The first exposure is called the *anticipation interval.* During this interval, subjects attempt to respond with the R element that has been paired with the exposed S element. In Canestrari's study the anticipation interval lasted either 1.5 seconds, 3 seconds, or an amount determined by each subject individually. The second exposure is called the *study interval.* During this interval, subjects have the opportunity to rehearse the S and R elements, thereby adding to the strength of the connection between those elements. The study interval in Canestrari's study also lasted either 1.5 seconds, 3 seconds, or an amount determined by each subject individually. Most important, the durations of the two intervals were yoked together. Thus, the 1.5 second anticipation interval was always accompanied by the 1.5-second study interval, the 3-second anticipation interval with the 3-second study interval, and the self-paced anticipation interval with the self-paced study interval. Consequently, the effect of varying rate on age differences in task proficiency could be due to either or both rate manipulations.

That effect is shown in Figure 8.16 for mean errors made in learning the list. The interaction apparent in this figure indicates a multiplicative relationship between age and rate (if necessary, review the material on multiplicative relationships in Chapter 5). That is, the age deficit in proficiency decreased as overall performance improved across the levels of the rate variable for both age groups. Our inference, therefore, is that the process altered by rate variation is age sensitive. That process could be the aforementioned speed of responding to S elements. The adverse effects of slower responding by elderly subjects simply become less pronounced as the duration of the anticipation interval increases. On the other hand, the age-sensitive process could be one that is affected by variation of the study interval. A possible candidate in this event is the rate of emitting rehearsal responses. According to this hypothesis, the slower rehearsal rate of elderly subjects is at least partially compensated for by lengthening the study interval, thereby giving them added time to rehearse S and R elements. Again, the yoked nature of the variation in the two intervals does not permit us to distinguish between these alternatives.

To untangle the confounding present in these early studies, Monge and Hultsch (1971) wisely employed a complete factorial design in which duration of each interval was varied separately. There were three levels of each variable: 2.2 seconds, 4.4 seconds, and 6.6 seconds. Thus, nine groups were required at each age level—those receiving 2.2-2.2, 2.2-4.4, 2.2-6.6, 4.4-2.2, and so on combinations of anticipation-study interval durations. In agreement with the performance-deficit hypothesis, Monge and Hultsch found a significant interaction between age and duration of the anticipation interval, as illustrated in the top panel of Figure 8.17 (a similar outcome occurred in an earlier study by Arenberg, 1965, in which duration of the anticipation interval was varied while the duration of the study interval was held constant). It may be seen that the

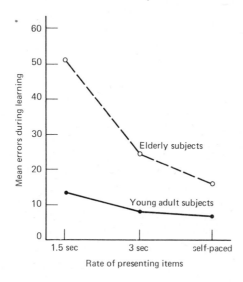

Figure 8.16. Age differences in paired-associate learning proficiency as affected by rate of presenting items. (Adapted from Canestrari, 1963, Table 2.)

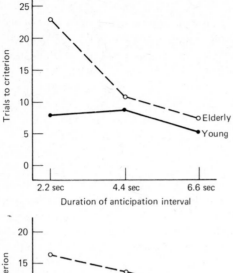

Figure 8.17. Age differences in paired-associate learning proficiency as affected separately by variation in duration of the anticipation interval (top panel) and study interval (bottom panel). (Adapted from data in Monge & Hultsch, 1971.)

age deficit was much greater with a fast rate (2.2 seconds) than with a slower rate (either 4.4 or 6.6 seconds). The resulting multiplicative relationship implies that an age-sensitive process is tapped by variation in the length of the antici-pation interval. The likely candidate, of course, seems to be speed of responding.

On the other hand, the interaction between age and duration of the study interval, shown in the bottom panel of Figure 8.17, did not attain statistical significance. In other words, the magnitude of the age deficit in learning proficiency was about as great with a brief study interval (2.2 seconds) as it was with longer intervals (4.4 or 6.6 seconds). The absence of an interaction between age and duration of study intervals was also found in a study by Hulicka, Sterns, and Grossman (1967). In their study, the anticipation method was replaced by a method in which study trials alternate with test trials. During each study trial, S-R pairs are presented successively for study with no performance being demanded of subjects. Each study trial is then followed by a test trial in which each S element is presented alone and subjects attempt to recall the R element paired with it. This method avoids the confusion, especially for elderly subjects (Kausler, 1963), created in the anticipation method by the constant alternation of performance (i.e., anticipation) and learning (i.e., study) periods. The absence of an interaction between age and study interval duration in both Monge and Hultsch's (1971) study and Hulicka et al.'s (1967) study indicates an additive relationship between age and duration of study intervals. The implication of this kind of relationship (see Chapter 5) is that the process altered by the manipulable independent variable is age insensitive. If that process is rote-rehearsal activity, then it is unlikely that age differences in this process account for age differences in paired-associate learning proficiency. At the same time, it is obvious that some process is altered, independently of age variation, by variation in the duration of study intervals. Note in the bottom panel of Figure 8.17 that performance proficiency for both age groups improved progressively as duration increased, that is, there was a main effect for variation-of-study intervals.

Our analysis does not rule out, however, the probable involvement of an age-sensitive learning process as a major factor contributing to adult-age differences in paired-associate learning proficiency. It simply indicates that whatever that process is, it is not affected by the duration of study intervals. A strong candidate for age sensitivity, as we will soon see, is engagement in mediated rehearsal (e.g., the use of imagery to related S and R elements together). Young-adult subjects are more likely than elderly subjects to initiate mediated rehearsal regardless of the duration of the study interval.

One other finding in this area of aging research is worth mentioning. Under complete self-pacing conditions, elderly subjects do take more total time to learn a list than do young-adult subjects (Canestrari, 1963). Moreover, this disparity in total time remains about the same regardless of the specific pacing conditions that are introduced (Kinsbourne & Berryhill, 1972). For each age level, it takes about the same amount of total time to learn a list regardless of the specific pacing condition employed. For example, about three times as many trials are needed to learn a list with a 2-second rate of presentation than with a 6-second rate, but the total time involved stays invariant.

Research with Manipulable Independent Variables: Mediational Instructions.
The use of mediators to relate S and R elements together is widely practiced by young adults during paired-associate learning. For example, Underwood and Schulz (1960) discovered that nearly three fourths of the pairs learned by their subjects were acquired through the use of a mediator of some kind. Our reference is to the spontaneous use of mediators, that is, use without any special prodding or instructions. Our discussion in the preceding section implied that elderly adults are far less likely than young adults to use mediators spontaneously and that it is this age differential in spontaneous mediation that accounts for much of the age difference found in paired-associate learning proficiency. An age difference in spontaneous mediation has indeed been found in several studies (Hulicka, 1965; Hulicka & Grossman, 1967). For example, Hulicka and Grossman found that only 36% of their elderly subjects reported using mediation during practice on a paired-associate list, compared to 68% of their young subjects. Moreover, young and elderly subjects also differ in the kinds of me-

diators they employ. Young adults are more likely to use imaginal mediators (i.e., constructing mental pictures of S and R elements interacting together) than verbal mediators (i.e., constructing phrases or sentences combining S and R elements), whereas elderly adults show the opposite pattern. This is another important factor contributing to age deficits in paired-associate learning. In general, imaginal mediators are more effective than verbal mediators in promoting paired-associate learning (Paivio, 1971). Interestingly, bizarre images are no more effective as mediators than are common-event images, either for young adults (Nappe & Wollen, 1973) or elderly adults (Poon & Walsh-Sweeney, 1981). On the other hand, the complexity of mediators, once they are elicited, does not seem to differ greatly between young and elderly adults (Marshall, Elias, Webber, Gist, Winn, King, & Moore, 1978).

The remaining issue is the extent to which the age difference in the spontaneous use of mediators can be overcome by instructions and training. At stake is the important question of whether or not elderly adults have a true *mediational deficiency* relative to young adults (Kausler, 1970). The deficiency would presumably be the consequence of biological degeneration. If such a deficiency does exist, then it is highly unlikely that any amount of instruction or training could restore mediational proficiency to the level characteristic of young adulthood. Alternatively, elderly adults may be experiencing only a *production deficiency,* or performance decrement, brought about, most likely, by the lack of practice in mediation once they have left formal educational settings. If only a production deficiency is involved, then age deficits in paired-associate learning should be largely overcome through the effective use of instructions and training. There is, in fact, evidence (Treat, Poon, Fozard, & Popkin, 1978) indicating that elderly people do begin to use imaginal mediators spontaneously after practice on a number of paired-associate lists.

This issue has been examined in several additional studies employing instructions as a manipulable independent variable. One of these studies (Hulicka & Grossman, 1967) was touched upon in Chapter 1 (also see Figure 1.2). We discovered then that training in the use of an imaginal mediator improved the performance of elderly subjects by 18% (from 35% of the pairs recalled without special training to 53% with special training). We also discovered that young adults also improved with special training, but to a smaller degree than elderly adults (11%; from 70% to 81%). The resulting multiplicative relationship between age levels and training conditions implies that mediation, the process varied by training, is age sensitive. The experimental-training condition in this case encouraged subjects to generate their own imaginal content, linking S and R elements together. There were other training conditions involved in this study as well. In one, the investigators supplied both young and elderly subjects with a suggested content for each image. For example, with *army-bank* as a pair, the suggestion was to form an image of any army attacking a bank. Relative to the control, or noninstructed, condition, performance proficiency improved for both age groups (45% and 78% of the pairs being recalled by elderly and young subjects respectively). Note, however, that the gain in proficiency was less pronounced than when subjects supplied their own imaginal content (10% gain for the elderly subjects, 8% for the young subjects). A final condition employed in this study consisted of training and instructions in the use of verbal mediators. Specifically, suggestions as to content of connecting phrases were given (e.g., *army* attacks *bank*). Relative to the control condition, elderly subjects improved somewhat in proficiency of recall (a 12% gain; from 35% to 47%), whereas young subjects showed virtually no gain (1% from 70% to 71%).

A similar pattern of results was obtained by Canestrari (1968). There were three instructional conditions: (1) a control with no special instructions, (2) an experimental condition in which subjects were urged to use images corresponding to pictures shown that depicted interacting S and R elements, and (3) an experimental condition in which subjects were urged to use phrases corresponding to those given to them by the experimenter. The results, expressed as mean errors made in learning the list, are plotted in Figure 8.18 for both young adults (interestingly, male prisoners averaging 20.2 years of age) and elderly adults (male residents of a Veterans' Administration facility averaging 62.4 years of age—the two age groups were comparable in educational levels, socioeconomic backgrounds, and vocabulary-test scores). A multiplicative relationship may again be observed, although in this case it may be complicated by a ceiling effect for the young subjects. The elderly subjects clearly benefited from both verbal and imaginal instructions, but, as in Hulicka and Grossman's (1967) study, more so for the latter. The improvement in both studies for instructed elderly subjects clearly indicates that part of the age deficit in paired-associate learning proficiency is the consequence of a production deficiency (or, perhaps more appropriately, a production inefficiency; Reese, 1976) that can be at least partially overcome by training and practice. However, it seems likely that some true loss of mediational ability in late adulthood is involved as well. Even with mediational prodding, paired-associate learning proficiency of elderly subjects remains well below the level of young-adult subjects. Of course, it is conceivable that psychologists have yet to discover a fully effective means of overcoming production inefficiencies. Some hope of this possibility emerged in a complex study by Treat and Reese (1976). Mediational conditions were varied together with several rate-of-presentation variables. With long anticipa-

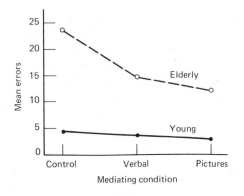

Figure 8.18. Age differences in paired-associate learning proficiency as affected by variation in mediational instructions. (Adapted from Canestrari, 1968, Figure 1.)

tion intervals, their elderly subjects performed as well as their young-adult subjects, but only when all of the subjects were encouraged to generate their own imagery content (see Poon, Walsh-Sweeney, & Fozard, 1980, for an extensive discussion of training programs for enhancing the use of imaginal mediation).

Finally, it should be noted that research varying the rated imagery values of S and R elements is in basic agreement with our hypothesis that an imaginal deficit underlies much of the difficulty encountered by elderly people in paired-associate learning. We discovered earlier (Chapter 5; also see Figure 5.8) that the age difference favoring young adults is greater for S and R elements composed of abstract nouns (and, therefore, low-imagery arousing) than it is for S and R elements composed of concrete nouns (and, therefore, high-imagery arousing) (Rowe & Schnore, 1971). As we indicated at the time, this multiplicative relationship implies the age sensitivity of imaginal mediation.

Adult-Age Difference in Verbal Learning: Serial Learning

The psychology of verbal learning had its historical origin in research on serial learning. The originator was Hermann Ebbinghaus (1885). He served as his own subject, learning list after list of nonsense syllables. The task he introduced was basically a form of serial learning in which a subject studies a series of items and then attempts to reproduce the series in the order the items were presented. What makes Ebbinghaus's research especially intriguing to us is the fact that, at age 33, the only subject (Ebbinghaus himself) was not exactly a young-adult learner.

Despite this promising start, interest in serial learning by noncollege-age subjects lagged well behind the same kind of interest in other kinds of learning. Perhaps the first formal study of adult-age differences in serial learning with verbal elements was that of Bromley (1958). By then, the task format preferred by investigators had shifted from that of serial reproduction to that of serial anticipation. With this revised format, items, usually words, are presented consecutively. As each item is exposed, subjects both study that item and anticipate what the next item in the series will be. Thus, each exposure of an item doubles as an anticipation interval as well as a study interval.

Bromley's study revealed cross-sectional adult age differences in serial-learning proficiency, favoring young adults. A number of subsequent cross-sectional studies (e.g., Eisdorfer, Axelrod, & Wilkie, 1963; Eisdorfer & Service, 1967) have replicated this finding. Typically, these studies employed young and elderly groups of subjects that were carefully matched with respect to educational levels and vocabulary scores, thus making it unlikely that the age deficit in learning proficiency was attributable to cohort effects. Further support for this conclusion comes from the impressive longitudinal study by Arenberg and Robertson-Tchabo (1977). Their evidence indicating a true age change in serial-learning proficiency closely parallels the evidence found in the same study indicating a true age change in paired-associate learning proficiency (see Chapter 3 and Figure 3.13). As in paired-associate learning, longitudinal decrements in serial learning were generally found to be comparable to intracohort cross-sectional decrements over the same age range.

Bromley (1958) also found no age difference in what is called the serial-position effect. The effect is in reference to the distribution across ordinal positions in the list of the total number of errors made while learning the list. With young-adult subjects, many studies (see Kausler, 1974, pp 276–288) have revealed that very few errors are made for the beginning items in the list and slightly more errors are made for the items at the end of the list. The highest concentration of errors occurs for those items embedded in the middle of the list, peaking at some point closer to the end of the list than to the beginning. Bromley's evidence (later replicated by Eisdorfer et al., 1963) indicates that elderly subjects distribute their errors in the same pattern. Many explanations of the serial-position effect have been offered over the years, none of which are completely satisfactory (Kausler, 1974, pp. 276–288). An especially appealing one, however, argues that the distribution of errors simply reflects the order in which subjects learn ordinal placements of items in the list (Jensen, 1962a). That is, early items are learned first, then end items, and, finally, midlist items. The absence of an age difference in the overall pattern of error distribution suggests that elderly adults apply the same basic strategy that young adults apply in learning a serial list.

Beyond the simple reporting of age differences in rate of serial learning and the absence of an age difference in the serial position effect most studies have been concerned with the effect of varying rate of presentation on age differences in serial-learning proficiency. The results of one of these studies (Eisdorfer & Service, 1967) were given in Chapter 5 (also see Figure 5.9). The pattern found in this study, namely, decreasing age differences as the duration of item exposure increases, is fairly representative of this effect. As a further example, the results obtained by Arenberg (1967a) are shown in Figure 8.19.

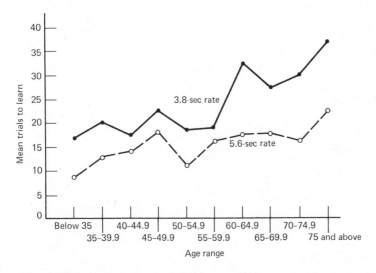

Figure 8.19. Age differences in serial-learning proficiency as affected by variation in duration of item exposure. (Adapted from Arenberg, 1967a, Table 2.)

His procedure called for exposing each word of a 12-item list for 2 seconds, followed by a blank interval of either 1.8 seconds or 3.6 seconds. Thus, subjects at each of many age levels had a total time of either 3.8 seconds or 5.6 seconds to anticipate what the next word in the series would be. Note that age differences in mean trials to learn the list were considerably less pronounced with the slower pacing condition than with the faster pacing condition. Much of this decrease in the overall age deficit undoubtedly resulted from overcoming some of the adverse performance factors experienced by elderly subjects under a fast-pacing condition. Strong support for this argument comes from the study by Eisdorfer et al. (1963). Some of their elderly subjects began practice on a serial list under a fast-pacing condition and were switched on later trials to a slower pacing condition. After the switch, their performance improved considerably, reaching the level of proficiency attained by other elderly subjects who received the slower rate throughout practice. If rate-of-presentation markedly affected the amount learned, then the subjects with the originally faster rate should have continued to lag behind the subjects with the originally slower rate after the switch.

As in paired-associate learning, the presence of performance deficits does not rule out the existence of learning deficits as well. Even with a very slow rate of item presentation, such as the 10-second rate employed by Eisdorfer and Service (1967), a sizable age deficit in serial-learning proficiency remains (see Figure 5.9). The specific age-sensitive serial-learning process remains unknown however. We observed in Chapter 6 that the nature of serial learning per se is far from being understood. Nevertheless, the age-sensitive process is probably one that is closely allied to the age-sensitive mediational process entering into paired-associate learning. Indirect evidence in support of this hypothesis was provided in the previously mentioned study by Arenberg (1967a). His subjects learned a paired-associate list as well as a serial list. Of interest are the correlations between paired-associate learning scores and serial-learning scores. For each age range of subjects and for both fast- and slow-pacing conditions, the correlation coefficient was moderately high (r of about .60). It seems likely that learning processes shared by the two kinds of tasks at each age level account for much of the covariation between task proficiencies. A likely candidate for a shared process is mediation. We should note, however, that the correlation coefficients reported in Arenberg's study are unusually high. Other investigators (e.g., Jensen, 1962b), working only with college-age subjects, have found the correlation between paired-associate and serial-learning scores to be considerably lower than .60.

The efficacy of mediation in facilitating serial learning may be demonstrated by training subjects to use a plan, or strategy, while learning an ordered list of items. In effect, the plan provides a means of converting the serial list into a paired-associate list. For this conversion, the to-be-learned serial items become R elements, each of which is associated with an S element inherent within the plan itself. Two such plans have been widely employed in research with young-adult subjects. The first utilizes what is called a *pegword system* (Miller, Galanter, & Pribram, 1960). The initial step taken by a subject is to learn fully a simple rhyme involving the numbers 1 through 10. Each number is associated with a word that may be readily transformed into a mental picture. For example, the first line of the rhyme is "one is a bun." The user of the pegword system imagines a distinctive-looking picture of the first word in the series, one that is interacting with a "bun." For example, if the first word in the list is *car,* the subject might create an image of a "Detroit sandwich" (or, perhaps, a "Japanese sandwich") in which a car is squeezed into a bun along with lettuce, mustard, and what have you. Each successive line of the rhyme serves a similar function, that is, it provides a pegword for constructing a compound image that includes a picture of a to-be-remembered item in the serial list. At recall, subjects then recite the line to themselves. With "one is a bun," the appropriate image containing a car is recovered, thus identifying the first item in the list. This procedure continues until the last line, "10 is a hen," is recited, and the 10th item of the list is recovered by means of its representation in an interaction with a hen. Young adults who are taught to use this system learn 10-item serial lists much more readily than control subjects who are left to their own devices (e.g., Bugelski, Kidd, & Segmen, 1968).

The second plan utilizes what is called the *method of loci.* Here, the serial learner imagines a trip through a familiar environs, such as the learner's own home. At successive distinctive locations in the environs, an image of each successive word in the serial list is placed. Thus, if the first stop on the trip is a familiar chair in the living room, the learner might construct an image of a *car* (again, the first item in the serial list) seated comfortably with the front tires resting on an ottoman. To recover the words in the list, the subject travels the route again, this time naming the object found at each location. As with the pegword system, the method of loci promotes rapid serial learning by young adults (e.g., Bower, 1970).

Our concern, of course, is with the effectiveness of these two methods for elderly subjects. For the pegword system, Smith (1975a; Mason & Smith, 1977) found no gain in learning proficiency when it was applied by either middle-age or elderly subjects. On the other hand, young-adult subjects in these studies manifested the expected benefit. A somewhat more promising outcome, however, was reported by Hellebusch (1976) who found elderly subjects as well as young subjects to benefit from the use of the system. However, the gain relative to control subjects was apparent only immediately after studying the list for the elderly subjects. By contrast, experimental young subjects continued to excel relative to control subjects, even after a two-week retention interval. Finally, a study by Robertson-Tchabo, Hausman, and Arenberg (1976) demonstrated that elderly subjects are able to apply successfully the method of loci. The question of whether or not they apply it as well as young adults do could not be answered in this study. Robertson-Tchabo et al. also discovered that their elderly subjects did not apply the newly learned method unless they were specifically instructed to do so. That is, unfortunately, there appeared to be no gain in the spontaneous use of the method. Despite the conflicting findings of these studies, training in the use of either method does seem to offer a promising means of improving the serial-learning proficiency of elderly people, even though the improvement may not bring them to the level of proficiency characteristic of younger learners.

We will have more to say about serial learning in Chapter 11. There, we will discover that the serial-learning task has been a popular medium for testing hypotheses about the effects on learning of age differences in intelligence.

Adult-Age Differences in Retention

Problems in Assessing Age Differences. Learning's contributions to the overall adaptability of the human organism are hindered by another of life's inevitabilities—forgetting. Once material is learned, there is no assurance of its permanent retention. Our interest centers on adult-age differences in the rate of forgetting previously learned material. A common assumption among laypersons and psychologists alike, as we noted in Chapter 6, is that elderly adults forget recently learned material more rapidly than do young adults. The reason usually given for this suspected age differential in rate of forgetting is the greater interference proneness of elderly adults relative to young adults.

The notion of an age difference in interference proneness apparently originated in Welford's (1958) review of early studies contrasting retention between young and elderly subjects. Illustrative of these early studies is one by Cameron (1943). A three-digit number was read three times to both young and elderly subjects. A one-minute retention interval then followed. During this interval, experimental subjects of both ages performed another task (backward spelling), while control subjects of both ages simply rested. No age difference in retention was found for control subjects. By contrast, a pronounced age difference, favoring young adults, was found for experimental subjects. The age deficit in retention supposedly resulted from the greater interference produced by the interpolated task for the elderly subjects than for the young subjects. (Interestingly, generalizability of this age deficit is highly limited by the fact that Cameron's elderly subjects were all diagnosed as being senile and suffering from memory defects.)

There are two important interpretative problems inherent in Cameron's study and in other early studies on age differences in retention as well. The first is the failure of the investigator to equate age groups in degree of learning for the to-be-retained material. From what we know about age differences in rate of learning, young adults are almost certain to have learned more than elderly adults after a fixed number of exposures to the elements of a learning task. Thus, after three readings of a number, young adults are likely to be able to recall immediately more of that number than are elderly adults. Of all the variables that could affect the retention of learned material, the most important by far is the degree to which that material has been learned prior to the onset of the retention interval—the more thoroughly the material has been learned, the more resistant it is to forgetting (Underwood, 1954). Consequently, unless age differences in amount of original learning are eliminated, an age deficit in amount retained is virtually certain to occur.

More recent studies of age differences in retention have been cognizant of this problem, and they have involved a valiant effort to equate age groups in degree of original learning. The standard solution has been to take all subjects to the same criterion of mastery. For example, practice continues over trials until an errorless trial occurs (or, perhaps, two consecutive errorless trials). A subject's learning score is the number of trials required to reach the particular criterion set in advance. The mean number of trials for elderly subjects is likely to be somewhat greater than the mean number for young-adult subjects. Just how satisfactory this procedure is for equating age groups in degree of original learning is debatable (Kausler, 1970). A potential problem exists in the possibility of an age difference in the amount of overlearning received by the easiest components of the learning task. These are the components of the total task that are learned early in practice. Because elderly subjects usually take more trials to learn the entire task, they have more opportunity than young subjects to overlearn these initially learned components. In general, overlearning serves to increase resistance to forgetting. Consequently, greater overlearning by elderly subjects than by young subjects could lead to an underestimation of the true extent of an age deficit in retention. There are other methods available for equating groups in degree of original learning (Underwood, 1964), but, unfortunately, these methods have yet to be applied in experimental aging research.

Even if age groups could be equated for degree of original learning, there is a related issue to be considered. We discovered earlier that young adults are more likely than elderly adults to learn by means of the use of associative mediators. This presents a problem in evaluating age differences in retention in that there is convincing evidence with young-adult subjects to indicate that paired-associates learned by means of either verbal or imaginal mediators are more resistant to forgetting than are associations learned rotely (e.g., Adams & Montague, 1967; Bugelski, 1968). Consequently, elderly adults might be expected to forget more than young adults simply because the products of original learning differ between the two groups. If elderly adults could be prodded to use mediation during original learning to the same extent as young adults, then their inferior retention may disappear or, at least, improve drastically.

The second interpretative problem arises from the failure of early investigators to deal with the processes accounting for forgetting in the first place. From our discussion in Chapter 6, we realize that these processes are commonly viewed to be those of interference theory. According to this theory, forgetting occurs through the existence of an interference relationship between each to-be-retained association and another association having the same S element but a different R element. Through this interference relationship, the processes of unlearning and competition at recall become operative. It is difficult to see how spelling backwards, the interpolated task in Cameron's (1943) study, bears an interference relationship with a three-digit number (the to-be-retained material). Consequently, the greater forgetting manifested by elderly subjects in Cameron's experimental condition is impossible to interpret. The age difference in amount retained may have been only a performance difference. Specifically, the unfamiliar nature of spelling backwards may have produced sufficient stress among the elderly subjects to depress their performance on the following activity (i.e., recalling the original number).

Retroactive and Proactive Inhibition. More recent studies on age differences in retention have conformed to the task conditions required by interference theory. To understand these conditions, we must first understand the unique symbolic system used to describe the relationship between the associations of successively learned lists. Our model will be provided by paired-associate learning, the standard task employed in basic research on retention/forgetting.

The first of two lists entering into an interference relationship is identified as the A-B list, with A symbolizing all of the S elements within that list and B all of the R elements. The specific pairs of that list may, therefore, be labeled as A_1-B_1, A_2-B_2, and so on. The second list in the relationship is identified as the A-C list, with A noting the fact that the S elements are identical to those of the first list and C the fact that the R elements are unrelated to the R elements of the first list. The specific pairs of this list are therefore A_1-C_1, A_2-C_2, and so on. For example, *apple-table* may be the A_1-B_1 pair of the first list and *apple-pencil* the A_1-C_1 pair of the second list. As shown in the top panel of Figure 8.20, the amount of first-list (A-B) forgetting produced by unlearning and competition at recall is evaluated by comparing recall scores for subjects in an experimental condition with recall scores for subjects in a control condition. Experimental subjects learn initially the A-B list, followed, usually immediately, by the learning of the A-C list (which, therefore, functions much like the interpolated task in Cameron's (1943) study—but in a known, interference-producing role). Recall of A-B content is then tested after some specified retention interval. Control subjects learn only the A-B list, therefore, bypassing the unlearning and competition at recall (see the top panel of Figure 8.20) produced by the interpolated A-C list. These subjects are also tested for recall of A-B content following the retention interval. Inferior recall of the A-B content by experimental subjects relative to control subjects defines the phenomenon of *retroactive inhibition*. Its presence presumably results from the interference processes operating only in the experimental condition or, at least, to a greater extent in the experimental condition than in the control condition (retention is usually less than perfect in the control condition as we will see shortly). Alternatively, as illustrated in the bottom panel of Figure 8.20, an investigator may be interested in the retention of the A-C, or second-, list content manifested by subjects in the experimental condition. In this case, subjects in the control condition receive only the A-C list (i.e., a list identical in content to the second list received by experimental subjects). Recall of A-C content is then tested following the retention interval for subjects in both conditions. Inferior recall by experimental subjects, again relative to control subjects, defines the phenomenon of *proactive inhibition*. Its presence is also presumed to result from interference processes present only in the experimental condition (or to a greater extent in the experimental condition than in the control condition).

Our interest is in aging studies that have made use of these standard procedures to determine the presence or absence of age differences in interference proneness and, therefore, in the rate of forgetting. The popular choice in these studies has been to use the sequence defining retroactive inhibition. A heterogeneous factorial study is employed in which age variation is combined with variation in list sequence (i.e., a control condition receiving only an A-B list and an experimental condition receiving successive A-B, A-C lists). If el-

Time →

Sequence

Condition	Learn List 1	Learn List 2	Recall List 1

Top panel:

Experimental $A_1 \to B_1$ $A_1 \to C_1$ $\nearrow B_1$ (some unlearning) (Retention interval) $A_1 \to B_1$ $\nearrow C_1$ (competition at time of recall)

Control $A_1 \to B_1$ (Retention Interval) $A_1 \to B_1$

Difference favoring control condition = Retroactive inhibition

Time →

Sequence

Condition	Learn List 1	Learn List 2	Recall List 1

Bottom panel:

Experimental $A_1 \to B_1$ $A_1 \to C_1$ $\nearrow B_1$ (some unlearning) (Retention interval) $A_1 \to C_1$ $\nearrow B_1$ (competition at time of recall)

Control $A_1 \to C_1$ (Retention Interval) $A_1 \to C_1$

Difference favoring control condition = Proactive inhibition

Time →

Figure 8.20. Schematic representation of the procedures defining retroactive inhibition (top panel) and proactive inhibition (bottom panel).

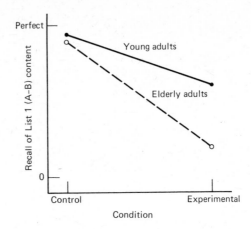

Figure 8.21. Outcome of a hypothetical study on age differences in retroactive inhibition based on the principle that elderly adults are more interference prone than young adults.

derly adults are indeed more interference prone than young adults, then an outcome of the general kind shown in Figure 8.21 is expected. The critical component of this hypothetical outcome is a statistically significant interaction effect between age and the list-sequence condition. The age difference for subjects in the control condition should be slight, whereas the age difference for subjects in the experimental condition should be pronounced (with superior retention of A-B content being manifested by young adults). In other words, a multiplicative relationship should emerge, one implying the age sensitivity of the process varied by the manipulable independent variable. That process, of course, is susceptible to the interference produced by the interpolated learning of the A-C list.

Tests of age differences in the amount of retroactive inhibition have been reported by Gladis and Braun (1958), Wimer and Wigdor (1958), and Hulicka (1967b). In none of these studies was a significant interaction effect found when all subjects were taken to the same criterion of mastery on the A-B list. The results for two of these studies are plotted in Figure 8.22. The top panel shows the outcome of Wimer and Wigdor's study. Their experimental subjects, both young and elderly, learned a four-pair A-B list to a criterion of one errorless trial; next they learned a four-pair A-C list to a criterion of two successive errorless trials. Then 15 minutes after learning the first list (with much of this time being spent learning the second list), they were tested for recall of the B responses (i.e., first list) when cued by the A stimulus elements. Their control subjects, both young and elderly, also learned the A-B list to a criterion of one errorless trial, and 15 minutes later (the time being filled by performance on a nonlearning task to prevent further rehearsal of the A-B pairs), they, too, were tested for recall of B responses. Note in the top panel of Figure 8.22 that pronounced retroactive inhibition occurred at both age levels. That is, for each age group, recall in the experimental condition was well below recall in the control condition, as predicted by interference theory. More important, however, the amount of retroactive inhibition was certainly no greater for elderly subjects than for young subjects. Thus, there was no hint of the interaction effect predicted on the basis of greater interference proneness for elderly adults

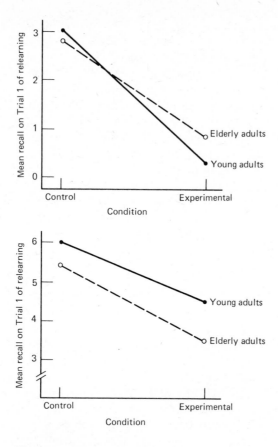

Figure 8.22. Results obtained in tests of age differences in amount of retroactive inhibition. (Top panel: Adapted from Wimer & Wigdor, 1958, Table 2. Bottom panel: Adapted from Hulicka, 1967b, Table 3.)

than for young adults. In fact, if anything, the amount of retroactive inhibition was slightly greater for their young subjects than for their elderly subjects (see the top panel of Figure 8.22).

The bottom panel of Figure 8.22 shows the outcome of Hulicka's (1967b) study. Although the age difference in amount recalled, favoring young subjects, was greater in the experimental condition than in the control condition, the disparity was not large enough to permit rejection of the null hypothesis for the interaction effect. Of interest is a study by Arenberg (1967b) employing a partial retroactive inhibition design in which only the experimental condition (A-B, A-C) was included. Significantly poorer retention of the A-B list was found for elderly subjects but only with a fast rate-of-item-presentation for content of the two lists. With a slower rate of presentation, the age difference did not reach statistical significance.

There does not appear to be a pronounced adult-age difference in rate of forgetting, at least as far as forgetting is studied under the conditions yielding retroactive inhibition. Of course, the age equality in rate of forgetting occurs only when the age groups are taken to the same criterion of mastery on the to-be-retained material. To achieve this equality, the elderly subjects in both Wimer and Wigdor's (1958) study and Hulicka's (1967b) study required nearly twice as many trials as the young adult subjects. As indicated earlier, the additional study opportunity given elderly subjects probably results in considerable overlearning for some components of the to-be-retained material. Given this overlearning, the retention found for elderly adults appears to approximate that of young adults. It is a different matter, however, when the same amount of limited practice on the first list is given to both age groups. This condition was included in a second experiment by Hulicka (1967b). All of her subjects received the same number of practice trials on the A-B list (six), with experimental subjects then learning the second list to a criterion of one errorless trial. Here the interaction effect was clearly statistically significant, with the age difference, favoring young adults, being more pronounced in the experimental condition than in the control condition.

Single-List Retention. Of additional interest is the possibility of an age difference in the forgetting of a single list's content. Retention of a single list is required of control subjects in a study on retroactive inhibition. Note in Figure 8.22 that the control subjects, whether young or elderly, in both retroactive inhibition studies exhibited some forgetting. That is, recall of that list was less than maximum (4 in the top panel, 7 in the bottom panel), even though the retention interval lasted only minutes and there was no interpolated learning of an interfering list. Interference theorists (Underwood, 1957; Underwood & Postman, 1960) view such forgetting as resulting from proactive inhibition. The prior interfering list is hypothesized to consist of associations learned in the real world. For example, consider *apple-table* as one of the A-B pairs learned by control subjects. Many responses to apple may be assumed to have been learned outside of the laboratory, such as apple → fruit and apple → pie. According to interference theory, these associations have to be temporarily unlearned, or suppressed, while learning the novel apple → table association. Over the duration of the retention interval, the prior associations recover and intrude at recall with the newly learned association, thus producing some degree of proactive inhibition. An age difference in interference proneness again leads to the prediction of greater forgetting of a single list's content by elderly subjects than by young subjects. This does not seem to be true, at least when the retention spans only minutes. In both of our retroactive inhibition studies, the amount of forgetting for the single list (control condition) was about the same for young and elderly subjects (see Figure 8.22).

But what about longer retention intervals? Are age differences still absent when retention of a single list is tested after hours have lapsed? Weeks? Here we find conflicting evidence. Hulicka and Weiss (1965) evaluated age differences in retention after intervals of 20 minutes and one week. Surprisingly, their elderly subjects (mean age, 68 years) retained more than their younger subjects (mean age, 38 years). On the other hand, significantly greater forgetting by elderly subjects was found by both Davis and Obrist (1966) and Harwood and Naylor (1969). In the study by Davis and Obrist, paired associates made up the single list and the retention interval was 48 hours. In the study by Harwood and Naylor, free recall of names of common objects made up the single list and the retention interval was four weeks. Although a statistically significant age difference in amount retained was found in both studies, the absolute magnitude of this age difference was actually fairly small. Our conclusion, once more, is that the retention of recently learned material is relatively unaffected by aging, provided the to-be-retained material is well learned by the elderly.

Real-Life Forgetting. Laboratory research indicates that aging has little effect on the retention of new material that has been learned fairly thoroughly. There is an important question left unanswered by this research, however, namely the generalizability of the absence of a major age difference to material learned in the real world. Our concern here is intensified by the fact that laboratory evidence clashes strongly with a popular notion about human aging. The notion is that recently learned material is poorly retained by elderly people, while material learned years earlier is remarkably preserved. Support for this notion has come from both clinical studies of senile individuals (Ribot, 1882; Shakow, Dolkart, & Goldman, 1941) and anecdotes provided by elderly people themselves. A good example of the latter is a comment made by composer Aaron Copland in describing the problems he encountered while writing his autobiography: "I have no trouble remembering everything that happened 40 or 50 years ago—dates, places, faces, music. But I'm going to be 90 my next birthday, Nov. 14, and I find I can't remember what happened yesterday" (*Time,* 1980, p. 57). Our faith in Copland's analysis of his difficulties with retaining current events is enhanced by the fact that he would really be only 80 years old on his next birthday.

In this section, we will review research studies that have attempted to test for the retention of events, names, and so on, learned in real-life situations (see Erber, 1981, for additional review). Obviously, research of this kind has to rely on methods other than controlled laboratory assessments. Our first objective is to discover what truth there is to the notion that early learning experiences are remarkably preserved as one gets older.

Probably the first study on this topic was by Schonfield (1969a). Adults ranging in age from their 20s to their 70s were simply asked to recall the names of all their grade and high school teachers. Learning of teachers' names is a learning experience shared by all of us. Also shared by all of us is the steadily increasing amount of interference we encounter as we continually learn new names over the years. Schonfield's results, expressed in terms of the mean proportion of teachers' names recalled, are plotted in Figure 8.23. Note that by the time his subjects had reached their 20s, they had already forgotten a third of the names of their teachers. Beyond that age, forgetting began to slow down considerably. Nevertheless, for people age 70 and beyond, more than half of the names had been forgotten. Fairly comparable rates of forgetting over the years were found later by Bahrick, Bahrick, and Wittlinger (1975) for names of

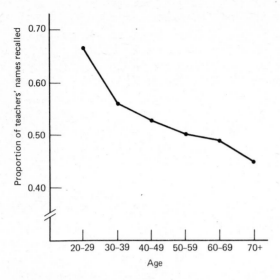

Figure 8.23. Retention of names of teachers as assessed over the adult lifespan. (Adapted from data in Schonfield, 1969a.)

high school classmates, by Bahrick (1979) for names of streets in the city housing the college attended by the subjects, by Squire and Slater (1975) for names of television shows, and by Bartlett and Snelus (1980) for titles of songs. For example, the retention-time function observed by Bahrick (1979) for names of streets is plotted in Figure 8.24. The independent variable in this case is the number of years passing since graduation from college. Retention scores were adjusted, or corrected, for the number of visits made to the city in question during the intervening years. The similarity to the retention-time (expressed as age) function obtained by Schonfield (1969a) is striking. Again, the rate of forgetting is rapid for the first few years following the learning experience, followed by a general leveling off for the amount retained. Generalizing from these studies, the notion that remote learning experiences are remarkably immune to forgetting does not appear to be true. Of course, it is still remarkable, considering all of the retroactive inhibition produced by 50 or so years of new learning experiences, that retention does hold up as well as it does in late adulthood.

A somewhat different strategy was developed by Warrington and Silberstein (1970) for the study of the retention of events varying in degree of remoteness. Instead of testing for the retention of personalized learning experiences, such as learning the names of teachers, they tested the retention of newsworthy events. Their procedure has the advantage of studying the effect on retention of the age of an event as well as the effect of the age of the individuals being tested for retention. At the same time, the procedure is loaded with methodological problems that confound possible ontogenetic changes in retention with changes linked to other potentially causative factors. Before we examine these methodological problems, we will review briefly the highly conflicting results obtained with Warrington and Silberstein's procedure.

In the original study by Warrington and Silberstein, remoteness of events extended only to 18 months prior to the time of testing. No adult-age differences in retention were found within this limited degree of remoteness. In a more comprehensive study by Warrington and Sanders (1971), individuals ranging in age from 40 to 80 years were tested for the retention of events occurring during two-year periods, beginning with 1967–1968 and ending with 1930–1931. The popular notion mentioned earlier predicts that the oldest members of the total group should excel for retention of the most remote events (those of 1930–1931), whereas the youngest members should excel for retention of the most recent events (1967–1968; remember the study was conducted around 1970). Contrary to this notion, Warrington and Sanders (1971) discovered that retention decreased progressively with increasing age for all degrees of remoteness. That is, their oldest subjects retained less of early events as well as more recent events. These results were subsequently replicated by Squire (1974). However, other studies have reported quite different outcomes. Botwinick and Storandt (1974b) found no overall age differences for the retention of events occurring from the 1890s to the 1960s, whereas Perlmutter (1978b) found significantly superior retention overall (i.e., combining all the time periods being tested) by her older subjects. To complete the confusion, Poon, Fozard, Paulshock, and Thomas (1979) found no age differences for the retention of relatively recent events and superior retention by elderly adults for more remote events!

The absence of adult-age differences in the retention of relatively recent events (Poon et al., 1979; Warrington & Silberstein, 1970) should not be surprising, despite the fact that this null outcome conflicts with the popular notion about aging's effects on retention. The null effect is in agreement with the null effect generally found in laboratory studies on adult-age differences in retention. The implication is that elderly adults study current events as thoroughly as young adults. Having learned them as well, they also retain them as well over retention intervals that are of the same duration for each age level. What is

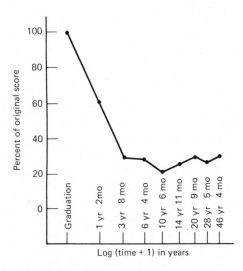

Figure 8.24. Retention of names of streets in the city housing the college attended, plotted as a function of years intervening since graduation. (Adapted from Bahrick, 1979, Figure 1.)

surprising is that some studies (e.g., Warrington & Sanders, 1971) found inferior retention for relatively recent events by elderly subjects. It seems likely that the elderly subjects in these studies suffered more from an initial learning than from a subsequent retention deficit. Given less learning, poorer retention is the expected consequence.

Interpretation of whatever adult-age differences exist in the retention of truly remote newsworthy events is especially difficult. Given the potential presence of causative factors other than age level at the time retention is assessed, it is little wonder that some investigators have found an age difference in retention favoring elderly subjects (Poon et al., 1979), whereas other investigators have found age differences favoring younger subjects (Warrington & Sanders, 1971). A potentially critical factor is the age of individuals at the time a newsworthy event occurs. Consider, for example, a retention test conducted in 1980 for events that occurred in 1950. Subjects who are 80 years old at the time of the test were 50 years old at the time the events happened, whereas subjects who are 50 years old at the time of the test were only 20 years old at the time the events happened. To the extent that learning proficiency is superior at age 20 than at age 50, the events of 1950 were learned initially more thoroughly by present 50-year-old subjects. Consequently, differences in retention between 50- and 80-year-old subjects may actually be an irrelevant factor. What really matters is the degree of original learning, a factor laboratory studies consistently identify as a critical one influencing the subsequent course of retention. There is, in fact, some evidence to indicate, at least for some kinds of real-life events, that age at the time of occurrence does greatly influence the amount retained years later (Storandt, Grant, & Gordon, 1978).

Another complicating factor is the historical time period in which remote events took place. Events taking place in some years, or period of years, are far more dramatic and worthy of attention than the events taking place in other years. Consider, for example, the world events transpiring in 1941–1942 versus those in 1961–1962. To those individuals who lived through them as young adults, the years 1941–1942 included unique events that are likely to be retained forever. The events occurring during 1961–1962 were not nearly as unique. A retention test conducted years after these events should reveal superior recall scores for 1941–1942 than for 1961–1962. Consider the likely outcome of a retention study designed to measure retention of 40-year-old events. Scores are likely to be higher if the test is administered in 1981–1982 (therefore, assessing retention of events during 1941–1942) than if it is administered in 2001–2002 (therefore, assessing retention of events during 1961–1962). Our conclusion regarding the effects of aging on remote retention is certain to be influenced strongly by this variation in time of measurement.

These complications do not enter into assessments of retention of names of teachers, names of streets in one's college town, and so on. Regardless of their age at the time retention is assessed, all subjects were about the same age at the time the to-be-retained material was learned. Moreover, there is no reason to expect age differences in retention to be affected greatly by the historical time period in which the events occurred. Neither teachers nor streets are likely to have been more distinctive in, say, the 1940s than in the 1930s or 1950s. Consequently, the course of forgetting over years of living for these kinds of events provides a more reliable picture of age changes in the retention of remote events than does the course of forgetting for so-called newsworthy events. That picture indicates diminishing retention as the cumulative effects of interference increase with years of intervening learning activities. Most important, the real-life picture is much like that portrayed in laboratory research on retention. Studies such as that of Hulicka and Weiss (1965) typically show rapid forgetting early in the overall retention interval followed by a more gradual loss over the remainder of the interval, both for young and elderly subjects. For example, their elderly subjects had forgotten 15% of the material learned originally after only 20 minutes but only an additional 18% over the next week (their young subjects showed a fairly comparable rate of forgetting). In effect, laboratory studies offer a time compressed simulation of forgetting in the real world. The course of forgetting over weeks for artificial laboratory material corresponds closely to the course of forgetting over years for material learned outside of the laboratory.

Adult-Age Differences in Transfer

In the real world, learning rarely occurs in a vacuum. Usually, learning of a particular task is affected by the learning of prior tasks. For some new tasks, prior learning hinders present learning, resulting in negative transfer, whereas for other tasks, prior learning facilitates present learning, resulting in positive transfer. Transfer varies not only in direction (i.e., positive versus negative) but also in amount for each direction. Our interest in the final section of this chapter is mainly with the possibility of age differences in the amount of transfer, whether positive or negative. However, we cannot ignore the possibility of age differences in direction of transfer, at least for some kinds of transfer conditions.

Specific Versus Nonspecific Transfer: Implications for Age Differences. Tests of age differences in transfer effects are complicated by the existence of two distinctive sources of transfer—*specific* and *nonspecific*. Specific transfer results from a relationship of some kind between the S and R elements of the transfer task and the prior learning task that affects acquisition of the transfer task. One form of relationship is the already familiar one of interference theory in which the two tasks have identical S elements and unrelated R elements. That is, the tasks form an A-B, A-C relationship with one another (with the A-C list forming the transfer task and the A-B list the prior learning task). Interference generated by intruding $A \rightarrow B$ associations during practice on new $A \rightarrow C$ associations is expected to retard acquisition of the new associations. In principle, the previously learned $A_1 \rightarrow B_1$ association inhibits rehearsal of the $A_1 \rightarrow C_1$ association, the previously learned $A_2 \rightarrow B_2$ association inhibits rehearsal of the $A_2 \rightarrow C_2$ association, and so on. Thus, negative specific transfer for the A-C list joins forgetting of the A-B list as an adverse consequence of the interference relationship inherent in an A-B, A-C list sequence. Our old friend, the suspected age differential in interference proneness, makes the possibility of greater amounts of negative transfer for elderly subjects than for young-adult subjects of considerable interest to experimental aging psychologists.

Another form of interlist relationship of special interest to us is one in which successive lists continue to have identical S elements and different R elements, but this time the R elements of the two lists are related in some way. In transfer terminology, related R elements are symbolized as B and B'. With these symbols in mind, our new transfer condition may be identified as involving the learning of A-B, A-B' lists. As an example, consider *apple-table* as the A_1-B_1 pair (first list) and *apple-chair* as the A_1-B_1' pair (second, or transfer, list). Real-life A-B, A-B' sequences do exist. Owners of professional athletic teams seem to be especially fond of them. For example, the Milwaukee Bucks have existed for some years as a men's professional basketball team. When a women's professional basketball team was formed in Milwaukee, the owners, surely not coincidentally, named the team the Does. Note that Milwaukee → Bucks corresponds to an A → B association in a transfer sequence and Milwaukee → Does to an A → B' association.

The relatedness between B and B' elements makes it possible to use the first list association to mediate the learning of the new association in the transfer list. That is, intrusion of a B element during practice on the new list should enhance rather than hinder learning of the new set of associations. The net effect should be positive specific transfer, but only if mediation is indeed operative during learning of the transfer list's associations. It is this contingency that makes the A-B, A-B' transfer condition intriguing to experimental aging psychologists (Kausler, 1970). Elderly subjects are less likely than young subjects to engage spontaneously in mediation during practice on A-B' pairs, and they should, therefore, be less likely to display specific positive transfer in this condition. There is, in fact, the possibility that related B and B' elements may be treated as if they are unrelated B and C elements. If true, the A-B, A-B' condition would become equivalent to an A-B, A-C condition. The consequence should then be specific negative transfer of the kind generated by an interference relationship.

Nonspecific transfer is always positive in direction. It occurs whenever successive tasks are of the same general format. For example, the tasks may all require paired-associate learning or they may all require serial learning. In either case, prior learning of one task is expected to facilitate acquisition of subsequent tasks, even when the S and R elements of the successive tasks are unrelated to one another. The primary reason for this facilitation is the occurrence of what is called learning-to-learn. It is a general process that is independent of a task's specific content. During practice on the first task, subjects are learning not only the content of that task but also the kinds of skills demanded for proficient performance on it and other tasks. When the task format is that of paired-associate learning, one of these general skills is the use of mediation to link S and R elements together. The advantage gained by seeking out and utilizing mediators may not be discovered until a subject is deeply immersed in practice on the first paired-associate task. Once discovered, however, the skill should become operative immediately on all subsequent paired-associate tasks. These later lists should, therefore, be learned more easily than the initial list, thus yielding nonspecific positive transfer. Another reason for the presence of nonspecific positive transfer stems from the fact that it often takes subjects time to warm up to performing on a laboratory task, much the way it takes an athlete time to warm up before an athletic contest. Performance on a first task may be affected adversely by the failure of subjects to have warmed up sufficiently. This should not be true for subsequent tasks, thereby eliminating a potentially debilitating factor for performance on these later tasks.

The existence of nonspecific positive transfer complicates any attempt to evaluate the direction and magnitude of a specific transfer effect (i.e., an effect attributable to the relatedness of items across tasks). Consider, for example, transfer in the A-B, A-C condition. The hindrance in learning A-C pairs that is produced by negative specific transfer is compensated, at least in part, by the facilitation that is produced by positive nonspecific transfer. The resultant is a reduction in the magnitude of the overall negative transfer that would otherwise be present in the absence of the positive contribution made by nonspecific transfer.

The standard means of assessing a specific transfer effect at any age level calls for the use of experimental and control groups of subjects. The experimental group receives the list sequence defining the specific transfer condition, such as an A-B first list and an A-C second, or transfer, list. The control group receives a list sequence that permits an adjustment for the contribution made by nonspecific transfer to an overall transfer effect. That sequence consists of an A-B first list and a C-D transfer list. C and D in this context refer to the S and R elements of the transfer list respectively. The letters symbolize the fact that these elements are unrelated to the S and R elements of the first list. For example, given *apple-table* as the A_1-B_1 pair of the first list, *book-jewel* could function as the C_1-D_1 pair of the transfer list.

With this design, experimental and control subjects have an equal opportunity to benefit from nonspecific positive transfer. That is, subjects in both groups should profit, and in approximately equal amounts, from the learning-to-learn and warm up occurring during first-list practice. Whatever difference is then observed in second-list performance between the two groups must be attributable to the specific transfer present only in the experimental group. Inferior performance for the experimental group relative to the control group identifies the presence of negative specific transfer, whereas superior performance identifies the presence of positive specific transfer. In addition, the magnitude of the difference in performance between the two groups identifies the magnitude of the specific negative or positive transfer effect. These procedures are summarized in Figure 8.25 for both the A-B, A-C transfer condition and the A-B, A-B' condition. Our interest, of course, is in age differences in transfer effects. From our preceding analyses, predictions are fairly straightforward—the amount of specific negative transfer (control group > experimental group; see top panel of Figure 8.25) should be greater for elderly subjects than young

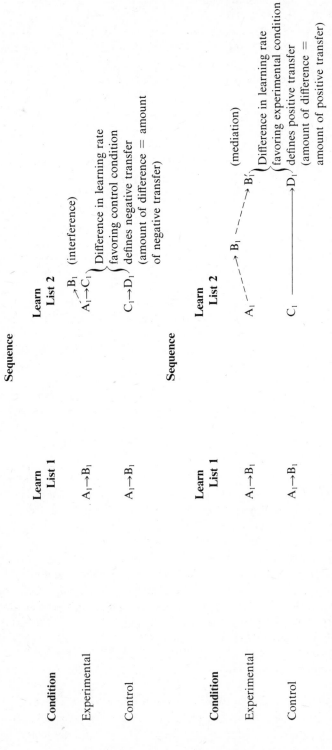

Figure 8.25. Schematic representation of the procedures defining specific negative transfer (top panel) and specific positive transfer (bottom panel).

subjects, whereas the amount of specific positive transfer (experimental group
> control group; see bottom panel of Figure 8.25) should be greater for young
subjects.

Laboratory Studies of Specific Transfer. Studies of retroactive inhibition (e.g.,
Hulicka, 1967b) always include the appropriate experimental group for evaluating specific negative transfer, namely, one receiving an A-B, A-C list sequence. However, the single-list control group in these studies, although
appropriate for assessing the effects of interference on retention, fails to provide a baseline for equating contributions from nonspecific transfer. Consequently, it is impossible to interpret age differences of the kind illustrated in
Figure 8.26. The top panel shows the mean number of trials to learn the A-B
and A-C lists by experimental subjects in Arenberg's (1967b) study, whereas
the bottom panel shows the comparable means in Hulicka's (1967b) study. In
both studies, young subjects improved in proficiency from the A-B list to the
A-C list, whereas elderly subjects either showed no gain (top panel) or a decrease in proficiency (bottom panel). Thus, the age difference favoring young
adults was greater in both studies for the A-C list than for the A-B list. Unfortunately, however, the obvious Age × List interaction effect could be due

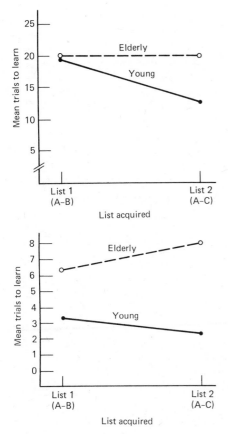

Figure 8.26. Age differences in trials to learn the first and second lists of an A-B, A-C sequence. (Top panel: Adapted from Arenberg, 1967b, Table 1. Bottom panel: Adapted from Hulicka, 1967b, Table 3.)

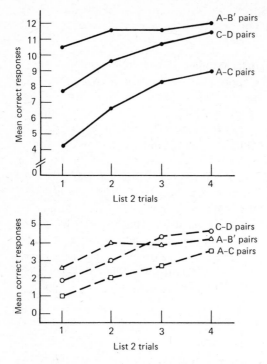

Figure 8.27. Correct responses by young-adult (top panel) and elderly (bottom panel) subjects over trials on List 2 for various transfer conditions. (Adapted from Freund & Witte, 1976, Figures 1, 2.)

either to greater specific negative transfer for elderly subjects or to greater nonspecific positive transfer for young subjects. The absence of an A-B, C-D control group at each age level prohibits a distinction between these alternative explanations of the age differences.

The only study of age differences in specific negative transfer that did include the appropriate control groups appears to be that of Freund and Witte (1976). Rate-of-item presentation was also included as an independent variable in their study. We will consider only the results obtained with a moderately fast rate, a rate comparable to that used in most transfer studies with young adults. Both experimental and control groups learned the A-B list to a criterion of one errorless trial. They then received four trials on the second list (A-C or C-D). The results, expressed in terms of mean number of correct responses on each trial of List 2 practice are shown in Figure 8.27 (maximum score = 12 for young subjects, 6 for elderly subjects; list length was intentionally made shorter for the elderly subjects). Note initially that negative transfer did occur at both age levels. That is, performance on the C-D list clearly exceeded performance on the A-C list for both young and elderly subjects on each trial. Of greater importance to us, however, is the absence of any sign of more negative transfer for elderly subjects than for young subjects. This pattern is in agreement with that found in aging studies on retroactive inhibition. In the A-B, A-C list sequence, there is no reason to believe that elderly adults are more interference prone than young adults.

We now have good reason to believe that the Age $\times$ List interaction apparent in both panels of Figure 8.26 resulted from an age difference in the amount of nonspecific positive transfer. Age differences in nonspecific transfer were touched on in our earlier review of secondary performance factors and their contributions to age differences (Chapter 3). At that time, we discovered that some investigators (e.g., Taub, 1973) have found an age difference favoring young subjects in amount of nonspecific transfer, whereas other investigators (e.g., Freund & Witte, 1979) found no systematic trend relating amount of nonspecific transfer to variation in age. The issue of age differences in nonspecific transfer remains an important one (Goulet, 1972) that is yet to be fully explored.

The possibility of age differences in amount of specific negative transfer does not end with the A-B, A-C transfer condition. There are other transfer conditions that involve interference during practice on the transfer list. One of these conditions entered into a study by Lair, Moon, and Kausler (1969). Interference in this case was created by real-life associative learning. The A-B list in this study was a phantom one in the sense that it really was not learned in the laboratory. It consisted of word pairs, such as *table-chair*, that were strong word associates and, therefore, highly likely to have been well learned in the real world. Experimental subjects were then required to learn what is called an A-Br list. The A and B symbolize the fact that the S and R elements of the transfer list are the same elements contained in the first list; the r symbolizes the fact that these elements are re-paired in the transfer list. The nature of this re-pairing is illustrated in Table 8.3. Note that the experimental subjects must inhibit, or suppress, their prior table $\rightarrow$ chair association while acquiring the new table $\rightarrow$ queen association. Such suppression is made difficult by the presence of the word, chair, as the R element of another to-be-learned association in the laboratory list. Control subjects were required to learn a list containing the same R elements as the list learned by experimental subjects but with different S elements. The replacements were neutral with respect to prior associative connections with the R elements, thus eliminating interference from previously learned associations (see Table 8.3). Lair et al. found their experimental list to be acquired much more slowly than their control list by both middle-age and elderly subjects. However, the disparity in learning rates was far more pronounced for their elderly subjects. This study implies that there are transfer conditions in which elderly adults do seem to be more interference prone than younger adults.

There is another negative transfer condition that should be of interest in aging research. It is one in which experimental subjects receive an A-B, C-B list sequence (whereas control subjects continue to receive an A-B, C-D list sequence). A C-B list carries over the R elements from the first list but replaces the prior S elements with new elements. For example, *apple-table* may serve as the A_1-B_1 pair, whereas *anchor-table* serves as the C_1-B_1 pair. Negative specific transfer is often found in the C-B condition when young adults serve as sub-

Table 8.3 Examples of the Kinds of Pairings Used in the Study of Age Differences in Transfer for the A-B, A-Br Condition

	List 1 (learned preexperimentally) All Subjects		List 2 (learned in the laboratory) Experimental Subjects		Control Subjects	
Pair	S element	R element	S element	R element	S element	R' element
A_1-B_1	Table	Chair	Table	Queen	Tennis	Queen
A_2-B_2	Fast	Slow	Fast	Chair	Flag	Chair
$A_n$$B_n$	King	Queen	King	Slow	Kind	Slow

jects (e.g., Kausler & Kanoti, 1963). Its presence is explained by interference generated from competing R-S, or backward, associations during practice on C-B pairs (see Kausler, 1974, pp. 228–237, for elaboration). Note that a backward association from the first list, such as table → apple, does form the equivalent of an A-B, A-C interference relationship with the backward association of its second-list counterpart, such as table → anchor. What should make this transfer condition intriguing to gerontological psychologists is our earlier observation that elderly subjects generally manifest less R-S learning than do young-adult subjects during practice on a paired-associate task. Given this diminished amount of R-S learning, elderly subjects should experience less backward interference than young-adult subjects during practice on C-B pairs, and they should, therefore, show less specific negative transfer than the young subjects. This possibility has yet to be tested adequately in the laboratory. There have, however, been several studies (Boyarsky & Eisdorfer, 1972; Traxler & Britton, 1970) that have included the A-B, C-B condition in tests of age differences in retroactive inhibition. Interference theory maintains that there is a close relationship between the amount of retroactive inhibition for the first list and the amount of negative transfer for the second list during practice on lists bearing any kind of interference relationship with one another. Conditions that alter the amount of negative transfer should also alter the amount of retroactive inhibition. In this case, age is the critical condition. Because elderly subjects are expected to show less negative transfer than young-adult subjects for a C-B list, they are also expected to show less retroactive inhibition for the A-B list preceding the C-B list. Unfortunately, methodological problems inherent in the aforementioned studies make it impossible to evaluate age differences in amount of retroactive inhibition found with an A-B, C-B list sequence (see Arenberg & Robertson-Tchabo, 1977, for further discussion of these problems).

Finally, what little is known about age differences in specific positive transfer comes from the previously mentioned study by Freund and Witte (1976). Included in their study were experimental groups receiving A-B, A-B′ list sequences. The groups differed with respect to the degree of relatedness, high versus low, between B and B′ response elements. We will consider only the condition employing a high degree of relatedness (defined in terms of word-association norms). The results obtained for this condition at each age level are plotted in Figure 8.27 along with the results obtained for the A-C and C-D groups. The scores are again the number of correct responses for each of four trials (again maximum values = 12 and 6 for young and elderly subjects respectively). Note that positive transfer was clearly present for the young subjects early in practice on A-B′ pairs (see the top panel of Figure 8.27). The amount of positive transfer diminished with continuing practice, as indicated by the eventual convergence with performance on C-D pairs. The decrement in positive transfer surely resulted from an early ceiling effect found for A-B′ pairs. A very different picture emerged for performance on A-B′ pairs by elderly subjects (see the bottom panel of Figure 8.27). Here, the amount of specific positive transfer was not distorted by a ceiling efect. Only slight positive transfer relative to C-D pairs appeared early in List 2 practice, and it eventually disappeared by the end of practice. Mediation on a transfer list seems to be as age sensitive as it is on an initial learning list.

Just as specific negative transfer extends to conditions other than the standard A-B, A-C condition, specific positive transfer extends to conditions other than the standard A-B, A-B' condition. For example, one such extension involves successively learned associations having identical R elements and related S elements (i.e., an A-B, A'-B condition). Positive transfer is the general rule for young-adult subjects receiving this sequence (see Kausler, 1974, pp. 235–236). Generalizing from what little is known about age differences in positive transfer with A-B' pairs is, of course, risky, but, in the absence of any research on age differences in other positive transfer conditions, there is no alternative. Comparable age deficits are likely to be found in these other conditions, probably because of an age deficit in the proficiency of a mediating process. Gaining knowledge of the extent of these age deficits should be an important objective of future experimental aging research. Much of everyday learning at all age levels does involve positive transfer from past learning. Once it is established that there are age deficits in such transfer, ways of compensating for these deficits may then be pursued. There is good reason to be optimistic that compensatory procedures will be discovered. In real-life positive transfer situations, elderly adults should have an important advantage over young adults, namely, a greater store of accumulated knowledge. Surely, ways will be found of utilizing this factor as a means of compensating for whatever deficits exist in specific transfer mechanisms (e.g., mediation).

Final Comments. Many studies have been reviewed in this chapter. Collectively, they have contributed a great deal to our knowledge and understanding of age differences in learning, retention, and transfer. We discovered that adult-age differences do exist on most kinds of learning tasks and that the age-sensitive processes accounting for many of these differences have been identified. We also discovered that age differences in long-term retention and in many transfer phenomena are slight and often nonexistent, given equal degrees of learning at all age levels.

At the same time, we discovered that there remain significant gaps in our knowledge about age differences for various learning, retention, and transfer phenomena. In fact, for some phenomena, such as stimulus selection in learning and transfer in the A-B, C-B and A-B, A'-B conditions, there really have not been studies directed at demonstrating the presence or absence of adult-age differences. Unfortunately, these gaps are unlikely to be filled in the foreseeable future. They exist in areas that are viewed traditionally as belonging to associationism and the mechanistic metamodel. The prevailing conceptual model in experimental psychology, including its gerontological extensions, is undoubtedly that of information processing. Research linked to associationism is seen as being part of experimental psychology's less than fruitful past. Our belief throughout this chapter has been that this position is unduly pessimistic. Psychology has not reached a stage of development as a science in which any one conceptual model is clearly the correct one. Experimental aging research that has had its origins in associative concepts and principles has enriched our understanding of the effects of aging on learning, retention, and transfer phenomena. Many of these effects do have important implications for adaptability to the world outside of the laboratory. Serious students of human aging should be as familiar with the contributions made in these areas as they are with the contributions made in other areas by information-processing psychologists. Hopefully, some of these serious students will someday fill in the missing pieces needed for full description and understanding of adult-age differences/changes in learning, retention, and transfer.

Summary

Learning and its related phenomena of retention and transfer are essential activities for the adaptability of the human organism. Deficits in these activities would, therefore, have important adverse consequences for the adaptability of elderly people to their environments. Learning itself is a diverse phenomenon. Its diversity is reflected by the existence of four broad areas of learning: conditioning, instrumental learning, motor-skill learning, and verbal learning. Retention and transfer phenomena are relevant to all four areas. However, they have been investigated primarily in the context of verbal learning.

There are two variants of conditioning: classical (Pavlovian) and operant. In classical conditioning, control over the elicitation of a response is shifted from its natural stimulus element (the unconditioned stimulus) to an originally neutral stimulus element (the conditioned stimulus). The response being conditioned is called an unconditioned response when elicited by its natural stimulus and a conditioned response when elicited by the conditioned stimulus. Conditioning takes place through trials in which the conditioned stimulus and the unconditioned stimulus are presented in close temporal proximity. Several studies using standard classical conditioning laboratory tasks (e.g., conditioning an eyeblink to a change in visual brightness as the conditioned stimulus) have revealed that elderly subjects condition at a considerably slower rate than young-adult subjects and also extinguish at a slower rate once conditioning has been established. The age deficit in classical conditioning has a number of practical implications. Many fears and attitudes are viewed as being learned through classical conditioning. In addition, classical conditioning is widely used in various forms of therapy, both physical and psychological. These therapies are likely to be less successful with elderly adults than with young adults.

Operant conditioning involves emitted behavior that is followed by a reinforcing stimulus. With a positive reinforcer, rate of emitting the prior behavior increases; with punishment, rate of emitting the prior behavior decreases. Relatively little operant research has been conducted with normally aging individuals. However, studies with elderly psychotic patients and individuals with senile dementia have indicated that their behavior can be modified by positive reinforcers. In general, adult-age differences in rate of operant conditioning with positive reinforcement are likely to be much less pronounced than adult-age differences in rate of classical conditioning. Of particular interest in the psychology of aging is the possibility of age deficits in avoidance learning, a more complex form of operant conditioning. In avoidance learning, an individual learns to make a response when cued by the presence of a warning stimulus. If the response occurs in time, the individual avoids receiving a noxious, or aversive, stimulus. A popular theory of avoidance learning stresses the presence of a preliminary stage involving the classical conditioning of fear to the warning stimulus. Given their slower rate of classical conditioning, elderly adults are likely to be less proficient in avoidance learning than young adults. Animal research does indicate slower avoidance learning by old rats than by young rats, with the age deficit increasing in magnitude as the complexity of the task increases.

Although conditioning requires learning a single response, instrumental learning requires learning a sequence of responses. The traditional task for studying instrumental learning is the multiple-choice maze. Here the learner's task is to learn the correct path leading to a goal. There has been little research on maze learning by noncollege-age human subjects. What has been done has contrasted middle-age and young adults. A moderate deficit in maze-learning proficiency does seem to be present by middle age. By contrast, many studies have compared the maze-learning proficiency of young and old rats. These studies indicate that old rats are slower maze learners than young rats only when the maze itself is a complex one involving many choice-points. Moreover, even this deficit largely disappears when old rats are guided through the maze and are, therefore, prevented from making response errors.

Both response-centered and perception-centered theories of maze learning have been offered over the years. The perception-centered theory views maze learning as the acquisition of a cognitive map of the spatial environment rather than the acquisition of a series of turning responses, each linked to stimuli present at a choice-point (the response-centered theory). The perceptual view has been emphasized in recent years. It has been extended to the acquisition of cognitive maps for novel spatial environments, such as that of a new neighborhood or a new residence. There is evidence indicating that nursing home residents manifest considerable difficulty in acquiring a cognitive map of their relatively indistinctive environment. Extensions of this kind of research to spatial cognitive learning by other elderly individuals is likely to become popular in the near future.

Early aging studies on motor-skill learning focused on age differences over a narrow segment of the adult lifespan for real-life activities, such as archery and typing. These studies revealed little effect of adult-age variation on motor-skill learning proficiency. More recent studies have contrasted young and elderly adults on artificial laboratory tasks, such as the line-drawing task and the pursuit-rotor task, thereby controlling for possible age differences in preexperimental familiarity with the task being investigated. These laboratory tasks fall into two broad categories, those requiring discrete responses (e.g., drawing a line of a specified length) and those requiring continuous responses (e.g., tracing a figure or maintaining contact with a rotating target).

Experimental aging studies employing the line-drawing task or other similar tasks (e.g., moving a hand a specified distance) have indicated that young adults benefit more from knowledge of results (i.e., feedback regarding accuracy of prior responses) than do elderly adults in terms of improving accuracy of responding over trials. Elderly subjects also perform less proficiently than young adults on the pursuit-rotor task. The age deficit on this task is much more pronounced when mirror vision is needed to maintain visual contact with the rotating target than when direct vision is needed. This evidence suggests that age deficits in motor-skill learning increase as the involvement of cognitive processes (e.g., the translation of mirror images to direct images) increases.

Of additional interest in motor-skill learning is the retention over the adult lifespan of highly skilled activities (e.g. playing the piano or typing), activities that appear to be programmed and flow smoothly without feedback from proprioceptive stimuli. What little evidence there is indicates that such motor programs acquired early in the lifespan remain relatively intact through late adulthood.

The paired-associate task has served as the medium for most studies investigating age differences in verbal learning. Early studies with this task revealed substantial age differences in performance proficiency favoring young adults. Of interest is the question of whether or not the age deficit results from an age change in rate of learning. Alternatively, elderly subjects may simply start off at a lower level of performance than young subjects but then progress at the same rate as young subjects. In general, most studies that have compared learning curves for young and elderly subjects have reported a slower rate of performance increments for the elderly subjects.

Why an age deficit in the rate of paired-associate learning? Traditionally, the age-sensitive process has been considered to be S-R associative learning. Stage analysts have expanded on this conceptualization by identifying additional learning processes that may be age sensitive. These additional processes are response learning, stimulus learning, and R-S, or backward, associative learning. Evidence does indicate that both response learning and R-S learning are age sensitive. To date, the age sensitivity of stimulus learning, defined in terms of selecting a functional stimulus from a nominal stimulus element, has not been tested.

A number of experimental aging studies have combined variation of a manipulable independent variable with variation of age level. These studies have served to identify mediation of S to R associations as a major age-sensitive process. One of these manipulable variables is the rate of presenting study-list items. Increasing the duration of the anticipation interval, that is, the time allowed for responding to stimulus elements exposed alone, reduces the magnitude of age differences in paired-associate learning proficiency. The implication is that some of the age deficit is a performance deficit attributable to the slower responding of elderly subjects. By contrast, variation in the duration of the study interval, that is, time allowed to rehearse simultaneously exposed stimulus and response elements, has little effect on the magnitude of age differences. The implication is that age differences in the quantity, or amount, of rote rehearsal is not a critical factor contributing to age deficits in verbal learning. Instead, the probable source of a true learning deficit is a difference in the quality, or kind, of rehearsal activity—mediated versus rote. This conclusion is supported by studies indicating that elderly subjects report less spontaneous use of mediators in paired-associate learning than do young subjects. When instructed as to the use of mediators, elderly subjects show an improvement in rate of learning but usually remain below the level of proficiency manifested by young subjects. Thus, a production deficiency in the use of mediators accounts for at least part of age differences in paired-associate learning. Whether or not a true mediational deficiency exists above and beyond this production deficiency remains unresolved.

Elderly subjects are also less proficient than young subjects in rate of serial learning. However, there are no apparent age differences in serial position effects (i.e., the distribution of errors across ordinal positions of items). Studies varying rate-of-item-presentation indicate that the age deficit in learning proficiency is much less pronounced with a slow rate than with a fast rate. However, a deficit remains even with a slow rate, implying the presence of an age-sensitive learning process, most likely mediational in nature.

Laboratory tests of age differences in retention/forgetting have generally employed paired-associate lists and a retroactive inhibition design. Within this design, both young and elderly experimental subjects receive successive lists conforming to an A-B, A-C interference relationship (identical stimulus elements and different and unrelated response elements across lists). Both young and elderly control subjects receive only the A-B list. After a designated retention interval, all subjects are tested for retention of the

A-B list. Superior retention by control subjects, regardless of age level, defines retroactive inhibition. The principle of an age differential in interference proneness (i.e., increasing interference with increasing age) predicts greater amounts of retroactive inhibition for elderly subjects than for young subjects. Evidence from a number of studies does not support this prediction. Rate of forgetting appears to be independent of age, provided the degree of A-B learning is equated for young and elderly subjects.

Some studies of real-life forgetting have examined retention over many years for such material as the names of one's school teachers. These studies reveal that the rate of forgetting is fairly rapid over the first few years following acquisition and then progresses at a much slower rate. Other studies have examined retention over the years of newsworthy events. Conflicting results have emerged in these studies. However, in general, they fail to provide any convincing support for the notion that remotely learned material is better retained by elderly people than is more recently learned material.

Analysis of age differences in transfer effects is complicated by the presence of both specific and nonspecific transfer. Specific transfer produced by relatedness between the transfer task and prior learning tasks may be either positive or negative, whereas nonspecific transfer produced by learning-to-learn and warming up is always positive. Tests of age differences in direction and amount of specific transfer require a design in which experimental groups, both young and elderly, receive successive lists bearing relatedness in some form between stimulus and response elements, whereas control groups, both young and elderly, receive unrelated lists. Superior performance by control subjects defines specific negative transfer, whereas superior performance by experimental subjects defines specific positive transfer. An age differential in interference proneness predicts that elderly subjects will show more specific negative transfer than young subjects for an A-B, A-C list sequence (i.e., the same sequence given experimental subjects in the retroactive inhibition design). However, what little evidence there is indicates that the age difference in specific negative transfer is negligible, which is in agreement with the evidence indicating no substantial age difference in amount of retroactive inhibition. Other conditions expected to yield specific negative transfer (e.g., an A-B, C-B list sequence) have not been tested for the occurrence of adult-age differences in amount of negative transfer.

An age difference in the spontaneous use of mediators predicts that young subjects will show more specific positive transfer than elderly subjects. There is some evidence to support this prediction with an A-B, A-B' (identical stimulus elements and different, but related, response elements across lists) transfer condition. Other positive transfer conditions (e.g., A-B, A'-B) have not been tested for the presence or absence of age differences in amount of transfer.

CHAPTER 9

Memory

What did you have for lunch a week ago? Assuming your diet is somewhat more varied than a daily hamburger, a reasonable guess is that you do not remember what you did have to eat. In fact, if you grace various food establishments with your presence, you probably have difficulty remembering where you ate that day. Of course, if you happened to have dropped your tray in a cafeteria on that occasion, you may find the entire episode, including the contents of the tray, to be distinctive enough to be readily accessible for recall. This is far from being an isolated incident. What about the attempt at humor one of your professors made in class the other day? You may remember the gist of the humor, but not the finer details. Even a vigorous search of your memory system will probably fail to retrieve those missing details. How much do you remember of the last commercial you watched on television? Of the last sporting event you attended?

Human memory is obviously imperfect, and its imperfection is manifested throughout the lifespan. The ubiquitousness of memory failure may be seen in the results obtained in an interesting study by Cavanaugh and Perlmutter (1979). Their subjects, who ranged in age from 20 to 60 years, maintained a memory diary for a period of time. In it, they kept a daily record of their failures to remember such things as appointments they had scheduled. There was a pronounced age difference in the concern expressed by subjects about their memory failures. The older members of this sample reported themselves to be more upset with their failures than did the younger members. This observation agrees with our earlier one that elderly people commonly view memory problems to be a major difficulty encountered in everyday living. Surprisingly, however, no age difference was found in the frequency of reported memory failures. The fact that no age difference was found does not necessarily mean that elderly people are unrealistic in their concern about memory problems. In the first place, the oldest subjects (age 60) in this study were not really old. If people in their 70s and 80s had been included in this study, the outcome would probably have been quite different. Moreover, we have to question the extent to which diary keeping really captures the full scope of memory problems. Most important, there may well be an age difference in the number of times a memory failure is itself forgotten before it can be recorded in a diary. Nor can the self-reports of elderly people be accepted as being fully reliable indices of their own memory capabilities. In fact, the correlation between severity of memory complaints and actual performance on laboratory memory tasks is, for all practical purposes, zero (Zarit, Cole, & Guider, 1981).

Not all memories are as trivial as remembering what one ate for lunch or remembering a professor's joke. Many memories greatly affect our everyday activities. Memory of a weather forecast determines the degree of preparation for a heavy snowstorm. Memory of someone's birthday influences the nature of interactions with that person for some time. Memory of a dinner date determines just how prepared you are to welcome a guest. Memory of a stranger's face may make you either an excellent eyewitness or a poor eyewitness to a crime. Our list could go on and on. There is an obvious need to understand the processes mediating what we earlier called episodic memory. Nor does the need end here. There is also the need to evaluate the extent of age changes in the proficiency of episodic memory and to determine the reasons for these changes. Conceivably, training procedures could then be found to reduce whatever deficits do occur in late adulthood. If such procedures fail to materialize, then there is need for an alternative strategy. Specifically, elderly people could be encouraged to employ memory surrogates as much as possible. Many of these surrogates are already widely used by people of all ages who do not quite trust their memory systems.They include copious note taking at meetings to assure important details are not forgotten, carrying an appointment book to record the time and place of all future commitments, listing all expenditures in a daily log, and so on. Objective records of this kind compensate considerably for at least some shortcomings of the human memory system. Surely their value as memory surrogates will be expanded greatly by the eventual widespread use of home computers.

Our main concern in the present chapter is in adult-age differences/changes in episodic memory. Unfortunately, what is known about age differences in learning has little relevance for age differences in episodic memory. Although one could argue (e.g., Smith, 1980) that the encoding of episodic information is actually learning, there is good reason, as we tried to convey in Chapter 6, for maintaining a distinction between learning and memory. Traditional learning theories, namely, those derived from associationism, have contributed little, if anything, to our understanding of memories for personally experienced events. By contrast, information-processing psychology has made episodic memory a focal point of its analysis of human behavior.

Accordingly, our review of age differences/changes in episodic-memory proficiency will focus on research instigated by information-processing models of the human memory system. As we discovered in Chapter 6, these models stress both storage structures and the processes governing the encoding of information for storage and the retrieval of information from storage. Shared by each model is the concept of an initial sensory store where informational inputs are retained briefly and are then either lost or transmitted in some encoded format to a subsequent store. Consequently, our review will begin with age differences in sensory-memory phenomena. Our further review of episodic memory is complicated by the fact that there are different information-processing models of the human memory system. Two of these models have been especially efficacious in stimulating experimental aging research (Chapter 6). The first is the dual-store model with its emphasis on separate short-term and long-term postsensory components of the total memory system. Research guided by this model has attempted to analyze separately age differences in primary-memory phenomena (i.e., phenomena attributable to the short-term component) and in secondary-memory phenomena (i.e., phenomena attributable to the long-term component). We will turn to this research after we have completed our review of sensory-memory studies. The other model that concerns us is that of levels of processing. The distinction between primary and secondary memory is abandoned in this model. Instead, variability in the proficiency of episodic memory, including variability associated with increasing age, is conceptualized in terms of disparities in depth of processing. Experimental aging research guided by this model has been booming in the last few years. Our review will, therefore, move on to include a detailed examination of the contributions made by these studies.

Four additional topics will be included in the present chapter. The first deals with organizational phenomena in episodic memory. Two forms of organization, categorical (or taxonomic) and subjective, have been of interest to basic-memory researchers for some years. We have touched on the concept of subjective organization at various places. In this chapter, the concept will receive closer scrutiny. Categorical organization refers to the utilization of information stored in generic memory to enhance the episodic memory of to-be-remembered items. The processes regulating organizational phenomena have been conceptualized somewhat independently of both the dual-store model and the levels-of-processing model (and can be readily accommodated by either model). Accordingly, age differences in these phenomena will be considered separately in the present chapter. The second topic deals with age differences in memory for connected discourse, such as sentences and paragraphs. Here the emphasis is on memory for integrated semantic content rather than on memory for a series of discrete episodic events. The processes postulated to mediate this important aspect of human memory can be viewed independently of any formal model of the total memory system. The third topic deals with age differences in memory processes that are often presumed to be automatic and are, therefore, immune to aging deficits in their proficiencies (this topic was touched upon earlier). As with the processes mediating memory for connected discourse, automatic memory processes can be viewed independently of any commitment to a formal model of the total memory system. The final topic deals with age differences in generic-memory phenomena. The concept of a generic store of knowledge is essential for all information-processing models of a total memory system. Of considerable interest to gerontological psychologists is the possibility of adult-age differences in the proficiency of retrieving information stored in generic form.

Adult-Age Differences in Sensory Memory

Iconic Memory. Does information held in a sensory receptor terminate as soon as the originating stimulus terminates? With visual stimuli, there is good reason to believe that it does not. Consider an array of letters flashed briefly (say for 50 milliseconds) by means of a tachistoscope. A subject's task is to identify, or name, as many of the letters as possible. The amount of information that can be seen in a glance is known as the *span of apprehension.* For young adults, the span has been known for many years to be four or five letters (Woodworth, 1938). (There is some evidence, Schonfield & Wenger, 1975, indicating a modest decline in late adulthood.) However, it has also been known for many years that subjects typically report to the experimenter that they actually see more than four or five letters—the problem is that the image of what they have seen seems to have faded away by the time they have named four or five letters. Most important, they report that images of the letters persist briefly after the visual stimulus ceases. Subjectively, they feel they are naming the letters seen in these persisting images, and they continue to do so until the images disappear. Thus, it appears as if the retina of the eye retains information briefly, with the information being in the form of an image, or icon, of a just-terminated visual stimulus. Not surprisingly, this form of sensory memory has been labeled *iconic memory* (Neisser, 1967).

   Iconic memory plays an important adaptive role in information processing. It prolongs the time information is available for perceptual analysis and identification. That is, the processes of pattern recognition are not necessarily restricted to operating on information that is presently reaching the receptors of the retina, they may continue to operate on the memory of that information. The time extension permitted by iconic memory probably enhances the operations of selective attention as well. As observed by Solso:

> By preserving the complete sensory impression for a brief period we can scan the immediate events, picking out those stimuli which are most salient, and fitting them into the tangled matrix of human memory. When all works properly, no more or no less information is coded, transformed, or stored than is necessary for humans to carry on a normal existence. (1979, p. 48)

Three questions come to mind immediately concerning iconic memory. The first concerns its locus. Is it really a peripheral phenomenon produced by continuing activity of retinal receptors (i.e., rods and cones)? Or is it a central phenomenon that reflects the encoding of information into some postsensory, or nonphysical, format? Here we find considerable division of opinion among basic researchers who have been investigating the nature of iconic memory. On the one hand, there is evidence to indicate that iconic memory stems from persisting activity of both rods (Sakitt, 1975) and cones (Adelson, 1978). On the other hand, there is also evidence to indicate that postsensory factors are at least partially responsible for the existence of iconic memory (Holding, 1975; Merikle, 1980; Sakitt & Appelman, 1978). The second question concerns the duration of iconic memory. Here we cannot trust the subjective reports of subjects. What is needed are methods that permit rigorously controlled assessments of an icon's duration. Fortunately, two such methods have appeared in the past 20 years. The third question, the one that concerns us most directly, follows naturally from the second: Are there adult-age differences in the duration of iconic memory? To the extent that iconic memory is determined by the persisting activity of photoreceptor cells in the retina, we should expect duration to be longer for elderly adults than for young adults. This is simply one more prediction derived from the principle of an age difference in stimulus persistence. The advent of methods to assess the duration of iconic memory has made it possible to test the validity of this prediction.

The first of these methods was introduced in a famous study by Sperling (1960). The method is basically an expanded version of the method used for years to measure the span of apprehension for letters. We noted earlier that this method consists of exposing an array of letters briefly and having subjects name as many of the letters as possible. Sperling continued to use this procedure, requiring his subjects on some trials to give what he called a whole report. Specifically, an array of 12 letters was exposed for 50 milliseconds. As illustrated in the top panel of Figure 9.1, the array was arranged in three rows of four letters each. Immediately after the termination of the array's exposure, subjects in the whole-report condition began naming as many of the 12 letters as they could. In agreement with many early studies, Sperling found that his young-adult subjects could name, on the average, about 4.5 letters. Stated somewhat differently, they could recall about 40% of what they had seen. Sperling's innovative touch consisted of the inclusion of another condition, one in which subjects gave a partial report rather than the traditional whole report. In a partial report, only the letters in a single row had to be named. His subjects did not know in advance on any partial-report trial which one of the three rows was the one to be named. That knowledge came only *after* the physical display itself had terminated, and it came in the form of a tone that signaled which of the three rows was the target for that trial (the rows varied randomly in being signaled over trials). A high-frequency tone signaled name the top row, a medium-frequency tone signaled name the middle row, and a low-frequency tone signaled name the bottom row. One other highly innovative feature was added to the partial-report condition. Sperling varied the interval separating termination of the visual display and the signal cuing which row to name. This interval was set at 0 milliseconds on some trials (i.e., the signal sounded as the display

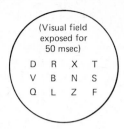

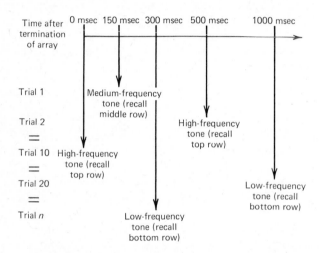

Figure 9.1. Top panel: Typical array of letters exposed briefly for a Sperling task in which subjects give either a full report (all letters) or a partial report (a single row). Bottom panel: Example of the procedure followed in the partial-report condition of a Sperling task.

went off), and at 150, 300, 500, or 1000 milliseconds on other trials. The nature of this procedure is summarized in the bottom panel of Figure 9.1.

Sperling's results with the partial-report condition are shown in Figure 9.2. Performance is expressed in terms of the percentage of row letters correctly named (i.e., out of the four letters in a row). Note that about 80% of the letters in a signaled row could be identified after a 0 delay. His subjects, of course, did not know on any given trial which row would be signaled for identification. Thus, if 80% of the designated row could be identified, then the implication is that 80% of each of the other two rows could also have been identified. A reasonable estimate, therefore, is that the actual capacity of the iconic memory store is about 9.6 letters (i.e., 80% of 12) rather than 4.5 letters as estimated by the whole-report procedure. The reason why the capacity of the store appears less in the whole-report condition is that information stored in the form of icons or images fades as the subject begins to name the letters. By the time 4 or 5 letters are named, the icons have disappeared completely, thereby prohibiting any further recall of what had been seen. Now consider what happens with the partial-report procedure when the signal is delayed 100 or more milliseconds.

During the delay, iconic information is fading rapidly, making fewer and fewer letters available for identification. By 500 milliseconds the percentage was down to 50% (See Figure 9.2), and by 1000 milliseconds it had reached the 40% level found with the whole-report procedure. A reasonable argument is that as long as partial-report recall exceeds full-report recall (percentagewise), some iconic memory remains. Thus, a comparison of partial and full-report scores provides an estimate of the duration of iconic memory. Sperling's results (Figure 9.2) indicate that the duration for young adults is at least 500 milliseconds but less than 1 second.

Sperling's ingenious method offers a potentially valuable means of examining adult-age differences in the capacity of the iconic store as well as in the duration of iconic memory. Unfortunately, however, its use with elderly subjects encounters a number of perhaps insurmountable obstacles (see Walsh and Prasse, 1980, for a detailed discussion). Indicative of these obstacles is the fact that 8 out of the 10 elderly subjects entering into a study by Walsh and Thompson (as reported in Walsh, 1975) were unable to perform under a partial-report condition. Apparently, their difficulty was one of attention rather than the absence of iconic memory per se. A partial report demands the rapid focusing of attention on a segment of the information held in the iconic store. With increasing age, the rapid shifting of attention becomes increasingly more difficult to accomplish. Another kind of problem encountered by the elderly was demonstrated in a study by Salthouse (1976). His elderly subjects were characterized by an inefficient strategy in adapting to partial-report conditions. Specifically, they tended to focus their attention on only the top row of the letters in an array. This is fine as long as recall of the top row is signaled. However, it makes the letters in another row virtually impossible to recall when that row is

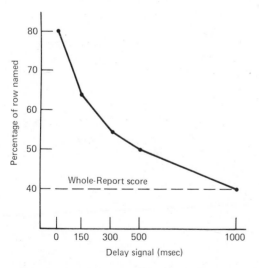

Figure 9.2. Percentage of the letters reported in a row (partial report) as a function of the delay between termination of the visual display and onset of the signal cuing which row to report. (Adapted from data in Sperling, 1960.)

signaled. By contrast, his young-adult subjects displayed a far more flexible strategy. A method with far fewer attentional demands seems to be needed to provide information about adult-age differences in iconic-memory phenomena.

The second method, one introduced by Eriksen and Collins (1967), does satisfy this requirement. The method itself was described in Chapter 7. Briefly, in review, the method calls for the brief exposure of successive visual stimuli with a temporal interval separating the two exposures. The experimenter, then, determines the maximum interstimulus interval (ISI) for which the temporally separated stimuli are perceived as being continuously one stimulus event. The ability to integrate the information from the second stimulus with the information conveyed by the first stimulus is seemingly dependent on the presence of iconic memory of the first stimulus at the time the second stimulus is exposed. Thus, the maximum ISI promoting a continuously perceived event should provide an effective estimate of the duration of iconic memory. Moreover, there is no unusual attentional demand required to perform this task.

The experimental aging studies that employ this method were reviewed in Chapter 7. At that time, we discovered that there are conflicting results regarding both the estimated duration of iconic memory and the direction of whatever age difference exists in duration. With a flashing light as the successive, and temporally separated, stimuli, the duration is estimated to be less than 100 milliseconds for both young and elderly subjects, and it is estimated to be slightly longer for elderly subjects than for young subjects (Amberson, Atkeson, Pollack, and Malatesta, 1979). The direction of the age difference is, of course, in agreement with the stimulus-persistence principle. With a single letter as the stimulus source, the duration is estimated to be slightly less than 300 milliseconds for both young and elderly subjects, and it is estimated to be either moderately longer for young subjects than for elderly subjects (Walsh & Thompson, 1978) or moderately longer for elderly subjects than for young subjects (Kline & Schieber, 1981). In these studies, the estimated time for young adults is somewhat less than the time estimated by Sperling (1960). More important, these studies imply that there is no major change over the adult lifespan in the proficiency of iconic memory, at least with respect to its continuing existence and to its duration. Unfortunately, however, this second method, unlike Sperling's method, does not permit an assessment of the iconic store's capacity. Thus, there is no way of using this second method to evaluate potential age changes in capacity. However, given the fact that iconic memory is largely a retinal-based phenomenon and the fact that the retina itself changes little with aging, there is no reason to expect any major age change in capacity. Our conclusion is that iconic memory is largely insensitive to any pronounced changes over the adult lifespan.

Echoic Memory. There is an auditory equivalent of iconic memory, namely *echoic memory* (Neisser, 1967). It, too, has been widely investigated with young-adult subjects. As with iconic memory, it refers to the persistence of an image of a physical stimulus. In this case, the image appears to preserve the sound features of an originating auditory stimulus. Solso has given us a clear description of the importance of echoic memory, or the preperceptual auditory store in his terms, to information processing:

> Preperceptual auditory store (PAS) is similar to preperceptual visual store (PVS; i.e., iconic memory) in the sense that the raw sensory information is held in it with true fidelity (in order that the pertinent features can be extracted and further analyzed) for a very short time. As in PVS, which allows us an additional time to view fleeting stimuli, PAS allows us additional time to hear an auditory message. If we consider the complex process of understanding common speech, the utility of PAS becomes obvious. Auditory impulses that make up speech are spread over time. Information contained in any small fraction of speech, music, or other sound is meaningless unless placed within the context of other sounds. PAS, by briefly preserving auditory information, provides us with immediate contextual cues for comprehension of auditory information. (1979, p. 45)

Two methods have been introduced as means of assessing directly the duration of echoic memory. Each, in principle, has the potential for extension to experimental aging research for the purpose of evaluating age differences in duration. However, implementing these methods is not easy to accomplish with elderly subjects (see Crowder, 1980, for a detailed account). One obvious problem is the fact that many elderly people experience hearing problems at the direct sensory level. Consequently, there has been little experimental aging research dealing directly with echoic memory.

One method for assessing duration is the auditory analogue of Sperling's (1960) partial-report versus whole-report procedure (e.g., Darwin, Turvey, & Crowder, 1972; Moray, Bates, & Barnett, 1965). Three auditory messages (e.g., strings of digits) are presented simultaneously from three different spatial locations. In the whole-report condition, the subject attempts to recall as many digits as possible from all three locations immediately after hearing them. In the partial-report condition, a visual cue signals to the subject which one of the three locations is to be reported. Once more, the time between termination of the messages and the onset of the signal is a critical independent variable. A superior partial-report score relative to a whole-report score is viewed as indicating the continuing presence of echoic memory. With young adults, this superiority continues for at least a full second. Thus, echoic memory is believed to have a somewhat longer duration than iconic memory. Use of this method with elderly subjects is confronted by the same problems encountered in partial-report research on iconic memory. Consequently, it is of little use in the experimental psychology of aging.

The second method is a novel one. Subjects are given a number of serial-recall lists, each of which is presented aurally. In serial recall, a string of items, such as digits or letters, is presented for a single-study trial and subjects are required to recall the items in the exact order presented. In effect, the task is much like that of a memory-span task, except for the fact that the number of items exceeds the number ordinarily spanned without error. To test the duration of echoic memory, a simple addition is made to half of the lists a subject receives (Crowder & Morton, 1969). The addition is that of a suffix in the form of an additional element heard at the end of the list. The suffix may be either another digit or letter that is not part of the memory list or a completely unrelated element, such as the sound *uh.* Whatever its nature, the suffix itself is not to be recalled. No suffix is added to the remaining lists (i.e., control lists). The presence of a suffix has a startling effect on recall of the to-be-remembered items. Specifically, the probability of recalling the last few items in the list is markedly below the level manifested for those same positions in the control list. For other positions in the list, the decrement produced by the suffix is much less pronounced and may even be nonexistent. The suffix effect presumably occurs because the tacked-on sound at the end blots out the echoic memory of the last few items in the list. It is this persisting sound content that enables subjects to recall many of the items near the end of the list. A similar blotting out does not occur, of course, for a control list.

To assess the duration of echoic memory requires one additional critical step—varying the time interval between the last list item and the onset of the suffix. If a suffix effect (i.e., a recall decrement in the suffix condition relative to the control condition) is present after X number of seconds, then our conclusion is that echoic memory persists for at least X number of seconds. This strategy was employed in a study by Watkins and Watkins (1980). Their results suggest that echoic memory for young adults has a duration of at least 4 seconds. That is, a suffix effect was manifested even after a 4-second delay separating the last item in their list and the suffix.

There has been one interesting study with the suffix method (Parkinson & Perey, 1980) that provides some information about the proficiency of echoic memory in late adulthood. Young-adult and elderly subjects who were matched for digit-span performance scores were given a number of serial-recall lists, each composed of seven digits. In their suffix condition, *uh* followed the last digit after an interval of half a second (no *uh,* of course, occurred in the control condition). The results obtained for their young subjects are shown in the top panel of Figure 9.3, and the results obtained for their elderly subjects are shown in the bottom panel. Note that their elderly subjects exhibited a suffix effect that did not differ greatly from that of their young subjects. Apparently, echoic memory does continue into late adulthood, and it has a duration of at least half a second. Unfortunately, however, this study does not permit an evaluation of age differences in duration of echoic memory. To accomplish this objective, additional experimental aging studies are needed in which the length of the interval separating the last-list item and the onset of the suffix is varied systematically.

Echoic memory also enters into an episodic-memory phenomenon of considerable importance. The phenomenon is known as the *modality effect.* It refers to the difference in recall, whether serial or free, between list items presented auditorily and list items presented visually (and at the same exposure rate for each modality). The nature of the effect may be seen in Figure 9.4. The results are those obtained by Madigan (1971) with young-adult subjects and a

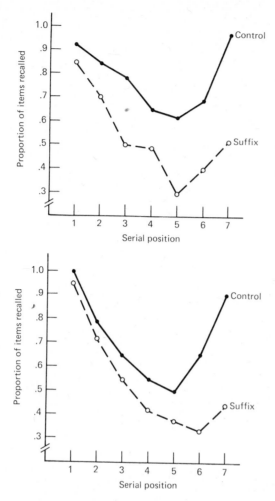

Figure 9.3. Magnitude of the suffix effect (depressed recall of end items relative to a control condition receiving no redundant suffix at the end of the list) for young-adult (top panel) and elderly (bottom panel) subjects. (Adapted from Parkinson & Perey, 1980, Figure 2.)

serial-recall task. Note that recall of items near the end of the list was much higher when those items were presented auditorily than when they were presented visually. It is this superiority for auditory presentation that defines the modality effect. By contrast, there was little difference attributable to modality of presentation for items occurring earlier in the list. Why a modality effect for end items? According to Watkins and Watkins:

> The modality effect might have been predicted from the very fact of echoic memory as a psychological phenomenon. With auditory presentation, echoic information corresponding to the final few list items should persist after list presentation and so facilitate their recall. Of course, a corresponding sensory store, referred to

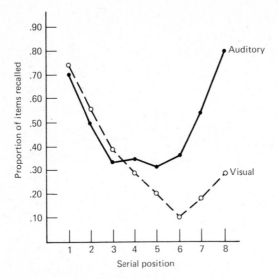

Figure 9.4. Superior recall for end items when presented auditorily than for end items when presented visually (the modality effect). (Adapted from Madigan, 1971, Figure 1.)

as iconic memory (again after Neisser, 1967) is usually assumed for visual presentation. But iconic information is, by most estimates, too transitory to be of any practical consequence in a typical immediate recall procedure (Sperling, 1960). Recency recall should therefore show positive effects of echoic memory but not of iconic memory. In this way, the concept of sensory storage provides a ready explanation of the modality effect. (1980, p. 252)

The appearance of a modality effect for elderly subjects, therefore, offers an alternative to a suffix effect for demonstrating the continuation of echoic memory during late adulthood. Such a demonstration was given by Arenberg (1976). Both young and elderly subjects received a series of free-recall lists, each containing 16 words with either auditory or visual presentation. The results are shown in the top (young subjects) and bottom (elderly subjects) panels of Figure 9.5. At both age levels there was a modest, but consistent, modality effect spread over the last four items (i.e., the last four items in the input sequence for each free-recall list). The effect seems to be as pronounced for the elderly subjects as for the young subjects. (On the other hand, the probability of recalling items at *all* input positions, disregarding modality of presentation, was clearly higher for young subjects than for elderly subjects—an important point that we will return to in the next section.) Other studies (Arenberg, 1968b; McGhie, Chapman, & Lawson, 1965; Taub, 1972) have also reported an advantage of auditorily presented items over visually presented items that was as pronounced for elderly subjects as for young subjects. In Arenberg's (1968b) study, the task required detecting which digit in a series was a repetition of a previously presented digit; in Taub's (1972) study, the task was a standard digit-span task. As with iconic memory, there is no reason to believe that there

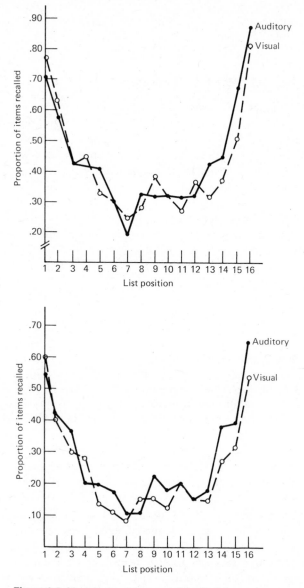

Figure 9.5. Magnitude of the modality effect found for young adults (top panel) and elderly adults (bottom panel). (Adapted from Arenberg, 1976, Figure 1.)

are major age changes in echoic memory, at least for elderly adults without serious hearing dysfunctions.

Other Senses. The equivalent of iconic or echoic memory for each of the other senses has received relatively little attention. Of these other senses, the strongest case thus far for the existence of a sensory memory can be made for touch (e.g., Gilson & Baddeley, 1969). To date, however, there apparently have been no studies dealing with age differences in memory for touch or any other of the remaining senses.

Adult-Age Differences in Episodic Memory: Dual-Store Model

For information held in a sensory store to become an episodic-memory trace, it must first be transformed (by means of the operations of pattern recognition) from its physical format into a mental representation. According to the dual-store model of human memory, this representation, usually in the form of sound or phonemic attributes, is then transmitted to a short-term store. Here, it resides briefly and is then either lost (or forgotten), recalled directly, or encoded further for transmission to a long-term store for more permanent storage. The short-term, or primary, component of the total memory system obviously plays a critical role in regulating episodic-memory phenomena. Most important, the primary-memory component offers a number of possible sources of adult-age differences in episodic-memory proficiency. Our review of experimental aging research conducted from the perspective of the dual-store model will begin with primary-memory phenomena. We will then turn to the evidence regarding age differences in the secondary memory (long-term) component of the total memory system.

Primary Memory: Short-term Storage Capacity. Age differences in primary-memory proficiency may result from an age change in the capacity of the short-term store. In principle, the number of bins in which information can be held temporarily may be less for elderly adults than for young adults. Such shrinkage would account nicely for the modest, but consistently found, age deficit on memory-span tasks. Many memory theorists (e.g., Craik, 1977; Watkins, 1977), however, believe that performance on memory-span tasks is not determined exclusively by the capacity of the short-term store. In fact, the actual capacity of this store is viewed as being less than the seven or so items spanned, on the average, on a digit-span task or even the five or so items spanned on a word-span task. Why should memory span exceed the capacity of the short-term store, presumably the store from which the to-be-remembered items are directly recalled? The most likely explanation is that at least part of the span is mediated by secondary-memory processes, processes that increase the number of items that may be recalled beyond the limitation set by the capacity of the store itself. The involvement of secondary-memory processes greatly complicates attempts to evaluate age changes in the capacity of the short-term store. Age differences in performance may well be the consequence of age-sensitive secondary-memory processes rather than an age change in primary-memory capacity.

There are two ways by which secondary-memory processes may supplement the direct recall of information from the short-term store. One is through extra rehearsal given to some items in a string, thereby enhancing the probability that these items enter the long-term store. Once they enter the long-term store, these items may then be available for direct recall from that store. The requisite extra rehearsal needed for this transmission from short-term to long-term memory is likely to be greater for young adults than for elderly adults, therefore, inflating span scores more for young than elderly subjects. The alternative way is through the chunking of items that are components of a to-be-remembered string (Miller, 1956). Chunking is an encoding process akin to subjective organization. Through it, successive items in a string are related in some manner to one another. The advantage of chunking is that several items rather than only one may then occupy the space of a single bin in the short-term store. The requisite process, one presumably part of the secondary-memory system, is again more likely to be present for young adults than for elderly adults, once more inflating span scores more for young subjects than for elderly subjects.

Some evidence in support of the above account was given in Chapter 5 (also see Figure 5.14). There, we discovered that word span is greater for both young and elderly subjects when the intrastring items are high-frequency words than when they are low-frequency words. We also discovered that the age deficit in span length is greater for high-frequency words than for low-frequency words. In principle, span length should be independent of word frequency (assuming all of the words are known to subjects) if it is determined solely by the capacity of the short-term store. One word, regardless of its frequency of occurrence, should occupy each bin in the store. We noted at the time, however, that high-frequency words are more likely to be chunked than are low-frequency words. Diminished proficiency in chunking with increasing age seemingly accounts, therefore, for the observed interaction between age and word frequency. Additional evidence for an age deficit in chunking comes from a study by Taub (1974). Young, middle-age, and elderly subjects were given 12 letters to recall in serial order. In a low-chunking condition, the letters provided little opportunity for chunking (e.g., *PBSKOJUHRMGA* as a series). In a high-chunking condition, successive groups of four letters each formed a meaningful word (e.g., *JUMPHOGSBARK*). All subjects participated in both conditions, and they had no advance information describing the presence of words in the high-chunking condition. The means for number of letters recalled for both conditions and all three age groups are plotted in Figure 9.6. Note that age differences favoring young adults were far greater in the high-chunking condition than in the low-chunking condition, in agreement with our preceding analysis.

The evaluation of age differences in short-term memory capacity clearly requires a method that eliminates contributions of secondary-memory processes to the recall of to-be-remembered items. One method suggested by the very nature of the dual-store model (e.g., Glanzer & Cunitz, 1966) involves the assessment of what is called the *recency effect* in the free recall of word lists. The recency effect emerges when subjects are given a number of successive free-recall lists, each for a single study-test trial. When the probability of recalling list items for all of the lists combined is plotted across the ordinal position of those items during study trials, the resulting function takes the form shown in

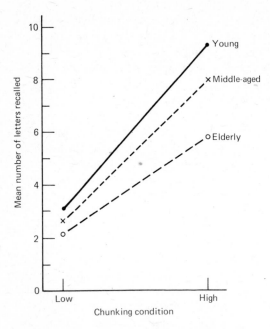

Figure 9.6. Age differences in recall of letter series as a function of chunking present within the series. (Adapted from Taub, 1974, Figure 1.)

Figure 9.7. The last few items in study trials have an unusually high probability of recall relative to midlist items, a disparity that defines the recency effect. Variation in the magnitude of the recency effect may be either in the magnitude of the heightened probability or in the number of items from the end of the list over which the heightened probability spreads. The effect is presumed to result from the direct recall of item information held in the short-term store. Items at and near the end of the list are still in the store at the time item presentation ceases, and they are, therefore, in residence at the time recall of items begins. That is, there are no additional items to displace them from the store, making them available for direct recall from the short-term store. By contrast, earlier items in a list are followed by a number of additional items, and they must, therefore, be booted out of the store to make room for new incoming information. These items must be recalled from the long-term store if they are to be recalled at all. The first few items in a list have a greater probability of being transmitted to the long-term store than do midlist items. Consequently, there is also a *primacy effect* in free recall, defined in terms of the heightened probability of recalling early list items relative to midlist items (see Figure 9.7). We will turn to the importance of the primacy effect in experimental aging research later in this section.

Primacy and recency effects in free recall clearly resemble the serial-position effects that characterize serial-anticipation learning. For each task, performance is superior for the items at the two ends of a list than for items in the middle of the same list. The resemblance ends there however. Quite different

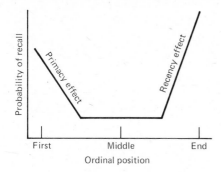

Figure 9.7. The nature of primacy and recency effects in the recall of items from free-recall lists.

processes are postulated to underlie the superficially similar phenomena. In serial-anticipation learning, subjects must acquire information pertaining to each item's position in the total list as well as acquire information regarding what specific words serve as list items. It is the former process that presumably accounts for serial-position effects. That is, order, or position, information is learned earlier for items at the two ends of the list than for items in the middle of the list. The availability of the items themselves is not presumed to vary across serial positions (Jensen, 1962a). In free recall, separate components of the total memory system are responsible for the heightened performances at the two ends of a list—the short-term store for one and the long-term store for the other. (Alternatively, different levels of processing are postulated for terminal items than for beginning and middle items—an alternative analysis of free recall that will be discussed more thoroughly later in this chapter.)

The nature of the recency effect for elderly subjects is of great interest. If its attributes match those found for the recency effect manifested by young subjects, then the argument may be made that the capacity of the short-term store is basically unaltered by aging. The results here are conflicting however. Craik (1968), in a careful analysis of age differences in the recency effects obtained with various kinds of words, concluded that the capacity of the short-term store is about the same for elderly adults as it is for young adults. Raymond (1971) came to the same conclusion. Only elderly subjects participated in her free-recall study. The recency effect manifested by these subjects is illustrated in Figure 9.8. Raymond compared the attributes of this effect (i.e., its height and its extension from the end of the list toward the middle of the list) with those reported in a number of studies with young-adult subjects (e.g., Glanzer & Cunitz, 1966) and found few, if any, differences. Craik (1971) also found little effect attributable to age variation when a recognition test substituted for a recall test.

On the other hand, the recency effects for young and elderly subjects apparent in the study by Arenberg (1976) cited earlier do show an important difference. For his young subjects (top panel of Figure 9.5), the proportions of last and next-to-last items recalled averaged (combined over modalities) about .85 and .57, respectively. For his elderly subjects, the comparable proportions were about .60 and .37. From the perspective of the dual-store model, these

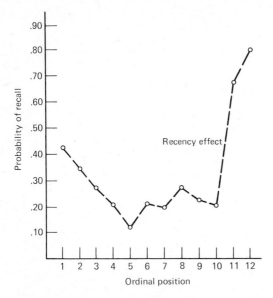

Figure 9.8. Magnitude and extent of the recency effect found for elderly subjects. (Adapted from data in Raymond, 1971.)

disparities could be viewed as indicating a diminished storage capacity in late adulthood. Salthouse (1980a) has also reported results from a free-recall study that revealed a pronounced age deficit in the probability of recalling recency items.

A similar age deficit was found by Parkinson (1980) with a running memory-span task instead of a free-recall task. His young and elderly subjects received strings of digits that varied in length from trial to trial. Following the presentations of the last digit on a given trial, subjects tried to recall the last five items in the string, starting with the terminal item. No age difference was found for the very last item. However, beginning with the next-to-last item and extending through all of the remaining items, young subjects clearly recalled a higher proportion of items than elderly subjects. This deficit also implies a diminished storage capacity in late adulthood.

In general, the evidence from various sources suggests that there may be a modest decline in the capacity of the short-term store by late adulthood. Our conclusion must be tempered, however, by our awareness that not all memory theorists hold to the concept of a limited capacity short-term store. Again, we will discover in the next section that these other theorists have an alternative way of explaining such phenomena as the recency effect in free recall.

Primary Memory: Rate of Loss of Information. Age differences in primary-memory proficiency may also result from an age change in the rate with which information is lost, or forgotten, from the short-term store. Short-term forgetting, that is, forgetting over intervals of seconds instead of minutes, hours, or days, is widely studied in basic-memory research through the use of a procedure introduced around the same time by Brown (1958) and Peterson and Peterson (1959) and, therefore, commonly referred to as the Brown-Peterson procedure. The strategy is a simple but potent one. Subjects are given a single nonsense syllable to hold in memory over a retention interval that varies across trials from 0 to 18 seconds. To prevent rehearsal of that syllable during the retention interval (and, therefore, to prevent its constant reentry into the short-term store), subjects are required to count backwards by threes, starting with a three-digit number that is given immediately after the syllable is presented. Each subject receives many trials, with each trial involving the retention of a different nonsense syllable. On some trials the retention interval is set at 0 seconds (i.e., subjects recall the syllable immediately after its presentation), on some trials at 3 seconds (filled with counting backwards), and still other trials at longer intervals, up through 18 seconds. Performance may then be measured in terms of the proportion of subjects recalling syllables at each of the retention intervals.

The results obtained by the Petersons (1959) with young-adult subjects are plotted in the top panel of Figure 9.9. Note the very rapid forgetting of information presumably held in the short-term store at the onset of the retention interval. Memory psychologists have proposed various explanations for the rapid rate of forgetting found with a Brown-Peterson-type of task. To some (e.g., Brown, 1958) it results from the spontaneous decay of information residing in the short-term store; to others it results from either the displacement of letters from the store by the numbers recited in counting backwards (e.g., Reitman, 1971) or the kind of interference postulated by interference theorists to account for proactive inhibition (Keppel & Underwood, 1962). The reason for the rapid forgetting is of less importance to us than is the possibility that there may be major age differences in the rate of forgetting. That this is unlikely to be true was demonstrated in two important studies by Kriauciunas (1968) and Schonfield (1969b). In both studies, the procedure basically replicated that of the Petersons (1959), except for the fact that elderly subjects as well as young-adult subjects participated. The results obtained by Schonfield are shown in the bottom panel of Figure 9.9 (comparable results were obtained in the other study). Note that the rate of forgetting was essentially the same for the two age groups. Recall simply began at a higher level (i.e., at the 0.5-second retention interval) for the young subjects, probably because they encoded the linguistic element more proficiently than did the elderly subjects. The age difference remained about the same, however, at each successive retention interval, indicating that the rate of losing information in the short-term store was about the same for each age group. If elderly subjects forget at a faster rate, we would expect the magnitude of the age difference in amount recalled, favoring young adults, to increase as the retention interval increased. An absence of an age difference in rate of short-term forgetting was also found by Keevil-Rogers and Schnore (1969) with digits as the to-be-remembered items and color-naming as the interpolated rehearsal-preventing activity.

Other evidence indicating the absence of adult-age differences in the rate of short-term forgetting comes from studies employing a variation of the

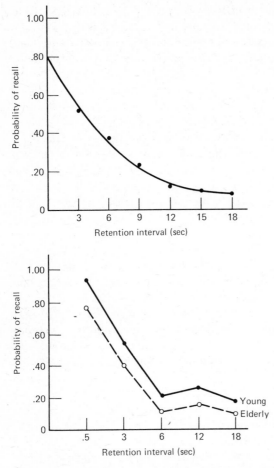

Figure 9.9. Top panel: Rate of forgetting in short-term memory as found by the Petersons for young-adult subjects. (Adapted from Peterson & Peterson, 1959, Figure 3.) Bottom panel: Age differences in rate of short-term memory forgetting. (Adapted from Schonfield, 1969b, Table 3.)

Brown-Peterson procedure that was introduced by Wickens (e.g., Wickens, Born, & Allen, 1963). With this modified procedure, triplets of words serve as the to-be-remembered items. After each triplet is presented, subjects perform on a rehearsal-preventing activity during a specified retention interval (e.g., 18 seconds) and then attempt to recall the three words. In a control condition, the triplets have the same form of relatedness on each of four consecutive trials. For example, each triplet may consist of the names of three different animals (fox, lion, bear on the first trial; zebra, monkey, seal on the second trial; and so on). With young-adult subjects, recall of the words declines progressively over the four trials. That is, proactive inhibition increases steadily from trial to trial. In an experimental condition, the only change is in the nature of the triplet presented on the critical fourth trial. Instead of animal names, words from a different taxonomic category (e.g., vegetables) now make up the triplet (e.g., lettuce, corn, turnip). With young-adult subjects, proactive inhibition again increases over the first three trials. However, there is typically a release-from-proactive-inhibition effect on the critical fourth trial. That is, recall of the words is dramatically higher than recall of the words given on the same trial for subjects in the control condition.

Several studies (Elias & Hirasuna, 1976; Mistler-Lachman, 1977; Puglisi, 1980) have contrasted young and elderly subjects in their performances on a Wickens-like task. The results have been virtually identical in these studies. Plotted in Figure 9.10 are the results obtained by Elias and Hirasuna (1976). Note that proactive inhibition increased (i.e., amount recalled decreased) at about the same rate for young and elderly subjects in the control condition. Moreover, the extent of the release from proactive inhibition was about the same for the two age groups. That is, the greater recall in the experimental condition relative to the control condition on Trial 4 was about the same for elderly subjects as for young adults. Once more, we have no reason to suspect that short-term forgetting is markedly affected by age over the adult lifespan. The only age difference favoring young adults was in the overall level of recall that was apparent on the first trial and continued over the remaining trials (see Figure 9.10). This superiority is most likely attributable to the more proficient encoding of the triplets by young subjects at the time the items are presented.

In general, the evidence is quite convincing—the rate of forgetting for information held in the short-term store is resistant to any major age change.

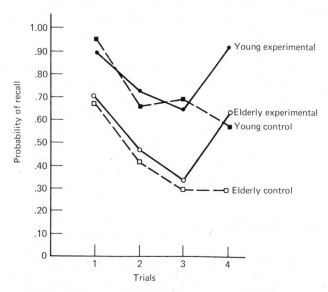

Figure 9.10. Magnitude of release from proactive inhibition (experimental minus control) for young and elderly subjects. (Adapted from Elias & Hirasuna, 1976, Figure 1.)

Interestingly, this is the same conclusion we reached with regard to the rate of forgetting over far longer retention intervals for materials acquired with practice (i.e., the products of learning).

Primary Memory: Flexibility of Representation. We observed earlier that information held in the short-term store consists ordinarily of sound representations of inputs into our sensory registers. For example, if the letter *V* is a visually presented list item, it is the sound *ve* that is likely to enter the short-term store. Support for this position comes from studies (e.g., Conrad, 1964) in which strings of letters make up the items for a Brown-Peterson-type task. With retention intervals of several seconds, it is not unusual to discover errors of recall involving letters that are phonemically similar to to-be-remembered items. For example, *V* may be recalled as *B*. On the other hand, it is unusual to discover errors involving letters that are orthographically similar but phonemically dissimilar to to-be-remembered items (e.g., recalling *Y* instead of *V*). At the same time, there does seem to be considerable flexibility in the kind of representation that may be stored in short-term memory. For young adults, visual representations of sensory inputs are capable of residing in the short-term store for at least several seconds. One way of demonstrating visual short-term memory is through the use of the Posner (Posner, Boies, Eichelman & Taylor, 1969) method described in Chapter 7. Subjects again receive pairs of letters having the same name. In one condition, the letters are of the same case (e.g., *AA*); in another condition, they are different in case (e.g., *Aa*). In either condition, the correct decision is same. To test for the presence of visual representations in the short-term store, the investigator also varies the time separating the exposures of the two letters in a pair. When that time is no more than 2 seconds, decision time is faster for *AA*-type pairs than for *Aa*-type pairs (Posner et al., 1969). A visual image of *A*, the first letter exposed, seems to be retained over this 2-second interval, thus making it possible to match the second *A* with that stored information. Such a match is not possible when the second letter is *a*. Here the decision of sameness can be made only on the basis of a common name for the two letters. When the retention interval is longer than several seconds, there is no longer visual information available in the short-term store, information that would be necessary to permit direct matching. Consequently, the decision can be made only on the basis of the common name, just as it is in the *Aa* condition, and there is no longer an advantage to be gained for *AA* pairs. A retention interval of 2 seconds, of course, implies the underlying process cannot be that of iconic memory (it persists for less than 1 second) and must, therefore, be a postsensory, or short-term memory, process.

The overall difficulty that elderly people have with imaginal activity implies that they may also have difficulty in constructing visual representations for short-term storage. There have been no experimental aging studies, however, that have employed either the above method or one of several alternative methods (e.g., Kroll, Parks, Parkinson, Bieber, & Johnson, 1970). Consequently, we do not know if the flexibility for short-term memory offered by visual representations diminishes in late adulthood. However, there have been a number of experimental aging studies (e.g., Adamowicz, 1976, 1978; Adam-owicz & Hudson, 1978; Arenberg, 1977, 1978) in which short-term retention (i.e., retention over seconds) has been tested with such visual stimuli as mosaic patterns and geometric designs. These studies have found pronounced age defi-cits in short-term memory as measured by both recognition of the visual stimuli and reproduction of those stimuli. Interpretation of these deficits is difficult however. They could be the consequence of poorer visual representations in short-term memory for elderly subjects than for young subjects, but they could also be the consequence of poorer translation of visual stimuli into verbal representations by elderly subjects than by young subjects. This is an important problem area, one that merits further investigation of age differences with the kind of methodology described earlier.

Primary Memory: Search of Content. Finally, age differences in primary-mem-ory proficiency may result from an age change in the rate with which the short-term store is searched for the presence or absence of specific information. This is the kind of activity we touched on in Chapter 6 when we described the problem confronting an individual who, after hearing the names of today's baseball winners, is asked if a particular team won that day. Our assumption is that the winners' names reside in the short-term store at the time the question is asked. To answer the question, the store's content must be searched, or scanned, name by name to determine if the queried name is present.

The nature of short-term memory scanning has been one of the most thoroughly studied topics in basic-memory research over the past 15 or so years. Interest in the topic began with several striking discoveries by Sternberg (1966, 1969b). The task introduced by Sternberg (subsequently labeled the Sternberg task) was itself highly original. His young-adult subjects received a memory set of items (usually digits but sometimes letters or words) on each of many trials. The size of the set varied from trial to trial. On some trials, a single digit was presented for study and transmission to the short-term store. On other trials, the set was expanded to 2, 3, 4, 5, or 6 digits shown in succession (with an exposure rate slightly greater than 1 second per digit). Following exposure of the last digit in a memory set, his subjects received a test stimulus. On half of the trials for each set size, the test stimulus was a digit that had been part of the just-presented memory set (e.g., 7 1 3 as a memory set and 1 as a test stimulus); on the other half, the test stimulus was not part of the prior memory set (2 as the test stimulus for the 7 1 3 set). On each trial, a subject's task was to respond yes or no to the test stimulus—pushing one button for yes, a differ-ent button for no—to indicate whether or not that stimulus was a member of the memory set. The dependent variable was the reaction time in pressing the appropriate button (errors are unusual—subjects rarely press the wrong but-ton). Sternberg's striking discoveries may be seen in the top panel of Figure 9.11 where mean reaction time is plotted as a function of the set size (i.e., number of digits in the set). The first discovery is that it really made no differ-ence for each set size whether the test stimulus was positive (yes) or negative (no)—mean reaction time was about the same for each kind of stimulus. The

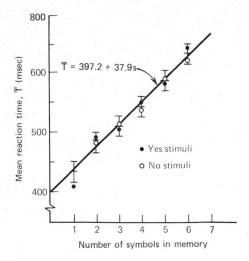

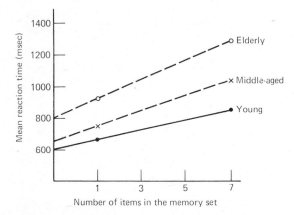

Figure 9.11. Top panel: Sternberg's results for reaction time to a test stimulus as a function of the number of items searched in the short-term store. (Adapted from Sternberg, 1966, Figure 1.) Bottom panel: Age differences in reaction time on the Sternberg task. (Adapted from Anders et al., 1972, Figure 1.)

second is that reaction time increased linearly as the size of the set increased. Because positive and negative test stimuli did not differ in reaction times, they were combined for purposes of plotting the best fitting line (top panel of Figure 9.11) to represent the relationship between reaction time and variation in set size. Not apparent from Figure 9.11 is another one of Sternberg's discoveries. For positive stimuli, he found reaction time to be independent of a stimulus's position in the preceding memory set. Thus, if the memory set consisted of 7 1 3, then reaction time was about the same for 7 as the test stimulus as it was for either 1 or 3 as the test stimulus.

Collectively, these results revealed to Sternberg the fundamental nature of a search through the content of the short-term store. Specifically, the search appears to be both *serial* and *exhaustive*. It is serial in the sense that the items in the store are searched consecutively at a constant rate to determine the presence of the test stimulus. The rate of progression through the series is roughly the same in going from the first to second representation as it is from the second to third representation, and so on. The net effect is the linear increment in total reaction time as the number of items in a set increases. The search is exhaustive in the sense that it continues even after the test stimulus itself has been matched with a representation of an item in the store. Thus, for our 7 1 3 set, a subject continues to examine representations of 1 and 3 in the store even when 7 is the test stimulus. It is the equality of reaction times for positive and negative test stimuli at each set size that convinces us that the search must be exhaustive. If it were self-terminating (i.e., ending as soon as the representation of a positive test stimulus is located in the store), then mean reaction time would be expected to increase more steeply as set size increases for negative stimuli than for positive stimuli. Sternberg (1969b) has argued quite effectively that an exhaustive search actually leads to more proficient memory operations than does a self-terminating search.

Quantitatively, two measures were introduced by Sternberg (1966) to summarize the attributes of a search, both are most useful in evaluating age differences in the proficiency of the underlying processes. The first is the slope of the best fitting line shown in the top panel of Figure 9.11. From that slope, the rate of scanning information in the short-term store may be estimated for the average member of a group of subjects. The slope of the line in the top panel of Figure 9.11 indicates that the average young adult scans at the rate of about 25 digits per second—obviously a high-speed operation. The second measure is the point at which the straight line intersects the ordinate. From the top panel of Figure 9.11 it may be seen that this intercept is about 400 milliseconds. A widely held belief is that this value estimates the average time it takes a young adult to encode the test stimulus in preparation for its trip through the short-term store to seek out its equivalent in that store.

Does the nature of a memory search change over the adult lifespan? Studies by Anders, Fozard, and Lillyquist (1972) and Eriksen, Hamlin, and Daye (1973) suggest strongly that the qualitative attributes of a memory search are unaltered by age. Thus, for elderly adults, reaction time continues to be about the same for positive and negative test stimuli, it continues to increase linearly as memory set size increases, and it is independent of the serial position occupied by a positive stimulus in the memory set. In other words, the search remains both serial and exhaustive. On the other hand, there are important changes with aging in the quantitative attributes of a memory search. These changes may be seen in the bottom panel of Figure 9.11 for the elderly subjects included in the study of Anders et al. (1972) (comparable results were obtained in the study of Eriksen et al. (1973)). The changes are obvious when slope and intercept values found for elderly subjects are compared with the values found in the same study for young (and middle-age) subjects. The slopes indicate that elderly subjects scan items at a much slower rate, about 14 items per second, than young subjects, about 26 items per second (in close agreement with Sternberg's, 1966, earlier finding). Middle-age subjects also appear to scan at a much slower rate than young subjects, averaging about 16 items per second. Intercept values indicate that elderly subjects encode a test stimulus more slowly than do young subjects, averaging about 800 milliseconds, relative to the 600 or so milliseconds taken by young subjects (an estimate somewhat greater than that of Sternberg, 1966). By contrast, encoding time for middle-age subjects seems to be about the same as that of young subjects. The overall pattern fits the concept of a general slowing down of mental activities in late adulthood, a slowing down that affects the scanning of the short-term store as well as many other activities.

Thus far our discussion has concerned only searching, or scanning, under a condition in which the content of the memory set items varies from trial to trial. This condition corresponds closely to the varied mapping condition employed in visual-search research (see Chapter 7). However, the Sternberg (1966) task may also be structured so that it corresponds to the consistent mapping condition employed in visual-search research. One way of accomplishing this objective is to use a fixed-memory set (Sternberg, 1969b). That is, the same items, whether digits, letters, or any other kind of item, constitute the to-be-remembered set on each trial. With a fixed-set procedure, representations of the repeated items should eventually be stored in the long-term episodic store and secondary-memory processes should become involved in yes-no decisions (Atkinson & Juola, 1973; Waugh & Anders, 1973). In consistent mapping for visual targets, we discovered in Chapter 7 that the search process eventually becomes automatic. A similar outcome is expected for a memory search task (Schneider & Shiffrin, 1977). Automaticity in this case should be manifested by a zero-slope line fitting the reaction-time-set size function. That is, reaction time for a yes-no decision should be as fast for a set of, say, five items as it is for a set of, say, two items.

Age differences under fixed-set conditions have been examined by Anders and Fozard (1973) and Madden and Nebes (1980). Faster decision times for young adults continued to be manifested in both studies. Madden and Nebes (1980) also found a trend toward automaticity for both young and elderly subjects with extended practice on the fixed-set of items. That is, slope values decreased systematically over many trials, but, even for young adults, they did not reach zero.

Another variation of the basic Sternberg (1966) task involves memory sets that are components of generic memory. Consider, for example, this question: Is Montreal in the Eastern Division of baseball's National League? The generic memory store of a baseball fan includes the information that Chicago, Montreal, New York, Philadelphia, Pittsburgh, and St. Louis are the six cities having teams in the National League's Eastern Division. Conceivably, a test stimulus such as Montreal, is answered affirmatively following a high-speed search of information in the generic store. A laboratory counterpart of this task was used in an interesting study by Thomas, Waugh, and Fozard (1978). Their generic set of items consisted of the letters *A B C D E F,* a set organized sequentially in the same way it is likely to be organized in generic memory. Age differences in reaction times to both positive (e.g., *C*) and negative (e.g., *X*) stimuli were far less pronounced than they were to a fixed set of letters that violated the kind of organization extant in generic memory (e.g., *P G K T R I* as a fixed set of scrambled letters). This outcome is consistent with other evidence indicating the relative absence of age changes in generic memory phenomena.

Secondary Memory: The Primacy Effect and Transmission of Information to the Long-Term Store. Our analysis to this point suggests that primary-memory deficits are marginal in late adulthood. The implication, therefore, is that secondary-memory processes are responsible for most aging deficits found in episodic memory.

A phenomenon commonly viewed as being one of secondary memory and, therefore, an appropriate one for examining age differences in secondary-memory proficiency is that of the primacy effect in free recall (see Figure 9.7). Some idea of the magnitude of the age difference in the primacy effect may be gathered by comparing the probabilities of recalling the first few list items for the young and elderly subjects included in the study by Arenberg (1976) described earlier (see Figure 9.5). For his young subjects, the proportions of first and second items recalled averaged (combined over modalities) about .75 and .60 respectively. For this elderly subjects, the comparable proportions were about .58 and .40. Age disparities this large have also been found in several other studies (e.g., Craik, 1968; Salthouse, 1980a).

To understand the reason for these age deficits, we must first consider the explanation of the primacy effect given by proponents of the dual-store model. They view the primacy effect as simply reflecting a gradient in the amount of rehearsal items receive while they are residing in the short-term store. The argument is that the probability of transmission of information from the short-term store to the long-term store increases linearly as the amount of rehearsal increases. As that probability increases, so does the probability of recalling information from the long-term store. The early items in a list are assumed to be rehearsed more than later items, with the amount of rehearsal decreasing progressively from the first item on. Indirect support for this position comes from studies (e.g., Glanzer & Cunitz, 1966) in which rate of presenting free-recall items is varied. A slow rate results in heightened probability of recall for all items of the list other than those near the end (although even these items may be affected; see Bernbach, 1975) relative to a fast rate of presentation. A slow rate provides more rehearsal time and, therefore, more rehearsal responses throughout the list. The result is increased transmission of item information to the long-term store, except for items near the end of the list where recall is mediated largely, if not entirely, by the short-term store. More direct support comes from studies (e.g., Rundus & Atkinson, 1970) in which subjects are required to rehearse overtly, or out loud, during a study trial. By tape recording

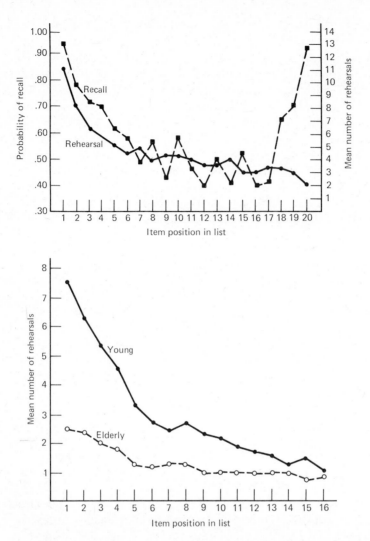

Figure 9.12. Top panel: Results obtained by Rundus and Atkinson for both the probability of recalling items as a function of their input positions and the number of rehearsals per item as a function of input position. (Adapted from Rundus & Atkinson, 1970, Figure 1.) Bottom panel: Age differences in number of rehearsal responses. (Adapted from Sanders, Murphy, Schmitt, & Walsh, 1980, Figure 2.)

each subject's overt rehearsal activity, it becomes possible to count the actual number of rehearsal responses each item in the list receives. The results obtained by Rundus and Atkinson (1970) with this procedure and with young adults as subjects are plotted in the top panel of Figure 9.12. Shown in this figure are both the mean number of rehearsal responses each item received and the probability that that item was recalled. Note that the number of rehearsal responses decreased from the first input position in a list through the sixth input position—and so did the probability of recalling the items at those positions. Beyond this gradient of decreasing recall (the primacy effect), the number of rehearsal responses leveled off at a modest value—and so did the probability of recall, at least until the recency segment of recall emerged at the 18th-input position (with direct recall from the short-term store presumably taking over).

Increasing the number of rehearsal responses seemingly increases the probability of transmission to, and the retrieval from, the long-term store. There are several possible reasons for the direct covariation between number of rehearsal responses and proficiency of recall (see Crowder, 1976, for a detailed discussion). One possibility is that the number of rehearsal responses determines the strength of an item's representation as a single trace in the long-term store. Another is that each rehearsal response transmits a different copy of that item's representation in the store (i.e., multiple traces rather than a single trace varying in strength). The ease of recalling an item from the store may be assumed to increase directly as either its strength increases or its number of copies increases. In either case, there is a ready explanation for the age deficit in secondary-memory proficiency as such proficiency is evaluated by probabilities of recalling nonrecency items for free recall. Elderly subjects are likely to emit fewer rehearsal responses than young adults at each nonrecency position in a list of to-be-remembered items. The overall decrement in number of rehearsal responses should be revealed when elderly subjects as well as young-adult subjects are required to rehearse overtly and their responses are tape recorded. The expected age differential in number of rehearsal responses was indeed found by Sanders, Murphy, Schmitt, & Walsh (1980). Their results may be seen in the bottom panel of Figure 9.12. Note that elderly subjects averaged fewer responses at each position in the list, with the age differential being especially pronounced at the nonrecency positions.

Explanation of the age deficit in secondary memory in terms of an age deficit in number of rehearsal responses fits nicely the conception of a general slowing down of activities in late adulthood, including those activities relevant to memory phenomena (Salthouse, 1980a; Waugh & Barr, 1980). In effect, age deficits in memory are reduced to quantitative changes, such as those involved in rate-of-rehearsal responses, much like the changes presumed by classical associationists to underlie age deficits in paired-associate learning. We discovered earlier, however, that quantitative changes in rehearsal activity are less likely than qualitative changes in that activity to be responsible for age differences in associative learning. A similar possibility exists in the encoding of information for transmission to long-term episodic memory (Kausler, 1978). That is, the critical factor underlying age deficits in secondary memory may be the kind of processes in which young and elderly subjects engage. This position is the one advocated by proponents of a levels-of-processing approach to age differences in secondary memory, and it will be discussed in detail in the next section. Initially, however, we should report some evidence favoring this interpretation, evidence that comes from studies employing the externalized rehearsal procedure of Rundus and Atkinson (1970). Specifically, our interest

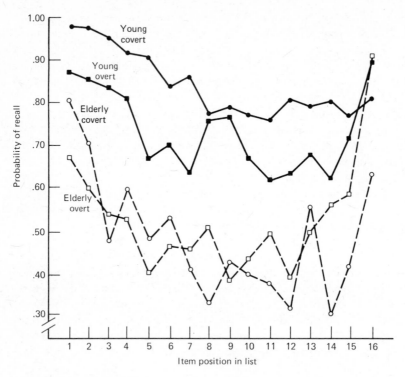

Figure 9.13. Age differences in recall as a function of the type of rehearsal activity (overt or covert). (Adapted from Sanders, Murphy, Schmitt, & Walsh, 1980, Figure 1.)

rests in the question: How does recall under the overt rehearsal condition compare with recall under the standard covert rehearsal condition (i.e., silent rehearsal of the kind usually employed in free recall research)?

This comparison was made by Kellas, McCauley, and McFarland (1975) with young-adult subjects. Recall without overt rehearsal was clearly superior to recall with overt rehearsal. Similar contrasts were made for both young and elderly subjects by Sanders et al. (1980). Their results are shown in Figure 9.13. In agreement with the results obtained earlier by Kellas et al. (1975), recall proficiency for young subjects deteriorated when overt rehearsal was demanded (see Figure 9.13). Note that recall with covert rehearsal exceeded recall with overt rehearsal at every position in the list except the last. By contrast, no systematic difference favoring covert rehearsal was found for elderly subjects. The implication is that overt rehearsal by young adults forces the rote repetition of items, thereby prohibiting the more efficacious kind of elaborative rehearsal engaged in by young adults when they are left on their own (as in the covert condition). On the other hand, elderly adults are unlikely to engage in elaborative rehearsal even when rehearsal is covert. Consequently, the restriction placed on rehearsal by making it overt makes little difference. However, there is evidence indicating that the failure of elderly people to use elaborative

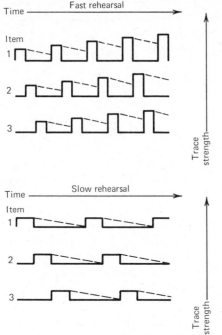

Figure 9.14. Postulated effects of rate of rehearsal on strength of memory traces. (Adapted from Salthouse, 1980a, Figure 2.2.)

rehearsal is largely a production deficiency that can be overcome with appropriate training (Schmitt, Murphy, & Sanders, 1981).

Finally, the concept of slower rehearsal activity by elderly subjects than by young subjects has led to an intriguing alternative explanation by Salthouse of age deficits in secondary memory:

> We postulated that the memory process that would most likely be affected by age-related speed loss was rate of rehearsal. A speculative model indicating the manner in which rate of rehearsal might affect memory performance is illustrated in Figure [9.14]. Assumptions implicit in the processes portrayed in Figure [9.14] are:
>
> 1. That rehearsal of items is continuous with both fast and slow rehearsal;
> 2. That item strength increases a fixed amount with each rehearsal and decays at a constant rate between rehearsals regardless of rehearsal speed; and
> 3. That the strength of an item trace accumulates if residual strength remains from the proceding rehearsal.
>
> As can be seen in the two panels of the figure, these assumptions lead to items rehearsed at a fast rate having a greater trace strength over the same period of time as items rehearsed at a slow pace. (1980a, p. 56)

What makes this hypothesis intriguing is that it shifts the reason for the age deficit in memory away from an age difference in the number of rehearsal responses per se to an age difference in the time separating successive rehearsal responses. The slowing down of rehearsal rate in late adulthood means a longer separation between consecutive responses. Consequently, more decay of the trace built by prior responses should occur for elderly subjects than for young subjects (see Figure 9.14). The core of this hypothesis, of course, is the concept of spontaneous decay of a memory trace over time, a concept that many memory psychologists find difficult to accept (see Kausler, 1974).

Secondary Memory: Retrieval and Recall Versus Recognition. Our emphasis thus far has been on an age difference in the encoding of information. More information about an item's inclusion in a list is presumed to be transmitted to the long-term store by young adults than by elderly adults. Thus, at the end of a study trial, more information about item content resides in storage for young adults than for elderly adults, thus accounting for the superior free-recall performance by young adults, particularly for nonrecency positions. Although encoding storage of information is a probable factor in producing age differences in such phenomena as the primacy effect, it is unlikely to be the only factor. Performance on such tasks as free recall depends on the proficiency of retrieving information from the store as well as the proficiency of getting information into the store. In principle, it is conceivable that a retrieval deficit is the major factor responsible for age deficits in free-recall performance and could even be the *only* factor underlying performance deficits.

The nature of retrieval in secondary-memory phenomena becomes apparent when recall of to-be-remembered items is compared with recognition of those items. Recall demands an active search of the long-term store's contents (Atkinson & Shiffrin, 1968). Once a trace is located, a decision must then be made as to whether or not the trace matches the content of a prior to-be-remembered item. Recognition presumably bypasses the necessity of searching the store. Test items are given, some of which correspond to previously studied items (i.e., they are old), whereas others are new in the sense of their exclusion from the study list. Recognition tests, therefore, offer the means of determining whether or not the age deficits manifested in recall are due to inefficient encoding processes or inefficient search processes. If age defects disappear when a recognition test replaces a recall test, then it is apparent that the search process is the only age-sensitive process (see Chapter 6). However, if age deficits remain even on recognition tests, then it is reasonable to conclude that less information is encoded and placed in storage by elderly adults than by young adults.

Of considerable interest then are age comparisons on recognition tests of memory. Some studies have reported either no adult-age differences in recognition test performance (Schonfield & Robertson, 1966) or only slight age differences (Craik, 1971; Gordon & Clark, 1974a). However, most studies have reported a modest decrement in recognition-memory proficiency with increasing age. Representative of these studies is one by Erber (1974). She administered a multiple-choice test to her young and elderly subjects in which each old item (a word) from a prior study list was combined with four new items (or distractors) and subjects had to select the old item from each combination.

Correct identifications of old items averaged 80.7% and 69.2% for young and elderly subjects respectively. Other investigators have employed a different testing format, but they have found essentially the same outcome as that reported by Erber. For example, Rankin and Kausler (1979) administered what is called a continuous recognition memory task to their subjects. Here subjects receive a lengthy list of items (words), some of which are repeated at later points in the sequence. As each item is exposed, subjects decide if it is old (i.e., repeated) or new (i.e., exposed for the first time). Young, middle-age, and elderly subjects averaged respectively a 93.9%, 80.8%, and 76.4% accuracy in identifying truly old items as old. Superior continuous recognition-memory scores for young-adult subjects relative to elderly subjects was also found by Erber (1978). Signal-detection methodology has been employed by still other investigators (Gordon & Clark, 1974b; Harkins, Chapman, & Eisdorfer, 1979; Wickelgren, 1975) as a means of evaluating age differences in recognition-memory scores. Again, superior scores (expressed as d' values) by young adults have been found. Superior recognition-memory scores for young adults have also been reported when list items are nonverbal in content. Included have been faces as items (Ferris, Crook, Clark, McCarthy, & Rae, 1980) and even recorded bird calls and tactual stimuli (Riege & Inman, 1981). Incidentally, superior recall scores by young adults relative to elderly adults have also been found when items other than words are to be remembered (e.g., location of digits in a matrix or grid; see Schear & Nebes, 1980).

The use of signal-detection methodology to evaluate the nature of adult-age differences in performance on recognition-memory tests is especially important. There is the possibility that greater cautiousness by elderly subjects than by young subjects is responsible for many of the lower accuracy scores found for elderly subjects. That is, elderly subjects may be reluctant to respond old to a test item unless they are absolutely certain of its oldness. A conservative response bias of this nature would serve to lower considerably the overall number of old items identified as being old. There would be another important consequence of this conservative bias as well, namely, a lower false alarm rate for elderly subjects than for more liberal young-adult subjects. That is, elderly subjects would be expected to respond old to new test items less often than would young subjects. Surprisingly, this is not the case. If anything, elderly subjects have been found in a number of studies (e.g., Ferris et al., 1980; Harkins et al., 1979; Rankin & Kausler, 1979) to have a higher false alarm rate than young-adult subjects.

These studies of age differences in recognition memory leave little room for doubt. Age deficits in secondary-memory proficiency do not disappear when a recognition test substitutes for a recall test. At least some of the overall decline in secondary-memory proficiency during late adulthood must be due to the less efficient encoding of item information by elderly adults than by young adults. At the same time, we cannot deny the fact that retrieval as a search process also enters into age deficits in secondary-memory proficiency. In those studies that have tested subjects for both recall and recognition-of-item content (e.g., Erber, 1974; Schonfield & Robertson, 1966; Shaps & Nilsson, 1980), the magnitude of the age difference favoring young adults is greater for a recall test than for a recognition test. Again, the critical difference between recall and recognition-of-item content rests in the inclusion of an active search process in recall but not in recognition. The diminished proficiency of the search process in late adulthood must, therefore, be considered a contributor to the overall age deficit in secondary-memory proficiency.

Secondary Memory; Another Form of Recognition Memory. Thus far we have considered recognition memory only for conditions in which single items are studied one item at a time. There is, however, another form of recognition memory that has important implications for the psychology of aging, namely, that of multiple-item recognition memory (or verbal discrimination as it is often called; Kausler, Pavur, & Yadrick, 1975). The procedure calls for exposing two or more items at the same time during a study trial. In each exposure, one of the items is arbitrarily designated correct by the investigator, whereas the other item(s) is designated incorrect. The distinction between correct and incorrect items is made by simply underlining the correct item of each combination of items. On a subsequent test trial, subjects attempt to identify which items had been previously designated correct when confronted by the item combinations in the absence of the distinctive markings.

What makes this procedure intriguing to experimental aging psychologists is the nature of the different roles played by correct and incorrect items. In effect, correct items may be viewed as conveying relevant information, whereas incorrect items covery irrelevant information. The most effective strategy for mastering a multiple-item recognition list is to focus attention on only correct items during each study trial. To the extent that attention is divided between correct and incorrect items, performance proficiency should deteriorate. From our discussion in Chapter 7, we know that elderly subjects are more readily distracted by irrelevant information than are young subjects. Moreover, the extent of the age difference in distractability increases as the amount of irrelevant information increases. Consequently, the magnitude of the age deficit in multiple-item recognition memory is expected to increase as the number of incorrect items combined with each correct item increases. This prediction was tested by Kausler and Kleim (1978). Their young and elderly subjects received study lists in which correct items were combined with either one or three incorrect items. Their results, expressed in terms of mean number of errors made in mastering the lists, are plotted in Figure 9.15. Note that an age difference favoring young subjects was clearly present in both conditions. However, as predicted by the expected age differential in susceptibility to distraction by irrelevant stimuli, the magnitude of the age difference increased as the number of distracting items increased. Elderly subjects were far less proficient when multiple distractors were present than when only one distractor was present. On the other hand, young subjects, if anything, increased in proficiency as the number of distractors increased. This seemingly paradoxical outcome has been found with young subjects by other investigators (e.g., Radtke, McHewitt, & Jacoby, 1970). Actually, the outcome is readily explained by the prevailing

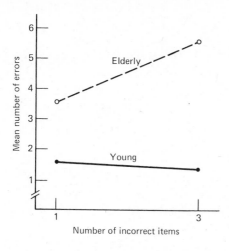

Figure 9.15. Age differences in multiple-item recognition memory as a function of number of incorrect items paired with each correct item. (Adapted from Kausler & Kleim, 1978, Table 1.)

theory of multiple-item recognition memory (Ekstrand, Wallace, & Underwood, 1966). The theory itself does not concern us here. What does concern us is the fact that we have uncovered yet another situation in which the susceptibility of elderly people to the interference produced by irrelevant stimuli reduces considerably their proficiency in performing the task at hand.

Secondary Memory: Output Interference. There is a remaining alternative route that may be taken in explaining age deficits in secondary-memory phenomena. Some years ago Tulving and Arbuckle (1963) postulated the existence of what they called *output interference* in the recall of long-term episodic-memory traces. Briefly, the outputting, or active recalling, of some items from the long-term store is expected to decrease the retrievability of the other items that remain in the store and await recall. Some evidence of greater proneness to output interference by elderly adults than by young adults was reported by Taub and Walker (1970). In one of their conditions, subjects had to respond with a redundant item on each list prior to recalling the items that were specific to a given list. In effect, responding with this prefix item may be expected to generate output interference for the recall of the list-specific items. Performance of their elderly subjects suffered more from this added requirement (relative to a control condition in which the redundant prefix was absent) than did their young subjects, which is in agreement with the hypothesis of an age change in proneness-to-output interference.

A more rigorous test of this hypothesis by Smith (1975a), however, failed to provide support. In his study, the to-be-remembered items were eight paired associates that were presented for a single-study trial. Tulving and Arbuckle (1963) had used the same materials and procedure in their earlier study with young adults. They argued that paired-associate learning may be viewed as an episodic-memory phenomenon. A trace of paired items may be transmitted to the long-term store, just as a trace of a single item may be transmitted. Returning to Smith's (1975a) study, after the single-study trial was over, stimulus

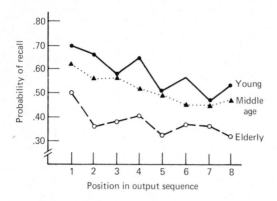

Figure 9.16. Age differences in output interference. (Adapted from Smith, 1975a, Figure 1.)

elements of the pairs were presented as cues for recalling their paired response elements. The order of these stimulus elements was systematically varied so that pairs that were first in the input sequence (i.e., during the study trial) were sometimes tested first in the output sequence, sometimes second, and so on, through the eighth output position. Similarly, pairs in the second input position were tested from the first through eighth output positions, and so on. Smith's results, showing recall probability as a function of position in the output sequence (as averaged over all eight input positions) are illustrated in Figure 9.16. Output interference was clearly present for young, middle-age, and elderly subjects. That is, for all three age groups, there was a progressive decline in recall as the number of prior items recalled (or outputted) increased. More important, however, there was no significant interaction between age and output position. Thus, output interference was no greater for elderly subjects than for younger subjects. It seems likely that the age differential in output interference reported by Taub and Walker (1970) was actually due to the confusion created by having to preface each recall sequence with the prefix item. That is, the adverse effect of this confusion was probably greater for elderly subjects than for young subjects.

Overall Evaluation of the Dual-Store Model. From the perspective of the dual-store model, what are the reasons for memory problems in late adulthood? Clearly, the results of many aging studies have indicated that the problems associated with the short-term memory component are slight. What problems there are appear to be due either to the failure of elderly people to perceive information appropriately *prior* to its entry into the short-term store or to the slower search rate of elderly people for the content of the short-term store. The first problem may be compensated in the real world by simply slowing down the rate at which to-be-remembered information is presented to elderly people, thus allowing more time for encoding the phonemic content of that information. Once that material has been encoded, there is no reason to suspect that it will be forgotten more rapidly by elderly people than by younger people. The deficit in the search operation is largely of academic interest only. Even with the slower rate of searching, the operation remains relatively fast to the point that little content is likely to be forgotten over the extra time taken by elderly people. This conclusion is warranted by the fact that recognition errors on the Sternberg (1966) task are only modestly greater for elderly subjects than for young subjects.

It is a different matter with the long-term memory component however. Moderate deficiencies of long-term memory phenomena for elderly subjects have been reported in numerous studies. Undoubtedly, these deficiencies reflect those found in the real world. Our review has implicated both encoding processes and retrieval processes in this overall age-related decline in the proficiency of long-term memory. It is here that the shortcomings of the dual-store model become apparent. Both encoding and retrieval processes are treated rather superficially by proponents of the model. Little effort is made to distinguish between quantitive and qualitative changes in processes. The possibility that age deficits in episodic memory may be due to qualitative changes that may be modified by appropriate training is largely ignored. It is with such qualitative changes that the levels of processing model has been most useful.

Adult Age Differences in Episodic Memory: Levels-of-Processing Model

The basic characteristics of the levels-of-processing model were described in Chapter 6. Briefly, in this model, the emphasis shifts from memory stores to encoding processes. Traces of items differ in their recallability not because they reside in separate short-term and long-term stores, but rather because the items themselves differ in the nature of the encodings they receive. Distinctions between shallow and deep processing and maintenance and elaborative rehearsal replace the distinctions between primary and secondary memory indigenous to the dual-store model. In this section, we will examine the basic procedures used in testing hypotheses derived from the levels-of processing model, and we will review the studies that used these procedures to evaluate age differences in processing activities.

Orienting Tasks and Variation in Depth of Processing. For some years, researchers (e.g., Saltzman, 1953) have known that incidental memory-of-item content need not be below the level of intentional memory of that same content. The critical factor is not the presence or absence of intent to commit to memory, but rather the nature of the processing of information at the time it is being perceived. A widely cited study by Hyde and Jenkins (1969) provided a convincing demonstration of how processing activities influence the memorability of items. Three groups of young-adult subjects, each performing under an incidental memory condition (i.e., the subjects were not informed in advance that they would eventually be tested for memory of item content), differed with respect to the orienting task they performed during exposure to each item (a word) of a 24-item list. An orienting task is an activity a subject performs to assure attention is directed at each list item. The first orienting task required

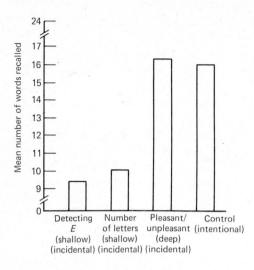

Figure 9.17. Results obtained by Hyde and Jenkins for the recall of items as a function of the depth of processing they received. (Adapted from Hyde & Jenkins, 1969, Table 1.)

subjects to evaluate each item in terms of the pleasant or unpleasant feeling that item aroused. The second task required a decision for each item as to whether or not it contained the letter E, whereas the third task required an estimate of the number of letters contained in each item. In addition, there was another group of subjects performing under a control condition, that is, with intent to commit the list items to memory (and without an orienting task to perform). The mean number of items recalled in each condition is shown in Figure 9.17. Note that recall was as high with the first orienting task (plea-sant/unpleasant decisions) as it was with intentional memory. On the other hand, recall with the other two orienting tasks was well below the level found with intentional memory.

Why should incidental memory following pleasant/unpleasant evaluations be equivalent to intentional memory? According to the levels-of-processing model, a decision about a word's emotional connotation requires an examina-tion of that word's meaning as it is stored in generic memory. To make this examination, subjects must first encode the item per se deeply, that is, in terms of its meaning, This is the kind of encoding operation postulated by the model to lead to a relatively permanant memory trace, quite independently of any intent to memorize that item. Consequently, a trace of that operation is likely to be available for recall after the orienting task is completed. Most important, this is the same kind of deep processing engaged in by young adults when they study a list of words with the intent to recall those words. Thus, there should be little difference between incidental and intentional memory when the orienting task guiding incidental memory forces the deep processing of incoming items. The processing demand is very different, however, for the other two orienting tasks employed by Hyde and Jenkins (1969). Only shallow processing is needed to determine either the presence/absence of a specific letter or the number of letters in a word. The result in each case is a more fragile memory trace and, therefore, lower recall scores than expected with either intentional memory or incidental memory following deep processing.

The Hyde and Jenkins procedure has considerable relevance for testing alternative hypotheses about age deficits in episodic-memory phenomena. The alternatives closely approximate the meditational-deficit-versus-production-deficit hypothesis encountered earlier in our analysis of age differences in learning. On the one hand, elderly adults may be viewed as being less proficient than young adults in memory because the former have suffered a true decrement in the ability to engage in deep processing. On the other hand, elderly adults may simply be less likely than young adults to initiate deep processing spontaneously. In either case, recall of items under an intentional memory condition is expected to favor young adults. The critical condition is for incidental memory with an orienting task that forces deep processing. If the age difference in recall disappears, then it is obvious that the deficit present under intentional memory is only a production deficit. That is, once deep processing is prodded by an appropriate orienting task, episodic memory would appear to be as proficient for elderly adults as it is for young adults. Consequently, the age deficit apparent in intentional memory would appear to be due simply to the failure of elderly people to engage spontaneously in deep processing.

These alternative hypothesis were tested initially in an important study by Eysenck (1974) that followed closely the procedural guidelines set by Hyde and Jenkins (1969). There were four incidental memory groups, two receiving shallow-processing orienting tasks and two receiving deep-processing orienting tasks. One shallow task required subjects to count the number of letters in each item (word), whereas the other required them to name a rhyming word for each item. One deep task required subjects to form an image of each item and then rate the vividness of each image, whereas the other required them to name a modifying adjective for each item. In addition, an intentional memory condition was included for both young and elderly subjects. The results found for total number of items recalled from the 27-item list are shown in Figure 9.18. Shallow processing clearly led to inferior performance relative to both intentional memory and incidental memory by means of deep processing at both age levels. Moreover, recall following shallow processing did not differ between the two age levels. Thus, there appears to be no change with aging in the ability to conduct shallow processing. Most important, the deep-processing tasks did not eliminate the age deficit found with intentional memory (see Figure 9.18), although the magnitude of the age deficit was reduced somewhat. The same pattern has since been found in a number of other studies with familiar words as items (Erber, Herman, & Botwinick, 1980; Lauer, 1976; Mason, 1979; Perlmutter, 1979; Smith, 1979a; S. White, as reported in Craik, 1977). That is, no age difference was found with shallow processing, whereas a pronounced age deficit was found both with intentional memory and with deep-processing incidental memory. The one exception occurred in a study by Barrett and Wright (1981). They employed a rather unique list of words. The words were old-fashioned ones, such as *pompadour, doily,* and *Victrola,* which are likely to be

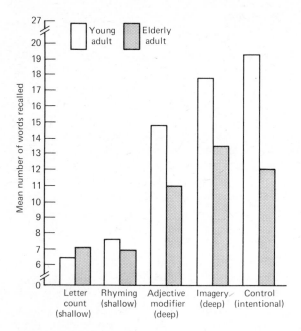

Figure 9.18. Age differences in recall of items as a function of depth of processing. (Adapted from Eysenck, 1974, Table 1.)

more familiar to elderly people than to young adults. In fact, many of the words are probably equivalent to nonsense syllables to contemporary young adults. Not surprisingly, a reverse age differences was found. That is, incidental recall following a deep-processing orienting task was greater for the elderly subjects than for the young subjects. In the other studies on age differences in depth of processing, the words were common ones certain to be familiar to adult subject of all ages and were, therefore, unlikely to favor recall by any specific age group.

The implication is that a true decrement in processing proficiency does occur by late adulthood. Unresolved, however, is the question of the locus of the age deficit. In their formulation of the levels-of-processing model, Craik and Lockhart (1972) stressed the distinction between both shallow and deep processing and maintenence and elaborative rehearsal. One posssibility for the age deficit found under intentional memory and incidental memory with deep-processing orienting tasks is that elderly adults cease engaging in deep processing as it is defined by the semantic encoding of items. This possibility seems highly unlikely, however. One line of evidence indicating that elderly adults do indeed encode items semantically is provided by studies demonstrating release from proactive inhibition by elderly subjects. Release occurs when items for one taxonomic category are followed by items from another taxonomic category. It would not be possible unless semantic information (i.e., category membership) is encoded by elderly subjects at the time the relevant items are studied. A second line of evidence comes from experimental aging studies employing the *false-recognition procedure* (Rankin & Kausler, 1979; Smith, 1975c). This is a modification of a recognition test in which two classes of new test items (or distractors) are employed by the investigator. One class consists of words that are unrelated to prior study-list words (as in the kinds of recognition-memory studies we discussed earlier). The other class consists of words that are related through synonymity to prior study-list words (e.g., *late* as a study-list item, *tardy* as a test-list item). Of interest is the difference in false alarm rates between these two classes of new items. A higher false alarm rate for synonyms that for unrelated words, a *false-recognition* effect, reveals that subjects have been misled by the commonality in meaning between a study-list item and a test-list that is semantically related to that study-list item. Both Rankin and Kausler (1979) and Smith (1975c) found a clear false-recognition effect for their elderly subjects. This effect would be possible only if elderly subjects do encode both study-list items and test-list items semantically.

The second possibility is a more realistic one. It argues that elderly adults engage in less elaborative rehearsal, that is, rehearsal defined in terms of generating images of study-list items and generating associations to those items, than do younger adults. Elaborative rehearsal is expected to yield especially durable memory traces. With fewer elaborated memory traces, elderly subjects would be expected to have lower recall scores than younger subjects. This explanation, of course, is in close harmony with the explanation offered earlier for many of the verbal-learning deficits manifested by older subjects.

Elaborative rehearsal, whether it occurs in a learning or a memory context, is a highly effortful cognitive process. Consequently, it is believed to place a considerable demand on the limited capacity of the central processor. During late adulthood, this capacity is likely to decrease somewhat, thus decreasing the capability of older individuals to rehearse elaboratively (Craik & Simon, 1980; Simon, 1979). On the other hand, a decrease in processing capacity is unlikely to affect less demanding, or effortful, activities, such as shallow processing and maintenence rehearsal.

Recall Versus Recognition: Noncued Versus Cued Recall. Our analysis thus far has ignored an important issue, namely, the issue we faced earlier in distinguishing between encoding deficits and retrieval deficits in secondary-memory phenomena. What roles does a retrieval deficit play in determining the age deficits observed for the recall of elaboratively encoded items? In principle, these deficits could result from an elderly subject's inefficient search of the episodic store rather than from that subject's diminished encoding proficiency. One way of determining the extent to which retrieval as a search process is responsible for the age deficits found with the Hyde and Jenkins (1969) procedure with a deep orienting task is to use the by now familiar strategy of replacing a recall test with a recognition test. If elderly adults are indeed deficient in deep, elaborative rehearsal and encoding, then the deficiency should continue to be observed on a recognition test. This strategy has now been used in a number of studies in which depth of processing was varied by means of an orienting task. Some of these studies (Erber et al., 1980; Perlmutter, 1979; S. White, as cited in Craik, 1977) found little, if any, any age difference on a recognition test that followed a deep-processing orienting task, whereas other studies (Mason, 1979; Smith & Winograd, 1978) found a pronounced age difference favoring young adults.

Incidentally, the study by Smith and Winograd (1978) is of sufficient interest to merit additional comment. It demonstrated that the age deficit found for the deep processing of words as study-list items applies equally to the deep processing of pictures of faces. Deep processing during incidental memory was stimulated by having subjects decide for each study-list face if it appeared friendly, whereas shallow processing was stimulated by having subjects decide if each face had a big nose. Surprisingly, an age difference favoring young adults in the hit rate for recognizing old faces as old was found with shallow processing as well as with words (again, the age difference with words as items is found for deep processing but not for shallow processing). Smith and Winograd's results have important implications for a number of real-world phenomena (see Winograd & Simon, 1980 and Yarmey & Kent, in press, for further discussion). One of these implications pertains to possible age differences in the reliability of eyewitness testimony. Witnessing a criminal commit his crime often occurs under incidental-memory conditions and often with shallow processing of the events transpiring. The ability of an eyewitness to recognize the face of the criminal depends, of course, on how well that face had been processed and encoded at the time of the crime. The diminished proficiency of elderly people in encoding faces for later recognition, regardless of the level of processing involved, suggests that they may be even less reliable eyewitnesses than young adults (who themselves are far from being infallible eyewitnesses; see Baddeley, 1979).

The conflicting results obtained for age differences on recognition tests make it imperative to consider alternative ways of eliminating, or greatly reducing, the involvement of the search process in studies attempting to identify the reason for age differences in episodic-memory proficiency. A commonly used alternative in basic-memory research is to provide subjects with a retrieval cue, or aid, for each study-list item at the time that memory proficiency is being assessed (Tulving & Pearlsone, 1966). Recall proficiency may then be compared with these cues (i.e., *cued recall*) and without these cues (i.e., *noncued recall*). In noncued recall, failure to recall items could result from either (or both): (1) inadequate encoding during a study trial, with no registration of traces in the episodic store or (2) inadequate searching during a test trial of those traces that were encoded and registered in the store. In cued recall, retrieval cues presumably gain access to stored traces, just as old items do on a recognition test. Consequently, recall failure in this condition is the result of an encoding deficit. If an age deficit manifested in noncued recall persists in cued recall, then encoding per se is identified as an age-sensitive process. However, if the deficit is eliminated in cued recall, then encoding appears to be insensitive to an age change. The underlying logic is obviously much like that entering into comparisons between recognition tests and noncued recall tests. Experimental aging studies that compare age differences found with cued and noncued recall have employed several different kinds of retrieval cues, and they have involved both incidental memory and intentional memory.

One form of retrieval cue consists of synonyms for previously studied items. For example, with *late* as a study-list item, *tardy* may be the retrieval cue given as an aid to recall the prior item. In a study involving incidental memory and a deep-orienting task, Simon (1979) found that these cues enhanced the recall scores of young adults relative to a noncued recall condition, but they did not enhance the scores of elderly adults. Consequently, the performance deficit found for elderly subjects in noncued recall was even greater in cued recall. Retrieval cues, of course, cannot aid recall unless information has been adequately encoded and placed in storage in the first place. Simon's results clearly support the notion that a decrement in encoding proficiency, as mediated by elaborative rehearsal, underlies many of the memory problems experienced in late adulthood.

Somewhat different outcomes were reported by Drachman and Leavitt (1972) and Smith (1977) with quite different conditions than those found in Simon's (1979) study. Intentional memory rather than incidental memory provided the format for both studies. In Drachman and Leavitt's study, a 35-item free-recall list was presented for three study-test trials, with cued recall being compared with noncued recall on each test trial. The retrieval aids in the cued-recall condition consisted of the first letter of each study-list item (e.g., l as the cue for recalling *late*). The results are summarized in the top panel of Figure 9.19. Note that, in contrast to the outcome of Simon's (1979) study, retrieval cues enhanced recall scores for elderly subjects as well as for young subjects. However, the extent of the age difference favoring young subjects was as great with cued recall as with noncued recall.

In Smith's study, a 20-item list was presented for a single study-test trial. For each item, the retrieval aid in the cued-recall condition consisted of the taxonomic category, or superordinate, subsuming each study-list item. For example, with *robin* as a study-list item, the retrieval cue was, *a bird*. The results are summarized in the bottom panel of Figure 9.19. Note that this time retrieval cues aided the recall of older subjects more than they aided the recall of young subjects. Nevertheless, a pronounced age difference favoring young subjects persisted in cued recall as well as in noncued recall. The continuation of the age deficit in cued recall found in both studies implies that there is indeed an encoding deficit in late adulthood. In addition, Smith's study implies that the retrieval process is also age sensitive. The implication follows from the fact that the age deficit in recall was less pronounced with cued recall (retrieval eliminated or reduced) than with noncued recall.

This picture is muddled, however, by still other evidence. Craik and Masani (1969) found that the age deficit in recall is largely eliminated under a condition that approximated that of cued recall. They concluded that a retrieval deficit accounts for much of the age difference commonly reported on free-recall tasks. That is, encoding per se is largely insensitive to an age change. Adding to the confusion is the outcome found in another part of Smith's study.

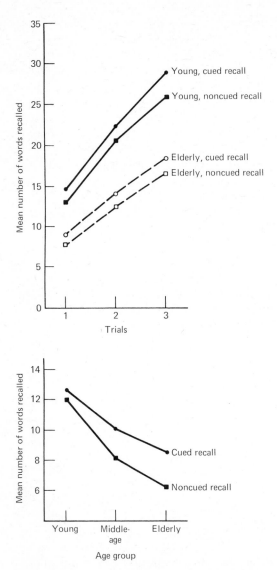

Figure 9.19. Top panel: Age differences for cued versus noncued recall in which first letters of items served as retrieval cues. (Adapted from Drachman & Leavitt, 1972, Figure 2.) Bottom panel: Age differences for cued versus noncued recall in which category names served as retrieval cues. (Adapted from Smith, 1977, Figure 1.)

Subjects in a modified condition were given the same list of items received by other subjects. This time, however, they were informed in advance of the nature of the items. That is, they were told that one item would be an instance of *a bird,* another item would be an instance of a *a fruit,* and so on. In addition, the category names served as retrieval cues during the test trial. The advance information had little effect on recall scores for young adults relative to the previously described cued-recall condition (i.e., the one omitting the advance information), but it did lead to vastly improved scores for both middle-age and elderly subjects. Apparently, older subjects were prodded into the use of elaborative rehearsal when they were given an appropriate context for using it (i.e., categorical information about each item). This outcome supports the notion that older subjects experience a production deficit in the use of elaborative rehearsal and not necessarily a true deficit in the ability to engage in such rehearsal activity. Because young subjects engage spontaneously in elaborative rehearsal, they benefit little from the extra prodding provided by advance categorical information.

The conflicting results obtained in the various studies in which recognition and cued recall have been compared with noncued recall make interpretation extremely difficult. There are about as many studies indicating an age deficit in encoding-storage proficiency at the level of elaborative rehearsal as there are studies indicating the absence of an age deficit. Our best guess is that there is a modest age deficit in encoding proficiency, and the degree of that deficit has been overestimated in a number of studies. Why the overestimation? Our best guess, here, is that any task involving the recall of a lengthy list of items is viewed suspiciously by many elderly subjects as being trivial and of dubious ecological relevance. We will have more to say about this a bit later.

Primary Memory and the Recency Effect Reconsidered. One of the hallmarks of the levels of processing approach to episodic-memory phenomena is its elimination of the distinction between primary and secondary memory. Phenomena attributable to the primary- (short term) memory system by dual-store theorists must be explained solely by means of processes consonant with the concepts of levels of processing. Illustrative of these phenomena is the recency effect so clearly manifested in free recall by both young and elderly subjects. To dual-store theorists, the recency effect is the product of the direct recall of item information from the short-term store, and an age deficit in the effect results from a diminished capacity of this store in late adulthood. How satisfactory is this account? Not very, according to Craik and Lockhart (1972) in their highly influential introduction of the levels-of-processing model.

The reason for their concern begins with a consideration of the procedure typically used in studies dealing with the recency effect (e.g., Glanzer & Cunitz, 1966; Raymond, 1971). The procedure calls for giving subjects many free-recall lists, often as many as 14 or 15, each with a single study-test trial. The probabilities of recalling items in end positions of these lists are then determined by pooling together all of the lists and finding the average probability at each list position. What happens when each list is analyzed separately? In principle, each list, including the first one received, should yield a recency effect of the approximate magnitude found when all of the lists are pooled together. From the perspective of the dual-store model, nothing changes over the successive lists. For each list, the recency effect reflects direct recall from the limited-capacity short-term store. Because the capacity of that store does not change from list to list, the magnitude of the recency effect should not change either.

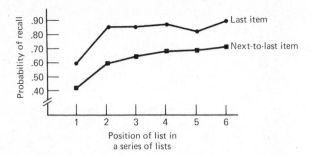

Figure 9.20. Probability of recalling end items of a free-recall list as a function of position in a series of lists. (Adapted from Keppel & Mallory, 1969, Figure 2.)

The invariance of the recency effect over lists is not the case, however, as demonstrated initially by Keppel and Mallory (1969). They analyzed separately each of the six successive free-recall lists their subjects received, determining for each list the probability of recalling the last few items in that list. Their results for the last and the next-to-last item are charted in Figure 9.20. Note that the probability of recall was far from being constant over lists. It was moderate for the last item of the first list, but it increased dramatically for the last item of the second list (and remained high for the last item of each remaining list). In addition, probability of recall for the next-to-last item increased regularly from the first through the sixth list. Comparable results with young-adult subjects have since been reported by other investigators (e.g., Maskarinec & Brown, 1974).

To account for these changes in the magnitude of the recency effect, proponents of the levels of processing model argue that subjects change the nature of their rehearsal strategy during the course of receiving successive free-recall lists (e.g., Watkins & Watkins, 1974). For the first few lists, subjects attempt to rehearse each item elaboratively, including end items. However, with later lists, they switch to maintenance rehearsal for end items while continuing to use elaborative rehearsal for earlier list items. Maintenance rehearsal yields shallow processing and, therefore, results in fragile memory traces of a sensory-content format. To make these fragile traces available for immediate recall, the switch in rehearsal strategy is accompanied by a switch in retrieval, or outputting, strategy (Maskarinec & Brown, 1974). For the first few lists, early items tend to be retrieved and recalled before end items. For later lists, end items assume a higher priority in the order with which items are retrieved and recalled. That is, the end items are recalled immediately after the study trial terminates and, therefore, while their fragile traces are still available for recall. The outcome is the eventual emergence of a pronounced recency effect.

A recent study by Wright (in press) revealed that this switch in strategy is as characteristic of elderly subjects as it is of young-adult subjects. Her young and elderly subjects received 10 consecutive free-recall lists. The order of recalling items by subjects of both age levels is illustrated in the top panel of Figure 9.21. Positive scores (maximum value = +1) indicate recall of items early in an output sequence; negative scores (maximum value $= -1$) indicate recall of items late in an output sequence. For convenience, mean-order scores are plotted for the first two lists averaged together, the fifth and sixth lists averaged together, and the last two lists averaged together. Both age groups clearly reversed their outputting strategy as they progressed from the initial lists to the final lists. For the initial lists, primacy items were recalled early in the output sequence, that is, prior to recency items. For the final lists, recency items were recalled early in the sequence, whereas primacy items were among the last ones to be outputted. Most important, the interaction between age and lists fell far short of statistical significance. Thus, no age change was apparent in the overall shift in the order of outputting items. The consequence of this change in output strategy is illustrated in the bottom panel of Figure 9.21. For both age groups, the magnitude of the recency effect *increased* progressively from initial to final lists. This outcome is in complete agreement with the results obtained by Keppel and Mallory (1969), which are graphed in Figure 9.20. At the same time, it may be seen from Figure 9.21 that the magnitude of the primacy effect *decreased* progressively from initial to final lists. This outcome is also in agreement with the results obtained by Keppel and Mallory. Holding back on the

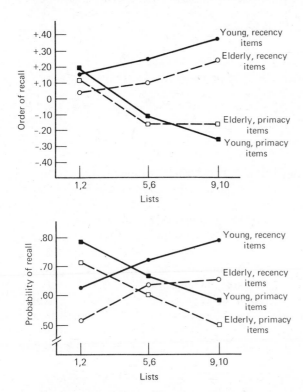

Figure 9.21. Top panel: Age differences in the order of recalling primacy and recency items as a function of position in a series of lists. Bottom panel: Age differences in probability of recalling primacy and recency items as a function of position in a series of lists. (Adapted from data in Wright, in press.)

outputting of primacy items until recency items have been recalled means that the primacy items are subjected to increasing amounts of output interference across lists, thus accounting for the decreasing probabilities of recalling these early list items from the initial to the final lists.

The results obtained by Wright (in press) suggest strongly that the age deficit in the magnitude of the overall recency effect found when lists are pooled together, as in Arenberg's (1976) study (see Figure 9.5), are attributable to some factor other than different outputting strategies by young and elderly subjects. Most likely, the deficit is simply the product of more maintenance-rehearsal responses of end items by young subjects than by elderly subjects. There is evidence in basic-memory research to indicate that increments in the number of rote rehearsal responses do yield more durable memory traces and, therefore, higher probabilities of recall (e.g., Nelson, 1977).

Overall Evaluation. The levels-of-processing model offers a fresh and attractive perspective for the understanding of age changes in episodic-memory phenomena. The intent of the model is to provide a broad conceptualization of the human memory system, one that has implications for age changes in a wide range of everyday memory experiences. Not surprisingly, many experimental aging psychologists have been attracted to the model as their framework for examining age changes in episodic memory. In all fairness, however, we must note that several basic principles of the model have been severely criticized by basic-memory researchers in recent years (e.g., Baddeley, 1978; Morris, Bransford, & Franks, 1977; Nelson, 1977). Foremost among the principles under attack is that of the fragility of memory traces composed of sensory attributes (i.e., the products of shallow processing). A number of studies over the past five or so years have indicated that sensory-based memory traces can be robust and, therefore, can be available for retrieval long after a study phase is completed. Some of the relevant evidence on this point will be presented in our later discussion of automatic encoding processes. These various criticisms of the model have led to a number of refinements in its components. For example, much of the current thinking deals with structural differences between the traces produced by shallow and deep processing rather than temporal, or durability, differences (e.g., Hunt & Elliott, 1980). Briefly, sensory-based traces are usually less distinctive than are semantic-based traces. Phonemically encoded traces are bound to share many attributes with each other, given the limited number of phonemes there are in a spoken language. By contrast, semantically encoded traces are far less restricted in their content, given the many meanings that are communicated by words. Thus, semantically encoded traces have a decided advantage in retrievability over sensorily encoded traces. These refinements in the levels-of-processing model have not really affected aging research to date, and they will, therefore, not be pursued further.

Of additional concern is the ecological validity of levels-of-processing research for understanding the everyday memory problems characteristic of late adulthood. Again, the model itself is intended to apply to a wide range of human memory phenomena. Yet, tests of the model have been nearly exclusively limited to memory phenomena indigenous to the multiple-item free-recall task. (Of course, tests of the dual-store model have also focused largely on free-recall phenomena.) How representative of real-world episodic-memory experiences, especially those of older people, are the episodes generated by encounters with free-recall lists? Most likely, not very. The closest real-world counterpart to a free-recall list would seem to be a shopping list you carry in your head to the supermarket (age deficits have been found when a shopping list provides the material for a laboratory free recall task; e.g., McCarthy, Ferris, Clark, & Crook, 1981). Even then, the list is unlikely to exceed six or seven items. Moreover, most shoppers prefer to write down the items they plan to purchase rather than trust their memory systems. The verisimilitude of the free-recall task as a paradigm for studying everyday episodic memory is challenged even more when the task is expanded to include list after list given to the same subjects. Rarely in the everday world do we encounter such concentrated series of to-be-remembered events. Instead, the new items, or episodes, we need to commit to memory are distributed over time—an appointment at one time, a new face at another time, a funny joke at still another time, and so on. Of course, it may be argued, and it usually is by the experts, that the processes studied in free recall are highly general ones. The task itself simply provides a convenient means of capturing these processes and studying them carefully under tightly controlled conditions.

To understand age changes in these processes is, therefore, to understand age changes in most everyday memory activities. Perhaps. The present author is far less confident about the ecological relevance of free-recall research to the real world than he is about the ecological relevance of most of the other laboratory tasks we described in earlier chapters, such as those used in the study of motor-skill learning and verbal learning.

Experimental aging research badly needs innovative laboratory tasks that simulate more closely everyday episodic-memory activities. The free-recall task attempts to simulate memory of external events. However, many of our everyday memory problems involve events that are self-generated rather than extrinsically generated (Linton, 1975). For example, while working in his office, the present author often instructs himself to take home a particular journal that evening, and then discovers that he forgot to do so. Such memory mishaps probably result from the failure to engage in elaborative rehearsal at the time of self-instruction, which is in agreement with the basic principles of the levels-of-processing model (and, therefore, supporting the generalizability of research with the free-recall task). Nevertheless, it would be of great value to the psychology of aging to test the validity of this generalizability in a task context that more closely approximates everyday self-generated memory activities.

Adult-Age Differences in Episodic Memory: Organizational Processes

Thus far we have considered episodic-memory traces that are independent of one another. A trace is a transformation of a discrete item into a memorial representation of that item. The transformation is in terms of information, whether it be sensory or semantic in format, about the item that is stored in generic memory. This information is encoded and transmitted as a single-memory trace to the episodic store. Memory traces need not involve just single items, however. A memory trace for one item may be related to the memory trace of another item or to the traces of several other items. That is, two or more discrete items may be organized into a complex memory trace that preserves some inherent relatedness among those items (Mandler, 1967, 1979). The existence of organizational processes has attracted considerable interest in experimental aging research. In this section, we will review the contributions that have been made to our understanding of age changes in two kinds of organization, categorical and subjective.

Categorical Organization. Consider a free-recall list containing the 20 items shown in Table 9.1. The items are grouped in five sets, each containing four items. Within a set, the items are all instances of the same taxonomic category. The five categories represented in the list are also identified in Table 9.1. The items/instances are scattered randomly through the list during a study trial, whereas the category names themselves are omitted from the list. Following the study trial, subjects are free to recall the items in any order they wish. Beginning with a famous study by Bousfield (1953), many studies (see Kausler, 1974, for a review) have observed an intriguing phenomenon in the output sequences of young-adult subjects for this kind of list. The phenomenon is that of *cate-*

Table 9.1 Example of the Kind of Material Used to Test the Presence of Categorical Organization

Category	Items/Instances	Order of Items in Study Trial
A bird	Robin	Chair
	Sparrow	Robin
	Cardinal	Apple
	Canary	Sofa
A fruit	Apple	Canary
	Plum	Horse
	Pear	Copper
	Banana	Lamp
An article of	Chair	Lion
furniture	Sofa	Sparrow
	Desk	Banana
	Lamp	Gold
A metal	Iron	Plum
	Tin	Dog
	Gold	Desk
	Copper	Iron
A four-footed	Dog	Bear
animal	Horse	Tin
	Lion	Cardinal
	Bear	Pear

gorical clustering—items from the same taxonomic category tend to be recalled consecutively despite their separation during the study trial.

The implication of these studies is that information stored in episodic memory emulates the structure of its storage in generic memory. That structure, at least to many memory theorists, is hierarchical, as we discovered in Chapter 6, with superordinates subsuming subordinates. Episodic-memory traces may be similarly organized (Tulving & Pearlstone, 1966). Given multiple instances of the same category, subjects construct episodic structures in which the category name is the superordinate, or higher order unit, with the list instances forming subordinate units. The resulting episodic traces extant at the end of the input series are hypothesized to be much like those shown in Figure 9.22. At output, retrieval processes take over. According to Tulving (1968), retrieval of organized-memory traces is a two-stage process. The first stage consists of gaining access to the higher order units (i.e., category names). Once a higher order unit is retrieved, the subordinate units (i.e., items/instances) stored with it are then searched and recalled. The net effect is the successive recall of related items (i.e., clustering), as illustrated in Figure 9.22. Categorical organization does appear to enhance recall, at least for young-adult subjects. That is, recall scores tend to be higher for a list of categorically related items than for a list of unrelated items (e.g., Puff, 1970).

Performance proficiency on a categorized list is multiply determined. It is contingent on the ability to encode information in a structured format (i.e., as illustrated in Figure 9.22), the ability to retrieve higher order units from each structure (i.e., category names), and the ability to retrieve the specific-item traces stored with each higher order unit. Any one of these component processes may be age sensitive. Tests of the age sensitivity of these various processes involve comparisons between age groups on a categorizable list under

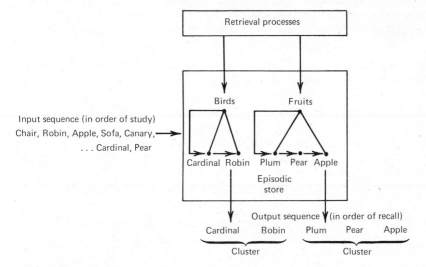

Figure 9.22. Schematic representation of organization for a list of items that are instances of various taxonomic categories.

both noncued- and cued-recall conditions. The reason for the use of both non-cued- and cued-recall conditions should be apparent by now. The contrast in recall scores between the two conditions offers a means of distinguishing, hopefully, age-sensitive encoding-storage processes from age-sensitive retrieval processes.

Before reviewing the relevant studies that have used this procedure, we should point out the existence of a potentially confounding methodological factor. The problem rests in the comparability of categorical instances for adults of different ages. For example, are elderly subjects as likely to view *canary* as an instance of *a bird* as are young-adult subjects? If not, then age differences in performance on a categorized list could be due to this factor rather than to age differences in either encoding or retrieval processes. The problem is much like the one encountered earlier when we discussed age comparisons in learning paired items that differed in preexperimental associative strength. Fortunately, the problem is not a serious one (nor was the earlier one). This may be seen in the responses given when young and elderly subjects are asked to name instances of various categories (e.g., name a bird). The responses of elderly subjects (Howard, 1980) are much like those of young adults (Battig & Montague, 1969).

In the first study to evaluate age differences in performance on a categorical list, Laurence (1967) compared noncued recall with cued recall in which the category names were available during the test trial that followed a single-study trial. Young adults were clearly superior to elderly adults on the noncued-recall test. However, the age difference all but disappeared on the cued-recall test. The resulting interaction effect between age and type of test suggests that the encoding of categorical information is age insensitive, whereas gaining later access to the higher order units is age sensitive. Category names as retrieval cues presumably lead to stored information that is otherwise inaccessible through a direct search of the store.

A different outcome was obtained in a more thorough study by Hultsch (1975). His study list contained 40 items, 4 instances from each of 10 taxonomic categories. The proportion of words recalled from this list by three age groups under both noncued- and cued-recall conditions are plotted in the top panel of Figure 9.23. It can be seen that, contrary to Laurence's (1967) results, recall by young subjects exceeded that of older subjects with cued recall as well as with noncued recall. Conceivably, the older subjects in this study encoded and, therefore, stored less higher order categorical information than the young subjects. As a result, retrieval cues failed to eliminate age differences in recall scores. However, the improbability of this account of the age deficit manifested in cued free recall was revealed by two additional analyses conducted by Hultsch.

The first analysis compared his age groups on the proportion of the 10 categories retrieved during recall. A category was considered to be retrieved in both the noncued- and the cued-recall condition if at least one item/instance of that category was recalled. Thus, if *robin* was recalled by a subject, then it was assumed that the subject had gained access to a successfully encoded and

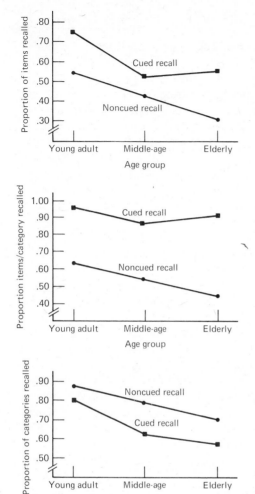

Figure 9.23. Age differences in total items recalled (top panel), category names recalled (middle panel), and instances per category recalled (bottom panel). (Adapted from Hultsch, 1975, Tables 1, 2, 3.)

stored higher order unit, namely that of *a bird*. The proportions of such higher order units retrieved by the three age groups are plotted in the middle panel of Figure 9.23. An interaction is apparent—age differences were found for noncued recall but *not* for cued recall. The overall age deficit in encoding and storage does not have its locus in the encoding and storage of the higher order units. If it were, then cued recall should be as ineffective as noncued recall for older subjects. Again, if information has not been encoded and stored successfully, then no amount of retrieval aid can recover it. However, older subjects do appear to have greater difficulty than young subjects in locating these higher order units in storage, a difficulty that is eliminated when category names per se serve as retrieval cues.

The second analysis examined the proportion of items/instances recalled from each category. If a subject recalled two names of birds that had been in the study list, then the subject's score for that category would be .50 (i.e., two out of four instances). Mean scores for this measure (averaged over all 10 categories) are plotted in the bottom panel of Figure 9.23. It may be seen that age differences, favoring young subjects, existed for both noncued- and cued-recall conditions. One interpretation of this outcome is that the encoding of specific instances declines in proficiency with increasing age, in contrast to the encoding of higher order information which, as noted earlier, appears to be age insensitive. There is an alternative interpretation, however, one suggested by the fact that more instances per category were retrieved at all age levels with noncued recall than with cued recall (see the bottom panel of Figure 9.23). Basic memory researchers (e.g., Rundus, 1973) have identified a form of output interference that occurs when category names serve as retrieval cues. The nature of this interference will not concern us, however, in that it does not seem to be any greater for elderly subjects than for young-adult subjects (Hultsch & Craig, 1976). Our best conclusion is that it is indeed the inefficient encoding and ensuing storage of specific items/instances that accounts for the diminished performance scores of elderly subjects on categorizable lists.

Relationships among items may involve attributes other than common categorical membership. For example, *chair* as a to-be-remembered item may be related to *share* as another to-be-remembered item because of the fact that the two items rhyme. Research with young-adult subjects has revealed that rhyming words tend to cluster together during recall trials, even though the words are widely separated during study trials (see Kausler, 1974). Organizational processes again seem to account for the emergence of this form of clustering. Mueller, Rankin, and Carlomusto (1979) demonstrated that elderly subjects display both less total-item recall and less clustering for rhyming words than do young subjects. Moreover, the age deficit in number of items recalled occurred for both noncued- and cued-recall conditions, which is in general agreement with Hultsch's (1975) results obtained with categorically related items.

Another form of clustering commonly found for young-adult subjects occurs when pairs of synonyms (e.g., *ocean* and *sea*) serve as to-be-remembered items of a free-recall list (see Kausler, 1974). As with rhyming words, synonyms tend to be recalled together, even though the words were widely separated in the study list. Denney (1974a) compared middle-age and elderly subjects in their performances on such a list. Her middle-age subjects emulated the performance of young-adult subjects by showing a statistically significant amount of synonym clustering. Moreover, there was a substantial positive correlation between the amount of clustering and the total number of words recalled. By contrast, her elderly subjects failed to show a significant amount of clustering, nor were their clustering scores significantly correlated with their recall scores. Not surprisingly, the middle age subjects recalled significantly more words than the elderly subjects. Again, the implication is that of an age deficit in the proficiency of encoding processes under organizational conditions. In support of this conclusion, Howard, McAndrews, and Lasaga (1981) also found a trend toward a greater clustering effect for young-adult subjects than for elderly subjects. In addition, they also found a substantial positive correlation between the amount of clustering and the total number of words recalled for their elderly subjects as well as for their young subjects.

This pessimistic picture of age deficits in organizational processes is mitigated somewhat by the results obtained by Hultsch (1969). His study is relevant to our analysis of the relationship between intelligence and the content areas of experimental psychology, and it will, therefore, be examined in detail in Chapter 11.

Subjective Organization. Organization of list items is by no means limited to items that are preexperimentally related to one another. Even items that are seemingly unrelated, at least to the investigator who selected them as components of a study list, can become unitized. That is, young-adult subjects often find a connecting link between so-called unrelated words. The connecting link may then serve as a higher order unit for subsuming the traces of the discrete items. For example, consider *late* and *robin* as items in a study list. A clever subject might find a link between them by reversing an old proverb (i.e., the *late robin* never gets the worm). The modified proverb would become the higher order unit for accommodating both list items. During the test trial, a search of the episodic store would retrieve the higher order unit first, followed by retrieval of the traces of the specific items nested under that unit. Consequently, *late* and *robin* would be recalled consecutively, even though the items may have been widely separated in the study list.

We have described what is called *subjective organization* by basic-memory researchers (Tulving, 1962, 1964). Its existence is established by the fact that the probability of recalling items like *late* and *robin* consecutively increases steadily as the number of study-test trials on the same list increases. Most important, increments in the amount of subjective organization with practice are expected to increase the number of items recalled from the list. Thus, subjective organization is viewed as being a potent process underlying increments in total-recall scores with continuing practice on a list of so-called unrelated items (Tulving, 1962, 1964).

One of the studies used as an example in our earlier review of methodological issues was the first to evaluate age differences in subjective organization. In it, Laurence (1966) found lower total-item recall scores by her elderly subjects than by her young-adult subjects, even though the two age groups did not differ in amount of subjective organization. This finding contradicts the principle that it is increments in subjective organization that make possible increments in total-item recall scores. However, there was a methodological problem inherent in Laurence's study. The scoring system used to measure subjective organization was a crude one that did not take into account subjective units that incorporated more than two items. With many study-test trials on a given list, subjects have the opportunity to unitize three or more items. For example, the item *meal* could eventually be linked to *late* and *robin* in the reverse early bird proverb functioning as a higher order unit. A more recent study by Hultsch (1974) made use of a more sophisticated scoring system, one taking into account longer sequences of linked items. This time an age deficit was found for amount of subjective organization as well as for total number of items recalled. Further evidence indicating a decrement in proficiency of subjective organization with increasing age was reported by Smith (1979).

In addition, Hultsch (1969) demonstrated that the age decrement in subjective organization reflects more than just a production deficit. Instructions that prodded subjects to organize items in some manner did not eliminate the age deficit in subjective organization found for subjects with low verbal ability. That deficit appears to be the result of a true age change in organizational ability (to be discussed further in Chapter 11).

Age differences in subjective organization have also been investigated through the use of a method introduced by Mandler (e.g., Mandler & Pearlstone, 1966). Subjects are given a stack of cards, each card contains a word that is unrelated to the words on the other cards. The subject's task is to sort the cards/words into two or more piles. Each pile represents an artificial category shared in some way by the words sorted into that pile. Thus, subjects must find connections of some kind among the words assigned to the same category. This forced categorization leads to organizational structures that enhance the later (and unexpected) recall of the individual words relative to control subjects who either simply study the individual words without sorting them or sort them into piles designated by people other than themselves (and, therefore, into categories that are not relevant to their own subjective organizations). This procedure was applied in an aging study by Hultsch (1971b). An age deficit in number of words recalled was found with both the relevant-sorting task and the control task. However, relevant sorting improved recall scores for elderly subjects as well as for young subjects and, in fact, more so for the elderly subjects. Consequently, the age deficit in recall was less pronounced in the sorting condition than in the control condition. Perhaps elderly subjects do construct higher order subjective units as proficiently as do young subjects. The main reason for the lower total-recall scores of elderly subjects is probably their reduced capacity for encoding specific items and storing them as lower order units associated with a given higher order unit. In addition, the effect of the encoding deficit is likely to be magnified by a retrieval deficit as well.

Adult-Age Differences in Episodic Memory: Connected Discourse

Memory psychologists do not devote all of their time and effort in research involving memory of discrete items in a list. For many years, memory of connected discourse was a topic of modest interest (e.g., F. C. Bartlett, 1932). This interest has intensified greatly in recent years (e.g., Anderson & Bower, 1973; Kintsch, 1974). Accompanying the increase in basic research has been an increase in research directed at age differences in memory for connected discourse, that is, memory for meaningful series of words at the levels of individual sentences, paragraphs, and stories.

Some gerontological psychologists (e.g., Hulicka, 1967a; 1967c; Kay, 1955) have argued that age differences favoring young adults should be less pronounced for the meaningful material characteristic of, say, sentences than for the meaningless material characteristic of, say, free-recall lists. The argument is a familiar one, elderly subjects are presumed to be less motivated when confronted by meaningless material than when confronted by meaningful material. Consequently, adverse performance factors are less pronounced for elderly subjects with meaningful material than with meaningless material. Other gerontological psychologists (e.g., Craik & Masani, 1967), however, have argued that, if anything, age deficits should be greater for meaningful material than for meaningless material. They believe that the differential rests in age-sensitive organizational processes that enter into memory of meaningful material but not into memory of meaningless material. In defense of their argument, Craik and Masani cited evidence reported by Heron and Craik (1964). In that study, no age deficit in digit span was found when the digits were read in Finnish, but an age deficit was found when the digits were read in English (the subjects' native language). The contrast between Finnish and English digits was regarded by Craik and Masani (1967) as being simply one form of the more general contrast between meaningless and meaningful material. They, therefore, expected the effect of this kind of contrast on age differences to apply to other kinds of material that may vary in meaningfulness, including word strings.

Sentence Memory. One way of testing these opposing views of the interaction between age and the degree of meaningfulness is to compare young and elderly subjects in their memories for material that ranges from being a random string of words to being a completely meaningful sentence. Do age differences favoring young adults increase or decrease as the meaningfulness of the strings increases? A useful set of materials for such tests was constructed by Miller and Selfridge (1950). They prepared strings of words that varied in their order of approximation to meaningful English text. A zero-order string consists of randomly selected and randomly ordered words. Successively higher order approximations increase progressively in their conformity to English syntax and in their likelihood of conveying a meaningful content. This may be seen in Table 9.2 where 20 word strings of zero-, first-, third-, and fifth-order approximations are listed along with another string that constitutes meaningful English text (i.e., it is a syntactically and semantically legitimate sentence). Material of this nature (only the strings were 30 words in length rather than 20) were read to young-adult and elderly subjects by Craik and Masani (1967). Means for the number of words recalled by each age group in each approximation condition are plotted in Figure 9.24. Note that both age groups improved greatly in number of words recalled as the strings increased progressively in their approximations to text. However, the magnitude of the age difference favoring young adults also increased progressively. The result is a divergent relationship (see Chapter 5). That is, the magnitude of the age deficit increased as overall performance scores increased. The implication is that different age-sensitive organizational processes become involved in the transition from meaningless to meaningful material. Zero-order strings are equivalent to a free-recall list composed of unrelated items. Consequently, the organizational processes governing the encoding of the material are those that govern subjective organization. Increasing the approximation to textual material means that both syntax and semantic content become increasingly involved. The constraints offered by normal syntax provide an effective organization for ordering words correctly and should, therefore, lead to a major reduction in the number of errors made in recalling the string. For example, the sequence *has been paid* in the textual string listed in Table 9.2 follows that of normal syntax. To recall it as *been has paid* would clearly violate the rules of syntax. Similarly, the constraints offered by semantic content provide an effective organization for ordering words correctly. If the content of the textual string in Table 9.2 is encoded correctly, it would make no sense, for example, to reverse the positions of *diet* and *disease* in recalling the sentence—the meaning would be altered drastically. The divergent relationship found by Craik and Masani suggests that syntactic/semantic organizational processes suffer a greater decrement in proficiency from early to late adulthood than do subjective organizational processes of the kind described earlier.

An age deficit in the recall of normal sentence content has also been found by Gordon (1975) and Whitbourne and Slevin (1978). The study by Whitbourne and Slevin is especially informative. Two kinds of sentences were constructed. In one kind, the subject and object of each sentence were concrete nouns of high-imagery value, whereas in the other kind, they were abstract

Table 9.2   Word Strings of Varying Approximations to English Text

Zero-order
betwixt trumpeter pebbly complication vigorous tipple careen obscure attractive consequence expedition pane unpunished prominence chest sweetly basin awoke photographer ungrateful

First-order
tea realizing most so the together home and for were wanted to concert I posted he her it the walked

Third-order
family was large dark animal came roaring down the middle of my friends love books passionately every kiss is fine

Fifth-order
road in the country was insane especially in dreary rooms where they have some books to buy for studying Greek

Text
more attention has been paid to diet but mostly in relation to disease and to the growth of young children

Source: Adapted from Miller and Selfridge, 1950.

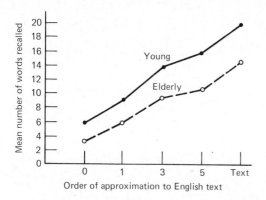

Figure 9.24. Age differences in words recalled as a function of approximation to meaningful text. (Adapted from data in Craik & Masani, 1967.)

nouns of low-imagery value. A number of studies with young-adult subjects (e.g., Begg & Paivio, 1969) have found far superior recall of content for sentences containing high-imagery words than for sentences containing low-imagery words. Presumably, imaginal representations of a sentence's content enhance recall of that content. Such representations, of course, are more likely to occur with high-imagery words than with low-imagery words. As illustrated in Figure 9.25, Whitbourne and Slevin's results indicated that elderly subjects benefited as much from high-imagery words as did young subjects. Consequently, the age difference in recall scores favoring young subjects was no greater for sentences containing low-imagery words than for sentences containing high-imagery words. The additive nature of the relationship between age variation and imagery variation suggests that the use of imagery to encode sentence content changes little over the course of the adult lifespan. By contrast, the ability to employ imagery with other kinds of material, such as paired associates, does appear to decline with advancing age.

Another interesting finding was reported by Botwinick and Storandt (1974b). Their subjects received foolish sentences, that is, word strings that were syntactically sound but semantically meaningless. For example, one of their sentences was, "The Declaration of Independence sang overnight while the cereal jumped by the river." If the age-related decrement in recall of sentence content is due only to an age change in the ability to utilize semantic constraints, then age differences in recall should disappear when those constraints are no longer relevant. That is, young subjects should be as disadvantaged as elderly subjects when confronted by foolish sentences. Our reasoning, of course, follows from the application of the deletion method. However, Botwinick and Storandt did not find the age deficit in recall to disappear. Nevertheless, the magnitude of the deficit was not as pronounced as the magnitude found with normal sentences (Figures 9.24, 9.25). Apparently, semantic organization is an age-sensitive process. Of further interest would be a study comparing age groups on distorted sentences that are semantically valid but syntactically out of order, such as, "Neighbors sleeping noisy wake parties"

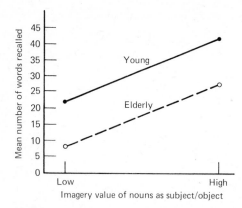

Figure 9.25. Age differences in words recalled from sentences of low- and high-imagery value. (Adapted from Whitbourne & Slevin, 1978, Table 1.)

(Marks & Miller, 1964). Comparisons of age deficits found with these kinds of sentences and with foolish sentences would offer a means of evaluating the relative contributions of syntactic and semantic organizational processes to age changes in memory for normal sentences.

Paragraph Memory. A paragraph relates consecutive sentences together into an integrated content. A number of ideas of the kind illustrated in Table 9.3 are represented in a single paragraph. Memory proficiency for the content of this paragraph may be evaluated by determining how many of the 16 ideas embedded within it are recalled after reading it once. Whether or not the individual ideas are recalled in exactly the same words present in the paragraph is unimportant. What is important is recall of the basic ideas and not their specific phrasings. For example, recall of the last idea in the paragraph ("no casualities were reported") would be scored as being correct if it took the form, "there were no casualities."

Age differences in memory proficiency may then be evaluated by comparing mean-idea recall scores for various age groups. This simple procedure was applied in an early study by Wechsler (1945). He found a modest decline by age 50 in the number of ideas recalled from paragraphs of the kind illustrated in Table 9.3. A later study by Hulicka (1966) used the materials from Wechsler's study and extended the age to people in their 80s. The decline observed by

Table 9.3   Paragraph Used to Test Age Differences in Memory for Connected Discourse[a]

> Thousands of persons/ have been evacuated/ from their homes/ in two/ Mexican states/ after more than forty-eight hours/ of rains/ that have caused/ disastrous floods./ Several lowland sections/ in three cities/ were reported under water./ One flooding river/ has covered/ almost a half million acres./ No casualities were reported.

[a]Slash marks denote separate ideas, each given a score of 1 if recalled.
Source: Botwinick and Storandt, 1974b.

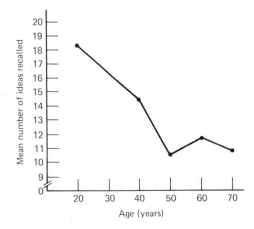

Figure 9.26. Age differences in ideas recalled from paragraphs. (Adapted from Botwinick & Storandt, 1974b, Figure 11.)

Wechsler was found to continue steadily through late adulthood with subjects in their 80s recalling about one-fourth fewer ideas than subjects in their 20s. A more precipitous decline was found by Botwinick and Storandt (1974b). The paragraph shown in Table 9.3 is one of two received by their subjects. The second paragraph contained 25 ideas, thus making 41 the maximum possible recall score for the two paragraphs combined. It can be seen from the mean recall scores, as plotted in Figure 9.26, that the performance proficiency of 70-year-old subjects was about half that of 20-year-old subjects. An age deficit has also been reported when a recognition test replaces a recall test (Gordon & Clark, 1974; Taub, 1976).

Most of the other studies concerned with age differences in memory for the content of a paragraph have centered on the issue of the modality of presentation for the to-be-remembered material. That is, is the magnitude of the age deficit affected by the visual versus auditory mode of presenting the content? One of these studies (Taub, 1975) was touched on in Chapter 5 (also see Figure 5.11). There we discovered that, regardless of age level, the mean number of ideas recalled is greater following visual presentation than following auditory presentation. However, we also discovered that the magnitude of the age deficit was about the same for each modality. We should point out that Taub's procedure allowed subjects to review the paragraph while reading it. That is, as each new idea occurred, a subject could refer back to earlier segments of that paragraph. This review was not possible with auditory presentation. When review is prohibited with visual presentation, Taub (Taub & Kline, 1976) discovered that recall of paragraph content is not affected by modality of presentation, again regardless of age level. In other studies, Taub (Taub, 1976; Taub & Kline, 1978) compared age differences in paragraph-recall scores when subjects read silently versus reading aloud. This variation was found to have virtually no effect on memory scores for either young or elderly subjects. Consequently, the age difference favoring young adults was about the same in each condition.

Why an age deficit in memory for the ideas embedded in relatively short paragraphs? This question has received surprisingly little attention. The one possibility that has been examined (Taub, 1979) is that elderly adults comprehend fewer ideas in a paragraph than do young adults. If true, then elderly adults would store fewer ideas (and more verbatim content) in memory than young adults, and they would, therefore, be able to recall fewer ideas. The possibility of an age difference in comprehension of textual material was approached in Chapter 1 (also see Figure 1.3). We discovered there that the age difference in comprehension favoring young adults is modest when subjects are tested for verbatim knowledge of a paragraph's content (G. Cohen, 1979). A modest age difference in verbatim comprehension was also found by Taub (1979), and little age difference in comprehension was found by Belmore (1981) when subjects were tested with paraphrases of a paragraph's content immediately after reading that paragraph. Most important, however, Taub found no age difference in memory for the ideas of a paragraph when his young and elderly subjects were equated in their ability to comprehend the content of that paragraph. The implication is that it is an encoding deficit that underlies much of the difficulty encountered by many elderly people in recalling ideas from a paragraph.

The importance of comprehension as a potential age-sensitive process was nicely demonstrated in a study by Till and Walsh (1980). Their procedure followed closely that of Hyde and Jenkins (1969). Memory was tested following various orienting tasks, such as giving a pleasant/unpleasant rating to each study-list item. The items, however, were sentences rather than individual words. Most important, each sentence carried with it an implication that had to be inferred from its content. For example, one sentence was, "The chauffeur drove on the left side." The implication is that the action took place in England. Full comprehension of the sentence would include this implication as well as knowledge of who did the driving. Following the study list, subjects received either a noncued-recall test or a cued-recall test for sentence content. The retrieval cue for each sentence in the cued-recall condition was a single word relevant to the implication of that sentence. Thus, *England* was the retrieval cue for the previously given sentence. Young-adult subjects recalled more sentences than elderly subjects in both recall conditions. More important, however, the magnitude of the age deficit was greater in the cued-recall condition than in the noncued condition. In fact, the young subjects had higher recall scores when cued than when noncued, whereas the opposite was true for elderly subjects. The implication of each sentence was seemingly comprehended to a greater degree by young than by elderly subjects, which is in agreement with G. Cohen's (1979) conclusion regarding the inferential content of sentences. Consequently, the implications were more likely to be represented in the memory traces of young subjects than in the memory traces of elderly subjects. Without such storage of implications, the retrieval cues could not be effective.

In a second experiment, Till and Walsh (1980) demonstrated that the age deficit found in their first experiment could be overcome by giving elderly subjects an appropriate orienting task during the study trial. Rather than rating sentences on the pleasant/unpleasant dimension, subjects now had to write down for each sentence a single word that summarized the implication of that sentence. When then tested by implication retrieval cues, elderly subjects recalled as many sentences as did young subjects. The failure to comprehend the deeper meanings of sentences by many elderly people seems to be more of a production deficit than a true deficit in the ability to comprehend the deeper meanings. In agreement with Taub's (1979) results, once comprehension is assured, the age deficit in memory disappears.

Memory for Stories and Other Longer Discourses. In the real world, memory for connected discourse usually involves sequences that are much longer than single paragraphs. The discourse is likely to be in the form of a story, novel, essay, newspaper or magazine article, and so on. Memory of individual ideas for this kind of material is less important than the ability to integrate the ideas together as a superordinate to subordinate hierarchy of propositions, or summary statements, about the material's content (Anderson & Bower, 1973). At the top of the hierarchy is a representation of the material's central theme. Below it is an organization of interrelated subordinate propositions.

While reading or listening to, say, a story, an individual who is comprehending that story's content is abstracting various ideas and integrating them together as a summary proposition. The final product of this abstraction process is a schematic representation, or *schema,* of the story's content that is stored in episodic memory as a complex memory trace. On retrieval of the schema from the store, the individual attempts to reproduce the story's content. However, the result is likely to be a reconstruction of the story rather than a true reproduction. Again, a schema is only an abstraction of the story's content. To fill in the details, the individual must tell the story in his or her own words. Moreover, the abstraction process itself may be influenced by the attitudes and beliefs of the individual reader or listener. The resulting schematic representation would then reflect those attitudes and beliefs rather than those of the story's author. Consequently, the individual's reconstruction of the story's content may well contain many distortions, inferences, and embellishments (Bartlett, 1932).

Theories about the nature of the schematic abstraction process have stimulated considerable basic research on memory for stories in recent years (see Solso, 1979, for a highly readable review). Unfortunately, however, little attention has been directed at adult-age differences in the proficiency of schematic abstraction. Notable exceptions have been studies by Walsh and Baldwin (1977) and Walsh, Baldwin, and Finkle (1980). These studies are of great interest in that they suggest the possibility of little age change in the abstraction process. Both studies were extensions of a well-known study by Bransford and Franks (1971). In that study, young-adult subjects were exposed to a series of sentences that collectively communicated the four ideas shown in the bottom segment of Table 9.4 (i.e., the one-idea sentences). A number of sentences were exposed during a study trial, one sentence at a time. Some, but not all, of the one-idea sentences were included in the study phase. Similarly, some, but not all, of the two-and three-idea sentences were also included in the study phase. Collectively, the study-list sentences conveyed all four of the ideas shown in Table 9.4. The study phase was followed by a recognition-test phase containing

Table 9.4   Materials Used by Bransford and Franks (1971) to Study the Abstraction Process in the Memory of Connected Discourse

Four-Idea Sentence
The ants in the kitchen ate the sweet jelly
   which was on the table. (Test only)
Three-Idea Sentences
The ants ate the sweet jelly which was on
   the table. (Study only)
The ants in the kitchen ate the sweet jelly.
   (Test only)
Two-Idea Sentences
The ants ate the sweet jelly. (Both study and
   test)
The sweet jelly was on the table. (Test only)
One-Idea Sentences
The jelly was on the table. (Study only)
The ants were in the kitchen. (Study only)
The jelly was sweet. (Test only)
The ants ate the jelly. (Test only)

Source: Bransford and Franks (1971), Table 1.

both old and new sentences, some from each class (i.e., one-, two-, and three-idea sentences). Most important, the four-idea sentence (top segment of Table 9.4) was shown in the test phase only, and it was, therefore, a new item. Nevertheless, there was a high false alarm rate for incorrectly recognizing this sentence as being old. Bransford and Franks (1971) reasoned that subjects abstract ideas from separate but interrelated (as in a story) sentences. These abstractions are integrated together and stored as a holistic representation (or schema) of the overall content. The four-idea sentence conforms to this holistic representation of the four ideas conveyed by the sentences actually exposed during the study phase. Consequently, this higher order sentence is readily but falsely identified as being old.

Walsh and Baldwin (1977) found that this false-recognition effect was as pronounced for their elderly subjects as for their young-adult subjects. Later Walsh and Baldwin (1980) also discovered little sign of an age difference when abstract ideas (e.g.,"the attitude was arrogant") substituted for the concrete ideas of the kind shown in Table 9.4. The implication is that elderly adults are as proficient as young adults in abstracting ideas and integrating them together into holistic representations. However, relatively few ideas were involved in these studies. Whether or not the absence of an age change in abstraction/integration generalizes to more complex and longer materials, such as stories, is an important question.

There is also reason to question the generalizability of Walsh and Baldwin's (1977, 1980) findings to a different kind of integration, one in which a picture's content is integrated with the content of a sentence relevant to that picture. There is evidence (Pezdek, 1980) to indicate that elderly subjects are less proficient than young subjects in this form of integration.

Aging research on memory for longer discourses has been largely exploratory to date. Unfortunately, the results obtained in several such exploratory studies have been highly conflicting (see Hartley, Harker, and Walsh, 1980, for a detailed review). We are talking about memory for the content of discourse that contains hundreds of words rather than discourse of the kind ordinarily used in research on memory for paragraph content (e.g., Table 9.3). In their studies of age differences in prose memory, Gordon and Clark (1974b) and G. Cohen (1979) employed 300-word passages. Superior memory scores were found in both studies for young adults. G. Cohen's study is especially important in that an attempt was made to score recall protocols for both higher order, or summary, propositions and lower order, or modifying, propositions. That is, the scoring system allowed age comparisons to be made for various levels in the presumed hierarchical organization of story content. Young adults excelled in memory for both higher order and lower order units. With a still longer passage (over 600 words) but with a content analysis similar to that of G. Cohen (1979), Meyer, Rice, Knight, & Jessen (1979) found a quite different outcome. There was little difference among age groups for superordinate units, whereas older subjects recalled *more* subordinate units than younger subjects. There is, however, an important methodological difference between the studies. G. Cohen's subjects *listened* to their passage, while subjects of Meyer et al. *read* their passage. As noted earlier, older subjects are especially likely to benefit from reading material relative to listening to material. Again, self-paced reading permits subjects to refer back to earlier content while they attempt to comprehend present content. Finally, Zelinski, Gilewski, and Thompson (1980) also found no age difference in the recall of superordinate content. However, in contrast to the earlier finding of Meyer et al., elderly subjects recalled fewer subordinate units than did young-adult subjects. Research in this area has been handicapped by the difficulty in establishing a reliable scoring system for analyzing recall protocols in terms of hierarchical units. As progress is made in refining this analysis, a more complete understanding of whatever age differences exist in memory for lengthy discourses will eventually emerge.

Adult-Age Differences in Episodic Memory: Automatic Encoding Processes

Breadth of Encoding. Episodes on laboratory tasks typically consist of single words. Subjects are exposed to the words in either their printed form (visual presentation) or spoken form (auditory presentation). In either case, as we have seen throughout this chapter, it is the *content,* or name, of each visual or auditory input that is usually tested for later recall or recognition. For example, with *king* as a list item, a subject attempts to recall or recognize the fact that the word, *king,* had been part of a prior study list. Our encoding processes, however, are seldom restricted to only the content of inputs. They often register additional information that accompanies attended-to inputs (Underwood, 1969). The breadth of encoding is dramatically illustrated by the millions of Americans who give such accounts as "I was shopping in the supermarket when

I heard the news that President Kennedy had been shot" and "I was driving west on Broadway when I heard the news bulletin about Pearl Harbor" (see Linton, 1975). The memory trace in each case clearly extended beyond content (a news bulletin) to include environmental information that coincided with, but was independent of, that content. Less dramatic, but just as convincing, is the memory trace for the student who tells us, "In my psych class yesterday I heard this male voice behind me whisper, 'Shut up—I can't hear the lecture:' " Encoding of the episode obviously included the sex of the complainer as well as the content of the complaint.

More prosaic but still quite convincing are the experiences of subjects on laboratory simulations of the breadth of encoding phenomenon. The nature of one such simulation is illustrated in Table 9.5. A series of study-list words is presented with half of the words printed in uppercase letters, the other half in lowercase letters. Subjects are informed in advance of the study trial that they will be given a memory test for the content of the list. However, the test they receive is somewhat different than the one expected (see Table 9.5). On an answer sheet is a list of words printed in both uppercase and lowercase format along with the term, new. Some of the test words are old (i.e., carried over from the study list), whereas the remaining words are new. Subjects respond to each test word by encircling one of the three options. If they do not remember a test word, then they encircle new. If they remember a test word as being old, then they encircle either its uppercase or lowercase format, contingent on its appearance as they remember it in the study list (see Figure 9.27). How accurate are subjects in their identifications of case format? A number of studies (e.g., Hintzman, Block, & Inskeep, 1972; Light & Berger, 1976) have revealed that the hit rate for young adults is well above the level of chance expectancy (i.e., .50).

A similar memory phenomenon has been found when items are presented auditorily. Here, the items are varied with respect to the sex of the voice reading the items during a study trial—half of the items in a man's voice, half in a woman's voice. As with case recognition in the visual modality, the hit rate for

Table 9.5 Study-Test Procedure Used to Measure Memory for Uppercase/Lowercase Format of Study-List Items. Correct Responses Are Encircled on the Test List.

Study List		Test List			
Item I:	APPLE	Item 1:	WINDOW	(window)	NEW
Item 2:	TABLE	Item 2:	GERM	germ	(NEW)
Item 3:	king	Item 3:	(PARTY)	party	NEW
Item 4:	pencil	Item 4:	KING	(king)	NEW
Item 5:	TIGER	Item 5:	SONG	song	(NEW)
Item 6:	window	Item 6:	(APPLE)	apple	NEW
—		—			
—		—			
—		—			
Item n:	PARTY	Item n:	PENCIL	(pencil)	NEW

identifying the sex of voice of prior study-list items is well above chance expectancy for young-adult subjects (e.g., Geiselman & Bellezza, 1976, 1977).

Interest in memory for such nonsemantic attributes of study-list items as their case and sex of voice has been stimulated greatly by the possibility that the underlying encoding processes may be *automatic* (e.g., Geiselman & Bellezza, 1976). An automatic encoding process is one that draws little, if at all, upon the limited capacity of the organism's central processor (Hasher & Zacks, 1979; Posner & Snyder, 1975). By contrast, the encoding processes mediating the storage of item content are considered to be *cognitively effortful.* These processes do place a strain on the organism's limited processing capacity. What makes the distinction between automatic and effortful processes of concern to gerontological psychologists is the possibility that the capacity of the central processor decreases over the course of the adult lifespan (Hasher & Zacks, 1979). This diminished capacity would be expected to affect adversely memories that are encoded by cognitively effortful processes, such as memory for item content, but not memories that are encoded by automatic processes, such as memory for the nonsemantic attributes of items. Consequently, memory for nonsemantic attributes, unlike memory for item content, is expected to be insensitive to adult-age changes. In this section, we will review those aging studies that have tested the validity of the hypothesis that memory for nonsemantic attributes is age insensitive.

Nonsemantic attributes of items are not the only ones commonly hypothesized to be encoded automatically and that are, therefore, immune to adult-age changes in their memorability. In Chapter 2, we discovered that the frequency of occurrence of items in a series may be encoded automatically. Additional evidence dealing with this issue will also be reviewed in this section, as will the evidence dealing with the recency of occurrence of items in a series, another attribute often hypothesized to be encoded automatically.

Nonsemantic Attributes of To-be-remembered Items. Age differences in memory for case format were examined in two studies by Kausler and Puckett (1980b, 1981b). In the first study, young and elderly subjects received three different lists. The lists differed with respect to the attribute subjects were instructed to remember for a subsequent memory test. For the first list, the attribute was item content (i.e., a traditional recognition-memory test). For the second list, the attribute was the uppercase/lowercase format of each item; for the third list, the attributes were both content and case. Mean hit rates for the three lists are graphed in Figure 9.27. Note that an age deficit was apparent for both content as the only instructed attribute and case format as the only instructed attribute. A comparable outcome was found in the second study by Kausler and Puckett 1981b), this time with a somewhat differently structured task. The age-related decline in encoding proficiency commonly found for item content seems to apply equally well to encoding proficiency for a visual nonsemantic attribute of to-be-remembered items. On the other hand, no age differences were found between young and middle-aged adults (Kausler & Puckett, in press).

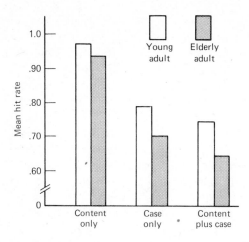

Figure 9.27. Age differences in recognition scores for content of items, case format of items, and content plus case. (Adapted from Kausler & Puckett, 1980b, Table 1.)

The age sensitivity of memory for an auditory nonsemantic attribute, sex of voice, has also been amply demonstrated. Kausler and Puckett (1981a) gave young-adult and elderly subjects successive tasks, each requiring memory of the content in 20 sentences. For each task, half of the sentences in the list were read in a man's voice, half in a woman's voice (randomly ordered). The tasks differed in one fundamental way. The first was administered with incidental-memory instructions, the second with intentional-memory instructions. The incidental/intentional distinction in this context refers only to the sex of voice attribute. For both tasks, memory of sentence content was intentional. That is, the subjects knew in advance that they would be tested for item content. This test involved cued recall in which the verb of each sentence served as the retrieval cue for recalling the two nouns (subject and object of the sentence) linked with it. For the first task (incidental memory), subjects did not know in advance that they would also be tested for recognition of the sex of voice of each sentence during the study phase. For the second task (intentional memory), they were informed in advance that they would be tested for both sentence content and the sex-of-voice attribute. The incidental/intentional contrast is an important one. One of the major criteria for establishing an encoding process's automaticity is its insensitivity to variation in instructions (Hasher & Zacks, 1979). That is, memory proficiency for an automatically encoded attribute is expected to be no greater with intentionality than without it.

Mean sentence-recall scores (maximum, 40) reported by Kausler and Puckett, (1981a) are plotted in the top panel of Figure 9.28, whereas mean sex-of-voice-recognition scores (maximum, 20) are plotted in the bottom panel. An age deficit was clearly present for sex-of-voice scores as well as for sentence-recall scores, regardless of the instructional condition. In addition, voice-recognition scores were higher at both age levels in the intentional condition than in the incidental condition. In fact, voice identification by the elderly subjects did not exceed chance expectancy (10 out of 20) in the incidental condition. On the other hand, sentence recall was poorer in the intentional condition than in the incidental condition. The disparity between conditions, however, was considerably more pronounced for the elderly subjects than for the young subjects. A very similar pattern was found in the other study by Kausler and Puckett (1981b). This time the content task involved word recognition rather than sentence recall. The pattern found in these two studies suggests a trade-off effect between the encoding of content and the encoding of nonsemantic information accompanying that content (Light, Berger, & Bardales, 1975). When informed of a forthcoming test for memory of a nonsemantic attribute (i.e., the intentional condition), subjects utilize a segment of their processing capacity for encoding that attribute. The resulting exertion of cognitive effort enhances memory of that attribute relative to memory found when subjects are tested incidentally. At the same time, processing capacity available for the effortful encoding of item content is reduced. Consequently, content scores decrease from the incidental- to the intentional-memory condition, whereas nonsemantic attribute scores increase across conditions (i.e., a trade-off occurs). Given the relatively large processing capacity of the young adult, the adverse effect of the trade-off on content memory is slight for young subjects. Given the reduced capacity of the elderly adult, the magnitude of the trade-off effect is more pronounced (see the top panel of Figure 9.28).

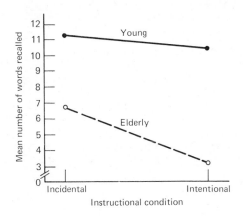

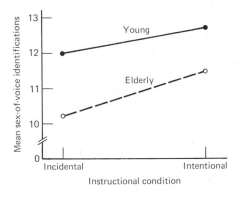

Figure 9.28. Age differences in recall of sentence content (top panel) and in recognition of sex of voice of those sentences (bottom panel). (Adapted from Kausler & Puckett, 1981a, Tables 1, 2.)

In summary, aging studies offer little support for the argument that the nonsemantic attributes of content items are encoded automatically. Instead, these attributes, like content itself, appear to be encoded effortfully. Consequently, the age deficit commonly found for semantic information (i.e, content) generalizes to nonsemantic information. It should be noted that the elderly subjects employed in the series of studies by Kausler and Puckett (1980b, 1981a, 1981b), were superior ones with respect to such dimensions as vocabulary level and educational level. Attributing the moderate age deficits in nonsemantic memory found in these studies to cohort effects seems inappropriate. Rather, the deficits appear to be the consequence of a true reduction in processing capacity, however modest, during late adulthood.

Frequency and Recency Judgments. The nature of the frequency-judgment task was described in Chapter 2 (also see Figure 2.9). At that time, we described a study by Kausler and Puckett (1980a) in which no age difference was found for relative frequency judgments (i.e., subjects select which member of a test pair occurred more frequently in a study list). What was not mentioned is the fact that the scores plotted in Figure 2.9 were obtained under an incidental-memory condition. The subjects were simply asked to study items in a list in preparation for a subsequent and unspecified memory test. Nor did we mention the fact that the same subjects then received a second frequency-judgment task. This time they were fully aware during the study trial of what the memory test would be like. That is, the second task was administered under an intentional-memory condition. Intentionality, however, had no effect on the accuracy of relative frequency judgments. Most important, the absence of an age difference in accuracy scores was as obvious with intentionality as it was without it. An identical outcome, that is, no effect for variation in either age or instructions, was reported by Attig and Hasher (1980). In addition, others (e.g., Hasher & Chromiak, 1977) have found a similar absence of an age effect when children's frequency judgments are compared with those of young adults.

Given such results, it is little wonder that Hasher and Zacks (1979) concluded that the encoding of frequency-of-occurrence information is an automatic process and, therefore, immune to age changes. Frequency-of-occurrence information is assumed to be highly important for maintaining efficient contact with the stream of environmental events. Its importance has assured, presumably through innate factors, the continuous proficiency of the underlying encoding operation over the lifespan.

Our feeling, however, is that it may be too early to conclude that the encoding of frequency information is truly insensitive to an age change in proficiency over the adult segment of the lifespan. There are two reasons for our hesitation in accepting its age insensitivity. First, age differences have been found repeatedly for frequency judgments when the test required absolute rather than relative judgments (Attig & Hasher, 1979; Freund & Witte, 1978; Warren & Mitchell, 1980). Illustrative of these age differences are those reported by Freund and Witte. Their young and elderly subjects received a study list in which words were exposed either one, two, three, or five times. They were

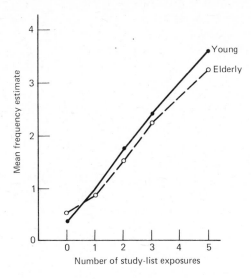

Figure 9.29. Age differences in absolute frequency-judgment scores as a function of number of study-list exposures. (Adapted from Freund & Witte, 1978, Figure 1.)

then asked on the test trial to estimate how many times they had seen each item. Included on the test trial were zero-frequency items, that is, words that had not been part of the prior study list. Their results, expressed as mean judged frequencies, are plotted in Figure 9.29. Note the absence of age differences for words having low frequencies of exposure. At the same time, note that their elderly subjects clearly underestimated the frequency of high-frequency words to a greater extent than did their young subjects. Conceivably, the observed age difference simply reflects a more conservative, or cautious, response bias by the elderly subjects. That is, they may be less likely than young subjects to respond with larger frequency scores. This explanation seems strained, however, in light of the fact that elderly subjects are no more conservative than young subjects on other kinds of recognition-memory tasks. Second, a modest, but statistically significant, age difference favoring young subjects was found by Kausler, Hakami, and Wright (in press) on a relative judgment task in which instances of taxonomic categories were presented with varying frequencies in a study list. For example, there may have been five men's first names, three names of states, and only one name of a religion. Judgments were then made in terms of which category of a pair (e.g., men's names versus state's names) had more representations within the study list. Thus, the presence or absence of an age deficit seems to depend on the nature of the representations that vary in their frequencies of occurrence.

Finally, recency-of-occurrence judgments are also commonly viewed as being mediated by an automatic encoding process. The task in this case begins with a study trial in which a number of words (or pictures) are each exposed once. On the following test trials, subjects are given pairs of words from the study list, and they are asked to judge which word occurred more recently in the study-list series. There is limited evidence (Perlmutter, Metzger, Nezworski, & Miller, 1981) indicating the absence of age differences in the accuracy of such judgment scores. However, considerably more evidence will be required before we can conclude that the kind of temporal information needed to make recency judgments is truly encoded automatically and is, therefore, immune to age changes in proficiency.

Adult-Age Differences in Generic Memory

A recurring theme throughout this chapter has been the central role played by the generic memory system in mediating episodic-memory phenomena. The content of an episodic memory trace is usually influenced strongly by generic knowledge pertinent to the input initiating that trace. To elaborate imaginally on *king* as a to-be-remembered free-recall item demands knowing something about the meaning of that word. Similarly, maintenance of *king* in the short-term store by means of repeating the word rotely is greatly facilitated by prior familiarity with *king's* phonemic representation in generic memory. Contrast *king* as a free-recall item in a recency position with, say, *mujik,* a word that is unlikely to have a phonemic representation in most generic-memory stores. Generic memory even enters into such encodings as that of sex of voice in the sense that the maleness or femaleness of the voices communicating episodic information approximate a prototype of each sex stored generically.

The importance of generic memory to our everyday activities, however, goes far beyond its role in episodic memory. As we discovered in Chapter 7, generic memory plays an equally important role in assigning meanings to our perceptions of objects and events. In addition, there are frequent occasions when we must retrieve information directly from generic memory to answer questions directed at us, such as "What does the word *nuance* mean?" "What is the capital city of Illinois?", and so on.

Given the importance of generic memory, it is essential that we consider possible age changes in its structures and retrieval operations. Structural changes could include decrements in either the amount of information stored generically or the organization of that information. The possibility of age changes in amount of stored information is an issue faced in assessments of age differences in intelligence. Vocabulary tests, as indices of the amount of information stored in the internal lexicon, have long been popular components of more general intelligence tests. So have tests of general information, information presumably stored in generic memory. Accordingly, we will delay a detailed review of age differences in performance on tests of generic knowledge until Chapter 11. However, a strong hint of the absence of any decrement in the content of knowledge with normal aging was offered in Chapter 2. The organization of generic information also seems to remain intact during late adulthood. It would have to be intact to have categorical clustering emerge in elderly subjects' recall from episodic memory. Again, clustering is viewed as reflecting the hierarchical organization inherent in generic memory.

Research on adult-age differences in the retrieval of information from generic memory is in its infancy. However, several studies have already demonstrated that the retrieval operations characteristic of generic memory are remarkably insensitive to any major adverse age changes. To date, these studies have focused on the retrieval of information from the internal lexicon, the storehouse of knowledge about words. One indication of the robustness of retrieval operations during late adulthood comes from studies by Howard (Howard, Lasaga, & McAndrews, 1980; Howard et al., 1981) dealing with potential age differences in a phenomenon known as *spreading activation* (Collins & Loftus, 1975). The phenomenon refers to the indirect activation of a word's representation in generic memory by the direct activation of a related word. That is, the activation of one word spreads to other words that are semantically related to the activated word. The net effect is to prime subjects for rapid responding to the indirectly activated word when it is actually exposed. A procedure that has worked well in demonstrating spreading activation with young adults involves a modification of the basic Stroop test (Warren, 1972). Briefly, reaction time in identifying the name of a color is increased when the color is that of the ink a word is printed in relative to naming the same color in isolation. Reading the word occurs automatically, thereby competing with, and interfering with, the identification of the color name. The competition is especially pronounced when the word is the name of a color other than that of its own print. Nevertheless, the interference is substantial when a neutral word, such as *bird,* is printed in the to-be-named color. This interference may be increased still more by the indirect activation of *bird* prior to its exposure. To accomplish this objective, subjects are given a set of relevant instances, such as *canary, sparrow,* and *pigeon,* to hold in memory prior to their exposure to *bird.* The memory-set words are then recalled after naming the color ink of *bird.* The amount of interference created by spreading activation is determined by contrasting reaction time for color naming in the relevant instance condition with reaction time in a control condition. The appropriate control condition is one in which subjects receive an irrelevant set of words (e.g., *valley, river,* and *canyon*) to hold in memory prior to their exposure to *bird.* In their use of this procedure, Howard et al. (1980) found that the increase in mean reaction time from irrelevant to relevant instances was as great for elderly subjects as for young-adult subjects (Figure 9.30). The age equality in the inter-

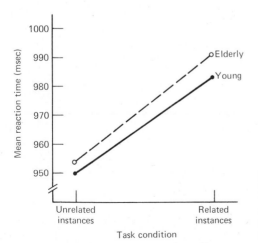

Figure 9.30. Age differences in reaction times for naming the print color of words that are either unrelated or related to words previously stored in memory. (Adapted from Howard, Lasaga, & McAndrews, 1980, Table 3.)

ference effect implies that spreading activation operates no differently in late adulthood than in early adulthood. (See, however, Burke & Light, 1981, for a move negative evaluation.)

The absence of age changes in retrieval operations is also apparent when those operations are tested more directly (Eysenck, 1975; Mueller, Kausler, & Faherty, 1980). Eysenck's procedure was one used earlier by Freedman (Freedman & Loftus, 1971; Loftus, Freedman, & Loftus, 1970) with young-adult subjects. It calls for presenting a category name for which subjects must name an instance beginning with a letter that is presented simultaneously. For example, given *fruit* as the category, the letter might be either *A* or *K*. With young subjects, reaction time is considerably faster for the *A* than for the *K*. The letters are selected deliberately to be cues for retrieving instances of the category that vary in their familiarity. Thus, *A* is a cue for retrieving *apple,* a high-familiarity instance of *fruit,* whereas *K* is a cue for retrieving *kumquat,* a far less familiar instance. Eysenck (1975) discovered that the disparity in reaction time is as characteristic of elderly subjects' performance on this kind of task as it is of young subjects' performance. Moreover, he found no age difference in mean reaction time for either kind of cue. Mueller et al. (1980) employed a quite different procedure. In an experimental condition, both young and elderly subjects had to decide whether or not simultaneously exposed words were members of the same taxonomic category (e.g., *apple-plum* and *apple-river* as yes-and-no pairs respectively). Mean reaction times were compared with mean reaction times in a control condition where simultaneously exposed words were simply judged as being the same word twice or two different words (e.g., *apple-apple* and *apple-river* as yes and no pairs respectively). The increase in mean reaction time from the control to the experimental condition was found to be no greater for their elderly subjects than their young subjects.

Finally, a number of contemporary psychologists view another set of mental operations as being components of generic memory. The operations are collectively known as those of *metamemory*. Metamemory means knowing about remembering, that is, knowing what one's own memory system can and cannot accomplish. Through such knowledge, we are able to assess somewhat realistically just how much new episodic information we can assimilate in a given time period, we are able to evaluate somewhat realistically just how likely previously encoded information is retrievable, we are able to know what memory strategies we have available and how to deploy those strategies contingent on the requirements of various tasks, and so on. Considerable research with children has demonstrated that this form of self-knowledge increases dramatically from early to late childhood (see Flavell & Wellman, 1977). An important remaining question is: "Does metamemory decrease dramatically from early to late adulthood?"

Several studies (e.g., Lachman, Lachman, & Thronesbery, 1979; Perlmutter, 1978) have revealed that some aspects of metamemory are remarkably robust and resistant to age changes over the adult lifespan. These aspects are those relevant to knowledge about facts stored in generic memory. That is, elderly adults are as aware of what facts they know and what facts they do not know as are young adults. However, metamemory may not be nearly as robust with respect to knowledge regarding the skills needed to store information episodically. In an interesting study by Murphy, Sanders, Gabriesheski, & Schmitt, (1981), young and elderly subjects were given a series of pictures of common objects to study with the objective being to recall the names of the objects in serial order. Some of the series were of memory-span length, others were of subspan length (two items less), and still others of supraspan length (two items more). Most important, the subjects were allowed as much time as they wanted to study each string before they felt ready to recall it without error. The results are plotted in Figure 9.31 for both the proportion of strings recalled at each length and the mean time spent studying each type of string. Note that the elderly subjects spent considerably less time than the young subjects in studying both the span-length and supraspan-length strings and that the adverse effects are clearly reflected in the poorer recall performance of the elderly subjects for each length. Apparently, the elderly subjects failed to assess realistically the strain placed on their episodic-memory systems by the longer series of items, and they, therefore, failed to spend sufficient time rehearsing those series. Stated somewhat differently, the elderly subjects were less cautious than the young subjects in evaluating their readiness for recalling without error. As with other aspects of performance on memory tasks, this finding conflicts with the generally held notion that elderly adults are more cautious than young adults.

In a second experiment, Murphy et al. employed a forced-time condition in which elderly subjects had to spend at least as much time studying to-be-recalled strings as the young adults averaged studying those length strings in the first experiment. Thus, for span-length and supraspan-length strings, they had to spend at least 32 and 59 seconds respectively (i.e., the mean times

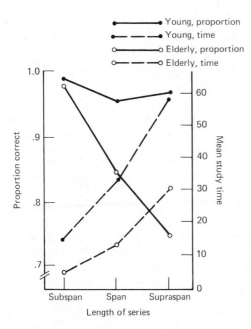

Figure 9.31. Age differences in proportion of serial strings recalled and mean time spent in studying the strings before feeling readiness to recall without error. (Adapted from Murphy, Sanders, Gabriesheski, & Schmitt, 1981, Figure 1, Table 1.)

observed in the first experiment; see Figure 9.31). With these expanded study periods, their elderly subjects recalled as many strings without error as did the young subjects in the first experiment.

This study has important implications for interpreting age deficits found in both the laboratory and real-life settings. For example, in the laboratory, we discovered in Chapter 8 that elderly subjects perform less proficiently than younger subjects on paired-associate learning tasks even when practice is self-paced. Conceivably, elderly subjects simply overestimate their own competence and, therefore, fail to allow themselves the full amount of extra rehearsal time they really need to master such tasks. Similarly, in the real world, many elderly people may have the tendency to terminate their rehearsal of to-be-remembered episodic information too soon. With a little more time and effort devoted to rehearsal activity, they may well discover considerable increments in their memory proficiency. From this perspective, it is to the advantage of elderly people to stress to them the existence of moderate declines in the proficiency of memory processes with aging. Once they confront this knowledge realistically, they may be better prepared to work harder to enhance the memorability of episodic information.

Summary

Episodic memory, that is, memory for personally experienced events, or episodes, is clearly imperfect, as confirmed by our everyday observations of our own memory failures. Memory problems are by no means restricted to elderly people. However, it is commonly assumed that memory proficiency does decline in late adulthood. In addition, concern about memory problems is more intense among elderly people than it is among younger people. How pronounced is the decline in episodic-memory proficiency over the course of the adult lifespan? What are the age-sensitive processes that are responsible for whatever decrease there is? In this chapter, we attempted to answer these questions by reviewing the many studies that have dealt with age differences and changes in episodic-memory phenomena.

An analysis of episodic memory begins with the concept of sensory memory. Considerable research with young-adult subjects has revealed that sensory information persists in a physical form for a brief duration following termination of the originating stimulus. Such persistence is an important phenomenon in that it prolongs the time that information is available for processing and transformation into memory traces. The most widely studied forms of sensory memory are those of iconic, or visual, memory and echoic, or auditory, memory. If the durations of iconic- and echoic-memory representations are less for elderly adults than for young adults, then elderly adults would be handicapped by having less processing time than young adults have. Various laboratory procedures are available for measuring the duration of both iconic and echoic memory. These procedures indicate that, for young adults, the duration of iconic memory is less than 1 second, whereas the duration of echoic memory is 2 seconds or more. Applications of these procedures with elderly subjects indicate that any age change in duration for either sensory-memory component is slight. Thus, it seems unlikely that age changes in sensory memory account for the the memory problems commonly associated with old age. In addition, the continuation of echoic memory into late adulthood accounts for the fact that elderly subjects show the same modality effect found for young-adult subjects in the recall of a list of items. The modality effect refers to the fact that items at the end of the list are recalled better following auditory presentation than following visual presentation. There is reason to believe that auditorily presented items are recalled directly from information still residing in echoic memory. The much briefer duration of iconic memory makes direct recall from it virtually impossible.

What happens to information held in the sensory store once it has been processed by the operations of pattern recognition? The answer is contingent on the particular model serving to conceptualize the episodic-memory system. A popular conceptualization is that of the dual-store model. According to this model, a mental representation of the information held in a sensory store is transmitted to the short-term store where it may reside briefly and is then either lost (or forgotten), recalled directly, or rehearsed and encoded into a memory trace that is transmitted to the more permanent long-term store.

The structures and operations of the short-term, or primary-memory, component of the total system offer a number of possible sources of adult-age differences in episodic-memory proficiency. One possibility is that the capacity of the store diminishes progressively with increasing age, thus enabling elderly people to recall less information than younger people over brief time periods. Tests of this hypothesis are complicated by the probable involvement of secondary-, or long-term, memory processes on many kinds of tasks, such as memory span, that superficially appear to measure the capacity of the short-term store. To dual-store theorists, the problem is resolved by the use of the free-recall task. End items of a free-recall list are viewed as being recalled directly from the short-term store. The ready availability of these items creates a recency effect, defined as the higher probability of recalling the end items than recalling midlist items. The magnitude and extent of this effect offers a means of estimating the capacity of the store and also age changes in that capacity. However, studies comparing the recency effect for young and elderly subjects have yielded conflicting findings—some have found no age difference, whereas others have found a modest decrement in both magnitude and extent of the effect. Whatever loss there is in storage capacity during late adulthood appears to be slight.

Other possible sources of age differences in primary memory rest in the rate of loss of information from the short-term store, in the format of information transmitted to the store, and in the attributes of searching the content of the store. Rate of losing information is determined through the use of the Brown-Peterson procedure. Here, a to-be-remembered item is studied and then recalled following a retention interval of varying duration that is filled with a rehearsal-preventing activity. Studies comparing the amount recalled by young and elderly subjects after 0, 3, 6, and so on, seconds have revealed no significant age difference in the rate of forgetting (i.e., the rate of losing information from the store). Various studies with young-adult subjects have indicated that information held in the short-term store is usually phonemic in the format of its representation. However, there appears to be considerable flexibility in format. That is, visual representations may supplement or even replace phonemic representations with certain task demands. Little is known about the continuation of this flexibility in late adulthood. Finally, the nature of a young adult's search of the short-term store's contents has been determined through the use of the Sternberg task. Here, a memory set that varies in the number of items it contains is studied and then followed by a test item that may or may not have been included in the prior memory set. Decision times for yes and no test items reveal that young adults search the store's content rapidly. Moreover, the search is typically one that is both serial (i.e., it progresses from item to item in the store at a constant rate) and exhaustive (i.e., it continues until the last item in the store has been examined). Aging studies have demonstrated that the serial, exhaustive nature of the search continues through late adulthood. However, the rate of searching the store's content is considerably slower for elderly subjects than for young-adult subjects.

According to the dual-store model, rehearsal of items is essential for their transmission from the short-term to the long-term store—the greater the amount of rehearsal, the greater the probability of transmission to, and recall from, the long-term store. The nature of the relationship between amount of rehearsal and probability of recall is clearly seen in the primacy effect in free recall. The beginning items of a list are rehearsed more than midlist items and, therefore, have a higher probability of recall than midlist items (the primacy effect). Age differences in the proficiency of secondary memory may be evaluated by comparing the magnitudes and extents of primacy effects for young and elderly subjects. These comparisons support the hypothesis that rehearsal and storage processes for long-term memory are age sensitive. Moreover, the fact that age deficits in performance are greater on recall tests, where an active retrieval search of the long-term store is required, than on recognition tests, where the search process may be bypassed, indicates that retrieval itself is an age-sensitive process. In addition, the fact that age deficits in performance exist for recognition tests as well as recall tests provides further support for the position that rehearsal and storage processes are age sensitive.

The major alternative to the dual-store model is the levels-of-processing model. According to this model, age differences in episodic-memory proficiency are attributable mainly to age differences in encoding processes. Elderly adults usually encode items less deeply than do young adults, and they, therefore, generate less durable memory traces. Variation in depth of processing is accomplished in the laboratory by giving subjects different orienting tasks to perform on items under incidental memory conditions. When the orienting task prods shallow processing, there are no age differences in the number of items that can subsequently be recalled. On the other hand, an orienting task that prods deep processing yields superior recall by young adults, a superiority that parallels that found with intentional memory and without an orienting task. The implication is that there is a true age change in the ability to engage in the kind of elaborative rehearsal that promotes deep processing. The adverse effect of the age change is clearly apparent on intentional-memory tasks. Here the greater use of elaborative rehearsal by young subjects than by elderly subjects results in superior recall scores by the young subjects. The fact that the age deficit in elaborative rehearsal is more than a production deficit is indicated by the fact that age deficits in performance persist even when elderly subjects are prodded to use deep processing (i.e., with an appropriate orienting task). However, at least part of elderly subjects' difficulty in recalling items following deep processing results from their diminished ability to retrieve previously stored memory traces.

Of further interest to experimental aging psychologists are possible age deficits in organizational processes, in memory for connected discourse and in memory processes that are commonly believed to be automatic in the sense of placing no demand on the limited capacity of the central processor. Organization involves the detection and utilization of relationships between individual episodic events, such as the items of a free-recall list. Through organizational processes, the traces of the separate items are integrated into more complex traces that reflect the nature of their relationship. Once stored together as an integrated memory structure, the related items are likely to be recalled consecutively, even though they may have been widely scattered during a study phase.

One form of organization emerges when list items consist of multiple instances, or exemplars, of various taxonomic categories. Traces of these items/instances appear to be organized as hierarchical structures composed of superordinates (category names) as higher order units and subordinates (category instances) as lower order units. Retrieval of the episodic information translates into a two-stage process. The first stage consists of gaining access to the higher order units, the second of gaining access to the lower order units. Experimental aging studies have revealed lower recall scores on categorizable lists by elderly subjects than by young-adult subjects. The age deficit, however, does not appear to be the product of an inability to encode and store higher order units. Instead, the deficit results from age-related declines in the ability to encode and store lower order units (i.e., the specific instances of each category included in a list). Another form of organization occurs even when the items of a list are seemingly unrelated to one another. Inventive subjects are able to discover their own relationships between such items, yielding what is called subjective organization. The ability to organize items into such subjective units, however, does appear to decline in late adulthood.

Do the age deficits found for memory of lists composed of random words apply to memory of lists that form connected discourse (i.e., sentences, paragraphs, and so on). Contrary to the argument that age deficits in episodic memory should diminish as material increases in meaningfulness, laboratory evidence indicates the opposite. That is, the magnitude of the age deficit appears to increase as word strings increase in their degree of approximation to meaningful sentences. In general, young adults also excel in memory for the ideas embedded in a paragraph. However, the age deficit virtually disappears when comprehension of the ideas is equated between young and elderly age groups. In addition, elderly subjects are perfectly capable of integrating ideas into more complex representations (or schemas), at least when only a few ideas are involved. Whether or not the ability to integrate the ideas of lengthier material, such as a story, is adversely affected by aging is uncertain. Studies in this area have been largely exploratory, and they have yielded conflicting results regarding age differences.

Of further interest is the extent to which the age deficits in memory found for item content generalize to other attributes of items, such as their format (e.g., whether presented in uppercase or lowercase letters) and their frequencies of occurrence in a series. Some memory theorists believe that these attributes are encoded automatically and are, therefore, unaffected by the diminished processing capacity believed to be characteristic of late adulthood. Given such automaticity, no age differences are expected in memory scores for these attributes. However, the evidence indicates that age deficits are present for memory of nonsemantic attributes, including both case format and the sex of voice of auditorily presented items. The evidence for automaticity and the absence of adult-age differences is more ambiguous for the encoding of frequency-of-occurrence information, with some studies reporting no age differences and other studies reporting modest age differences favoring young adults.

Finally, episodic memory is largely contingent on information stored in generic memory as the basis for encoding various episodic events. The possibility of age differences in the structures and operations of generic memory has received considerable attention in recent years. A number of studies have indicated that the generic-memory system, unlike the episodic-memory system, is immune to any major change over the course of the adult lifespan, at least with respect to the retrieval of its stored knowledge. However, another component of generic memory, referred to as metamemory, may show age changes, particularly in terms of self-knowledge regarding how well episodic information has been mastered.

CHAPTER 10

Thinking

Pondering the meaning of a black hole, solving the daily scrambled word or anagram puzzle in your local newspaper, and deducing what your bridge partner has in mind with that last strange bid. These are everyday examples of the three main activities experimental psychologists study under the general heading of *directed thinking:* concept formation (the black hole example), problem solving (the scrambled-word example), and reasoning (the bridge example). In directed thinking, symbols, whether words or images, are manipulated covertly to achieve a particular objective. These manipulations clearly involve higher order processes, that is, processes that are more complex than the lower order processes governing perception, memory, and so on.

Consider, for example, what took place when you finally understood the meaning of a strike in baseball. To do so, you had to form a disjunctive concept. Three different stimulus events had to be identified and each event had to be independently associated with the same response, that of saying strike. The first consists of the batter swinging and missing, the second of the batter failing to swing when the umpire says he should have, and the third of the batter hitting the ball but the ball lands outside of the playing field. Your learning in this case was surely more complex than the simple paired-associate learning that occurred when you identified the name *Royals* with Kansas City.

Concept acquisition is largely concentrated in childhood. It is then that we form concepts of a person, a tree, a building, and other stable concepts that permit us to classify the objects and events of our environment and, therefore, provide an organizational structure for our generic memories. Nevertheless, our constantly changing society makes concept formation a lifespan activity. Over the past century, adults have encountered such novel concepts as an automobile, an airplane, fascism, a hippie, rock and roll, and gas guzzler. Each new concept must be mastered by adults of all ages, including elderly people, if they are to stay in step with social changes. Similarly, adults of all ages encounter problems to be solved and dilemmas to be reasoned through. In fact, the list is virtually endless—finding a way to enter your locked apartment when you do not have the key, figuring out what car to buy that best fits your needs and budget, and so on. Proficient problem solving and reasoning are obviously as important for the adjustment of older people to their environments as they are for the adjustment of younger people to their environments.

Many elderly people are as concerned about their presumed decline in thinking ability as they are about their presumed decline in memory. "I just don't think as clearly as I used to" is a remark we often hear made by elderly people. In this chapter, we will review the relatively little that is known about age changes in directed thinking activities. Our review will focus initially on concept formation, problem solving, and reasoning. Progress in understanding age changes in these activities has lagged behind the progress made in understanding age changes in the lower order (but still complex in their own right) activities of perception, learning, retention/transfer, and memory. Part of the lag is the consequence of the complexities of the higher order processes. These complexities have made it difficult both to conceptualize the underlying processes in terms of comprehensive theories and to isolate in the laboratory those processes that have been adequately conceptualized. Unfortunately, experimental aging psychologists have also contributed substantially to the lag. The contribution comes from their general adherence to what Giambra and Arenberg (1980) have called a "Gee-whiz, look at the age differences mentality" (p. 257). Experimental aging researchers have typically employed tasks in procedures that accomplish little more than revealing the existence of adult-age differences in, for example, the proficiency of problem solving. That is, their studies often yield little insight into the reasons for those age differences. The tasks employed are frequently invented by the investigators themselves without regard for their analytical capacities for identifying age-sensitive processes. Moreover, age is the only independent variable included in many adult studies on directed thinking. The identification of age-sensitive processes, of course, is highly contingent on the presence or absence of an interaction between age and a manipulable independent variable known from basic research to alter the contribution of a particular process to performance on a higher order task.

Two other topics will also be reviewed in this chapter. The first deals with age differences/changes in the ability to perform what has become known as a mental rotation. It is an important ability in that it focuses on the involvement of imaginal processes in thinking. The suspected decrement in the use of imagery by older people has made research on age differences in this ability a topic of considerable interest to the experimental psychology of aging. The second topic is one we discussed briefly in Chapter 6. It deals with age changes in logical thinking as viewed from the perspective of Jean Piaget's stage theory of cognitive development.

Finally, we should note that there is one other higher order activity, decision making, that is of interest in the experimental psychology of aging. Our review of aging research on this activity will be reserved for Chapter 11. Research in this area has been concerned mainly with the effects of age differences in personality on age differences in decision-making characteristics.

Adult Age Differences in Concept Formation

Classification of Concepts. Before we can examine age differences in concept formation, we must first be familiar with the nature of concepts per se and with the nature of basic research on concept formation. We will begin with an overview of the various types of concepts we acquire and the means by which these types are simulated in the laboratory.

Most objects and events in our environment are instances of one or more concepts. A given concept, such as *a car,* is defined with respect to both its attribute values on *relevant stimulus dimensions* and the *rule* that specifies the way these attributes must be combined to form a positive instance of the concept. Consider what is required for a vehicle to be an instance of *a car.* The relevant stimulus dimensions include the vehicle's power source and number of wheels. The possible attribute values are mechanically powered versus animal powered on the first dimension and four wheels versus two wheels on the other dimension. For a vehicle to be an instance of a car, it must have both mechanical power *and* four wheels. Otherwise, the vehicle could be either a wagon (animal power, four wheels) or a motorcycle (mechanical power, two wheels). In this case, we have what is called a *conjunctive concept.* The rule for a conjunctive concept specifies that all positive attribute values must be present before an object/event can be considered an instance of that concept. By contrast, a strike in baseball, as we discovered earlier, exemplifies a disjunctive concept. For a disjunctive concept, the rule specifies that the presence of any one of the concept's positive attribute values is sufficient to define an instance of that concept.

The instances of a given concept need to be alike only with respect to their values on relevant stimulus dimensions. That is, they are free to vary in their values on other *irrelevant stimulus dimensions.* For a car, irrelevant stimulus dimensions include both size and color. A Volkswagen whether red, white, or blue is as much an instance of a car as is a Lincoln Continental. Similarly, a called strike in baseball is a strike whether the ball had been thrown by a right-handed or a left-handed pitcher. In principle, most concepts, once they have been formed, must be capable of generalization across a wide range of irrelevant stimulus dimensions to fulfill their organization role in human thinking.

To study conjunctive and disjunctive concept formation as well as the formation of still other types of concepts in the laboratory, basic researchers commonly make use of the kinds of objects illustrated in Figure 10.1. In actual studies, the objects are usually depicted individually on cards. For the sake of simplicity, only three stimulus dimensions, each with only two attribute values, are represented in the objects shown in this figure. The first dimension is form, with square and triangle as attribute values, the second dimension is brightness, with black and white as attribute values, and the third dimension is size, with large and small as attribute values. In many studies, there may be additional

Objects

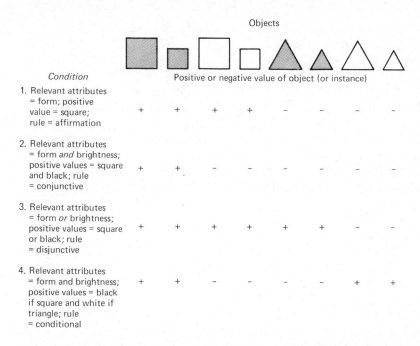

Condition	Positive or negative value of object (or instance)							
1. Relevant attributes = form; positive value = square; rule = affirmation	+	+	+	+	−	−	−	−
2. Relevant attributes = form *and* brightness; positive values = square and black; rule = conjunctive	+	+	−	−	−	−	−	−
3. Relevant attributes = form *or* brightness; positive values = square or black; rule = disjunctive	+	+	+	+	+	+	−	−
4. Relevant attributes = form and brightness; positive values = black if square and white if triangle; rule = conditional	+	+	−	−	−	−	+	+

Figure 10.1. Representative objects and conditions for defining various types of concepts.

dimensions, such as the presence of absence of a border around a depicted object or there may be additional attribute values for a given dimension, such as a circle as well as a square and a triangle for the form dimension.

The simplest type of concept to be formed from the kinds of objects shown in Figure 10.1 is one in which there is only one relevant stimulus dimension. One attribute value of that dimension then defines all positive instances of the concept, whereas all other attribute values define negative instances of the same concept. For example, form, as indicated in Figure 10.1, may be the relevant dimension, with squareness assigned the positive value and triangularity the negative value. The resulting four objects that are positive instances of the squareness concept are indicated in Figure 10.1. Note that brightness and size have become irrelevant dimensions. That is, it does not matter if a square is black or white, large or small, it remains a positive instance of the to-be-discovered concept. The rule for any single-dimension concept is simply one of affirmation—an object is a positive instance as long as it possesses the positive value of that one dimension. Our laboratory-based squareness concept functions much the way the real-world squareness concept functions. Objects in the real world are square whether they be tiles, windows, or walls.

More complex concepts are ones having two or more relevant dimensions. For example, with reference to the objects in Figure 10.1, both form and brightness may be relevant dimensions, thus making size the only irrelevant dimension. In Figure 10.1, square and black have been assigned the roles of positive attributes for these dimensions. Given these values, the type of concept that may be formed depends on the kind of rule relating the attributes to one another. For a conjunctive concept, the rule demands an *and* relationship—both squareness and blackness must be present in an object for it to be defined as a positive instance of the concept. Consequently, only two of the objects in Figure 10.1 are positive instances of the to-be-discovered concept, the remaining six objects are all negative instances of the concept. The processes entering into the formation of an artificial conjunctive concept, like a black square, presumably approximate the processes entering into the formation of real-world conjunctive concepts, such as that of a car. For a disjunctive concept, we may retain the same positive values, but we now change the rule to that of an either/or relationship between those values. That is, *either* squareness *or* blackness present in an object is sufficient to define a positive instance of the now disjunctive concept. Six of the eight objects shown in Figure 10.1 would, therefore, qualify as positive instances of this concept. Again, the processes entering into the formation of an artificial disjunctive concept, like square or black, presumably approximate the processes entering into the formation of real-world disjunctive concepts, such as that of a strike in baseball.

There is one other type of concept that may be formed from the objects shown in Figure 10.1. It involves a rule that it considerably more complex than either a conjunctive rule or a disjunctive rule. It is a conditional, or *if/then,* rule. For example, with form and brightness as the relevant stimulus dimensions, the rule could be: if the form is a square, then it must be black to be a positive instance of the concept; however, if the form is a triangle, then it must be white to be a positive instance of the concept. As indicated in Figure 10.1, four of the eight objects qualify as positive instances of this conditional concept. In the real world, a familiar example of a conditional rule is one that expands and qualifies on the concept of a strike in baseball. If a batter has fewer than two strikes, then a foul ball adds another strike to his count; however, if a batter has two strikes, then a foul ball adds nothing to his count.

Nature of Basic Research on Concept Formation. Suppose subjects are given the task of identifying one of the concepts derivable from the objects in Figure 10.1. The typical procedure for studying their proficiency on this task would follow what is called the reception paradigm. A stack of cards is prepared, each containing either a positive or a negative instance of the to-be-identified concept. The cards are arranged in a predetermined order by the investigator who then administers them one by one to the subjects. As the subjects study each card, they are required to classify the card as containing a positive or negative instance of the concept. After each classification, they are given feedback regarding its correctness. This procedure continues until some specified criterion, such as 10 consecutive instances classified without error, is attained. The number of errors made in reaching this criterion commonly serves as the primary dependent variable used to assess the proficiency of concept formation. This dependent variable may be supplemented by another dependent variable that requires subjects to verbalize both the positive attributes of the concept in question and the rule regarding the combination of those attributes. With an alternative procedure, called the selection paradigm (Bruner, Goodnow, & Austin, 1956), all of the possible positive and negative instances of the concept are exposed simultaneously. Initially, a positive instance is pointed to by the experimenter. After studying that instance, subjects are allowed to make their own choices of what they believe are positive instances, receiving feedback as to their correctness after each choice. Their selections continue until they reach the specified criterion.

The selection paradigm is especially useful in determining the strategy a subject seems to be applying in identifying a concept. The strategy used by many young adults is called the conservative focusing strategy. An as example, consider an array of instances, or objects, constructed by varying the attributes of the three stimulus dimensions of size, brightness, and form. Suppose the initial positive instance identified by the experimenter is a large black square. On the subject's first selection of an instance, the conservative focusing strategy calls for varying the attribute value of one of the three dimensions, while retaining the attribute values of the other two dimensions. For example, the subject might vary only the size-dimension attribute, therefore, selecting a *small* black square. If told that this too is a positive instance of the concept, then the subject should know that size is an irrelevant stimulus dimension. That is, the largeness or smallness of the object does not matter. If told that the new selection is a negative instance, then the subject should know that largeness is one of the positive attributes of the to-be-identified concept. There are, of course, other possible strategies, such as the focus-gambling strategy in which a subject varies attribute values for two or more stimulus dimensions simultaneously (e.g., selects a *small white* square). With this strategy the subject risks gaining little new information when the selected instance is negative. Either one of the varied attributes could have a positive value. There is no way of knowing which one without making an additional selection of an instance and receiving feedback regarding its correctness. For this reason, the focus-gambling strategy is ordinarily not a very popular one with young adults.

In most studies employing either the reception paradigm or the selection paradigm, subjects have to discover on their own both the to-be-identified concept's positive attribute values and the rule (e.g., conjunctive or disjunctive) regarding those values to identify the concept. There is, however, an important modification of this standard procedure in which subjects are told in advance what the positive attribute values are for the to-be-identified concept. Therefore, their only requirement in this modified procedure is to discover the rule that governs the way those values combine to form the concept. For example, they may be told that black and square are the positive values and then respond to instances until they discover that the governing rule is a disjunctive one. It is through studies (e.g., Haygood & Bourne, 1965) employing this modified procedure that we know that rules vary in difficulty—again, the affirmation rule being the easiest to discover, followed by the conjunctive, disjunctive, and conditional.

Given the standard procedure in which subjects have to discover both the positive attributes and the rule and either the reception or the selection para-

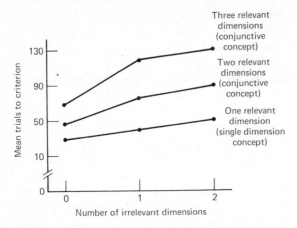

Figure 10.2. Representative results when the number of relevant and the number of irrelevant stimulus dimensions of a concept-learning problem are varied simultaneously. (Adapted from Bulgarella & Archer, 1962, Figure 1.)

digm, variation in some important task condition may be readily introduced in an experiment, and the effect of that variation on the proficiency of concept identification may then be determined (see Bourne, 1966; Bourne, Dominowski, & Loftus, 1979, for detailed reviews of basic research on concept identification). Illustrative of this kind of research are studies varying the number of relevant and irrelevant stimulus dimensions. Suppose, for example, that there are five different stimulus dimensions entering into the construction of possible positive and negative instances of a concept. For a simple unidimensional concept, such as blackness or squareness, the single relevant dimension could be combined with one, two, three, or four irrelevant dimensions in forming positive and negative instances. For either a conjunctive or a disjunctive concept, there could be two, three, or four relevant stimulus dimensions combined respectively, with three, two, or one irrelevant stimulus dimensions. Many studies with young adults have revealed the general pattern of results illustrated in Figure 10.2 (Bulgarella & Archer, 1962). Note that difficulty increases progressively as the number of dimensions, both relevant and irrelevant, increases.

Another popular variation calls for holding constant the number of relevant and irrelevant dimensions while varying the number of attributes within each dimension. For example, with form as one of the dimensions, the number of attributes could vary from two to five or more (e.g., square, triangle, circle, diamond, and rectangle). As the number of attributes increases systematically from two to five, the number of positive attribute values remains fixed at one, whereas the number of negative values increases from one to four. Not surprisingly, the difficulty of reaching a criterion of mastery increases progressively as the number of negative values for each stimulus dimension increases.

Associative Theories of Concept Acquisition and Their Extensions to Age Deficits. The identification of age-sensitive processes in concept attainment is possible only to the extent that the processes governing concept formation per se have been adequately conceptualized. In this section and the next, we will examine briefly the kinds of associative and cognitive theories that have attempted over the years to conceptualize these processes (see Bourne et al., 1979, and Solso, 1979, for more comprehensive reviews). We will also indicate how these theories may be extended to account for age deficits in the proficiency of concept acquisition.

Classical associationism offers a rather sterile but, nevertheless, fairly complete conceptual base for analyzing the processes of concept acquisition. The basic nature of this analysis is illustrated in Figure 10.3 with respect to a single dimensional concept, that of squareness. For simplicity's sake, only one irrelevant dimension, brightness, is included in this illustration, and both the relevant and the irrelevant dimension have been given only two attribute values (square and triangle for the relevant dimension and black and white for the irrelevant dimension). Consequently, only the four objects shown in Figure 10.3 are received by a subject, one per trial. As each object is received, the subject responds yes or no to indicate whether or not that object is believed to be a positive instance of the to-be-identified concept. Feedback is then given

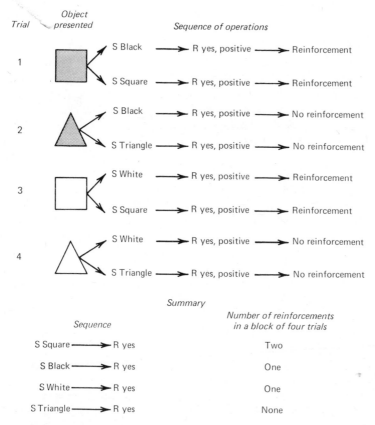

Figure 10.3. Analysis of the acquisition of a simple concept from the perspective of classical associationism.

regarding the correctness of that response. Positive feedback following a correct yes response serves as a reinforcement to strengthen the associations between the stimulus features present in the object (e.g., squareness and blackness) and the response of saying yes. The subject's task is essentially one of discrimination learning (Restle, 1955). That is, the subject must learn to give one response, saying yes, to any object possessing one of those features, squareness, while learning to give a different response, saying no, to any object that does not possess that stimulus feature. Note in Figure 10.3 that in each block of four trials, a yes response to the square feature receives two reinforcements, whereas yes responses to black and white features each receive one reinforcement, and a yes response to the triangle feature receives no reinforcements. Over a number of such blocks of trials, the yes response to triangularity should eventually be extinguished, whereas the yes response to squareness should gain (because of its higher rate of reinforcement) more associative strength than the yes response to either blackness or whiteness. If now asked to identify the concept, the subject should reply squareness simply because the yes response to any object containing that stimulus feature has accrued discriminably greater strength than the comparable response to all objects that are devoid of that feature.

Why should difficulty increase considerably when the to-be-identified concept is more complex than a single-dimension concept? The probable reason is illustrated in Figure 10.4 for the conjunctive concept of a black square. Note that a yes response to each of the positive stimulus features, blackness and squareness, receives only one reinforcement in each block of trials. Moreover, these responses also receive one nonreinforcement in each trial block, as do the responses to the negative stimulus features, whiteness and triangularity. With fewer reinforcements per block of trials to positive stimulus features combined with the added factor of some nonreinforced responses to those same features, the disparity in overall strength of connection to the yes response favoring the positive stimulus object over the negative stimulus objects grows at a slower rate than when the concept involves only one dimension. Consequently, discrimination on the basis of associative strength takes more trials to accomplish than it does in the case of the simpler one-dimensional concept. Our analysis also implies that discrimination on the basis of disparities in associative strengths for different stimulus objects should increase in difficulty as the number of stimulus dimensions or attributes increases, which is in agreement with the usual experimental findings.

There are two possible directions a gerontological psychologist may take to explain age deficits in the proficiency of concept acquisition from the perspective of classical associationism's analysis of the underlying processes. The first direction stresses attention and perception as the basis for age deficits in mastering the kinds of concepts illustrated in Figures 10.3 and 10.4. In effect, an object, such as a black square, is a compound stimulus that must be perceived in terms of its component elements or features (e.g., a black square is both black and a square) if concept acquisition is to occur. Conceivably, elderly adults are slower in their segmentation of such compounds into their elements

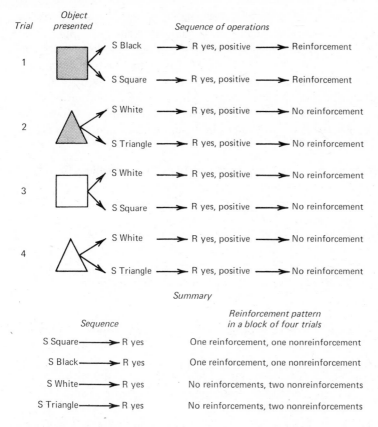

Figure 10.4. Analysis of the acquisition of a conjunctive concept from the perspective of classical associationism.

than are young adults. If true, the consequence, of course, would necessarily be a slower rate of concept acquisition for elderly subjects than for young subjects. The second direction stresses basic learning processes as the locus of age deficits in concept formation. One possibility rests in the now-familiar principle that elderly adults have a slower rehearsal rate than young adults. Following a positive feedback to a yes response, subjects are likely to rehearse the stimulus elements just perceived in conjunction with the response yes or its equivalent. This rehearsal activity should strengthen further the connections between the stimulus features and the yes response. However, the slower rehearsal rate of elderly subjects should result in smaller increments in strength than the increments found for young subjects. Another possibility is that of a greater difference threshold for elderly subjects than for young subjects. If true, then the disparity in strengths for associations involving positive- and negative-stimulus objects would have to be greater for elderly subjects than for young subjects for the discrimination between strengths to become reliable. Of course, it is conceivable that both perceptual and learning processes are involved in the age deficits commonly found in research on concept acquisition.

Concept acquisition may also be approached from the perspective of stage analysis. Here the emphasis is placed on a subject's ability to apply verbal mediators—particularly the names associated with the stimulus dimensions and stimulus features embedded within the positive and negative instances of the concept—to short-circuit the rote acquisition of the solution (e.g., Kendler & Kendler, 1962). Mediational theory has been especially important in stimulating research on age differences in transfer on various kinds of concept-oriented tasks. We will examine this theory in greater detail when we review this specific area of research.

Cognitive Theories of Concept Attainment and Their Extensions to Age Deficits. Cognitive psychologists have long argued that subjects are active participants in forming concepts rather than passive accumulators of associative strengths as pictured by classical associationism's analysis of concept attainment. Their active nature is manifested largely in their ability to formulate hypotheses, or reasoned guesses, concerning the attribute or attributes defining the to-be-identified concept. Moreover, subjects are capable of abandoning a given hypothesis when it proves to be incorrect and substituting another hypothesis in its place.

An early hypothesis-testing theory of concept acquisition was that of Bower and Trabasso (1964). They postulated that subjects approach objects of the kind described in Table 10.1 with a pool of all possible hypotheses regarding the stimulus feature or features defining the concept in question. To demonstrate the basic nature of their theory, we will deal only with a single dimensional concept assigned to the eight objects described in Table 10.1. We will assume that the experimenter has made size the relevant stimulus dimension and with large the positive attribute value or stimulus feature. Moreover, we will assume that subjects have been informed in advance that the concept in question is a single dimensional one. Knowing this, an active and reasonable subject would construct a pool of the six possible hypotheses (indicated in Table 10.1) regarding the specific stimulus feature designated by the experimenter to be the defining feature. On presentation of the first object, a small black square, the subject selects randomly one of the six hypotheses from the pool. We have assumed in Table 10.1 that "black is the positive feature" is the first hypothesis selected. This hypothesis is then applied to the first object, serving as the basis for a yes or no decision. Because that object is black, the subject responds, "Yes, it is a positive instance of the concept." However, the experimenter's feedback informs the subject that this response is incorrect. That is, the object is a negative instance of the concept. At this point, the subject abandons the first hypothesis and samples from the pool to select a second hypothesis, namely, "White is the positive feature." This hypothesis is then applied to the second object presented, a large white triangle. Because this object is white, the subject responds, "Yes," and receives feedback revealing that this response is correct (but, of course, for the wrong reason). Now there is no reason to abandon the on-going hypothesis, and it is applied to the next object presented, a large black triangle. Given the absence of whiteness in the object, the subject responds, "No." However, the experimenter's feedback re-

Table 10.1   Hypothetical Series of Trials for a Subject on a Single-Dimension Concept Problem[a]

Pool of Objects	Pool of Hypotheses
Large black square, small black square, large white square, small white square, large black triangle, small black triangle, large white triangle, small white triangle	Black is the positive feature White is the positive feature Square is the positive feature Triangle is the positive feature Large is the positive feature Small is the positive feature

Trial	Object Presented	Hypothesis Sampled	Subject's Response	Feedback	Fate of Hypothesis
1	Small black square	Black is positive	Yes	Incorrect	Abandoned (returned to pool)
2	Large white triangle	White is positive	Yes	Correct	Retained
3	Large black triangle	White is positive	No	Incorrect	Abandoned (returned to pool)
4	Small white triangle	Triangle is positive	Yes	Incorrect	Abandoned (returned to pool)
5	Large black square	Small is positive	No	Incorrect	Abandoned (returned to pool)
6	Small black triangle	Large is positive	No	Correct	Retained (solution has been attained)
7	Large white square	Large is positive	Yes	Correct	Retained
8	Small white square	Large is positive	No	Correct	Retained

[a] The objects received are given at the top (largeness is the experimenter-designated positive stimulus feature) as are the hypotheses formulated by the subject. The subject's performance is based on predictions derived from Bower and Trabasso's (1964) hypothesis-testing theory of concept acquisition.

veals that this response is incorrect, forcing the subject to abandon the second hypothesis and select a third one from the pool for testing the next object. This process continues until the subject finally selects the correct hypothesis from the pool (Trial 6, Table 10.1). Once this hypothesis is selected, all decisions based on it will be correct. Consequently, there is no reason to abandon this hypothesis—the problem at hand has been solved.

From this analysis we may see that Bower and Trabasso's theory has three distinguishing characteristics or principles. First, progress toward acquiring the concept in question takes place only on trials in which a subject makes an error in responding to an object or instance. Then, and only then, is an incorrect hypothesis eliminated and an opportunity is created for selecting the correct hypothesis. Second, acquisition of the concept proceeds in an all-or-none manner. The concept is acquired only when the correct hypothesis is sampled— prior to that time the subject is performing at a chance level (i.e., correctness is contingent solely on the coincidental correlation between the subject's erroneous hypothesis and the object the experimenter assigned for presentation). By contrast, associationism's account holds to the principle that concept acquisition occurs gradually through steady increments in associative strength. Finally, and most surprisingly, the theory postulates a memoryless subject. Once an incorrect hypothesis is rejected, it is returned to the original pool from which it may again be sampled and applied all over again (and, of course, rejected again). That is, there is no episodic memory trace of a given hypothesis's incorrectness, and there is, therefore, no mechanism for avoiding its reselection and reapplication.

These principles have been only moderately successful in accounting for the results obtained in the many basic research studies reported on concept acquisition. A far more successful hypothesis-testing theory is one introduced by Levine (e.g., 1975). Its principles are considerably more in line with those of information-processing psychology than are the principles of Bower and Trabasso's (1964) theory. Most important, episodic memory is assumed to play an important role in attaining the correct hypothesis. Specifically, hypotheses, once they have been formulated, are transmitted as memory traces to episodic memory. There the traces become organized into two subsets as practice on the concept task progresses. The first subset contains only traces of those hypotheses that have already been tested and found to be incorrect. The second subset contains traces of only those hypotheses that have yet to be tested and, therefore, remain viable with respect to identifying the critical positive feature. Whenever a new hypothesis needs to be selected, it is retrieved randomly from the second subset. Optimal performance in concept acquisition, thus, demands a perfect memory system, a demand that is, of course, virtually impossible to fulfill.

There are other important principles of Levine's (1975) theory that depart from those of Bower and Trabasso's (1964) theory. For example, a subject is viewed as being capable of testing at one time more than one hypothesis from the total pool of viable hypotheses. How this is possible is described in Table 10.2 for the same materials and initial pool of hypotheses found in Table 10.1. On Trial 1 the subject again selects the hypothesis, "Black is the positive feature" and applies it to the small black square object (large remains the experimenter-defined positive feature). By discovering that this object is not a positive instance of the to-be-identified concept, the subject now has the evidence to rule out not only the initial hypothesis but also two other hypotheses, namely, "Small is the positive feature" and "Square is the positive feature." That is, these tag along hypotheses could not possibly be correct and still have a *small* black *square* be a negative instance of the concept. Consequently, the subject may now organize the six hypotheses into subsets of the three hypotheses already rejected and the other three hypotheses that remain potentially

Table 10.2 Restructuring of the Events Shown in Table 10.1, this Time from the Perspective of Levine's (1975) Hypothesis-Testing Theory of Concept Acquisition

Pool of Objects					Pool of Hypotheses
Same as those shown in Table 10.1					Same as those shown in Table 10.1

Trial	Object	Hypothesis Sampled	Response	Feedback	Outcome
1	Small black square	Black is positive	Yes	Incorrect	Store "black is positive," "small is positive," and "square is positive" as a subset of incorrect hypotheses in episodic memory; store "white is positive," "large is positive," and "triangle is positive" as a different subset of potentially correct hypotheses
2	Large white triangle	White is positive	Yes	Correct	No change in information stored in episodic memory
3	Large black triangle	White is positive	No	Incorrect	Add "white is positive" to subset of incorrect hypotheses in episodic memory; only "triangle is positive" and "large is positive" remain in subset of potentially correct hypotheses
4	Small white triangle	Triangle is positive	Yes	Incorrect	Add "triangle is positive" to subset of incorrect hypotheses; only "large is positive" remains in subset of potentially correct hypotheses and must, therefore, be correct (solution has been attained)
5	Large black square	Large is positive	Yes	Correct	Hypothesis retained
6	Small black triangle	Large is positive	No	Correct	Hypothesis retained

correct. It is from this second subset of three that the subject selects randomly the next hypothesis to be tested on the second object presented by the experimenter (a large white triangle). Note that the probability of selecting the correct hypothesis (one out of three or .33) is considerably greater than predicted by Bower and Trabasso's (1964) theory (one out of six or .167—remember a rejected hypothesis is returned to the original pool and that the pool size for selection is always six hypotheses for the present materials). The second hypothesis selected is assumed to be, "White is the positive feature." When this hypothesis is applied to the second object, the subject must respond "Yes," therefore, receiving feedback revealing the response is correct (but, again, for the wrong reason). Thus, there is no reason to change the hypothesis for testing the third object presented (a large black triangle). However, the feedback following the subject's "No" response indicates that this hypothesis is incorrect and should, therefore, be added to the subset of incorrect hypotheses in episodic memory. At this point, the only hypothesis remaining in the still viable subset is the correct one, "Large is the positive feature"—and the solution has been attained.

Age deficits in concept acquisition may be explained from the perspective of a hypothesis-testing theory in terms of either, or both, lower order or higher order age-sensitive processes. Lower order processes include both the encoding of stimulus features embedded in the objects/instances received for study and episodic memory of hypotheses that have already proved to be incorrect. The encoding deficit possibility is one shared with classical associationism's analysis of potential sources of age sensitivity. Again, the ability to segment, or encode, an object such as a black square into its component features of black and square is an indispensable preliminary step for acquiring a concept. An age-related decline in the proficiency of feature analysis could, therefore, account for much of an age-related decline in the proficiency of concept acquisition. The memory source of possible sensitivity is unique to Levine's (1975) cognitive information-processing theory of concept acquisition. Given an age-related decrement in episodic-memory proficiency, we would expect elderly subjects to have greater difficulty than young subjects in segregating traces of tested and rejected hypotheses and still viable hypotheses into appropriate subsets. In effect, subjects with poor episodic-memory proficiency would be expected to perform on a concept task in the manner predicted by Bower and Trabasso's (1964) memoryless-subject theory. By contrast, subjects with excellent episodic-memory proficiency would be expected to perform in the manner predicted by Levine's perfect-memory theory. As observed earlier, a clear superiority in rate-of-concept acquisition is predicted for those subjects who at least approximate a perfect memory system.

The most likely higher order process to be considered for age sensitivity is the ability to formulate hypotheses per se. Memory of a rejected hypothesis involving adequately encoded features is impossible unless subjects actually generate a pool of hypotheses to guide their search for the positive-stimulus feature. Elderly subjects may simply view a concept-acquisition problem as if it were one of rote learning. Consequently, they may make little, if any, effort to generate formal hypotheses. The slow, incremental acquisition of the solution predicted by classical associationism's analysis of concept acquisition would be the result. That is, elderly adults may simply be manifesting a production deficiency, a deficiency that could be overcome with appropriate training and practice on the skill of formulating hypotheses. Alternatively, the ability to generate hypotheses may suffer a true decrement from early to late adulthood. If true, then training and practice would not be able to overcome the deficit.

Classification of Objects. Before we review studies dealing directly with age differences in concept acquisition, we will touch on studies dealing with age differences in a closely related behavior. The behavior is that of classifying, or categorizing, diverse objects in some systematic manner. Skill in this behavior often plays an important role in many kinds of cognitive activities (Bruner, 1966). Basically, what is required on a classification task is the ability to discover similarities among objects, much as similarities among positive instances must be discovered in concept acquisition.

Representative of research on age differences in classifying behavior are studies by Kogan (1974), Cicirelli (1976), Denney (1974b), and Denney and Lennon (1972). The studies by Kogan and Cicirelli employed the same materials, a stack of 50 pictures of common objects, such as a fork, a cup, a book, and a pipe. Both young and elderly subjects sorted the stack after being instructed to group the objects depicted into "the most comfortable number of categories." Of initial interest is the number of categories, or groups of objects, to which the pictures were assigned. Elderly subjects were found by both Kogan and Cicirelli to assign the pictures to fewer categories than did the young subjects. In Cicirelli's (1976) study, there were three groups of elderly subjects, the first consisting of people in their 60s, the second of people in their 70s, and the third of people in their 80s. The trend toward the use of fewer categories in late adulthood was found to increase in magnitude from the 60s through the 80s. At the same time, more pictures/objects were left unclassified, or ungrouped, by elderly subjects than by young subjects in both studies. Of greater interest, however, are the qualitative differences among age groups in the nature of their invented categories. One class of categories, referred to as categorical-inferential, consists of superordinates (e.g., kitchen utensils as the inferred basis for grouping a fork and a cup together). Another class, referred to as relational-thematic, consists of placing objects together simply because of their meaning relationship to one another (e.g., a match and a pipe). Sorting into relational-thematic categories is generally considered to be a less mature, less abstract mode of thinking than is sorting into categorical-inferential categories. In both studies, a smaller percentage of the total number of invented categories was found to consist of categorical-inferential categories for elderly subjects than for young subjects, whereas the reverse was true for the percentage of relational-thematic categories. It may be seen in Figure 10.5 that these trends were especially apparent in very late adulthood. Similar trends were found in the studies by Denney (1974b; Denney & Lennon, 1972), but with different kinds of objects (geometric figures) to be sorted.

Do these trends reflect "regressive age changes in certain categorization behaviors?" (Cicirelli, 1976, p. 67). Interestingly, the investigators in these studies believe not. Kogan (1973, 1974) attributed the increased use of relational responding by elderly subjects to their willingness to try something more ad-

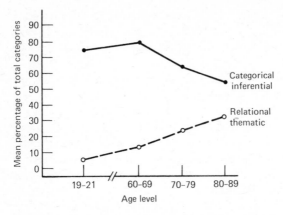

Figure 10.5. Age differences in sorting objects into categorical-inferential classes (a relatively abstract form of thinking) and relational-thematic classes (a less abstract form of thinking). (Adapted from Cicirelli, 1976, Table 1.)

venturous and less conventional. In effect, an age difference in cognitive style is held responsible for the age differences in cognitive behavior. We will have more to say about age differences in cognitive style in Chapter 11. Denney (1974b) discovered that many of her elderly subjects who did not sort at the higher level (i.e., categorical-inferential) could be trained to do so through the use of a brief modeling procedure. The implication, of course, is that the cognitive deficit found in these studies is really the consequence of a production deficit and not the product of a true decrement in overall cognitive ability during late adulthood. Finally, in sympathy with Denney's position, Cicirelli concluded that the "environment of many elderly people is not one which requires the use of logical classification, and thus such responses would not tend to appear unless there was some clear demand for their use" (1976, p. 680). Nevertheless, more evidence is clearly needed before we can conclude definitely that categorization ability does not suffer a true age change.

Descriptive Studies on Age Differences in Concept Acquisition. There have been a number of purely descriptive studies on adult-age differences in the proficiency of concept acquisition. The nature of the materials used in these studies has varied greatly. In some studies (e.g., Botwinick & Birren, 1963; Hopkins & Post, 1955; Mack & Carlson, 1978; Thaler, 1956; Vega & Parsons, 1967) the materials consisted of forms varying along other dimensions (e.g., size and color). Thus, the positive and negative instances of the to-be-identified concept were much like those used in most basic research studies on concept acquisition with only young adults as subjects. In other studies (e.g., Wetherick, 1964; Wiersma & Klausmeier, 1965), the investigators made up their own materials. Typically, the to-be-identified concept in these descriptive studies has been a single dimensional one. However, conjunctive and disjunctive concepts were involved in some of these studies. Regardless of type of concept to be acquired, inferior performance—whether measured by trials to a criterion, time to attain a criterion, or errors made in attaining a criterion—for older subjects relative to younger subjects has been the typical outcome. An important exception, however, occurred in the study by Wetherick (1964). No age differences were found in this study for the acquisition of either a simple single-dimension concept or a more complex disjunctive concept. Interestingly, Wetherick's young and elderly subjects had been carefully matched in scores on a test (Raven Progressive Matrices Test) commonly believed to measure level of fluid intelligence. We will return to this point in Chapter 11.

To illustrate the general nature of descriptive aging studies on concept acquisition, we will examine in some detail the study by Wiersma and Klausmeier (1965). The selection paradigm was used for an array of 64 instances, constructed from four stimulus dimensions, two of which had four attribute values and two had two attribute values. The to-be-identified concepts were conjunctive ones in which one of the two-value dimensions provided one of the positive features and one of the four-value dimensions provided the other positive feature. Thus, there were two relevant and two irrelevant dimensions involved in each of four different to-be-identified concepts. The dimensions themselves were made to conform to stimulus conditions likely to exist in a classroom setting (e.g., the kind of teaching method used and the type of subject content being taught; the subjects were education students). There were three age groups: a young adult group, ranging in age from 20 to 24 years, a slightly older group, ranging in age from 25 to 34 years, and a middle-age group, ranging in age from 35 to 51 years. The differences in performance proficiency over this restricted segment of the adult lifespan are plotted in Figure 10.6 for both time taken to identify concepts and the total number of errors made during acquisition. It can be seen that, with either dependent variable score, proficiency declined as age increased (although only the age

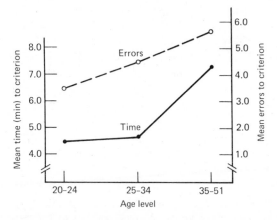

Figure 10.6. Age differences in performance scores (errors made in identifying the concept and time taken to identify the concept) on a conjunctive concept problem. (Adapted from data in Wiersma & Klausmeier, 1965.)

difference in the time score was statistically significant). A reasonable expectancy is that the rate of decline would have accelerated considerably if older age levels had also been included in the study.

Unfortunately, as observed by Arenberg (1973), Wiersma and Klausmeier's (1965) study offers no information about why solution time increases with increasing age. The longer time taken by the oldest group could have resulted from either, or both, an increase in time per selection or an increase in the number of selections required to identify a given concept. The absence of independent variables other than age makes an analysis of the sources of age sensitivity impossible, a limitation shared with the other purely descriptive studies.

Process-Oriented Studies on Age Differences in Concept Acquisition. There has been a smattering of studies that go beyond the "Gee whiz, look at the age differences" approach to research on the effects of aging on the proficiency of concept acquisition. In this section, we will review what these studies have revealed about the reasons for age deficits in ease of concept acquisition. Although these studies do offer valuable insights into age-sensitive processes, they have also yielded conflicting evidence regarding some of these processes.

Our assumption, of course, is that there are indeed age-sensitive processes that account for the age deficits reported in the purely descriptive studies. This is not necessarily true however. The age deficits observed in these studies may merely be the consequence of adverse performance factors that, once removed, would eliminate the age deficits.

As with classification behavior, appropriate responses by elderly subjects may not appear spontaneously unless there is "some clear demand for their use" (Cicirelli, 1976, p. 680). The relative void in spontaneous use of appropriate responses could be the result of years of exposure to an environment that rarely demands responses to the kinds of abstract stimuli employed in most laboratory studies of concept acquisition. The results of studies on age differences could, therefore, be quite different if more concrete and more realistic stimuli conveyed the positive and negative instances of the to-be-acquired concept. This approach was taken by Arenberg (1968a) in his study cited in Chapter 3. The concept may be viewed as a single dimensional one in which there are many values of the single relevant dimension (specific food substances) and there are no irrelevant dimensions. The subject's task was to discover the positive attribute of the single dimension (i.e., the poisoned food; see Table 3.2). (Alternatively, the problem could be viewed as involving one relevant stimulus dimension [e.g., beverages with one positive value, such as tea, and two negative values, such as coffee and milk] and two irrelevant dimensions, each with three values [vegetables—rice, corn, and peas; and meat—beef, veal, and lamb]). Despite the use of highly concrete stimulus events, pronounced age differences favoring young adults continued to be manifested, just as they are in studies employing abstract-stimulus events. Interestingly, the age deficit in Wiersma and Klausmeier's (1965) study also occurred despite the use of relatively concrete stimulus events (i.e., classroom conditions).

Perhaps the nature of the stimulus event is less important than the opportunity given elderly people to regain the use of latent but rusty-from-disuse cognitive skills. An early study by Crovitz (1966) hinted at the effectiveness of training on improving the quality of performance of elderly subjects on a simple concept-acquisition task. Her elderly subjects in a training group observed the experimenter sort the instances of the single-dimensional concept. While watching, they were required to verbalize on what basis the instances were being classified. These subjects were found to master a subsequent concept problem considerably more readily than control-group subjects given no observation-verbalization experience.

A series of more recent studies by Sanders (Sanders, Sterns, Smith, & Sanders, 1975; Sanders, Sanders, & Sielski, 1976; Sanders & Sanders, 1978) has indicated further that the performance of elderly subjects on concept-oriented tasks can indeed be markedly improved by appropriate training and experience. The strategy calls for a sequence of tasks arranged so that the initial concepts encountered are very easy ones to acquire. These problems are followed by progressively more difficult ones. Experimental elderly subjects are guided through these training problems and have their errors pointed out and the reasons for the selections of correct instances clearly described. By contrast, control elderly subjects receive practice on the problems without intervention from the experimenter. The training procedure was found to improve performance substantially for experimental subjects relative to control subjects on both single-dimensional test problems (Sanders et al., 1975) and conjunctive problems (Sanders et al., 1976). Moreover, Sanders and Sanders (1978) discovered that their experimental subjects who had participated in their single-dimensional training program also displayed superior performance relative to control subjects on conjunctive problems, even though the new test problems were not received until a year after the original training program had been completed. Labouvie-Vief and Gonda (1976) also found considerable improvement for elderly subjects on a task related to concept acquisition following a training and modeling program.

The impact of these studies is diminished considerably, however, by the fact that there were no experimental and control groups of young-adult subjects. We discovered in Chapter 3 that, when these groups are included in training/modification studies, it is not unusual to find that young subjects receiving the special training benefit as much as the elderly subjects. The net effect is to find age differences favoring young subjects that are as pronounced with training as without training.

Turning to process-oriented research per se, we will consider first those studies that have attempted to determine the contribution of age deficits in memory processes to age deficits in concept acquisition. The earliest of these studies was by Wetherick (1965). His subjects, like those in Arenberg's (1968a) study, simply had to acquire a single-dimensional concept for which there was no irrelevant stimulus dimensions. The relevant dimension consisted of letters of the alphabet. For purposes of illustration, we will assume the positive-stimulus value to be a single letter, say *B,* whereas the negative values are three other

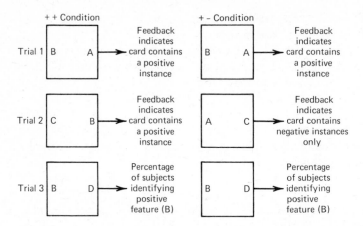

Figure 10.7. Procedure employed by Wetherick, 1965, to vary the sequence of instances (+ + and + − conditions) received by subjects on a simple-concept learning problem.

letters, say *A, C,* and *D.* (Wetherick's actual problems were somewhat more difficult than our demonstration problem). Subjects received a series of three trials on the problem, with the nature of the materials exposed on each trial being illustrated in Figure 10.7. The critical independent variable was the sequence of instances given on Trials 1 and 2. Young and elderly subjects in one condition received a positive instance (*B*) of the concept on each trial that was in each case paired with a different negative instance (*A* on Trial 1, *C* on Trial 2). This sequence is labeled a + + sequence. The subjects in a second condition also received a positive instance on the first trial (again paired with a negative instance), but they received only negative instances on the second trial (see Figure 10.7). This sequence is labeled a + − sequence. The dependent variable consisted of the percentage of subjects in each condition correctly naming the concept on Trial 3. Surprisingly, an age deficit was found only in the + − condition.

This outcome is surprising in that, from the perspective of Levine's (1975) hypothesis-testing theory, there is no reason to expect a difference between + + and + − conditions, given an efficient episodic-memory system. On Trial 1, in both conditions, the "*A* is the positive feature" and the "*B* is the positive feature" hypotheses should both be stored in memory as being potentially correct hypotheses. The comparable hypotheses for *C* and *D* should be stored in memory as being incorrect (i.e., neither letter could be the positive feature and still have the first card contain a positive instance). On Trial 2, in the + + condition, the "B is the positive feature" hypothesis is confirmed by means of *B*'s presence combined with *A*'s absence in a card for which feedback indicates the presence of a positive instance. However, confirmation should also take place on Trial 2 in the + − condition by means of *A*'s presence and *B*'s absence on a card for which feedback indicates the presence of only negative instances. Thus, in both conditions, the correct hypothesis should be the only one remaining in the subset of potentially correct hypotheses following Trial 2.

Nevertheless, there is an important difference between these two conditions in the extent to which they place a demand on memory. In the $+ +$ condition, the possibility of B being the positive feature (as established on Trial 1) is reaffirmed by its physical presence on Trial 2. This reaffirmation does not occur on Trial 2 in the $+ -$ condition—B is *not* physically present. Consequently, the viability of the correct hypothesis is contingent on its residence as a trace in episodic memory. The presence of an age deficit with a $+ -$ sequence but not with a $+ +$ sequence necessarily implies that retaining information about previously tested hypotheses is the *only* age-sensitive process in concept acquisition, at least for single-dimensional concept acquisition. If other processes were involved, then an age deficit in proficiency of acquisition would be expected for the $+ +$ sequence as well as the $+ -$ sequence (with the magnitude of the deficit being greater, however, for the $+ -$ sequence, given its added requirement of an age-sensitive memory process).

The contrast between $+ +$ and $+ -$ sequences was pursued further in Arenberg's (1968a) poisoned-food study. There was an important departure, however, from the procedure followed in Wetherick's (1965) study. In the earlier study, the instances presented on a given trial were removed from the subject's view prior to receiving the next trial's instances (a procedure commonly followed with the reception paradigm). The result is an "out of sight, out of mind" principle for testing hypotheses in the $+ -$ sequence. The demand placed on memory should disappear, however, if the instances and their outcomes for a given trial remain visible to the subject on all subsequent trials. In effect, performance should now become equivalent for elderly subjects in the $+ +$ and $+ -$ conditions. With the memory requirement seemingly equated across conditions, Arenberg did, indeed, find equivalent performance scores for elderly subjects in the two conditions. However, he also found an age deficit in *both* conditions (again, Wetherick found a deficit only in the $+ -$ condition). The implication is that memory processes are by no means the only processes that are age sensitive in concept acquisition. Elimination of the memory requirement should not affect the involvement of these other processes.

Considered together, the conditions present in Wetherick's (1965) study and Arenberg's (1968a) study follow the basic logic of the deletion method. That is, the memory requirement involved in the first study was deleted in the second study. Our preference, however, is to find a single study in which all of the necessary steps of the deletion method were carried out. Fortunately, there is such a study, namely, one by Brinley, Jovick, and McLaughlin (1974). This time there was no evidence to support the age sensitivity of memory as a major contributor to age deficits in proficiency of concept acquisition. As in the earlier studies, a $+ -$ sequence of trials, a sequence that normally has a strong memory requirement, was followed by a critical-test trial. In this case, however, the to-be-identified concept was a conjunctive one. The relevant dimensions were letters of the alphabet and the uppercase/lowercase format of those letters. A sample problem in which a is the solution is illustrated in Figure 10.8. For the time being, our concern is only with the top columns in the left half of this figure. Note that the column on the far left is labeled, low retention. In this

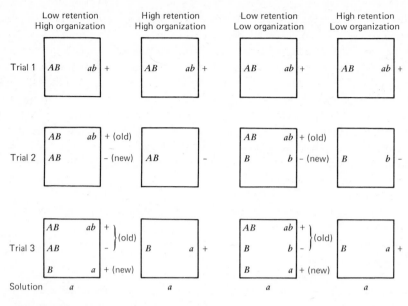

+ = positive instance present on card
− = only negative instances present on card

Figure 10.8. Procedure employed by Brinley, Jovick, and McLaughlin (1974) to vary the memory demand (high- and low-retention conditions) on a conjunctive concept problem. (Adapted from Brinley et al., 1974, Figure 1.)

condition, the memory requirement was deleted by having the information conveyed by Trial 1's card repeated on Trial 2's card (along with the new instances given on Trial 2). Similarly, the information from both Trial 1 and Trial 2 was repeated on Trial 3's card (again, along with the new instances for that trial). Consequently, subjects did not have to rely on memory to retrieve information from prior trials while performing on a given trial. Repetition of prior information was eliminated in the high-retention condition, thus forcing subjects in this condition to retrieve that information from memory while responding on a given trial. Surprisingly, neither the main effect for retention condition nor interaction effect of the age × retention condition approached statistical significance. That is, the age deficit was as pronounced in the low-retention, or deletion, condition as in the high-retention, or nondeletion, condition. Deletion of a presumably age-sensitive process should surely be expected to yield a large reduction in the magnitude of age differences favoring young-adult subjects.

Further research on the question of memory's involvement in age deficits on concept problems is badly needed. A potentially valuable direction to pursue by future investigators would be to assess episodic-memory proficiency independently of performance on a concept-acquisition task. The identification of high- and low-proficiency elderly subjects could be accomplished by means of scores earned on several of the memory tasks described in Chapter 9. If episodic-memory deficits play a critical role in determining age deficits in concept acquisition, then we would expect to find a large positive correlation between memory-task scores and scores on subsequent concept-acquisition tasks.

The remaining evidence has concentrated on the possible age sensitivity of the various higher order processes that enter into concept acquisition. The initial evidence comes from a study by Wetherick (1966). He discovered that elderly subjects are more likely than young subjects to misinterpret features that are shared by positive and negative instances of the same single-dimensional concept. Consider, for example, *AB* and *BC* as positive instances of a to-be-identified concept and *AC* and *DC* as negative instances of the same concept. The to-be-identified concept is, of course, *B*, the only feature shared by both positive instances. However, *A* is a feature shared by a positive instance and a negative instance. It is representative of the kind of feature more likely to be identified erroneously by elderly subjects than by young subjects as the concept's positive feature.

A similar confusion seemingly occurs for many elderly subjects when redundant information occurs over trials, as demonstrated in Arenberg's poisoned-food study (1968a). The meaning of redundant information in this context is shown in Table 10.3. Note that after Trial 2, only tea and corn remain viable as potentially correct positive features. These options are not changed by the information presented on Trial 3, thus making that information redundant. Similarly, the options are not changed by the information presented on Trial 4, again making that information redundant. In principle, both tea and corn should remain as viable after Trial 4 as they were after Trial 2. Nevertheless, Arenberg's elderly subjects but not his young subjects revealed an alarming propensity to reject tea and corn after Trial 4 and to substitute instead the new, and necessarily negative features, presented in the redundant information (e.g., milk and beef; see Table 10.3).

A similar tendency for elderly subjects to abandon still viable hypotheses was reported by Offenbach (1974), even though redundant information was not involved. The materials consisted of the more traditional geometric forms (square and circle) that differed in both color (red and blue) and size (large and small). The to-be-identified concept was a single dimensional one with, for

Table 10.3   Representative Concept Problem Involving Redundant Information

	Instances	Informational Condition	Feedback: Lived (−) or Died (+)	Possible Positive Feature
Trial 1	Tea, Lamb, Corn	Nonredundant	+	Tea, Lamb, Corn
Trial 2	Coffee, Lamb, Rice	Nonredundant	−	Tea, Corn
Trial 3	Milk, Beef, Rice	Redundant	−	Tea, Corn
Trial 4	Tea, Beef, Corn	Redundant	+	Tea, Corn
Trial 5	Coffee, Veal, Corn	Nonredundant	−	Tea

Source: Adapted from Arenberg, 1968, Table 1.

example, form as the relevant dimension (square $= +$, circle $= -$) and color and size as irrelevant dimensions. Subjects examined two simultaneously presented instances, such as a large red square and a small blue circle, on Trial 1 and selected which of the two they believed to be the positive instance, and they received feedback indicating the correctness of their selection. They were then asked to identify their hypothesis regarding the positive feature. Suppose a subject at this point identified redness as the potentially correct feature. The subject's hypothesis is certainly a reasonable one after discovering that an object containing redness (the large red square) is a positive instance of the concept. The subject then received another pair of instances, say a large blue square and a small red circle, on Trial 2. We should now expect our hypothetical subject to have selected the small red circle as the positive instance—a selection that is consistent with the still viable hypothesis, "Red is the positive feature." Offenbach found that this was indeed the case for young-adult subjects. Nearly 90% of them based their Trial 2 selection on the still viable hypothesis. By contrast, only 50% of the elderly subjects held on to their original and still viable hypothesis. Thus, their selections were seemingly determined more by random guessing than by the systematic application of hypothesis testing.

The possible involvement of encoding processes in age deficits on concept-acquisition problems was examined in the previously mentioned study by Brinley et al (1974) and also in studies by West, Odom, and Aschkenasy (1978) and Hoyer, Rebok, and Sved (1979). Brinley et al. varied what they called organization. The nature of their organizational conditions may be seen in Figure 10.8. As can be seen in the two columns in the left half of that figure, subjects in their high-organization condition could encode the information presented on Trial 2 homogeneously with respect to case format. That is, both letters presented on that trial were of the same case and, therefore, did not have to be encoded differentially in terms of their case values. On the other hand, subjects in their low-organization condition (the two columns in the right half of Figure 10.8) had to encode case format as well as letter content. That is, the two letters presented on Trial 2 differed in case format. Organizational variation was found to have little effect on the proficiency of concept acquisition for young-adult subjects. However, it did have a pronounced effect on the performance of elderly subjects. They solved the problems with high organization more readily than they solved the problems with low organization. Consequently, the age deficit in concept acquisition was considerably more pronounced in the low-organization condition than in the high-organization condition.

The perceptual salience, or noticeability, of the relevant dimensions of a conjunctive concept was varied by West et al. (1978). For both young-adult and elderly subjects, the ease of concept acquisition was greater for high-salient dimensions than for low-salient dimensions, as might be expected. More important, there was no interaction effect between age and level of saliency. That is, the age difference favoring young subjects was as pronounced for the high-salient dimension as for the low-salient dimension. Increasing the salience of the relevant dimension, therefore, does not appear to be a means of overcoming age deficits in the proficiency of concept acquisition.

Hoyer et al. (1979) provided greatly needed information about the effect of variation in the number of irrelevant dimensions on the magnitude of age deficits in proficiency of concept acquisition. As we indicated earlier (see Figure 10.2), difficulty of concept acquisition increases as the number of irrelevant stimulus dimensions increases. Most important, there is good reason to suspect that the adverse effect of increasing irrelevant information will be much greater for elderly adults than for young adults. We discovered in Chapter 7 that elderly subjects are more readily distracted by irrelevant stimuli than are young subjects. A similar effect on a concept task would be expected to detract more from the encoding of relevant dimension features for elderly subjects than for young subjects and would, therefore, be expected to contribute substantially to observed age deficits on those concept tasks involving irrelevant stimulus dimensions. This conclusion received strong support from the outcome of the study of Hoyer et al. (1979). A single relevant stimulus dimension was combined with 0, 1, 2, or 3 irrelevant stimulus dimensions. As can be seen in Figure 10.9, a multiplicative relationship emerged, that is, as overall difficulty increased with increments in the number of irrelevant dimensions so did the magnitude of the age deficit.

In summary, age-sensitive higher order processes appear to be especially important contributors to age deficits in the proficiency of concept acquisition. Of great concern is the possible reversibility of adverse age changes in these higher order processes. The training studies by Sanders (e.g., Sanders et al.,

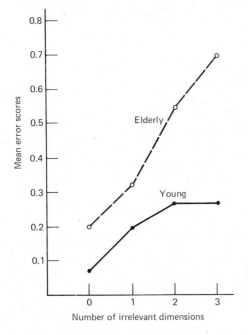

Figure 10.9. Age differences in the effect of variation of the number of irrelevant stimulus dimensions on concept identification. (Adapted from Hoyer, Rebok & Sved, 1979, Figure 2.)

1976) and Labouvie-Vief and Gonda (1976) described earlier offer considerable hope of improving the proficiency of these processes through effective guidance and practice. Whether or not elderly adults, on the average, can be brought to the level of proficiency manifested by young adults, on the average, remains to be demonstrated.

Solution-Shift Studies. Thus far we have reviewed only process-oriented studies that are related to cognitive theories of concept acquisition. There have also been, however, a handful of studies that bear upon associationism's analysis of concept acquisition. These studies have all dealt with the identification of age-sensitive processes through age differences in performance on so-called *solution-shift tasks* (Kendler & Kendler, 1962). The traditional forms of these tasks are illustrated in Figure 10.10. Subjects perform on an original-concept task and then receive a transfer task that requires either a *reversal shift* of solution or a *nonreversal shift* of solution. On the original task, subjects acquire a single-dimension concept that usually involves only a bilevel relevant stimulus dimension and a single bilevel irrelevant stimulus dimension. For the problem shown in Figure 10.10 the relevant and irrelevant dimensions are form (square $= +$, triangle $= -$) and brightness (black and white) respectively. After the solution of this problem is attained, subjects are shifted unexpectedly and without interruption to either the reversal-shift problem or the nonreversal-shift problem, both of which are illustrated in the bottom segment of Figure 10.10. The transfer problem in both cases involves the same stimulus objects, or instances, presented on the original task (top segment of Figure 10.10). However, in the reversal-shift condition, form remains the relevant stimulus dimension, but triangle becomes the positive value and square the negative value, whereas in the nonreversal-shift condition, brightness becomes the relevant stimulus dimension (e.g., with black designated the positive value) and form the irrelevant stimulus dimension.

The contrast between the two shift conditions is of great interest to associationists. From the perspective of classical associationism, a nonreversal-shift solution should be easier to accomplish than a reversal-shift solution. Note that one of the two positive instances following a nonreversal shift (the black square) had also been a positive instance on the original task (i.e., it possesses both the positive feature, squareness, of the original task and the positive feature, blackness, of the transfer task). Therefore, a yes response to this stimulus (S_2 in Figure 10.10) has already accrued considerable associative strength prior to the shift, strength that carries over to the new task. As a result, subjects need learn only to give a yes response to the other stimulus object (S_4 in Figure 10.10) to solve the transfer problem. By contrast, neither of the positive instances (S_3 and S_4) following a reversal shift had been a positive instance on the original task. Therefore, there is no previously accrued associative strength to transfer to the new task and the yes response to each new positive instance must start from scratch. Again, the net effect should be to make a nonreversal shift easier than a reversal shift.

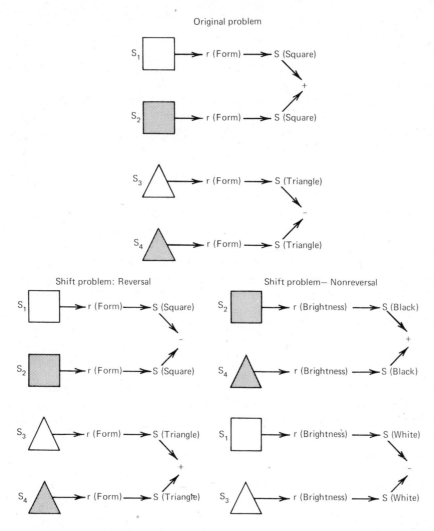

Figure 10.10. Representative objects and conditions for introducing reversal and nonreversal shifts on a concept-learning task.

A very different outcome is expected, however, from the perspective of stage analysis and its emphasis on mediation as a means of connecting S and R elements. Exposure to the instances of the original-task results in a mediating verbal chain that begins with the response that names the relevant dimension (form in Figure 10.10). This response produces its own stimulus consequences, the words square and triangle, that, in turn, become associated with positive (yes response) and negative (no response) values (top of Figure 10.10). On the reversal-transfer problem, there is no need to unlearn, or inhibit, the mediating verbal response of form—it still identifies the relevant stimulus dimension. All a subject has to do is reverse the positive and negative values for the two stimulus consequences of this mediating response (bottom left of Figure 10.10). This is not the case for a subject confronted by a nonreversal shift. Now the original mediating response is no longer appropriate, and it must be either extinguished or actively inhibited. At the same time, a new mediating verbal response, one that names brightness as the relevant dimension, must be established, and its stimulus consequences must be differentially associated with positive and negative values (bottom right of Figure 10.10). The net effect is the prediction that a reversal shift should be easier to master than a nonreversal shift.

A number of studies have revealed that older children and young adults solve reversal-shift problems more readily than nonreversal shifts, whereas the opposite is true for young children (Kendler & Kendler, 1962). The implication is quite clear. Older children and young adults engage in the higher order process of mediation during performance on a concept-acquisition task, whereas young children engage in the lower order process of rote rehearsal. What about elderly adults? If they regress to the processes characteristic of early childhood, then they would be expected to relinquish the use of mediation and to revert to the rote acquisition of a concept. The advantage of a reversal shift over a nonreversal shift would, therefore, be expected to disappear. Unfortunately, the only study that provided a direct contrast between reversal- and nonreversal-shift proficiency for elderly subjects yielded inconclusive results. Rogers, Keyes, and Fuller (1976) found both kinds of shift problems to be very difficult for their elderly subjects—40% failed to solve the reversal-shift problem and 53% the nonreversal-shift problem. Moreover, for the few remaining subjects who did attain shift solutions, the reversal shift was easier for some kinds of stimulus materials and the nonreversal shift for other kinds.

There have been several aging studies, however, that have made effective use of modified versions of the traditional reversal- and nonreversal-shift conditions. The modification of the reversal shift results in what is called an *intra-dimensional-shift* problem. Here, the relevant and irrelevant dimensions from the original task are unaltered on the transfer task (as is also true for the reversal shift per se), but the attribute values from the original task are replaced by new attribute values on the transfer task. For example, consider an original task in which form is the relevant dimension, with square and triangle the positive and negative values respectively, and color is the irrelevant dimension, with red and green as the attribute values. On the transfer task, form remains the relevant stimulus dimension but with new attribute values, say circle (+) and diamond (−). Color remains the irrelevant stimulus dimension but also with new attribute values, say blue and yellow. The modification of the nonreversal shift results in what is called an *extradimensional shift*. As in a traditional nonreversal shift, the previous relevant stimulus dimension becomes irrelevant, whereas the previous irrelevant dimension becomes relevant. However, the attribute values of the original task are replaced by new attribute values on the transfer task, as in an intradimensional-shift problem. Thus, color would become the relevant dimension, with blue (+) and yellow (−) as new attribute values; form would become the irrelevant dimension, with circle and diamond as new attribute values. The predictions regarding these modified transfer tasks parallel those for the traditional tasks from which they are derived. Most important, young adults are expected to master an intradimensional shift more easily than an extradimensional shift. The mediating verbal response (e.g., form) remains operative in an intradimensional shift, but it must be extinguished and replaced by a new mediating response (e.g., color) in an extradimensional shift. This expectancy has been confirmed in a number of studies (e.g., P. J. Johnson, 1967). In addition, an intradimensional shift is mastered about as easily as a traditional reversal shift, even though new attribute values are involved in the former (e.g., P. J. Johnson, 1967).

The transition to modified shift tasks is an important step to be taken in experimental aging research. The traditional shift tasks are likely to be especially confusing to many elderly subjects through their continued use of the same instances employed in the original-concept-acquisition task, but with new decisions to be made for those old instances. Such confusion is avoided in the modified task conditions through the use of new instances that are quite distinctive from the old instances. Nevertheless, the studies employing these modified shift tasks have demonstrated convincingly that elderly subjects find an intradimensional shift to be no easier to make than an extradimensional shift (Coppinger & Nehrke, 1972; Nehrke, 1973; Nehrke & Coppinger, 1971). Moreover, the absence of an advantage for what should be a short-circuited condition (i.e., mediation) persists even after many overlearning trials on the original task (Nehrke & Sutterer, 1978). We will use as our representative example of research in this area an especially informative study by Witte (1971). His subjects were preschool children, young adults, "young" elderly adults (median age, 65 years), and "old" elderly adults (median age, 74.5 years). Subjects at each age level received, unexpectedly, new instances (e.g., a blue circle, a blue diamond, a yellow circle, and a yellow diamond) after attaining the solution to an original problem (e.g., with a red square, a red triangle, a green square, and a green triangle as instances). Of interest are the percentages of subjects, plotted in Figure 10.11, responding as if the new instances conformed to an intradimensional-shift condition. Note that the percentage of the "old" elderly adults was well below that of both young adults and "young" elderly adults. In

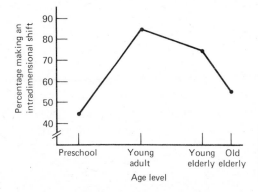

Figure 10.11. Age differences in the percentage of subjects manifesting an intradimensional shift on a concept-learning task. (Adapted from data in Witte, 1971.)

fact, the percentage approached that of presumably mediationally deficient preschool children.

The implication of these solution-shift studies is that many elderly people do experience a mediational deficit in concept acquisition, just as they apparently do in paired-associate learning. A mediational deficit does not mean, of course, that new concepts cannot be learned by most elderly people. It simply means that the rate of acquisition is likely to be slower than the rate characteristic of most young adults who do engage actively in mediation. Again, mediational activity is expected to short-circuit the slow process of learning any task by rote rehearsal. In addition, there remains the possibility that at least part of the loss of mediational ability with aging may be reversible. We discovered in Chapter 8 that some success has occurred in overcoming the age decrement commonly found for imaginal mediation in paired-associate learning.

Adult-Age Differences in Problem Solving

> Problems come in all shapes and sizes but generally share the characteristic that the individual must discover what to do in order to achieve a goal. Whether looking for the screwdriver that isn't where it's supposed to be, searching for a friend's house in an unfamiliar neighborhood, trying to figure out why the car won't start, or working on a mathematics exam in school, a person faces a situation in which the correct response is somewhat uncertain. (Bourne et al., 1979, p. 232)

A problem is essentially a stimulus situation for which an individual has no immediate response and must, therefore, discover an appropriate response. There is obviously some commonality between concept formation and problem solving. However, there is also an important distinction, as pointed out by Ellis, Bennett, Daniel, & Rickert:

> Concept formation, then, can be characterized as involving a large number of different stimuli to which a very limited and completely specified set of responses must be made. Problem solving, on the other hand, typically involves a single stimulus (albeit a complex stimulus) to which an unspecified, large number of responses can be made. Some, one, or none of these responses may be the correct response. (1979, pp. 406–407)

Bourne et al. (1979) reminded us that real-life problems come in all shapes and sizes. Earlier we observed that these real-life problems are faced by adults of all ages. Our concern is with what happens to problem-solving proficiency over the course of the adult segment of the lifespan and with what accounts for age changes in proficiency. To study problem-solving behavior in the laboratory, psychologists have introduced a number of specific-problem situations that are intended to simulate the myriad of problem situations encountered in the real world. Several of these problems are given in Table 10.4. Our initial step will be to examine the processes that have been postulated by both associationists and cognitive psychologists to enter into the solving of these kinds of problems (see Bourne et al., 1979; Glass, Holyoak, & Santa, 1979; and Newell

Table 10.4   Representative Problem Situations Used in Basic Research on Problem Solving. (Answers Found in Text)

ANAGRAMS: Rearrange the letters in each set to make an English word.

EFCTA

IAENV

BODUT

LIVAN

IKCTH

TWO-STRING PROBLEM: Two strings hang from the ceiling in a large, bare room. The strings are too far apart to allow a person to hold one and walk to the other. On the floor are a book of matches, a small screwdriver, and a few pieces of cotton. How could the strings be tied together?

NUMBER PROBLEM: The price of a notebook is four times that of a pen. The pen costs 30¢ less than the notebook. What is the price of each *item*?

MATCHING PROBLEM: Sitting at a bar, from left to right, are George, Bill, Tom, and Jack. Based on the following information, figure out who owns the Cadillac.

1. George has a blue shirt.
2. The man with a red shirt owns a VW.
3. Jack owns a Buick.
4. Tom is next to the man with a green shirt.
5. Bill is next to the man who owns the Cadillac.
6. The man with a white shirt is next to the Buick owner.
7. The Ford owner is farthest away from the Buick owner.

WATER-JAR PROBLEM: A person goes to the river with three jars having the pint capacities listed below. How should the person go about measuring the desired amount in each problem?

	Capacity			*Desired Amount*
	A	B	C	
(1)	17	7	4	2
(2)	22	9	3	7
(3)	30	19	3	5
(4)	20	7	5	3
(5)	28	7	5	11
(6)	17	7	3	4

Source: Adapted from Bourne, Dominowski, and Loftus, 1979, Figure 8-1 and Table 8-4.

& Simon, 1972, for more detailed reviews). Along the way we will indicate likely candidates for age sensitivity.

Process Analysis and Age Sensitivity. Associationism's analysis of problem solving keeps faith with the belief that complex activities are reducible to simpler associative processes. This analysis has been most effectively applied to anagrams as to-be-solved problems (see Maltzman, 1955, for associative analyses of other problem-solving tasks). Consider, for example, the anagram BODUT listed in Table 10.4. The subject's task is to unscramble these letters and find the word composed of those same letters. From the perspective of stage analysis, an anagram may be considered a nominal stimulus element upon which the stimulus selection process operates, as illustrated in Figure 10.12. The initial selection is likely to yield one or two letters, for example, "TO", from the nominal element to serve as a transitory functional stimulus. These letters elicit words as responses, each word beginning with "TO." However, a matching of the letter content of these words with the letter content of the nominal stimulus (i.e., the anagram) indicates that no word beginning with "TO" solves the problem (Figure 10.12). Thus, the subject selects a different functional stimulus (e.g., "TU" in Figure 10.12) and repeats the word-generation matching process. Again finding no match, the subject repeats the process until a solution is attained (see Figure 10.12). This analysis predicts that performance on an anagram task should increase in proficiency as the familiarity of the solution words (and, therefore, their availabilities as responses to functional stimuli) increases, a prediction generally confirmed with young-adult subjects (e.g., Mayzner & Tresselt, 1958). A prediction of special significance to us is the expected adverse effect of a subject's rigidity in the stimulus-selection process. Subjects who show little flexibility in selecting different letter combinations to begin a solution word are likely to fail solving an anagram problem. A common hypothesis in gerontology is that elderly people are more rigid than young adults (to be discussed more thoroughly in Chapter 11). If true, this

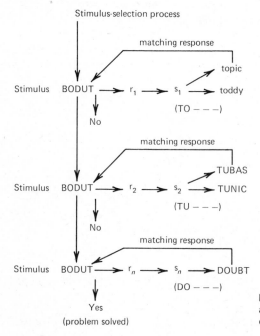

Figure 10.12. Analysis of solving an anagram problem from the perspective of stage analysis.

hypothesis implies that the proficiency of solving anagrams should decrease with increasing age.

An early cognitive approach to analyzing problem-solving behavior was that of Gestalt psychologists. Their emphasis was on the perceptual reorganization of the stimulus situation confronting the problem solver. Once accomplished (exactly how was not specified), the solution (i.e., emitting the appropriate response) should follow quite naturally. This process, known as *insight,* gained considerable attention through Köhler's research (1925) on the problem solving of apes. The standard procedure called for placing both a banana and a long stick outside of an ape's cage and beyond the ape's reach. Inside the cage was a short stick that was not long enough to reach the banana. However, it was long enough to rake in the long stick which, in turn, the ape could use to rake in the banana. After much trial-and-error effort to reach the banana, some apes displayed insight into the relationship between the two sticks and the banana. That is, they reorganized their perception of these objects and, by so doing, solved the problem. The Gestalt approach bears some similarity to the functional stimulus analysis of associationism. That is, environmental objects (the nominal stimulus) must be reorganized to yield an effective functional stimulus. The suspected rigidity of older people would, therefore, have to be considered once more a major detriment to solving problems.

The difficulty with the insight principle is its vagueness and its inability to relate to manipulable independent variables. In its place, cognitive psychologists have increasingly turned in recent years to the more analytical approach of information processing. Information-processing psychologists stress the possible involvement of many different processes during problem solving. The precise processes are contingent on the specific kind of problem being solved. However, the processes for any problem's solution can be organized into three sequential general stages: *preparation, production,* and *judgment* (see Figure 10.13).

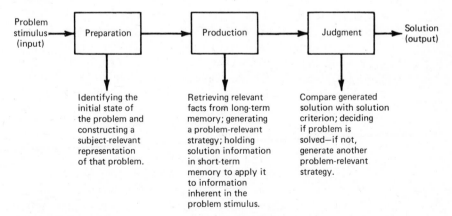

Figure 10.13. Stages of problem solving as identified by an information-processing analysis of problem solving.

Preparation refers mainly to a subject's reconstruction of the stimulus information inherent in a problem. The objective is to form an internal representation of that problem that promotes subsequent attainment of a solution. Consider, for example, the number problem described in Table 10.4. The stimulus information is given in the form of verbal statements or propositions. To solve this problem, most of us are likely to transform this verbal information into an algebraic representation whereby x = the cost of a pen and 4x = the cost of the notebook. Once in that form, our knowledge of the rules of algebra should take over and the second stage of problem solving should begin. For the two-string problem in Table 10.4, the solution is almost entirely dependent on a subject's ability to construct a particular representation of the environmental objects. Visualize one of the strings hanging from the ceiling as being something other than mere string, namely, consider it to be a potential pendulum. All that is then needed is to suggest converting it into a pendulum by tying the screwdriver to its loose end. Once this representation is constructed, the problem is virtually solved. Reconstruction in this sense is obviously related to what the Gestalt psychologists believed to underlie the phenomenon of insight. For the matching problem, there are several ways of representing the given information. One way is to construct two-way matrices (column/row) to record known outcomes with variations in events. For example, one matrix consists of the four men's names as one dimension and shirt color as the other. We know that George has a blue shirt, a fact that rules out the possibility of this shirt color for the other three men. We also know that Tom does not have a green shirt (he is seated next to the man who does). These bits of information may then be combined with the bits of information found in the other matrices (e.g., color of shirt and type of car as dimensions) to yield the solution that Tom owns the Cadillac. Studies with young-adult subjects (e.g., Schwartz, 1971) have revealed that a matrix form of representation yields more proficient solutions to matching problems than do various other forms of representation.

Failure to construct an adequate representation of the information inherent in a problem is a possible reason for age deficits in problem-solving proficiency. In some cases, the failure could result from the general tendency of elderly people to pay inordinate amounts of attention to irrelevant information, such as the presence of the book of matches and the pieces of cotton in the two-string problem (see Table 10.4). In other cases, the failure could be the consequence of increased rigidity in late adulthood and the resulting inability of many elderly subjects to alter the representational format indigenous to the problem statement, such as the verbal statement in the number problem given in Table 10.4.

During the production stage, a problem solver's main activities are to generate a strategy for processing the general kind of information inherent in the present problem's representation and then apply that strategy to the problem's specific content. Information-processing psychologists distinguish between two general classes of solution strategies, *algorithms* and *heuristics*. An algorithm is a solution strategy that, if followed through completely, is certain to solve the problem at hand. An anagram problem is one for which an algorithm would work. The algorithm would simply generate all possible orders of the letters contained in the anagram. For a five-letter anagram, such as BO-DUT, our problem solver would have to produce 119 additional orders of the five letters. For an eight-letter anagram, 40,319 additional orders would have to be produced! Regardless of how many there are, the orders would have to be checked individually to see which one matches a word stored in the problem solver's generic memory. Reliance on an algorithm is obviously likely to be a time-consuming and impractical activity, except for a computer simulating a human problem solver. Here, all possible orders may be generated and checked with information stored in the computer's memory bank in a matter of a few seconds. Human problem solvers usually prefer a heuristic as their method of producing a solution. In effect, heuristics are "selective or restricted solution methods which usually reduce cognitive strain" (Bourne et al., 1979, p. 241). The initial strategy selected may solve the problem—if the subject is lucky. If not, then this strategy must be dropped and an alternative strategy substituted. A problem solver faced by the anagrams in Table 10.4 might begin with the heuristic of searching for words that begin with a consonant-vowel combination, as many English words do. This heuristic would eventually solve the first three anagrams in that table (*facet, naive,* and *doubt*). However, it would not succeed for the remaining anagrams whose solution words (*anvil* and *thick*) do not begin with consonant-vowel combinations. Alternative heuristics would, therefore, have to be tried until solutions were found.

A heuristic for an anagram solution is really a segment of the algorithm that could, in principle, be applied to the problem. For many problems, however, there is no preexisting algorithm to serve as the base for deriving restricted heuristics. This is likely to be true for the two-strings problem in Table 10.4. The solution is dependent largely on the problem solver's ability to retrieve task-relevant information that is stored in generic memory. Specifically, the subject needs to retrieve the knowledge that a string is analogous in some ways to a pendulum when it is suspended from the ceiling. Once retrieved, all that is needed to produce the solution is to recognize the role the screwdriver can play in making the analogy a reality. An algorithm is also unlikely to be available for solving the water-jar problem given in Table 10.4. However, most problem solvers do have generic knowledge about formulas and how formulas serve to symbolize operations about objects. Now what is needed is the abstraction of the specific operations needed in combining the three jars to attain the solution. This abstraction should lead eventually to the formula $A - B - 2C$ (fill the A jar; from its content fill the B jar once and the C jar twice; what is left in the A jar is the desired amount of water). This formula offers the means of solving each of the six problems (although a simpler formula may be applied to the sixth problem, namely $B - C$; the fact that elderly subjects persist more than younger subjects in continuing to apply the more complex formula on the sixth problem is commonly accepted as evidence for increasing rigidity with increasing age, a topic to be discussed in Chapter 11).

Once a strategy has been activated, its implementation often depends on the problem solver's limited capacity for processing information and retaining the outcome of that processing in short-term memory. This is especially the case when a solution requires a sequence of steps in which the outcome of the first step influences the choice of action in the next step. The strain on short-term memory is especially apparent in playing chess, a highly complex problem-solving activity:

> Any of a number of pieces might be moved, and considering many different moves (scanning) is quite sensible. In determining the consequences of a particular move, it would be better to see what might happen one, two, or three moves later (searching) rather than relying solely on the immediate effects. The major difficulty in completing an adequate search-scan scheme lies in the person's limited capacity for processing current information and maintaining the outcomes of that processing. To reduce the load on STM, people sometimes choose moves on the basis of local considerations, minimizing search and tending not to plan ahead. In searching down a particular path, people tend not to remember all of the intermediate steps taken: rather they tend to return to some "initial or early state" if the path proves unproductive. Since choosing the best move might require more processing and remembering than can easily be accomplished, the problem solver might engage in *satisficing* which is choosing the first move which seems "good enough" (Newell & Simon, 1972).
>
> In various ways, people adopt strategies which minimize the load on STM, typically with the result that problem solving is less efficient. (Bourne et al., 1979, pp. 260–261)

Interestingly, master chess players are capable of chunking, or organizing, considerably more information found on a chess board than less gifted players, and they are, therefore, able to hold considerably more information in short-term memory at any given moment of a game than are other players (Chase & Simon, 1973).

Our analysis of the production stage implies a number of possible reasons for age deficits on various kinds of problem-solving tasks. Lower order memory processes involving either or both short-term memory and generic memory could be involved. And so could higher order processes. Specifically, elderly adults may have greater difficulty than young adults in discovering task-appropriate heuristics. More generally, the age sensitivity of both lower order and higher order processes in problem solving could be the consequence of the overall limited processing capacity of the human organism and the fact that this capacity diminishes by late adulthood, if not earlier.

For many problems, the judgment stage is uncomplicated, and it is unlikely to be a contributer to age deficits in problem solving. These are problems for which there is an objective criterion for evaluating the correctness of a proposed solution. This is the case with an anagram problem, where the criterion consists of a match between letters of the anagram and letters of the solution word. For other problems, however, there is no objective criterion for evaluating the correctness of a proposed solution. This is true, for example, for the matching problem in Table 10.4. The only basis for confidence in the proposed solution that Tom owns the Cadillac is one's confidence in the steps taken to come up with that solution. The suspected increase in cautiousness from early to late adulthood (Chapter 11), therefore, offers another possible explanation of age deficits in problem solving. Elderly subjects may have relatively little confidence in what are really correct solutions; they may, therefore, be more willing than young-adult subjects to forsake these solutions and to continue searching for other solutions.

Process-Oriented Studies on Age Differences in Problem Solving. Age differences in problem-solving proficiency for a wide range of tasks have been examined in a number of studies over the past 30 or so years. Inferior proficiency for elderly subjects relative to younger subjects has been found for number problems (Brinley, 1965; Brinley & Fichter, 1970; Clay, 1954; Wright, 1981); matching problems requiring subjects to figure out the correspondence between lights and buttons (Jerome, 1962; Young, 1966, 1971); matching problems involving verbal information (Rimoldi & Vander Woude, 1969) and haptic (touch) information (Kleinman & Brodzinsky, 1978); the water-jar problem (Heglin, 1956); and target identification by means of asking questions (Denney & Denney, 1973) (see Agruso, 1978, Botwinick, 1967, and Rabbitt, 1977, for additional reviews). In addition, other studies will be reviewed in Chapter 11 in terms of their implications for age changes in intelligence or personality.

There have been some notable exceptions however. It will be recalled from Chapter 3 that Arenberg (1974) reported cross-sectional age deficits for the light/button matching task. However, longitudinal reassessments of the same subjects revealed age changes in problem-solving proficiency only for subjects age 70 or greater at the time of the initial assessment. In addition, Heyn, Barry, and Pollack (1978) found no age difference for a word-problem task between young and elderly subjects, however, both groups solved fewer problems than a middle-age group of subjects (a group superior to the other two age groups in years of formal education). A further complication encountered in an attempt to generalize the adverse effect of aging on problem-solving proficiency is presented by the results obtained by Young (1971). The age change in proficiency noted above was true only for the men subjects. Comparable levels of performance were reported for women in their 40s, 50s, and 60s. Furthermore, Hayslip and Sterns (1979) found an absence of age differences in solving anagrams. Nevertheless, there is sufficient evidence for a true age change in problem-solving proficiency to force our consideration of the age-sensitive processes responsible for that change.

Some investigators have made effective use of supplementary dependent-variable scores as a means of gaining information about age-sensitive processes (Chapter 5). Rimoldi and Vander Woude (1969) gave their subjects 10 questions that could be answered in whatever order a given subject selected. Each question in the subject-determined sequence was then answered, with the answer presumably providing information relevant to the to-be-solved problem (determining the number of girls at a school who sell tickets to a dance). The questions, however, varied considerably in terms of the pertinence of their answers to the attainment of the solution. The most effective heuristic consisted of a specific pattern of selecting questions that needed answers. Subjects who

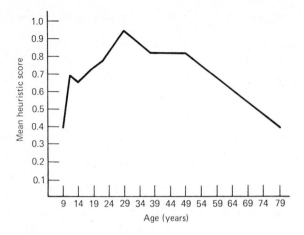

Figure 10.14. Age differences in the effectiveness of the heuristic (strategy) employed by subjects on a problem-solving task. (Adapted from Rimaldi & Vander Woude, 1969, Figure 2.)

displayed this exact pattern received heuristic scores of 1. Other patterns of selections were downgraded in value to the extent they approximated the ideal pattern (a 0 score indicated a random pattern of selecting questions). Mean heuristic, or strategy, scores were obtained for groups of subjects ranging in average age from 9.4 to 78.4 years. These means are plotted in Figure 10.14. Note that adults in their 20s were characterized by the occurrence of nearly optimal strategies. The effectiveness of the heuristic declined progressively beyond that age, reaching by the late 70s a level of heuristic performance that corresponded to that of 9-year-old children.

Further evidence of an age-related decline in the level of heuristics employed in problem solving comes from studies by Kleinman and Brodzinsky (1978) and Denney and Denney (1973). Kleinman and Brodzinsky had their subjects solve a problem in which a standard stimulus form had to be matched by touch alone with comparison forms, one of which was equated with the standard form. A representative problem in their study is shown in the top panel of Figure 10.15. Age differences in the mean number of such problems solved (out of four problems received) may be seen in the middle panel of Figure 10.15. No difference in problem-solving proficiency was observed between young-adult and middle-age subjects. However, both of these groups were clearly superior to the group of elderly subjects (see Figure 10.15). Although part of the age deficit manifested by elderly subjects in problem-solving proficiency probably resulted from their diminished tactile sensitivity, much of the deficit was undoubtedly the result of the poor quality of the heuristics employed by the elderly subjects. Records were kept of how subjects went about comparing the standard stimulus with the various comparison stimuli. An effective heuristic for this task is the use of congruent-feature comparison, that is, the simultaneous comparison of a feature on the standard with a spatially congruent feature on a comparison stimulus. By contrast, a highly ineffective heuristic is the use of mirror-image feature comparison, that is, simultaneous comparison of a feature on the standard with a feature on a comparison stimulus that is located in a mirror-image position. Plotted in the bottom panel of Figure 10.15 are the mean proportions for these two strategies (out of all strategies employed) at each age level. Note that the elderly subjects were characterized by both a decrease in the use of the effective strategy and an increase in the use of the ineffective strategy relative to the younger subjects.

Denney and Denney's (1973) middle-age and elderly subjects participated in a variation of the venerable 20-questions game. Their task was to identify which one of 42 pictures of common objects (e.g., a doll and a saw) placed in front of them was the target designated by the investigator. They were allowed

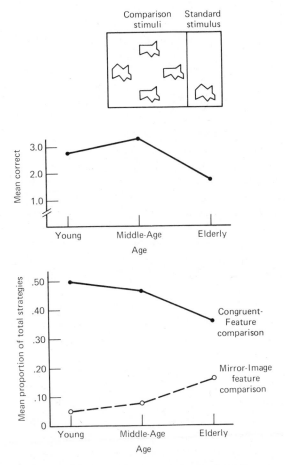

Figure 10.15. Top panel: Sample of material used in a problem in which a standard stimulus is matched by means of touch alone with a comparison stimulus. Middle panel: Age differences in the mean number of problems solved. Bottom panel: Age differences in the use of an effective heuristic (a congruent-feature comparison strategy) and an ineffective heuristic (a mirror-image comparison strategy). (Adapted from Kleinman & Brodzinsky, 1978, Figure 1 and Tables 2, 6.)

to ask only questions that could be answered yes or no. The objective, of course, was to identify the target object with as few questions as possible. The most effective heuristic for this task is to ask questions that, when answered negatively, eliminate an entire class of objects. An example is the question, "Is it a living thing?" The percentage of such questions asked by their middle-age subjects far exceeded the percentage asked by their elderly subjects (58.3% to 3.5%). The preponderence of questions asked by their elderly subjects were ones that would eliminate only one object at a time, such as "Is it the doll?"

Although these studies strongly suggest that an age decrement in heuristic effectiveness underlies many of the age deficits found on problem-solving tasks, they are not without their ambiguities. It is conceivable that the lower quality of heuristics employed by elderly subjects follows quite naturally from their failure to construct effective representations of the given information. That is, the true causative factor may rest at the level of the preparation stage rather than at the level of the production stage. This complication may be most clearly seen with reference to Denney and Denney's (1973) study. To ask hypothesis-testing questions (i.e., of the "Is it a living thing?" variety), subjects must first represent the objects shown to them in terms of their relationships to superordinates stored in generic memory (e.g., the superordinate of living things). Without the retrieval of this hierarchical generic information during the preparation stage of problem solving, there is no hope of activating the hypothesis-testing heuristic during the production stage. Thus, the age deficit reported by Denney and Denney could well be the consequence of less adequate preparation by elderly subjects than by younger subjects. To resolve such interpretative problems, Giambra and Arenberg (1980) proposed that future investigators add an important supplementary performance measure in their studies on problem solving. The measure is obtained from the thinking-aloud procedure that has been used successfully in basic research on problem solving (Newell & Simon, 1972) but that has been rarely employed in experimental aging studies on problem solving. Subjects are asked to verbalize all of the thoughts they experience while working on a problem. The result is a set of statements that often provide valuable insights into the nature of problem-solving processes. Applied to Denney and Denney's task, we would know the extent to which elderly subjects fail to represent objects as deeply as do younger subjects.

Most studies on age differences in problem solving have included variation in at least one manipulable independent variable. One of the favorite variables in these studies has been that of task complexity, defined with respect to the attributes of the to-be-solved problem in each study. For example, with Kleinman and Brodzinsky's (1978) haptic matching problem, complexity was defined in terms of the number of comparison stimuli with which the standard stimulus had to be compared to find a match. In addition to the four-choice situation, illustrated in Figure 10.15, they also included two-choice and three-choice situations. Not surprisingly, the number of correct matches decreased progressively for each age group as the number of comparison stimuli increased. However, there was no interaction effect between age and the number of stimuli. The additive relationship implies that the process altered in this case by variation in task complexity is age insensitive. Our interest is mainly in those studies that did find an interaction effect between age and the complexity attribute. The resulting multiplicative relationships should enhance our understanding of why age deficits are so commonly found on problem-solving tasks.

Representative of these studies are those of Clay (1954, 1956). In Clay's initial study, subjects had to fill in the squares of a checkerboard matrix with counters. Each counter had a numerical value of 1, 2, 3, or 4. The objective was to obtain the sums indicated for the rows and columns of the matrix. Complexity was increased by increasing the size of the matrix: 3 × 3 in the first problem, 4 × 4 in the second, 5 × 5 in the third, and 6 × 6 in the fourth. The nature of the problems and their solutions are illustrated in Figure 10.16 for the 3 × 3 and 5 × 5 matrices. To solve a given problem, subjects have to obtain, by arranging the counters in the appropriate squares, the sums given in the margins of the matrix. An effective plan for solving each problem is to begin by listing all of the possible ways a designated sum (e.g., 10 for the top row and left-hand column of the 3 × 3 matrix) may be obtained with counters having values of 1, 2, 3, and 4. These possibilities are listed in Figure 10.16 for all of the sums needed to solve the 3 × 3 matrix. It may be seen that there are two possible ways of combining counters to arrive at a sum of 10. One of these ways must then be combined with one of the three ways of obtaining the sum of 9 and one of the two ways of obtaining the sum of 8 (permitted by the counters available) to solve the total problem. If the first combination selected fails, then a subject must try other combinations until one is found that works.

Interestingly, Clay (1954) found no sign of an age deficit for the simplest, or 3 × 3, problem. However, age deficits of progressively increasing magnitudes were found as the matrices expanded in size, as may be seen in Figure 10.17 (percentage of subjects at each age level solving each kind of problem). Why the emergence of what is clearly a multiplicative relationship between age and problem complexity? We could argue that elderly adults are simply less accurate than young adults in adding columns or rows of numbers, and the punitive effect of this diminished accuracy increases as the amount of addition required increases (as it must in progressing from a 3 × 3 to a 6 × 6 matrix). There is, in fact, evidence indicating that, in general, elderly people are less accurate than young adults in adding columns of numbers (Birren, Allen, & Landau, 1954). However, the addition required to solve Clay's matrix problems is so simple that it seems unlikely that an age decrement in accuracy of addition could account for the large decrement found in problem-solving proficiency. Nor does it seem likely that the age decrement in proficiency could have resulted from the failure of elderly subjects to seek out a plan to solve the matrix problems, such as the list plan given in Figure 10.16. If the absence of planning were an important factor, then an age deficit should have been found even for the relatively simple matrix. This clearly was not the case. Clay's own analysis identified what is probably the true causative factor, not only for the matrix problem but also for any problem-solving task that demands the organization of subject-generated data. In the matrix problem, a sequence of numbers (i.e., data) generated by a subject to fill one row or column has to be organized with

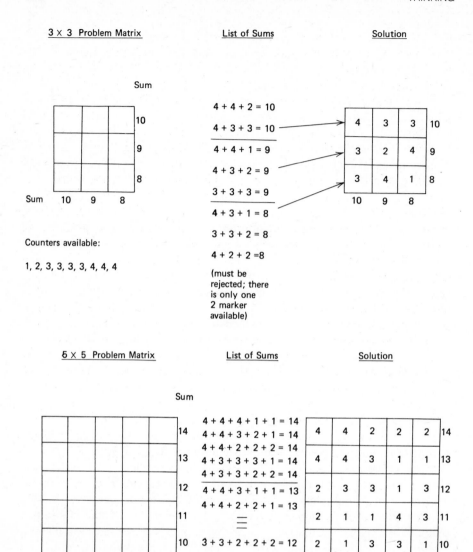

Figure 10.16. Representative matrix-addition problems employed by Clay, 1954.

the sequences that will fill the other rows and columns. Most important, the previously generated data must be held in memory storage while new data are being generated. Clay (1956) later demonstrated that the age deficit disappeared for the 5 × 5 matrix problem when the amount of data demanding organization was greatly reduced. The reduction was accomplished by requiring subjects to solve the matrix only for rows or columns, not for both simultaneously.

A somewhat similar outcome was reported years later by Brinley and Fichter (1970). Their young and elderly subjects performed on simple addition problems. In one form of their task, a typical problem was: 19 + 4 = 22 ( ) 24 ( ) 23 ( ). The subject checked the correct answer for each such problem. No age difference was found, either in errors made or in time taken per problem to complete the task. In another form of their task, a typical problem was: 19 + ? = 22 ( ) 24 ( ) 23 ( ). Now subjects not only had to add a number to the base number (19) to obtain the solution, they also had to remember *what number* to add to the base. Suppose they had been informed in advance that the addend must be either 1, 4, or 7. Retrieval of this previously stored information should signal the fact that 23 must be the solution to the given problem. With this greater task complexity, elderly subjects both made more errors and took more time per problem than did the young subjects.

What seems to be age sensitive in problems of the kind investigated by Clay (1954) and Brinley and Fichter (1970) is what contemporary information-processing psychologists call *working memory,* a system that "consists of a limited capacity 'work space' which can be divided between storage and control processing" (Baddeley & Hitch, 1974, p. 76). To the extent that performing on a problem requires memory storage of data, the work space available for oper-

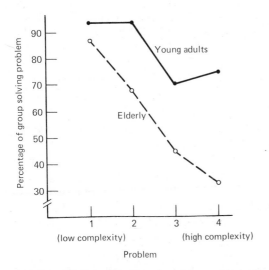

Figure 10.17. Age differences in solving matrix problems as a function of problem complexity. (Adapted from data in Clay, 1954.)

ating on new information and generating new data from that information is diminished. The concept of a limited capacity for processing information is a familiar one to us. And so is the concept of a reduction in total capacity from early to late adulthood. What is novel is the application of these concepts to age deficits in problem solving. The requirement of storing past data takes up work space, thus decreasing the amount of space available for generating new data. The trade off should have relatively little effect on the problem proficiency of young adults, given the large capacity of their working memory. By contrast, the trade off should have a considerably larger adverse effect on the problem-solving proficiency of elderly adults, given their age-related decrement in total capacity of the work space.

Although the concept of working memory is a fairly recent addition to information-processing psychology's analysis of problem solving, the nature of the concept's relevance to explanations of age deficits in problem-solving proficiency had been brilliantly anticipated years earlier by Inglis (1959), Talland (1965), and especially Welford (1958). Welford's recent comments on the role played by working memory in age deficits on problem-solving tasks are well worth repeating here:

> Be this as it may, there is clear evidence that temporary storage is often a source of limitation in problem solving, especially among older subjects. They have little difficulty, compared with younger subjects, at tasks such as adding where, in essence, the solution involves relating A to B to make C, then relating C to D to make E, and so on. The difficulty cannot, therefore, be due to inability to make the leap that A + B = C. Rather, difficulty appears when the task involves an operation such as relating A to B to make C and then holding C while D is related to E to make F, which has then to be related to C. The difficulty seems to arise with the intermediate storage. Older people have been found in a number of problem-solving tasks to forget intermediate solutions or data held while gathering further data. As a result, they may have to obtain the same data several times before reaching a solution (for examples, see Jerome, 1962; Welford, 1958, Chapter 8). (Welford, 1980, pp. 13–14)"

As long as the division between storage and processing is manageable within the capacity of the elderly subject's work space, there is no reason to expect an age deficit in the proficiency of problem solving. However, with progressively increasing demand placed on this capacity, there is reason to expect an age deficit as the capacity of the elderly subject is exceeded before the capacity of the young subject is exceeded. This important hypothesis received convincing support in a study by Wright (1981). Her young adult and elderly subjects received a series of addition problems. Each problem required summing a two-digit number and a three-digit number. The demand placed on capacity was altered by variation of two different manipulable independent variables. The first consisted of variation in memory load, that is, variation in the amount of information that had to be held in storage to perform the requisite operations of addition. For one fourth of the problems, both addends were clearly visible while subjects performed the operations, thus making the storage load equal to zero. For another fourth of the problems, only the three-digit addend was visible, with the two-digit addend presented auditorily. Here, the memory load consisted of two digits, namely, those of the auditorily presented addend. For still another fourth, the two-digit addend was visible, whereas the three-digit addend was presented auditorily, thus making the memory load consist of three digits. For the remaining problems, both addends were presented auditorily, thus increasing the memory load to five digits. The effect of this variation on accuracy of problem solving (i.e., correct additions) is shown in the top panel of Figure 10.18 for one of the levels of Wright's second manipulable independent variable (the carry-10s condition described in the next paragraph; the effect of variation in memory load was much the same for each of the other levels of this second independent variable). Note that no age deficit in problem-solving proficiency was apparent for either the zero-load or two-load condition (in fact, the elderly subjects were slightly superior to the young subjects). By contrast, an age deficit was clearly present for both the three-

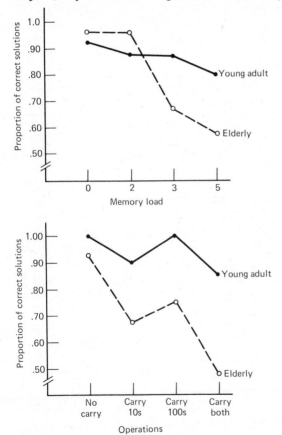

Figure 10.18. Top panel: Age differences in solving carry-10s addition problems as a function of memory load (number of digits). Bottom panel: Age differences in solving addition problems varying in complexity (number of operations) while maintaining a three-digit memory load. (Adapted from data in Wright, 1981.)

digit-load and the five-digit-load conditions. Stated somewhat differently, a decline in problem-solving proficiency did not occur for young subjects until the memory load reached five digits, and even then it was a modest decline. On the other hand, the decline occurred sooner for elderly subjects, that is, at a memory load of three digits, and, when it did, it was much greater than that found for young subjects (see Figure 10.18).

Wright's second manipulable variable consisted of variation in the carrying operations demanded by the addends in an addition problem. The least demand on work space required no carrying from one column to the next (e.g., 534 and 25 as addends); the greatest demand required carrying both from the units column to the 10s column and from the 10s column to the 100s column (e.g., 534 and 87 as addends). Intermediate demands were set by requiring either carrying only from the units column to the 10s column (e.g., 534 and 28 as addends) or from the 10s column to the 100s column (e.g., 534 and 82 as addends). The effect of this variation is shown in the bottom panel of Figure 10.18 for the three-digit memory-load condition of the first manipulable variable. With few operations, no age deficit was apparent; with additional operations, an age deficit emerged. This outcome closely parallels that found when memory load increased. When working memory's capacity is exceeded at one age level but not at another age level, an age deficit in problem-solving proficiency is the consequence. It does not matter what is responsible, an excessive memory load or an excessive number of operations, for the strain placed on working memory's capacity.

Our treatment of age-sensitive processes has focused entirely on processes indigenous to cognitive/information-processing analyses of problem-solving activities. Our intention has not been to slight those processes that are relevant to associative analyses of problem solving. The fact is, however, that, unlike research on age differences in concept acquisition, there has been virtually no research on age differences in problem solving that is amenable to associative analysis. The one problem-solving task that does lend itself nicely to a breakdown into associative component processes is that of unscrambling anagrams—and it is a task that seems immune to any major loss in proficiency over the course of the adult lifespan (Hayslip & Sterns, 1979). As we shall see in Chapter 11, the stability of performance on the anagrams task has been linked to the absence of age changes in crystallized intelligence (Hayslip, 1977).

Of further concern in this section is the possibility of modifying age-related deficiencies in problem-solving processes. It is conceivable that some problem-solving abilities appear to deteriorate in late adulthood simply because there is a lack of environmental press for elderly people to use those abilities in their everyday activities (Denney & Denney, 1974). The argument is that these abilities suffer from disuse, but they do not experience irretrievable loss. Consequently, these abilities should regain considerable proficiency, given appropriate training, support, and reason for their use. One of these abilities appears to be the use of the hypothesis-testing strategy called for on the 20-questions task. Denney (Denney & Denney, 1974; Denney, Jones, & Krigel, 1979) succeeded in increasing substantially the rate with which elderly subjects asked constraint-seeking questions by providing them with an effective model to follow, such as an experimenter who explained the efficacy of asking appropriate questions. It seems likely that this procedure works because it draws a subject's attention to the hierarchical manner by which objects can be represented. There are other problem-solving activities, of course, for which there is unlikely to be a lack of environmental press. Surely addition problems engage these kinds of activities—and balancing checkbooks and figuring out a budget are demands placed on adults of all ages.

There remain important issues regarding age differences in problem solving for which nothing appears to be known. Are there adult-age differences in the retention of a problem's solution? In the transfer of a solution from one problem to a similar problem? In the everyday world, a problem once solved does not disappear as it does in the laboratory. It may well be encountered again in its original form at a later time or it may be encountered in a somewhat modified form. The ease of solving a problem on its reoccurrence is contingent on the degree of retention of its original solution; the ease of solving a modified version is contingent on the degree of positive transfer from the original problem. As we have seen, age deficits in memory processes involved in solving a problem for the first time can play a critical role in producing age deficits in solving that problem. Retention is quite different than memory, however. We discovered in Chapter 8 that retention seems to be largely unaffected by aging, provided original learning has been equated at each age level. Therein lies the problem. How certain can we be of equality in learning a solution for young and elderly subjects, even when they all attained solution of the problem? Moreover, with young-adult subjects, the degree of retention of a problem's solution seems to be related to the nature of the processes leading to that solution (e.g., Jacoby, 1978). Any significant disparity in the problem-solving processes engaged in by young and elderly subjects may, therefore, yield significant age differences in the degree of retention. As to potential age differences in transfer effects for problem-solving tasks, so little is known about age differences on simpler learning tasks that we are reluctant to speculate about more complex tasks. Hopefully, more will become known about the answers to these important questions in the near future.

Originality and Creativity in Problem Solving. Solutions to some problems are judged with regard to their originality rather than their correctness. Originality means that the solution responses are uncommon, while, at the same time, they are relevant to the problem at hand (Wilson, Guilford, & Christensen, 1953). Consider, for example, the problem of giving six uses for a newspaper, other than its primary use for reading. Some responses on this unusual-uses test (Wilson et al., 1953) (e.g., to start a fire) would be given by many people and would, therefore, not qualify as being original. Other responses (e.g., to provide words for constructing a kidnap-ransom note) would be given by considerably fewer people and would, therefore, qualify as being original.

Originality deals with problem-solving situations that require *divergent,* or productive, thinking in contrast to the *convergent thinking* commonly called for on the problem-solving activities discussed in the previous section (Guilford, 1956). In the latter situations, subjects must zero in on a particular solution or answer (as in number problems) rather than produce an original solution (as in the unusual-uses task). Our initial interest in the present section concerns possible age changes in originality. Unfortunately, there has been little research on the important topic of age changes in originality. What has been done with standard laboratory or psychometric tasks (Bromley, 1956, 1967; Renner, Alpaugh, & Birren, 1978) does imply the existence of a decline in originality with increasing age over the adult lifespan.

Bromley's subjects were given four wooden blocks that could be arranged in a number of different orders according to their heights, weights, number of sides, shades of grayness, and so on. After subjects finished arranging the blocks in one logical order, they were asked to find another logical order. This continued until they could produce no further orders. His elderly subjects produced far fewer orders than did his young subjects. However, the reduction in number occurred mainly for original, or infrequent, response orders. For the least frequent and, therefore, the most original responses, the rate of production of elderly subjects was only about half that of younger subjects. More traditional tests of divergent thinking (i.e., of the unusual-uses variety) were employed by Renner et al (1978). Age differences continued to be present nevertheless. That is, their elderly subjects gave more conventional answers and fewer original ones than did their young-adult subjects.

Originality for real-world activities has been examined largely in the context of performance on skilled games, particularly chess. An analysis of tournament-level chess players indicates that they peak in performance at about age 36. Although players in their 60s do show less proficiency than players in their 30s, the older tournament players are, nevertheless, as proficient as tournament players in their early 20s (Elo, 1965). A recent study by Charness (1981) gave some important insights into the reasons why skilled chess players experience relatively little loss in skill as they grow older. Chess is a complex game that draw heavily upon both memory ability and problem solving ability. Although the memory ability component appears to show diminished proficiency with aging, problem solving ability, as reflected by the time taken to make effective moves, remains remarkably robust (Charness, 1981).

Our main concern in this section, however, is with age differences in creativity. Originality by itself does not define creativity in problem solving. What is needed besides originality is a response to a problem situation that is "appropriate, useful, and (usually) ingenious rather than logical" (Weiner, Runquist, Runquist, Raven, Meyer, Leiman, Kutscher, Kleinmuntz, & Haber, 1977, p. xxvii). Defined in this way, creativity becomes the discovery of solutions to problems of significance to society, a discovery that comes out of the blue. We have in mind the solutions of problems that lead to advancements in science, mathematics, philosophy, and, yes, even psychology. Are these discoveries largely the contributions of young adults? In other words, does creativity diminish greatly from early to late adulthood? This is a question, of course, of great social significance.

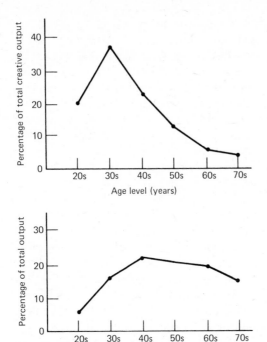

Figure 10.19. Top panel: Age differences in creative contributions combined for many academic disciplines. (From data in Lehman, 1953, as adapted by Botwinick, 1967.) Bottom panel: Age differences in total contributions to science independently of their creativity. (Adapted from data in Dennis, 1966, as adapted by Botwinick, 1967.)

The classic analysis by Lehman (1953) suggests that creativity does decrease considerably by middle age. Lehman examined the contributions of many eminent people to various disciplines, such as chemistry, physics, and mathematics, over many years. He attempted initially to evaluate the quality of these contributions. This was accomplished in several ways, including determining the frequency with which a specific contribution was cited in textbooks of the discipline in question. The next step was to determine the ages of the contributors of these high-quality works at the time they were produced. Shown in the top panel of Figure 10.19 are his results as presented in general summary form (i.e., combined for many disciplines). They chart the percentage of highly creative contributions made at various age levels. Note that 20% were contributed by people in their 20s, nearly 40% by people in their 30s, and slightly more than 20% by people in their 40s. Thus, 80% of the high-quality contributions were made by people younger than age 50. Earlier analyses had revealed a very similar pattern for artists, such as painters, (Lehman, 1942), philosophers (Lehman & Gamertsfelder, 1942), and inventors (Alexander, 1945), whereas later analyses revealed a similar pattern for psychologists (Lyons, 1968; Zusne, 1976).

The implication of these analyses is clear—creativity is largely the product of the young mind. However, a number of criticisms have been directed at Lehman's (1953) methodology and results, primarily by Dennis (1956a, 1956b, 1958, 1966) (see Botwinick, 1967, for a more detailed review). One criticism was of Lehman's procedure of pooling together the contributions of people having differential longevities. Conceivably, all of the contributors lived to age 40, but progressively fewer attained each successive decade of the lifespan, meaning that relatively few reached their 70s. Consequently, the contributions made by people in their 70s would have to be infrequent in an absolute sense, even if these septuagenarians maintained a high level of creativity. In his own reanalysis of Lehman's data, Dennis (1966) plotted the productivity of only those contributors to a discipline who lived long lives. After all, if creative people died in their 40s, they could scarcely make creative contributions in their 70s. His results for contributions to science are shown in the bottom panel of Figure 10.19. Contrary to Lehman's analysis, productivity was found to remain fairly constant from the 30s through the 70s. However, Lehman's (1956, 1958, 1960) rebuttal to this criticism was a reasonable one. His original analysis of contributions to a discipline concerned only their quality and not their quantity. Older scientists, mathematicians, and so on do not cease contributing to their disciplines. Nevertheless, they do contribute less substantively than do younger scientists, mathematicians, and so on. Moreover, Lehman argued that the age disparity in quality of contributions remains even when the confounding attributed to longevity is eliminated.

Why are there age differences in creativity? There are a number of possible explanations. One possibility stresses a factor that happens to coincide with increasing age, namely the advancement of creative people as they grow older to positions that remove them from active participation in their disciplines or, at least, reduce greatly the time they have available for creative activity (Bjorksten, 1946). In other words, a number of them are wasted as college deans, industrial administrators, and so on. Another possibility is the probable relatedness between certain personality characteristics and creativity (D.M. Johnson, 1972). Creativity does appear to be related to such characteristics as flexibility and tolerance of ambiguity (e.g., MacKinnon, 1962). Conceivably, age changes in these characteristics are responsible for much of the age-related decline in creative productivity. There is also the complicating factor of the long delay that often separates a highly creative work and the recognition justifiably given that work. This may be seen most dramatically in the lag of many years commonly separating the completion of highly significant research and the awarding of a Nobel Prize for that research (Manniche & Falk, 1957). Delaying the reward that follows a behavior is hardly an effective means of maintaining that behavior, even when it consists of highly creative problem solving.

Most pessimistically, age differences in creativity could be the consequence of a true decline with aging of the higher order processes that mediate originality. This possibility is suggested by the results obtained by Bromley (1956, 1967) and by Renner et al. (1978). However, there is an alternative explanation for age-related declines on divergent thinking tasks, as proposed by Renner et al. It emphasizes the by-now familiar environmental-press hypothesis. The environment of many elderly people may be such that it forces thinking processes to become convergently biased. The implication is that divergent-thinking processes may actually change little with advancing age, only the demand for their services diminishes. Considerably more research employing a wide variety of personality tests, tests of originality, and training procedures is needed before any firm conclusion can be reached regarding the true causative factor(s) for the appearance of adult-age differences in creativity.

Adult-Age Differences in Reasoning

The objective of logical reasoning is to draw valid inferences or conclusions from facts that either are known to be true or are assumed to be true. Bourne et al. aptly characterized logical reasoning as determining "what follows from what" (1979, p. 270). The distinction between logical reasoning and both concept acquisition and problem solving is not an easy one to make. Formulating hypotheses during performance on a concept task is actually a form of reasoning. What follows from the assumed fact that a particular attribute defines a concept (i.e., a specific to-be-tested hypothesis) is the conclusion that any instance containing that attribute must be positive. Of course, we may view concept acquisition as being devoid of logical reasoning and being promoted only by rote-associative processes. In addition, logical reasoning can be considered to be only a special case of problem solving, just as creativity is considered to be only a special case. Specifically, a reasoning problem is one in which logical relations between events and objects are given and the solution requires a true or false conclusion, or solution response, based on the nature of these relations. Most psychologists working in the area of higher order mental processes feel that reasoning is a sufficiently unique form of problem solving to justify its study independently as logical thinking rather than as problem solving per se.

In this section, we will describe initially both the kinds of tasks typically employed in research on reasoning and the processes generally assumed to mediate reasoning (and which are, therefore, potentially age sensitive). We will then turn to a review of the few studies that have examined adult-age differences in reasoning.

Tasks and Processes. Most basic research on logical reasoning has been conducted with verbal problems called *syllogisms*. A syllogism is an argument composed of two or more premises. Syllogistic reasoning is arriving at a *logical conclusion* from these premises. Consider, for example, the following premises, Statements 1 and 2, and a conclusion, Statement 3, derived from these premises:

1. All psychologists are scientists.
2. All scientists are expert computer technologists.
3. All psychologists are, therefore, expert computer technologists.

A subject's task is to decide whether the conclusion is true or false. Most subjects would have no trouble deciding it is true. The truth of the conclusion has nothing to do with the truth of the separate premises. The subject must assume their truth for the purpose of responding to the conclusion. We would, in fact, have good reason to question the validity of both premises in the real world. The decision for this syllogism is relatively easy because the concept, all, means in formal logic what it means in our everyday use of the concept, namely, each and every case with no exceptions. Now consider a different set of premises and conclusion:

1. All psychologists are scientists.
2. Some scientists are expert computer technologists.
3. Not all psychologists are expert computer technologists.

The temptation is strong to respond true to Statement 3. In our everyday language, some means part but not all of the cases in question. In formal logic, however, some means at least one case and perhaps all cases in question. Thus, the correct answer to this syllogism is "cannot say" (as it must be for any other firm conclusion, such as "all psychologists are expert computer technologists"). That is, the premises lead to an indeterminate solution that should be apparent to someone who understands the meaning of some in formal logic (and subjects in syllogistic research studies are fully informed as to the meaning of such terms before they respond to a set of syllogisms).

In some basic-research studies, syllogisms are presented in propositional form whereby the premises and conclusions are given as verbal statements having concrete subjects and predicates. This is the case for our examples using psychologists, scientists, and computer technologists. In other studies, the premises and conclusions are expressed abstractly. That is, letters of the alphabet replace the concrete objects or events found in propositional syllogisms. Examples of different abstract syllogistic problems (out of the many possible) are given in Table 10.5. Of special interest to psychologists are those problems for which the premises lead to an indeterminate, or "cannot say" conclusion (examples 2, 4, 7, and 8 in Table 10.5). Subjects who answer either true or false to conclusions for these problems are presumed to be thinking illogically.

Why do subjects make illogical errors on indeterminate problems? Several hypotheses have been offered over the years. One of the earliest hypotheses, and still very much a viable one, attributes errors to what is called an *atmosphere effect* (Woodworth & Sells, 1935). The argument is that subjects reach conclusions based on the atmosphere, or global impression, created by the premises of a syllogism. When both premises contain the term, all, subjects are viewed as being likely to accept as true any conclusion that also contains the term, all, even though the conclusion is indeterminate. This is the case for Example 7 in Table 10.5. That is, "All A are C" is likely to be accepted as being true, even though the conclusion is actually nonsensical. Acceptance of this conclusion is tantamount to concluding that all dogs are cats! Note that all dogs are animals is equivalent to all A are B, whereas all cats are animals is

Table 10.5 Examples of Syllogisms Employing Abstract Premises and the Logical Conclusions They Permit

	Premises	Logical Conclusion
(1)	All A are B All B are C	All A are C
(2)	All A are B Some B are C	Cannot say
(3)	No A are B All C are B	No A are C
(4)	No B are A Some B are not C	Cannot say
(5)	Some A are B All B are C	Some A are C
(6)	Some B are A No B are C	Some A are not C
(7)	All A are B All C are B	Cannot say
(8)	All B are A No B are C	Cannot say

equivalent to all C are B. Similarly, when one of the premises contains the term, some, subjects are viewed as being likely to accept as true any conclusion that also contains the term, some, even though the conclusion is indeterminate. There is evidence (Begg & Denny, 1969) to indicate that errors made by young adults on syllogisms do follow the distribution predicted by the atmosphere effect. Age deficits in syllogistic, or logical, reasoning would, therefore, have to be attributed to an especially pronounced atmosphere effect for elderly subjects. If true, elderly subjects should adhere more closely to the error pattern predicted by the atmosphere hypothesis than do young adults.

The major rival of the atmosphere-effect hypothesis is the premise-conversion hypothesis (Chapman & Chapman, 1959). According to this hypothesis, people are prone to the misinterpretation of premises. However, once premises are misinterpreted, they are then viewed as being acted on as logically as possible. Thus, the premise "All A are B" may be misinterpreted to mean "All B are A" as well, whereas the premise "Some A are B" may be misinterpreted to mean "Some A are *not* B" as well. There is evidence that supports the validity of the premise-conversion hypothesis, evidence that at the same time is inconsistent with the atmosphere-effect hypothesis. For example, illogical conclusions are less likely to be made with concrete propositional syllogisms than with abstract syllogisms (Revlis, 1973), an outcome that is in agreement with the conversion hypothesis. Thus, "All Slobbovians are communists" (i.e., "All A are B") is ulikely to be misinterpreted to mean "All communists are Slobbovians," whereas the misinterpretation does occur when the premises are in abstract form. By contrast, an atmosphere effect should be present regardless of a problem's concrete/abstract format. From this perspective, age deficits in syllogistic reasoning would have to be attributed to a higher rate of premise conversions by elderly subjects than by younger subjects, a disparity in rates that may extend to concrete premises as well as abstract premises.

There is the distinct possibility that both hypotheses may be valid (see Bourne et al., 1979, for elaboration). Some subjects commit errors on syllogisms because of the atmosphere effect, whereas other subjects commit errors because of conversion effects. Similarly, both factors may be contributors to age deficits in logical reasoning.

Thus far we have considered only logical reasoning as represented by responses to syllogisms. There are, however, other important forms of reasoning. The only other form we will consider is *functional reasoning* (Collins, Warnock, Aiello, & Miller, 1975) or reasoning through the use of analogy. Its nature is apparent in our ability to interpret the meaning of proverbs, such as "Don't cry over spilt milk." A proverb offers a concrete analogy for a more general set of circumstances that the interpreter attempts to describe. The cognitive nature of interpreting proverbs is apparent from the fact that this task has long been a component of the Stanford-Binet Intelligence Test. Functional reasoning is also involved in the ability to interpret the meaning of metaphors, such as "Inflation is eating our savings." The meaning of "is eating" in this sentence is certainly intended to be nonliteral. However, we should be able to recognize the analogy, namely, that the effect of inflation on savings is similar to the effect of eating on food (i.e., in both cases, something is being devoured). The possibility of age deficits in functional reasoning is an important one in the psychology of aging, one that is just beginning to receive appropriate attention. Metaphors, in particular, are common forms of expression in our everyday communication. Diminished proficiency in thinking by analogy could, therefore, reduce the communicative skills of elderly people.

Aging Research. Early studies on age differences in reasoning were descriptive and psychometric in format. Adult-age differences in scores on the various components of the Watson-Glaser Critical Thinking Appraisal (Watson & Glaser, 1952) were reported by Burton and Joël (1945) and Friend and Zubek (1958). Included among these components is a test of deductive thinking ability that is essentially a test of syllogistic reasoning. The results obtained by Friend and Zubek are especially informative in that they tested a large group of subjects over a wide age range (12 to 80 years). As may be seen in Figure 10.20, the mean score (expressed in standard score form, with 50 being the norm or average) increased steadily from adolescence through age 35. However, beyond age 35 performance showed a rapidly accelerated decline, eventually reaching a level for subjects in their 70s that was below that of adolescents. It seems unlikely that the decline resulted from pronounced age differences in the magnitude of the conversion effect. The problems in the Watson-Glaser test are all in propositional form and contain concrete premises and conclusions. These are conditions that should minimize the tendency to convert premises. In the absence of any information about the types of error made at different age levels, it is impossible to determine the extent to which age differences in the magnitude of the atmosphere effect contributed to the decline in test scores

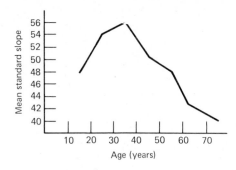

Figure 10.20. Age differences in performance on a test of syllogistic reasoning. (Adapted from data in Friend & Zubek, 1958.)

from early to late adulthood. Friend and Zubek themselves attributed the decline largely to adverse attitudinal and emotional factors present only in late adulthood. These factors were assumed to make older subjects less likely than younger subjects to perceive some problems as having indeterminate solutions. Implied in their analysis is that the age differences apparent in Figure 10.20 are largely performance differences and that the cognitive abilities mediating logical reasoning are not necessarily affected adversely by aging to any great extent.

A complicating factor in Friend and Zubek's study is the lower educational level of their older subjects relative to their younger subjects. Conceivably, the older subjects would have scored at a lower level than the younger subjects even if the former had been tested when they themselves were younger. This problem did not enter into the carefully controlled laboratory study of Wright (1981). Her young adult and elderly subjects were nicely equated for both educational level and scores on the vocabulary test of the Wechsler. This study is the same one we discussed earlier in connection with problem solving. A second task was administered to all of Wright's subjects. This task required true/false decisions on what are called *linear syllogisms* (D.M. Johnson, 1972). For each problem, verbal information is given in a study frame that describes the order in which abstract events occur, such as "A precedes B" or "B is not followed by A." A test frame follows in which a linear order is specified (e.g., AB or BA), and a decision must be made as to the order's correspondence to that given in the study frame. Age deficits on linear syllogisms like age deficits on the more traditional form of syllogisms, are presumably the consequence of age deficits in logical reasoning ability.

Most important, Wright (1981) viewed age deficits in logical-reasoning ability from the same perspective she viewed age deficits in problem-solving ability. That is, working memory space may diminish with increasing age, thereby reducing the elderly subject's ability to engage in proficient logical reasoning as well as problem solving. The negative effect of this diminished capacity is manifested, however, only when it is strained by the conditions extant at the time of solving logical-reasoning problems. The working-memory hypothesis offers a testable alternative to the other hypotheses that may be extended to explain age deficits in logical reasoning.

Wright's procedure followed closely the procedure used in the problem-solving component of her study. Specifically, age differences were examined under variations of task conditions that were expected to alter the demand placed on the capacity of working memory. With little demand, little or no age deficit was expected in performance on linear syllogisms. As the demand increased, the magnitude of the age deficit in performance was expected to increase.

Demand was altered by variation of two different manipulable independent variables: the first varied memory load, the second task complexity (as in the problem-solving component). This time memory load was defined independently of the primary task (in this case, performing on linear syllogisms). In advance of receiving a syllogism problem, subjects were given a string of digits to hold in storage until a true/false decision had been made, at which time the digits were to be recalled. Thus, the total task called for divided attention between the memory-span component and the reasoning component. The length of the string varied from two to six for different subgroups of syllogism problems. Task complexity was defined in terms of the type of linear syllogism to be answered (Baddeley & Hitch, 1974). The simplest problems (i.e., those involving the fewest cognitive operations) were expressed as active positive sentences (e.g., "A follows B"), whereas the most complex problems (i.e., those involving the greatest number of cognitive operations) were expressed as passive negative sentences (e.g., "B is not followed by A"). At intermediate levels of complexity, the sentences were either passive positive (e.g., "A is preceded by B") or active negative (e.g., "B does not precede A"). Representative results are illustrated in Figure 10.21. The top panel shows the effect of variation in memory load on the proportion of subjects answering correctly for passive positive syllogisms (roughly comparable results were obtained for each of the other sentence types). Note the absence of an age deficit when the demand on working memory capacity was slight (two and three digits) and the presence of a pronounced deficit when demand was large (five and six digits). The bottom panel shows the effect of variation in task complexity when the memory load consisted of six digits. Note that an age deficit was absent for the simplest task even with a six-digit memory load. However, as task complexity increased, the reduced working space brought about by the large memory load in combination with a more difficult syllogism task resulted in a pronounced decrement in reasoning proficiency for elderly subjects relative to the modest decrement found for young subjects. Clearly, decrements in logical reasoning are not necessarily the consequences of aging. They seem to be present only under conditions that are highly demanding cognitively.

The results obtained by Wright (1981) for her reasoning task are strikingly similar to the results found with her problem-solving task. And with good reason. Working memory is postulated to be a general cognitive space. Its diminished capacity in late adulthood should affect performance on *any* task that strains its capacity.

Age differences in functional reasoning have been examined for the interpretations given to both proverbs (Bromley, 1957) and metaphors (Boswell,

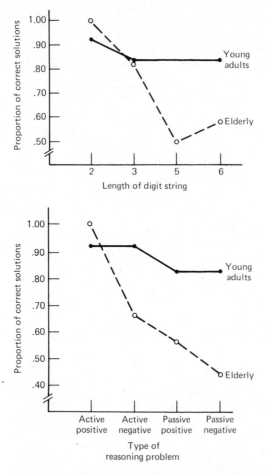

Figure 10.21. Top panel: Age differences in solving passive positive syllogisms as a function of simultaneous memory load (a digit string). Bottom panel: Age differences in solving different types of syllogisms while carrying simultaneously a six-digit memory load. (Adapted from data in Wright, 1981.)

1978). Bromley scored his subjects in terms of whether or not they abstracted principles from proverbs and then generalized these principles to analogous everyday situations or events. A smaller proportion of his older subjects than his younger subjects accomplished these abstractions/generalizations. On the other hand, Boswell found older subjects gave more integrative interpretations of metaphors than did high school students. In a different kind of metaphor study, Labouvie-Vief, Campbell, Weaver, & Tannenhaus (1979) compared young and elderly subjects in memory for metaphors that were the to-be-remembered items of a study list. In one condition, subjects attempted to recall the verbatim content of each metaphor, whereas in another condition they attempted to recall only the meaning of each metaphor. Young adults excelled in verbatim recall and elderly adults in recall of meaning.

The studies on metaphors imply that functional reasoning is maintained at a high level of proficiency in late adulthood. This implication conflicts, of course, with the one that may be drawn from Bromley's (1957) results on the proverb-interpretation task. Conceivably, proverbs and metaphors involve different forms of functional reasoning that differ in their age sensitivity. Of interest would be the degree of covariation between scores on a proverb-interpretation task and scores on a metaphor-interpretation task. If separate reasoning abilities are indeed involved, then the correlation would be expected to be quite low for both young adults and elderly adults. At any rate, considerably more research is needed before a firm conclusion can be reached regarding the effects of aging on functional reasoning.

Adult-Age Differences in Mental Rotation

Our earlier analysis of age differences in problem-solving proficiency concentrated on problems for which solutions are likely to be attained through the manipulation of linguistic symbols. There is the distinct possibility, however, that some problems are solved through the manipulation of imaginal representations of objects rather than linguistic representations. Consider, for example, this simple problem: True or false—Oregon's outline on a map is more similar to Colorado's outline than it is to West Virginia's outline? How did you arrive at your answer? If you had a map in front of you, you would have been able to compare directly the physical outlines of these states. In the absence of a map, many people report they compare mental images of these outlines in much the way they compare physically present outlines. In other words, the relationship between imaginal representations and operations on those representations closely approximate the relationships between their physical counterparts and operations on those counterparts (Shepard, 1968). Thus, the decisions regarding outlines of states arrived at by means of imaginal operations are virtually identical to the decisions arrived at by means of direct physical operations (Shepard & Chipman, 1970).

The close parallel between imaginal operations and physical operations was pursued further by Shepard and his colleagues in a series of remarkable experiments involving the mental rotation of objects. The nature of one of his rotation tasks is illustrated in the top panel of Figure 10.22. Pairs of objects, with each object consisting of 10 cubes joined together in a unique configuration, are exposed simultaneously. On half of the trials, the paired objects have identical configurations (rows A and B in Figure 10.22); on the remaining trials, the paired objects are mirror images of one another (row C). The subject's task is to respond, as quickly as possible, "same" for identical configurations and "different" for mirror-image configurations. The primary independent variable is the degree to which the object on the right is rotated from the orientation of the object on the left, with the amount of rotation varying from 0° to 180° in steps of 20°. Two kinds of rotation are employed—the one in the surface plane (as in row A), the other in depth, that is, toward or away from the viewer (as in row B). To respond "same" or "different" a subject

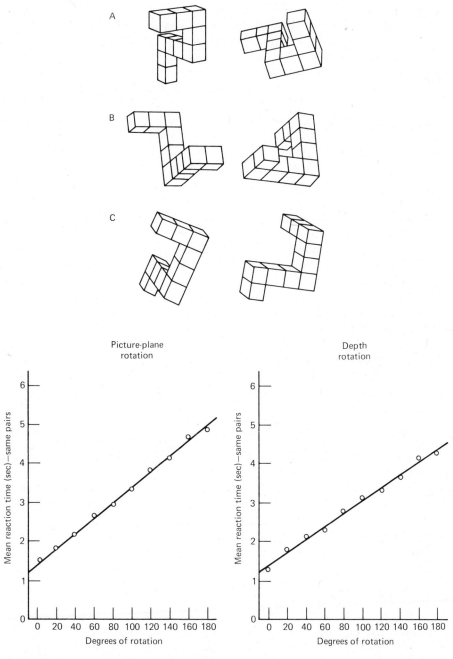

Figure 10.22. Top panel: Representative standard (left) and comparison (right) stimulus objects that have either identical configurations (rows A and B) or mirror-image configurations (row C) and require either a picture-plane rotation (row A) or a depth rotation (row B). Bottom panel: Mean reaction times obtained with young-adult subjects as a function of the degree of rotation required. (Adapted from material in Shepard & Metzler, 1971.)

must rotate the object on the right mentally the number of degrees it departs from the orientation of the object on the left to see if the two figures are congruent. This mental operation is equivalent to the physical operation a subject would perform if three-dimensional objects were available to manipulate. With these objects, reaction time should increase progressively as the number of degrees of rotation increases. Shepard's evidence (Metzler & Shepard, 1974; Shepard & Metzler, 1971), as illustrated in the bottom panel of Figure 10.22 for the two kinds of "same" problems, indicated that the same linear increments in time occur when the objects have to be rotated mentally instead of physically. This is the outcome that must occur if imaginal operations truly parallel physical operations.

Other studies (e.g., Cooper & Shepard, 1973) demonstrated a comparable progressive increment in reaction time when the to-be-rotated object was either a letter of the alphabet, such as ↘, or a mirror image of that letter, such as ↙. The primary independent variable was the degree of rotation an object received, again ranging from 0° to 180°. For each problem, a subject simply had to indicate whether the object shown was a true letter or a mirror-image letter. Making this decision seemingly forces a subject to rotate the object mentally until it is in an upright position. In agreement with the results obtained with the mental rotation of more complex objects, reaction time increased progressively as the departure from the upright position increased from 0° through 180°.

Mental-rotation problems present a far more effective test of imaginal thinking than do comparison problems involving state outlines. It is difficult to conceive of how rotation problems could be solved without imaginal operations that are analogous to the operations conducted on physical objects. By contrast, outline comparison could be based solely on the retrieval of linguistic information stored in generic memory. This information might describe Oregon's shape as being regular, West Virginia's shape as being irregular, and so on. Comparisons of this information could yield decisions about the degree of similarity between the outlines of any two specific states.

Given their unique imaginal content, mental-rotation problems have captured the attention of contemporary experimental psychologists and the attention of experimental aging psychologists as well. The booming interest in mental research has been part of the overall surge of interest expressed by contemporary psychologists in mental imagery. As we discovered earlier, another form of this interest has been in the study of imaginal mediational processes on the acquisition of verbal-learning tasks. The surge of interest followed years of suppression of concern about imagery, a suppression brought about largely by the refusal of early behaviorists (e.g., Watson, 1919) to consider imagery to be an appropriate topic for experimental psychologists to investigate.

Aging Research. Age differences in proficiency on mental-rotation tasks were first investigated by Gaylord and Marsh (1975). Young-adult and elderly subjects received rotation problems employed earlier by Shepard and Metzler

(1971). As may be seen in Figure 10.23, mean reaction time increased linearly for both age groups as the degree of rotation for the comparison object increased. Age differences are clearly apparent for two components of the straight-line charting the course of the time/degree of rotation relationship. The first is the rate-of-rotation component. For a given age group, it corresponds to the slope of the line shown in Figure 10.23 for that group. The average time per degree of rotation (i.e., slope of the line) was significantly greater for the elderly subjects (17.7 milliseconds) than for the young subjects (8.1 milliseconds). The second component is the total time required to complete the nonrotational aspects of the problem-solving task. That is, it is the time taken to encode the stimulus objects plus the time taken to respond after completing the rotation. For a given age group, the nonrotational time corresponds to the point of intersection of that group's straight-line function with the ordinate. The average time was again significantly greater for the elderly subjects (3640 milliseconds) than for the young subjects (1520 milliseconds). The dual nature of slowing down in late adulthood for the mental-rotation task corresponds closely to the dual nature of the slowing down found for the memory-scanning, or Sternberg, task. As observed by Gaylord and Marsh, "Whether this similarity is fortuitous or whether it indicates a similar decline for all serial processing relying upon recent memory processes remains to be determined" (1975, p. 678).

In addition, Gaylord and Marsh compared error rates in decisions for their two age groups. The rate was found to be significantly greater for their elderly subjects (11.04%) than for their young subjects (5.43%; a rate that approximated the 3% rate found by Shepard and Metzler [1971] for their young subjects). The age deficit in error rate was present even though the two objects to be evaluated for congruity were present simultaneously. Consequently, there was no demand placed on memory. Suppose, however, that the first object is removed from sight before the second object, that is, the to-be-rotated object is

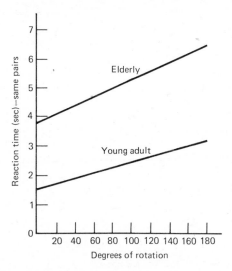

Figure 10.23. Age differences in mean reaction times for varying degrees of mental rotation for the kinds of material illustrated in Figure 10.22 (row B). (Adapted from Gaylord & Marsh, 1975, Figure 2.)

exposed. Under these conditions, a congruity decision would have to be based on a comparison between the memory trace of the first object and a rotated image of the second object. Given this heavy memory demand, it seems likely that the age deficit in error rate would be considerably greater than the deficit reported by Gaylord and Marsh. With comparison objects (nonsense shapes)— considerably simpler than the configurations employed by Gaylord and Marsh—Krauss, Quayhagen, and Schaie (1980) did find a substantial increase in the error rate for elderly subjects under a successive exposure condition (i.e., with a memory requirement) relative to a simultaneous exposure condition (i.e., without a memory requirement). Unfortunately, they did not include young-adult subjects in their study. Thus, the magnitude of the increase in the age difference brought about by the successive exposure of objects could not be determined.

A somewhat different outcome was obtained by Jacewicz and Hartley (1979) with the letter-rotation problem employed originally by Cooper and Shepard (1973). Their results for two age groups (mean ages, 21.6 and 55.9 years) are plotted in Figure 10.24. Although the slope value for their older subjects was greater than the slope value for their younger subjects, the age difference was not statistically significant. Jacewicz and Hartley (1979) reasoned that the presence/absence of true age differences on rotation problems is contingent on the extent to which the stimulus objects are familiar to older subjects. With familiar objects, such as letters, there is little, if any, slowing down of imaginal operations. In further agreement with this hypothesis, Herman and Coyne (1979) reported an absence of age differences for the rotation of familiar household objects placed in an array. It is a different matter, however, when the stimulus objects are highly unfamiliar, such as the block configurations employed by Gaylord and Marsh (1975). With unfamiliar objects, age deficits are expected to be pronounced, as they were in Gaylord and

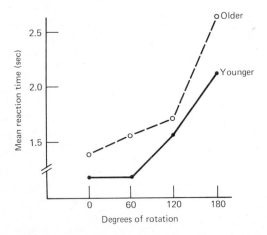

Figure 10.24. Age differences in mean reaction times for varying degrees of mental rotation for English letters as stimulus objects. (Adapted from Jacewicz & Hartley, 1979, Figure 1.)

Marsh's study and also in Jacewicz and Hartley's study when unfamiliar Greek letters replaced English letters as stimulus objects. Unfortunately, the use of relatively "young" older subjects by Jacewicz and Hartley did not permit a rigorous test of their hypothesis. Conceivably, the trend toward increasing slope and intersection values with increasing age on English-letter problems would have attained statistical significance with still older subjects.

It seems logical to assume that the ability to solve mental-rotation problems is related to the spatial ability assessed on various intelligence tests (e.g., the Primary Mental Abilities Test [PMA]). Consequently, age changes in performance on mental-rotation tasks would be expected to correlate positively with age changes in performance on tests of spatial ability. In support of this expected covariation, Krauss et al. (1980) did find that performance on a mental-rotation task is affected by several variables in the same way performance on the PMA spatial test is affected.

Stage Theory of Cognitive Development and Age Changes in Thinking

Stage Regression. Age deficits in concept-learning proficiency, problem-solving proficiency, and reasoning proficiency are readily accommodated by the quantitative model of development. The various lower and higher order processes mediating performance on these tasks simply deteriorate in proficiency as biological changes occur from early to late adulthood. But are there broader cognitive changes as well? That is, are there sweeping qualitative changes that, in effect, force many elderly people to regress to the more primitive cognitive operations characteristic of their preadulthood stages of development? As we noted in Chapter 6, "Is it possible that an adult once capable of functioning at the level of formal operations now finds it difficult to function at the level of concrete operations?"

From our discussion in Chapter 6, we know that regressive changes in thinking are antithetical to the Piagetian stage theory of cognitive development, at least as that theory has been commonly conceptualized. Cognitive development is seen as progressing irreversibly through the sensorimotor stage (roughly birth to 2 years of age), the preoperational stage (roughly 2 to 7 years of age), the concrete operational stage (roughly 7 to 11 years of age), culminating in the formal operational stage (adolescence and adulthood). Some psychologists (e.g., Arlin, 1975; Gruber, 1973) have advanced the notion that there is a fifth stage of cognitive development, one that is gained by only a segment of the adult population. The fifth stage is basically a refinement of the formal operational stage. According to Arlin, it goes beyond the problem-solving characteristics of the fourth stage and results in problem-finding thinking (e.g., raising general questions from ill-defined problems) for those who attain it. Other psychologists (e.g., Cropper, Meek, & Ash, 1977; Fakouri, 1976) have questioned the existence of a stage that is truly qualitatively different from the formal operational stage. The number of adult stages is irrelevant, however, to the concept of irreversibility of stages. That concept has been questioned seriously in recent years by several developmental psychologists (e.g., Hooper,

1973; Hooper, Fitzgerald, & Papalia, 1971; Hooper & Sheehan, 1977). The implication is that an adult who once functioned at the level of formal operations may indeed find it difficult to think at the level of concrete operations. The qualitative regression, however, is presumed to be the consequence of the same kind of biological/neurological degeneration generally held accountable for quantitative changes in directed thinking activities (Hooper et al., 1971).

In this final section of Chapter 10, we will review briefly the evidence relevant to the important issue of cognitive-stage regression. Our interest centers on studies comparing young adults and healthy, community-dwelling elderly adults in performance on the kinds of tasks traditionally used to assess the operations associated with the various stages of cognitive development, particularly the concrete operational stage. Not surprisingly, a number of studies have revealed considerable deterioration of performance on many Piagetian tasks by elderly people suffering from senility (e.g., Ajuriaguerra, Muller, & Tissot, 1960) and prolonged institutionalization (e.g., Rubin, 1973).

Aging Studies. The favorite tasks used in tests of age regression from a Piagetian perspective have been those involving understanding of the principles of conservation. An early study by Sanders, Laurendeau, and Bergeon (1966) contrasted young (20 to 39 years of age), middle-age (45 to 59 years of age), and elderly (60 years of age and over; mean age, 72.3 years) subjects in performance on a space-conservation task. The materials consisted of two pieces of green cardboard, equal in area, each serving as a grazing field for a toy cow placed on the surface as well as a number of blocks serving as houses built in each field. Each house placed in a field, of course, reduces the grazing surface for that field's resident cow. For conservation problems, the number of houses in each field was the same. However, the houses were placed close together in one field, whereas they were widely scattered in the other field. Subjects had to decide if the cows had the same or different amounts of grazing space. Age differences in the full understanding of the conservation principle (i.e., responding same— and explaining why they are the same) were extremely large: 84% of the young-adult subjects and 72.1% of the middle-age subjects, but only 22.6% of the elderly subjects demonstrated complete mastery.

The age deficit on a space-conservation task was subsequently replicated by Papalia, Kennedy, and Sheehan (1973). In addition, other investigators (Papalia, 1972; Rubin, 1976; Storck, Looft, & Hooper, 1972) have found comparable age deficits on weight-, volume-, and substance-conservation tasks (see Papalia & Bielby, 1974, for a detailed review). For example, the percentages demonstrating full understanding were 62, 50, and 6 for elderly subjects and 100, 100, and 50 for young-adult subjects on substance-, weight-, and volume-conservation tasks respectively.

Comprehension of conservation concepts requires understanding that objects may be transformed without necessarily altering a basic property of those objects. A child who has progressed through the concrete operational stage has achieved competence in understanding and utilizing these transformations. By contrast, the preoperational child is unable to integrate and coordinate information in a way that permits understanding of conservation. For example, liquid poured from one beaker to another is viewed as increasing in volume if the second beaker is narrower and taller than the first. The level of the liquid in the second beaker is, therefore, higher than it was in the first beaker. It is this physical disparity that deludes the preoperational child into believing that volume per se has increased. The concrete operational child integrates information about the height and weight of the beakers and, through this integration, realizes that volume does not change with this simple transformation. The failure of many elderly subjects to master conservation problems presumably results from their loss of the necessary integrating operations and, therefore, signifies their regression to the preoperational stage of cognitive functioning.

Regression to the preoperational stage implies that afflicted individuals will manifest other attributes of that stage as well as the loss of conservation principles. Foremost among these other attributes is egocentrism or thinking solely from one's self-perspective (see Looft, 1972, for a more detailed discussion). Preoperational children can think about many environmental events from their own point of view, but they have difficulty thinking about and describing those events from someone else's perspective. Spatial egocentrism is one manifestation of egocentrism in which an individual has difficulty imagining how a visual object looks to someone who has a different view of that object. One of the kinds of problems used to assess degree of spatial egocentrism is illustrated in Figure 10.25. The subject examines a stimulus object of the kind shown in the top segment of this figure. The subject's task is to select from among the alternatives shown in the bottom segment of Figure 10.25 the one that corresponds to what the experimenter (seated across the table from the subject) sees simultaneously. For the specific problem in Figure 10.25, the correct answer is B, whereas the egocentric answer is D. Although alternatives A and C are wrong answers, they are not egocentric answers. With problems of this kind, several investigators (Bielby & Papalia, 1975; Rubin, 1974; Rubin,

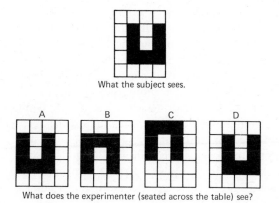

What the subject sees.

What does the experimenter (seated across the table) see?

Figure 10.25. Representative problem for testing egocentrism in which subjects select from the four alternatives what the stimulus pattern (top) looks like to the experimenter. (Adapted from Schultz & Hoyer, 1976, Figure 1.)

Attewell, Tierney, & Tumolo, 1973) have reported inordinately large proportions of elderly subjects performing egocentrically. Communicative egocentrism is another form of egocentrism in which an individual has difficulty
comprehending how information transmitted by that individual is perceived by
another person. To assess communicative egocentrism, subjects are assigned
one of several available stimulus objects (e.g., cards containing different geometric designs) as a target. Their task is to transmit information about the
target to other people, information that will enable them to identify which
object is the target. Here, too, several investigators (Looft & Charles, 1971;
Rubin, 1974) have reported inordinately large proportions of elderly subjects
performing egocentrically.

The net effect of these aging studies on conservation and on egocentrism is
a gloomy picture of late adulthood. Elderly people are seen as having a high
probability of regressing cognitively to the preoperational stage. There are reasons to believe, however, that the previously cited studies grossly exaggerate the
extent of qualitative changes with aging in thinking.

One reason is the failure of these investigators to consider the probable
involvement of adverse performance factors in determining age deficits on Piagetian tasks. As observed by Hornblum and Overton, "Such factors include
lack of familiarity with the testing situations, irrelevance of the tasks, a con-
stricting life space, disuse of relevant skills or strategies, memory limitations,
and preferential modes of thinking" (1976, pp. 68-69). The irrelevance of the
task, for example, is clearly apparent in the study by Sanders et al. (1966). The
material (toy cow, blocks, and so on) was designed for research on children's
ability to solve conservation problems. Elderly subjects are likely to resent
being treated as if they were children, and their negative attitudes are likely to
be reflected in inattention to stimulus materials and task demands. Most important, there is convincing evidence of the effectiveness of training programs
in elevating the performance levels of previously deficient elderly subjects to
the point where they demonstrate comprehension of conservation principles
(Hornblum & Overton, 1976) and they exhibit few errors on tests of egocentrism (Schultz & Hoyer, 1976). Thus, age deficits on both kinds of tasks seem to
result more from production deficiencies than from deficiencies in competence.

There is also evidence to indicate that some observed age deficits in spatial
egocentrism may be the result of the diminished proficiency of episodic memory in late adulthood rather than the result of the diminished proficiency of
higher order processes. The evidence comes from a clever study by Ohta,
Walsh, and Krauss (1981). Their young and elderly subjects judged the accuracy of slides depicting views of three miniature buildings placed on a circular
cardboard in front of the subjects. In a memory condition, the subjects had
previously viewed the buildings from their own position and then from other
positions around the circumference of the circular area anchoring the buildings.
Subsequent recognition of the buildings' relationships to one another, as depicted in the slides (some of which were accurate reproductions, whereas others
were distortions, including distortions as they would appear if the buildings
were being perceived egocentrically), was presumed to be determined by a

subject's memory of what had actually been seen while moving around the circular area. Under this memory condition, a significantly greater proportion of total errors were egocentric errors for the elderly subjects than for the young subjects. In another condition, the subjects examined the buildings from their judgment position only. That is, they were not allowed to move about the circle and view the buildings from other spatial perspectives. Consequently, accuracy of judgments was contingent on the subject's ability to imagine the view from other spatial perspectives around the circle. Under this condition, the age difference in the proportion of total errors that were egocentric in nature disappeared.

The nature of the subject populations is another probable contributor to the pronounced age deficits found on many Piagetian tasks. One problem, as noted by Chance, Overcast, and Dollinger (1978), is the failure of some investigators to include young-adult subjects in their stage-oriented aging studies. The assumption is that young-adults, particularly college students, would earn perfect scores on most conservation and egocentrism tasks. Therefore, a less-than-perfect score by elderly subjects would be accepted as indicating an age deficit. In reality, errors on both kinds of tasks are far from being uncommon among young-adult subjects (Chance et al., 1978; Neimark, 1975). Another potential problem rests in the vagueness of the descriptions of the samples of elderly subjects entering into a number of the Piagetian aging studies. Consequently, in some cases at least, it is difficult to determine the health status and educational level of the elderly subjects. Both of these non-age attributes are likely to covary positively with scores on Piagetian tasks. In question is the comparability of young and elderly subjects on these important non-age attributes in Piagetian aging studies. Interestingly, Chance et al. (1978) found no age deficits on conservation tasks with an elderly sample that was roughly comparable in health status and educational level to their young-adult sample. In addition, Krauss and Schaie (1976) found that disparities in educational level accounted for a large proportion of the age deficit in scores on their test of egocentrism; Tesch, Whitbourne, and Nehrke (1978) found no age differences in egocentrism for adult-age groups that were homogeneous with respect to a number of non-age attributes.

Finally, evidence reviewed in Chapter 9 argues effectively against the notion that there is any serious loss of ability to solve conservation problems in late adulthood. The principles involved in conservation, once mastered in pre-adulthood, are surely stored in generic memory as part of permanent knowledge about the world. We know that generic knowledge is highly resistant to loss in normal aging. It seems unlikely that conservation rules would be an exception. Moreover, solving problems on a spatial egocentrism task is somewhat analogous to solving mental-rotation problems. Note that recognition of the correct answer in Figure 10.25 requires a mental rotation of the stimulus object facing the subject. The objective is to find an alternative answer that is congruent with the rotated object. Although error rates on mental-rotation problems do appear to be greater for elderly subjects than for young subjects, especially for unfamiliar stimulus objects, the age disparity is far from being large enough to suggest the presence of a major qualitative age change in the underlying cognitive process.

Our best estimate is that adult-age changes in directed thinking, as viewed from the perspective of Piagetian stage theory, are confined to quantitative changes in the proficiency of those processes commonly identified with the formal operational stage (Flavell, 1970). These changes are seemingly comparable to the changes described earlier in this chapter quite independently of stage progression/regression theory.

Summary

Concept learning, problem solving, and reasoning are directed thinking activities that are mediated to a large extent by the so-called higher order mental processes. That is, the processes are more complex than those mediating perception, learning, and memory. Directed thinking activities are important to adults of all ages for their adjustments to their everyday environments. For example, concept learning has no age limits. New concepts are continually being introduced by society—concepts such as black hole and gas guzzler. There is the strong possibility of age changes in directed thinking, especially in light of the commonly expressed complaint by elderly people that "they don't think as well as they once did." Consequently, research on age differences/changes in directed thinking is an important part of the experimental psychology of aging. However, advancement in this area has been slower than in other areas, such as age differences/changes in memory. Much of the difficulty rests in the complexity of the higher order processes and the resulting relatively slow progress in developing adequate theories to represent their operations and their interactions with other processes.

The first area of directed thinking examined in this chapter was that of concept learning. A concept is defined with respect to both its attribute values on relevant stimulus dimensions and the rules that determine the way these attributes must be combined to form a positive instance of that concept. Positive instances usually vary, however, with respect to their values on other irrelevant stimulus dimensions. Simple concepts have only one relevant stimulus dimension, with a single attribute of that dimension defining positive instances. More complex concepts have more than one relevant dimension, with the positive attributes of those dimensions being combined by either a conjunctive, a disjunctive, or a conditional rule to form positive instances of the concept.

Associative theories of concept learning stress either the rote or the mediated acquisition of connections between the stimulus features, or attributes, of a concept's instances and responses identifying instances as being exemplars of the concept. These connections gain greater strength with practice for positive instances of the concept than for negative instances. Age deficits in concept learning may then be postulated to result from either the slower rote rehearsal rate of elderly subjects or the reduced use of mediators by elderly subjects—in either case relative to younger subjects. Cognitive theories of concept learning stress the formulation by subjects of hypotheses regarding which stimulus feature or combination of features defines the concept. Especially influential in basic research on concept learning has been Levine's (1975) hypothesis-testing theory. According to this theory, information pertaining to hypotheses previously tested and found to be incorrect and information pertaining to untested, and, therefore, still viable hypotheses are stored as separate subsets in episodic memory. From this perspective, age deficits in concept learning are largely due either to the inefficiency of the episodic-memory system in late adulthood or to the reduced ability of elderly subjects to formulate viable hypotheses identifying potentially positive stimulus attributes.

A number of descriptive studies have reported the existence of age deficits in the acquisition of both simple and complex concepts. Of greater importance, however, are the relatively few studies that included variation in some manipulable independent variable, thus providing insight, by means of interaction effects, into the age-sensitive processes accounting for age deficits in concept-learning proficiency. One of these manipulated variables is the sequence in which instances of the concept are presented. In general, age deficits in concept learning are greater when the sequence places a demand on memory than when it does not. The implication is that an inefficient episodic-memory system is indeed a potent contributor to age deficits in the proficiency of concept learning. Elderly subjects have also been found to establish less stable hypotheses than younger subjects. For example, elderly subjects are more likely than younger subjects to abandon still viable hypotheses following the receipt of redundant information during performance on a concept-learning task. In addition, the adverse effect of increasing the number of irrelevant stimulus attributes on concept-learning proficiency is greater for elderly subjects than for younger subjects.

A further area of concept-learning research has involved what are called intradimensional- and extradimensional-solution shifts. The nature of transfer effects on shift tasks indicates whether subjects acquired an original concept rotely or through mediation. Aging research with these shift tasks implies that the involvement of mediational acquisition processes is greater for young-adult subjects than for elderly subjects, whereas the involvement of rote-acquisition processes is greater for elderly subjects than for young-adult subjects.

On problem-solving tasks, subjects encounter a stimulus situation for which they have no immediate response, and they must, therefore, discover an appropriate response. Most basic research on problem-solving has been guided by an information-processing analysis of problem-solving activities. According to this analysis, the processes for any problem's solution can be organized into three general stages, preparation, production, and judgment. Preparation refers to the preliminary activity whereby a subject forms an internal representation of the problem itself. Age deficits in problem-solving proficiency could involve the preparation stage through such factors as the tendency of elderly subjects to direct inordinate attention to irrelevant components of a problem situation and, therefore, direct insufficient attention to relevant components. Production refers to the subject's generation of a strategy, or heuristic, for processing information inherent in a problem's representation. Diminished ability to generate effective heuristics may also account, in part, for age deficits in problem-solving proficiency. Moreover, the implementation of a strategy in solving a problem often requires memory storage of prior problem-relevant data while applying the strategy to gather further data. Consequently, age deficits in episodic-memory processes may well be contributors to age deficits in problem-solving proficiency. The judgment stage requires a subject to evaluate the correctness of a proposed solution. Excessive cautiousness by elderly subjects may reduce the proficiency of their problem solving by giving them little confidence in their solutions, even when they are correct, thereby leading unnecessarily to searching for other solutions.

Process-oriented aging research on problem solving does indicate that elderly subjects employ heuristics that are less effective than the heuristics employed by younger subjects. However, at least part of this heuristic difficulty probably stems from the poorer representations of problems constructed by elderly subjects than by younger subjects. In general, experimental aging research indicates that the magnitude of age deficits in problem-solving proficiency does increase progressively as the memory demand placed on the problem solver increases. This relationship between memory demand and magnitude of the age deficit in problem-solving proficiency is readily explained in terms of the concept of a working-memory system. The work space of this system is presumed to diminish in capacity from early to late adulthood. As the memory demand of a problem-solving task increases, a decreasing amount of work space remains for processing the remaining components of the problem. The diminished capacity of elderly subjects is expected to lead to problem-solving deficits only when a problem requires committing a large portion of the work space to the storage of prior data. Predictions derived specifically from the working-memory concept have received recent confirmation.

A unique form of problem-solving activity is that of creativity. In creative problem solving, individuals must give original, or uncommon, responses that have social significance and relevance. Research on originality per se (i.e., the ability to give uncommon responses in a problem situation independently of their social significance) reveals that elderly subjects tend to give fewer unique responses than do younger subjects. With respect to actual creativity, a classic study by Lehman (1953) suggests that creative contributions to science, mathematics, philosophy, and so on (as analyzed by number of citations in books) are made primarily by individuals younger than age 50. Various explanations have been offered for declining creativity with increasing age, including the advancement of creative people to other assignments (e.g., administrative) as they gain experience while growing older, the increasing inflexibility of problem solvers as they grow older, the exposure of many elderly people to environments that are biased against the use of creative thought, and the probable presence of true declines in original thinking ability with advancing age.

The objective of logical reasoning is to draw valid conclusions that either are known to be true or are assumed to be true. Logical reasoning is commonly studied through performance on syllogisms. Of special interest is performance on syllogism problems that have indeterminate solutions. The occurrence of illogical errors on these problems is commonly explained in terms of either the atmosphere-effect hypothesis or the premise-conversion hypothesis. However, neither of these hypotheses is effective in explaining age deficits in performance on syllogism problems. A more general explanation is in terms of the diminished work space of elderly people for solving problems of any kind that demand considerable processing capacity. Recent evidence has supported the application of the working-memory concept to age deficits in performance on syllogisms.

Functional reasoning, or reasoning through the use of analogy, is another important form of directed thinking activity. It is commonly studied by having subjects interpret the meanings of proverbs and metaphors. There is little evidence regarding the existence of adult-age differences in the proficiency of functional reasoning. What there is indicates the presence of age deficits for the interpretation of proverbs but not for the interpretation of metaphors.

A novel form of problem solving that has been of great interest to basic researchers in recent years is one in which subjects are required to rotate a stimulus object mentally. Subjects rotate the object imaginally to determine whether or not it is congruent with a comparison object. Reaction time, or time taken to decide on congruity, has been found to increase progressively for young adults as the degree of deviation from congruence increases. The underlying mental operation on mental-rotation problems is a form of imaginal thinking, and it appears to be equivalent to the physical operation a subject would perform if the requisite object could be rotated physically instead of mentally.

Given the suspected decrement in imaginal ability over the course of the adult lifespan, the extent of age differences on mental-rotation problems has assumed considerable importance to experimental aging psychologists. Elderly subjects have been found to perform more slowly than younger subjects on mental-rotation problems, in terms of both the rate of rotation and the time to complete nonrotational components of the problems. The magnitude of the age deficits is greater when unfamiliar objects (e.g., Greek letters) must be rotated mentally rather than familiar objects (e.g., English letters). In addition, the magnitude of age deficits on mental-rotation problems appears to be greater when the comparison object must be held in memory rather than being present simultaneously with the to-be-rotated object.

Finally, age changes in directed thinking activities were examined from the perspective of Piagetian stage theory of cognitive development. Recent evidence pertaining to adult-age differences on both conservation tests and tests of egocentrism has implied a cognitive regression in late adulthood to the preoperational stage of cognitive functioning. However, many of the reported deficits appear to be attributable to adverse performance factors present in late adulthood only rather than to true qualitative regressive age changes in cognitive abilities. A more realistic appraisal is that late adulthood is characterized merely by quantitative changes in the proficiency of those operations identified with the formal operational stage of development. These changes are comparable to the ones reported by experimental aging psychologists for concept-learning, problem-solving, and reasoning tasks.

CHAPTER 11

Intelligence, Personality, and Social Behavior

Sensory psychologists study the processes of the sensory system, memory psychologists the processes of the memory system, and so on. But it is people, not isolated systems, who participate in laboratory studies of sensory processes, memory processes, and other processes of direct concern to experimental psychologists. People bring their intelligences, their personalities, and their social predispositions with them into the laboratory. Age differences in these important characteristics of human behavior can scarcely be ignored by experimental psychologists of aging. We discovered in earlier chapters that age differences in such characteristics as cautiousness and rigidity do indeed influence the magnitude of age differences on sensory, memory, and problem-solving tasks. Conceivably, age differences in other characteristics, generally subsumed under the heading of individual-differences variables by psychologists, also affect performance on many laboratory tasks. Of course, even if these variables do not interact with sensory, perceptual, and learning processes among others, there would still be good reason for anyone interested in human aging, including experimental aging psychologists, to be familiar with research dealing with age differences in intelligence, personality, and social behavior. Surely, many of our everyday behaviors are determined by our various intellectual abilities, cognitive styles, compliances to authorities, and so on.

Our overall coverage will, therefore, be broadened in this chapter by reviewing research evaluating age differences/changes in intelligence, personality, and social behavior. Some of this research has been of an experimental nature, in the sense that intellectual, personality, or social variables served as the dependent variables in laboratory-based studies. Most aging studies in these areas, however, have been psychometrically oriented. That is, age differences for the characteristic in question were assessed by means of an intelligence test, a personality test, or an attitude test. Our review will survey highlights of these nonexperimental aging studies.

Adult–Age Differences in Intelligence

Intelligence and the Experimental Psychology of Aging: Overview. The concept of intelligence has played a critical role in the evolution of gerontological psychology. For many years, virtually all of the gerontological research conducted by psychologists was concerned with adult-age differences in performance on various intelligence tests (Jones, 1959). Even today, a sizable proportion of gerontological research deals in some way with adult-age differences in intelligence (Botwinick, 1977). It is largely through the early gerontological research on intelligence that issues concerning true age changes in behavior, as opposed to mere age differences in behavior, arose. Our frequent choice in Chapters 2, 3, and 4 of studies dealing with intelligence was far from being coincidental. These issues, of course, are by no means limited to performance on intelligence tests.

In this chapter, our initial objective is to offer a more formal coverage of research dealing with age differences/changes in intelligence as they are evaluated by traditional intelligence tests (see Baltes & Labouvie, 1973; Botwinick, 1967, 1977; Jones, 1959; Schaie, 1973, 1975, 1980; and Willis & Baltes, 1980, for additional reviews and discussions of critical issues). Only a small segment of this research can be classified as being truly part of the experimental psychology of aging through its use of experimental methodology. These are largely studies (some of which were encountered in Chapter 3) that attempted either to distinguish between true age changes in intellectual competence as opposed to age changes attributable to performance factors or to demonstrate the extent to which performance decrements can be alleviated by appropriate practice and training conditions. These studies provide us with some justification for including intelligence in our review of the experimental psychology of aging. There is an even more important reason however. Intelligence is generally viewed as being the "aggregate or global capacity of the individual to act purposefully, to think rationally and to deal effectively with his environment" (Wechsler, 1944, p. 3). Thus, intelligence subsumes the abilities to learn, to solve problems, and to reason—abilities of great interest in the experimental psychology of aging, and abilities, as we have seen, that are widely studied by experimental psychologists of aging.

The overlap between the psychometric study of individual differences in intellectual abilities and the laboratory-based study of cognitive abilities is accentuated by the number of tasks incorporated into intelligence tests that have their laboratory counterparts. In Chapter 4, we observed the common interest of intelligence testers and experimental psychologists in performance on memory-span tasks. Since then we have encountered a number of other laboratory tasks for which there are striking parallels in components of many intelligence tests. For example, laboratory assessments of generic-memory proficiency are not far removed from psychometric assessments of generic memory through the use of vocabulary tests and tests of general information. Similarly, the problem-solving tasks described in Chapter 10 are functionally very similar to such tests as the Arithmetic and Picture Arrangement subtests of the Wechsler Adult Intelligence Scale (WAIS). Our present review of research on age differences in intelligence should, therefore, complement our earlier reviews of research on age differences for a number of cognitive abilities. Most important, our present review should offer an independent means of evaluating the degree and nature of true age changes in these higher order abilities.

Of particular interest to us will be those aging studies that have examined covariations between cognitive abilities assessed psychometrically and cognitive abilities assessed by performance on learning and problem-solving tasks among others. As we will see, the nature of these covariations is of great importance in contemporary conceptualizations of intelligence and cognition (e.g., Hunt, Frost, & Lunneborg, 1973). It seems likely that age differences in the patterns and degrees of these covariations will eventually play an important role in guiding thinking about the nature of age changes in cognitive abilities and activities.

Psychometric Assessment Beyond Early Adulthood. As every introductory psychology student knows, the first successful intelligence test was constructed by Alfred Binet (Binet & Simon, 1905). Binet's creative efforts were stimulated by a very practical need, namely, to devise a procedure for identifying school-age children who were potentially slow learners and, therefore, required special education classes. Accordingly, Binet constructed a test that equated intelligence with educational aptitude. He believed that intelligence, as a dominant factor in determining school success, is a general ability that expresses itself in a number of different abilities, abilities that collectively determine the potential to learn and benefit from formal academic training. Accordingly, his test contained many kinds of questions and problems for which the total score (i.e., mental age) yielded an overall assessment of general intelligence as defined in terms of academic aptitude. Most important, scores on his test were expected to correlate positively with scores on an external criterion, namely, school grades. The positive correlation was expected simply because performance on the test and performance in school called for the same mediating abilities. To Binet's everlasting credit, his prediction received strong confirmation. His general intelligence test turned out to predict grades in school with considerable success.

Binet's test, and its American successor, the Stanford-Binet, provided the model for constructing later adult intelligence tests, such as the Army Alpha and the WAIS. As with Binet's test, these tests were considered to be successful only to the extent that they resolved some practical need. Accordingly, they were constructed with the intent of predicting performance on some external criterion. By so doing, they would permit decisions, based on test performance, regarding who would and who would not be successful with respect to the external criterion. But what criterion? Here, too, Binet's test provided the model. The criterion became performance in some educational setting, whether it be college or a training program established by industry or the military. High scorers on the test were to be considered better risks of benefiting from training than low scorers. Thus, adult intelligence testing continued in the tradition of assessing educational aptitude.

A serious problem arises, however, whenever adult intelligence tests are to be applied to adults (including most elderly people) who are far removed from academic settings. Of what value is it to evaluate academic aptitude for these individuals? The dilemma facing the adult intelligence tester was aptly described by Schaie:

> When intellectual functioning is considered beyond young adulthood, external validity problems become exacerbated, as it is unlikely that one can suggest a plausible single criterion situation comparable to that of educational aptitude, nor will tasks retain their ecological validity when the situational context of the individual to be assessed changes as a function of developmental progressions as well as idiosyncratic changes in individual life situations and roles (also see Fisher, 1973). (1978, pp. 695–696)

We will examine the criterion problem and its potential resolutions in the next section. Before we do, however, we should note that there is another serious problem associated with the transition from intelligence testing of young adults to intelligence testing of older adults. Adult intelligence tests, such as the WAIS, have traditionally placed a considerable premium on speed of responding. Bonus points are commonly awarded for responses that excel some time criterion. Alternatively, a time limit is set for performance on some component of the test, and points are awarded only for correct responses emitted within that time limit. The slowing down of responding during late adulthood implies that elderly people are unduly handicapped on these components of intelligence. Presumably, a fairer form of assessment would be by means of power tests, that is, intelligence tests without time limits. We will examine this issue more thoroughly in a later section.

The Criterion Problem. Valid intelligence tests for use with most adults are those that relate "to our coping in a competent manner with the problems of daily living (i.e., the situations in which intellectual abilities are to be applied and assessed)" (Schaie, 1978, pp. 696–697). Ecologically valid intelligence tests should be constructed with real-life situational criteria in mind. These criteria, however, are likely to change over the course of the adult lifespan. That is, the situations calling for intellectual competence in late adulthood are almost certain to differ from those in earlier stages of adulthood. The single criterion of educational aptitude is probably a fair one to apply in evaluating the validity of intelligence tests when they are used with young adults. However, this criterion is relatively meaningless when applied to older adults. In fact, no single criterion is sufficient for evaluating the validity of intelligence tests when they are to be used with older individuals.

Schaie and his colleagues (Schaie, 1978; Scheidt & Schaie, 1978) have taken the first step needed to develop ecologically valid intelligence tests for older adults. That step consists of identifying many of the real-life situations that seemingly call on the utilization of intellectual competence. These situations are classified in terms of various broad dimensions, such as whether the situations are common or uncommon, whether they require high activity or low activity, whether they involve social or nonsocial activity, and whether they are supportive or depriving in nature. Representative real-life situations conforming to these combinations of dimensions are given in Table 11.1. According to Schaie, the ultimate objective of psychologists studying age differences in intelligence should be to construct intelligence tests that correlate substantially with both self-ratings of older people and the ratings given to older people by others for current competence in these various situations. Unfortunately, fulfillment of this objective seems to be many years away.

We should note that other psychologists in the past have been dissatisfied with the status of intelligence tests for use with older people and have attempted to correct the problem by constructing their own versions of more ecologically relevant tests. Foremost among these pioneers were Demming and Pressey (1957). Unhappy with intelligence tests that asked older people such esoteric questions as "Who wrote Faust?" and "What is an iguana?," they substituted their own kinds of questions. Their questions tapped a person's knowledge of how to use the yellow pages of a telephone directory to solve a

Table 11.1 Examples of Specific Situations Relevant to Manifestations of Intellectual Competence Classified in Terms of Several Broad Dimensions

	Social	*Nonsocial*
High Activity		
Common-Supportive	Arguing with person about important point	Doing weekly shopping in crowded supermarket
Common-Depriving	Pressured by salesperson to buy merchandise	Cleaning apartment or household
Uncommon-Supportive	Traveling around city looking for new residence	Preparing large meal for friends
Uncommon-Depriving	Returning faulty or defective merchandise to store	Driving auto during rush-hour traffic
Low Activity		
Common-Supportive	Seeking aid/advice from friend or family member	Making plans for future
Common-Depriving	Hearing from friend that he/she is considering suicide	Worrying about ability to pay a debt
Uncommon-Supportive	Entering darkened nightclub to take dinner	Recording day's events in diary
Uncommon-Depriving	Opening door to stranger selling product or soliciting opinion	Discovering you locked keys in car while shopping

Source: Adapted from Scheidt and Schaie, 1978, Table 1.

Table 11.2   Examples of Questions Found in Demming and Pressey's (1957) Practical Test of Adult Intelligence

Use of the Yellow Pages of a Telephone Directory
  "Where in the yellow pages of the telephone directory would you look if you wanted to buy an Airedale? Under heating equipment, kennels, shoe stores, real estate, dairy equipment?"

Common Legal Terms
  "A document controlling disposition of one's property at death is called a bond, title, contract, will, equity?"

People to Get to Perform Services in Everyday Life
  "The person to baptize a baby is a naturalist, notary public, nurseryman, magistrate, clergyman?"

problem, their knowledge of legal terms having practical significance, and their knowledge of occupations that could provide helpful services to that person (an example of each kind is given in Table 11.2). However, Demming and Pressey had no external situational criteria for evaluating the validity of their intriguing test. Consequently, the degree of covariation of scores on the test with competence manifested in real-life situations of the kind given in Table 11.1 is unknown. Nevertheless, it is interesting that subjects in their 40s and 50s scored higher on Demming and Pressey's tests than did younger subjects. A similar age trend (i.e., scores peaking in middle age) was reported by Denney and Palmer (1981) when subjects were given practical, everyday problems to solve rather than problems of an abstract nature.

A more recent effort to construct an intelligence test geared for adults removed from academic settings was made by Gardner and Monge (1977). Among the components of their test are subtests dealing with knowledge about disease and death, knowledge about transportation, and knowledge about finance. Age differences on some of these components were found to be quite different from the age differences commonly found with intelligence tests that are geared for use with young adults in formal educational settings. For example, the results obtained with men on the disease/death and finance subtests are plotted in Figure 11.1 (similar results were obtained with women). Note that in

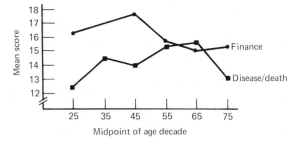

Figure 11.1. Age differences in components of a test designed to assess knowledge of events having relevance to success in everyday living. (Adapted from Gardner & Monge, 1977, Figures 3a, 5.)

neither case was the maximum average score the one earned by young adults. In fact, for the disease/death subtest, the highest average score was obtained by men in their 60s, for the finance subtest, it was by men in their 40s. Moreover, relatively little decline in average scores was found for men older than the ones scoring the highest. The problem confronting this test, however, is the same one that confronted Demming and Pressey (1957). Nothing is known about how well scores on this test relate to performance by older people in real-life non-educational settings and situations. Nevertheless, the test seems promising. Hopefully, future investigators will find a way of determining its validity with respect to ecologically meaningful external criteria.

The dubious criterion validity of adult intelligence tests, at least when these tests are applied to older individuals, has not prevented a number of investigators from examining adult-age differences in performance on these tests. We will review the evidence regarding the magnitude of these age differences in the following sections. Our interest rests in what this evidence reveals about age differences and, ultimately, about age changes in intellectual competence. However, we should keep in mind the important question: Competence for doing what?

Psychometric Assessment: Global-Age Comparisons. Adult intelligence tests, such as the Army Alpha, usually consist of subtests, each purporting to measure a separate intellectual ability (e.g., reasoning). Of initial concern to us, however, are the total scores earned on these tests. Conceptualizing intelligence as a global capacity implies that there is a general ability, or g, factor (Spearman, 1927), that affects performance to some degree on all tasks involving each separate ability. A person's total score, as a summation of scores on the individual subtests, is assumed to estimate that person's general intellectual ability relative to that of other people. Age differences in general, or overall, intelligence may then be determined by comparing the average total scores earned by people of different ages.

The first systematic study of adult-age differences in general intelligence was made possible by the administration of the Army Alpha test to nearly 2 million American soldiers during World War I. Age comparisons of total scores were reported, however, only for officers (Yerkes, 1921). The results of these comparisons are shown in the top panel of Figure 11.2. Average scores are expressed here in standard deviation units relative to the average score earned by 18-to-20-year-old officers. The pronounced decline in average score with increasing age was subsequently found in a number of later studies as well, both with the Army Alpha (e.g., Jones & Conrad, 1933) and other tests (e.g., the Otis Self-Administering Test of Intelligence; Miles & Miles, 1932). Of these other studies, the best known is that of Jones and Conrad. They tested over 1000 subjects between the ages of 10 and 60 years, all of whom lived in New England rural communities and were, therefore, from relatively homogeneous socioeconomic backgrounds. Their results are shown in the bottom panel of Figure 11.2.

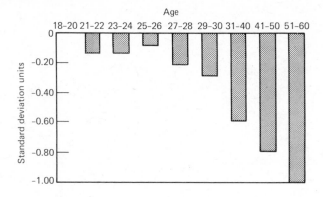

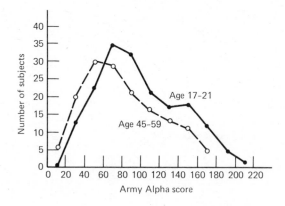

Figure 11.2. Top panel: Age differences in scores on the Army Alpha test for army officers in World War I. (Adapted from Jones, 1959, Figure 1.) Bottom panel: Age differences in scores on the Army Alpha test for over 1000 residents of New England rural communities. (From data in Jones & Conrad, 1933, as adapted by Jones, 1959, Figure 3.)

The concept of general intelligence received an important modification in Wechsler's (1944) monumental contribution to the assessment of adult intelligence. Wechsler believed that abilities that are not fully cognitive influence individual intellectual achievements. Rather than allow these abilities to remain uncontrolled and, therefore, confound measures of pure intellect, Wechsler introduced separate overall tests, or scales, one to measure pure verbal intelligence and the other to measure these noncognitive, or performance, factors. The result was the famous Wechsler-Bellevue test. It consisted of two separate groupings of subtests, one of which yielded a verbal-intelligence score (the verbal scale), the other a performance-intelligence score (the performance scale)—a feature that remained in the Wechsler-Bellevue's later replacement, the still popular WAIS. The original test was administered to nearly 2000 people, ranging in age from 10 to 59 years of age, living in and around New

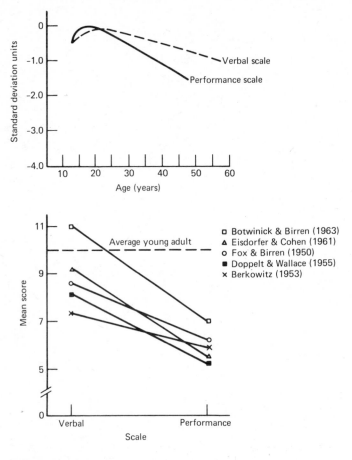

Figure 11.3. Top panel: Age differences in scores on the verbal and performance scales of the Wechsler. (Adapted from Jones, 1959, Figure 5.) Bottom panel: Magnitudes of the age deficits on the verbal and performance scales of the Wechsler as reported in various studies. (Adapted from Botwinick, 1967, Figure 3.)

York City. Age differences in average scores (expressed in standard deviation units relative to the maximum average score earned at a particular age) are shown in the top panel of Figure 11.3 for Wechsler's total standardization sample. Wechsler's results clearly replicated those of earlier investigators in demonstrating cross-sectional decrements in total scores with increasing age. However, he also demonstrated that the age-related decrements were considerably more pronounced for the performance component of his total test than for the verbal component.

Later investigators extended considerably the older age limit tested with Wechsler's verbal and performance scales (e.g., Berkowitz, 1953; Botwinick & Birren, 1963; Doppelt & Wallace, 1955; Eisdorfer & Cohen, 1961; Fox & Birren, 1950). In general, these studies indicated that the progressive declines apparent in the top panel of Figure 11.3 continue during late adulthood, and, if anything, they increase in their rate of decline during the sixth and seventh decades of life. They also provided corroboration of Wechsler's finding that the decline is greater for scores on the performance scale than for scores on the verbal scale. Shown in the bottom panel of Figure 11.3 are overall mean scores (expressed with respect to 10 as the mean score earned by young adults of average intelligence) obtained by these investigators for their age-60-and-beyond subjects on the two scales. Note that the mean score is considerably less on the performance scale than on the verbal scale in each study. However, the disparity in scale means does reveal variability among studies. Note further that not all investigators found an age deficit in mean score on the verbal scale. In fact, Botwinick and Birren (1963) reported a mean score for their elderly subjects that was well above that of the average young-adult subject (see the bottom panel of Figure 11.3). Moreover, the extent of the deficit in verbal-scale score varied considerably even among those studies that did report a deficit. On the other hand, an age deficit in mean-performance score was clearly present in each study.

There is one other test of general intelligence that has figured prominently in aging research. It is the Primary Mental Abilities Test (PMA) (Thurstone & Thurstone, 1941, 1947), the one that entered so often in our earlier discussion of Schaie's (1965) sequential analysis of developmental changes in intelligence. The pattern of age decline in composite scores for the PMA appears to be somewhat different from the pattern commonly reported for both the Army Alpha test and the Wechsler tests. Schaie (1958, 1959) administered the test to 500 people, 50 in each five-year interval from the 20s through the 60s. Mean scores, expressed in terms of composite standard scores (T values), are plotted in Figure 11.4 for five-year age ranges. Note that overall scores remain quite stable through age 50 and then begin a precipitous decline. By contrast, the onset of the decline in mean scores appears much earlier for both the Army Alpha test (see Figure 11.2) and the Wechsler tests (see Figure 11.3).

From our discussion in Chapters 2 and 3, we realize that cross-sectional age differences in intelligence do not necessarily mean an age change in intelligence (a rereading of those chapters would be helpful at this point). Most

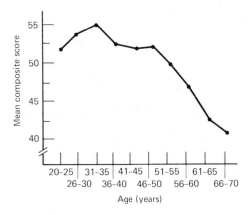

Figure 11.4. Age differences in composite scores on the Primary Mental Abilities Test (PMA). (Adapted from Botwinick, 1977, Figure 2, as derived from data in Schaie, 1959.)

important, the samples at each age level selected by both Jones and Conrad (1933) and Wechsler (1944) were intended to be representative of their overall populations. In fact, Wechsler's samples were intended to provide normative values for interpreting individual scores on his test. Consequently, the age groups in these studies differed on many important non-age attributes, particularly years of formal education. We discovered in Chapter 2 that cross-sectional age differences in intelligence test scores are, in fact, considerably reduced when a concerted effort is made to equate age groups in years of education. The implication is that true age changes in general intelligence are considerably more moderate than are the changes implied by the outcomes of descriptive cross-sectional studies. This conclusion receives strong support from the longitudinal study by Owens (1966) discussed in Chapter 3 and from other longitudinal studies of age changes in intelligence (e.g., Bayley & Oden, 1955). Also worth rereading at this point is our earlier discussion of how level of ability during early adulthood affects the subsequent rate of decline in intelligence test performance with increasing age.

Psychometric Assessment: Special-Ability Age Comparisons. Do the separate abilities that collectively make up general intelligence show equivalent age differences? To answer this question, we must first consider the kinds of abilities that are evaluated on traditional intelligence tests. In some cases, the abilities are the products of the test constructor's own logical analysis of what enters into human intelligence. This is true for both the Army Alpha test and the WAIS. Once these abilities have been identified, the constructor then devises a separate subtest to assess each ability. For the Army Alpha, these subtests are those of Arithmetic, Analogies, Synonyms-Antonyms, and so on; for the WAIS, these subtests are those of Vocabulary, General Information, and so on in the verbal test, and Digit Symbol, Picture Arrangement, and so in the performance test. In other cases, however, the abilities are those identified by the complex statistical method of factor analysis. This is true for the PMA. Here, too, a separate subtest is devised for each separate ability or factor. As we discovered in Chapter 4, these subtests for the PMA are those of Verbal Meaning, Space, Reasoning, Number, and Word Fluency.

Our first concern is with the considerable variability shown in the magnitude of age differences for the subtest, or ability, scores of the Army Alpha. One of the earliest comparisons was that of Willoughby (1927). Included in this study were the Arithmetic and Analogies subtests. Little change in mean score was found for the Arithmetic subtest from roughly 20 years of age to 60 years of age. By contrast, mean score for the Analogies subtest declined progressively and steeply with increasing age beyond the peak score earned at about age 20. Later cross-sectional studies (Garfield & Blek, 1952; Gilbert, 1935) reported similar pronounced age differences favoring younger adults in performance on tests of verbal analogies. Interestingly, Owen's longitudinal study (1966) yielded only a partial replication of Willoughby's (1927) earlier cross-sectional study. A modest decline with increasing age was again found for numerical ability (or arithmetic). However, reasoning scores (derived largely from the

Analogies subtest) actually increased with increasing age (see Figure 3.5), an increase Owens attributed to a cultural change.

Considerable variability in the magnitude of age differences for the subtest, or ability, scores of the WAIS has also been found in a number of studies (e.g., Berkowitz, 1953; Howell, 1955). In general, however, scores on the verbal subtests tend to show less decline with increasing age than do scores on the performance subtests. Representative results (Berkowitz, 1953) for the vocabulary and information subtests of the verbal scale are plotted in Figure 11.5. Note that vocabulary scores are about the same for adults in their 60s and 70s as they are for adults in their 20s and 30s. An early study by Beeson (1920), with the vocabulary test of the Stanford-Binet, revealed that vocabulary scores are remarkably robust even for institutionalized elderly people. There is one disturbing note to sound however. A detailed analysis by Botwinick and Storandt (1974c) of definitions given to WAIS vocabulary words by young and elderly subjects suggested that there may actually be age declines in vocabulary proficiency, at least as proficiency is evaluated qualitatively. That is, their young-adult subjects gave more superior definitions of the test words than did their elderly subjects, even though the two age groups differed little in terms of quantitative score on the test.

Information scores (Figure 11.5) also are about the same for adults in their 60s and 70s as they are for younger adults. An interesting question, however, is why there are not reverse age differences in information scores. Elderly people,

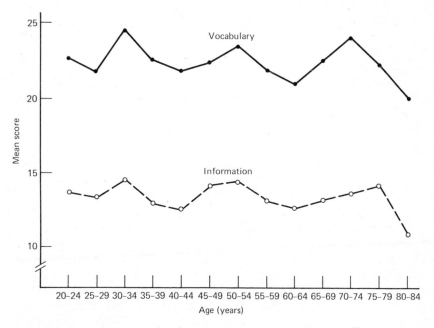

Figure 11.5. Age differences in scores on the vocabulary and information subtests of the Wechsler. (Adapted from data in Berkowitz, 1953.)

having lived longer and, therefore, having had a greater opportunity to accumulate knowledge than young adults, might be expected to excel young adults in scores on the information subtest. Part of the reason why this expectancy has not been fulfilled in most studies employing the WAIS information subtest probably rests in the nature of the questions asked (another reason may be the decline in fluid intelligence with aging). Many of the questions are of the esoteric kind criticized by Demming and Pressey (1957). They deal with information that has a reasonably high probability of being acquired while people reside in a formal educational setting, but a low probability of acquisition while residing in noneducational settings. It is the latter, of course, that characterizes most of adulthood, thus accounting for the overall absence of systematic increases in information scores with increasing age, at least for the kind of material included on the WAIS. Interestingly, Demming and Pressey did find increasing mean scores with increasing age, at least through middle age, for the more practical kinds of information they included in their test. Of further interest is the fact that many of their subjects were prisoners. Corsini and Fassett (1953) also employed prisoners in their study with the WAIS information subtest—and they, too, found increasing scores with increasing age. They argued that prisoners represent an ideal population of subjects for conducting aging research. That is, they tend to be more cooperative and eager to participate in research studies than do most adults selected from the civilian population. Their study was a cross-sectional one. It seems even more reasonable to argue that prisons would make ideal settings for conducting longitudinal studies.

Other subtests included in the WAIS verbal scale are the digit-span, arithmetic, comprehension (e.g., "What is the thing to do in such and such emergency?"), and similarities (e.g., "In what way are X and Y the same?") subtests. Both digit-span and arithmetic resemble the vocabulary and information subtests in the sense of revealing relatively little age-related decrements in mean scores (e.g., Berkowitz, 1953; Howell, 1955). The general robustness of performance on the digit-span subtest is in agreement, of course, with the results of laboratory studies on age differences in memory span. By contrast, age-related declines have been commonly found on both the comprehension subtest and the similarities subtest, both for civilians (e.g., Berkowitz, 1953; Howell, 1955) and prisoners (Corsini & Fassett, 1953). The disparities in age differences and age-related declines for the various verbal subtests implies that these subtests may be measuring two separate broad abilities, one that "holds" with aging and one that "doesn't hold" (W.L. Hunt, 1949). We will return to this point in a later section.

Representative results (Berkowitz, 1953) for the Digit Symbol and Picture Arrangement (a series of randomly ordered pictures must be arranged in the correct order to tell a story) subtests of the performance scale are plotted in Figure 11.6. Note the continuous and steep declines in mean scores with increasing age. These declines are clearly more pronounced than the declines found for any of the verbal subtests. Comparable age-related declines have also

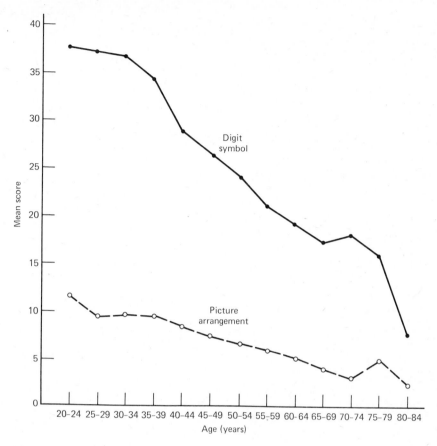

Figure 11.6. Age differences in scores on the Digit Symbol and Picture Arrangement subtests of the Wechsler. (Adapted from data in Berkowitz, 1953.)

been found for other digit-symbol tests (e.g., Weisenburg, Roe, & McBride, 1936). The age-related decline for the block design subtest (arranging colored blocks to conform to a designated design) has been found to be comparable to the declines shown in Figure 11.6. However, the age-related declines for the object-assembly subtest (much like working on a jigsaw puzzle) and picture-completion subtest (pictures are shown with a to-be-identified missing piece) have been found to be much less pronounced, approximating those found for the comprehension and similarities verbal subtests.

The pattern for age differences on tests measuring pure factors of intelligence is much like that found for age differences on the subtests of the WAIS. That is, there is considerable variability among the tests in the magnitude of age-related declines in mean scores. Most of the relevant research has involved the PMA. Age-related declines, when assessed cross-sectionally, tend to be relatively slight for number, verbal-meaning, and word-fluency tests, and relatively large for space and reasoning tests (Kamin, 1957; Schaie, Rosenthal, &

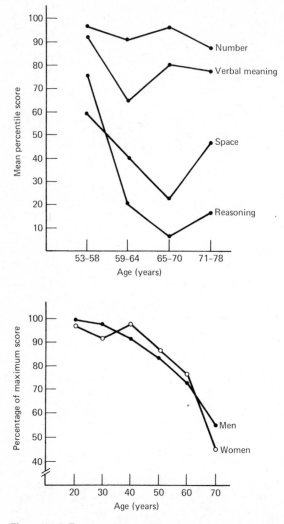

Figure 11.7. Top panel: Age differences in scores on the factor components of the Primary Mental Abilities Test (PMA). (Adapted from Schaie, Rosenthal, & Perlman, 1953, Figure 2.) Bottom panel: Age differences in scores on the Raven Progressive Matrices Test. (Adapted from data in Heron & Chown, 1967.)

Perlman, 1953; Strother, Schaie, & Horst, 1957). (See the top panel of Figure 11.7 for representative results, expressed relative to the average 17-year-old.) These age-related declines, of course, are those manifested by conventional cross-sectional research. As we discovered in Chapter 4, Schaie's (1965) sequential studies imply that these age-related declines are due largely to nonontogenetic factors, such as cohort effects.

Spatial ability is measured on the PMA by giving subjects standard figures, such as J. These figures then have to be compared with other figures that are either rotations of the standard figure (e.g., $\backslash$) or of its mirror image (e.g., $\swarrow$). The special ability being measured by this subtest is obviously similar to the ability entering into laboratory research on mental rotation. Pronounced age-related declines in spatial ability have also been reported for other tests of spatial ability that have also been derived through the use of factor analysis (e.g., Bilash & Zubek, 1960; Heston & Cannell, 1941).

Reasoning is measured on the PMA by giving subjects series of letters, such as *"a b m c d m e f m g h m,"* for which they have to discover a rule and then apply the rule to select from among alternatives the next letter in the sequence. Pronounced age-related declines in reasoning have also been found for standardized tests of so-called nonverbal reasoning. Foremost among these tests is the Raven Progressive Matrices Test (Raven, 1951) in which subjects are given visual designs from which pieces are missing. For each design, the missing piece is selected from several alternatives. Representative age differences found for men and women on the Raven test (Heron & Chown, 1967) are plotted in the bottom panel of Figure 11.7.

One other observation needs to be made of the variability in age differences for tests of special abilities. As may be seen from the age-performance relationships illustrated in Figures 11.5, 11.6, and 11.7, there is obvious variability in the age at which age-related declines in test scores first become apparent. An interesting hypothesis regarding the age of onset of decline was proposed by Trembly and O'Connor (1966). The hypothesis states that the age of onset for a given ability is related to the age at which peak performance is attained for that ability. Abilities that peak early in the lifespan are hypothesized as having their declines begin at older ages than abilities that peak later in the lifespan. Unfortunately, Trembly and O'Connor offered very limited data in support of their hypothesis. The hypothesis is surely important enough, however, to continue testing its validity.

Relationship Between Special Abilities: The Differentiation/De-differentiation Hypothesis. Another issue of great interest to gerontological psychologists concerns possible age changes in the nature of the relationship between general intelligence, or *g*, and special abilities. The abilities measured by the subtests of the WAIS correlate moderately with one another. For example, with education held constant, the correlations varied from .15 (vocabulary and digit symbol) to .68 (vocabulary and information) for over 900 subjects, aged 25 to 64 years, in the original standardization sample of the WAIS (Birren & Morrison, 1961). Why these positive correlations? One plausible explanation is that each subtest taps *g* to some degree as well as its own special ability. It is this sharing of *g* that accounts for the presence of intertest correlations. What interests gerontological psychologists, however, is possible changes in the magnitudes of these intertest correlations over the course of the adult lifespan. The presence of such changes would imply major alterations in the structure of intelligence from early to late adulthood.

Interest in this issue has been motivated by an extension of the differentiation hypothesis (Burt, 1954; Garrett, 1946). The hypothesis, as expressed by

Garrett, takes the following form: "Abstract or symbol intelligence changes in its organization as age increases from a fairly unified and general ability to a loosely organized group of abilities or factors (p. 373)." The reference is to changes in the structure of intelligence from early childhood to early adulthood. As illustrated in Figure 11.8, structure is viewed as being dominated by *g* early in childhood. Special abilities (the oval figures numbered 1 to 10 in Figure 11.8) have not yet emerged as special entities. Performance on a test measuring each special ability is, therefore, assumed to be determined largely by a child's level of *g*. A high level of *g* should mean high scores (for that child's age level) on each test, whereas a low level of *g* should mean low scores on each test. Consequently, intertest scores should be very high.

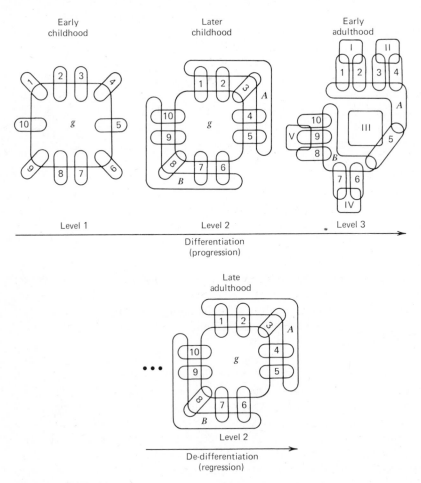

Figure 11.8. Schematic representation of the changes in relationships among general intelligence (*g*), broad factors of intelligence (Roman numerals), and specific abilities (Arabic numerals) hypothesized to take place from the perspective of differentiation/de-differentiation theory.

Later in development, broader factors (A and B in Figure 11.8) have separated from *g*. Some special abilities are governed by one of these broad factors (e.g., abilities 1 to 5 by Factor A in Figure 11.8), whereas other abilities are governed by a different factor (e.g., abilities 6 to 10 by Factor B in Figure 11.8), although all cognitive abilities continue to draw somewhat from *g* per se. The differentiation of abilities means that intertest correlations, considered overall, should be lower later in childhood than they are earlier in childhood. An individual may have different levels of competence for the separate broad factors of intelligence. Thus, scores may be higher for those abilities governed by Factor A than for those abilities governed by Factor B, thereby leading to lower correlation coefficients overall.

Differentiation is presumed to continue to progress through early adulthood. By then, what are called *primary factors* (I to V in Figure 11.8) have separated from each broad factor (or *secondary factor*). In practice, the secondary factors are identified as being crystallized intelligence and fluid intelligence, whereas the primary factors are spatial ability, reasoning, and so on. At this stage of development, special abilities are assumed to depend on *g* to an even smaller degree than they did in childhood. Consequently, intertest correlations should be lower than they are in late childhood. The expected lowering of intertest correlations with increasing age through early adulthood has received empirical support in a number of studies. However, it has also failed to be supported in just about as many other studies (see Reinert, 1970, for a review of these studies).

Our main concern, of course, is with whatever structural changes occur beyond early adulthood. To accommodate the expected changes, the differentiation hypothesis was extended by Balinsky (1941) to include a *de-differentiation* component. Older adult are expected to revert cognitively to the structure of intelligence characteristic of childhood, as illustrated in Figure 11.8. If true, the pattern of intertest correlations for special abilities should become like that of childhood (i.e., high correlations) during late adulthood. Balinsky's own data provided support for the occurrence of de-differentiation, as have the data provided by some other investigators (e.g., Green & Berkowitz, 1964; McHugh & Owens, 1954). On the other hand, a number of other investigators (e.g., J. Cohen, 1957; Weiner, 1964) have failed to find validating evidence for the de-differentiation hypothesis (see Reinert, 1970, for a detailed review).

Although its empirical support batting average is no better than .500, the differentiation/de-differentiation hypothesis has not exactly been placed in limbo. It has resurfaced in recent years with respect to the relationship between crystallized and fluid intelligence, a resurfacing we will discuss in the next section.

The hypothesis does have some interesting additional implications. Consider, for example, the familiar concept of memory span. It may be tested through the use of either digits or words (or, for matter, letters, nonsense syllables, and so on). If memory span is a general ability, then the materials used to assess its length should not matter. Individuals who have a large span for one kind of material should also have a large span for other kinds of material relative to other people. On the other hand, if memory span overall is a collection of moderately correlated special abilities, then individuals who score highly for one type of material need not score highly for another type of material. According to the differentiation/de-differentiation hypothesis, the correlation between length of digit span and length-of-word span should be modest for young adults who have progressed to the level of relatively independent span abilities. The correlation should be much higher, however, for elderly adults who have reverted to a more general span ability. This is exactly the pattern found by Friedman (1974). The correlation coefficient (r) between digit-span scores and word-span scores was only .33 for young adults, whereas it was .74 for elderly adults.

By contrast, what little evidence there is offers no convincing support for de-differentiation in learning ability. Here the differentiation/de-differentiation hypothesis predicts that correlations between scores on different kinds of learning tasks, such as paired-associate learning and serial-learning tasks, should be greater in late adulthood than in early adulthood. We discovered in Chapter 8, however, that this does not seem to be the case. That is, the correlation between learning proficiency scores was found to be relatively independent of age level. Nevertheless, in fairness to the differentiation/de-differentiation hypothesis, further investigation of age differences in correlations across tasks, for example, concept-learning and problem-solving tasks, should be encouraged. There simply has been little research conducted thus far on this important topic.

Crystallized and Fluid Intelligence. A useful elaboration of the concept of general intelligence was proposed some years ago by R. B. Cattell (1940, 1963) (an elaboration, however, that has not been devoid of criticism; see Guilford, 1980). Rather than being a single entity, general intelligence was viewed as consisting of two broad factors, crystallized intelligence, or Gc, and fluid intelligence, or Gf. The distinction between the two factors has been nicely clarified by Horn (1970, 1978), one of Cattell's early collaborators and a pioneer in investigating age changes in the two broad factors. Here is his definition of the factors:

> 1. Gf is characterized by processes of perceiving relationships, educing correlates, maintaining span of immediate awareness in reasoning, abstracting concept formation, and problem solving. It is measured in unspeeded as well as speeded tasks involving figural symbolic or semantic content, but tasks in which relatively little advantage accrues from intensive or extended education and acculturation.
> 2. Gc also involves the processes of perceiving relationships, educing correlates, reasoning, etc., just as does Gf, and Gc, too, can be measured in unspeeded tasks involving various kinds of content (semantic, figural, symbolic) but the content of the tasks that best characterizes Gc indicates relatively advanced education and acculturation either in the fundaments of the problems or in the operations that must be performed on the fundaments (Horn, 1978, pp. 220–222).

There seems to be an obvious connection between the postulation of two broad intellectual abilities, or factors, and the pattern of correlations for tests and subtests of special intellectual abilities. As we have seen, there is considerable variability in the correlations between subtest scores on the WAIS. Such variability is to be expected if some of the subtests assess special abilities subsumed by Gc, whereas other subtests assess special abilities subsumed by Gf. In fact, the verbal scale subtests of the WAIS appear to draw on Gc and are, therefore, largely "hold" subtests with respect to the effects of aging, whereas the performance scale subtests appear to draw on Gf and are, therefore, largely "don't hold" subtests with respect to the adverse effects of aging. This segregation of WAIS subtests seemingly accounts for the fact that the correlation between scores on the vocabulary and information subtests is considerably larger (both draw on Gc) than the correlation between scores on the vocabulary and digit-symbol subtests (one draws on Gc, the other on Gf). Even primary factors of intelligence, as assessed for example by the PMA, are not completely independent of one another. For example, Schaie et al. (1953) reported intertest correlation coefficients ranging between .06 (space and number) and .31 (space and reasoning). The implication is that certain primary factors are subsumed under one secondary factor (e.g., Gf), whereas other primary factors are subsumed under the other secondary factor (e.g., Gc). Considerable research by Horn and Cattell (e.g., 1967) by means of the methods of factor analysis has provided support for this heirarchical structure of human intelligence (i.e., from secondary factors to primary factors and from primary factors to specific special abilities)—but, again, see Guilford, 1980, for a counter argument. Horn and Cattell's (1967) analyses have also indicated that there are some primary factors—and, therefore, various special abilities governed by those factors—that are derived in part from both Gf and Gc. A representative sample of primary abilities they believe to be Gf related, Gc related, and Gf-Gc related is given in Table 11.3.

From Horn's description of the two secondary factors, it is apparent that one's optimal level of Gf is determined largely by heredity, whereas one's optimal level of Gc is determined largely by environmental conditions and personal experiences. Developmentally, the capacity of Gf is assumed to increase throughout the prematurity segment of the lifespan as neurological maturation increases with increasing age. However, the reverse is likely to occur over the remainder of the lifespan as neurological degeneration increases with increas-

Table 11.3 Representative Primary Factors of Intelligence That Are Derived Separately from Gf (Fluid Intelligence) and Gc (Crystallized Intelligence) and From Gf and Gc Together

Secondary-Factor Composition		
Gf	Gc	Gf *and* Gc
Inductive reasoning	Verbal comprehension	General reasoning
Deductive reasoning	Information	(arithmetic)
Figural relations	Experiential evaluation	Semantic relations
Memory span	Mechanical knowledge	(verbal analogies)

Source: Adapted from material in Horn and Cattell, 1967.

ing age (Horn & Cattell, 1967). That is, the capacity of Gf is expected to decrease with increasing age. By contrast, the capacity of Gc is expected to increase throughout the lifespan as experiences steadily accumulate. Nevertheless, the rate of growth for Gc is expected to decrease progressively beyond early adulthood. The reason for this deceleration is that

> it is only through the exercise of fluid intelligence that crystallized intelligence is built up. Therefore in the face of postulated age-related decline in fluid intelligence, the increments in crystallized intelligence in old age are progressively smaller. (Cunningham, Clayton, and Overton, 1975, p. 53).

These postulated relationships between age and fluid/crystallized intelligence are illustrated in the top panel of Figure 11.9.

Support for the postulated decline with aging in Gf comes from studies comparing age groups on standardized tests purporting to measure fluid intelligence. One of these tests is the previously mentioned Raven Progressive Matrices Test. Cunningham et al. (1975) found that the magnitude of the age

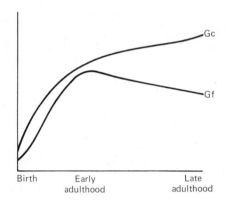

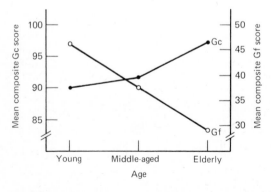

Figure 11.9. Top panel: Hypothesized age changes for crystallized intelligence (Gc) and fluid intelligence (Gf). Bottom panel: Age differences in composite scores on tests of Gc and Gf. (Adapted from Hayslip & Sterns, 1979, Table 2.)

difference favoring young over old subjects was much greater for scores on the Raven test than it was for scores on the WAIS vocabulary subtest (presumably measuring Gc), even though the age groups were roughly comparable in educational level. Among the other tests of fluid intelligence are those constructed by Horn (1975). One of these tests, a test of figural relations, was found by Kausler and Puckett (1980a) to yield significantly lower scores for elderly subjects than for young-adult subjects, even though the opposite was true for scores on the WAIS vocabulary test. In a more comprehensive study, Hayslip and Sterns (1979) compared young, middle-age, and elderly adults on separate batteries of tests, one battery supposedly assessing Gf, another Gc. The results, as can be seen in the bottom panel of Figure 11.9, clearly indicate progressive and steep decrements in Gf scores and progressive, but modest, increments in Gc scores with increasing age, which is in agreement with the hypothesized relationships between aging and the two broad intellectual abilities (compare these results with those predicted in the top panel of Figure 11.9).

What is the nature of the relationship between Gf and Gc? They surely cannot be completely independent abilities. To gain from experience and, therefore, to add to Gc, seemingly demands utilization of one's fluid intelligence. Consequently, some degree of positive correlation is expected between scores on tests assessing Gf and scores on tests assessing Gc. Our concern, however, is mainly with possible adult-age differences in the degree of this relationship. Cunningham et al. (1975) argued strongly that the degree of correlation should *decrease* with increasing age, an argument that has the support of Horn (1978). The decrease is expected on the basis of the relatively steep decline in Gf with increasing age combined with the relative stability of Gc over the same age range. As a result, Gf and Gc are assumed to become increasingly independent of one another as one progresses over the course of the adult lifespan.

Results in agreement with this interpretation were reported by Cunningham et al. (1975) and Kausler and Puckett (1980a). Cunningham et al. found the correlation coefficient (r) between Raven test scores and vocabulary test scores to be .67 for their young-adult subjects, but only .39 for their elderly subjects. Similarly, Kausler and Puckett found the correlation coefficient (r) between figural relations test scores and vocabulary test scores to be higher for their young-adult subjects (.43) than for their elderly subjects (.18), although in neither case did the coefficient attain statistical significance. This interpretation, and the correlational evidence supporting it, obviously contradicts what is expected on the basis of the age differentiation/de-differentiation hypothesis. This hypothesis seemingly predicts a convergence of a kind for Gf and Gc by late adulthood. That is, individuals are expected to revert to an undifferentiated state of general intelligence, thus leading to increasing correlations between Gf and Gc test scores with increasing age. In fairness to this hypothesis, it should be noted that both Arnold (1973) and Hayslip and Sterns (1979) did find such increases in correlation coefficients for their measures of Gf and Gc. These major disparities in outcomes of correlational studies indicate that we have a long way to go before we fully comprehend the nature of Gf and Gc—much less the relationship between the two.

Intelligence in the Laboratory: Performance on Laboratory Tasks as an External Criterion. Our perspective changes considerably in this and the following sections. We will move from issues concerning the nature of intelligence per se to issues concerning the relationships between intelligence and the content areas of experimental psychology. These relationships demonstrate the important ways by which psychometric assessments of intelligence and laboratory assessments of cognitive processes complement one another.

One such relationship concerns covariations between intelligence test scores and scores on the various laboratory tasks employed by experimental psychologists. For example, are individuals who are high in assessed verbal or crystallized intelligence better learners than individuals who are low in the same ability? Better problem solvers? These kinds of questions have aroused considerable interest among contemporary experimental psychologists, thanks largely to the fascinating research being conducted by E. Hunt (e.g., E. Hunt, 1978; E. Hunt et al., 1973). E. Hunt's approach consists of comparing college students who are high and low in verbal ability as measured by such tests as the Scholastic Aptitude Test on tasks that call for rather clearly defined cognitive processes. By so doing, we can gain a better understanding of what variation in verbal ability means in terms of variation in the proficiencies of specific cognitive processes. For example, is verbal ability related to the speed with which people conduct feature analysis and the other component processes of pattern recognition? E. Hunt's research (1978) indicates that it is. Through the use of chronometric analysis, high-verbal-ability young adults have been found to be faster than low-verbal-ability young adults, both when the paired letters are physically identical and when they have the same name but are physically different (i.e., one is uppercase, the other lowercase). Not surprisingly, the advantage of being high verbal is especially large for same name decisions, decisions that are based on central rather than peripheral cognitive processes. This finding has added something to our understanding of how high-verbal people differ from low-verbal people, and the added understanding is at the level of a specific process or activity of the organism.

Our interest, however, is in age differences or the absence of age differences in these covariations. Are measures of intellectual abilities better predictors of performance on laboratory tasks for young adults than they are for elderly adults? To answer this question, we must replace the traditional external criteria for evaluating the validity of an intelligence test with a new external criterion. Instead of achievement in either a formal educational setting or in an everyday coping situation, our criterion must be achievement on some laboratory task mediated by some specific psychological process. Unfortunately, there has not been much aging research of this kind. Moreover, most of what has been done has involved gross phenomena, such as overall learning proficiency, and, therefore, leaves unknown the specific process or processes accounting for the covariation with scores on an intelligence test.

Pioneers in this important area of experimental aging research were Eisdorfer and Service (1967). Their serial-learning study was described briefly in Chapter 5. At the time, our interest was in only one of the non-age independent variables included in their study, namely, the rate of exposing study-list items (fast, 4 seconds per item, or slow, 10 seconds per item). We discovered then that the age difference in total errors, favoring young adults, was much greater with the fast rate than with the slow rate. However, we told only part of the story at the time. An additional non-age independent variable in this study was level of verbal ability as determined by scores on the WAIS vocabulary test. Half of the subjects at each age level were people having average vocabulary scores; the other half were people having above average scores. Shown in Figure 5.9 are the mean number of errors for only those subjects who were average in verbal ability. Mean scores for all four groups are plotted in the top panel of Figure 11.10. Note that the elderly subjects of high-verbal ability were clearly superior in learning proficiency with respect to the elderly subjects of average verbal ability, but only under the fast rate of exposure. Under the slower rate, the two groups did not differ in learning proficiency (in fact, if anything, the elderly subjects of average verbal ability were slightly superior). By contrast, young-adult subjects of high-verbal ability were clearly superior in learning

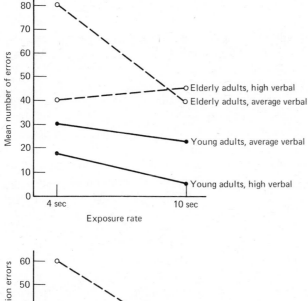

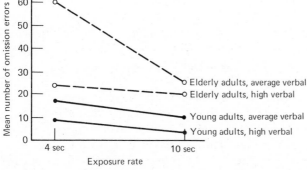

Figure 11.10. Age differences in total errors (top panel) and errors of omission (bottom panel) on a serial-learning task for young and elderly subjects of high and average verbal ability. (Adapted from Eisdorfer & Service, 1967, Figures 1, 2.)

proficiency to their counterparts of average verbal ability, regardless of rate of exposure.

Possible reasons for this interesting pattern of results became apparent when Eisdorfer and Service (1967) analyzed separately errors of omission (i.e., failure to respond errors), the most common type of error in serial learning. As may be seen in the bottom panel of Figure 11.10, elderly subjects of average verbal ability made many more such errors with the fast pacing than with the slow pacing. On the other hand, variation in rate of exposure had little effect on learning proficiency for elderly subjects of high verbal ability. Verbal ability in late adulthood may affect serial-learning proficiency either in terms of the speed of processing item information (i.e., analyzing each item's content) or in terms of speed of responding with the name of each item when required. Those of high verbal ability may be able to process item information at a rate not far removed from that of young adults with average verbal ability. This may not be true of elderly adults having average verbal ability. Their slower rate of processing would, therefore, be a handicap on a learning task when the to-be-learned items are presented rapidly. Their slower rate would not be a handicap, however, when the items are presented slowly. Alternatively, elderly adults of high verbal ability may simply be faster responders than elderly adults of average verbal ability. This would be an advantage for the former individuals only when the pacing of items on a learning task is fairly rapid. Other results provided by Eisdorfer (1965; Wilkie & Eisdorfer, 1977) suggest that the second explanation may be the more valid one.

In a similar manner, age differences in verbal ability were related to age differences in performance on a free-recall task by Hultsch (1969). Included in this study were young-adult subjects (16 to 19 years of age), early middle-age subjects (30 to 39 years of age), and late middle-age subjects (45 to 54 years of age) of both high and low verbal ability (as assessed by scores on a vocabulary test). An additional independent variable consisted of variation in the instructions regarding the use of organization as a memory strategy. In a control condition, subjects at each age level and verbal-ability level were given no instructions urging the use of organization to master the list. In two experimental conditions, the subjects were given either general instructions regarding the advantage of using an organizational plan without specifying any kind of plan or specific instructions urging the use of a particular plan (the use of each item's initial letter). There were no significant age differences in the number of words recalled for subjects of high-verbal ability under any of the instructional conditions. By contrast, there were significant differences favoring the younger subjects of low-verbal ability under the control and general instructional conditions, but not under the specific instructional condition. The implication is that an age-related deficit in organizational ability occurs primarily for individuals of low-verbal ability who apparently are unlikely to activate spontaneously organizational processes of the kind that enhance memory of list items. That deficit can be largely overcome, however, by providing older subjects of low-verbal ability with an appropriate organizational strategy. High-verbal individuals, at least through late middle age, presumably engage spontaneously in organizational processes and, therefore, do not have to be prodded into their use.

Measures of both crystallized and fluid intelligence were related to a variety of perceptual and memory phenomena by Horn (1980; Horn, Donaldson, & Engstrom, 1981). With regard to perceptual activities, some degree of positive covariation was found between Gf and both the ability to divide attention and to ignore irrelevant stimuli. With regard to memory phenomena, Gf was found to covary positively with working-memory capacity, the magnitude of the recency effect in free recall, and the proficiency of organization in free recall. In addition, Gc was found to covary positively with the magnitude of the primacy effect in free recall. Hultsch's results described above also imply that Gc, along with Gf, is related to organizational proficiency in free recall. The involvement of both crystallized and fluid intelligence in episodic memory phenomena does seem reasonable. Events have to be encoded with respect to information stored in generic memory. The encoding component would seem to call on fluid intelligence, whereas the existence of appropriate information in generic memory would seem to call on crystallized intelligence. These are important relationships, but ones that require considerably more evidence before we are able to evaluate their validities. Moreover, the question of what happens to these relationships over the course of the adult lifespan remains largely unknown. Horn's subjects did range in age from 20 to 60 years, however, and apparently there was no indication of any systematic change in the pattern of any covariation with increasing age.

Of particular interest are relationships between intelligence test scores and performance scores on various problem-solving tasks. Especially intriguing are the results obtained by Kesler, Denney, and Whitely (1976). Their middle-age and elderly subjects were tested on the block-design and picture-completion subtests of the WAIS, tests that presumably measure largely Gf. As expected, the middle-age subjects were superior to the elderly subjects in performance on the intelligence tests. All subjects also received a battery of problem-solving tasks that included written problems (e.g., arithmetic word problems) and the 20-questions game. Again, as expected, the middle-age subjects were superior to the elderly subjects in performance on each component of the battery. Our interest, however, lies mainly in the whopping positive correlation coefficient (r = .72) Kesler et al. found between a composite score on the intelligence tests and a composite score on the problem-solving battery. They proceeded to demonstrate that when their age groups were adjusted for differences in educational level and level of fluid intelligence (or performance intelligence with respect to Wechsler's terminology), there was no longer an age difference in problem-solving proficiency. (The adjustment procedure is a form of the deletion strategy described in Chapter 5—the objective is to demonstrate the age sensitivity of a process by eliminating age differences through the absence of that process.) Their comments on this important point are worth repeating here:

> However, this does not mean that age is of no importance to problem solving. It
> simply means that there were no age effects over and above those accounted for by

education and nonverbal intelligence scores. This supports an earlier study by
Wetherick (1964) in which very few age differences were found when age groups
were matched for nonverbal intelligence. (Kesler et al., 1976, p. 317)

A similar outcome occurred in a study by Kausler and Puckett (in press).
In this case, the laboratory task was that of recognition memory and the age
comparison was between young and middle-age adults. Previous studies (e.g.,
Rankin & Kausler, 1979) had indicated a significant decline in recognition-
memory proficiency from early adulthood to middle age. However, in these
earlier studies, no attempt had been made to equate the age groups with respect
to fluid intelligence. In Kausler and Puckett's (in press) study, the age groups
were indeed quite comparable in scores earned on a standard test of fluid
intelligence. Given this comparability, the age deficit usually found for this
kind of laboratory task disappeared. Whatever the nature of a task, we cannot
attribute age deficits in performance to disparities in age per se. It is the diminishing proficiency of some process with increasing age that accounts for an age
deficit. If subjects of different ages are equated for proficiency on that process,
then there should obviously be no age difference in performance on a task
mediated solely by that process. Equating groups varying in age in their level of
fluid intelligence seemingly assures comparability of process proficiency for at
least some kinds of laboratory tasks and, therefore, should assure the absence
of age differences in performance on those tasks.

Returning to the question of the relationship between intelligence and
problem-solving proficiency, there remains the distinct possibility that scores
on Gc tests may also covary with scores on certain kinds of problem-solving
tasks. Horn and Cattell's (1967) analysis (see Table 11.3) indicated, for example, that certain kinds of reasoning problems demand both Gf and Gc. A recent
study by Hayslip and Sterns (1979) appears to confirm this analysis. Two broad
classes of problem-solving activities were identified (derived from an earlier
analysis by G. A. Davis, 1966). One class consists of problems for which solution responses are well known to the subjects in advance of receiving the actual
problems. Because prior experience seems essential for solving this kind of
problem, Gc is hypothesized to be more strongly correlated than Gf with the
proficiency of solving such problems. Anagrams were selected to represent this
class of problem-solving activities. Here one's knowledge of words (a component of Gc) should be clearly related to the ability to find solution words that
match the letter content of anagrams. The other class consists of problems
having abstract, unfamiliar stimulus elements and solution responses that, initially, are unknown to the subjects. Gf is hypothesized to be more strongly
correlated than Gc with the proficiency of solving these kinds of problems. A
concept-learning task with geometric forms, colors, and number of objects as
stimulus dimensions, was selected by Hayslip and Sterns (1979) to represent
this class of problems. The correlation coefficients found for young-adult, middle-age, and elderly subjects between intelligence test scores, for both Gc and
Gf, and scores on both laboratory tasks are listed in Table 11.4. A positive
correlation for the anagram task indicates a positive covariation between intel-

Table 11.4 Correlation Coefficients (r's) Between Scores on Gf and Gc Tests and Scores on Problem-Solving Tasks

Correlated Variables		Age		
		Young Adult	Middle-Age	Elderly
Gf and number of anagrams solved		.64[a]	.24[a]	.48[a]
Gc and number of anagrams solved		.34[a]	.23[a]	.50[a]
	t	3.03 (significant)	.04 (not significant)	.19 (not significant)
Gf and number of concept-learning errors		− .14	− .01	− .38[a]
Gc and number of concept-learning errors		.30[a]	− .20	− .23
	t	1.38 (not significant)	1.36 (not significant)	1.64 (not significant)

[a] Correlation coefficient significantly greater than 0.
Source: Adapted from Hayslip and Sterns, 1979, Table 3.

ligence test scores and problem-solving scores, whereas a negative correlation for the concept-learning task (score equals number of errors made in learning the concept) indicates a positive covariation between intelligence test scores and problem-solving scores. Also listed in this table are the outcomes of t tests comparing the magnitudes of correlation coefficients involving Gf and Gc in each age/task condition.

Note first that Gc was a fair predictor of proficiency on the anagram task at each age level. But so was Gf! In fact, for young adults, Gf scores were a better predictor of number of anagram solutions than were Gc scores. In general, solving anagrams seems to call on fluid intelligence, just as the word problems and 20-questions problems employed by Kesler et al. (1976) call on fluid intelligence. Note further that Gf scores were a fair predictor of success on the concept-learning task, but only for the elderly subjects. Obviously, much remains to be discovered about the relationships between intelligence and problem-solving proficiencies, including the effects of aging on those relationships.

The studies reviewed thus far in this section were unusual in the sense of introducing some component of intelligence as an independent variable in conjunction with performance on a laboratory task. In most experimental aging studies, however, an assessment of intelligence serves only as a matching variable for age groups, if it is involved at all. Young and elderly age groups are often equated in verbal ability, usually defined by score on a vocabulary test. This matching procedure entered, for example, into the paired-associate learning study by Kausler and Puckett (1980a) and the paired-associate retention study by Hulicka and Weiss (1965) described in earlier chapters. In the former study, elderly subjects were inferior to young-adult subjects in learning proficiency despite the superiority of the elderly subjects overall in vocabulary-test scores; in the latter study there were no age differences in either retention scores or vocabulary-test scores. More important, at least for present purposes, the matching procedure offers an indirect means of examining possible age differences in the relationship between verbal ability, or Gc, and task proficiency. This may be done simply by determining the correlation coefficient at each age level between vocabulary and laboratory-task scores. Unfortunately, these correlations are rarely reported by those investigators who use vocabulary-test scores as a matching variable. The studies by Kausler and Puckett and Hulicka and Weiss were exceptions however. A positive correlation was found between verbal ability and learning proficiency for both young and elderly subjects, although the magnitude of the correlation coefficient was somewhat greater for the young subjects than for the elderly subjects (Kausler & Puckett, 1980a), no statistically significant correlation coefficient was found between verbal ability and retention proficiency at either age level (Hulicka & Weiss, 1965).

In addition, Kausler and Puckett reported a significant positive correlation between Gf scores and frequency-of-occurrence-judgment scores for their young-adult subjects but not for their elderly subjects. The age disparity in correlation was subsequently replicated by Kausler, Hakami, and Wright (in press) with a modified form of the frequency judgment task. Frequency judgment is commonly assumed to be mediated by automatic memory processes that are insensitive to age changes in proficiency. Such automaticity does not seem to mean, however, that individual differences in proficiency are independent of individual differences in fluid intelligence, at least for young adults. Why there may be an age difference in covariation between fluid intelligence and frequency-judgment proficiency remains an unanswered question.

Finally, an interesting question centers on the common practice of matching age groups on the basis of verbal ability or some other component of crystallized intelligence: Why bother when the laboratory task under investigation seemingly calls on Gf rather than Gc? There is good reason for following this matching procedure however. If elderly subjects can be demonstrated to be equal and perhaps even superior to young-adult subjects on Gc, then we have a reasonable case for arguing that the level of fluid intelligence manifested by these elderly subjects when they themselves were young adults did not differ greatly from the level presently manifested by the young adults serving as subjects in the same study. This reasoning follows from the overall positive correlation known to exist between Gc and Gf scores. Whatever age deficit is found on the laboratory task in question can then be attributed with greater certainty to the effect of aging per se rather than to a confounding produced by having elderly subjects who, owing perhaps to their cohort membership, never did have the competence of the present young-adult subjects. In other words, selecting contemporary elderly subjects who are comparable to contemporary young-adult subjects in crystallized intelligence (a "hold" component of intelligence) assures approximate comparability of the two age groups during their respective young adulthoods in fluid intelligence (a "doesn't hold" component of intelligence).

Intelligence in the Laboratory: Identification of Age-Sensitive Processes. The relationship between age differences in intelligence and the content areas of experimental psychology may also be investigated by research directed at the process analysis of an intelligence test or subtest. Performance on a given subtest of the WAIS, for example, may be conceptualized in terms of perceptual, learning, memory, or higher order processes. A logical analysis of Subtest A may suggest that performance is mediated by Processes X and Y. The age sensitivity of these processes with respect to their responsibility for age deficits on Subtest A may then be identified by examining interaction effects between age and manipulable independent variables for performance scores on Subtest A. The critical manipulable independent variables are those known either to delete Process X's involvement on Subtest A or to alter the proficiency of Process X on Subtest A. In other words, the strategy calls for applying one of the analytical methods for detecting age-sensitive processes described in Chapter 5.

To date, this strategy has been restricted to the Digit Symbol subtest of the WAIS, which shows especially pronounced age deficits in performance. These deficits are for a gross phenomenon. What accounts for them? At stake are questions concerning what processes mediate performance on this test and which ones are age sensitive. Answers to these questions and eventually all other components of general intelligence tests as well should greatly enhance our understanding of age differences/changes in intelligence.

An important first step in the analysis of a digit symbol test is to distinguish between probable noncognitive and cognitive contributors to age deficits in performance on that test. Noncognitive factors are involved largely because a digit-symbol test is a speed test rather than a power test. Again, a speed test is one with a time limit and, therefore, rewards rapid performance, whereas a power test is one without a time limit. Consequently, your score on a speed test, but not on a power test, depends partly on the rapidity of your performance. As noted by Jones:

> In a timed mental test, scores are obviously influenced by individual differences in speed or in the number of items which can be completed in a given time. This is often thought of as a superficial aspect of mentality, related to personal "style" rather than to actual ability. (1959, p. 722)

The "superficial aspect" means that scores are reflecting a secondary performance factor rather than an "actual ability" factor (i.e., competence). Most important, it has long been recognized (e.g., Lorge, 1936; C. C. Miles, 1934) that the slowing-down characteristic of late adulthood should contribute substantially to the age deficit found in performance on any speed test of intelligence, such as a digit-symbol test.

The speed component by itself does not account, however, for the full extent of the age deficit manifested in performance on a digit-symbol test. This was demonstrated in a recent study by Storandt (1976). Her young and elderly subjects performed both on the standard (timed) Digit Symbol subtest of the WAIS in which they had to code digits into their paired symbols and on an altered form of this test in which subjects simply copied the symbols for the same amount of time (90 seconds) allotted for the standard test. The number of digits copied per second provided an index of the speed or noncognitive component of performance on the Digit Symbol test. Not surprisingly, her elderly subjects were clearly inferior on this speed component. The difference between this number and the number per second answered on the standard form of the test provided an index of the cognitive component. Here, too, her elderly subjects were clearly inferior to her young-adult subjects. Overall, the noncognitive and cognitive components contributed about equally at each age level to scores on the standard form of the test. Given this outcome, it is obvious that the age deficit on the test cannot be attributed solely to an age deficit in the noncognitive speed component. A later study by Storandt (1977) demonstrated further that age deficits on other WAIS subtests having a heavy speed-of-performance requirement (e.g., the Picture Arrangement subtest) do not disappear when the speed element is eliminated. Thus, the age deficit found for these tests must also be due in part to age differences in cognitive components or processes.

Our present concern is with whatever cognitive processes enter into performance on a digit-symbol test and may, therefore, be age sensitive. (This does not mean that speed per se is unimportant as a contributor to intellectual achievement; see Witt and Cunningham, 1979, for elaboration.) A clue as to one probable process was given in Chapter 8. At that time, we discovered that a digit-symbol test can be conceptualized as a paired-associate learning task in which the digits are the stimulus elements and the symbols the response elements. In fact, we noted then that a test of incidental learning following performance on a digit-symbol task reveals less digit-symbol learning by elderly subjects than by young-adult subjects. Superior scores on the digit-symbol task per se should result for those subjects who learn which symbol goes with which digit. By contrast, inferior scores should result for those subjects who resort to translating each digit into its symbol substitute by referring to the code printed at the top of the test booklet. Thus, to the extent that learning does occur, performance on a digit-symbol test should be enhanced. Learning of the digit-symbol paired associates is made difficult, however, by the unfamiliar nature of the response elements (i.e., the symbols). We observed in Chapter 8 that response learning is an age-sensitive process and that elderly subjects are especially handicapped when the response elements have low familiarity and meaningfulness. A reasonable hypothesis, therefore, is that the response-learning process is the primary cognitive locus for age deficits in performance on a digit-symbol test.

Early support for this hypothesis came from a study by Schonfield and Robertson (1968). Elderly subjects earned considerably higher scores when the task required coding digits (stimulus elements) into other digits (response elements) rather than into abstract symbols. Digits surely are more readily available as to-be-associated responses than are symbols, thus markedly reducing the amount of response learning needed for proficient performance. Unfortunately, young-adult subjects were not employed in this study, making it impossible to determine the effect on age differences of reducing the response-learning requirement. Young-adult subjects were included, however, in a later study by Salthouse (1978) that also offered partial support for the response-learning hypothesis. Salthouse's strategy called for varying the number of stimulus-response pairs composing the digit-symbol task. His young and elderly subjects performed initially on the standard WAIS subtest. Nine different digit-symbol pairs are involved in this task. The subjects received separate tasks involving, in one case, only one digit-symbol pairing (i.e., each box involved the same to-be-coded digit and the same to-be-filled-in symbol); in other cases, either three, six, or nine digit-symbol pairings (with the last condition duplicating that of the WAIS subtest). His results, expressed in terms of the average number of seconds per symbol completed in each task condition, are shown in Figure 11.11. Increasing scores in this figure mean decreasing performance proficiency. Note that the magnitude of the age deficit diminished as performance increased across task conditions for both age groups, thus indicating the presence of a multiplicative interaction effect. The implication, therefore, is that the process altered by variation in number of digit-symbol pairs is indeed age sensitive. Our best guess is that this process is the number of responses held available while coding digits into symbols. However, a firm conclusion is made impossible by the fact that the number of S-R associations (i.e., digit → symbol associations) also varied across conditions. Conceivably, the associative learning stage also contributes to age deficits in performance on any digit-symbol test. In addition, Salthouse observed that the magnitude of the age deficit did not vary across task conditions when scores were expressed relative to performance on the standard form of the WAIS Digit Symbol test. The reason for the presence of an age × conditions-interaction effect with absolute scores but not with relative scores is unclear. However, Salthouse suspected that the invariant age deficit present with relative scores indicates that a learning process is not responsible for age deficits on the digit-symbol test. He postulated that the age-sensitive cognitive processes are likely to be either perceptual or decisional in

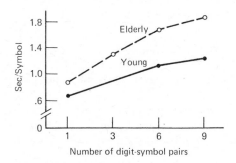

Figure 11.11. Age differences in rate of completing digit-symbol pairs as a function of number of different pairs on the task. (Adapted from Salthouse, 1978, Figure 1.)

nature. More recently, Erber, Botwinick, and Storandt (in press) reached the same conclusion.

Further research on age-sensitive processes for the digit-symbol task is clearly needed to resolve these ambiguities. Even more badly needed is comparable research on other major subtests of omnibus tests, such as the WAIS (e.g., the Picture Arrangement subtest). There are subtests, however, for which this kind of research seems unnecessary. This is particularly true for the information and vocabulary subtests of the WAIS. Here the underlying *age-insensitive* process seems to be retrieval of information from generic memory. The age insensitivity of this process has been well documented by laboratory research.

Intelligence in the Laboratory: Plasticity Theory and Intervention. Over the years, many gerontological psychologists have believed that the age deficits apparent in scores on intelligence tests are due more to secondary performance factors than to true declines in intellectual competence. Diminished speed of motor responses is one of these factors. However, we discovered in the previous section that deemphasizing speed does not make age deficits go away. Other secondary factors believed to be largely responsible for age deficits in performance on intelligence tests have included age differences in motivation and in fatigue susceptibility. Again, if age differences in these factors could be eliminated, or at least drastically reduced, then age differences on intelligence tests should largely disappear. A number of studies directed at this objective were reviewed in Chapter 3. We discovered then that the magnitude of age deficits on intelligence tests is usually not reduced by improving these secondary performance factors. In fact, it is not unusual to find that the age deficit increases as test scores increase for both young and elderly subjects. Nevertheless, these studies do demonstrate one very important point—elderly adults often perform on intelligence tests under standard conditions at a level that is below their actual level of competence. Perhaps competence per se does suffer little with increasing age over the adult lifespan—we just have yet to find the means of fully reversing the performance loss brought about for many elderly people by prolonged exposure to impoverished intellectual environments.

Belief in the restorableness of intelligence to its former level of performance is the core part of *plasticity theory* (Baltes & Schaie, 1976). The theory's basic premise is illustrated in Figure 11.12. Note that much of the loss in performance is viewed as being reversible. That is, there is a certain degree of plasticity or modifiability in late adulthood. Given appropriate environmental experience, intellectual performance can be restored to its latent high level of competence. The emphasis on experience is in line with what is known as the *environmental docility hypothesis* (Lawton & Simon, 1968). The hypothesis stresses that as performance in general decreases with aging, the proportion of behavior attributable to environmental characteristics, as opposed to personal characteristics, increases.

Plasticity theory implies that constructive environmental intervention for elderly people should be beneficial in modifying their decrements in intellectual performance. In the long run, this means providing individuals with stimulating

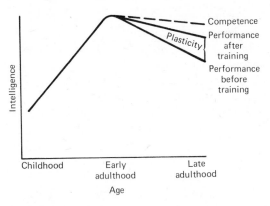

Figure 11.12. Changes in intelligence produced by positive training experiences as expected from the perspective of plasticity theory.

and challenging environments as they progress over the adult lifespan, especially beyond middle age. The objective, of course, is to forestall environmentally linked performance decrements. In principle, intervention with a more immediate payoff should also be possible through the use of effective training programs. These programs have ranged from those involving simple positive-reinforcement principles (e.g., Bellucci & Hoyer, 1975) to those involving intensive efforts much like those used to modify decrements in performance on concept learning and problem solving (e.g., Plemons, Willis, & Baltes, 1978). Although reinforcement for efficient performance has had moderate success in improving level of performance for elderly subjects, it usually has failed to narrow the gap between young and elderly subjects. The reason, of course, is that young adults, like elderly adults, tend to perform at levels below their actual competence unless they are stimulated by special environmental conditions. A more thorough training program was found by Plemons et al. (1978) to increase scores earned by elderly subjects on a figural relations test (a measure of one form of fluid intelligence). However, the effect of this training program on tests measuring other components of fluid intelligence (e.g., number series) was negligible. Moreover, the absence of young-adult subjects in this study again makes it impossible to evaluate the effect of the training program on age differences in figural-relations test performance, much less its effect on competence in fluid intelligence overall.

Alternatively, of course, training programs geared toward renewed cognitive competence in late adulthood could stress physiological rather than psychological intervention. This is the approach taken in biofeedback programs that attempt to increase brain-wave frequencies, programs that thus far have had only modest success.

Plasticity theory does gain support from the fact that there is little commonality in performance on intelligence tests between normally aging elderly people and younger adults known to have diffuse brain damage (Goldstein & Shelly, 1975; Hicks & Birren, 1970). The major exception appears to be for tests that have a heavy motor-skill involvement. If there were considerable commonality, then the implication would be that normally aging people, in general, experience the same kind of irreversible loss in brain functioning produced at younger ages by diffuse brain lesions. Similarly, normally aging people are clearly distinguishable in intelligence test performance from elderly people diagnosed as suffering from an organic brain syndrome (Overall & Gorham, 1972). Whatever brain changes with normal aging seem to be quite different from the brain changes that occur with disease or injury at any age. The advent of tomographic brain scans as a diagnostic test of brain functioning should greatly facilitate understanding of these normal changes with aging. At any rate, the absence of pronounced brain changes, comparable to those found with pathology, does lend hope to the possibility of reversing performance losses in intelligence. This hope is abetted by the fact that physical intervention programs, through the use of rigorous exercise programs, have had considerable success in reversing much of the age loss commonly experienced for vital lung capacity, oxygen transport capacity, physical work capacity, and both systolic and diastolic blood pressure (deVries, 1975). Hopefully, comparable reversals of cognitive decrements will eventually become possible through the intervention of vigorous mental exercise programs.

Finally, there is one particular form of age decline in intelligence test scores that appears to be especially serious. The phenomenon in question was described by Botwinick, West, and Storandt (1978):

> A growing body of research since the early 1960's indicates that psychological test performance of elderly people may be used to predict ensuing death: poor test performance may signal death within the next five years. If this be true, the research is of obvious importance—preventive and remedial efforts can be compared, life-styles may be adjusted. (1978, p. 755)

The phenomenon, commonly known as *terminal drop*, was first reported by Kleemeier (1962). He observed that older individuals who manifested a sharp decline in intelligence test scores from one test session to a second test session had an inordinately high probability of death within a relatively short period of time following the retesting. The poor test performance referred to by Botwinick et al. (1978) is, therefore, defined with respect to longitudinal decline in intelligence that grossly exceeds the decline expected through normal aging. The implication is that neurological decrements, forewarners of impending death, are present in these individuals and are reflected by their scores on an intelligence test. In support of this analysis, it does seem to be true that elderly people near death do show significant neurological changes, such as the slowing down of brain-wave frequencies, that are well beyond the level usually found in old age (e.g., Müller, Grad, & Engelsmann, 1975).

Kleemeier's (1962) original observation has received support in a number of other studies (e.g., Jarvik & Falek, 1963; Lieberman, 1965; Reimanis & Green, 1971; Riegel & Riegel, 1972; Steuer, LaRue, Blum, & Jarvik, 1981). There has been considerable disagreement, however, as to which components of intelligence tests serve as valid predictors of terminal drop. For example, Jarvik and Falek (1963) found decrements in scores on the Vocabulary, Digit Symbol, and Similarities subtests of the WAIS to be better predictors of impending death than decrements in scores on the other subtests of the WAIS. By contrast, Reimanis and Green (1971) found total scores on the WAIS, both verbal and performance, to be especially valid. To complicate matters further, Botwinick et al. (1978) found no supportive evidence for longitudinal decline in test scores as a predictor of death. On the other hand, they found that absolute scores earned by elderly people on a battery of tests correlated substantially (.47) with subsequent survival/death over a subsequent five-year period. Low scorers on this battery, which included the WAIS Digit Symbol subtest, a paired-associate learning test, and a self-health rating scale, simply had a higher probability of death than did high scorers. Interestingly, a similar correlation for elderly adults between scores on another battery of tests and degree of positive adjustment to living in a residence requiring self-care and independence had been reported by Storandt, Wittels, and Botwinick (1975).

Research on the terminal-drop phenomenon has often been hindered by a number of methodological problems (see Botwinick, 1977; Palmore and Cleveland, 1976; and Siegler, 1975, for elaboration). The presence of methodological confoundings seemingly serves to exaggerate the magnitude of the terminal-drop phenomenon. In an exceptionally well-designed and controlled study that eliminated most of these confoundings, Palmore and Cleveland (1976) found the magnitude of the phenomenon to be slight but statistically significant nonetheless. The probable presence of a terminal drop does present a real challenge to plasticity theory and to the efficacy of intervention with intellectual decline.

Adult-Age Differences in Personality

Representative of how psychologists conceptualize personality are the following comments by Darley, Glucksberg, Kamin, & Kinchla:

> There is no one accepted definition of personality; there are many, each resting on different assumptions and stressing different aspects of being. A key theme uniting many definitions, however, is that personality is the organized and distinctive pattern of behavior that characterizes an individual's adaptation to a situation and endures over time. . . . The range of concerns in the study of personality thus includes ideas, motives, attitudes, emotions, life crises, beliefs, values, and the processes by which people try to understand their own behavior, that of others, and the world. (1981, p. 397)

Our concern rests in the assumption that personality "endures over time." Does personality indeed remain stable over the adult lifespan? Stated somewhat differently, is personality characterized by continuity or discontinuity from early to late adulthood? Interest in answering this question has stimulated much of the research conducted on personality by gerontological psychologists (Neugarten, 1977). In the past, a number of gerontologists hypothesized that personality undergoes pronounced changes for most people in their transitions from early to middle adulthood and from middle adulthood to late adulthood. For example, a popular belief has been that people tend to become increasingly introverted as they grow older (Botwinick, 1973). As we will soon see, this belief is apparently one of the myths of aging, at least for normally aging people. Our review will focus largely on adult-age differences/changes (or their absence) in personality (see Riegel, 1959; Schaie & Marquette, 1972; and Schein, 1968, for additional reviews of early gerontological studies of personality; also Lawton, Whelihan, and Belsky, 1980, for a thorough discussion of the methodological problems encountered in gerontological research on personality). It is complicated by the fact that there is no single approach to the study of personality. Instead, the study of personality has been guided by many different theories that involve different views of the human organism and different methodologies for studying personality in general and age differences in personality in particular. Several of these theories will provide the framework for our review of age differences/changes in personality (see Cartwright, 1974, for detailed descriptions of these theories).

We will also attempt to review what little research has been directed at the relationships between personality changes with aging and performance on tasks of concern to experimental aging psychologists. In earlier chapters, we observed that people are commonly believed to change in personality in ways that could affect signal-detection performance, memory performance, problem-solving ability, creativity, and so on. Especially prominent have been the beliefs that rigidity and cautiousness increase with increasing age, and the related beliefs that these increments affect performance of elderly people on a variety of laboratory tasks. We will examine these issues carefully in the following sections.

Trait Theory. A trait is viewed as being a structure in personality that accounts for relatively enduring dispositions and consistencies in an individual's behavior over time. An example is Extroversion-Introversion. An individual classified as being introverted on this trait supposedly behaves in the same way across many variations in situations and contexts.

The essence of trait theory is in psychometric measurement. By means of personality inventories, questionnaires, or tests, individuals may be assessed on a number of traits, usually those that have been identified as component structures of personality through the statistical method of factor analysis. Age differences in trait scores may then be investigated by applying one or more of the traditional developmental methods.

The cross-sectional method, however, was the only one used in early studies of these age differences (Bendig, 1960; Craik, 1964). The age differences in trait scores revealed cross-sectionally may well be due to cohort effects rather than to true age changes in personality. As we observed in Chapter 4, personality traits are likely to be susceptible to early environmental influences, and they may, therefore, vary considerably over generations. Nor is the longitudinal method a panacea for eliminating confoundings of age changes in personality traits by uncontrolled non-age factors. Personality traits could be altered by major cultural changes, thus confounding age effects with time-of-measurement effects in conventional longitudinal assessments of traits. The causative factors underlying age differences in traits can be isolated only through the use of sequential designs and analysis. Fortunately, there have been several studies in the past 10 years that have made effective use of these designs. Our review of age differences on personality traits will be restricted to these studies. Three different personality inventories have been involved: the Guilford-Zimmerman Temperament Survey (Guilford & Zimmerman, 1949); the Sixteen Personality Factor Questionnaire (Cattell & Eber, 1957); and the California Psychological Inventory (Gough, 1964). The traits assessed by these three tests do vary somewhat. Nevertheless, there is considerable commonality in their trait content.

The Guilford-Zimmerman Temperament Survey provides scores on each of the 10 personality traits listed in Table 11.5. The survey was employed in the study by Douglas and Arenberg (1978) that was discussed briefly in Chapters 3 and 4. In review, the survey was administered to 915 men (participants in the Baltimore Longitudinal Study) who ranged in age from 18 to 98 years at the time of initial assessment. This assessment was followed by a second one from 5.6 to 9.9 years later. The wide age range and the fairly lengthy time interval separating assessments made it possible to examine age differences both cross-sectionally and longitudinally and, most important, to conduct sequential analyses with age, cohort membership, and time of measurement as independent variables. The overall results of these analyses are summarized in Table 11.5. Note that age variation had relatively little effect on trait scores. In fact, Masculinity and General Activity were the only traits for which age differences could be attributed to true age, or maturational, changes. The maturational decline in Masculinity is in agreement with the familiar notion that men progress from active to passive mastery of the environment as they grow older (Gutmann, 1977). The maturational decline in General Activity is certainly not surprising, given the overall physical slowing down that occurs with normal aging. By contrast, both cohort variation and cultural variation over a relatively short historical time period appeared to be causative factors for changes in several personality traits. The probable roles played by cohort membership and cultural changes in producing individual differences in personality merit serious attention by trait theorists and by constructors of trait-oriented personality tests.

The traits measured by the Guilford-Zimmerman Temperament Survey may be considered primary factors of personality, just as Reasoning and Spatial Ability may be considered primary factors of intelligence. As with the primary factors of intelligence, the primary factors of personality cluster together to form fewer, broader based, secondary factors that are analogous to Gc and Gf of intelligence. Costa and his colleagues (Costa, McCrae, & Arenberg, 1980; McCrae, Costa, & Arenberg, 1980) have conducted this cluster analysis for the traits of the Guilford-Zimmerman Temperament Survey. Through it, they identified three broad factors: a General Neuroticism factor; Social Activity factor; and a Thinking Introversion factor. Most important,

Table 11.5   Traits Included on the Guilford-Zimmerman Temperament Survey and the Effects of Developmentally Relevant Variables on Scores for Each Trait

Factor or Trait	Meaning of High Scores	Developmental Effects
General Activity	High energy, liking for speed	Age effect (less activity with increasing age); no cohort effect; no cultural change
Restraint	Deliberate, serious minded	No age effect; cohort effect (earlier cohorts more serious than later cohorts); no cultural change
Ascendance	Leadership, social assertiveness	No age effect; cohort effect (earlier cohorts less assertive than later cohorts); no cultural change
Emotional Stability	Composure, evenness of mood	No effect for age, cohort, or cultural change
Objectivity	Freedom from suspiciousness	No effect for age, cohort, or cultural change
Friendliness	Respect for others, toleration of hostility	No age effect; cohort effect (earlier cohorts friendlier than later cohorts); cultural change (from more to less)
Thoughtfulness	Reflective, introverted, meditative	No age effect; no cohort effect; cultural change (from more to less introversion)
Personal Relations	Tolerance of people, freedom from faultfinding and self-pity	No age effect; no cohort effect; cultural change (from more to less tolerance)
Masculinity	Interest in traditional masculine activities (e.g., hunting)	Age effect (less activity with increasing age); no cohort effect; no cultural change
Sociability	Having many friends, liking social activities	No effect for age, cohort, or cultural change

Source: Adapted from material in Douglas and Arenberg, 1978.

scores on these broader factors, when analyzed by sequential methods, were also found to show no sign of major maturational changes over the course of the adult lifespan.

As you might suspect, the Sixteen Personality Factor Questionnaire measures individual differences on 16 different personality traits (e.g., Dominance and Radicalism). This test was the instrument used by Siegler, George, and Okun (1979) in a major sequentially designed study. What makes this study especially interesting is that women as well as men were included as subjects. The subjects ranged in age from 54 to 70 years, and they were tested four times over an 8-year period. No maturational changes in trait scores were found. Moreover, there were only a few changes attributable to either cohort variation or cultural variation over the 8-year period. By contrast, there were some major sex differences in trait scores, with women appearing less reserved, more submissive, more tenderminded, more naive, and more tense than men, regardless of age. Of course, no young adults were included in this study. It would be of great interest to see if these sex differences interacted with cohort membership more broadly extended to include the current generation of young adults. A reasonable expectancy is that at least some of the sex differences would be far less pronounced for this generation.

Overall stability in trait scores was also reported in Schaie and Parham's (1976) sequential study. The personality inventory used in this study was constructed by the investigators. However, the inventory did have considerable overlap with the trait content of the Sixteen Personality Factor Questionnaire. The age range and cohort range of their subjects were considerably greater than those found in the study of Siegler et al. (1979) study (age range, 22 to 84 years). With these extended ranges, more trait changes attributable to cohort variation were found than in the study of Siegler et al. However, little effect attributable to true age changes continued to be the case.

The Sixteen Personality Factor Questionnaire has also been subjected to a cluster analysis by Costa (Costa & McCrae, 1976, 1977, 1978, 1980) to identify secondary personality factors. In common with the comparable analysis performed on the Guilford-Zimmerman Temperament Survey, three broad factors were discovered: Anxiety-Adjustment; Introversion-Extroversion; and Open-Closed Experiential Style. Like the secondary factors of the earlier inventory, these broad factors were found to be relatively stable maturationally and, therefore, resistant to major maturational changes over the course of the adult lifespan.

The outcome of a sequentially designed study with the California Psychological Inventory was much like that of the outcomes of the studies using other personality tests. Woodruff and Birren (1972) tested students averaging 19.5 years of age in 1944 and then retested them in 1969 when their average age was 44.5 years. At the time of retesting, they also tested for the first time a number of high school and college students. Thus, they had the necessary data for performing a sequential analysis of test scores. In agreement with the studies using other tests, maturational changes in trait scores were found to be quite small. By contrast, there were pronounced cohort effects. For example, members of the 1924 cohort (i.e., subjects 44.5 years of age in 1969) scored higher than members of both the 1948 (college students in 1969) and 1953 (high school students in 1969) cohorts on social adjustment.

The presence of cohort effects for various personality traits means that widely separated age groups of subjects in an experimental aging study are likely to differ on those traits, not because of their differences in age (again, there seems to be little effect for age per se), but rather because of their differences in generational memberships. This could create a problem in interpreting age differences in performance on various cognitive tasks but only if personality trait scores correlate with scores on those cognitive tasks. Given this correlation, the difference between age groups in personality rather than in age per se could be the true causative factor responsible for age differences in task scores. This is the kind of potential confounding we discussed at length in Chapter 2 with educational level as the potentially confounding non-age variable. At that time, we discovered that the solution to such problems is to balance, or match, the age groups with respect to scores on the non-age variable. Thus, if performance on a particular cognitive task is known to be higher, on the average, for introverts than for extroverts, then the age groups being contrasted in performance on that task should be matched with respect to scores on the introversion-extroversion trait.

How pronounced are the relationships between such personality traits as introversion-extroversion and performance on, among others, perceptual, learning, memory, and problem-solving tasks? Considerable evidence with young adults as subjects (see Eysenck, 1977) suggests that modest relationships do exist, at least for some laboratory tasks. Some idea of the magnitude of these relationships and how these magnitudes are affected by age variation may be gained by examining the results obtained by Costa, Fozard, McCrae, and Bosse (1976). Subjects of various age levels were administered both the Sixteen Personality Factor Questionnaire and batteries of cognitive tests. The personality test was scored with respect to the three secondary factors indigenous to that test (i.e., Anxiety-Adjustment, Introversion-Extroversion, and Open-Closed Experiental Style). High scorers and low scorers were identified for each of these secondary factors, thus yielding Adjusted versus Anxious, Introverted versus Extroverted, and Open versus Closed subgroups for each total-age group. One of the cognitive test batteries, labeled Information Processing Ability, assesses cognitive skills comparable to those of crystallized intelligence, whereas the other battery, labeled Pattern Analysis Capability, assesses skills comparable to those of fluid intelligence. The results for the various subgroups, expressed in mean deviation units above or below average score on each battery, are plotted in Figure 11.13. Note first that age variation had little effect on test scores for the battery reflecting crystallized intelligence, but it did have a pronounced adverse effect on scores for the battery reflecting fluid intelligence. This pattern, of course, agrees with what is known about the differential effects of aging on the two broad components of intelligence. Our main interest, however, is the effect variation in personality had on cognitive test scores and also in the nature of the interaction between personality and aging. It may be seen in Figure 11.13 that introverts and extroverts performed, at each age level, approximately the same on the tests tapping crystallized intelligence, but that introverts outscored extroverts, again at each age level, on the tests tapping

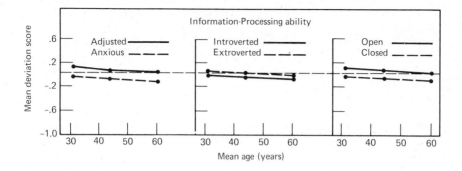

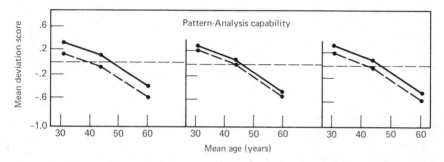

Figure 11.13. Age differences in performance on a task assessing crystallized intelligence (top panel) and a task assessing fluid intelligence (bottom panel) as affected by individual differences on three different personality traits. (Adapted from Costa, Fozard, McCrae, & Bosse, 1976, Figure 1.)

fluid intelligence. In addition, adjusted individuals and open-to-experience individuals outscored, at each age level, anxious individuals and closed-to-experience individuals, respectively, on the tests tapping both crystallized and fluid intelligence. Although the absolute effects of personality variation were found to be slight, they were large enough to suggest that such variation could distort the magnitude of age differences on intelligence tests if left uncontrolled.

Lewin's Personality Theory: The Rigidity Concept. Another early personality theory that offers a foundation for conceptualizing potential age changes in personality is that of Kurt Lewin (1935, 1951). (See Hall and Lindzey, 1957, for an overview of Lewin's theory; see Riegel, 1959, for a broader discussion of the theory's implications for the psychology of aging). The core concept of Lewin's theory is an individual's *life space* as composed of both that person's internal environment (or personality) and external environment. According to Lewin, the life space is differentiated into regions that, as described by Hall and Lindzey, have varying degrees of communication across their boundaries:

> A third way of representing the interconnections between regions is to take into account the nature of the medium of a region. The medium of a region is the floor or surface quality. Lewin has distinguished several properties of the medium, the most important of which is the *fluidity-rigidity* dimension. A fluid medium is one

that responds quickly to any influence that is brought to bear upon it. It is flexible and pliant. A rigid medium resists change. It is stiff and inelastic. Two regions that are separated from each other by a region whose surface quality is extremely rigid will not be able to communicate with one another. It is analogous to a person trying to cross a swamp or make his way through heavy underbrush. (1957, pp. 216–217)

What makes Lewin's theory attractive to gerontologists is the fact that human aging is commonly hypothesized to be accompanied by increasing degrees of rigidity or inflexibility. Rigidity in this context means the inability to shift from one behavioral activity to another even though the shift may be advantageous to the individual. The increased behavioral rigidity of elderly people, if true, would explain, in part at least, why they have greater difficulty than younger people in solving reversal-shift problems, tracing figures while viewing them in a mirror, and other activities for which proficiency is seemingly hindered by an individual's inability to abandon a once-effective behavior that is no longer effective. The most widely cited evidence for age differences in behavioral rigidity, however, is that provided by Heglin (1956). (See Botwinick, 1959, 1978, for reviews of other studies employing both human and animal subjects). One of the tasks in Heglin's study was the water-jar task described in Chapter 10. As observed earlier, elderly subjects were less likely than younger subjects to shift from a complex formula to a simpler formula in solving problems. A comparable age difference was also found for finding a pathway through a maze. Elderly subjects continued to select long and tortuous paths, even though shorter routes were available, following exposure to a number of mazes in which the complex paths were the only ones possible.

Unfortunately, behavioral rigidity tells us little about either age differences/changes in rigidity as a personality characteristic or the causative role played by rigidity in determining age differences/changes in concept learning, problem solving, and so on. We could argue that elderly people are poorer concept learners or problem solvers than younger people because they are more rigid, or we could argue that elderly people simply appear to be more rigid than younger people because they are poorer concept learners or problem solvers. Understanding of the relationships between rigidity, as a personality characteristic presumably affected by aging, and performance on various laboratory tasks is possible only to the extent that individual differences in rigidity can be assessed independently of individual differences on behavioral tasks presumably affected by rigidity. Various psychometric tests have been constructed over the years to accomplish this objective (Chown, 1961; Riegel & Riegel, 1960; Schaie, 1958; Shields, 1958). These tests are all oriented toward the view that there are multiple forms of rigidity, with each form requiring separate assessment. For example, Schaie's test provides measures for three factors of rigidity. The first factor, Motor-Cognitive Rigidity, concerns effective adjustment to shifts in familiar patterns and to continuously changing situational demands; the second factor, Personality-Perceptual Rigidity, concerns effective adjustment to unfamiliar surroundings and new situations; and the third factor, Psychomotor Speed, concerns rate of emission of familiar cognitive responses.

There is no doubt that there are large adult-age differences in scores on rigidity tests, with rigidity increasing as age increases. The magnitude of these age differences may be seen in Figure 11.14 (decreasing scores indicate increasing rigidity) for Schaie's (1958) Personality-Perceptual Rigidity factor (comparable age differences have been reported for the other two factors and for the rigidity tests employed by other investigators). But do these age differences necessarily mean that people become increasingly more rigid as they advance through adulthood? That is, is there a maturational or otogenetic change in rigidity?

Two problems are encountered in attempts to answer this question. The first is created by the moderately high correlation found between intelligence test scores and rigidity test scores (Chown, 1961; Schaie, 1958; Shields, 1958). People of high intelligence appear to be less rigid than people of low intelligence. Because intelligence test scores decline with increasing age, adult-age differences in rigidity could be accounted for by the increasingly larger proportion of people with lower intelligence test scores as age increases. The important question then is: Do age differences in rigidity persist when adjustments are made for age differences in intelligence? Here, we find conflicting evidence. Analyses by Schaie (1958) and Shields (1958) of their data indicated that age differences in rigidity do indeed persist, whereas Chown's (1961) analysis revealed that age differences in rigidity largely disappeared. The second problem is the familiar one associated with cross-sectional research: How do we know the age differences are not really due to cohort effects? Later sequential analyses by Schaie (Schaie, Labouvie, & Buech, 1973; Schaie & Labouvie-Vief, 1974) provided substantial evidence for the potency of cohort effects for all three of his rigidity factors. Members of earlier generations appear to be more rigid than members of later generations. By contrast, little, if any, true maturational change was found for any of the rigidity factors.

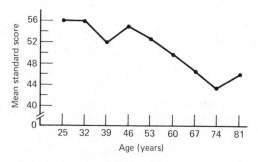

Figure 11.14. Age differences in scores on a test of rigidity. (Adapted from data in Schaie, 1958.)

If age differences in rigidity represent a potential confounding factor in an experimental aging study, then the investigator should exercise care in matching the age groups in scores on rigidity tests. This practice is made necessary by the fact that widely separated age groups differ in generational membership and are, therefore, likely to differ in psychometrically assessed rigidity. Just how widespread this matching procedure should be is difficult to determine however. Little is known about the relationship between rigidity and performance on conventional laboratory tasks, that is, tasks for which rigidity is not ordinarily considered to be a major determiner of performance scores.

Information-Processing Theory of Personality: Cognitive Style. The connection between information-processing theories of human cognition and personality characteristics is made clear in the following comments by Cartwright:

> As part of the general topics of thinking and problem solving, the means by which a person comprehends the nature and implications of the world around him become of focal interest to students of personality who adopt a cognitive approach. Varieties of human intelligence become varieties of the cognitive aspects of personality. Cognitive styles, such as augmenting versus reducing of incoming signals (stimulus inputs) are shown to influence a wide range of personality characteristics. (1974, p. 301)

The core concept in information processing's analysis of personality is that of *cognitive style.* One basic form of cognitive style, alluded to by Cartwright, refers to an individual's manner of perceiving environmental stimuli. For example, how sensitive is an individual to contextual stimuli while attending to some specific stimulus? To irrelevant stimuli while attending to relevant stimuli? The information-processing personality theorist views individual differences in sensitivity to contextual and irrelevant stimuli in terms of a broad cognitive style dimension called *field independence-field dependence* (Witkin, Dyk, Faterson, Goodenough, & Karp, 1962). In general, people classified as being field-dependent are believed to rely primarily on external stimuli in making perceptual judgments and to experience their environments in a global, relatively undifferentiated way. By contrast, people classified as being field independent are believed to rely largely on internal stimuli in making perceptual judgments and to experience their environments in a relatively differentiated way. Field-dependent people are, therefore, more likely than field-independent people to be distracted by irrelevant stimuli and to suffer attentional problems when confronted by multiple stimulus inputs. Some personality psychologists have extended the differences between field-dependent and field-independent people to include such nonperceptual characteristics as sociability (Witkin et al., 1962). For our purposes, the extension of greatest interest concerns the covariation between chronological age and field independence-field dependence. Child psychologists have discovered that young children are largely field dependent. However, children become increasingly field independent as they mature perceptually. The popular notion of adult-age regression leads naturally to the hypothesis that people become progressively more field dependent as they advance over the adult segment of the lifespan. That is, they are expected to revert to more childlike perceptual activities.

The evaluation of the age-regression principle obviously requires a reliable means of assessing individual differences in field independence and dependence. The two most widely employed means of making these assessments have been with the rod-and-frame test and the embedded-figures test. The former (see the top panel of Figure 11.15) tests subjects in a darkened room with an apparatus composed of a luminescent rod surrounded by a luminescent square. The subject's task is to move the rod until, on some trials, it is vertical with respect to the floor or, on other trials, it is horizontal with respect to the floor. The task is made difficult by tilting the square background (see Figure 11.15), thus making accuracy, as measured by degrees of deviation from verticality or horizontality, contingent on the subject's ability to ignore the distorting context offered by the tilted square. In the embedded-figures test, subjects attempt to find simple geometric figures hidden within more complex designs. Accuracy is again contingent on a subject's ability to ignore contextual information, in this case information provided by elements of the complex designs.

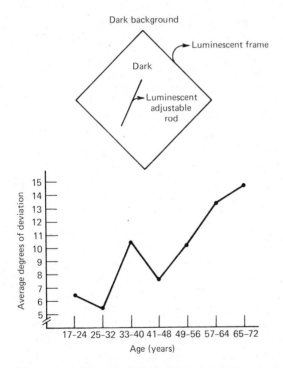

Figure 11.15. Top panel: Task structure used to assess individual differences in field independence-field dependence. Bottom panel: Age differences in deviation scores for vertical and horizontal settings of a rod (shown in top panel) with increasing scores that indicate increasing field dependency. (Adapted from Panek, Barrett, Sterns, & Alexander, 1978, Table 1.)

The rod-and-frame and embedded-figures tests have been used in a number of aging studies. These studies have generally supported the hypothesis that field dependence increases from early to late adulthood (Comalli, Wapner, Werner, 1959; Eisner, 1972; Kogan, 1973; Lee & Pollack, 1978; Markus, 1971; Panek, Barrett, Sterns, & Alexander, 1978; Schwartz & Karp, 1967). Age differences on the rod-and-frame test obtained in one of the most comprehensive of these studies, that of Panek et al. (1978), are shown in the bottom panel of Figure 11.15. It may be seen that increasing age was indeed accompanied by fairly regular increments in deviation (i.e., degree of deviation from verticality or horizontality) scores. Comparable age differences were also found in this study with the embedded-figures test. The implication is that field dependency does increase as adults grow older. However, the study of Panek et al., like the other ones in this area of investigation, made use only of conventional cross-sectional analysis of age differences. It could be argued that the age differences manifested in this and the other studies are the consequence of cohort differences and that this aspect of cognitive style, in common with a number of other personality characteristics, is relatively immune to true maturational change. Lee and Pollack (1978) have argued quite convincingly, however, that ontogenetic changes in various components of the perceptual system represent the more likely reason for the pronounced increments in field dependency commonly observed to accompany increments in chronological age. These increments do offer an explanation of why elderly people perform so poorly on various perceptual tasks in which performance is likely to be hindered by inordinate attention directed at irrelevant stimuli. In the real world, one of these tasks consists of driving an automobile. Independently of age, automobile accident rates are higher for field-dependent individuals than for field-independent people (e.g., Mihal & Barrett, 1976). The high accident rate of elderly drivers may, therefore, be accounted for, at least in part, by the large proportion of elderly drivers likely to be field dependent.

To test this hypothesis, young and elderly subjects who are matched in scores on the rod-and-frame test could be compared on laboratory tasks that involve distractability by irrelevant stimuli, such as the card-sorting tasks described in Chapter 7. If the hypothesis of an age differential in field dependency is valid and if this differential accounts for the age difference in susceptibility to distraction by irrelevant stimuli, then the customary deficits exhibited on these sorting tasks by elderly adults should be greatly reduced, if not eliminated entirely. That is, the process responsible for age differences in distractability, namely field dependency, should now be equated across age groups. In effect, the strategy is equivalent to the one described earlier in connection with age differences in fluid intelligence.

Another dimension of cognitive style that has special importance in the experimental psychology of aging is that of *cautiousness*. In this, the personality characteristic at stake affects the decision-making level of information processing instead of the attentional and perceptual levels. To repeat a point made numerous times in earlier chapters, a long-time popular belief has been that elderly people are more cautious and, therefore, less willing to take risks than are younger people. Behavioral evidence in support of increasing cautiousness with increasing age has been somewhat conflicting however. Strong support comes from the finding that elderly subjects are more cautious than younger subjects on signal-detection tasks. Additional support is in the form of the higher proportion of omission errors made by elderly subjects than by younger subjects on verbal-learning tasks. On the other hand, false alarm rates on recognition-memory tasks tend to be higher for elderly subjects than for younger subjects, therefore, implying less cautiousness in old/new decision making by the elderly subjects.

As in the analysis of age changes in rigidity, what is needed are assessments of individual differences of cautiousness/risk taking that are made independently of tasks for which age differences in cautiousness offer an explanation of age differences in task performance. An early test designed with this objective in mind is the Choice Dilemmas Questionnaire of Wallach and Kogan (1961). On this test, subjects are given descriptions of life situations involving an individual who is faced with a decision. For example, an individual must decide whether or not to leave the employment of a company that offers long-term security but a low salary to join another company that offers a high salary but an uncertain security owing to its shaky financial condition. Answers are given in terms of the lowest probability of financial soundness the subject considers acceptable for the individual in question to change jobs. The choices range from 1 in 10 to 9 in 10 that the company will prove to be financially sound. The 9 in 10 choice, of course, indicates low risk taking (i.e., high cautiousness), whereas the 1 in 10 indicates high risk taking (i.e., low cautiousness). Wallach and Kogan discovered that their elderly subjects scored substantially higher in cautiousness than did their young adult subjects. Gaffney and Lair (1979) reported a similar outcome with a revised questionnaire that varied the conditions under which a decision had to be made. They discovered that their elderly subjects remained quite cautious, regardless of the conditions present for the companies involved in the job switch, whereas their younger subjects varied considerably in their cautiousness, contingent on the specific employment conditions. Unfortunately, the usefulness of the Choice Dilemmas Questionnaire is tainted considerably both by its apparent low reliability (Okun, Stock, & Ceurvorst, 1980) and by problems inherent in the format of the responses required of subjects (Botwinick, 1966, 1969).

An alternative procedure for assessing individual differences in cautiousness/risk taking is one in which individuals choose from among levels of a particular task the single level they wish to receive for actual performance (Atkinson, 1957). The levels of the task differ in difficulty so that the probability of being successful ranges from being very high for the first level to very low for the last level. Most important, the payoff, or reward for each correct response, may also be structured so that increasingly more points (which may later be cashed in for money) are received as the probability of success decreases. This intriguing procedure was first employed in an aging study by Okun and DiVesta (1976). Their young and elderly subjects initially were given a vocabulary test covering a wide range of difficulty. Based on their subjects'

Table 11.6 Formats of Risk-Taking Tasks Used to Evaluate Age Differences in Cautiousness

Task Level	Probability of Success	Payoff (Points per Correct Answer)	Expected Value
	Expected Value Equal at All Task Levels		
1	1.00	10	10.0
2	.90	11	9.9
3	.80	12	9.6
4	.70	14	9.8
5	.60	17	10.2
6	.50	20	10.0
7	.40	25	10.0
8	.30	33	9.9
9	.20	50	10.0
	Expected Value Increases as Task Difficulty Increases		
1	1.00	1	1.0
2	.90	3	2.7
3	.90	6	5.4
4	.70	10	7.0
5	.40	22	8.8
6	.30	37	11.1
	Expected Value Decreases as Task Difficulty Increases		
1	1.00	11	11.0
2	.90	10	9.0
3	.90	8	7.2
4	.70	7	4.9
5	.40	8	3.2
6	.30	3	0.9

Source: Adapted from material in Okun & DiVesta, 1976; Okun & Elias, 1977.

performances on this test, Okun and DiVesta constructed a second vocabulary test with levels that varied in terms of probability of successful answers. These probabilities and the number of points awarded for each correct answer at each level of difficulty are listed in the top segment of Table 11.6. Also listed in this table is the expected value associated with each level of task difficulty. It represents the number of points a subject could expect to earn by choosing a specific difficulty level, and it is found by multiplying the probability of success by the number of points awarded for each correct answer. Note that the task levels are essentially equal with regard to expected value. Thus, there is no particular advantage to selecting one level of task difficulty over any other level of difficulty. Nevertheless, the elderly subjects in this study were more cautious than the younger subjects. The age disparity was apparent in the higher mean probability of success for the levels of difficulty selected by the elderly subjects (.68) than for the levels of difficulty selected by the young-adult subjects (.50). The greater cautiousness manifested by elderly subjects is in agreement with the results obtained by Wallach and Kogan (1961) with a very different testing procedure as well as with the results obtained in a real-life study in which older executives were found to be more conservative in risk taking than were younger executives (Vroom & Pahl, 1971).

There is, however, limited generalizability for the results obtained by Okun and DiVesta (1976). As observed by Okun and Elias (1977), the problem rests in the constant expected values as level of difficulty increases. Given this constancy, there really is no incentive for taking greater risks—the outcome in terms of points earned should be about the same, regardless of the risk taken. To correct this situation, Okun and Elias revised the payoff structure inherent in the earlier study. This time the payoff awarded for each correct response varied in a way, as shown in the middle segment of Table 11.6, that made the expected value increase directly as the probability of success decreased. The age difference in mean level of difficulty selected was now found to be slight and statistically nonsignificant (4.47 for the young subjects and 4.44 for the elderly subjects). Okun and Elias also reversed the payoff structure, as shown in the bottom segment of Table 11.6, so that the expected value decreased as the probability of success decreased. The age difference in level of difficulty selected was again found to be slight and statistically nonsignificant (1.92 for the young subjects, 2.27 for the elderly subjects). Okun and Elias concluded that there is no reason to believe that elderly people are more cautious than younger people when the total reward is commensurate with the degree of risk involved. The capability of elderly people to reduce their cautiousness when the reward for taking risks is increased received dramatic support in a study by Birkhill and Schaie (1975). These investigators discovered that scores on the Primary Mental Abilities test increase greatly for elderly subjects when monetary incentives are offered in a way that makes omissions of answers more unrewarding than incorrect answers. Presumably, failure to answer a question on an intelligence test reflects cautiousness, just as an omission error on a learning task reflects cautiousness. On the other hand, the flexibility manifested by elderly subjects with Okun and Elias's (1977) risk-taking procedure conflicts with the stereotyped cautiousness manifested by elderly subjects with Gaffney and Lair's choice dilemma procedure.

Okun and Elias provided us with a quite reasonable summary of the confusing status of age differences in cautiousness:

> In conclusion, the research on age differences on cautiousness has yielded equivocal results (Botwinick, 1973; Okun, 1976). Age effects are clearly sensitive to variations in tasks and procedures. Thus generalizations from such results must be held in abeyance pending research which focuses on (a) establishing convergent validity among risk-taking measures across the adult life-span and (b) developing paradigms which distinguish motivational, cognitive, and situational components of age differences in cautiousness. (1977, p. 455)

An important first step in "establishing convergent validity among risk-taking measures across the adult life-span" was taken by Okun, Siegler, and

George (1978). Their young and elderly subjects received both the Choice Dilemmas Questionnaire and Okun and DiVesta's (1976) risk-taking test. At both age levels, the correlation between scores on these separate measures of cautiousness was essentially 0. Thus, cautiousness appears to be a multidimensional characteristic. Consequently, neither standard measure of cautiousness is likely to suffice as a means of evaluating individual differences in all dimensions of cautiousness. The fact that both measures of cautiousness do relate to cautiousness manifested on a laboratory task was attested to by the positive, but modest (r's around .30), correlation coefficients found between scores on each test and omission errors made while mastering a serial-learning task. Interestingly, Okun et al. (1978) found that an age deficit in serial-learning proficiency persisted even after adjustments were made to equate statistically their age groups in cautiousness as evaluated by a composite score derived from the two psychometric tests. This is another example of the strategy that calls for equating age groups on some variable suspected of causing age differences in performance on a laboratory task. In this case, the age deficit did not disappear, thus implying that age deficits in serial-learning proficiency are largely the consequence of age differences in some factor other than age differences in cautiousness.

Finally, studies on age differences in cautiousness have all made use of the traditional cross-sectional method. Consequently, there remains the interesting possibility that whatever age differences do exist in cautiousness are the products of cohort differences in cautiousness rather than a true age change in cautiousness. That is, members of earlier generations may be characterized by greater cautiousness than members of later generations.

Expectancy Theory: Locus of Control. Expectancy theory (Rotter, 1966; Rotter, Chance, & Phares, 1972) views an individual's behavior as being contingent on: (1) the likelihood, or expectancy, of that behavior's success in attaining some incentive or objective; and (2) the attractiveness, or reinforcement value, of that incentive or objective to the individual who is considering emitting that behavior. In other words, people behave in a certain way if they believe their behavior will yield a positive experience or effect. The theory's main impact rests in one of its major concepts, that of *locus of control.* Locus of control varies along an internal-external dimension. If individuals believe that positive experiences, rewards, and (perhaps most important) the avoidance of negative experiences and punishments are contingent on their own actions and behaviors, then they are classified as having internal control. Internals have high expectancies for their abilities to control their own destinies. By contrast, if individuals believe that positive experiences, rewards, and aversive effects are the consequences of luck, chance, and the actions of other people, then they are classified as having external control. Externals have low expectancies for their abilities to control their own destinies. Stated somewhat differently, internals are likely to make an active attempt to control their own lives, whereas externals are likely to believe there is relatively little they can do to control their own lives.

A popular hypothesis is that adjustment to environmental stresses is affected by individual's beliefs about their locus of control so that maladjustment and failure to cope with personal problems are more likely for externals than for internals. There is, in fact, considerable evidence with young adults in support of this hypothesis (see Lefcourt, 1976). Nor are community-dwelling, healthy elderly people an exception to the covariation between locus of control and degree of adjustment. Several studies (e.g., Kuypers, 1972; Palmore & Luikart, 1972; Wolk & Kurtz, 1975) have found that elderly people scoring as internals on standard tests of locus of control score higher on measures of adjustment and satisfaction with life than do elderly people scoring as externals. Our reference study is the one by Wolk and Kurtz. Their elderly subjects (median age, 68 years) were evaluated on several indices of adjustment, including a widely used one, the Life Satisfaction Index (to be described in detail later). Scores on this index range from 0 to 18, with higher scores indicating greater satisfaction with life. Mean scores on this index are plotted in Figure 11.16 separately for men and women who qualified as internals and externals on the basis of their scores on the locus of control test. It may be seen that life-satisfaction scores were indeed considerably higher, regardless of sex, for internals than for externals. Fairly comparable differences between internals and externals were found for the other indices of adjustment employed by Wolk and Kurtz.

A follow-up study by Wolk (1976) suggested, however, that there may be a limit to the generalization that elderly internals are better off psychologically than externals. Two samples of elderly subjects were employed in this study. The members of the first sample were residents of a retirement village who supervised their own activities and were responsible for their own actions. For these subjects, the relationship between locus of control and adjustment replicated that found for the subjects in Wolk and Kurtz's (1975) earlier study. The members of the second sample were residents of a retirement home in which the rules and regulations regarding daily activities were established by and governed by the home's staff. For this sample, there was no sign of a relationship between locus of control and adjustment. Wolk (1976) proposed that the critical factor determining whether or not internals adjust better than externals is the constraint offered by the environmental setting in which elderly people

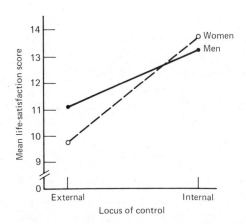

Figure 11.16. Relationship between locus of control and life-satisfaction test scores for elderly subjects. (Adapted from data in Wolk & Kurtz, 1975.)

find themselves. With a high-constraint setting, as in a staff-ruled retirement center, of what use is it to be an internal? The environment is so structured that it removes virtually all opportunity to assert personal control over one's fate. Perhaps the ultimate in constraint is the environment offered by a professional nursing home. Here it could be argued that externals among the residents may actually be better adjusted than internals. That is, internals may become disturbed and agitated by the fact that they no longer control their own regimens, whereas externals become content with having others control their lives. The evidence on this point is conflicting, however. Felton and Kahana (1974) did find superior adjustment, as evaluated both by self-ratings and staff ratings, to an institutionalized setting by externals than by internals. On the other hand, Reid, Haas, and Hawkings (1977) found the opposite relationship, that is, superior adjustment by internals.

An intriguing further question concerning the locus-of-control/degree-of-adjustment issue for institutionalized people is: "What happens to their well-being if they are provided the opportunity to control an important component of their lives?" A fascinating study by Schulz (1976) sheds some light on this important practical question. His subjects were residents of a church-affiliated home. Three groups of subjects each received visitors (undergraduate students at a nearby university) on a regular basis over a 2-month period. Members of one of the groups (the control-visits group) were able to control the time and duration of the visits, whereas members of a second group (the predict-visits group) could not control the time and duration, but they did know precisely when the visits would take place. The members of the third group (the random-visits group) had neither control over the visits nor predictability of the visits (i.e., the visits were announced in advance and were randomly scheduled). Finally, there was a fourth group (the nontreatment group) whose members received no visits at all. Members of both the control-visits and predict-visits groups exhibited significant (and comparable) improvements in health status, activity levels, and psychological well-being over the 2-month period, whereas members of the other two groups did not. Some degree of control over important environmental events, or at least the knowledge of when these events will occur, does seem to be an effective means of improving the physical and psychological welfare of elderly people who are forced to follow highly routinized daily schedules.

The opportunity to assert control over events may also affect positively performances on many cognitive activities, including many of those studied in the laboratory. A possible example of these effects is the benefit gained by self-pacing in practice on a paired-associate learning task. Self-pacing of item presentations leads to more proficient performance than experimenter-provided pacing for both young and elderly subjects, but the advantage is especially pronounced for elderly subjects (see Figure 8.16). One reason for the advantage of self-pacing could simply be the transfer of control over practice conditions from the experimenter to the subjects themselves. However, there are other explanations for the self-pacing advantage, as discussed in Chapter 8, that are independent of locus-of-control mechanisms. Other procedures for offering subjects control over laboratory events are clearly needed. One such procedure has been to allow subjects to choose their own response elements on a paired-associate learning list. For each stimulus element, they are shown several potential response elements, and they choose the one they want to associate with that stimulus element. This choice procedure has been found to yield more proficient learning by young adults relative to other young adults who have no choice over which word is paired with which stimulus element (Perlmuter & Monty, 1977). A recent study by Fleming and Lopez (1981) demonstrated that the advantage of control over response content applies equally well to elderly subjects.

One other issue concerning locus of control and adjustment needs to be considered. The issue centers on the concept of *learned helplessness*. The concept, as we discovered earlier, refers to the adoption of a what's-the-use attitude following prolonged exposure to unavoidable aversive stimuli. The aversive consequences appear to be inevitable in that their avoidance seems to be beyond the control of the individual concerned. Individuals showing learned helplessness seem to be unmotivated even for an activity in which they can control the outcome by means of effective performances. Laboratory research with only young-adult subjects (e.g., Hiroto, 1974) indicates that externals are more prone to manifestations of learned helplessness than are internals. This should not be surprising in that externals carry with them into the laboratory the belief that aversive consequences are largely beyond their control—the laboratory experience simply adds to this belief. In addition, experimental aging research (Krantz & Stone, 1978) indicates that, independently of variation in locus of control, elderly subjects are more prone to manifestations of learned helplessness than are young subjects. Given this pattern of results, we might expect elderly adults who have an external locus of control to be especially vulnerable to the debilitating effects of learned helplessness, such as prolonged periods of depression, in the real world. The problems facing these elderly people are especially serious in that the unfriendly and unsupportive environment often confronting them should be particularly conducive to acquiring learned helplessness.

Our main concern, however, is in the possibility of adult-age differences in locus of control. Here, the evidence to date is highly ambiguous. Some investigators (e.g., Bradley & Webb, 1976) have found elderly adults to be more external in their locus of control than younger adults, whereas other investigators have found either the opposite age effect (e.g., Staats, & Experimental Psychology Class, 1974) or no age effect at all (e.g., Duke, Shaheen, & Nowicki, 1974; Kuypers, 1972). Our best estimate is that there is relatively little change in locus of control over the adult lifespan for the total population of adults. People who are internals or externals early in adulthood are likely to remain internals and externals respectively during middle and late adulthood. Thus, locus of control probably joins several other important dimensions of personality in being relatively stable with advancing age. It seems unlikely, therefore, that age differences in locus of control represent a potential source of confounding by a non-age attribute in most experimental aging studies testing hypotheses about age differences/changes in, among others, sensory, perceptual, and learning processes.

Disengagement Versus Engagement: Life Satisfaction. A theory uniquely directed at adjustment in late adulthood is the *disengagement theory* of Cumming and Henry (1961). According to this theory, society gives its "permission" to elderly people to reduce their number and variety of roles (e.g., their occupational role). In effect, society expects elderly people to disengage from social activity. Successfully aging people, therefore, should be those who conform to this expectancy and reduce their role activities and their activities in general.

If nothing else, disengagement theory managed to stir up considerable controversy, largely because it contradicted the then prevailing theory of successful aging, namely, engagement or activity theory (e.g., Maddox, 1964). Engagement theory is the polar opposite of disengagement theory. According to it, successful aging depends on remaining active despite the normal role reduction that is normally forced on elderly people. Activity may take the form of volunteer work, interacting with and visiting with friends and relatives, and so on.

Tests of the validities of these rival positions require first establishing some means of defining and measuring "successful aging." The standard approach taken by most gerontologists has been through the assessment of life satisfaction. Scores on tests of life satisfaction may then be correlated with various indices of activity to determine the relationship between the two (see Larson, 1978, for a detailed review of the many studies dealing with life satisfaction during late adulthood). Engagement theory, of course, predicts a high positive correlation, whereas disengagement theory predicts a 0 correlation, if not a negative correlation.

The most widely used test of life satisfaction has been the Life Satisfaction Index introduced by Neugarten, Havighurst, and Tobin (1961). It contains 20 questions (but shorter versions of it are often used), a sample of which is given in Table 11.7—each question is answered by agree, disagree, or uncertain. Neugarten et al. intended the test to measure five different components of life satisfaction: (1) Zest for Life (as opposed to apathy); (2) Resolution and Fortitude (as opposed to resignation); (3) Congruence between Desired and

Table 11.7 Representative Items of the Life Satisfaction Index (Responses Indicating Life Satisfaction Are Underlined)

Item	*Response*		
I am just as happy as when I was younger	<u>Agree</u>	Disagree	?
Compared to other people, I get down in the dumps too often	Agree	<u>Disagree</u>	?
The things I do are as interesting to me as they ever were	<u>Agree</u>	Disagree	?
I feel old and somewhat tired	Agree	<u>Disagree</u>	?
As I look back on my life, I am fairly well satisfied	<u>Agree</u>	Disagree	?
When I think back over my life, I didn't get most of the important things I wanted	Agree	<u>Disagree</u>	?

Source: Adapted from material in Neugarten, Havighurst, and Tobin, 1961.

Achieved Goals; (4) Optimistic Mood Tone; and (5) Positive Self-Concept. Factor analyses of the test, however, have generally indicated that it measures fewer than the intended five components (e.g., D. L. Adams, 1969). Another popular test of life satisfaction has been the Philadelphia Geriatric Center Morale Scale (Lawton, 1975). Its format is much like that of the Life Satisfaction Index. In addition, some investigators prefer using a single global rating of life satisfaction, such as rating how satisfied you are with your life, on a 10–point scale (e.g., Palmore & Kivett, 1977). The intercorrelations among these various tests of life satisfaction are quite high (Lohmann, 1977), making them largely interchangeable with one another.

Engagement, or activity, theory has gained some modest support in several studies measuring the life satisfaction of elderly people. Both Edwards and Klemmack (1973) and Lemon, Bengston, and Peterson (1972) found a positive correlation between frequency of activities away from the home and magnitude of life satisfaction scores, but not for the frequency of either visiting relatives or the frequency of solitary activities and life-satisfaction scores. However, Hoyt, Kaiser, Peters, & Babchuk (1980) later demonstrated that these positive relationships apply to some components of life satisfaction but not to other components. George (1978) reported a slight, but significant, positive correlation between a composite score summarizing the weekly time spent in church attendance, doing volunteer work, and so on, and life-satisfaction scores. Interestingly, a positive correlation has also been found between the number of projected future activities over a week's time and life satisfaction scores (Schonfield, 1973). In addition, life-satisfaction scores tend to be higher for elderly people living in low-constraint settings than for elderly people living in high-constraint settings (Wolk & Telleen, 1976).

There is a problem, however, in accepting the direct causative role played by activity in determining degree of life satisfaction. High activity presumably requires both a sound financial status and a sound health status. There is, in fact, a high positive correlation between such activities as participating in volunteer associations and such personal attributes as health status and socioeconomic status (S. J. Cutler, 1973). Conceivably, these personal attributes are the direct determiners of both activity *and* life satisfaction. Highly sophisticated correlational analyses do, in fact, provide substantial support for the position that satisfaction with one's personal resources (i.e., health and standard of living) rather than activity per se is the major determiner of overall satisfaction with life for both elderly men and women (Elwell & Maltbie-Crannell, 1981; Medley, 1976). However, these analyses also reveal that the family resources of elderly people also strongly affect overall life satisfaction during late adulthood. Nor can the personality traits and characteristics of elderly people be ignored as potent variables linked to life satisfaction. Considerable research (Neugarten & Hagestad, 1976; Neugarten, Havighurst, & Tobin, 1968) has revealed that individuals possessing certain personality characteristics are more likely to find high life satisfaction by means of disengagement and diminished activity than with engagement and continuing activity, whereas individuals possessing other personality characteristics show the reverse pattern.

Experimental aging psychologists probably have little reason for fearing potential confoundings from age differences in life satisfaction. The evidence on adult-age differences in life satisfaction is much like the evidence for age differences in locus of control. Some cross-sectional studies have found slight increments in the magnitude of life satisfaction with increasing age (Campbell, Converse, & Rodgers, 1976; Soper, 1979), whereas others have found either slight decrements with increasing age (D. L. Adams, 1971; Wessman, 1957) or no age differences at all (Bortner & Hultsch, 1970). The overall pattern suggests that there is little age change in the total population of adults. This position is reinforced by further evidence indicating little longitudinal change over a period of 4 years in life-satisfaction scores for adults of various ages at the time of the first assessment (Palmore & Kivett, 1977). There is also evidence, however, indicating that the different components of life satisfaction contribute differentially to overall life satisfaction at different age levels (Cutler, 1979).

Incidentally, the stability of life satisfaction over the adult lifespan implies that there is relatively little change with increasing age in what personality psychologists call the *self-concept* (i.e., the overall positive or negative attitude an individual has toward his or her competence, personality, and so on). Adult-age differences in the self-concept have been studied independently of age differences in life satisfaction. A variety of assessment techniques have entered into these studies of self-concept. They include having subjects go over a lengthy list of adjectives and noting which ones seem descriptive of themselves. Another familiar procedure is to have individuals rate themselves on a series of bipolar adjectives that collectively make up what is called a semantic differential self-evaluation. Although some cross-sectional studies with these techniques have found the self to be viewed more negatively after age 50 than before age 50 (e.g., Bloom, 1961), other studies have found either the opposite effect (e.g., Hess & Bradshaw, 1970) or no age effect at all (e.g., Nehrke, 1974), or they have found some components of the self-concept to change but not other components (Monge, 1975). A longitudinal study (Pierce & Chiriboga, 1979), with adults of different ages at the time of the first assessment, found that some components of the self-concept (e.g., Amiability) were quite stable over a 5-year period, whereas other components (e.g., Assertion) manifested some degree of variability over the same time period.

The self-concept has also been found to increase positively with increasing age during late adulthood (i.e., higher for people in their 70s than for people in their 60s, and so on; Nehrke, Hulicka, & Morganti, 1980). Nehrke et al. interpreted these increments from the perspective of Erikson's (1959) psychosocial theory of development. According to this theory, the self undergoes development throughout the lifespan. However, it can do so only by resolving life crises associated with different stages of development. In late adulthood, the crisis is that of ego (or self) *integrity versus despair*. If elderly people have developed normally and have resolved all earlier crises, then they are prepared to face old age enthusiastically, with the feeling that they have lived satisfactorily. Ego integrity is the expected outcome. If this is not the case, then they are doomed to face old age with a feeling of despair. Nehrke et al. viewed their results as indicating that more and more individuals resolve this final crisis as they advance from the early to late stages of old age. Consequently, positive self-concept evaluations increase in frequency over the course of the final segment of the adult lifespan.

The one paradoxical bit of information that challenges the absence of any major age decline in life satisfaction from early to late adulthood concerns suicide rates. The stability of life satisfaction suggests that the suicide rate should be no greater for people age 65 and beyond than it is for younger people. However, this clearly is not the case. In 1970, the most recent year for which a full analysis of age differences in suicides is available (U.S. Public Health Service, 1974), the rate for the entire population of the United States was 11.6 per 100,000 people, whereas the rate for people 65 years of age and older was 36.9 per 100,000 people. Thus, the suicide rate for elderly people was more than three times that of the total population. Interestingly, the accelerated rate was restricted entirely to white males, a restriction that has persisted for a number of years (Marshall, 1978). For example, the suicide rate in 1970 for white males age 20 to 24 years was 19.3 per 100,000, whereas the rate for white males age 70 to 74 years was 40.4 per 100,000. Comparable young/elderly rates in the same age groups for white females, nonwhite males, and nonwhite females were 5.7 and 9.7, 19.4 and 8.2, and 5.5 and 3.9, respectively (see Pfeiffer, 1977, for further age analyses). Fortunately, the suicide rate for white males age 65 to 74 years has been steadily declining since the late 1940s, whereas the rate for the total population of the United States has stayed roughly constant (Marshall, 1978; see Figure 11.17). As observed by Marshall, the probable reason for the progressive decline is the progressive increment that has been occurring in the annual income of elderly people since the late 1940s. The connection between income and suicide rate for elderly men should

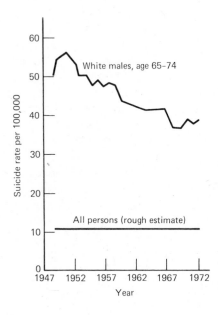

Figure 11.17. Declining suicide rates for white males from 1947 through 1972. (Adapted from Marshall, 1978, Figure 1.)

not be surprising, given the fact that degree of life satisfaction is clearly rated to degree of standard of living.

Psychopathology. Our focus is on personality as manifested in "normally" aging people. Our review thus far indicates that personality shows relatively little change from early to late adulthood. An important corollary of this stability is that personality disorders should also show few adult-age differences. A scattering of studies with the Minnesota Multiphasic Personality Inventory (MMPI) suggests that this is basically true. On this inventory, subjects answer a large number of true-false questions about themselves (e.g., "No one seems to understand me"). Their answers are compared with those given by individuals who had been diagnosed as having severe depression, paranoia, schizophrenia, and so on. Based on these comparisons, "normal" subjects can be assessed in terms of the extent to which they possess symptoms of depression, paranoia, and so on. Both cross-sectional and longitudinal studies (e.g., Brozek, 1955; Leon, Gillum, Gillum, & Gouze, 1979) have revealed few age differences in scores on the various scales of the MMPI (see Gynther, 1979, for a detailed review of these studies). Again, there is little reason to believe that there are pronounced age changes in personality over the course of the adult lifespan.

The one exception seems to be for scores on the depression scale. Here several studies (e.g., Harmatz & Shader, 1975; Leon et al., 1979; Pearson, Swenson, & Rome, 1965) have reported increasing symptoms of depression with increasing age. Clinical studies have also commonly reported more symptoms of depression for elderly patients than for younger patients (see Gurland, 1976). The high incidence of symptoms for elderly people, however, seems to be attributable to their frequent listing of somatic, or physical, complaints. Most important, there seem to be few age differences for affective or cognitive symptoms. This differential pattern may be seen in the results of a study by Zemore and Eames (1979). Mean ratings of symptom severity on a 0 to 3 scale (neutral to maximum) were obtained for both young adults (mean age, 18.9 years) and community-dwelling elderly adults (mean age, 79.9 years). The values for a representative sample of these symptoms are listed in Table 11.8. It may be seen that significantly greater severity for the elderly subjects was restricted largely to somatic symptoms. An increase in somatic problems, however, is part of aging, and an increase with increasing age in somatic complaints is, therefore, the norm rather than a sign of acute depression. Zemore and Eames concluded that "studies which have relied on symptom counts may have overestimated the severity of depression in the elderly" (p. 721).

Residents of a nursing home (mean age, 78.7 years) were also included in Zemore and Eames's study. They, too, had elevated depression scores only for somatic symptoms, leading Zemore and Eames to conclude that "no support was found for the widely held belief that old-age homes are breeding grounds for depression" (p. 721). Our best estimate is that personality disorders, like normal personality characteristics, are relatively free of adult-age differences.

Finally, the uniquely occurring forms of psychopathology in late adulthood are the various disorders resulting from brain dysfunctioning (i.e., organ-

Table 11.8 Representative Depression Subscale Mean Ratings for Young and Elderly Adults

Subscale	Young Adults	Elderly Adults	Age Comparison
Sadness	0.15	0.27	not significant
Pessimism	0.19	0.42	significant
Sense of failure	0.32	0.27	not significant
Guilt	0.19	0.25	not significant
Work difficulty	0.49	1.15	significant
Insomnia	0.46	0.83	significant
Fatigability	0.47	0.95	significant
Somatic preoccupation	0.21	0.27	not significant
Loss of libido	0.11	2.20	significant

Source: Adapted from Zemore and Eames, 1979, Table 2.

icity). Approximately half of the elderly population diagnosed as being behaviorally abnormal consists of people diagnosed as having one form or another of an organic brain syndrome (Pfeiffer, 1977). About 27% of the first admissions to mental hospitals are elderly adults meeting this diagnosis (Busse, 1959). Because people age 60 and over make up less than 40% of all first admissions to mental hospitals (Busse, 1959), it is clear that organic syndromes constitute the most prevalent form of debilitating psychopathology in old age. And, yet, the absolute incidence of such psychopathology is not very high. The probability at birth of ever being diagnosed as having senile psychosis, for example, is .023 for females and .018 for males. Of course, at advanced ages the probability increases strikingly—over .50 for those who attain age 90 (Gaitz, 1971).

There are three main classes of irreversible, or chronic, organic disorders. The most familiar is *senile psychosis* or *senile dementia*. It results from diffuse brain cell loss, and it has an unknown etiology. The onset of the disorder is usually after age 60, averaging about age 75. The disorder is found in nearly twice as many woman as men, most likely simply owing to the greater longevity of women. The behavioral symptoms may include impairment of judgment, impairment of comprehension, loss of memory, loss of orientation regarding time and place, and the appearance of shallow or flattened emotionality (Butler & Lewis, 1977). About half of the individuals afflicted with the disorder show simple deterioration of psychological functioning uncomplicated by other symptoms; the other half show additional symptoms akin to those of paranoia, mania, or schizophrenia. The time between onset of the disorder and death is quite variable and may be as short as 1 year or as long as 11 or more years (Busse, 1959). Another class of brain disorders in late adulthood is that of *presenile dementia*. The age of onset is usually in the late 40s or early 50s, averaging about age 54. This disorder, also of unknown etiology, is characterized by rapid mental deterioration, with death usually occurring within 5 years of onset. The most common form of presenile dementia is Alzheimer's disease.

Like senile dementia it is more prevalent in women than in men. The remaining class of organic disorders is that of *arteriosclerotic brain disease*. Here, the etiology has been well established, namely loss of brain functions owing to occlusive arterial or arteriolar disease. The average age of onset is around 65 years. Unlike the other disorders, it is more prevalent among men than among women. There are also cases of reversible organic disorders in old age. They are usually produced by such conditions as drug intoxication. The reversible disorders account for from 10% to 20% of all cases of organicity in old age (Pfeiffer, 1977).

Adult-Age Differences in Social Behavior

Social psychologists investigate a wide range of phenomena, including conformity to group pressure, obedience to authority, attribution of causation for people's successes and failures, cognitive dissonance, prejudice, and attitudes toward various political, social, and moral issues. Adult-age differences in these phenomena have received surprisingly little attention. The primary exceptions have been age differences in conformity and age differences in attitudes. Our final review will be limited to these phenomena.

Conformity. Beginning with the pioneering work of Sherif (1935), a number of investigators have discovered that the responses by young adults to many kinds of stimuli are influenced by the responses given by other individuals. That is, young adults have the tendency to bias their responses in directions conforming to group norms and pressure. What about older adults? The popular notion is that older adults are more conforming than younger adults. The question of such adult-age differences was finally tested empirically by Klein (1972; Klein & Birren, 1972). The two studies differed in terms of the type of task employed (tone detection in Klein and Birren's study, visual discrimination in Klein's study), but their outcomes were very similar. The visual discrimination study (Klein, 1972) will serve as our example.

The procedure closely followed that of Asch's (1951) classic study of social conformity. Asch's subjects were given pairs of lines differing in length, and they were asked to select the longer line in each pair. The judgments were made in a group context so arranged that each subject was the last member of the group to report each judgment. Unknown to each subject was the fact that the other members of the group were really stooges of the investigator. The situation was rigged so that for certain preselected pairs of lines all of the stooges reported the wrong judgment. That is, they said the discriminably shorter line was actually the longer one. A number of young-adult subjects were found to acquiesce to the pressure exerted by the group, and they agreed with the choice made by the other members. Asch also discovered that the proportion of subjects conforming to group pressure decreased as the physical distinctiveness between the paired stimuli increased.

In Klein's (1972) version of Asch's procedure, young and elderly subjects were shown pairs of discs differing in diameter, and they were asked to select

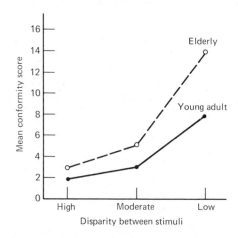

Figure 11.18. Age differences in conformity as influenced by stimulus disparity of judged stimulus pairs. (Adapted from Klein, 1972, Figure 1.)

the larger one of each pair. In a pretest phase of the study, all of the subjects made judgments in the absence of group pressure (i.e., they were tested alone). Here, the two age groups were equivalent in performance scores. Thus, subsequent age differences in conformity could not be attributed to the keener perceptual skills of the young subjects. During the conformity phase of the experiment, the subjects were told that they would repeat the judgment task, but this time as part of a four-member group. Not to our surprise, the subjects discovered that they were to be the last members of their groups to report judgments. They were then removed to isolation booths where they received the paired stimuli, heard over an intercom system the judgments given by the other members of their groups (all stooges, of course), and followed with their own judgments. On some of the trials, the stooges reported truthfully; on the other trials, they gave the wrong judgment. It is the latter trials that concerns us. On a third of these trials, the paired stimuli were low in discriminability (low disparity—a slight difference in diameter), on another third they were moderately discriminable (moderate disparity), and on the remaining third they were highly discriminable (high disparity—a large difference in diameters).

The results, expressed as mean conformity scores (maximum = 24), are plotted for both age groups in Figure 11.18. Note that, in agreement with Asch's (1951) earlier research, conformity at each age level decreased as the true difference between stimuli increased (i.e., as disparity increased from low to high). More important is the fact that conformity was greater for elderly subjects than for young subjects regardless of stimulus disparity. That is, the main effect for age was clearly significant. In addition, as can be seen in Figure 11.18, there was a clear interaction between age and stimulus disparity—the age difference in conformity increased progressively as stimulus disparity decreased.

Klein had some interesting speculations about his results:

There appears to be a need to utilize the data from conformity studies in a practical manner. Having found that the older individual is more conforming, perhaps, the older individual's conformity behavior could be modified when it is in conflict with his needs, interests, desires, and rights. In this way, the older person would cease to be targets for advertisements, demagoguery, and con games. (1972, pp. 233–234)

He also expressed concern that age differences in conformity may be task specific and limited, say, to only perceptual-judgment tasks. Thus, the age differences on this task may not reflect a general tendency of older people to conform more than younger people on many kinds of tasks. Furthermore, nothing is known about how age differences in conformity might affect age differences in performance on traditional sensory, learning, and memory tasks among others. Nor is it known whether or not age differences in conformity are the result of a true age change. Conceivably, they could be the consequence of cohort effects. Additional research on age differences/changes in conformity has been sorely lacking. There have been, however, two studies of marginal relatedness to conformity, both dealing exclusively with elderly adults. In one (Trimakas & Nicolay, 1974), elderly women with high positive self-concepts were found to be more susceptible to social influence in an altruistic situation (namely, expressed willingness to give away money they might have won in a lottery) than were elderly women with low positive self-concepts. In the other study (Kahana & Coe, 1969), institutionalized elderly people who were rated high in conformity to the staff's regulations were rated higher in adjustment by the staff than were elderly people who were rated low in conformity. This outcome should not be surprising. Conforming residents of an institution are the ones who are behaving in the way the staff members want them to behave. They, therefore, could be rated high in adjustment for that reason alone.

Attitudes and Attitude Change. Attitudes are "relatively enduring organizations of feelings, beliefs, and behavior tendencies toward other persons, groups, ideas, or objects" (Baron & Byrne, 1977, p. 95). They, therefore, have a cognitive component in the form of beliefs, an emotional component in the form of feelings, and a behavioral component in the form of predispositions, or tendencies, to react in certain ways toward the person, idea, or object involved.

Adult-age differences in attitudes toward political, social, and moral ideas or issues have been widely investigated. Most studies have employed the traditional cross-sectional method (e.g., Glamser, 1974; Riley & Foner, 1968). These studies have typically indicated the presence of more conservative attitudes among older people than among younger people. Our representative study is the one by Glamser. The subjects, all faculty wives at a university, were evaluated with respect to attitudes toward race, law enforcement, and patriotism. Overall, only 21% of the women in the 50-year-old-and-older range were classified as being liberal on the basis of their attitude test scores, in contrast to 55% of the women in the 20-to-29 year-old range. There is good reason to believe that such age differences are more the product of cohort effects than the products of true age changes from liberalism to conservatism over the course of the adult lifespan. That is, members of earlier generations were more likely to have acquired conservative positions on many issues than were members of later generations. This may be seen, for example, in analyses of allegiance to political parties. In recapitulation of material touched on in Chapter 1, several years ago, the proportion of elderly people who considered themselves Republicans was much greater than the proportion of young adults who considered themselves Republicans. This does not necessarily mean, however, that growing old converts Democrats into Republicans. The older Republicans were predominantly Republicans when they themselves were young adults (Cutler, 1969). Attraction to the Republican party simply diminished for members of later generations. In addition, sequential analysis reveals that age per se has little effect on views toward economic and foreign policy issues (Douglass, Cleveland, & Maddox, 1974).

There is also considerable evidence to indicate that elderly people change their attitudes in the liberal direction at the same rate as younger people do when society's values change. That is, as cultural shifts occur over time, they are likely to influence older people to the same extent they influence younger people. We discovered in Chapter 1 that this seems to be the case with attitudes about legalized abortion. Cutler, Lentz, Muha, & Riter (1980) compared attitude scores for members of four different generations as assessed from 1965 through 1977. Mean scores for their oldest generation (born in 1911 or before) and their youngest generation (born between 1936 and 1947) are shown in Figure 11.19. Two different scales were involved, one evaluating "hard" reasons for legalizing abortion (e.g., there is a strong chance of serious deficits in the child), the other "soft" reasons (e.g., the woman does not want to marry the man responsible for the child). Note that there was a pronounced increment in a favorable attitude toward legalized abortion, for both hard and soft reasons, from 1965 to 1972, with the more liberalized attitude remaining fairly stable

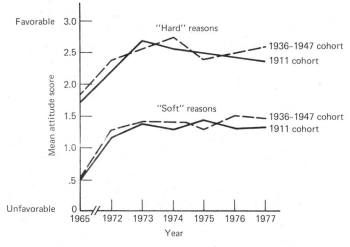

Figure 11.19. Attitude scores for "hard" (medical) and "soft" (nonmedical) reasons to legalize abortion obtained from the members of two widely separated cohorts over a number of years. (Adapted from Cutler, Lentz, Muha, & Riter, 1980, Figure 1.)

over subsequent years. Most important, the increment was as characteristic of members of the early generation as it was members of the late generation. Further evidence for liberalization comes from a longitudinal study by Willits, Bealer, & Crider (1977). Their subjects were assessed initially when they were all high school sophomores in rural areas of Pennsylvania, and they were reassessed 24 years later. Attitudes toward such adult-oriented moral issues as "working on Sunday" and "attending movies on Sunday" became considerably more liberal by the time these individuals had reached middle age. On the other hand, attitudes toward youth-oriented issues (e.g., "The matter of staying out late should be left up to the person involved") became more conservative with the transition to middle age (and probably the assumption of responsibility for an adolescent)!

Cultural shifts are not the only means by which attitudes may be changed. Persuasive communication is another way of accomplishing an attitude change—and in a short period of time. Messages sympathetic to a particular position on a specific issue can be effective, at least for some people, in bringing about some amount of change in attitude toward that issue. However, persuasive messages can be effective only to the extent that their contents are fully comprehended by their audience (McGuire, 1969). Given the reduced comprehension of aurally presented messages by elderly adults, a change of attitude evoked by persuasive communication might be expected to be less pronounced for elderly adults than for young adults. However, there is an opposing process operating here, one that favors greater attitude change by elderly adults than by young adults. The process is that of conformity. Elderly adults are seemingly more conforming than young adults, and the former should, therefore, be swayed more than the latter by the pressure of an effective argument, assuming the message is equally comprehended by the age groups.

A test of the consequences of these opposing processes was finally conducted by Herzog (1979). Young and elderly subjects were pretested on their attitudes toward childrearing settings. Both age groups expressed strong convictions that children were far better off if reared in homes than if reared in institutions. They were then exposed to a recorded message that offered effective arguments for the advantages of institutional child rearing. In agreement with the expected age differential in conformity, the elderly subjects changed their attitudes about child rearing after hearing the message to a greater extent than did the young subjects. However, the age difference in attitude change was found only when the message was presented at a moderate rate. At faster rates and, therefore, with poorer comprehension by the elderly subjects, the elderly subjects were no more prone to an attitude change than were the young adults. Thus, only with assurance of full comprehension does it seem likely that there will be age differences in attitude change through persuasive communication.

Two important questions remain concerning age differences in attitudes. The first is: "Are there age differences in the negative attitude directed at elderly people themselves?" We discovered in Chapter 1 that young adults generally view elderly people in terms of a negative stereotype. The magnitude of this stereotype is well dramatized in a study by Reno (1979). Young-adult subjects were given information pertaining to a fictitious person who had begun college after working for some years. Half of the subjects were informed that the new student was 25 years old; the other half of the subjects were informed that the new student was 63 years old. Subsequently, all of the subjects were told that the student did not make it through college, and they were asked to attribute probable causes for the student's failure. For the student perceived to be relatively young, the failure was attributed largely to motivational factors, such as not trying hard enough. By contrast, for the student perceived to be relatively old, the failure was attributed largely to cognitive factors, such as insufficient ability for college. Unfortunately, the negative attitude directed at elderly people is not limited to young people. Elderly individuals have the tendency to rate other elderly people as poorly as young individuals do (Bell & Stanfield, 1973). This outcome is somewhat paradoxical, given the fact that the self-concepts of elderly people tend to be as positive as those of younger people. The fact that many elderly people rate their peers so negatively is perhaps the best testimony of the pervasive and successful job society has done in perpetuating the negative stereotype of elderly people.

The second question is: "Are there age differences in attitudes toward death and dying?" Appropriately, our review of studies attempting to answer this question ends our total survey.

One approach to examining age differences in attitudes toward death is to ask adults of various ages the question: "If you were told that you had a terminal disease and six months to live, how would you want to spend the time?" This question was asked of over 400 people in the Los Angeles area by Kalish and Reynolds (1976). They classified responses to this question into various types. Older adults were clearly less concerned about altering their current life-styles than were younger adults, and they were more concerned about spending their remaining time in contemplative, reflective activities.

Another approach is to interview people of various ages about their fear of death and their frequency of thinking about death. Studies employing this approach generally agree that elderly people are less frightened by the prospect of death than are younger people (e.g., Feifel & Branscomb, 1973; Kalish & Reynolds, 1976). At the same time, these studies also reveal that elderly people think about death more often than do younger people (e.g., Riley, 1970). Kalish (1976) argued that the diminished fear of death in late adulthood is derived from one or more of three different factors: (1) elderly people often feel their chances for well-being (e.g., good health) are dim for the future anyway; (2) elderly people often feel they have already lived longer than they had expected and, therefore, are already living on borrowed time; and (3) elderly people have become habituated to death by the loss, over the years, of many relatives and friends, and they feel that death may even bring relief from prolonged bereavement.

There is another probable reason why elderly people fear death less than younger people. Considerable evidence indicates that there is a relationship between strength of religious conviction and fear of death. The relationship appears to be a complex one, however (Kalish, 1963). Very religious people tend to have the least fear of death, whereas very nonreligious people tend to have moderate levels of fear of death. It is people who are modestly committed to religious beliefs who tend to fear death most. The connection between age, religion, and fear of death should be obvious. Older people are more likely to be committed to religious beliefs and faith in an afterlife than are young adults (Riley & Foner, 1968). The implication is that this commitment alleviates fear of death. Many additional questions may be raised regarding the reasons for age differences in religious beliefs. Do they represent true age changes? Or do they reflect cohort effects? Nor can we ignore the probable existence of cultural shifts in religious beliefs. These intriguing questions and issues have been explored thoroughly by others (e.g., Ward, 1979). Our feeling is that further discussion here will take us too far astray from the experimental psychology of aging—and we have already detoured considerably from our main objective of acquainting you with what the experimental psychologist has informed us about human aging.

Summary

Our focus shifted in this chapter to topics and issues generally identified with the psychology of individual differences. The experimental psychologist of aging can scarcely ignore issues pertaining to age differences in intelligence, personality, and social behavior, the primary areas of concern in approaches to the study of individual differences. It is the entire person who enters the laboratory to perform on some sensory, learning, and memory, task and so on, bringing along his or her intellectual abilities, personality characteristics, and social predispositions. Nor can we ignore the fact that our understanding of age differences in intelligence, personality, and social behavior should contribute substantially to our understanding of age differences in adjustment to the problems of the everyday world.

The study of intelligence overlaps considerably with the study of cognitive processes conducted by experimental psychologists. Consequently, research on age differences in intelligence offers a means of complementing and enhancing the knowledge gained from laboratory studies of cognition.

Intelligence testing originated through the need to identify children who were likely to have difficulty in school. The emphasis on using intelligence tests to predict success on academic criteria eventually carried over to those intelligence tests that were constructed for the specific purpose of assessing individual differences in adult intelligence. Tests geared to predict academic success seem inappropriate, however, for measuring the intelligence of older people who are many years removed from an academic setting. For them, a more meaningful criterion for an intelligence test with which to correlate is success in adjustment to the problems encountered in the everyday world. Several tests have been constructed with this more meaningful criterion in mind. However, they have not yet received widespread application. Much of the problem rests in past failures to scale adjustment to everyday problems. Recently, significant advances have been made in analyzing the appropriate external criterion for evaluating the validity of adult intelligence tests.

One way of evaluating adult-age differences in intelligence is to compare age groups on global tests of intelligence, that is, tests measuring general ability (or g). Cross-sectional studies with the Army Alpha, the WAIS, and other tests of general intelligence have revealed substantial age differences in overall scores, favoring younger adults over older adults. Age differences have been examined further for the special ability components of general intelligence tests. Initially, these special abilities may be grouped, as they are on the WAIS, into verbal abilities and performance abilities. Composite scores for verbal abilities generally show far less decline with increasing age than do composite scores for performance abilities. When examined separately, the verbal abilities measured by the Vocabulary and Information subtests of the WAIS remain relatively stable over the adult lifespan (i.e., they are "hold" tests). By contrast, the nonverbal abilities measured by such subtests as Digit Symbol and Picture Arrangement decline considerably, at least cross-sectionally, with increasing age (i.e., they are "don't hold" tests). Somewhat similar variability in decline with increasing age is found for the abilities measured by tests constructed by means of factor analysis method (e.g., the Primary Mental Abilities (PMA) test).

Of interest to developmental psychologists are age changes in the nature of the relationship between the different special abilities and the relationship between general intelligence and the special abilities. The differentiation hypothesis states that intellectual functioning is strongly dominated by general intelligence during early childhood. Thus, high correlations are expected between scores on different special ability tests. However, in the progression to adulthood, the separate abilities become increasingly differentiated and independent of general intelligence. Consequently, low correlations are expected between tests of special abilities during early adulthood. De-differentiation is then expected to occur over the course of the adult lifespan, to the point that general intelligence again dominates intellectual functioning during late adulthood and the intercorrelations between tests of special abilities are again expected to be high. The evidence supporting this hypothesis is not very convincing however.

A more viable hypothesis about intelligence is that it is composed of two broad abilities, or secondary factors, each subsuming a number of special abilities or primary factors. One of these secondary factors, crystallized intelligence, is strongly influenced by education and acculturation and is considered to be largely insensitive to decrements from early to late adulthood. It is assessed by such tests as those of verbal comprehension (vocabulary), information, and mechanical knowledge. The other secondary factor, fluid intelligence, is largely uninfluenced by education and acculturation and is considered to show progressive decrements from early to late adulthood. It is assessed by such tests as those of reasoning and figural relations.

Age differences on both secondary factors of intelligence have been found to correlate with age differences on various cognitive tasks employed by experimental aging psychologists. For example, age differences in fluid intelligence account for much of the age deficit found on problem-solving tasks. When age groups are matched for scores on tests of fluid intelligence, age deficits in problem-solving proficiency seem to be eliminated.

Experimental psychologists are also involved in the analysis of the age-sensitive processes that underlie age deficits in performance on tests of special abilities. The Digit Symbol subtest of the WAIS has been the most frequent recipient of this analytical approach. The strategy calls for introducing critical independent variables that affect performance on this test, then determining the nature of the interactions these variables have with age variation. The results of studies employing this strategy indicate that the age-sensitive process is one akin to the response learning process of paired-associate learning, although not all psychologists agree with this interpretation. The analytical approach should eventually lead to fuller understanding of the specific cognitive processes accounting for age deficits on many other tests of special abilities.

Plasticity theory argues that the age deficits in fluid intelligence are largely modifiable, given appropriate training and environmental intervention. Thus far, short-term intervention by means of training programs has met with only modest success in improving the performance of elderly people on components of fluid intelligence tests. There remains the possibility, however, that long-term intervention programs, such as providing more stimulating environments for people as they grow older, will prove to be more successful.

Most of the gerontological interest in personality has centered on the issue of stability versus change of personality characteristics over the course of the adult lifespan. Research on this issue has been guided by many different personality theories, each of which stresses a different view of human personality and its assessment.

A long popular theory is one that stresses the existence of numerous personality traits. A trait is viewed as being a structure in personality that accounts for relatively enduring dispositions and consistencies in an individual's behavior over time. A number of personality inventories have been developed to measure such traits as introversion-extroversion, masculinity, and so on. Cross-sectional studies with these inventories generally reveal substantial age differences on many traits. However, sequential studies with the same inventories reveal that, with a few exceptions (e.g., masculinity), these age differences are the products of cohort effects. Sequential studies also indicate that cultural changes have occurred for certain personality traits over the years. Some personality traits have been found to correlate with performances on various tasks employed by experimental psychologists. Matching age groups in trait scores is probably a wise practice to follow when age differences are known to exist for that trait.

Another personality theory that has been of interest to gerontological psychologists is that of Kurt Lewin. Of particular interest is the theory's concept of fluidity-rigidity. A popular notion is that rigidity, or inflexibility of behavior and thought, increases as people grow older. Cross-sectional psychometric studies do reveal substantial increases in rigidity with increasing age. However, sequential analysis suggests that these increases are really the consequence of cohort differences in which members of earlier generations appear to be more rigid in personality than members of later generations.

Information-processing theory of personality stresses individual differences in cognitive style. One aspect of cognitive style refers to an individual's manner of attending to and perceiving environmental stimuli. The underlying dimension is that of field independence-field dependence. The reference is to the extent people are influenced by contextual stimuli in attending to a central stimulus. Elderly people have been found to be more field dependent (i.e., strongly influenced by contextual factors) than younger people. Some psychologists believe that this age difference is the consequence of a true ontogenetic change. The increased field dependency of elderly people seemingly accounts for the difficulties they have on laboratory tasks involving distractability by irrelevant stimuli. Another aspect of cognitive style is that of cautiousness while responding to environmental stimuli and while making decisions. Age differences in cautiousness have been reported on both psychometric tests and behavioral tasks involving risk-taking alternatives. However, age differences in risk-taking situations tend to disappear when the expected value for taking large risks is no greater than the expected value for taking small risks. In addition, the correlation for both young and elderly subjects between scores on these different measures of cautiousness is virtually 0, suggesting that the two procedures are evaluating relatively independent components of cautiousness. Whether age differences in cautiousness are due to true age changes or to cohort effects is unknown.

The concept of greatest interest to gerontological psychologists in Rotter's expectancy theory of personality is that of locus of control. Locus of control varies in terms of an internal-external dimension. Internals believe they are largely responsible for controlling their own significant experiences, while externals believe there is little they can do to control their own destinies. In general, elderly people who are assessed as being internal on tests of locus of control appear to be better adjusted and more satisfied with life than elderly people who are assessed as being externals. There is also evidence to indicate that institutionalized elderly people who are given the opportunity to control, or at least predict, a significant event in their lives improve in health status and overall well being. The adjustment problem for elderly externals is increased greatly by their potential susceptibility to learned helplessness. The evidence regarding overall age differences in locus of control is ambiguous however. Nevertheless, it seems likely that there are few age changes in locus of control during adulthood.

The most controversial personality theory of interest to gerontologists is that of disengagement theory. Its focus is exclusively on conditions affecting personality in late adulthood. The theory argues that elderly people's satisfaction with life is contingent on their ability and willingness to withdraw, as society expects them to do, from social and occupational activity. An opposing theory argues that continuing activity, or engagement, is essential for maintaining life satisfaction in old age. Activity theory has gained support from studies indicating that degree of life satisfaction for elderly people correlates positively with frequency of certain activities, such as doing volunteer work and visiting friends. However, frequency of activity also correlates substantially with both health and economic status. There is reason to believe that these status variables, rather than activity per se, bear the direct causative relationship with degree of life satisfaction. Most important, both cross-sectional and longitudinal studies reveal little change in degree of life satisfaction from early to late adulthood. Nor does there appear to be any major age change in the closely related personality dimension of self-concept.

The general stability of personality over the adult lifespan is strengthened further by the general absence of major age differences in various symptoms of functional psychopathology as measured by the MMPI. The main exception is for symptoms of depression, with elderly people manifesting more symptoms than younger people. However, the age difference here is due largely to the frequent somatic, or physical, complaints of elderly people, complaints that are probably normal with respect to the adverse biological problems associated with aging. There are, however, several forms of irreversible organic disorders, namely, senile dementia, presenile dementia, and arteriosclerotic brain disease, that are uniquely associated with aging.

Among the many phenomena of social psychology, only conformity and attitude toward political, social, and moral issues have received much investigation by gerontological psychologists. Conformity to group norms and pressure does seem to be greater for elderly subjects than for young adult subjects. Whether or not this age-related increment in conformity represents a true age change is unknown. A popular belief regarding attitudes is that people become more conservative as they grow older. However, the cross-sectional age differences that are commonly reported (indicating increments in conservatism with increasing age) are probably due to cohort variation rather than to true age changes. There is also reason to believe that as cultural changes to more liberal attitudes occur, elderly people shift in the direction of greater liberalism at the same rate younger people do. Unfortunately, elderly people tend to share the negative attitude that younger people have about old age. Finally, elderly people have a more positive attitude about death than do younger people. Several factors probably account for the diminished fear of death that occurs in late adulthood.

References

Abrahams, J. P.   Health status as a variable in aging research. *Experimental Aging Research,* 1976, *2,* 63–71.

Adam, J.   Statistical bias in cross-sequential studies of aging. *Experimental Aging Research,* 1977, *3,* 325–333.

———.   Sequential strategies and the separation of age, cohort and time of measurement contributions to developmental data. *Psychological Bulletin,* 1978, *85,* 1309–1316.

Adamowicz, J. K.   Visual short-term memory and aging. *Journal of Gerontology,* 1976, *31,* 39–46.

———.   Visual short-term memory, age, and imaging ability. *Perceptual and Motor Skills,* 1978, *46,* 571–576.

Adamowicz, J. K., & Hudson, B. R.   Visual short-term memory, response delay, and age. *Perceptual and Motor Skills,* 1978, *46,* 267–270.

Adams, D. L.   Analysis of a life satisfaction index. *Journal of Gerontology,* 1969, *24,* 470–474.

———.   Correlates of satisfaction among the elderly. *The Gerontologist,* 1971, *11,* 64–68.

Adams, J. A.   A closed-loop theory of motor learning. *Journal of Motor Behavior,* 1971, *3,* 111–149.

Adams, J. A., & Montague, W. E.   Retroactive inhibition and natural language mediation. *Journal of Verbal Learning and Verbal Behavior,* 1967, *6,* 528–535.

Adelson, E. H.   Iconic storage: The role of rods. *Science,* 1978, *201,* 544–546.

Agruso, V. M., Jr.   *Learning in the later years.* New York: Academic Press, 1978.

Aiken, L.   *Later life.* Philadelphia: Saunders, 1978.

Ajuriaguerra, J. de, Muller, M., & Tissot, R.   A propos de quelques problèmas posés par l'apraxie dans les démences. *Encéphale,* 1960, *5,* 375–406.

Alexander, C.   Youth and progress. *Journal of Social Psychology,* 1945, *22,* 209–213.

Allen, G. L., Siegel, A. W., & Rosinski, R. R.   The role of perceptual context in struc-
turing spatial knowledge. *Journal of Experimental Psychology: Human Learning and
Memory,* 1978, *4,* 617–630.

Amberson, J. I., Atkeson, B. M., Pollack, R. H., & Malatesta, V. J.   Age differences in
dark-interval threshold across the life-span. *Experimental Aging Research,* 1979, *5,*
423–433.

Anders, T. R., & Fozard, J. L.   Effects of age upon retrieval from primary and secondary memory. *Developmental Psychology,* 1973, *9,* 411–415.

Anders, T. R., Fozard, J. L., & Lillyquist, T. D.   Effects of age upon retrieval from
short-term memory. *Developmental Psychology,* 1972, *6,* 214–217.

Anderson, D. C., & Borkowski, J. G.   *Experimental psychology.* Glenview, Ill.: Scott,
Foresman, 1978.

Anderson, J. R.   *Cognitive psychology and its implications.* San Francisco: W. H. Freeman, 1980.

Anderson, J. R., & Bower, G. H.   *Human associative memory.* Washington, D.C.: Winston, 1973.

Ankus, M., & Quarrington, B.   Operant behavior in the memory disordered. *Journal of
Gerontology,* 1972, *27,* 500–510.

Anshel, M. H.   Effect of aging on acquisition and short-term retention of a motor skill.
Perceptual and Motor Skills, 1978, *47,* 993–994.

Arenberg, D.   Anticipation interval and age differences in verbal learning. *Journal of
Abnormal Psychology,* 1965, *70,* 419–425.

————.   Regression analyses of verbal learning on adult age differences at two anticipation intervals. *Journal of Gerontology,* 1967, *22,* 411–414. (a)

————.   Age differences in retroaction. *Journal of Gerontology,* 1967, *22,* 88–91. (b)

————.   Concept problem solving in young and old adults. *Journal of Gerontology,*
1968, *23,* 279–282. (a)

————.   Input modality in short-term retention of old and young adults. *Journal of
Gerontology,* 1968, *23,* 462–465. (b)

————.   Cognition and aging: Verbal learning, memory, and problem solving. In C.
Eisdorfer & M. P. Lawton (Eds.), *The psychology of adult development and aging.*
Washington, D.C.: American Psychological Association, 1973.

————.   A longitudinal study of problem solving in adults. *Journal of Gerontology,*
1974, *29,* 650–658.

————.   The effects of input condition on free recall in young and old adults. *Journal
of Gerontology,* 1976, *31,* 551–555.

————.   The effects of auditory augmentation on visual retention for young and old
adults. *Journal of Gerontology,* 1977, *32,* 192–195.

————.   Differences and changes with age in the Benton Visual Retention Test. *Journal of Gerontology,* 1978, *33,* 534–540.

Arenberg, D., & Robertson-Tchabo, E. A.   Learning and aging. In J. E. Birren & K. W.
Schaie (Eds.), *Handbook of the psychology of aging.* New York: Van Nostrand Reinhold, 1977.

Arlin, P. K.   Cognitive development in adulthood: A fifth stage? *Developmental psychology,* 1975, *11,* 602–606.

Arnold, W. R.   *Heart rate response measures related to human abilities: A cross-sectional
evaluation of fluid and crystallized intelligence.* Unpublished doctoral dissertation,
West Virginia University, 1973.

Aronoff, C.   Old age in prime time. *Journal of Communication,* 1974, *24,* 4.

Asch, S. E. Effects of group pressure upon the modification and distortion of judgment. In H. Guetzkow (Ed.), *Groups, leadership, and men.* Pittsburgh: Carnegie Press, 1951.

Atkeson, B. M. Differences in the magnitude of the simultaneous and successive Müller-Lyer illusions from age 20 to 79 years. *Experimental Aging Research,* 1978, *4,* 55–66.

Atkinson, J. W. Motivational determinants of risk-taking behavior. *Psychological Review,* 1957, *64,* 359–372.

Atkinson, R. C., & Juola, J. F. Factors influencing speed and accuracy of word recognition. In S. Kornblum (Ed.), *Attention and performance IV.* New York: Academic Press, 1973.

Atkinson, R. C., & Raugh, M. R. An application of the mnemonic keyword method to the acquisition of a Russian vocabulary. *Journal of Experimental Psychology: Human Learning and Memory,* 1975, *104,* 126–133.

Atkinson, R. C., & Shiffrin, R. M. Human memory: A proposed system and its control processes. In K. W. Spence & J. T. Spence (Eds.), *The psychology of learning and motivation* (Vol. 2). New York: Academic Press, 1968.

Attig, M., & Hasher, L. *Differences in memory processes among adults: Deterioration or response bias?* Paper presented at the annual meeting of the Eastern Psychological Association, Philadelphia, April 1979.

——. The processing of frequency of occurrence information by adults. *Journal of Gerontology,* 1980, *35,* 66–69.

Axelrod, S. Cognitive tasks in several modalities. In R. H. Williams, C. Tibbitts, & W. Donahue (Eds.), *Processes of aging* (Vol. 1). New York: Atherton, 1963.

Axelrod, S., Thompson, L. W., & Cohen, L. D. Effects of senescence on the temporal resolution of somesthetic stimuli presented to one hand or both. *Journal of Gerontology,* 1968, *23,* 191–195.

Ayllon, T., & Azrin, N. H. The measurement and reinforcement of behavior of psychotics. *Journal of Experimental Analysis of Behavior,* 1965, *8,* 357–383.

Baddeley, A. D. The trouble with levels: A reexamination of Craik and Lockhart's framework for memory research. *Psychological Review,* 1978, *85,* 139–152.

——. Applied cognitive and cognitive applied psychology: The case of face recognition. In L. Nilsson (Ed.), *Perspectives on memory research.* Hillsdale, N.J.: Lawrence Erlbaum, 1979.

Baddeley, A. D., & Hitch, G. Working memory. In G. H. Bower (Ed.), *The psychology of learning and motivation* (Vol. 8). New York: Academic Press, 1974.

Baer, D. M. An age-irrelevant concept of development. *Merrill-Palmer Quarterly,* 1970, *16,* 238–246.

Bahrick, H. P. Maintenance of knowledge: Questions about memory we forgot to ask. *Journal of Experimental Psychology: General,* 1979, *108,* 296–308.

Bahrick, H. P., Bahrick, P. O., & Wittlinger, R. P. Fifty years of memory for names and faces: A cross-sectional approach. *Journal of Experimental Psychology: General,* 1975, *104,* 54–75.

Balinsky, B. An analysis of the mental factors of various age groups from nine to sixty. *Genetic Psychology Monographs,* 1941, *23,* 191–234.

Baltes, M. M., & Zerbe, M. B. Re-establishing self-feeding in a nursing home resident. *Nursing Research,* 1976, *25,* 24–26.

Baltes, P. B. Longitudinal and cross-sectional sequences in the study of age and generation effects. *Human Development,* 1968, *11,* 145–171.

Baltes, P. B., & Goulet, L. R.   Status and issues of a life-span developmental psychology. In L. R. Goulet & P. B. Baltes (Eds.), *Life-span developmental psychology: Research and theory.* New York: Academic Press, 1970.

————.   Exploration of developmental variables by manipulation and simulation of age differences in behavior. *Human Development,* 1971, *14,* 149–170.

Baltes, P. B., & Labouvie, G. V.   Adult development of intellectual performance: Description, explanation, and modification. In C. Eisdorfer & M. P. Lawton (Eds.), *The psychology of adult development and aging.* Washington, D.C.: American Psychological Association, 1973.

Baltes, P. B., Nesselroade, J. R., Schaie, K. W., & Labouvie, E. W.   On the dilemma of regression effects in examining ability-level-related differentials in ontogenetic patterns of intelligence. *Developmental Psychology,* 1972, *6,* 78–84.

Baltes, P. B., Reese, H. W., & Nesselroade, J. R. *Life-span developmental psychology: Introduction to research methods.* Monterey, Calif.: Brooks/Cole, 1977.

Baltes, P. B., & Schaie, K. W.   On the plasticity of intelligence in adulthood and old age: Where Horn and Donaldson fail. *American Psychologist,* 1976, *31,* 720–725.

Baron, J., & Treiman, R.   Some problems in the study of differences in cognitive processes. *Memory & Cognition,* 1980, *8,* 313–321.

Baron, R. A., & Byrne, D.   *Social psychology: Understanding human interaction* (2nd ed.) Boston: Allyn & Bacon, 1977.

Barrett, G. V., Mihal, W. L., Panek, P. E., Sterns, H. L., & Alexander, R. A.   Information processing skills predictive of accident involvement for younger and older commercial drivers. *Industrial Gerontology,* 1977, *4,* 173–182.

Barrett, J. H.   *Gerontological psychology.* Springfield, Ill.: Charles C. Thomas, 1972.

Barrett, T. R., & Wright, M.   Age-related facilitation in recall following semantic processing. *Journal of Gerontology,* 1981, *36,* 194–199.

Bartlett, D. F.   Inflation: Our no. 1 enemy. *Catholic Golden Age Newsletter,* 1978, *2,* 1, 3.

Bartlett, F. C.   *Remembering: A study in experimental and social psychology.* Cambridge: At the University Press, 1932.

Bartlett, J. C., & Snelus, P.   Lifespan memory for popular songs. *American Journal of Psychology,* 1980, *93,* 551–560.

Basowitz, H., & Korchin, S. J.   Age differences in the perception of closure. *Journal of Abnormal and Social Psychology,* 1957, *54,* 93–97.

Battig, W. F., & Montague, W. E.   Category norms for verbal items in 56 categories: A replication and extension of the Connecticut category norms. *Journal of Experimental Psychology Monograph,* 1969, *80*(3, Pt. 2).

Baxt, N.   Ueber die Zeitwlche nötig ist, damit ein die Grösse (Extension) der bewussten Wahrnehmung bei einem Gesichtseindrucke von gegenbener Dauer. *Pfluegers Archiv fur die Gesamte Physiologie des Menschen und der Tiere* (Berlin), 1871, *4,* 325–336.

Bayley, N., & Oden, M. H.   The maintenance of intellectual ability in gifted adults. *Journal of Gerontology,* 1955, *10,* 91–107.

Beauvoir, S. de.   *The coming of age.* New York: Putnam, 1972.

Beeson, M. F.   Intelligence at senescence. *Journal of Applied Psychology,* 1920, *4,* 219–234.

Begg, I., & Denny, J. P.   Empirical reconciliation of atmosphere and conversion interpretations of syllogistic reasoning errors. *Journal of Experimental Psychology,* 1969, *81,* 351–354.

Begg, I., & Paivio, A.   Concreteness and imagery in sentence meaning. *Journal of Verbal Learning and Verbal Behavior,* 1969, *8,* 821–827.

Bell, B., Wolf, E., & Bernholz, C. D.   Depth perception as a function of age. *Aging and Human Development,* 1972, *3,* 77–88.

Bell, B. D., & Stanfield, G. G.   Chronological age in relation to attitudinal judgments: An experimental analysis. *Journal of Gerontology,* 1973, *28,* 491-496.

Beller, H. K.   Parallel and serial stages in matching. *Journal of Experimental Psychology,* 1970, *84,* 213-219.

Bellucci, G., & Hoyer, W. J.   Feedback effects on the performance and self-reinforcing behavior of elderly and young adult women. *Journal of Gerontology,* 1975, *30,* 456–460.

Belmore, S. M.   Age-related changes in processing explicit and implicit language. *Journal of Gerontology,* 1981, *36,* 316–322.

Bendig, A. W.   Age differences in the interscale factor structure of the Guilford-Zimmerman Temperament Survey. *Journal of Consulting Psychology,* 1960, *24,* 134–138.

Bennett, R., & Eckman, J.   Attitudes toward aging: A critical examination of recent literature and implications for future research. In C. Eisdorfer & M. P. Lawton (Eds.), *The psychology of adult development and aging.* Washington, D. C.: American Psychological Association, 1973.

Bergman, M., Blumfield, V. G., Cascado, D., Dash, B., Levitt, H., & Margulies, M. K.   Age related decrement in hearing for speech. *Journal of Gerontology,* 1976, *31,* 533–538.

Berkowitz, B.   The Wechsler-Bellevue performance of white males past 50. *Journal of Gerontology,* 1953, *8,* 76–80.

Bernbach, H. A.   Rate of presentation in free recall: A problem for two-stage memory theories. *Journal of Experimental Psychology: Human Learning and Memory,* 1975, *104,* 18–22.

Bielby, D. D., & Papalia, D. E.   Moral development and perceptual role-taking egocentrism: Their development and interrelationship across the life span. *International Journal of Aging & Human Development,* 1975, *6,* 293–307.

Bilash, I., & Zubek, J. P.   The effects of age on factorially "pure" mental abilities. *Journal of Gerontology,* 1960, *15,* 175–182.

Binet, A., & Simon, T.   The development of intelligence in children. *L'Année Psychologique,* 1905, 163–191.

Birkhill, W. R. & Schaie, K. W.   The effect of differential reinforcement of cautiousness in intellectual performance among the elderly. *Journal of Gerontology,* 1975, *30,* 578–583.

Birren, J. E.   *The psychology of aging.* Englewood Cliffs, N.J.: Prentice-Hall, 1964.

———.   Age changes in speed of behavior: Its central nature and physiological correlates. In A. T. Welford & J. E. Birren (Eds.), *Behavior, aging, and the nervous system.* Springfield, Ill.: Charles C. Thomas, 1965.

Birren, J. E., Allen, W. R., & Landau, H. G.   The relation of problem length in simple addition to time required, probability of success, and age. *Journal of Gerontology,* 1954, *9,* 150–161.

Birren, J. E., & Botwinick, J.   The relation of writing speed to age and to the senile psychoses. *Journal of Consulting Psychology,* 1951, *15,* 243–249.

Birren, J. E., & Clayton, V.   History of gerontology. In D. S. Woodruff & J. E. Birren (Eds.), *Aging: Scientific perspectives and social issues.* New York: Van Nostrand, 1975.

Birren, J. E., & Morrison, D. F.   Analysis of the WAIS subtests in relation to age and education. *Journal of Gerontology,* 1961, *16,* 363–369.

Birren, J. E., & Renner, V. J.   Research on the psychology of aging: Principles and experimentation. In J. E. Birren & K. W. Schaie (Eds.), *Handbook of the psychology of aging.* New York: Van Nostrand Reinhold, 1977.

Birren, J. E., Riegel, K. F., & Morrison, D. F.   Age differences in response speed as a function of controlled variations of stimulus conditions: Evidence of a general speed factor. *Gerontologia,* 1962, *6,* 1–18.

Birren, J. E. & Shock, N. W.   Age changes in rate and level of dark adaptation. *Journal of Applied Psychology,* 1950, *26,* 407–411.

Bjorksten, J.   The limitation of creative years. *Scientific Monthly,* 1946, *62,* 94.

Bloom, K. L.   Age and the self-concept. *American Journal of Psychiatry,* 1961, *118,* 534–538.

Blum, J. E., & Jarvik, L. F.   Intellectual performance of octogenarians as a function of education and initial ability. *Human Development,* 1974, *17,* 364–375.

Bolles, R. C.   *Learning theory* (2nd ed.). New York: Holt, Rinehart & Winston, 1979.

Bolton, C. F., Winkelmann, R. K., & Dyck, P. J.   A quantitative study of Meissner's corpuscles in man. *Neurology,* 1966, *16,* 1–9.

Borkan, G. A., & Norris, A. H.   Assessment of biological age using a profile of physical parameters. *Journal of Gerontology,* 1980, *35,* 177–184.

Bortner, R. W., & Hultsch, D. F.   A multivariate analysis of correlates of life satisfaction in adulthood. *Journal of Gerontology,* 1970, *25,* 41–47.

Boswell, D. A.   *Metaphoric processing in the mature years.* Paper presented at the annual meeting of the Gerontological Society, Dallas, Texas, November 1978.

Botwinick, J.   Drives, expectancies, and emotions. In J. E. Birren (Ed.), *Handbook of aging and the individual.* Chicago: University of Chicago Press, 1959.

———.   Cautiousness in advanced age. *Journal of Gerontology,* 1966, *21,* 347–353.

———.   *Cognitive processes in maturity and old age.* New York: Springer, 1967.

———.   Disinclination to venture response versus cautiousness in responding: Age differences. *Journal of Genetic Psychology,* 1969, *115,* 55–62.

———.   Sensory-set factors in age differences in reaction time. *Journal of Genetic Psychology,* 1971, *119,* 241–249.

———.   *Aging and behavior* (1st ed.). New York: Springer, 1973.

———.   Intellectual abilities. In J. E. Birren & K. W. Schaie (Eds.), *Handbook of the psychology of aging.* New York: Van Nostrand Reinhold, 1977.

———.   *Aging and behavior* (2nd ed.). New York: Springer, 1978.

Botwinick, J., & Arenberg, D.   Disparate time spans in sequential studies of aging. *Experimental Aging Research,* 1976, *1,* 55–61.

Botwinick, J., & Birren, J. E.   Cognitive processes: Mental abilities and psychomotor responses in healthy aged men. In J. E. Birren, R. N. Butler, S. W. Greenhouse, L. Sokoloff, & M. R. Yarrow (Eds.), *Human aging,* Public Health Service Publication No. 896. Washington, D.C.: U.S. Government Printing Office, 1963.

———.   A follow-up study of card-sorting performance in elderly men. *Journal of Gerontology,* 1965, *20,* 208–210.

Botwinick, J., Brinley, J. F., & Robbin, J. S.   Maintaining set in relation to motivation and age. *American Journal of Psychology,* 1959, *72,* 585–588.

Botwinick, J., & Kornetsky, C.   Age differences in the acquisition and extinction of GSR. *Journal of Gerontology,* 1960, *15,* 83–84.

Botwinick, J., Robbin, J. S., & Brinley, J. F.   Age differences in card-sorting performance in relation to task difficulty, task set, and practice. *Journal of Experimental Psychology,* 1960, 59, 10–18.

Botwinick, J., & Siegler, I.C.   Intellectual ability among the elderly: Simultaneous cross-sectional and longitudinal comparisons. *Developmental Psychology,* 1980, *16,* 49–53.

Botwinick, J., & Storandt, M.   Cardiovascular status, depressive affect, and other factors in reaction time. *Journal of Gerontology,* 1974, *29,* 543–548. (a)

———.   *Memory, related functions and age.* Springfield, Ill.: Charles C. Thomas, 1974. (b)

———.   Vocabulary ability in later life. *Journal of Genetic Psychology,* 1974, *125,* 303–308. (c)

Botwinick, J., West, R., & Storandt, M.   Predicting death from behavioral test performance. *Journal of Gerontology,* 1978, *33,* 755–762.

Bourne, L. E., Jr.   *Human conceptual behavior.* Boston: Allyn & Bacon, 1966.

Bourne, L. E. Jr., Dominowski, R. L., & Loftus, E. F.   *Cognitive processes.* Englewood Cliffs, N.J.: Prentice-Hall, 1979.

Bousfield, W. A.   The occurrence of clustering in the recall of randomly arranged associates. *Journal of General Psychology,* 1953, *49,* 229–240.

Bower, G. H.   Analysis of a mnemonic device. *American Scientist,* 1970, *58,* 496–510.

Bower, G. H., & Trabasso, T.   Concept identification. In R. C. Atkinson (Ed.), *Studies in mathematical psychology.* Stanford, Calif.: Stanford University Press, 1964.

Boyarsky, R. E., & Eisdorfer, C.   Forgetting in older persons. *Journal of Gerontology,* 1972, *27,* 254–258.

Bradley, R. H., & Webb, R.   Age-related differences in locus of control orientation in three behavioral domains. *Human Development,* 1976, *19,* 49–56.

Bransford, J. D., & Franks, J. J.   The abstraction of linguistic ideas. *Cognitive Psychology,* 1971, *2,* 331–350.

Braun, H. W., & Geiselhart, R.   Age differences in the acquisition and extinction of the conditioned eyelid response. *Journal of Experimental Psychology,* 1959, *57,* 386–388.

Brinley, J. F.   Cognitive sets, speed and accuracy of performance in the elderly. In A. T. Welford & J. E. Birren (Eds.), *Behavior, aging, and the nervous system.* Springfield, Ill.: Charles C. Thomas, 1965.

Brinley, J. F., & Fichter, J.   Performance deficits in the elderly in relation to memory load and set. *Journal of Gerontology,* 1970, *25,* 30–35.

Brinley, J. F., Jovick, T. J., & McLaughlin, L. M.   Age, reasoning, and memory. *Journal of Gerontology,* 1974, *29,* 182–189.

Broadbent, D. E.   *Perception and communication.* London: Pergamon, 1958.

Broadbent, D. E., & Gregory, M.   Some confirmatory results on age differences in memory for simultaneous stimulation. *British Journal of Psychology,* 1965, *56,* 77–80.

Broadbent, D. E., & Heron, A.   Effects of a subsidiary task on performance involving immediate memory in younger and older men. *British Journal of Psychology,* 1962, *53,* 189–198.

Bromley, D. B.   Some experimental tests of the effect of age on creative intellectual output. *Journal of Gerontology,* 1956, *11,* 74–82.

———.   Some effects of age on the quality of intellectual output. *Journal of Gerontology,* 1957, *12,* 318–323.

———.   Some effects of age on short term learning and remembering. *Journal of Gerontology,* 1958, *13,* 398–406.

————. Age and sex differences in the serial reproduction of creative conceptual responses. *Journal of Gerontology,* 1967, *22,* 32–42.

Bronfenbrenner, U. Toward an experimental ecology of human development. *American Psychologist,* 1977, *32,* 513–531.

Brown, J. A. Some tests of the decay theory of immediate memory. *Quarterly Journal of Experimental Psychology,* 1958, *10,* 12–21.

Brozek, J. Personality changes with age: An item analysis of the MMPI. *Journal of Gerontology,* 1955, *10,* 194–206.

Bruner, J. S. On cognitive growth. In J. S. Bruner, R. R. Olver, & P. M. Greenfield (Eds.), *Studies in cognitive growth.* New York: Wiley, 1966.

Bruner, J. S., Goodnow, J. J., & Austin, G. A. *A study of thinking.* New York: Wiley, 1956.

Bryden, M. P. Ear preference in auditory perception. *Journal of Experimental Psychology,* 1963, *65,* 103–105.

Bugelski, B. R. Images as mediators in one-trial paired-associate learning: II. Self-timing in successive lists. *Journal of Experimental Psychology,* 1968, *77,* 328–334.

Bugelski, B. R., Kidd, E., & Segmen, J. Image as a mediator in one-trial paired-associate learning. *Journal of Experimental Psychology,* 1968, *76,* 69–73.

Bühler, C. The curve of life as studies in biographies. *Journal of Applied Science,* 1953, *19,* 405–409.

Bulgarella, R. G., & Archer, E. J. Concept identification of auditory stimuli as a function of amount of relevant and irrelevant information. *Journal of Experimental Psychology,* 1962, *63,* 254–257.

Burke, D. M., & Light, L. L. Memory and aging: The role of retrieval processes. *Psychological Bulletin,* 1981, *90,* 513–546.

Burt, C. The differentiation of intellectual abilities. *British Journal of Educational Psychology,* 1954, *24,* 76–90.

Burton, A., & Joël, W. Adult norms for the Watson-Glaser Tests of Critical Thinking. *Journal of Psychology,* 1945, *19,* 43–48.

Buss, A. R. An extension of developmental models that separate ontogenetic changes and cohort differences. *Psychological Bulletin,* 1973, *80,* 466–479.

Busse, E. W. Psychopathology. In J. E. Birren (Ed.), *Handbook of aging and the individual.* Chicago: University of Chicago Press, 1959.

Busse, E. W., & Pfeiffer, E. *Behavior and adaptation in late life.* Boston: Little, Brown, 1977.

Butler, R. N. Age-ism: Another form of bigotry. *The Gerontologist,* 1969, *9,* 243–246.

————. *Why survive? Being Old in America.* New York: Harper & Row, 1975.

Butler, R. N., & Lewis, M. I. *Aging and mental health: Positive psychological approaches.* St. Louis: C. V. Mosby, 1973.

————. *Aging and mental health* (2nd ed.). St. Louis: C. V. Mosby, 1977.

Butterfield, G. B., & Butterfield, E. C. Lexical codability and age. *Journal of Verbal Learning and Verbal Behavior,* 1977, *16,* 113–118.

Calearo, C., & Lazzaroni, A. Speech intelligibility in relation to the speed of the message. *Laryngoscope,* 1957, *67,* 410–419.

Cameron, D. E. Impairment at the retention phase of remembering. *Psychiatric Quarterly,* 1943, *17,* 395–404.

Campbell, A., Converse, P. E., & Rodgers, W. L. *The quality of American life.* New York: Russell Sage Foundation, 1976.

Campbell, D. T., & Fiske, D. W. Convergent and disciminant validation by the multitrait-multimethod matrix. *Psychological Bulletin,* 1959, *56,* 81–106.

Campbell, D. T., & Stanley, J. C. Experimental and quasi-experimental designs for research on teaching. In N. L. Gage (Ed.), *Handbook for research on teaching.* Chicago: Rand McNally, 1963.

―――. *Experimental and quasi-experimental designs for research.* Chicago: Rand McNally, 1966.

Canestrari, R. E., Jr. Paced and self-paced learning in young and elderly adults. *Journal of Gerontology,* 1963, *18,* 165–168.

―――. Age differences in paired-associate learning as a function of response pretraining. Cited in J. Botwinick, *Cognitive processes in maturity and old age.* New York: Springer, 1967. [Unpublished, 1964.]

―――. The effects of commonality on paired-associate learning in two age groups. *Journal of Genetic Psychology,* 1966, *108,* 3–7.

―――. Age changes in acquisition. In G. A. Talland (Ed.), *Human aging and behavior.* New York: Academic Press, 1968.

Cartwright, D. S. *Introduction to personality.* Chicago: Rand McNally, 1974.

Cattell, J. McK. The time it takes to see and name objects. *Mind,* 1886, *11,* 63–65.

Cattell, R. B. A culture-free intelligence test. *Journal of Educational Psychology,* 1940, *31,* 161–179.

―――. Theory of fluid and crystallized intelligence: A critical experiment. *Journal of Educational Psychology,* 1963, *54,* 1–22.

Cattell, R. B., & Eber, H. W. *The Sixteen Personality Factor Questionnaire Test.* Champaign, Ill: Institute for Personality and Ability Testing, 1957.

Cavanaugh, J. C., & Perlmutter, M. *A diary study of adults' memory.* Paper presented at the annual meeting of the Gerontological Society, Washington, D.C., November, 1979.

Cerella, J., Poon, L. W., & Williams, D. M. A quantitative theory of mental processing time and age. In L. W. Poon (Ed.), *Aging in the 1980's: Selected contemporary issues in the psychology of aging.* Washington, D.C.: American Psychological Association, 1980.

Chance, J., Overcast, T., & Dollinger, S. J. Aging and cognitive regression: Contrary findings. *Journal of Psychology,* 1978, *98,* 177–183.

Chapman, C. M., & Jones, C. M. Variations in cutaneous and visceral pain sensitivity in normal subjects. *Journal of Clinical Investigation,* 1944, *23,* 81–91.

Chapman, L. J., & Chapman, J. P. Atmosphere effect reexamined. *Journal of Experimental Psychology,* 1959, *58,* 220–226.

Charness, N. Aging and skilled problem solving. *Journal of Experimental Psychology: General,* 1981, *110,* 21–38.

Chase, W. G., & Simons, H. A. The mind's eye in chess. In W. G. Chase (Ed.), *Visual information processing.* New York: Academic Press, 1973.

Cherry, C. Some experiments on the recognition of speech with one and two ears. *Journal of the Acoustical Society of America,* 1953, *25,* 975–979.

Chown, S. Age and the rigidities. *Journal of Gerontology,* 1961, *16,* 353–362.

Cicchetti, D. V., Fletcher, C. R., Lerner, E., & Coleman, J. V. The effects of a social medicine course on attitudes of medical students toward the elderly: A controlled study. *Journal of Gerontology,* 1973, *28,* 370–373.

Cicirelli, V. G. Categorization behavior in aging subjects. *Journal of Gerontology,* 1976, *31,* 676–680.

Clark, L. E., & Knowles, J. B. Age differences in dichotic listening performance. *Journal of Gerontology,* 1973, *28,* 173–178.

Clark, W. C., & Mehl, L. A sensory decision theory analysis of the effect of age and sex on d′, various response criteria, and 50% pain threshold. *Journal of Abnormal Psychology,* 1971, *78,* 202–212.

Clay, H. M. Changes of performance with age on tasks of varying complexity. *British Journal of Psychology,* 1954, *45,* 7–13.

———. An age difference in separating spatially contiguous data. *Journal of Gerontology,* 1956, *11,* 318–322.

Cohen, G. Language comprehension in old age. *Cognitive Psychology,* 1979, *11,* 412–429.

Cohen, J. The factorial structure of the WAIS between early adulthood and old age. *Journal of Consulting Psychology,* 1957, *21,* 283–290.

Colavita, F. B. Human sensory dominance. *Perception and Psychophysics,* 1974, *16,* 409–412.

Collins, A. M., & Loftus, E. F. A spreading activation theory of semantic processing. *Psychological Review,* 1975, *82,* 407–428.

Collins, A. M., & Quillian, M. R. Retrieval time from semantic memory. *Journal of Verbal Learning and Verbal Behavior,* 1969, *8,* 240–247.

Collins, A. M., Warnock, E. H., Aiello, N., & Miller, M. L. Reasoning from incomplete knowledge. In D. G. Bobrow & A. Collins (Eds.), *Representation and understanding.* New York: Academic Press, 1975.

Comalli, P.E., Jr., Wapner, S., & Werner, H. Perception of verticality in middle and old age. *Journal of Psychology,* 1959, *47,* 252–266.

———. Interference effects of Stroop color-word test in childhood, adulthood, and aging. *Journal of Genetic Psychology,* 1962, *100,* 47–53.

Comfort, A. *A good age.* New York: Simon & Schuster, 1976.

Conrad, R. Acoustic confusions in immediate memory. *British Journal of Psychology,* 1964, *55,* 75–84.

Cooper, L. A., & Shepard, R. N. The time required to prepare for a rotated stimulus. *Memory & Cognition,* 1973, *1,* 246–250.

Cooper, R. M., Bilash, M. A., & Zubek, J. P. The effect of age on taste sensitivity. *Journal of Gerontology,* 1959, *14,* 56–58.

Coppinger, N. W., & Nehrke, M. F. Discrimination learning and transfer of training in the aged. *Journal of Genetic Psychology,* 1972, *120,* 93–102.

Corsini, R. J., & Fassett, K. K. Intelligence and aging. *Journal of Genetic Psychology,* 1953, *83,* 249–264.

Corso, J. F. Age and sex differences in pure-tone thresholds. *Archives of Otolaryngology,* 1963, *77,* 385–405.

———. Sensory processes and age effects in normal adults. *Journal of Gerontology,* 1971, *26,* 90–105.

———. Auditory perception and communication. In J. E. Birren & K. W. Schaie (Eds.), *Handbook of the psychology of aging.* New York: Van Nostrand Reinhold, 1977.

———. *Aging sensory systems and perception.* New York: Praeger, 1981.

Cosh, J. A. Studies on the nature of vibration. *Clinical Science,* 1953, *12,* 131–151.

Costa, P. T., Jr., Fozard, J. L., McCrae, R. R., & Bosse, R. Relations of age and personality dimensions to cognitive ability. *Journal of Gerontology,* 1976, *31,* 663–669.

Costa, P. T., Jr., & McCrae, R. R. Age differences in personality structure: A cluster analytic approach. *Journal of Gerontology,* 1976, *31,* 564–570.

———. Age differences in personality structure revisited: Studies in validity, stability, and change. *International Journal of Aging and Human Development,* 1977, *8,* 261–275.

———. Objective personality assessment. In M. Storandt, I. C. Siegler, & M. F. Elias (Eds.), *The clinical psychology of aging.* New York: Plenum, 1978.

———. Still stable after all these years: Personality as a key to some issues in aging. In P. B. Baltes & O. G. Brim, Jr., (Eds.), *Life-span development and behavior* (Vol. 3). New York: Academic Press, 1980.

Costa, P. T., Jr., McCrae, R. R., & Arenberg, D. Enduring dispositions in adult males. *Journal of Personality and Social Psychology,* 1980, *38,* 793–800.

Cowart, D. A., Atkeson, B., & Pollack, R. B. Figural aftereffects in adulthood. *Bulletin of the Psychonomic Society,* 1979, *14,* 326–328.

Coyne, A. C., Eiler, J. M., Vanderplas, J. M., & Botwinick, J. Stimulus persistence and age. *Experimental Aging Research,* 1979, *5,* 263–270.

Craik, F. I. M. An observed age difference in response to a personality inventory. *British Journal of Psychology,* 1964, *55,* 453–462.

———. The nature of the age decrement in performance on dichotic listening tasks. *Quarterly Journal of Experimental Psychology,* 1965, *17,* 222–240.

———. The effects of aging on the detection of faint auditory signals. In *Proceedings of the 7th International Congress of Gerontology,* (Vol. 6), Vienna: Viennese Medical Academy, 1966.

———. Two components in free recall. *Journal of Verbal Learning and Verbal Behavior,* 1968, *7,* 996–1004.

———. Age differences in recognition memory. *Quarterly Journal of Experimental Psychology,* 1971, *23,* 316–323.

———. *Signal detection analyses of age differences in divided attention.* Paper presented at the annual meeting of the American Psychological Association, Montreal, Canada, August 1973.

———. Age differences in human memory. In J. E. Birren & K. W. Schaie (Eds.), *Handbook of the psychology of aging.* New York: Van Nostrand Reinhold, 1977.

Craik, F. I. M., & Lockhart, R. S. Levels of processing: A framework for memory research. *Journal of Verbal Learning and Verbal Behavior,* 1972, *11,* 671–684.

Craik, F. I. M., & Masani, P. A. Age differences in the temporal integration of language. *British Journal of Psychology,* 1967, *58,* 291–299.

———. Age and intelligence differences in coding and retrieval of word lists. *British Journal of Psychology,* 1969, 60, 315–319.

Craik, F. I. M., & Simon, E. Age differences in memory: The roles of attention and depth of processing. In L. W. Poon, J. L. Fozard, L. S. Cermak, D. Arenberg, & L. W. Thompson (Eds.), *New directions in memory and aging.* Hillsdale, N.J.: Lawrence Erlbaum, 1980.

Crandall, R. C. *Gerontology: A behavioral science approach.* Reading, Mass.: Addison-Wesley, 1980.

Crook, M. N., Alexander, E. A., Anderson, E. M. S., Coules, J., Hanson, J. A., & Jeffries, N. T. *Age and form perception* (Report No. 57–124). Randolph AFB, Tex.: USAF School of Aviation Medicine, 1958.

Cropper, D. A., Meek, D. S., & Ash, M. J. The relation between formal operations and a possible fifth stage of cognitive development. *Developmental Psychology,* 1977, *13,* 517–518.

Crossman, E. R. F. W., & Szafran, J. Changes with age in the speed of information-intake and discrimination. *Experimentia Supplementum IV.* Basel, Switzerland: Birkhauser, 1956.

Crovitz, E. Reversing a learning deficit in the aged. *Journal of Gerontology,* 1966, *21,* 236–238.

Crowder, R. G. *Principles of learning and memory.* Hillsdale, N.J.: Lawrence Erlbaum, 1976.

———. Echoic memory and the study of aging memory systems. In L. W. Poon, J. L. Fozard, L. S. Cermak, D. Arenberg, & L. W. Thompson (Eds.), *New directions in memory and aging.* Hillsdale, N.J.: Lawrence Erlbaum, 1980.

Crowder, R. G., & Morton, J. Precategorical acoustic storage (PAS). *Perception and Psychophysics,* 1969, *5,* 365–373.

Cumming, E., & Henry, W. E. *Growing old: The process of disengagement.* New York: Basic Books, 1961.

Cunningham, W. R., & Birren, J. E. Age changes in human abilities: A 28-year longitudinal study. *Developmental Psychology,* 1976, *12,* 81–82.

Cunningham, W. R., Clayton, V., & Overton, W. Fluid and crystallized intelligence in young adulthood and old age. *Journal of Gerontology,* 1975, *30,* 53–55.

Cunningham, W. R., Sepkoski, C. M., & Opel, M. R. Fatigue effects on intelligence test performance in the elderly. *Journal of Gerontology,* 1978, *33,* 541–545.

Curtis, H. J. *Biological mechanisms of aging.* Springfield, Ill.: Charles C. Thomas, 1966.

Cutler, N. E. Generation, maturation, and party affiliation: A cohort analysis. *Public Opinion Quarterly,* 1969, *33,* 583–588.

———. Age variations in the dimensionality of life satisfaction. *Journal of Gerontology,* 1979, *34,* 573–578.

Cutler, N. E., & Harootyan, R. A. Demography of the aged. In D. S. Woodruff & J. E. Birren (Eds.), *Aging: Scientific perspective and social issues.* New York: Van Nostrand, 1975.

Cutler, N. E., & Schmidhauser, J. R. Age and political behavior. In D. S. Woodruff & J. E. Birren (Eds.), *Aging: Scientific perspective and social issues.* New York: Van Nostrand, 1975.

Cutler, S. J. Voluntary association participation and life satisfaction: A cautionary research note. *Journal of Gerontology,* 1973, *28,* 96–100.

Cutler, S. J., Lentz, S. A., Muha, M. J., & Riter, R. N. Aging and conservatism: Cohort changes in attitudes about legalized abortion. *Journal of Gerontology,* 1980, *35,* 115–123.

Dalderup, L. M., & Fredericks, M. L. C. Colour sensitivity in old age. *Journal of the American Geriatric Society,* 1969, *17,* 388–390.

Danziger, W. L. Measurement of response bias in aging research. In L. W. Poon (Ed.), *Aging in the 1980's: Selected contemporary issues in the psychology of aging.* Washington, D.C.: American Psychological Association, 1980.

Danziger, W. L., & Botwinick, J. Age and sex differences in sensitivity and response bias in a weight discrimination task. *Journal of Gerontology,* 1980, *35,* 388–394.

Danziger, W. L., & Salthouse, T. A. Age and the perception of incomplete figures. *Experimental Aging Research,* 1978, *4,* 67–80.

Darley, J. M. Glucksberg, S., Kamin, L. J., & Kinchla, R. A. *Psychology.* Englewood Cliffs, N.J.: Prentice-Hall, 1981.

Darwin, C. J., Turvey, M. T., & Crowder, R. G. An auditory analogue of the Sperling partial-report procedure: Evidence for brief auditory storage. *Cognitive Psychology,* 1972, *3,* 255–267.

Davis, G. A. Current status of research and theory in human problem solving. *Psychological Bulletin.* 1966, *66,* 36–54.

Davis, R. H. Television communication and the elderly. In D. S. Woodruff & J. E.

Birren (Eds.), *Aging: Scientific perspectives and social issues.* New York: Van Nostrand, 1975.

Davis, S. H., & Obrist, W. D. Age differences in learning and retention of verbal material. *Cornell Journal of Social Relations,* 1966, *1,* 95–103.

Demming, J. A., & Pressey, S. L. Tests "indigenous" to the adult and older years. *Journal of Counseling Psychology,* 1957, *2,* 144–148.

Denney, D. R., & Denney, N. W. The use of classification for problem solving: A comparison of middle and old age. *Developmental Psychology,* 1973, *9,* 275–278.

Denney, N. W. Clustering in middle and old age. *Developmental Psychology,* 1974, *10,* 471–475. (a)

———. Classification abilities in the elderly. *Journal of Gerontology,* 1974, *29,* 309–314. (b)

Denney, N. W., & Denney, D. R. Modeling effects on the questioning strategies of the elderly. *Developmental Psychology,* 1974, *10,* 458.

Denney, N. W., Jones, F. W., & Krigel, S. H. Modifying the questioning strategies of young children and elderly adults with strategy-modeling techniques. *Human Development,* 1979, *22,* 23–36.

Denney, N. W., & Lennon, M. I. Classification: A comparison of middle and old age. *Developmental Psychology,* 1972, *7,* 210–213.

Denney N. W., & Palmer, A. M. Adult age differences on traditional and practical problem solving measures. *Journal of Gerontology,* 1981, *36,* 323–328.

Dennis, W. Age and achievement: A critique. *Journal of Gerontology,* 1956, *11,* 331–333. (a)

———. Age and productivity among scientists. *Science,* 1956, *123,* 724–725. (b)

———. The age decrement in outstanding scientific contributions: Fact or artifact? *American Psychologist,* 1958, *13,* 457–460.

———. Creative productivity between ages of 20 and 80 years. *Journal of Gerontology,* 1966, *21,* 1–8.

Deutsch, J. A., & Deutsch, D. Attention: Some theoretical considerations. *Psychological Review,* 1963, *70,* 80–90.

Devaney, K. O., & Johnson, H. A. Neuron loss in the aging visual cortex of man. *Journal of Gerontology,* 1980, *35,* 836–841.

deVries, H. A. Physiology of exercise and aging. In D. S. Woodruff & J. E. Birren (Eds.), *Aging: Scientific perspective and social issues.* New York: Van Nostrand, 1975.

Diamond, M. C. The aging brain: Some enlightening and optimistic results. *American Scientist,* 1978, *66,* 66–71.

Domey, R. G., McFarland, R. A., & Chadwick, E. Dark adaptation as a function of age and time: II. A derivation. *Journal of Gerontology,* 1960, *15,* 267–279

Donders, F. C. [On the speed of mental processes.] In W. G. Koster (Ed. and trans.), *Attention and performance II.* Amsterdam: North Holland, 1969. (Reprinted from *Acta Psychologica,* 1969, *30,* 412–431.)

Doppelt, J. E., & Wallace, W. L. Standardization of the Wechsler Adult Intelligence Scale for older persons. *Journal of Abnormal and Social Psychology,* 1955, *51,* 312–330.

Doty, B. A. Age and avoidance conditioning in rats. *Journal of Gerontology,* 1966, *21,* 287–290. (a)

———. Age differences in avoidance conditioning as a function of distribution of trials and task difficulty. *Journal of Genetic Psychology,* 1966, *109,* 249–254. (b)

Doty, B. A., & Doty, L. A. Effect of age and chlorpromazine on memory consolidation. *Journal of Comparative and Physiological Psychology,* 1964, *57,* 331–334.

Doty, B. A., & Johnston, M. M. Effects of post-trial eserine administration, age and task difficulty on avoidance conditioning in rats. *Psychonomic Science,* 1966, *6,* 101–102.

Douglas, K., & Arenberg, D. Age changes, cohort differences, and cultural change on the Guilford-Zimmerman Temperament Survey. *Journal of Gerontology,* 1978, *33,* 737–747.

Douglass, E. B., Cleveland, W. P., & Maddox, G. L. Political attitudes, age, and aging: A cohort analysis of archival data. *Journal of Gerontology,* 1974, *29,* 666–675.

Drachman, D., & Leavitt, J. Memory impairment in the aged: Storage versus retrieval deficit. *Journal of Experimental Psychology,* 1972, *93,* 302–308.

Duffy, E. *Activation and behavior.* New York: Wiley, 1962.

Duke, M. P., Shaheen, J., & Nowicki, S. The determination of locus of control in a geriatric population and a subsequent test of the social learning model for interpersonal distances. *Journal of Psychology,* 1974, *86,* 277–285.

Dunham, P. J. *Experimental psychology: Theory and practice.* New York: Harper & Row, 1977.

Ebbinghaus, H. *Uber das gedächtnis: Untersuchungen zur experimentellen psychologie.* Leipzig: Duncker and Humbolt, 1885.

Edwards, J. N., & Klemmack, D. L. Correlates of life satisfaction. *Journal of Gerontology,* 1973, *28,* 497–502.

Eichorn, D. The Institute of Human Development Studies: Berkeley and Oakland. In L. F. Jarvik, C. Eisdorfer, & J. E. Blum (Eds.), *Intellectual functioning in adults: Psychological and biological influences.* New York: Springer, 1973.

Eisdorfer, C. Changes in cognitive functioning in relation to intellectual level in senescence. In C. Tibbits & W. Donahue (Eds.), *Social and psychological aspects of aging.* New York: Columbia University Press, 1962.

———. Verbal learning and response time in the aged. *Journal of Genetic Psychology,* 1965, *107,* 15–22.

———. New dimensions and a tentative theory. *The Gerontologist,* 1967, *7,* 14–18.

Eisdorfer, C., & Axelrod, S. Senescence and figural aftereffects in two modalities: A correction. *Journal of Genetic Psychology,* 1964, *104,* 193–197.

Eisdorfer, C., Axelrod, S., & Wilkie, F. L. Stimulus exposure time as a factor in serial learning in an aged sample. *Journal of Abnormal and Social Psychology,* 1963, *67,* 594–600.

Eisdorfer, C., & Cohen, L. D. The generality of the WAIS standardization for the aged: A regional comparison. *Journal of Abnormal and Social Psychology,* 1961, *62,* 520–527.

Eisdorfer, C., Nowlin, J., & Wilkie, F. Improvement of learning in the aged by modification of autonomic nervous system activity. *Science,* 1970, *170,* 1327–1329.

Eisdorfer, C., & Service, C. Verbal rote learning and superior intelligence in the aged. *Journal of Gerontology,* 1967, *22,* 158–161.

Eisner, D. A. Developmental relationships between field independence and fixity-mobility. *Perceptual and Motor Skills,* 1972, *34,* 767–770.

Eisner, D. A., & Schaie, K. W. Age changes in response to visual illusions from middle to old age. *Journal of Gerontology,* 1971, *26,* 146–150.

Ekstrand, B. R., Wallace, W. P., & Underwood, B. J. A frequency theory of verbal discrimination learnings. *Psychological Review,* 1966, *73,* 566–578.

Elias, C. S., & Hirasuna, N. Age and semantic and phonological encoding. *Developmental Psychology,* 1976, *12,* 497–503.

Elias, J. W., & Elias, M. F.　Matching of successive auditory stimuli as a function of age and ear of presentation. *Journal of Gerontology,* 1976, *31,* 164–169.

Elias, M. F., & Elias, P. K.　Motivation and activity. In J. E. Birren & K. W. Schaie (Eds.), *Handbook of the psychology of aging.* New York: Van Nostrand Reinhold, 1977.

Ellis, H. C.　*Fundamentals of human learning, memory, and cognition.* (2nd ed.). Dubuque, Iowa: William C. Brown, 1978.

Ellis, H. C., Bennett, T. L., Daniel, T. C., & Rickert, E. J.　*Psychology of learning and memory.* Monterey, Calif: Brooks/Cole, 1979.

Elo, A. E.　Age changes in master chess performance. *Journal of Gerontology,* 1965, *20,* 289–299.

Elwell, F., & Maltbie-Crannell, A. D.　The impact of role loss upon coping resources and life satisfaction of the elderly. *Journal of Gerontology,* 1981, *36,* 223–232.

Emmerich, H. J.　Developmental differences in ratings of meaningfulness, concreteness, and picturability. *Developmental Psychology,* 1979, *15,* 464–466.

Engen, T.　Taste and smell. In J. E. Birren & K. W. Schaie (Eds.), *Handbook of the psychology of aging.* New York: Van Nostrand Reinhold, 1977.

Erber, J. T.　Age differences in recognition memory. *Journal of Gerontology,* 1974, *29,* 177–181.

————.　Age differences in learning and memory on a digit-symbol substitution task. *Experimental Aging Research,* 1976, *2,* 45–53.

————.　Age differences in a controlled-lag recognition. *Experimental Aging Research,* 1978, *4,* 195–206.

————.　*The effect of encoding instructions on recall and recognition memory.* Paper presented at the annual meeting of the Gerontological Society, Washington, D.C., November 1979.

————.　Remote memory and age: A review, *Experimental Aging Research,* 1981, *7,* 189–200.

Erber, J. T., Botwinick, J., & Storandt, M.　The impact of memory on age differences in digit symbol performance. *Journal of Gerontology,* in press.

Erber, J. T., Herman, T. G., & Botwinick, J.　Age differences in memory as a function of depth of processing. *Experimental Aging Research,* 1980, *6,* 341–348.

Eriksen, C. W., & Collins, J. F.　Some temporal characteristics of visual pattern perception. *Journal of Experimental Psychology,* 1967, *74,* 476–484.

Eriksen, C. W., Hamlin, R. M., & Breitmeyer, R. G.　Temporal factors in visual perception as related to aging. *Perception and Psychophysics,* 1970, *7,* 354–356.

Eriksen, C. W., Hamlin, R. M., & Daye, C.　Aging adults and rate of memory scan. *Bulletin of the Psychonomic Society,* 1973, *1,* 259–260.

Erikson, E. H.　Identity and the life cycle. *Psychological Issues,* 1959, *1* (Whole No. 1).

Estes, W. K.　The information-processing approach to cognition: A confluence of metaphors and methods. In W. K. Estes (Ed.), *Handbook of learning and cognitive processes,* (Vol. 6). Hillsdale, N.J.: Lawrence Erlbaum, 1978.

Everitt, A. V., & Burgess, J. A.　(Eds.) *Hypothalamus, pituitary and aging.* Springfield, Ill.: Charles C. Thomas, 1976.

Eysenck, M. W.　Age differences in incidental learning. *Developmental Psychology,* 1974, *10,* 936–941.

————.　Retrieval from semantic memory as a function of age. *Journal of Gerontology,* 1975, *30,* 174–180.

————.　*Human memory: Theory, research and individual differences.* Oxford: Pergamon, 1977.

Fakouri, M. E. "Cognitive development in adulthood: A fifth stage?" A critique. *Developmental Psychology,* 1976, *12,* 472.

Falk, J. L., & Kline, D. W. Stimulus persistence in CFF: Overarousal or underactivation? *Experimental Aging Research,* 1978, *4,* 109–123.

Farkas, M. S., & Hoyer, W. J. Processing consequences of perceptual grouping in selective attention. *Journal of Gerontology,* 1980, *35,* 207–216.

Farnham-Diggory, S. (Ed.) *Information processing in children.* New York: Academic Press, 1972.

Feifel, H., & Branscomb, A. B. Who's afraid of death? *Journal of Abnormal Psychology,* 1973, *81,* 282–288.

Felton, B., & Kahana, E. Adjustment and situationally-bound locus of control among institutionalized aged. *Journal of Gerontology,* 1974, *29,* 295–301.

Ferguson, E. D. *Motivation: An experimental approach.* New York: Holt, Rinehart & Winston, 1976.

Ferris, S. H., Crook, T., Clark, E., McCarthy, M., & Rae, D. Facial recognition memory deficits in normal aging and senile dementia. *Journal of Gerontology,* 1980, *35,* 707–714.

Finch, D. E., & Hayflick, L. (Eds.) *Handbook of the biology of aging.* New York: Van Nostrand Reinhold, 1977.

Fisher, J. Competence, effectiveness, intellectual functioning. *The Gerontologist,* 1973, *13,* 62–68.

Fitts, P. M. Perceptual-motor skill learning. In A. W. Melton (Ed.), *Categories of human learning.* New York: Academic Press, 1964.

Flavell, J. H. Cognitive changes in adulthood. In L. R. Goulet and P. B. Baltes (Eds.), *Life-span developmental psychology: Research and theory.* New York: Academic Press, 1970.

Flavell, J. H. & Wellman, H. W. Metamemory. In R. V. Kail & J. W. Hagen (Eds.), *Perspectives on the development of memory and cognition.* Hillsdale, N.J.: Lawrence Erlbaum, 1977.

Fleming, C. C., & Lopez, M. A. The effects of perceived control on the paired-associate learning of elderly persons. *Experimental Aging Research,* 1981, *7,* 71–77.

Ford, J. M., Hink, R. F., Hopkins, W. F., III., Roth, W. T., Pfefferbaum, A., & Kopell, B. S. Age effects on event-related potentials in a selective attention task. *Journal of Gerontology,* 1979, *34,* 388–395.

Foulds, G. A., & Raven, J. C. Normal changes in the mental abilities of adults as age advances. *Journal of Mental Science,* 1948, *94,* 133–142.

Fox, C., & Birren, J. E. The differential decline of subtest scores of the Wechsler-Bellevue Intelligence Scale in 60–69 year old individuals. *Journal of Genetic Psychology,* 1950, *77,* 313–317.

Fozard, J. L., Thomas, J. C., Jr., & Waugh, N. C. Effects of age and frequency of stimulus repetitions on two-choice reaction time. *Journal of Gerontology,* 1976, *31,* 556–563.

Fozard, J. L., Wolf, E., Bell, B., McFarland, R. A., & Podolsky, S. Visual perception and communication. In J. E. Birren & K. W. Schaie (Eds.), *Handbook of the psychology of aging.* New York: Van Nostrand Reinhold, 1977.

Freedman, J. L., & Loftus, E. F. The retrieval of words from long-term memory. *Journal of Verbal Learning and Verbal Behavior,* 1971, *10,* 107–115.

Freund, J. S., & Witte, K. L. Paired-associate transfer: Age of subjects, anticipation interval, association value, and paradigm. *American Journal of Psychology,* 1976, *89,* 695–705.

————. *Recognition and frequency judgments in young and elderly adults.* Paper presented at the annual meeting of the Psychonomic Society, San Antonio, Texas, November 1978.

————. *Learning-to-learn paired associates in young and elderly adults.* Paper presented at the annual meeting of the Gerontological Society, Washington, D.C., November 1979.

Friedman, H.   Interrelation of two types of immediate memory in the aged. *Journal of Psychology,* 1974, *87,* 177–181.

Friend, C. M., & Zubek, J. P.   The effects of age on critical thinking ability. *Journal of Gerontology,* 1958, *13,* 407–413.

Furry, C. A., & Baltes, P. B.   The effect of age differences in ability-extraneous performance variables on the assessment of intelligence in children, adults, and the elderly. *Journal of Gerontology,* 1973, *28,* 73–80.

Furry, C. A., & Schaie, K. W.   Pretest activity and intellectual performance in middle-aged and older persons. *Experimental Aging Research,* 1979. *53,* 413–421.

Gaffney, M., & Lair, C. V.   *The influences of individual differences and situational factors on the cautious behavior of young and elderly people.* Paper presented at the annual meeting of the Gerontological Society, Washington, D.C., November 1979.

Gaitz, C.   *Aging and the brain.* New York: Plenum, 1971.

Galton, F.   On the anthropometric laboratory at the late International Health Exhibition. *Journal of the Anthropological Institute,* 1885, *14,* 205–221, 275–287.

Gardner, E. F., & Monge, R. H.   Adult age differences in cognitive abilities and educational background. *Experimental Aging Research.* 1977, *3,* 337–383.

Garfield, S., & Blek, L.   Age, vocabulary level, and mental impairment. *Journal of Consulting Psychology,* 1952, *16,* 395–398.

Garrett, H. E.   A developmental theory of intelligence. *American Psychologist,* 1946, *1,* 372–378.

Gaylord, S. A., & Marsh, G. R.   Age differences in the speed of a spatial cognitive process. *Journal of Gerontology,* 1975, *30,* 674–678.

Geiselman, R. E., & Bellezza, F. S.   Long-term memory for speaker's voice and source location. *Memory & Cognition,* 1976, *4,* 483–489.

————. Incidental retention of speaker's voice. *Memory & Cognition,* 1977, *5,* 658–665.

George, L. K.   The impact of personality and social status factors upon levels of activity and psychological well-being. *Journal of Gerontology,* 1978, *33,* 840–847.

Giambra, L. M., & Arenberg, D.   Problem solving, concept learning, and aging. In L. W. Poon (Ed.), *Aging in the 1980's: Selected contemporary issues in the psychology of aging.* Washington, D.C.: American Psychological Association, 1980.

Gibson, E. J. & Yonas, A.   A developmental study of the effects of visual and auditory interference on a visual scanning task. *Psychonomic Science,* 1966, *5,* 163–164.

Gilbert, J. G.   Mental efficiency in senescence. *Archives of Psychology,* 1935, *27,* No. 188.

————. Memory loss in senescence. *Journal of Abnormal and Social Psychology,* 1941, *36,* 73–86.

————. Age changes in color matching. *Journal of Gerontology,* 1957, *12,* 210–215.

————. Thirty-five year follow-up study of intellectual functioning. *Journal of Gerontology,* 1973, *28,* 68–72.

Gilson, E. Q., & Baddeley, A. D.   Tactile short-term memory. *Quarterly Journal of Experimental Psychology,* 1969, *21,* 180–184.

Gladis, M., & Braun, H.   Age differences in transfer and retroaction as a function of intertask response similarity. *Journal of Experimental Psychology,* 1958, *55,* 25–30.

Glamser, F. D.   The importance of age to conservative opinions: A multivariate analysis. *Journal of Gerontology,* 1974, *29,* 549–554.

Glanzer, M., & Cunitz, A.   Two storage mechanisms in free recall. *Journal of Verbal Learning and Verbal Behavior,* 1966, *5,* 351–360.

Glass, A. L., Holyoak, K. J., & Santa, J. L.   *Cognition.* Reading, Mass.: Addison-Wesley, 1979.

Glenberg, A. M., & Adams, F.   Type I rehearsal and recognition. *Journal of Verbal Learning and Verbal Behavior,* 1978, *17,* 455–464.

Glenberg, A. M., & Bradley, M. M.   Mental contiguity. *Journal of Experimental Psychology: Human Learning and Memory,* 1979, *5,* 88–97.

Goldfarb, W.   An investigation of reaction time in older adults and its relationship to certain observed mental test patterns. *Contributions to Education* (No. 831). New York: Teachers College, Columbia University, 1941.

Goldstein, G. & Shelly, C. H.   Similarities and differences between psychological deficit in aging and brain damage. *Journal of Gerontology,* 1975, *30,* 448–455.

Goodrick, C. L.   Operant level and light-contingent bar presses as a function of age and deprivation. *Psychological Reports,* 1965, *17,* 283–288.

————.   Operant responding of nondeprived young and senescent male albino rats. *Journal of Genetic Psychology,* 1969, *114,* 29–40.

————.   Light- and dark-contingent bar pressing in the rat as a function of age and motivation. *Journal of Comparative and Physiological Psychology,* 1970, *73,* 100–104.

————.   Learning by mature-young and aged Wistar albino rats as a function of test complexity. *Journal of Gerontology,* 1972, *27,* 353–357.

Gordon, S. K.   Organization and recall of related sentences by elderly and young adults. *Experimental Aging Research,* 1975, *1,* 71–80

Gordon, S. K., & Clark, W. C.   Adult age differences in word and nonsense syllable recognition memory and response criterion. *Journal of Gerontology,* 1974, *29,* 659–665. (a)

————.   Application of signal detection theory to prose recall and recognition in elderly and young adults. *Journal of Gerontology,* 1974, *29,* 64–72. (b)

Gough, H. G.   *Manual for the California Psychological Inventory* (Rev. ed.). Palo Alto, Calif. Consulting Psychologists Press, 1964.

Goulet, L. R.   New directions of research on aging and retention. *Journal of Gerontology,* 1972, *27,* 52–60.

Granick, S., Kleban, M. H., & Weiss, A. D.   Relationships between hearing loss and cognition in normally hearing aged persons. *Journal of Gerontology,* 1976, *31,* 434–440.

Grant, E. A., Storandt, M., & Botwinick, J.   Incentive and practice in the psychomotor performance of the elderly. *Journal of Gerontology,* 1978, *33,* 413–415.

Green, D. M., & Swets, J. A.   *Signal detection theory and psychophysics.* New York: Wiley, 1966.

Green, R. F.   Age-intelligence relationship between ages sixteen and sixty-four: A rising trend. *Developmental Psychology,* 1969, *1,* 618–627.

Green, R. F., & Berkowitz, B.   Changes in intellect with age: II. Factorial analysis of Wechsler-Bellevue scores. *Journal of Genetic Psychology,* 1964, *104,* 3–18.

Gregory, R. L.   Increase in "neurological noise" as a factor in aging. In *Proceedings of the 4th Congress of the International Association of Gerontology; Merano, Italy, 1957.* Merano, Italy: International Association of Gerontology, 1957.

Griew, S.   Learning of statistical structure: A preliminary study in relation to age. In C.

Tibbitts & W. Donahue (Eds.), *Social and psychological aspects of aging.* New York: Columbia University Press, 1962.

———. Age and the matching of signal frequency in a two-channel detection task. *Journal of Gerontology,* 1968, *23,* 93–96.

Griew, S., Fellows, B. J., & Howes, R. Duration of spiral aftereffect as a function of stimulus exposure and age. *Perceptual and Motor Skills,* 1963, *17,* 210.

Gruber, H. E. Courage and cognitive growth in children and scientist. In M. Schwebel & J. Raph (Eds.), *Piaget in the classroom.* New York: Basic Books, 1973.

Grzegorczyk, P. B., Jones, S. W., & Mistretta, C. M. Age-related differences in salt taste acuity. *Journal of Gerontology,* 1979, *34,* 834–840.

Guilford, J. P. The structure of intellect. *Psychological Bulletin,* 1956, *53,* 267–293.

———. Fluid and crystallized intelligences: Two fanciful concepts. *Psychological Bulletin,* 1980, *88,* 406–412.

Guilford, J. P., & Zimmerman, W. S. *The Guilford-Zimmerman temperament survey: Manual of instructions and interpretations.* Beverly Hills, Calif.: Sheridan Supply Co., 1949.

Gurland, B. J. The comparative frequency of depression in various adult age groups. *Journal of Gerontology,* 1976, *31,* 283–292.

Guthrie, E. R. *The psychology of learning.* New York: Harper & Row, 1935.

Gutman, M. A. The effects of age and extraversion on pursuit rotor reminiscence. *Journal of Gerontology,* 1965, *20,* 346–350.

Gutmann, D. The cross-cultural perspective: Notes toward a comparative psychology of aging. In J. E. Birren & K. W. Schaie (Eds.), *Handbook of the psychology of aging.* New York: Van Nostrand Reinhold, 1977.

Gynther, M. D. Aging and personality. In J. N. Butcher (Ed.), *New developments in the use of the MMPI.* Minneapolis: University of Minnesota Press, 1979.

Hall, C. S., & Lindzey, G. *Theories of personality.* New York: Wiley, 1957.

Harkins, S. W., & Chapman, C. R. Detection and decision factors in pain perception in young and elderly men. *Pain,* 1976, *2,* 253–264.

———. The perception of induced dental pain in young and elderly women. *Journal of Gerontology,* 1977, *32,* 428–435.

Harkins, S. W., Chapman, C. R., & Eisdorfer, C. Memory loss and response bias in senescence. *Journal of Gerontology,* 1979, *34,* 66–72.

Harmatz, J. S., & Shader, R. I. Pharmacologic investigations in healthy elderly volunteers: MMPI depression scale. *Journal of the American Geriatric Society,* 1975, *23,* 350–354.

Harris, C. S. *Fact book on aging: A profile of America's older population.* Washington, D.C.: National Council on the Aging, 1978.

Hartley, J. T., Harker, J. O., & Walsh, D. A. Contemporary issues and new directions in adult development of learning and memory. In L. W. Poon (Ed.), *Aging in the 1980's: Some contemporary issues in the psychology of aging.* Washington, D.C.: American Psychological Association, 1980.

Hartley, J. T., & Walsh, D. A. The effect of monetary incentive on amount and rate of free recall in older and younger adults. *Journal of Gerontology,* 1980, *35,* 899–905.

Harwood, E., & Naylor, G. F. K. Recall and recognition in elderly and young subjects. *Australian Journal of Psychology,* 1969, *21,* 251–257.

Hasher, L., & Chromiak, W. The processing of frequency information: An automatic mechanism? *Journal of Verbal Learning and Verbal Behavior,* 1977, *16,* 173–184.

Hasher, L., & Zacks, R. T. Automatic and effortful processes in memory. *Journal of Experimental Psychology: General,* 1979, *108,* 356–388.

Hayflick, L.   The limited *in vitro* lifetime of human diploid cell strains. *Experimental Cell Research,* 1965, *37,* 614–636.

———.   Biomedical gerontology: Current theories of biological aging. *The Gerontologist,* 1974, *14,* 454; 458.

Haygood, R. C., & Bourne, L. E., Jr.   Attribute and rule-learning aspects of conceptual behavior. *Psychological Review,* 1965, *72,* 175–195.

Hays, W. L.   *Statistics for psychologists.* New York: Holt, Rinehart & Winston, 1963.

Hayslip, B., Jr.   Determinants of anagram problem solution in adulthood. *Experimental Aging Research,* 1977, *3,* 147–163.

Hayslip, B., Jr., & Sterns, H. L.   Age differences in relationships between crystallized and fluid intelligence and problem solving. *Journal of Geronotology,* 1979, *34,* 404–414.

Heglin, H.   Problem solving set in different age groups. *Journal of Gerontology,* 1956, *11,* 310–317.

Hellebusch, S. J.   On improving learning and memory in the aged: The effects of mnemonics on strategy, tra .sfer, and generalization. (Doctoral dissertation, University of Notre Dame, 1976). *Dissertation Abstracts International,* 1976, 1459-B. (University Microfilms No. 76–19, 496).

Herman, G. E., Warren, L. R., & Wagener, J. W.   Auditory lateralization: Age differences in sensitivity to dichotic time and amplitude cues. *Journal of Gerontology,* 1977, *32,* 187–191.

Herman, J. F., & Coyne, A. C.   *Mental transformation of spatial information in cognitive maps.* Paper presented at the annual meeting of the Gerontological Society, Washington, D.C., November 1979.

Heron, A., & Chown, S. M.   *Age and function.* London: Churchill, 1967.

Heron, A., & Craik, F. I. M.   Age differences in cumulative learning of meaningful and meaningless material. *Scandinavian Journal of Psychology,* 1964, *5,* 209–217.

Hertzog, C. K.   Applications of signal detection theory to the study of psychological aging: A theoretical review. In L. W. Poon (Ed.), *Aging in the 1980's: Selected contemporary issues in the psychology of aging.* Washington, D.C.: American Psychological Association, 1980.

Hertzog, C. K., Schaie, K. W., & Gribbin, K.   Cardiovascular disease and changes in intellectual function from middle to old age. *Journal of Gerontology,* 1978, *33,* 872–883.

Hertzog, C. K., Williams, M. V., & Walsh, D. A.   The effect of practice on age differences in central perceptual processing. *Journal of Gerontology,* 1976, *31,* 428–433.

Herzog, A. R.   Attitude change in older age: An experimental study. *Journal of Gerontology,* 1979, *34,* 697–703.

Hess, A., & Bradshaw, H. L.   Positiveness of self-concept and ideal self as a function of age. *Journal of Genetic Psychology,* 1970, *117,* 56–67.

Heston, J. C., & Cannell, C. F.   A note on the relation between age and performance of adult subjects on four familiar psychometric tests, *Journal of Applied Psychology,* 1941, *25,* 415–419.

Heyn, J. E., Barry, J. R., & Pollack, R. H.   Problem solving as a function of age, sex and the role appropriateness of the problem content. *Experimental Aging Research,* 1978, *4,* 505–519.

Hicks, L. H., & Birren, J. E.   Aging, brain damage, and psychomotor slowing. *Psychological Bulletin,* 1970, *74,* 377–396.

Hill, L. B.   A second quarter century of delayed recall or relearning at 80. *Journal of Educational Psychology,* 1957, *48,* 65–68.

Hines, T. M., & Posner, M. I. *Slow but sure: A chronometric analysis of the process of aging.* Paper presented at the American Psychological Association Symposium on Decision Making and Aging, Washington, D.C., August, 1976.

Hintzman, D. L. Apparent frequency as a function of frequency and the spacing of repetitions. *Journal of Experimental Psychology,* 1969, *80,* 139–145.

Hintzman, D. L., Block, R. A., & Inskeep, N. R. Memory for mode of input. *Journal of Verbal Learning and Verbal Behavior,* 1972, *11,* 741–749.

Hiroto, D. S. Locus of control and learned helplessness. *Journal of Experimental Psychology,* 1974, *102,* 187–193.

Hochberg, J. E. *Perception* (2nd ed.). Englewood Cliffs, N.J.: Prentice-Hall, 1978.

Hodgkins, J. Influence of age on the speed of reaction and movement in females. *Journal of Gerontology,* 1962, *17,* 385–389.

Holding, D. H. Sensory storage reconsidered. *Memory & Cognition,* 1975, *3,* 31–41.

Hooper, F. M. *Life-span analyses of Piagetian concept tasks: The search for nontrivial qualitative change.* Paper presented at the biennial meeting of the International Society for the Study of Behavioral Development, Ann Arbor, Michigan, June 1973.

Hooper, F. M., Fitzgerald, J., & Papalia, D. Piagetian theory and the aging process: Extensions and speculations. *Aging and Human Development,* 1971, *2,* 3–20.

Hooper, F M., & Sheehan, N. W. Logical concept attainment during the aging years: Issues in the neo-Piagetian research literature. In W. F. Overton & J. M. Gallagher (Eds.), *Knowledge and development: Vol. 1., Advances in research and theory.* New York: Plenum, 1977.

Hopkins, B., & Post, F. The significance of abstract and concrete behavior in elderly psychiatric patients and control subjects. *Journal of Mental Science,* 1955, *101,* 841–850.

Horn, J. L. Organization of data on life-span development of human abilities. In L. R. Goulet & P. B. Baltes (Eds.), *Life-span developmental psychology.* New York: Academic Press, 1970.

———. "Gf-Gc sampler." Mimeographed. Denver, Colo.: University of Denver, 1975.

———. Human ability systems. In P. B. Baltes (Ed.), *Life-span development and behavior* (Vol. 1). New York: Academic Press, 1978.

———. Concepts of intellect in relation to learning and adult development. *Intelligence,* 1980, *4,* 285–317.

Horn, J. L., & Cattell, R. B. Age differences in fluid and crystallized intelligence. *Acta Psychologica,* 1967, *26,* 107–129.

Horn, J. L., & Donaldson, G. On the myth of intellectual decline in adulthood. *American Psychologist,* 1976, *31,* 701–719.

———. Faith is not enough: A response to the Baltes-Schaie claim that intelligence does not wane. *American Psychologist,* 1977, *32,* 369–373.

Horn, J. L., Donaldson, G., & Engstrom, R. Apprehension, memory, and fluid intelligence decline in adulthood. *Research on Aging,* 1981, *3,* 33–84.

Hornblum, J. N., & Overton, W. F. Area and volume conservation among the elderly: Assessment and training. *Developmental Psychology,* 1976, *12,* 68–74.

Houston-Stein, A., & Baltes, P. B. Theory and method in life-span developmental psychology: Implications for child development. In H. W. Reese (Ed.), *Advances in child development and behavior* (Vol. 11). New York: Academic Press, 1976.

Hoving, K. L., Spencer, T., Robb, K. Y., & Schulte, D. Developmental changes in visual information processing. In P. A. Ornstein (Ed.), *Memory development in children.* Hillsdale, N.J.: Lawrence Erlbaum, 1978.

Howard, D. V. Category norms: A comparison of the Battig and Montague (1969) norms with the responses of adults between the ages of 20 and 80. *Journal of Gerontology,* 1980, *35,* 225–231.

Howard, D. V. Lasaga, M. I., & McAndrews, M. P. Semantic activation during memory encoding across the adult life span. *Journal of Gerontology,* 1980, *35,* 884–890.

Howard, D. V., McAndrews, M. D., & Lasaga, M. I. Semantic priming of lexical decision in young and old adults. *Journal of Gerontology,* in press.

Howell, R. J. Sex differences and educational influences on a mental deterioration scale. *Journal of Gerontology,* 1955, *10,* 190–193.

Hoyer, F. W., Hoyer, W. J., Treat, N. J., & Baltes, P. B. Training response speed in young and elderly women. *International Journal of Aging and Human Development,* 1978–1979, *9,* 247–253.

Hoyer, W. J., Labouvie, G. V., & Baltes, P. B. Modification of response speed deficits and intellectual performance in the elderly. *Human Development,* 1973, *16,* 233–242.

Hoyer, W. J., Rebok, G. W., & Sved, S. M. Effects of varying irrelevant information on adult age differences in problem solving. *Journal of Gerontology,* 1979, *14,* 553–560.

Hoyt, D. R., Kaiser, M. A., Peters, G. R., & Babchuk, N. Life satisfaction and activity theory: A multidimensional approach. *Journal of Gerontology,* 1980, *35,* 935–941.

Hubbert, H. B. The effect of age on habit formation in the albino rat. *Behavior Monographs,* 1915, *2.*

Hubel, D. H., & Wiesel, T. N. Receptive fields of single neurones in the cat's striate cortex. *Journal of Physiology,* 1959, *148,* 574–591.

Hulicka, I. M. *Age group comparisons for the use of mediators.* Paper presented at the annual meeting of the Southwestern Psychological Association, Oklahoma City, Oklahoma, April 1965.

————. Age changes and age differences in memory functioning. *The Gerontologist,* 1967, *7,* 46–54. (c)

————. Age differences in retention as a function of interference. *Journal of Gerontology,* 1967, *22,* 180–184. (b)

————. Age differences in Wechsler Memory Scale scores. *Journal of Genetic Psychology,* 1966, *109,* 134–145.

————. Short-term learning and memory efficiency as a function of age and health. *Journal of the American Geriatric Society,* 1967, *15,* 285–294. (a)

Hulicka, I. M., & Grossman, J. L. Age-group comparisons for the use of mediators in paired associate learning. *Journal of Gerontology,* 1967, *22,* 46–51.

Hulicka, I. M., Sterns, H., & Grossman, J. L. Age-group comparisons of paired-associate learning as a function of paced and self-paced association and response times. *Journal of Gerontology,* 1967, *22,* 274–280.

Hulicka, I. M., & Weiss, R. L. Age differences in retention as a function of learning. *Journal of Consulting Psychology,* 1965, *29,* 125–129.

Hull, C. L. Knowledge and purpose as habit mechanisms. *Psychological Review,* 1930, *37,* 511–525.

————. Goal attraction and directing ideas conceived as habit phenomena. *Psychological Review,* 1931, *38,* 487–506.

————. *Principles of behavior.* New York: Appleton-Century-Crofts, 1943.

Hultsch, D. F. Adult age differences in the organization of free recall. *Developmental Psychology,* 1969, *1,* 673–678.

————. Organization and memory in adulthood. *Human Development,* 1971, *14,* 16–29. (a)

————. Adult age differences in free-classification and free-recall. *Developmental Psychology,* 1971, *4,* 338–342. (b)

————. Learning to learn in adulthood. *Journal of Gerontology,* 1974, *29,* 302–308.

————. Adult age differences in retrieval: Trace-dependent and cue-dependent forgetting. *Developmental Psychology,* 1975, *11,* 197–201.

————. Changing perspectives on basic research in adult learning and memory. *Educational Gerontology,* 1977, *2,* 367–382.

Hultsch, D. F., & Craig, E. R. Adult age differences in the inhibition of recall as a function of retrieval cues. *Developmental Psychology,* 1976, *12,* 83–84.

Hultsch, D. F., & Plemons, J. K. Life events and life-span development. In P. B. Baltes & O. G. Brim, Jr. (Eds.), *Life-span development and behavior* (Vol. 2). New York: Academic Press, 1979.

Humphreys, L. G. Doing research the hard way: Substituting analysis of variance for a problem in correlational analysis. *Journal of Educational Psychology,* 1978, *70,* 873–876.

Hunt, E. Mechanics of verbal ability. *Psychological Review,* 1978, *85,* 109–130.

Hunt, E., Frost, N., & Lunneborg, C. Individual differences in cognition: A new approach to intelligence. In G. H. Bower (Ed.), *The psychology of learning and motivation* (Vol. 7). New York: Academic Press, 1973.

Hunt, R. R., & Elliott, J. M. The role of nonsemantic information in memory: Orthograpic distinctiveness effects on retention. *Journal of Experimental Psychology: General,* 1980, *109,* 49–74.

Hunt, W. L. The relative rates of decline of Wechsler-Bellevue "hold" and "don't hold" tests. *Journal of Consulting Psychology,* 1949, *13,* 440–443.

Husband, R. W. Certain age effects on maze performance. *Journal of Genetic Psychology,* 1930, *37,* 325–328.

Hutman, L. P., & Sekuler, R. Spatial vision and aging: II. Criterion effects. *Journal of Gerontology,* 1980, *35,* 700–706.

Hutto, G. L., & Smith, R. C. *The self-report of anxiety in adults: The effects of age and other variables on STAI scores.* Paper presented at the annual meeting of the Southwestern Psychological Association, Oklahoma City, April 1980.

Hyde, T. S., & Jenkins, J. J. Differential effects of incidental tasks on the organization of recall of a list of highly associated words. *Journal of Experimental Psychology,* 1969, *82,* 472–481.

Inglis, J. Learning, retention and conceptual usage in elderly patients with memory disorder. *Journal of Abnormal and Social Psychology,* 1959, *59,* 210–215.

Inglis, J., & Caird, W. K. Age differences in successive responses to simultaneous stimulation. *Canadian Journal of Psychology,* 1963, *17,* 98–105.

Jacewicz, M. M. & Hartley, A. A. Rotation of mental images by young and old college students: The effects of familiarity. *Journal of Gerontology,* 1979, *34,* 396–403.

Jacoby, L. L. On interpreting the effects of repetition: Solving a problem versus remembering a solution. *Journal of Verbal Learning and Verbal Behavior,* 1978, *17,* 649–667.

Jakubczak, L. F. Age and animal behavior. In C. Eisdorfer & M. P. Lawton (Eds.), *The Psychology of adult development and aging.* Washington, D.C.: American Psychological Association, 1973.

James, W. *Principles of psychology.* New York: Henry Holt, 1890.

Jarvik, L. F., & Falek, A. Intellectual stability and survival in the aged. *Journal of Gerontology,* 1963, *18,* 173–176.

Jensen, A. R. An empirical theory of the serial-position effect. *Journal of Psychology,* 1962, *53,* 127–142. (a)

———. Transfer between paired-associate and serial learning. *Journal of Verbal Learning and Verbal Behavior,* 1962, *1,* 269–280. (b)

Jernigan, T. L., Zatz, L. M., Feinberg, I., & Fein, G. Measurement of cerebral atrophy in the aged by computed tomography. In L. W. Poon (Ed.), *Aging in the 1980's: Selected contemporary issues in the psychology of aging.* Washington, D.C.: American Psychological Association, 1980.

Jerome, E. A. Age and learning—Experimental studies. In J. E. Birren (Ed.), *Handbook of aging and the individual. Chicago: University of Chicago Press, 1959.*

———. Decay of heuristic processes in the aged. In C. Tibbitts & W. Donahue (Eds.), *Social and Psychological aspects of aging.* New York: Columbia University Press, 1962.

Johnson, D. M. *Systematic introduction to the psychology of thinking.* New York: Harper & Row, 1972.

Johnson, P. J. Nature of mediational responses in concept-identification problems. *Journal of Experimental Psychology,* 1967, *73,* 391–393.

Jones, H. E. Intelligence and problem-solving. In J. E. Birren (Ed.), *Handbook of aging and the individual.* Chicago: University of Chicago Press, 1959.

Jones, H. E., & Conrad, H. S. The growth and decline of intelligence: A study of a homogeneous group between the ages of ten and sixty. *Genetic Psychology Monographs,* 1933, *13,* 223–298.

Jordan, T. C., & Rabbitt, P. M. A. Response times to stimuli of increasing complexity as a function of ageing. *British Journal of Psychology,* 1977, *68,* 189–201.

Kahana, E., & Coe, R. M. Dimensions of conformity: A multidisciplinary view. *Journal of Gerontology,* 1969, *24,* 76–81.

Kahneman, D. Method, findings, and theory in studies of visual masking. *Psychological Bulletin,* 1968, *70,* 404–425.

———. *Attention and effort.* Englewood Cliffs, N.J.: Prentice-Hall, 1973.

Kalish, R. A. An approach to the study of death attitudes. *American Behavioral Scientist,* 1963, *6,* 68–80.

———. Death and dying in a social context. In R. H. Binstock & E. Shanas (Eds.), *Handbook of aging and the social sciences.* New York: Van Nostrand Reinhold, 1976.

Kalish, R. A., & Reynolds, D. K. *Death and ethnicity: A psychocultural study.* Los Angeles: University of Southern California Press, 1976.

Kamin, L. J. Differential changes in mental ability in old age. *Journal of Gerontology,* 1957, *12,* 66–70.

Kausler, D. H. Comparison of anticipation and recall methods for geriatric subjects. *Psychological Reports,* 1963, *13,* 702.

———. Retention-forgetting as a nomological network for developmental research. In L. R. Goulet & P. B. Baltes (Eds.), *Life-span developmental psychology: Research and theory.* New York: Academic Press, 1970.

———. *Psychology of verbal learning and memory.* New York: Academic Press, 1974.

———. Comments on Winn and Elias: Testing the rehearsal deficit hypothesis. *Experimental Aging Research,* 1978, *4,* 343–347.

———. Imagery ratings for young and elderly adults. *Experimental Aging Research,* 1980, *6,* 185–188.

Kausler, D. H., Hakami, M., & Wright, R. E. Adult age differences in frequency judgments of categorical representations. *Journal of Gerontology,* in press.

Kausler, D. H., & Kanoti, G. A.   R-S learning and negative transfer effects with a mixed list. *Journal of Experimental Psychology,* 1963, *65,* 201–205.

Kausler, D. H., & Kleim, D. M.   Age differences in processing relevant versus irrelevant stimuli in multiple item recognition learning. *Journal of Gerontology,* 1978, *33,* 87–93.

Kausler, D. H., & Lair, C. V.   R-S ("backward") paired-associate learning in elderly subjects. *Journal of Gerontology,* 1965, *20,* 29–31.

———.   Associative strength and paired-associate learning in elderly subjects. *Journal of Gerontology,* 1966, *21,* 278–280.

Kausler, D. H., Pavur, E. J., Jr., & Yadrick, R. M.   Single-item recognition following a verbal discrimination study trial. *Memory & Cognition,* 1975, *3,* 135–139.

Kausler, D. H., & Puckett, J. M.   Effects of word frequency on adult age differences in word memory span. *Experimental Aging Research,* 1979, *5,* 161–169.

———.   Frequency judgments and correlated cognitive abilites in young and elderly adults. *Journal of Gerontology,* 1980, *35,* 376–382. (a)

———.   Adult age differences in recognition memory for a nonsemantic attribute. *Experimental Aging Research,* 1980, *6,* 349–355. (b)

———.   Adult age differences in memory for sex of voice. *Journal of Gerontology,* 1981, *36,* 44–50. (a)

———.   Adult age differences in memory for modality attributes. *Experimental Aging Research,* 1981, *7,* 117–125.

———.   Modality memory and frequency of occurrence memory for young and middle-aged adults. *Experimental Aging Research,* in press.

Kay, H.   The effects of position in a display upon problem solving. *Quarterly Journal of Experimental Psychology,* 1954, *6,* 155–169.

———.   Some experiments on adult learning. In *Old age in the modern world.* Edinburgh, Scotland: Livingstone, 1955.

Keele, S. W.   Movement control in skilled motor performance. *Psychological Bulletin,* 1968, *70,* 387–403.

Keevil-Rogers, P., & Schnore, M. M.   Short-term memory as a function of age in persons of above average intelligence. *Journal of Gerontology,* 1969, *24,* 184–188.

Kellas, G., McCauley, C., & McFarland, C. E.   Re-examination of externalized rehearsal. *Journal of Experimental Psychology: Human Learning and Memory,* 1975, *104,* 84–90.

Kendler, H. H., & Kendler, T. S.   Vertical and horizontal processes in human problem solving. *Psychological Review,* 1962, *69,* 1–18.

Kenshalo, D. R.   Age changes in touch, vibration, temperature, kinesthesis, and pain sensitivity. In J. E. Birren & K. W. Schaie (Eds.), *Handbook of the psychology of aging.* New York: Van Nostrand Reinhold, 1977.

Keppel, G., & Mallory, W. A.   Presentation rate and instruction to guess in free recall. *Journal of Experimental Psychology,* 1969, *79,* 269–275.

Keppel, G., & Underwood, B. J.   Proactive inhibition in short-term retention of single items. *Journal of Verbal Learning and Verbal Behavior,* 1962, *1,* 153–161.

Kesler, M. S., Denney, N. W., & Whitely, S. E.   Factors influencing problem solving in middle-aged and elderly adults. *Human Development,* 1976, *19,* 310–320.

Kessen, W.   Research design in the study of developmental problems. In P. H. Mussen (Ed.), *Handbook of research methods in child development.* New York: Wiley, 1960.

Kimble, G. A., & Pennypacker, H. W.   Eyelid conditioning in young and aged subjects. *Journal of Genetic Psychology,* 1963, *103,* 283–289.

Kimura, D. Cerebral dominance and the perception of verbal stimuli, *Canadian Journal of Psychology,* 1961, *15,* 166–171.

King, H. F. An age-analysis of some agricultural accidents. *Occupational Psychology,* 1955, *29,* 245–255.

Kinsbourne, M. & Berryhill, J. L. The nature of the interaction between pacing and the age decrement in learning. *Journal of Gerontology,* 1972, *27,* 471–477.

Kintsch, W. *The representation of meaning in memory.* Hillsdale, N.J.: Lawrence Erlbaum, 1974.

Kirchner, W. K. Age differences in short-term retention of rapidly changing information. *Journal of Experimental Psychology,* 1958, *55,* 352–358.

Klahr, D., & Wallace, J. G. *Cognitive development.* Hillsdale, N.J.: Lawrence Erlbaum, 1976.

Kleemeier, R. W. Intellectual change in the senium. In *Proceedings of the Social Statistics Section of the American Statistical Association,* 1962, *1,* 290–295.

Klein, R. L. Age, sex, and task difficulty as predictors of social conformity. *Journal of Gerontology,* 1972, *27,* 229–236.

Klein, R. L., & Birren, J. E. Age differences in social conformity on a task of auditory signal detection. In *Proceedings of the 80th Annual Convention* of the American Psychological Association, Washington, D.C. American Psychological Association, 1972.

Kleinman, J. M. & Brodzinsky, D. M. Haptic exploration in young, middle-aged, and elderly adults. *Journal of Gerontology,* 1978, *33,* 521–527.

Kline, D. W., Culler, M. P., & Sucec, J. Differences in inconspicuous word identification as a function of age and reversible-figure training. *Experimental Aging Research,* 1977, *3,* 203–213.

Kline, D. W., Hogan, P. M., & Stier, D. L. Age and the identification of inconspicuous words. *Experimental Aging Research,* 1980, *6,* 137–148.

Kline, D. W., & Nestor, S. Persistence of complementary afterimages as a function of adult age and exposure duration. *Experimental Aging Research,* 1977, *3,* 191–201.

Kline, D. W., & Orme-Rogers, C. Examination of stimulus persistence as the basis for superior visual identification performance among older adults. *Journal of Gerontology,* 1978, *33,* 76–81.

Kline, D. W., & Schieber, F. What are the age differences in visual sensory memory? *Journal of Gerontology,* 1981, *36,* 86–89.

Kline, D., & Szafran, J. Age differences in backward monoptic visual noise masking. *Journal of Gerontology,* 1975, *30,* 307–311.

Kogan, N. Creativity and cognitive style: A life-span perspective. In P. B. Baltes & K. W. Schaie (Eds.), *Life-span developmental psychology: Personality and socialization.* New York: Academic Press, 1973.

———. Categorization and conceptualizing styles in younger and older adults. *Human Development,* 1974, *17,* 218–230.

Köhler, W. *The mentality of apes.* New York: Harcourt, Brace & World, 1925.

König, J. Pitch discrimination and age. *Acta Oto-Laryngologica,* 1957, *48,* 473–489.

Korchin, S. J., & Basowitz, H. Age differences in verbal learning. *Journal of Abnormal and Social Psychology,* 1957, *54,* 64–69.

Krantz, D. S., & Stone, V. Locus of control and the effects of success and failure in young and community-residing aged women. *Journal of Personality,* 1978, *46,* 536–551.

Krauss, I. K., & Quayhagen, M. *Maximizing spatial task performance.* Paper presented at the annual meeting of the Gerontological Society, San Francisco, California, November 1977.

Krauss, I. K., Quayhagen, M, & Schaie, K. W.   Spatial rotation in the elderly: Performance factors. *Journal of Gerontology,* 1980, *35,* 199–206.

Krauss, I. K., & Schaie, K. W.   *Errors in spatial rotation in the elderly.* Paper presented at the annual meeting of American Psychological Association, Washington, D.C., September 1976.

Kriauciunas, R.   The relationship of age and retention interval activity in short term memory. *Journal of Gerontology,* 1968, *23,* 169–173.

Kroll, N. E. A., Parks, T., Parkinson, S. P., Bieber, S. L., & Johnson, A. L.   Short-term memory while shadowing: Recall of visually and aurally presented letters. *Journal of Experimental Psychology,* 1970, *85,* 220–224.

Kuhlen, R. G.   Social change: A neglected factor in psychological studies of the life-span. *School and Society,* 1940, *52,* 14–16.

Kuhn, T. S.   *The structure of scientific revolutions.* Chicago: University of Chicago Press, 1962.

Kuypers, J. A.   Internal-external locus of control, ego functioning and personality characteristics in old age. *The Gerontologist,* 1972, *12,* 168–173.

Kvale, S.   Dialectics and research on remembering. In N. Datan & H. W. Reese (Eds.), *Life-span developmental psychology: Dialectical perspectives on experimental research.* New York: Academic Press, 1977.

Labouvie-Vief, G., Campbell, S., Weaver, S., & Tannenhaus, M.   *Metaphoric processing in young and old adults.* Paper presented at the annual meeting of the Gerontological Society, Washington, D.C., November 1979.

Labouvie-Vief, G., & Chandler, M. J.   Cognitive development and life-span developmental theory: Idealistic versus contextual perspectives. In P. B. Baltes (Ed.), *Life-span development and behavior* (Vol. 1). New York: Academic Press, 1978.

Labouvie-Vief, G., & Gonda, J. N.   Cognitive strategy and intellectual performance in the elderly. *Journal of Gerontology,* 1976, *31,* 327–332.

Lachman, J. L., Lachman, R., & Thronesbery, C.   Metamemory through the adult life span. *Developmental Psychology,* 1979, *15,* 543–551.

Lachman, R., Lachman, J. L., & Butterfield, E. C.   *Cognitive psychology and information processing.* Hillsdale, N.J.: Lawrence Erlbaum, 1979.

Lair, C. V., & Moon, H. W.   The effects of praise and reproof on performance of middle aged and older subjects. *Aging and Human Development,* 1972, *3,* 279–284.

Lair, C. V., Moon, W. H., & Kausler, D. H.   Associative interference in the paired-associate learning of middle-aged and old subjects. *Developmental Psychology,* 1969, *1,* 548–552.

Lakowski, R.   Is the deterioration of colour discrimination with age due to lens or retinal changes? *Farbe,* 1962, *11,* 69–86.

Langer, E. J., Rodin, J., Beck, P., Weinman, C., & Spitzer, L.   Environmental determinants of memory improvement in late adulthood. *Journal of Personality and Social Psychology,* 1979, *37,* 2003–2013.

Larson, R.   Thirty years of research on the subjective well-being of older Americans. *Journal of Gerontology,* 1978, *33,* 109–125.

Lashley, K. S.   The acquisition of skill in archery. *Papers from the Tortugas Laboratory of the Carnegie Institution of Washington,* 1915, *7,* 105–128.

———.   The problem of serial order in behavior. In L. A. Jeffress (Ed.), *Cerebral mechanisms in behavior: The Hixon Symposium.* New York: Wiley, 1951.

Lauer, P. A.   The effects of different types of word processing on memory performance in young and elderly adults (Doctoral dissertation, University of Colorado, 1975) *Dissertation Abstracts International*, 1976, *36*, 5833-B. (University Microfilms No. 76-11, 591)

Laurence, M. W.   Age differences in performance and subjective organization in the free recall of pictorial material. *Canadian Journal of Psychology*, 1966, *20*, 388–399.

————.   Memory loss with age: A test of two strategies for its retardation. *Psychonomic Science*, 1967, *9*, 209–210.

Lawton, M. P.   The Philadelphia Geriatric Center Morale Scale: A revision. *Journal of Gerontology*, 1975, *30*, 85–89.

Lawton, M. P., & Simon, B. B.   The ecology of social relationships in housing for the elderly. *The Gerontologist*, 1968, *8*, 108–115.

Lawton, M. P., Whelihan, W. M., & Belsky, J. K. Personality tests and their uses with older adults. In J. E. Birren & R. B. Sloane (Eds.), *Handbook of mental health and aging*. Englewood Cliffs, N.J.: Prentice-Hall, 1980.

Layton, B.   Perceptual noise and aging. *Psychological Bulletin*, 1975, *82*, 875–883.

Lee, J. A., & Pollack, R. H.   The effect of age on perceptual problem-solving strategies. *Experimental Aging Research*, 1978, *4*, 37–54.

Leech, S., & Witte, K. L.   Paired-associate learning in elderly adults as related to pacing and incentive conditions. *Developmental Psychology*, 1971, *5*, 180.

Lefcourt, H. M.   *Locus of control: Current trends in theory and research*. Hilldale, N.J.: Lawrence Erlbaum, 1976.

Lehman, H. C.   The creative years: Oil paintings, etchings, and architectural works. *Psychological Review*, 1942, *49*, 19–42.

————.   *Age and achievement*. Princeton, N.J.: Princeton University Press, 1953.

————.   Reply to Dennis' critique of *Age and achievement*. *Journal of Gerontology*, 1956, *11*, 333–337.

————.   The influence of longevity upon curves showing man's creative production rate at successive age levels. *Journal of Gerontology*, 1958, *13*, 187–191.

————.   The age decrement in outstanding scientific creativity. *American Psychologist*, 1960, *15*, 128–134.

Lehman, H. C., & Gamertsfelder, W. S.   Man's creative years in philosophy. *Psychological Review*, 1942, *49*, 319–343.

Leibowitz, H., & Judisch, J. M.   Size constancy in older persons: A function of distance. *American Journal of Psychology*, 1967, *80*, 294–296.

Lemon, B., Bengston, V., & Peterson, J.   An explanation of the activity theory of aging: Activity tapes and life satisfaction among in-movers to a retirement community. *Journal of Gerontology*, 1972, *27*, 511–523.

Leon, G. R., Gillum, B., Gillum, R., & Gouze, M.   Personality stability and change over a 30 year period—middle age to old age. *Journal of Consulting and Clinical Psychology*, 1979, *47*, 517–524.

Levendusky, P. G.   Effects of social incentives on task performance in the elderly. *Journal of Gerontology*, 1978, *33*, 562–566.

Levine, M.   *A cognitive theory of learning*. Hillsdale, N.J.: Lawrence Erlbaum, 1975.

Levinson, D. J.   Middle adulthood in modern society: A sociopsychological view. In G. DiRenzo (Ed.), *Social character and social change*. Westport, Conn.: Greenwood Press, 1977.

————.   *The seasons of a man's life*. New York: Ballantine, 1978.

Lewin K.   *A dynamic theory of personality*. New York: McGraw-Hill, 1935.

————.   *Field theory in social science*. New York: Harper & Bros., 1951.

Lieberman, M. A. Psychological correlates of impending death: Some preliminary observations. *Journal of Gerontology,* 1965, *20,* 181–190.

Light, L. L., & Berger, D. E. Are there long-term "literal copies" of visually presented words? *Journal of Experimental Psychology: Human Learning and Memory,* 1976, *2,* 654–662.

Light, L. L., Berger, D. E., & Bardales, M. Trade-off between memory for verbal items and their visual attributes. *Journal of Experimental Psychology: Human Learning and Memory,* 1975, *104,* 188–193.

Linton, M. Memory for real-world events. In D. A. Norman & D. E. Rumelhart (Eds.), *Explorations in cognition.* San Francisco: W. H. Freeman, 1975.

Loftus, E. F., Freedman, J. L., & Loftus, G. R. Retrieval of words from subordinate hierarchies. *Psychonomic Science,* 1970, *21,* 235–236.

Loftus, G. R. On interpretation of interactions. *Memory & Cognition,* 1978, *6,* 312–319.

Logan, F. A. Hybrid theory of classical conditioning. In G. H. Bower (Ed.), *The psychology of learning and motivation: Advances in research and theory* (Vol. 11). New York: Academic Press, 1977.

Lohmann, N. Correlations of life satisfaction, morale, and adjustment measures. *Journal of Gerontology,* 1977, *32,* 73–75.

Longino, C. F., Jr., & Kitson, G. C. Parish clergy and the aged: Examining stereotypes. *Journal of Gerontology,* 1976, *31,* 340–345.

Looft, W. R. Egocentrism and social interaction across the life-span. *Psychological Bulletin,* 1972, *78,* 73–92.

———. Socialization and personality throughout the life span: An examination of contemporary psychological approaches. In P. B. Baltes & K. W. Schaie (Eds.), *Life-span development psychology: Personality and socialization.* New York: Academic Press, 1973.

Looft, W. R., & Charles, D. C. Egocentrism and social interaction in young and old adults. *Aging and Human Development,* 1971, *2,* 21–28.

Lorden, R., Atkeson, B. M., & Pollack, R. H. Differences in the magnitude of the Delboeuf illusion and Usnadze effect during adulthood. *Journal of Gerontology,* 1979, *34,* 229–233.

Lorge, I. The influence of the test upon the nature of mental decline as a function of age. *Journal of Educational Psychology,* 1936, *27,* 100–110.

Lowenthal, M. F., Berkman, P. L., Beuhler, J. A., Pierce, R. C., Robinson, B. C., & Trier, M. L. *Aging and mental disorder in San Francisco.* San Francisco: Jossey-Bass, 1967.

Lyons, J. Chronological age, professional age, and eminence in psychology. *American Psychologist,* 1968, *23,* 371–373.

Mack, J. L., & Carlson, N. J. Conceptual deficits and aging: The category test. *Perceptual and Motor Skills,* 1978, *46,* 123–128.

MacKinnon, D. W. The nature and nurture of creative talent. *American Psychologist,* 1962, *17,* 484–495.

Madden, D. J., & Nebes, R. D. Aging and the development of automaticity in visual search. *Developmental Psychology,* 1980, *16,* 377–384.

Maddox, G. L. Disengagement theory: A critical evaluation. *The Gerontologist,* 1964, *4,* 80–83.

Maddox, G. L., & Douglass, E. B. Aging and individual differences: A longitudinal analysis of social, psychological, and physiological indicators. *Journal of Gerontology,* 1974, *29,* 555–563.

Madigan, S. A.   Modality and recall order interactions in short-term memory for serial order. *Journal of Experimental Psychology,* 1971, *87,* 294–296.

Maltzman, I.   Thinking: From a behavioristic point of view. *Psychological Review,* 1955, *66,* 367–386.

Mandler, G.   Verbal learning. In G. Mandler, P. Mussen, N. Kogan, & M. A. Wallach (Eds.), *New directions in psychology III.* New York: Holt, Rinehart & Winston, 1967.

———.   Organization, memory, and mental structures. In C. R. Puff (Ed.), *Memory, organization and structure.* New York: Academic Press, 1979.

Mandler, G., & Pearlstone, Z.   Free and constrained concept learning and subsequent recall. *Journal of Verbal Learning and Verbal Behavior,* 1966, *5,* 126–131.

Manniche, E., & Falk, G.   Age and the Nobel Prize. *Behavioral Science,* 1957, *2,* 301–307.

Marinesco, G., & Kreindler, A.   Des réflexes conditionnels, troisième partie: application des réflexes conditionnels à certains problèmes clinques. *Journal Psychologie,* 1934, *31,* 722–791.

Marks, L. E., & Miller, G. A.   The role of semantic and syntactic constraints in the memorization of English sentences. *Journal of Verbal Learning and Verbal Behavior,* 1964, *3,* 1–5.

Marks, L. E., & Stevens, J. C.   Measuring sensation in the aged. In L. W. Poon (Ed.), *Aging in the 1980s: Selected contemporary issues in the psychology of aging.* Washington, D.C.: American Psychological Association, 1980.

Markus, E. J.   Perceptual field dependence among aged persons. *Perceptual amd Motor Skills,* 1971, *33,* 175–178.

Marsh, B. W.   Aging and driving. *Traffic Engineering,* 1960, 3–21.

Marshall, J. R.   Changes in aged white male suicide: 1948–1972. *Journal of Gerontology,* 1978, *33,* 763–768.

Marshall, P. H., Elias, J. W., Webber, S. M., Gist, B. A., Winn, F. J., King, P., & Moore, S. A.   Age differences in verbal mediation: A structural and functional analysis. *Experimental Aging Research,* 1978, *4,* 175–193.

Maskarinec, A. S., & Brown, S. C.   Positive and negative recency effects in free recall learning. *Journal of Verbal Learning and Verbal Behavior,* 1974, *16,* 328–334.

Mason, S. E.   Effects of orienting tasks on the recall and recognition performance of subjects differing in age. *Developmental Psychology,* 1979, *15,* 467–469.

Mason, S. E., & Smith, A. D.   Imagery in the aged. *Experimental Aging Research,* 1977, *3,* 17–32.

Massaro, D. W.   *Experimental psychology and information processing.* Chicago: Rand McNally, 1975.

Masters, W., & Johnson, V.   *Human sexual response.* Boston: Little, Brown, 1966.

Maule, A. J., & Sanford, A. J.   Adult age differences in multi-source selection behavior with partially predictable signals. *British Journal of Psychology,* 1980, *71,* 69–82.

Mayzner, M. S., & Tresselt, M. E.   Anagram solution times: A function of letter order and word frequency. *Journal of Experimental Psychology,* 1958, *56,* 376–379.

McCarthy, M., Ferris, S. H., Clark, E., & Crook, T.   Acquisition and retention of categorized material in normal aging and senile dementia. *Experimental Aging Research,* 1981, *7,* 127–136.

McCrae, R. R., Costa, P. T., Jr., & Arenberg, D.   Constancy of adult personality structure in males: Longitudinal, cross-sectional and times-of-measurement analyses. *Journal of Gerontology,* 1980, *35,* 877–883.

McFarland, R. A.   The sensory and perceptual processes in aging. In K. W. Schaie

(Ed.), *Theory and methods of research on aging*. Morgantown: West Virginia University Press, 1968.

McFarland, R. A., Domey, R. G., Warren, A. B., & Ward, D. C. Dark adaptation as a function of age: I. A statistical analysis. *Journal of Gerontology*, 1960, *15*, 149–154.

McFarland, R. A., & O'Doherty, B. M. Work and occupational skills. In J. E. Birren (Ed.), *Handbook of aging and the individual. Chicago: University of Chicago Press, 1959.*

McFarland, R. A., Tune, G. S., & Welford, A. T. On the driving of automobiles by older people. *Journal of Gerontology*, 1964, *19*, 190–197.

McGeoch, J. A. Studies in retroactive inhibition: I. The temporal course of the inhibitory effects of interpolated learning. *Journal of General Psychology*, 1933, *9*, 24–43.

McGhie, A. N., Chapman, J., & Lawson, J. S. Changes in immediate memory with age. *British Journal of Psychology*, 1965, *56*, 69–75.

McGuire, W. J. The nature of attitude and attitude change. In G. Lindzey & E. Aronson (Eds.), *The handbook of social psychology* (Vol. 3). Reading, Mass.: Addison-Wesley, 1969.

McHugh, R. B., & Owens, W. A. Age changes in mental organization—a longitudinal study. *Journal of Gerontology*, 1954, *9*, 296–302.

Meacham, J. A. A transactional model of remembering. In N. Datan & H. W. Reese (Eds.), *Life-span developmental psychology: Dialectical perspectives on experimental research.* New York: Academic Press, 1977.

Medley, M. L. Satisfaction with life among persons sixty-five years and older: A causal model. *Journal of Gerontology*, 1976, *31*, 448–455.

Melton, A. W., & Irwin, J. McD. The influence of interpolated learning on retroactive inhibition and the overt transfer of specific responses. *American Journal of Psychology*, 1940, *53*, 175–203.

Merikle, P. M. Selection from visual persistence by perceptual groups and category membership. *Journal of Experimental Psychology: General*, 1980, *109*, 279–295.

Metzler, J., & Shepard, R. N. Transformational studies of the internal representation of three-dimensional objects. In R. L. Solso (Ed.), *Theories in cognitive psychology: The Loyola Symposium.* Hillsdale, N.J.: Lawrence Erlbaum, 1974.

Meyer, B. J. F., Rice, G. E., Knight, C. C., & Jessen, J. L. Effects of comparative and descriptive types on the reading performance of young, middle, and old adults. *Research Report No. 7, Prose Learning Series.* Tempe: Department of Educational Psychology, Arizona State University, 1979.

Michalewski, H. J., Thompson, L. W., Smith, D. B. D., Patterson, J. V., Bowman, T. E., Litzelman, D., & Brent, G. Age differences in the contingent negative variation (CNV): Reduced frontal activity in the elderly. *Journal of Gerontology*, 1980, *35*, 542–549.

Mihal, W. L., & Barrett, G. V. Individual differences in perceptual information processing and their relation to automobile accident involvements. *Journal of Applied Psychology*, 1976, *61*, 229–233.

Miles, C. C. The influence of speed and age on intelligence scores of adults. *Journal of General Psychology*, 1934, *10*, 208–210.

Miles, C. C., & Miles, W. R. The correlation of intelligence scores and chronological age from early to late maturity. *American Journal of Psychology*, 1932, *44*, 44–78.

Miles, W. R. Psychological aspects of aging. In E. V. Cowdry (Ed.), *Problems of aging* (2nd ed.). Baltimore: Williams & Wilkens, 1942.

Milgram, S., Greenwald, J., Kessler, S., McKenna, W., & Walters, J. A psychological map of New York City. *American Scientist*, 1972, *60*, 194–200.

Miller, G. A. The magical number seven plus or minus two. Some limits on our capacity for processing information. *Psychological Review,* 1956, *63,* 81–97.

Miller, G. A., Galanter, E., & Pribram, K. H. *Plans and the structure of behavior.* New York: Holt, Rinehart & Winston, 1960.

Miller, G. A., & Selfridge, J. A. Verbal context and the recall of meaningful material. *American Journal of Psychology,* 1950, *63,* 176–185.

Miller, J. H., & Shock, N. W. Age differences in the renal tubular response to antidiuretic hormones. *Journal of Gerontology,* 1953, *8,* 446–450.

Misiak, H. Age and sex differences in critical flicker frequency. *Journal of Experimental Psychology,* 1947, *37,* 318–332.

Mistler-Lachman, J. L. Spontaneous shift in encoding dimensions among elderly subjects. *Journal of Gerontology,* 1977, *32,* 68–72.

Monge, R. H. Learning in the adult years: Set or rigidity? *Human Development,* 1969, *12,* 131–140.

————. Studies of verbal learning from the college years through middle age. *Journal of Gerontology,* 1971, *26,* 324–329.

————. Structure of the self-concept from adolescence through old age. *Experimental Aging Research,* 1975, *1,* 281–291.

Monge, R. H., & Gardner, E. F. A program of research in adult differences in cognitive performance and learning: Backgrounds for adult education and vocational retraining. Final Report, Project No. 6–1963. U.S. Department of Health, Education, and Welfare, 1972.

Monge, R. H., & Hultsch, D. F. Paired-associate learning as a function of adult age and the length of the anticipation and inspection intervals. *Journal of Gerontology,* 1971, *26,* 157–162.

Moore, J. J., & Massaro, D. W. Attention and processing recognition. *Journal of Experimental Psychology,* 1973, *99,* 49–54.

Moray, N. Attention in dichotic listening: Affective cues and the influence of instructions. *Quarterly Journal of Experimental Psychology,* 1959, *11,* 56–60.

Moray, N., Bates, A., & Barnett, T. Experiments on the four-eared man. *Journal of the Acoustical Society of America,* 1965, *38,* 196–201.

Morris, C. D., Bransford, J. D., & Franks, J. J. Levels of processing versus transfer appropriate processing. *Journal of Verbal Learning and Verbal Behavior,* 1977, *16,* 519–533.

Mueller, D. J., & Atlas, L. Resocialization of regressed elderly residents: A behavioral management approach, *Journal of Gerontology,* 1972, *27,* 390–392.

Mueller, J. H., Kausler, D. H., & Faherty A. Age and access time for different memory codes. *Experimental Aging Research,* 1980, *6,* 445–450.

Mueller, J. H., Rankin, J. L., & Carlomusto, M. Adult age differences in free recall as a function of basis of organization and method of presentation. *Journal of Gerontology,* 1979, *34,* 375–380.

Müller, H. F., Grad, B., & Engelsmann, F. Biological and psychological predictors of survival in a psychogeriatric population. *Journal of Gerontology,* 1975, *30,* 47–52.

Murphy, M. D., Sanders, R. E., Gabriesheski. A. S., & Schmitt, F. A. Metamemory in the aged. *Journal of Gerontology,* 1981, *36,* 185–193.

Murrell, F. H. The effect of extensive practice on age differences in reaction time. *Journal of Gerontology,* 1970, *25,* 268–274.

Myers, G. C., & Soldo, B. J. Older Americans: Who are they? In R. A. Kalish (Ed.), *The later years: Social applications of gerontology.* Monterey, Calif.: Brooks/Cole, 1977.

Nappe, G. W., & Wollen, K. A. Effects of instructions to form common and bizarre mental images on retention. *Journal of Experimental Psychology,* 1973, *100,* 6–8.

National Center for Health Statistics. Binocular visual acuity of adults, United States, 1960–1962. *Vital and Health Statistics,* Series 11, No. 3. Washington, D.C.: U.S. Government Printing Office, 1964.

Nebes, R. D. Vocal versus manual response as a determinant of age difference in simple reaction time. *Journal of Gerontology,* 1978, *33,* 884–889.

Nebes, R. D. & Andrews-Kulis, M. E. The effect of age on the speed of sentence formation and incidental learning. *Experimental Aging Research,* 1976, *2,* 315–331.

Nehrke, M. F. Age and sex differences in discrimination learning and transfer of training. *Journal of Gerontology,* 1973, *28,* 320–327.

———. *Actual and perceived attitudes toward death and self-concept in three-generational families.* Paper presented at the annual meeting of the Gerontological Society, Portland, Oregon, November 1974.

Nehrke, M. F., & Coppinger, N. W. The effect of task dimensionality on discrimination learning and transfer of training in the aged. *Journal of Gerontology,* 1971, *26,* 151–156.

Nehrke, M. F., Hulicka, I. M., & Morganti, J. B. Age differences in life satisfaction, locus of control, and self-concept. *International Journal of Aging and Human Development,* 1980, *11,* 25–33.

Nehrke, M. F., & Sutterer, J. R. The effects of overtraining on mediational processes in elderly males. *Experimental Aging Research,* 1978, *4,* 207–221.

Neimark, E. D. Intellectual development during adolescence. In F. D. Horowitz (Ed.), *Review of child development research* (Vol. 4). Chicago: University of Chicago Press, 1975.

Neisser, U. Decision-time without reaction-time: Experiments in visual scanning. *American Journal of Psychology,* 1963, *76,* 376-385.

———. Visual search. *Scientific American,* 1964, *210,* 94–102.

———. *Cognitive psychology.* New York: Appleton-Century-Crofts, 1967.

Nelson, T. O. Repetition and depth of processing. *Journal of Verbal Learning and Verbal Behavior,* 1977, *16,* 151–172.

Neugarten, B. L. Personality and aging. In J. E. Birren & K. W. Schaie (Eds.), *Handbook of the psychology of aging.* New York: Van Nostrand Reinhold, 1977.

Neugarten, B. L., & Hagestad, G. O. Age and the life course. In R. H. Binstock & E. Shanas (Eds.), *Handbook of aging and the social sciences.* New York: Van Nostrand Reinhold, 1976.

Neugarten, B. L., Havighurst, R. J., & Tobin, S. S. The measurement of life satisfaction. *Journal of Gerontology,* 1961, *16,* 134–143.

———. Personality and patterns of aging. In B. L. Neugarten (Ed.), *Middle age and aging.* Chicago: University of Chicago Press, 1968.

Newell, A., & Simon, H. A. *Human problem solving.* Englewood Cliffs, N.J.: Prentice-Hall, 1972.

Noble, S. G. The acquisition of skill in the throwing of basket goals. *School and Society,* 1922, *16,* 640-644.

Norman, D. A. Toward a theory of memory and attention. *Psychological Review,* 1968, *75,* 522-536.

O'Connell, A. N., & Rotter, N. G. The influence of stimulus age and sex on person perception. *Journal of Gerontology,* 1979, *34,* 220–228.

Offenbach, S. I. A developmental study of hypothesis testing and cue selection strategies. *Developmental Psychology,* 1974, *10,* 484–490.

Ohta, R. J. Spatial orientation in the elderly: The current status of understanding. In H. L. Pick, Jr., & L. P. Acvedolo (Eds.), *Spatial orientation: Theory, research, and application.* New York: Plenum, 1981.

Ohta, R. J., Walsh, D. A., & Krauss, I. K. Spatial perspective-taking ability in young and elderly adults. *Experimental Aging Research,* 1981, *7,* 45–63.

Okun, M. A. Adult age and cautiousness in decision: A review of the literature. *Human Development,* 1976, *19,* 220–233.

Okun, M. A., & DiVesta, F. J. Cautiousness in adulthood as a function of age and instructions. *Journal of Gerontology,* 1976, *31,* 571–576.

Okun, M. A., & Elias, C. S. Cautiousness in adulthood as a function of age and payoff structure. *Journal of Gerontology,* 1977, *32,* 451–455.

Okun, M. A., Siegler, I. C., & George, L. K. Cautiousness and verbal learning in adulthood. *Journal of Gerontology,* 1978, *33,* 94–97.

Okun, M. A., Stock, W. A., & Ceurvorst, R. W. Risk taking through the adult life span. *Experimental Aging Research,* 1980, *6,* 463–474.

Orgel, L. E. The maintenance of the accuracy of protein synthesis and its relevance to aging. *Biochemistry,* 1963, *49,* 517–521.

Overall, J. E., & Gorham, D. R. Organicity versus old age in objective and projective test performance. *Journal of Consulting and Clinical Psychology,* 1972, *39,* 98–105.

Overton, W. F., & Reese, H. W. Models of development: Methodological implications. In J. R. Nesselroade & H. W. Reese (Eds.), *Life-span developmental psychology: Methodological issues.* New York: Academic Press, 1973.

Owens, W. A., Jr. Is age kinder to the initially more able? *Journal of Gerontology,* 1959, *14,* 334–337.

———. Age and mental ability: A second follow-up. *Journal of Educational Psychology,* 1966, *57,* 311–325.

Paivio, A. *Imagery and verbal processes.* New York: Holt, Rinehart & Winston, 1971.

Paivio, A., Yuille, J. C., & Madigan, S. Concreteness, imagery, and meaningfulness values for 925 nouns. *Journal of Experimental Psychology Monograph,* 1968, *76,*(1, Pt. 2).

Palermo, D. S., & Jenkins, J. J. *Word association norms.* Minneapolis: University of Minnesota Press, 1964.

Palmore, E., & Cleveland, W. Aging, terminal decline and terminal drop. *Journal of Gerontology,* 1976, *31,* 76–81.

Palmore, E., & Kivett, V. Change in life satisfaction: A longitudinal study of persons aged 46–70. *Journal of Gerontology,* 1977, *32,* 311–316.

Palmore, E., & Luikart, C. Health and social factors related to life satisfaction. *Journal of Health & Social Behavior,* 1972, *13,* 68–80.

Panek, P. E., Barrett, G. V., Sterns, G. V., & Alexander, R. A. Age differences in perceptual style, selective attention, and perceptual-motor reaction time. *Experimental Aging Research,* 1978, *4,* 377–387.

Papalia, D. E. The status of several conservation abilities across the life-span. *Human Development,* 1972, *15,* 229–243.

Papalia, D. E., & Bielby, D. Cognitive functioning in middle and old age adults: A review of research based on Piaget's theory. *Human Development,* 1974, *17,* 424–443.

Papalia, D. E., Kennedy, E., & Sheehan, N. Conservation of space in noninstitutionalized old people. *Journal of Psychology,* 1973, *84,* 75–79.

Parkinson, S. R. *Information processing in the aged.* Paper presented at the Sandoz conference on Aging, Battelle Memorial Institute, Seattle, Washington, 1977.

————. Aging and amnesia: A running span analysis. *Bulletin of the Psychonomic Society,* 1980, *15,* 215–217.

Parkinson, S. R., Lindholm, J. M., & Urell, T. Aging, dichotic memory and digit span. *Journal of Gerontology,* 1980, *35,* 87–95.

Parkinson, S. R., & Perey, A. Aging, digit span, and the stimulus suffix effect. *Journal of Gerontology,* 1980, *35,* 736–742.

Pearson, J. S., Swenson, W. M., & Rome, H. P. Age and sex differences related to MMPI response frequency in 25,000 medical patients. *American Journal of Psychiatry,* 1965, *122,* 988–995.

Pepper, S. C. *World hypotheses.* Berkeley: University of California Press, 1942.

Perlmuter, L. C., & Monty, R. A. The importance of perceived control: Fact or fantasy? *American Scientist,* 1977, *65,* 759–765.

Perlmutter, M. *Age differences in the consistency of adults' associative responses.* Paper presented at the annual meeting of the Psychonomic Society, San Antonio, Texas, November 1978. (a)

————. What is memory the aging of ? *Developmental Psychology,* 1978, *14,* 330–345. (b)

————. Age differences in adults' free recall, cued recall, and recognition. *Journal of Gerontology,* 1979, *34,* 533–539.

Perlmutter, M., Metzger, R., Nezworski. T., & Miller, K. Spatial and temporal memory in 20 and 60 year olds. *Journal of Gerontology,* 1981, *36,* 59–65.

Peterson, L. R., & Peterson, M. J. Short-term retention of individual verbal items. *Journal of Experimental Psychology,* 1959, *58,* 193–198.

Pezdek, K. Life-span differences in semantic integration of pictures and sentences in memory. *Child Development,* 1980, *51,* 720–729.

Pfeiffer, E. Psychopathology and social pathology. In J. E. Birren & K. W. Schaie (Eds.), *Handbook of the psychology of aging.* New York: Van Nostrand Reinhold, 1977.

Pfeiffer, E., Verwoerdt, A., & Davis, G. Sexual behavior in middle life. *American Journal of Psychiatry,* 1972, *128,* 1262–1267.

Phillips, L. W., & Sternthal, B. Age differences in information processing: A perspective on the aged consumer. *Journal of Marketing Research,* 1977, *14,* 444–457.

Piaget, J. *The mechanisms of perception.* New York: Basic Books, 1969.

————. Structuralism. New York: Basic Books, 1970. (a)

————. Piaget's theory. In P. H. Mussen (Ed.), *Carmichael's manual of child psychology* (3rd. ed.). New York: Wiley, 1970. (b)

Pierce, R. C., & Chiriboga, D. A. Dimensions of adult self-concept. *Journal of Gerontology,* 1979, *34,* 8–85.

Planek, T. W., & Fowler, R. C. Traffic accident problems and exposure characteristics of the aging driver. *Journal of Gerontology,* 1971, *26,* 224–230.

Plemons, J. K., Willis, S. L., & Baltes, P. B. Modifiability of fluid intelligence in aging: A short-term longitudinal training approach. *Journal of Gerontology,* 1978, *33,* 224–231.

Plude, D. J., & Hoyer, W. J. *Adult age differences in visual search as a function of stimulus mapping and information load.* Paper presented at the annual meeting of the American Psychological Association, New York, September 1979.

Pollack, R. H., & Atkeson, B. M. Life-span approach to perceptual development. In P. B. Baltes (Ed.), *Life-span development and behavior* (Vol. 1). New York: Academic Press, 1978.

Poon, L. W., & Fozard, J. L. Speed of retrieval from long-term memory in relation to age, familiarity, and datedness of information. *Journal of Gerontology,* 1978, *33,* 711–717.

Poon, L. W., Fozard, J. L., Paulshock, D. R., & Thomas, J. C. A questionnaire assessment of age differences in retention of recent and remote events. *Experimental Aging Research,* 1979, *5,* 401–411.

Poon, L. W., Fozard, J. L., & Treat, N. J. From clinical and research findings on memory to intervention programs. *Experimental Aging Research,* 1978, *4,* 235–254.

Poon, L. W., Fozard, J. L., Vierck, V., Dailey, B. F., Cerella, J., & Zeller, P. *The effects of practice and information in feedback on age-related differences in performance, speed, variability, and error rates in a two-choice decision task.* Paper presented at the American Psychological Association Symposium on Decision Making and Aging, Washington, D.C., August 1976.

Poon, L. W., & Walsh-Sweeney, L. Effects of bizarre and interacting imagery on learning and retrieval of the aged. *Experimental Aging Research,* 1981, *7,* 65–70.

Poon, L. W., Walsh-Sweeney, L., & Fozard, J. L. Memory skill training for the elderly: Salient issues on the use of imagery mnemonics. In L. W. Poon, J. L. Fozard, L. S. Cermak, D. Arenberg, & L. W. Thompson (Eds.), *New directions in memory and aging.* Hillsdale, N.J.: Lawrence Erlbaum, 1980.

Posner, M. I., Boies, S. J., Eichelman, W., & Taylor, R. L. Retention of visual and name codes of single letters. *Journal of Experimental Psychology Monograph,* 1969, *79,* 1–16.

Posner, M. I., & Mitchell, R. F. Chronometric analysis of classification. *Psychological Review,* 1967, *74,* 392–409.

Posner M. I., & Synder, C. R. R. Attention and cognitive control. In R. L. Solso (Ed.), *Information processing and cognition.* Hillsdale, N.J.: Lawrence Erlbaum, 1975.

Postman, L. The present status of interference theory. In C. N. Cofer (Ed.), *Verbal learning and verbal behavior.* New York: McGraw-Hill, 1961.

Postman, L., & Greenbloom, R. Conditions of cue selection in the acquisition of paired-associate lists. *Journal of Experimental Psychology,* 1967, *73,* 91–100.

Postman, L., & Underwood, B. J. Critical issues in interference theory. *Memory & Cognition,* 1973, *1,* 19–40.

Potash, M., & Jones, B. Aging and decision criteria for the detection of tones in noise. *Journal of Gerontology,* 1977, *32,* 436–440.

Powell, D. A., Milligan, W. L., & Furchtgott, E. Peripheral autonomic changes accompanying learning and reaction time performance in older people. *Journal of Gerontology,* 1980, *35,* 57–65.

Prinz, P. N. Sleep patterns in the healthy aged: Relationship with intellectual function. *Journal of Gerontology,* 1977, *12,* 179–186.

Puff, C. R. Role of clustering in free recall. *Journal of Experimental Psychology,* 1970, *86,* 384–386.

Puglisi, J. T. Semantic encoding in older adults as evidenced by release from proactive inhibition. *Journal of Gerontology,* 1980, *35,* 743–745.

Rabbitt, P. M. A. Age and time for choice between stimuli and between responses. *Journal of Gerontology,* 1964, *19,* 307–312.

———. Age and discrimination between complex stimuli. In A. T. Welford & J. E. Birren (Eds.), *Behavior, aging and the nervous system.* Springfield, Ill.: Charles, C. Thomas, 1965. (a)

———. An age-decrement in the ability to ignore irrelevant information. *Journal of Gerontology,* 1965, *20,* 233–238. (b)

———. Changes in problem solving ability in old age. In J. E. Birren & K. W. Schaie

(Eds.), *Handbook of the psychology of aging.* New York: Van Nostrand Reinhold, 1977.

Rabbitt, P. M. A., & Birren, J. E.   Age and responses to sequences of repetitive and interruptive signals. *Journal of Gerontology,* 1967, *22,* 143–150.

Rabbitt, P. M. A., & Rogers, M.   Age and choice between responses in a self-paced repetitive task. *Ergonomics,* 1965, *8,* 435–444.

Radtke, R. C., McHewitt, E., & Jacoby, L.   Number of alternatives and rate of presentation in verbal discrimination learning. *Journal of Experimental Psychology,* 1970, *83,* 179–181.

Rajalakshmi, R., & Jeeves, M.   Changes in tachistoscopic form perception as a function of age and intellectual status. *Journal of Gerontology,* 1963, *19,* 275–278.

Rankin, J. L., & Kausler, D. H.   Adult age differences in false recognitions. *Journal of Gerontology,* 1979, *34,* 58–65.

Raven, J. C.   The comparative assessment of intellectual ability. *British Journal of Psychology,* 1948, *39,* 12–19.

———.   *Guide to using progressive matrices (1947). Sets A, Ab, B.* London: Lewis, 1951.

Raymond, B. J.   Free recall among the aged. *Psychological Reports,* 1971, *29,* 1179–1182.

Rees, J. N., & Botwinick, J.   Detection and decision factors in auditory behavior of the elderly. *Journal of Gerontology,* 1971, *26,* 133–136.

Reese, H. W.   Models of memory and models of development. *Human Development,* 1973, *16,* 397–416. (a)

———.   Life-span models of memory. *The Gerontologist,* 1973, *13,* 472–478. (b).

———.   The development of memory: Life-span perspectives. In H. W. Reese (Ed.), *Advances in child development and behavior.* New York: Academic Press, 1976.

Reese, H. W., & Lipsitt, L. P.   *Experimental child psychology.* New York: Academic Press, 1970.

Reese, H. W., & Overton, W. F.   Models of development and theories of development. In L. R. Goulet & P. B. Baltes (Eds.), *Life-span developmental psychology: Research and theory.* New York: Academic Press, 1970.

Reid, D. W., Haas, G., & Hawkings, D.   Locus of desired control and positive self-concept of the elderly. *Journal of Gerontology,* 1977, *32,* 441–450.

Reimanis, G., & Green, R. F.   Imminence of death and intellectual decrement in the aging. *Developmental Psychology,* 1971, *5,* 270–272.

Reinert, G.   Comparative factor analytic studies of intelligence throughout the human life-span. In L. R. Goulet & P. B. Baltes (Eds.), *Life-span developmental psychology: Research and theory.* New York: Academic Press, 1970.

Reitman, J. S.   Mechanisms of forgetting in short-term memory. *Cognitive Psychology,* 1971, *2,* 185–195.

Renner, V. J., Alpaugh, P. K., & Birren, J. E.   *Divergent thinking over the life-span.* Paper presented at the annual meeting of the Gerontological Society, Dallas, Texas, November 1978.

Reno, R.   Attribution of success and failure as a function of perceived age. *Journal of Gerontology,* 1979, *34,* 709–715.

Rescorla, R. A.   Informational variables in Pavlovian conditioning. In G. H. Bower (Ed.), *The psychology of learning and motivation: Advances in research and theory* (Vol. 6). New York: Academic Press, 1972.

Restle, F.   A theory of discrimination learning. *Psychological Review,* 1955, *62,* 11–19.

Revlis, R.   *Representation and set size in syllogistic reasoning.* Paper presented at the annual meeting of the Psychonomic Society, St. Louis, Missouri, November 1973.

Ribot, T. A. *The diseases of memory.* New York: Appleton, 1882.

Richman, J. The foolishness and wisdom of age: Attitudes toward the elderly as reflected in jokes. *The Gerontologist,* 1977, *17,* 210–219.

Riege, W. H., & Inman, V. Age differences in nonverbal memory tasks. *Journal of Gerontology,* 1981, 51–58.

Riegel, K. F. Personality theory and aging. In J. E. Birren (Ed.), *Handbook of aging and the individual.* Chicago: University of Chicago Press, 1959.

————.. History of psychological gerontology. In J. E. Birren & K. W. Schaie (Eds.), *Handbook of the psychology of aging.* New York: Van Nostrand, Reinhold, 1977.

Riegel, K. F., & Birren, J. E. Age differences in associative behavior. *Journal of Gerontology,* 1965, *20,* 125–130.

Riegel, K. F., & Riegel, R. M. A study of changes of attitudes and interests during later years of life. *Vita Humana,* 1960, *3,* 177–206.

————. Development, drop, and death. *Developmental Psychology,* 1972, *6,* 306–319.

Riegel, K. F., Riegel, R. M., & Meyer, G. Sociopsychological factors of aging: A cohort sequential analysis. *Human Development,* 1967, *10,* 27–56.

Riley, J. W., Jr. What people think about death. In O. G. Brim, Jr., H. E. Freeman, S. Levine, & N. O. Scotch (Eds.), *The dying patient.* New York: Russell Sage Foundation, 1970.

Riley, M., & Foner, A. *Aging and society: An inventory of research findings.* New York: Russell Sage Foundation, 1968.

Rimoldi, H. J. A., & Vander Woude, K. W. Aging and problem solving. *Archives of General Psychiatry,* 1969, *20,* 215–225.

Robertson-Tchabo, E. A., Hausman, C. P., & Arenberg, D. A classical mnemonic for older learners: A trip that works. *Educational Gerontology,* 1976, *1,* 215–226.

Rogers, C. J., Keyes, B. J., & Fuller, B. J. Solution shift performance in the elderly. *Journal of Gerontology,* 1976, *31,* 670–675.

Rosen, S., Bergman, M., Plester, D., El-Mofty, E., & Sath, M. Presbycusis study of a relatively noise-free population in the Sudan. *Annals of Otology,* 1962, *71,* 727–743.

Rosen, S., Plester, D., El-Mofty, E., & Rosen, V. H. High frequency audiometry in presbycusis: A comparative study of the Mabaan tribe in the Sudan with urban populations. *Archives of Otolaryngology,* 1964, *79,* 18–32.

Rotter, J. B. Generalized expectancies for internal versus external control of reinforcement. *Psychological Monographs,* 1966, *80*(1, Whole No. 609).

Rotter, J. B., Chance, J. E., & Phares, E. J. (Eds.). *Applications of a social learning theory of personality.* New York: Holt, Rinehart & Winston, 1972.

Rowe, E. J., & Schnore, M. M. Item concreteness and reported strategies in paired-associate learning as a function of age. *Journal of Gerontology,* 1971, *26,* 470–475.

Rubin, K. H. Decentration skills in institutionalized and non-institutionalized elderly. In *Proceedings of 81st Annual Convention of the American Psychological Association, Montreal, Canada, 1973.* Washington, D.C.: American Psychological Association, 1973.

————. The relationship between spatial and communicative egocentrism in children and young and old adults. *Journal of Genetic Psychology,* 1974, *125,* 295–301.

————. Extinction of conservation: A life span investigation. *Developmental Psychology,* 1976, *12,* 51–56.

Rubin, K. H., Attewell, P. W., Tierney, M. C., & Tumolo, P. Development of spatial egocentrism and conservation across the life span. *Developmental Psychology,* 1973, *9,* 432.

Ruch, F. L. Adult learning. *Psychological Bulletin,* 1933, *30,* 387–414.

————. The differentiative effects of age upon human learning. *Journal of General Psychology,* 1934, *11,* 261–286.

Rundus, D. Negative effects of using list items as recall cues. *Journal of Verbal Learning and Verbal Behavior,* 1973, *12,* 43–50.

Rundus, D., & Atkinson, R. C. Rehearsal processes in free recall: A procedure for direct observation. *Journal of Verbal Learning and Verbal Behavior,* 1970, *9,* 99–105.

Rychlak, J. F. Psychological science as a humanist sees it. In J. K. Cole (Ed.), *Nebraska Symposium on Motivation* (Vol. 23). Lincoln: University of Nebraska Press, 1975.

Sacher, G. A. Abnutzungstheorie. In N. W. Shock (Ed.), *Perspectives in experimental gerontology.* Springfield, Ill.: Charles C. Thomas, 1966.

Sakitt, B. Locus of short-term visual storage. *Science,* 1975, *190,* 1318–1319.

Sakitt, B., & Appelman, I. B. The effects of memory load and the contrast of the rod signal on partial report superiority in a Sperling task. *Memory & Cognition,* 1978, *6,* 562–567.

Salthouse, T. A. Age and tachistoscopic perception. *Experimental Aging Research,* 1976, *2,* 91–103.

————. The role of memory in the age decline in digit-symbol substitution performance. *Journal of Gerontology,* 1978, *33,* 232–238.

————. Age and memory: Strategies for localizing the loss. In L. W. Poon, J. L. Fozard, L. S. Cermak, D. Arenberg, & L. W. Thompson (Eds.), *New directions in memory and aging.* Hillsdale, N.J.: Lawrence Erlbaum, 1980. (a)

————. *Age and speed: A generalized slowing?* Unpublished manuscript, 1980. (b)

Salthouse, T. A., & Somberg, B. L. Isolating the age deficit in speeded performance. *Journal of Gerontology,* in press. (a)

————. Skilled performance: The effects of adult age and experience on elementary processes. *Journal of Experimental Psychology: General,* in press. (b)

Salthouse, T. A., Wright, R., & Ellis, C. L. Adult age and the rate of an internal clock. *Journal of Gerontology,* 1979, *34,* 53–57.

Saltzman, I. J. The orienting task in incidental and intentional learning. *American Journal of Psychology,* 1953, *66,* 593–597.

Sanders, J. A. C., Sterns, H. L., Smith, M., & Sanders, R. E. Modification of conceptual identification performance in older adults. *Developmental Psychology,* 1975, *11,* 824–829.

Sanders, R. E., Murphy, M. D., Schmitt, F. A., & Walsh, K. K. Age differences in free recall rehearsal strategies. *Journal of Gerontology,* 1980, *35,* 550–558.

Sanders, R. E., & Sanders, J. A. C. Long-term durability and transfer of enhanced conceptual performance in the elderly. *Journal of Gerontology,* 1978, *33,* 408–412.

Sanders, R. E., Sanders, J. A. C., & Sielski, K. A. Enhancement of conjunctive concept attainment in older adults. *Developmental Psychology,* 1976, *12,* 485–486.

Sanders, S., Laurendeau, M., & Bergeon, J. Aging and the concept of space: The conservation of surfaces. *Journal of Gerontology,* 1966, *21,* 281–285.

Schaie, K. W. Rigidity-flexibility and intelligence: A cross-sectional study of the adult life span from 20 to 70 years. *Psychological Monographs,* 1958, *72,*(9, Whole No. 462), 1–26.

————. Cross-sectional methods in the study of psychological aspects of aging. *Journal of Gerontology,* 1959, *14,* 208–215.

————. A general model for the study of developmental problems. *Psychological Bulletin,* 1965, *64,* 92–107.

————. A reinterpretation of age-related changes in cognitive structure and functioning. In L. R. Goulet & P. B. Baltes (Eds.), *Life-span developmental psychology: Research and theory.* New York: Academic Press, 1970.

————. Methodological problems in descriptive developmental research on adulthood and aging. In J. R. Nesselroade & H. W. Reese (Eds.), *Life-span developmental psychology: Methodological issues.* New York: Academic Press, 1973.

————. Age changes in adult intelligence. In D. S. Woodruff & J. E. Birren (Eds.), *Aging: Scientific perspectives and social issues.* New York: Van Nostrand, 1975.

————. Quasi-experimental designs in the psychology of aging. In J. E. Birren & K. W. Schaie (Eds.), *Handbook of the psychology of aging.* New York: Van Nostrand Reinhold, 1977.

————. External validity in the assessment of intellectual development in adulthood. *Journal of Gerontology,* 1978, *33,* 696–701.

————. Age changes in intelligence. In R. L. Sprott (Ed.), *Age, learning ability, and intelligence.* New York: Van Nostrand Reinhold, 1980.

Schaie, K. W., & Baltes, P. B. Some faith helps to see the forest. A final comment on the Horn and Donaldson myth of the Baltes-Schaie position on adult intelligence. *American Psychologist,* 1977, *32,* 1118–1120.

Schaie, K. W., & Labouvie-Vief, G. Generational versus ontogenetic components of change in adult cognitive behavior: A fourteen-year cross-sequential study. *Developmental Psychology,* 1974, *10,* 305–320.

Schaie, K. W., Labouvie, G. V., & Buech, B. U. Generational and cohort-specific differences in adult cognitive functioning. *Developmental Psychology,* 1973, *9,* 151–166.

Schaie, K. W., & Marquette, B. Personality in maturity and old age. In R. M. Dreger (Ed.), *Multivariate personality research: Contributions to the understanding of personality in honor of Raymond B. Cattell.* Baton Rouge, La.: Claitor's Publishing, 1972.

Schaie, K. W., & Parham, I. A. Stability of adult personality: Fact or fable? *Journal of Personality and Social Psychology,* 1976, *34,* 146–158.

————. Cohort-sequential analyses of adult intellectual development. *Developmental Psychology,* 1977, *13,* 649–653.

Schaie, K. W., Rosenthal, F., & Perlman, R. M. Differential mental deterioration of factorially "pure" functions in later maturity. *Journal of Gerontology,* 1953, *8,* 191–196.

Schaie, K. W., & Strother, C. R. A cross-sequential study of age changes in cognitive behavior. *Psychological Bulletin,* 1968, *70,* 671–680.

Scharf, B. Introduction. In B. Scharf (Ed.), *Experimental sensory psychology.* Glenview, Ill.: Scott, Foresman, 1975.

Schear, J. M., & Nebes, R. D. Memory for verbal and spatial information as a function of age. *Experimental Aging Research,* 1980, *6,* 271–281.

Scheidt, R. J., & Schaie, K. W. A taxonomy of situations for an elderly population: Generating situational criteria. *Journal of Gerontology,* 1978, *33,* 848–857.

Schein, V. E. Personality dimensions and needs. In M. W. Riley & A. Foner (Eds.), *Aging and society: Vol. 1. An inventory of research findings.* New York: Russell Sage Foundation, 1968.

Schemper, T., Voss, S., & Cain, W. S. Odor identification in young and elderly persons: Sensory and cognitive limitations. *Journal of Gerontology,* 1981, *36,* 446–452.

Schiffman, S. Food recognition by the elderly. *Journal of Gerontology,* 1977, *32,* 586–592.

Schluderman, E., & Zubek, J. P. Effect of age on pain sensitivity. *Perceptual and Motor Skills,* 1962, *14,* 295–301.

Schmitt, F. A., Murphy, M. D., & Sanders, R. E.   Training older adult free recall rehearsal strategies. *Journal of Gerontology*, 1981, *36*, 329–337.

Schneider, W., & Shiffrin, R. M.   Controlled and automatic human information processing: I. Detection, search, and attention. *Psychological Review*, 1977, *84*, 1–66.

Schofield, W.   *Psychotherapy: Purchase of friendship*. Englewood Cliffs, N.J.: Prentice-Hall, 1974.

Schonfield, D.   Age and remembering. Duke University Council on Aging and Human Development, Proceedings of Seminars. Durham, N.C.: Duke University, 1969. (b)

————.   Future commitments and successful aging: I. The random sample. *Journal of Gerontology*, 1973, *28*, 189–196.

————.   *In search of early memories*. Paper presented at the International Congress of Gerontology, Washington, D.C., July 1969. (a)

Schonfield, D., & Robertson, B. A.   Memory storage and aging. *Canadian Journal of Psychology*, 1966, *20*, 228–236.

Schonfield, D., & Robertson, E. A.   The coding and sorting of digits and symbols by an elderly sample. *Journal of Gerontology*, 1968, *23*, 318–323.

Schonfield, D., Trueman, V., & Kline, D.   Recognition tests of dichotic listening and the age variable. *Journal of Gerontology*, 1972, *27*, 487–493.

Schonfield, D., & Wenger, L.   Age limitation of perceptual span, *Nature*, 1975, *53*, 377–378.

Schultz, N. R., Dineen, J. T., Elias, M. F., Pentz, C. A., III., & Wood, W. G.   WAIS performance for different age groups of hypertensive and control subjects during the administration of a diuretic. *Journal of Gerontology*, 1979, *34*, 246–253.

Schultz, N. R., & Hoyer, W. J.   Feedback effects on spatial egocentrism in old age. *Journal of Gerontology*, 1976, *31*, 72–75.

Schulz, R.   Effects of control and predictability on the physical and psychological well-being of the institutionalized aged. *Journal of Personality and Social Psychology*, 1976, *33*, 563–573.

Schwartz, D. W., & Karp, S. A.   Field dependence in a geriatric population. *Perceptual and Motor Skills*, 1967, *24*, 495–504.

Schwartz, S. H.   Modes of representation and problem-solving: Well evolved is half solved. *Journal of Experimental Psychology*, 1971, *91*, 347–350.

Seeger, R. J.   Beyond operationalism. *Scientific Monthly*, 1954, *79*, 226–227.

Segall, M., Campbell, D., & Herskovits, M.   *The influence of culture on visual perception*. Indianapolis: Bobbs-Merrill, 1966.

Sekuler, R., & Hutman, L. P.   Spatial vision and aging: I. Contrast sensitivity. *Journal of Gerontology*, 1980, *35*, 692–699.

Sekuler, R., Hutman, L. P., & Owsley, C. J.   Human aging and spatial vision. *Science*, 1980, *209*, 1255–1256.

Seligman, M. E. P.   *Helplessness*. San Francisco: W. H. Freeman, 1975.

Shaffer, L. H.   Latency mechanisms in transcription. In S. Kornblum (Ed.), *Attention and performance IV*. New York: Academic Press, 1973.

Shakow, D., Dolkart, M. B., & Goldman, R.   The memory function in psychoses of the aged. *Diseases of the Nervous System*, 1941, *2*, 43–48.

Shaps, L. P., & Nilsson, L.   Encoding and retrieval operations in relation to age. *Developmental Psychology*, 1980, *16*, 636–643.

Shepard, R. N.   (Review of "Cognitive Psychology" by U. Neisser). *American Journal of Psychology*, 1968, *81*, 285–289.

Shepard, R. N., & Chipman, S.   Second-order isomorphism of internal representations: Shapes of states. *Cognitive Psychology*, 1970, *1*, 1–17.

Shepard, R. N., & Metzler, J.   Mental rotation of three-dimensional objects. *Science,* 1971, *171,* 701–703.

Sherif, M.   A study of some social factors in perception. *Archives of Psychology,* 1935, *27,* No. 187.

Sherman, R. A.   *Behavior modification: Theory and practice.* Monterey, Calif.: Brooks/ Cole, 1973.

Shields, E. A.   Rigidity in the aged. (Doctoral dissertation, Northwestern University, 1957). *Dissertation Abstracts,* 1958, *18,* 668–669.

Shiffrin, R. M., & Schneider, W.   Controlled and automatic human information processing: II. Perceptual learning, automatic attending, and a general theory. *Psychological Review,* 1977, *84,* 127–190.

Shmavonian, B. M., Miller, L. H., & Cohen, S. I.   Differences among age and sex groups in electro-dermal conditioning. *Psychophysiology,* 1968, *5,* 119–131.

———.   Differences among age and sex groups with respect to cardiovascular conditioning and reactivity. *Journal of Gerontology,* 1970, *25,* 87–94.

Shock, N. W.   The physiology of aging. *Scientific American,* 1962, *206,* 100–110.

———.   Biological theories of aging. In J. E. Birren & K. W. Schaie (Eds.), *Handbook of the psychology of aging.* New York: Van Nostrand Reinhold, 1977.

Siegler, I. C.   The terminal drop hypothesis: Fact or artifact? *Experimental Aging Research,* 1975, *1,* 169–185.

Siegler, I. C., & Botwinick, J.   A long-term longitudinal study of intellectual ability of older adults: The matter of selective subject attrition. *Journal of Gerontology,* 1979, *34,* 242–245.

Siegler, I. C., George, L. K., & Okun, M. A.   Cross-sequential analysis of personality. *Developmental Psychology,* 1979, *15,* 350–351.

Simon, E.   Depth and elaboration of processing in relation to age. *Journal of Experimental Psychology: Human Learning and Memory,* 1979, *5,* 115–124.

Singleton, W. T.   Age and performance timing on simple skills. In *Old age in the modern world.* Edinburgh, Scotland: Livingstone, 1955.

Sjostrom, K. P., & Pollack, R. H.   The effect of simulated receptor aging on two types of visual illusions. *Psychonomic Science,* 1971, *23,* 147–148.

Skinner, B. F.   *The behavior of organisms.* New York: Appleton-Century-Crofts, 1938.

Smith, A. D.   Aging and interference with memory. *Journal of Gerontology,* 1975, *30,* 319–325. (a)

———.   Interaction between human aging and memory. *Georgia Institute of Technology Progress Report No. 2,* 1975. (b)

———.   Partial learning and recognition memory in the aged. *International Journal of Aging and Human Development,* 1975, *6,* 359–365. (c)

———.   Adult age differences in cued recall. *Developmental Psychology,* 1977, *13,* 326–331.

———.   *Age-differences in memory as influenced by qualitatively different types of processing.* Paper presented at the annual meeting of the Gerontological Society, Washington, D.C., November 1979. (a)

———.   The interaction between age and list length in free recall. *Journal of Gerontology,* 1979, *34,* 381–387. (b)

———.   Age differences in encoding, storage, and retrieval. In L. W. Poon, J. L. Fozard, L. S. Cermak, D. Arenberg, & L. W. Thompson (Eds.), *New directions in memory and aging.* Hillsdale, N.J.: Lawrence Erlbaum, 1980.

Smith, A. D., & Winograd, E.   Adult age differences in remembering faces. *Developmental Psychology,* 1978, *14,* 443–444.

Smith, D. B. D., Thompson, L. W., & Michalewski, H. J. Averaged evoked potential research in adult aging—status and prospects. In L. W. Poon (Ed.), *Aging in the 1980's: Selected contemporary issues in the psychology of aging.* Washington, D.C.: American Psychological Association, 1980.

Snoddy, G. S. Learning and stability. *Journal of Applied Psychology,* 1926, *10,* 1–36.

Solso, R. L. *Cognitive psychology.* New York: Harcourt Brace Jovanovich, 1979.

Somberg, B. L. *Divided attention abilities in young and old adults.* Unpublished doctoral dissertation, University of Missouri, Columbia, 1981.

Soper, W. B. A brief note on a preliminary study of life satisfaction for male university faculty of differing chronological ages. *Experimental Aging Research,* 1979, *5,* 435–440.

Spear, N. E., Ekstrand, B. R., & Underwood, B. J. Association by contiguity. *Journal of Experimental Psychology,* 1964, *67,* 151–161.

Spearman, C. *The abilities of man.* New York: Macmillan, 1927.

Spence, K. W. A theory of emotionally based drive (D) and its relation to performance in simple learning situations. *American Psychologists,* 1958, *13,* 131–141.

Sperling, G. The information available in brief visual presentations. *Psychological Monographs,* 1960, *74*(11, Whole No. 498).

———. A model for visual memory tasks. In R. N. Haber (Ed.), *Information processing approaches to visual perception.* New York: Holt, Rinehart & Winston, 1969.

Spiker, C. C. Behaviorism, cognitive psychology, and the active organism. In N. Datan & H. W. Reese (Eds.), *Life-span developmental psychology: Dialectical perspectives on experimental research.* New York: Academic Press, 1977.

Spoor, A. Presbycusis values in relation to noise induced hearing loss. *International Audiology,* 1967, *6,* 48–57.

Squire, L. R. Remote memory as affected by aging. *Neuropsychologia,* 1974, *12,* 429–435.

Squire, L. R., & Slater, P. C. Forgetting in very long-term memory as assessed by an improved questionnaire technique. *Journal of Experimental Psychology: Human Learning and Memory,* 1975, *104,* 50–54.

Staats, A. W., & Staats, C. K. Attitudes established by classical conditioning. *Journal of Abnormal and Social Psychology,* 1958, *57,* 37–40.

Staats, S., & Experimental Psychology Class. Internal versus external locus of control for three age groups. *International Journal of Aging and Human Development,* 1974, *5,* 7–10.

Sternberg, S. High speed scanning in human memory. *Science,* 1966, *153,* 652–654.

———. The discovery of processing stages: Extensions of Donders' method. *Acta Psychologica,* 1969, *30,* 276–315. (a)

———. Memory Scanning: Mental processes revealed by reaction time experiments. *American Scientist,* 1969, *57,* 421–457. (b)

Steuer, J., LaRue, A., Blum, J. E., & Jarvik, L. F. "Critical loss" in the eighth and ninth decades. *Journal of Gerontology,* 1981, *36,* 211–213.

Stone, C. P. The age factor in animal learning: I. Rats in the problem box and the maze. *Genetic Psychology Monographs,* 1929, *5.*

Stone, J. L., & Norris, A. H. Activities and attitudes of participants in the Baltimore Longitudinal Study. *Journal of Gerontology,* 1966, *21,* 575–580.

Storandt, M. Speed and coding effects in relation to age and ability level. *Developmental Psychology,* 1976, *12,* 177–178.

———. Age, ability level, and scoring the WAIS. *Journal of Gerontology,* 1977, *32,* 175–178.

Storandt, M., Grant, E. A., & Gordon, B. C.   Remote memory as a function of age and sex. *Experimental Aging Research,* 1978, *4,* 365–375.

Storandt, M., & Hudson, W.   Misuse of analysis of covariance in aging research and some partial solutions. *Experimental Aging Research,* 1975, *1,* 121–125.

Storandt, M., Wittels, I., & Botwinick, J.   Predictors of a dimension of well-being in the relocated healthy aged. *Journal of Gerontology,* 1975, *30,* 97–102.

Storck, P. A., Looft, W. R., & Hooper, F. H.   Interrelationships among Piagetian tasks and traditional measures of cognitive ability in mature and aged adults. *Journal of Gerontology,* 1972, *27,* 461–465.

Stroop, J. R.   Studies of interference in serial verbal reactions. *Journal of Experimental Psychology,* 1935, *18,* 643–662.

Strother, C. R., Schaie, K. W., & Horst, P.   The relationship between advanced age and mental abilities. *Journal of Abnormal and Social Psychology,* 1957, *55,* 166–170.

Surwillo, W. W.   The relation of simple response time to brain wave frequency and the effects of age. *Electroencephalography and Clinical Neurophysiology,* 1963, *15,* 105–114.

———.   Timing of behavior in senescence and the role of the central nervous system. In G. A. Talland (Ed.), *Human aging and behavior.* New York: Academic Press, 1968.

Surwillo, W. W., & Quiller, R. E.   Vigilance, age, and response time. *American Journal of Psychology,* 1964, *77,* 614–620.

Szafran, J.   *Some experiments on motor performance in relation to aging.* Unpublished thesis, Cambridge University, 1953.

Tachibana, K.   On learning process of the aged. *Japanese Journal of Psychology,* 1927, *2,* 635–653.

Talland, G. A.   The effect of age on speed of simple manual skill. *Journal of Genetic Psychology,* 1962, *100,* 69-76.

———.   Initiation of response, and reaction time in aging, and with brain damage. In A. T. Welford & J. E. Birren (Eds.), *Behavior, aging, and the nervous system.* Springfield, Ill.: Charles C. Thomas, 1965.

———.   Visual signal defection, as a function of age, input rate, and signal frequency. *Journal of Psychology,* 1966, *63,* 105–115.

Taub, H. A.   A comparison of young adult and old groups on various digit span tasks. *Developmental Psychology,* 1972, *6,* 60–65.

———.   Memory span, practice, and aging. *Journal of Gerontology,* 1973, *28,* 335–338.

———.   Coding for short-term memory as a function of age. *Journal of Genetic Psychology,* 1974, *125,* 309–314.

———.   Mode of presentation, age, and short-term memory. *Journal of Gerontology,* 1975, *30,* 56–59.

———.   Method of presentation of meaningful prose to young and old adults. *Experimental Aging Research,* 1976, *2,* 469–474.

———.   Comprehension and memory of prose materials by young and old adults. *Experimental Aging Research,* 1979, *5,* 3–13.

Taub, H. A., & Kline, G. E.   Modality effects and memory in the aged. *Educational Gerontology,* 1976, *1,* 53–60.

———.   Recall of prose as a function of age and input modality. *Journal of Gerontology,* 1978, *33,* 725–730.

Taub, H. A., & Walker, J. B.   Short-term memory as a function of age and response interference. *Journal of Gerontology,* 1970, *25,* 177–183.

Tesch, S., Whitbourne, S. K., & Nehrke, M. F.   Cognitive egocentrism in institutionalized adult males. *Journal of Gerontology,* 1978, *33,* 546–552.

Thaler, M.   Relationships among Wechsler, Weigl, Rorschach, EEG findings, and abstract-concrete behavior in a group of normal aged subjects. *Journal of Gerontology,* 1956, *11,* 404–409.

Thomas, J. C., Fozard, J. L., & Waugh, N. C.   Age-related differences in naming latency. *American Journal of Psychology,* 1977, *90,* 499–509.

Thomas, J. C., Waugh, N. C., & Fozard, J. L.   Age and familiarity in memory scanning. *Journal of Gerontology,* 1978, *33,* 528–533.

Thornbury, J., & Mistretta, C. M.   Tactile sensitivity as a function of age. *Journal of Gerontology,* 1981, *36,* 34–39.

Thorndike, E. L.   *Human learning.* New York: Century, 1931.

Thorndike, E. L., Bregman, E. O., Tilton, J. W., & Woodyard, E.   *Adult learning.* New York: Macmillan, 1928.

Thumin, F. J.   Reminiscence as a function of chronological and mental age. *Journal of Gerontology,* 1962, *17,* 392–396.

Thurstone, L. L., & Thurstone, T. G.   *Factorial studies of intelligence.* Chicago: University of Chicago Press, 1941. (Psychometric Monograph No. 2)

————.   *Primary Mental Abilities Test.* Chicago: Science Research Associates, 1947.

Till, R. E.   Age-related differences in binocular backward masking with visual noise. *Journal of Gerontology,* 1978, *33,* 702–710.

Till, R. E., & Franklin, L. D.   On the locus of age differences in visual information processing. *Journal of Gerontology,* 1981, *36,* 200–210.

Till, R. E., & Walsh, D. A.   Encoding and retrieval factors in adult memory for implicational sentences. *Journal of Verbal Learning and Verbal Behavior,* 1980, *19,* 1–16.

Time.   People section. September 8, 1980, p. 57.

Timiras, P. S.   *Developmental physiology and aging.* New York: Macmillan, 1972.

————.   Biological perspectives on aging. *American Scientist,* 1978, *66,* 605–613.

Tolman, E. C.   *Purposive behavior in animals and men.* New York: Appleton-Century-Crofts, 1932.

Traxler, A. J., & Britton, J. H.   Age differences in retroaction as a function of anticipation interval and transfer paradigm. In *Proceedings of the 78th Annual Convention of the American Psychological Association,* Washington D.C.: American Psychological Association, 1970, *5,* 683–684.

Treat, N. J., Poon, J. L., Fozard, J. L., & Popkin, S. J.   Toward applying cognitive skill training to memory problems. *Experimental Aging Research,* 1978, *4,* 305–319.

Treat, N. J., & Reese, H. W.   Age, imagery, and pacing in paired-associate learning. *Developmental Psychology,* 1976, *12,* 119–124.

Treisman, A. M.   Contextual cues in selective listening. *Quarterly Journal of Experimental Psychology,* 1960, *12,* 242–248.

Treisman, A. M., & Davis, A.   Divided attention to ear and eye. In S. Kornblum (Ed.), *Attention and performance IV.* New York: Academic Press, 1973.

Trembly, D., & O'Connor, J.   Growth and decline of natural and acquired intellectual characteristics. *Journal of Gerontology,* 1966, *21,* 9–12.

Trimakas, K. A., & Nicolay, R. C.   Self-concept and altruism in old age. *Journal of Gerontology,* 1974, *29,* 434–439.

Troll, L. E., Saltz, R., & Dunin-Markiewicz, R.   A seven year follow-up of intelligence test scores for foster grandparents. *Journal of Gerontology,* 1976, *31,* 583–585.

Troyer, W. G., Eisdorfer, C., Bogdonoff, M. D., & Wilkie, F.   Experimental stress and learning in the aged. *Journal of Abnormal Psychology,* 1967, *72,* 65–70.

Tuddenham, R. D. Soldier intelligence in World Wars I and II. *American Psychologist,* 1948, *3,* 149–159.

Tulving, E. Subjective organization in free-recall of "unrelated words." *Psychological Review,* 1962, *69,* 344–354.

——. Intratrial and intertrial retention: Notes towards a theory of free recall verbal learning. *Psychological Review,* 1964, *71,* 219–237.

——. Theoretical issues in free recall. In T. R. Dixon & D. L. Horton (Eds.), *Verbal behavior and general behavior theory.* Englewood Cliffs, New Jersey: Prentice Hall, 1968.

——. Episodic and semantic memory. In E. Tulving & W. Donaldson (Eds.), *Organization of Memory.* New York: Academic Press, 1972.

Tulving, E., & Arbuckle, T. Y. Sources of intratrial interference in immediate recall of paired associates. *Journal of Verbal Learning and Verbal Behavior,* 1963, *1,* 321–334.

Tulving, E., & Pearlstone, Z. Availability versus accessibility of information in memory for words. *Journal of Verbal Learning and Verbal Behavior,* 1966, *5,* 381–391.

Turvey, M. T. On peripheral and central processes in vision: Inferences from an information-processing analysis of masking with patterned stimuli. *Psychological Review,* 1973, *80,* 1–52.

Underwood, B. J. Speed of learning and amount retained: A consideration of methodology. *Psychological Bulletin,* 1954, *51,* 276–282.

——. Interference and forgetting. *Psychological Review,* 1957, *64,* 49–60.

——. Stimulus selection in verbal learning. In C. N. Cofer & B. S. Musgrave (Eds.), *Verbal behavior and learning.* New York: McGraw-Hill, 1963.

——. Degree of learning and the measurement of forgetting. *Journal of Verbal Learning and Verbal Behavior,* 1964, *3,* 112–129.

——. Attributes of memory. *Psychological Review,* 1969, *76,* 559–573.

Underwood, B. J., & Postman, L. Extra-experimental sources of interference in forgetting. *Psychological Review,* 1960, *67,* 73–95.

Underwood, B. J., & Schulz, R. W. *Meaningfulness and verbal learning.* Philadelphia: Lippincott, 1960.

United Nations. *Demographic yearbook.* New York: United Nations, 1972.

U.S. Bureau of the Census. Population profile of the United States: 1974. *Current population reports,* Series P–20, No. 279. Washington, D.C.: U.S. Government Printing Office, 1975.

——. *Statistical analysis of the United States.* Washington, D.C.: U.S. Government Printing Office, 1978.

U.S. Department of Health, Education, and Welfare. *Health United States.* Washington, D.C.: U.S. Government Printing Office, 1975.

U.S. Health Survey. *Health statistics,* Series C, No. 4. Washington, D.C.: U.S. Government Printing Office, 1960.

U.S. Public Health Service. *Vital Statistics of the United States, 1970; Volume II, Mortality, Part A.* Rockville, Md: U.S. Public Health Service, 1974.

Vega, A., Jr., & Parsons, O. A. Cross-validation of the Halstead-Reitan tests for brain damage. *Journal of Consulting Psychology,* 1967, *31,* 619–625.

Vroom, V. H., & Pahl, B. Relationship between age and risk-taking among managers. *Journal of Applied Psychology,* 1971, *55,* 399–405.

Wallace, J. E., Krauter, E. E., & Campbell, B. Animal models of declining memory in the aged: Short-term and spatial memory in the aged rat. *Journal of Gerontology,* 1980, *35,* 355–363.

Wallach, M. A., & Kogan, N.   Aspects of judgment and decision making: Interrelationships and changes with age. *Behavioral Sciences,* 1961, *6,* 23–26.

Walsh, D. A.   Age differences in learning and memory. In D. S. Woodruff & J. E. Birren (Eds.), *Aging: Scientific perspectives and social issues.* New York: Van Nostrand, 1975.

———.   Age differences in central perceptual processing: A dichoptic backward masking investigation. *Journal of Gerontology,* 1976, *31,* 178–185.

Walsh, D. A., & Baldwin, M.   Age differences in integrated semantic memory. *Developmental Psychology,* 1977, *13,* 509–514.

Walsh, D. A., Baldwin, M., & Finkle, T. J.   Age differences in integrated semantic memory for abstract sentence, *Experimental Aging Research,* 1980, *6,* 431–444.

Walsh, D. A., Krauss, I. K., & Regnier, V. A.   Spatial ability, environmental knowledge, and environmental use: The elderly. In L. Liben, A. Patterson, & N. Newcombe (Eds.), *Spatial representation and behavior across the life span.* New York: Academic Press, 1981.

Walsh, D. A., & Prasse, M. J.   Iconic memory and attentional processes in the aged. In L. W. Poon, J. L. Fozard, L. S. Cermak, D. Arenberg, & L. W. Thompson (Eds.), *New directions in memory and aging.* Hillsdale, N.J.: Lawrence Erlbaum, 1980.

Walsh, D. A., & Thompson, L. W.   Age differences in visual sensory memory. *Journal of Gerontology,* 1978, *33,* 383–387.

Walsh, D. A., Till, R. E., & Williams, M. V.   Age differences in peripheral perceptual processing: A monoptic backward masking investigation. *Journal of Experimental Psychology: Human Perception and Performance,* 1978, *4,* 232–243.

Walsh, D. A., Williams, M. V., & Hertzog, C. K.   Age-related differences in two stages of central perceptual processes: The effects of short duration targets and criterion differences. *Journal of Gerontology,* 1979, *34,* 234–241.

Wapner, S., Werner, H., & Comalli, P. E., Jr.   Perception of part-whole relationships in middle and old age. *Journal of Gerontology,* 1960, *15,* 412–415.

Ward, R. A.   *The aging experience: An introduction to social gerontology.* Philadelphia: Lippincott, 1979.

Warren, L. R., & Mitchell, S. A.   Age differences in judging the frequency of events. *Developmental Psychology,* 1980, *16,* 116–120.

Warren, L. R., Wagener, J. W., & Herman, G. E.   Binaural analysis in the aging auditory system. *Journal of Gerontology,* 1978, *33,* 731–736.

Warren, R. E.   Stimulus encoding and memory. *Journal of Experimental Psychology,* 1972, *94,* 90–100.

Warrington, E. K., & Sanders, H. I.   The fate of old memories. *Quarterly Journal of Experimental Psychology,* 1971, *23,* 432–442.

Warrington, E. K., & Silberstein, M.   A questionnaire technique for investigating very long term memory. *Quarterly Journal of Experimental Psychology,* 1970, *22,* 508–512.

Watkins, M. J.   The intricacy of memory span. *Memory & Cognition,* 1977, *5,* 529–534.

Watkins, M. J., & Watkins, O. C.   Processing of recency items for free recall. *Journal of Experimental Psychology,* 1974, *101,* 448–493.

Watkins, O. C., & Watkins, M. J.   The modality effect and echoic persistence. *Journal of Experimental Psychology: General,* 1980, *109,* 251–278.

Watson, C. S., Turpenoff, M., Kelly, W. J., & Botwinick, J.   Age differences in resolving power and decision strategies in a weight discrimination task. *Journal of Gerontology,* 1979, *34,* 547–552.

Watson, G., & Glaser, E. *Watson-Glaser. Critical Thinking Appraisal: Manual.* Yonkers, N. Y.: World, 1952.

Watson, J. B. *Psychology from the standpoint of a behaviorist.* Philadelphia: Lippincott, 1919.

Waugh, N. C. Age-related differences in acquisition of a verbal habit. *Perceptual and Motor Skills,* 1980, *50,* 435–438.

Waugh, N. C., & Anders, T. R. Searching through long-term verbal memory. In S. Kornblum (Ed.), *Attention and performance IV.* New York: Academic Press, 1973.

Waugh, N. C., & Barr, R. A. Memory and mental tempo. In L. W. Poon, J. L. Fozard, L. S. Cermak, D. Arenberg, & L. W. Thompson (Eds.), *New directions in memory and aging.* Hillsdale, N.J.: Lawrence Erlbaum, 1980.

Waugh, N. C., Fozard, J. L., Talland, G. A., & Erwin, D. E. Effects of age and stimulus repetition on two-choice reaction time, *Journal of Gerontology,* 1973, *28,* 466–470.

Waugh, N. C., & Norman, D. A. Primary memory. *Psychological Review,* 1965, *72,* 89–104.

Weber, R. J., Brown, L. T., & Weldon, J. K., Cognitive maps of environmental knowledge and preference in nursing home patients. *Experimental Aging Research,* 1978, *3,* 157–174.

Wechsler, D. *The measurement of adult intelligence* (3rd ed.). Baltimore: Williams & Wilkins, 1944.

———. A standardized memory scale for clinical use. *Journal of Psychology,* 1945, *19,* 87–95.

———. *The measurement and appraisal of adult intelligence* (4th ed.). Baltimore: Williams & Wilkins, 1958.

Weinberger, L. E., & Millham, J. A multi-dimensional, multiple method analysis of attitudes toward the elderly. *Journal of Gerontology,* 1975, *30,* 343–348.

Weiner, B., Runquist, W., Runquist, P. A., Raven, B. H., Meyer, W. J., Leiman, A., Kutscher, C. L., Kleinmuntz, B., & Haber, R. N. *Discovering psychology.* Chicago: Science Research Associates, 1977.

Weiner, M. Organization of mental abilities from ages 14 to 54. *Educational and Psychological Measurement,* 1964, *24,* 573–587.

Weisenburg, T., Roe, A., & McBride, K. E. *Adult intelligence.* New York: The Commonwealth Fund, 1936.

Weiss, A. D. Auditory perception in relation to age. In J. E. Birren, R. N. Butler, S. W. Greenhouse, L. Sokoloff, & M. R. Yarrow (Eds.), *Human aging: A biological and behavioral study.* Bethesda, Md.: U.S. Department of Health, Education, and Welfare, 1963.

Welford, A. T. *Aging and human skill.* Oxford: Oxford University Press, 1958.

———. Psychomotor performance. In J. E. Birren (Ed.), *Handbook of aging and the individual.* Chicago: University of Chicago Press, 1959.

———. Changes in the speed of performance with age and their industrial significance. *Ergonomics,* 1962, *5,* 139–145.

———. Motor performance. In J. E. Birren & K. W. Schaie (Eds.), *Handbook of the psychology of aging.* New York: Van Nostrand Reinhold, 1977.

———. Memory and age: A perspective view. In L. W. Poon, J. L. Fozard, L. S. Cermak, D. Arenberg, & L. W. Thompson (Eds.), *New directions in memory and aging.* Hillsdale, N.J.,: Lawrence Erlbaum, 1980.

Welford, A. T., Norris, A. H., & Shock, N. W. Speed and accuracy of movement and their changes. *Acta Psychologica,* 1969, *30,* 3–15.

Werner, H. The concept of development from a comparative and organismic point of view. In D. B. Harris (Ed.), *The concept of development.* Minneapolis: University of Minnesota Press, 1957.

Wessman, A. E. A psychological inquiry into satisfaction and happiness. (Doctoral dissertation, Princeton University, 1956). *Dissertation Abstracts,* 1957, *17,* 1384–1385.

West, R. L., Odom, R. D., & Aschkenasy, J. R. Perceptual sensitivity and conceptual coordination in children and younger and older adults. *Human Development,* 1978, *21,* 334–345.

Wetherick, N. E., A comparison of the problem-solving ability of young, middle-aged and old subjects. *Gerontologia,* 1964, *9,* 164–178.

———. Changing an established concept: A comparison of the ability of young, middle-aged and old subjects. *Gerontologia,* 1965, *11,* 82–95.

———. The inferential basis of concept attainment. *British Journal of Psychology,* 1966, *57,* 61–69.

Wheeler, L. R. A comparative study of the intelligence of East Tennessee mountain children. *Journal of Educational Psychology,* 1942, *33,* 321–334.

Whitbourne, S. K. Test anxiety in elderly and young adults. *International Journal of Aging and Human Development,* 1976, *7,* 201–210.

Whitbourne, S. K., & Slevin, A. E. Imagery and sentence retention in elderly and young adults. *Journal of Genetic Psychology,* 1978, *133,* 287–298.

Whitehead, W. E., Lurie, E., & Blackwell, B. Classical conditioning of decreases in human systolic blood pressure. *Journal of Applied Behavior Analysis,* 1976, *9,* 153–157.

Wickelgren, W. A. Age and storage dynamics in continuous recognition memory. *Developmental Psychology,* 1975, *11,* 165–169.

Wickens, C. D. Temporal limits of human information processing: A developmental study. *Psychological Bulletin,* 1974, *81,* 739–755.

Wickens, D. D., Born, D. G., & Allen, C. K. Proactive inhibition and item similarity in short-term memory. *Journal of Verbal Learning and Verbal Behavior,* 1963, *2,* 440–445.

Wiersma, W., & Klausmeier, H. J. The effect of age upon speed of concept attainment. *Journal of Gerontology,* 1965, *20,* 398–400.

Wilder, C. S. Acute conditions: Incidence and associated disability: United States, July 1971 to June 1972. *Vital and Health Statistics,* Series 10, No. 80. Washington, D.C.: U.S. Government Printing Office, 1974.

Wilkie, F. L, & Eisdorfer, C. Sex, verbal ability, and pacing differences in serial learning. *Journal of Gerontology,* 1977, *32,* 63–67.

Williams, M. V. Receiver operating characteristics: The effect of distribution on between-group comparisons. In L. W. Poon (Ed.), *Aging in the 1980's: Selected contemporary issues in the psychology of aging.* Washington, D.C.: American Psychological Association, 1980.

Willis, S. L., & Baltes, P. B. Intelligence in adulthood and aging: Contemporary issues. In L. W. Poon (Ed.), *Aging in the 1980's: Selected contemporary issues in the psychology of aging.* Washington, D.C.: American Psychological Association, 1980.

Willits, F. K., Bealer, R. C., & Crider, D. M. Changes in individual attitudes toward traditional morality: A 24-year follow-up study. *Journal of Gerontology,* 1977, *32,* 681–688.

Willoughby, R. R. Family similarities in mental test abilities. *Genetic Psychology Monographs,* 1927, *2,* 235–277.

————. Incidental learning. *Journal of Educational Psychology,* 1929, *20,* 671–682.

Wilson, D. L. The programmed theory of aging. In M. Rockstein (Ed.), *Theoretical aspects of aging.* New York: Academic Press, 1974.

Wilson, R. C., Guilford, J. P., & Christensen, P. R. The measurement of individual differences in originality. *Psychological Bulletin,* 1953, *50,* 362–370.

Wimer, R. E., & Wigdor, B. T. Age differences in retention of learning. *Journal of Gerontology,* 1958, *13,* 291–295.

Winer, B. J. *Statistical principles in experimental design* (2nd ed.) New York: McGraw-Hill, 1971.

Winn, F. J., Jr., & Elias, J. W. Associative symmetry and item availability: Evidence for qualitative age differences in acquisition strategies. *Experimental Aging Research,* 1978, 4, 411–420.

Winn, F. J., Jr., Elias, J. W., & Marshall, P. H. Meaningfulness and interference as factors in paired-associate learning. *Educational Gerontology,* 1976, *1,* 297–306.

Winograd, E., & Simon, E. W. Visual memory and imagery in the aged. In L. W. Poon, J. L. Fozard, L. S. Cermak, D. Arenberg, & L. W. Thompson (Eds.), *New directions in aging.* Hillsdale, N.J.: Lawrence Erlbaum, 1980.

Witkin, H. A., Dyk, R. B., Faterson, H. F., Goodenough, D. R., & Karp, S. A. *Psychological differentiation.* New York: Wiley, 1962.

Witt, S. J., & Cunningham, W. R. Cognitive speed and subsequent intellectual development: A longitudinal investigation. *Journal of Gerontology,* 1979, *34,* 540–546.

Witte, K. L. Optional shift behavior in children and young and elderly adults. *Psychonomic Science,* 1971, *25,* 329–330.

————. Paired-associate learning in young and elderly adults as related to presentation rate. *Psychological Bulletin,* 1975, *82,* 975–985.

Witte, K. L, & Freund, J. S. Paired-associate learning in young and old adults as related to stimulus concreteness and presentation method. *Journal of Gerontology,* 1976, *31,* 186–192.

Wittels, I. Age and stimulus meaningfulness in paired-associate learning. *Journal of Gerontology,* 1972, *27,* 372–375.

Wolk, S. Situational constraint as a moderator of the locus of control-adjustment relationship. *Journal of Consulting & Clinical Psychology,* 1976, *44,* 420–427.

Wolk, S., & Kurtz, J. Positive adjustment and involvement during aging and expectancy for internal control. *Journal of Consulting and Clinical Psychology,* 1975, *43,* 173–178.

Wolk, S., & Telleen, S. Psychological and social correlates of life satisfaction as a function of residential constraint. *Journal of Gerontology,* 1976, *31,* 89–98.

Woodruff, D. S. A physiological perspective of the psychology of aging. In D. S. Woodruff & J. E. Birren (Eds.), *Aging: Scientific perspectives and social issues.* New York: Van Nostrand, 1975. (a)

————. Relationships among EEG alpha frequency, reaction time, and age: A biofeedback study. *Psychophysiology,* 1975, *12,* 673–681. (b)

Woodruff, D. S., & Birren, J. E. Age changes and cohort differences in personality. *Developmental Psychology,* 1972, *6,* 22–259.

Woodruff, D. S., & Kramer, D. A. EEG alpha slowing, refractory period, and reaction time in aging. *Experimental Aging Research,* 1979, *5,* 279–292.

Woodworth, R. S. *Experimental psychology.* New York: Henry Holt, 1938.

Woodworth, R. S., & Sells, S. B. An atmosphere effect in formal syllogistic reasoning. *Journal of Experimental Psychology,* 1935, *18,* 451–460.

Wright, J. M. von. An experimental study of human serial learning. *Societas scientiarum Fennica, Commentations humanarum litterarum,* 1957, *23,* No. 1.

Wright, L. L., & Elias, J. W. Age differences in the effects of perceptual noise. *Journal of Gerontology,* 1979, *34,* 704–708.

Wright, R. E. Aging, divided attention, and processing capacity. *Journal of Gerontology,* 1981, *36,* 605–614.

————. Adult age similarities in free recall output order and strategies. *Journal of Gerontology,* in press.

Yarmey, A. D., & Kent, J. Eyewitness identification by elderly and young adults. *Law and Human Behavior,* in press.

Yerkes, R. M. Psychological examining in the United States Army. Washington, D.C.: National Academy of Science, U.S. Government Printing Office, 1921.

Youmans, W. B. Growth. *The World Book Encyclopedia.* Chicago: Field Enterprises Educational Corporation, 1975.

Young, M. L. Problem-solving performance in two age groups. *Journal of Gerontology,* 1966, *21,* 505–509.

————. Age and sex differences in problem-solving. *Journal of Gerontology,* 1971, *26,* 330–336.

Zaretsky, H., & Halberstam, J. Age differences in paired-associate learning. *Journal of Gerontology,* 1968, *23,* 165–168. (a)

————. Effects of aging, brain damage, and associative strength on paired-associate learning and relearning. *Journal of Genetic Psychology,* 1968, *112,* 149–163. (b)

Zarit, S. H., Cole, K. D., & Guider, R. L. Memory training strategies and subjective complaints of memory in the aged. *The Gerontologist,* 1981, *21,* 158–164.

Zelinski, E. M., Gilewski, M. J., & Thompson., L. W. Do laboratory memory tests relate to everyday remembering and forgetting. In L. W. Poon, J. L. Fozard, L. S. Cermak, D. Arenberg, & L. W. Thompson (Eds.), *New Directions in memory and aging.* Hillsdale, N.J.: Lawrence Erlbaum, 1980.

Zemore, R., & Eames, N. Psychic and somatic symptoms of depression among young adults, institutionalized aged and noninstitutionalized aged. *Journal of Gerontology,* 1979, *34,* 716–722.

Zusne, L. Age and achievement in psychology: The harmonic mean as a model. *American Psychologist,* 1976, *31,* 805–807.

Acknowledgments

p. 1, Figure 1.1   A. N. O'Connell & N. G. Rotter. The influence of stimulus age and sex on person perception. *Journal of Gerontology,* 1979, *34,* 220–228. Adapted from Figure 2, p. 223, Adapted with permission.

p. 8, Figure 1.2   I. M. Hulicka & J. L. Grossman. Age-group comparisons for the use of mediators in paired-associate learning. *Journal of Gerontology,* 1967, *22,* 46–51. Adapted from Table 1, p. 48, with permission.

p. 10, Figure 1.3   G. Cohen. Language comprehension in old age. *Cognitive psychology,* 1979, *11,* 412–429. Adapted from Table 1, p. 417, with permission of Academic Press.

p. 12, Figure 1.4   B. W. Marsh. Aging and driving. *Transportation Engineering,* November, 1960. Adapted from data in text with permission of the Institute of Transportation Engineers.

p. 18, quotation   K. F. Riegel. History of psychological gerontology. In J. E. Birren & K. W. Schaie (Eds.), *Handbook of the psychology of aging.* New York: Van Nostrand Reinhold, 1977. Copyright © 1977 by Van Nostrand Reinhold Company. Reprinted with permission.

p. 20, Figure 1.6   A. T. Welford, A. H. Norris, & N. W. Shock. Speed and accuracy

of movement. *Acta Psychologica,* 1969, *30,* 3–15. Adapted from Table 2, p. 13, with permission of North-Holland Publishing Company.

p. 21, Figure 1.7   J. Botwinick & M. Storandt. *Memory, related functions and age.* Springfield, Illinois: Charles C. Thomas, 1974. Adapted from Figure 17, p. 132, courtesy of Charles C. Thomas.

p. 22, Figure 1.8   N. W. Shock. The physiology of aging. *Scientific American,* 1962, *206,* 100–110. Adapted from figure on page 110, with permission.

p. 23, Table 1.1   G. A. Borkan & A. H. Norris. Assessment of biological age using a profile of physical parameters. *Journal of Gerontology,* 1980, *35,* 177–184. Adapted from Table 1, p. 178, with permission.

p. 26   G. A. Borkan & A. H. Norris. Assessment of biological age using a profile of physical parameters. *Journal of Gerontology,* 1980, *35,* 177–184. Adapted from Figure 2, p. 181, with permission.

p. 28, quotation   R. N. Butler. *Why survive? Being old in America.* New York: Harper & Row, 1975. Reprinted with permission.

p. 54, Figure 2.9   D. H. Kausler & J. M. Puckett. Frequency judgments and correlated cognitive abilities in young and elderly adults. *Journal of Gerontology,* 1980, *35,* 376–382. Adapted from Table 1, p. 379, and from data on p. 380 with permission.

p. 55, Figure 2.10 D. H. Kausler & J. M. Puckett. Frequency judgments and correlated cognitive abilities in young and elderly adults. *Journal of Gerontology,* 1980, *35,* 376–382. Adapted from data on p. 381 with permission.

p. 71, Figure 2.19 R. F. Green. Age-intelligence relationship between ages sixteen and sixty-four: A rising trend. *Developmental Psychology,* 1969, *1,* 618–627. Adapted from Figure 1, p. 620, and Figure 3, p. 623. Copyright 1969 by the American Psychological Association. Adapted with permission of the publisher and author.

p. 80, Figure 3.2 P. B. Baltes & G. V. Labouvie. Adult development of intellectual performance: Description, explanation, and modification. In C. Eisdorfer & M. P. Lawton (Eds.), *The psychology of adult development and aging.* Washington, D.C.: American Psychological Association, 1973. From Figure 4, p. 172. Copyright 1973 by the American Psychological Association. Reprinted with permission of the publisher and authors.

p. 83, Figure 3.5 W. A. Owens, Jr. Age and mental ability: A second follow-up. *Journal of Educational Psychology,* 1966, *57,* 311–325. Adapted from Figure 1, p. 316. Copyright 1966 by the American Psychological Association. Adapted by permission of the publisher and author.

p. 84, Figure 3.6 I. C. Siegler & J. Botwinick. A long-term longitudinal study of intellectual ability of older adults: The matter of selective subject attrition. *Journal of Gerontology,* 1979, *34,* 242–245. Adapted from Figure 1, p. 243, with permission.

p. 86, Figure 3.7 I. C. Siegler & J. Botwinick. A long-term longitudinal study of intellectual ability of older adults: The matter of selective subject attrition. *Journal of Gerontology,* 1979, *34,* 242–245. Adapted from Figure 2, p. 244, with permission.

p. 90, Figure 3.9 J. Botwinick & J. E. Birren. A follow-up study of card-sorting performance in elderly men. *Journal of Gerontology,* 1965, *20,* 208–210. Adapted from Figure 1, p. 209, with permission.

p. 99, Table 3.1 D. Arenberg. A longitudinal study of problem solving in adults. *Journal of Gerontology,* 1974, *29,* 650–658. Adapted from Table 3, p. 654, with permission.

p. 101 D. Arenberg & E. A. Robertson-Tchabo. Learning and aging. In J. E. Birren & K. W. Schaie (Eds.), *Handbook of the psychology of aging.* New York: Van Nostrand Reinhold, 1977. Adapted from Figure 1, p. 422, with permission of the authors.

p. 107, Figure 3.16 S. K. Whitbourne. Test anxiety in elderly and young adults. *International Journal of Aging and Human Development,* 1976, *7,* 201–210. Adapted from Table 2, p. 206, with permission of Baywood Publishing Company. Copyright © 1976, Baywood Publishing Company, Inc.

p. 108, Figure 3.17 C. Eisdorfer, J. Nowlin, & F. Wilkie. Improvement of learning in the aged by modification of autonomic nervous system activity. *Science,* 1970, *170,* 1327–1329. Adapted from Figure 1, p. 1328. Copyright 1970 by the American Association for the Advancement of Science. Reprinted by permission of the publisher and the authors.

p. 111, Table 3.2 D. Arenberg. Concept problem solving in young and old adults. *Journal of Gerontology,* 1968, *23,* 279–282. Adapted from Table 1, p. 280, with permission.

p. 113, Figure 3.18 I. Wittels. Age and stimulus meaningfulness in paired-associate learning. *Journal of Gerontology,* 1972, *27,* 372–375. Adapted from Table 2, p. 373, with permission.

p. 114, Figure 3.19 E. A. Grant, M. Storandt, & J. Botwinick. Incentive and practice in the psychomotor performance of the elderly. *Journal of Gerontology,* 1978, *33,* 413–415. Adapted from Table 1, p. 414, with permission.

p. 119, Figure 3.20 C. A. Furry & K. W. Schaie. Pretest activity and intellectual performance in middle-aged and older persons. *Experimental Aging Research,* 1979, *5,* 413–421. Taken from *Experimental Aging Research, 5,* 1979, Table 1, p. 418, with permission of the authors and editor. Copyright Beech Hill Enterprises, Inc., 1979.

p. 120 Figure 3.21 H. A. Taub. Memory span, practice, and aging. *Journal of Gerontology,* 1973, *28,* 335–338. Adapted from Table 1, p. 337, with permission.

p. 121, quotation From *Life-span developmental psychology: Introduction to research methods* by P. B. Baltes, H. W. Reese, & J. R. Nesselroade. Copyright 1977 by Wadsworth Publishing Company, Inc.

Reprinted with permission of the publisher, Brooks/Cole Publishing Company, Monterey, California 93940.

p. 154, Figure 4.5   K. W. Schaie & C. R. Strother. A cross-sequential study of age changes in cognitive behavior. *Psychological Bulletin*, 1968, *70*, 671–680. From Figure 3, p. 675. Copyright 1968 by the American Psychological Association. Reprinted with permission of the publisher and the authors.

p. 157, Figure 4.6   D. A. Eisner & K. W. Schaie. Age changes in response to visual illusions from middle to old age. *Journal of Gerontology*, 1971, *26*, 146–150. From Figure 3, p. 149. Reprinted with permission.

p. 159, Table 4.10   J. Botwinick & D. Arenberg. Disparate time spans in sequential studies of aging. *Experimental Aging Research*, 1976, *1*, 55–61. Taken from *Experimental Aging Research, 1*, Table 1, with permission of the authors and editor. Copyright Beech Hill Enterprises Inc., 1976.

p. 161, Figure 4.7   J. Botwinick & I. C. Siegler. Intellectual ability among the elderly: Simultaneous cross-sectional and longitudinal comparisons. *Developmental Psychology*, 1980, *16*, 49–53. From Figure 1, p. 52. Copyright 1980 by the American Psychological Association. Reprinted by permission of the publisher and authors.

p. 163, Figure 4.8   P. B. Baltes. Longitudinal and cross-sectional sequences in the study of age and generation effects. *Human Development*, 1968, *11*, 145–171. From Figure 1, p. 152. Reprinted by permission.

p. 206, Figure 5.8   E. J. Rowe & M. M. Schnore. Item concreteness and reported strategies in paired-associate learning as a function of age. *Journal of Gerontology*, 1971, *26*, 470–475. Adapted from Figure 1, p. 472, with permission.

p. 207, Figure 5.9   C. Eisdorfer & C. Service. Verbal rote learning and superior intelligence in the aged. *Journal of Gerontology*, 1967, *22*, 158–161. Adapted from Figure 1, p. 159, with permission.

p. 209, Figure 5.11   H. A. Taub. Mode of presentation, age, and short-term memory. *Journal of Gerontology*, 1975, *30*, 56–59. Adapted from Table 1, p. 58, with permission.

p. 213, Figure 5.13   J. T. Erber. The effect of encoding instructions on recall and recognition memory. Paper presented at the annual meeting of the Gerontological Society, Washington, D.C., November, 1979. Adapted from Table 1 with permission of the author.

p. 214, Figure 5.14   D. H. Kausler & J. M. Puckett. Effects of word frequency on adult age differences in word memory span. *Experimental Aging Research*, 1979, *5*, 161–169. Taken from *Experimental Aging Research, 5*, text, p. 167, with permission of the authors and editor. Copyright Beech Hill Enterprises, Inc., 1979.

p. 228, Figure 5.20   P. N. Prinz. Sleep patterns in the healthy aged: Relationship with intellectual function. *Journal of Gerontology*, 1977, *12*, 179–186. Adapted from Table 2, p. 181, with permission.

p. 248, quotation   D. H. Kausler. *Psychology of verbal learning and memory.* New York: Academic Press, 1974. Reprinted with permission.

pp. 252–253, quotation   P. S. Timiras. Biological perspectives on aging. *American Scientist*, 1978, *66*, 605–613. Reprinted with permission of *American Scientist,* Journal of Sigma Xi, The Scientific Research Society.

p. 257, Figure 6.10   T. A. Salthouse. Age and speed: A generalized slowing? Unpublished manuscript, 1980. Adapted from table 1 with permission of the author.

p. 285, Figure 7.3   J. Botwinick. *Aging and behavior,* second edition. Figure 10.1, p. 148. Copyright 1978 by Springer Publishing Company, Inc., New York. Used with permission.

p. 286, Figure 7.4   J. König. Pitch discrimination and age. *Acta Oto-Laryngologica*, 1957, *48*, 473–489. Adapted from Figure 5, p. 482, with permission.

p. 287, Figure 7.5   R. G. Domey, R. A. McFarland, & E. Chadwick. Dark adaptation as a function of age and time: II. A derivation. *Journal of Gerontology*, 1960, *15*, 267–279. Adapted from Figure 12, p. 273, with permission.

p. 295, Figure 7.8   M. Potash & B. Jones. Aging and decision criteria for the detection of tones in noise. *Journal of Gerontology*, 1977, *32*, 436–440. Adapted from Table 1, p. 438, with permission.

p. 298, Figure 7.9   B. Bell, E. Wolf, & C. D. Bernholz. Depth perception as a function of age. *Aging and Human Development*, 1972, *3*, 77–88. From Figure 1, p. 79. Reprinted with permission of Baywood Publishing Company. Copyright © 1972, Baywood Publishing Company, Inc.

p. 299, Figure 7.10 R. Lorden, B. M. Atkeson, & R. H. Pollack. Differences in the magnitude of the Delboeuf illusion and Usnadze effect during adulthood. *Journal of Gerontology*, 1979, *34*, 229–233. Adapted from Figure 3, p. 232, with permission.

p. 302, Figure 7.12 D. W. Kline & C. Orme-Rogers. Examination of stimulus persistence as the basis for superior visual identification performance among older adults. *Journal of Gerontology*, 1978, *33*, 76–81. Adapted from Figure 2, p. 78, with permission.

p. 304, Figure 7.13 D. W. Kline & S. Nestor. Persistence of complementary afterimages as a function of adult age and exposure duration. *Experimental Aging Research*, 1977, *3*, 191–201. Taken from Figure 1, p. 197, with permission of the authors and editor. Copyright Beech Hill Enterprises, Inc., 1977.

p. 311, Figure 7.16 T. M. Hines & M. I. Posner. Slow but sure: A chronometric analysis of the process of aging. Paper presented at the American Psychological Association Symposium on Decision Making and Aging, Washington, D.C., August, 1976. Adapted with permission of the authors.

p. 312, Figure 7.17 L. W. Poon, J. L. Fozard, V. Dailey, B. F. Cerella, & P. Zeller. The effects of practice and information in feedback on age-related differences in performance speed, variability, and error rates in a two-choice decision task. Paper presented at the American Psychological Association Symposium on Decision Making and Aging, Washington, D.C., August, 1976. Adapted with permission of the authors.

p. 315, Figure 7.19 D. A. Walsh, M. V. Williams, & C. K. Hertzog. Age-related differences in two stages of central perceptual processes: The effects of short duration targets and criterion differences. *Journal of Gerontology*, 1979, *34*, 234–241. Adapted from Table 1, p. 237, with permission.

p. 316, Figure 7.20 C. K. Hertzog, M. V. Williams, & D. A. Walsh. The effect of practice on age differences in central perceptual processes. *Journal of Gerontology*, 1976, *31*, 428–433. Adapted from Table 1, p. 430, with permission.

p. 317, Figure 7.21 D. W. Kline & J. Szafran. Age differences in backward monoptic visual noise masking. *Journal of Gerontology*, 1975, *30*, 307–311. Adapted from Figure 1, p. 309, with permission.

p. 319, Figure 7.22 D. J. Plude & W. J. Hoyer. Adult age differences in visual search as a function of stimulus mapping and information load. Paper presented at the annual meeting of the American Psychological Association, New York, September 1979. Adapted with permission of the authors.

p. 323, Figure 7.23 W. K. Kirchner. Age differences in short-term retention of rapidly changing information. *Journal of Experimental Psychology*, 1958, *55*, 352–358. Adapted from Table 3, p. 355, with permission of the publisher and author.

p. 327, Figure 7.25 P. E. Comalli, Jr., S. Wapner, & H. Werner. Interference effects of Stroop color-word test in childhood, adulthood, and aging. *Journal of Genetic Psychology*, 1962, *100*, 47–53. Adapted from Figure 1, p. 49, with permission of the publisher and authors.

p. 328, Figure 7.26 P. M. A. Rabbitt. An age-decrement in the ability to ignore irrelevant information. *Journal of Gerontology*, 1965, *20*, 233–238. Adapted from Table 1, p. 235, with permission.

p. 330, Figure 7.27 M. S. Farkas & W. J. Hoyer. Processing consequences of perceptual grouping in selective-attention. *Journal of Gerontology*, 1980, *35*, 207–216. Adapted from Figure 2, p. 210, with permission.

p. 333, Figure 7.28 B. L. Somberg. Divided attention abilities in young and old adults. Unpublished doctoral dissertation, University of Missouri, Columbia, 1981. Adapted by permission of the author.

p. 335, Figure 7.29 (top panel) J. Inglis & W. K. Caird. Age differences in successive responses to simultaneous stimulation. *Canadian Journal of Psychology*, 1963, *17*, 98–105. Adapted from Figure 1, p. 104. Copyright 1963 , Canadian Psychological Association. Reprinted by permission.

p. 335, Figure 7.29 (bottom panel) L. E. Clark & J. B. Knowles. Age differences in dichotic listening performance. *Journal of Gerontology*, 1973, *28*, 173–178. Figure 1, p. 175. Reprinted with permission.

p. 338, Figure 7.30 L. E. Clark & J. B. Knowles. Age differences in dichotic listening performance. *Journal of Gerontology*, 1973, *28*, 173–178. Adapted from Table 2, p. 175. Adapted by permission of The Journal of Gerontology.

p. 350, Figure 8.3   H. W. Braun & R. Gieselhart. Age differences in the acquisition and extinction of the conditioned eyelid response. *Journal of Experimental Psychology,* 1959, *57,* 386–388. Adapted from Figure 1, p. 386, with permission of the publisher.

p. 357, Table 8.1   R. J. Weber, L. T. Brown, & J. K. Weldon. Cognitive maps of environmental knowledge and preference in nursing home patients. *Experimental Aging Research,* 1978, *4,* 157–174. Taken from Table 2, p. 166, with permission of the authors and editor. Copyright Beech Hill Enterprises, Inc., 1978.

p. 361, Figure 8.5   A. T. Welford. Psychomotor performance. In J. E. Birren (Ed.), *Handbook of aging and the individual.* Chicago: University of Chicago Press, 1959. Adapted from Table 21, p. 597, copyright 1959 by the University of Chicago. Adapted by permission of the publisher.

p. 363, Figure 8.6   F. L. Ruch. The differentiative effects of age upon human learning. *Journal of General Psychology,* 1934, *11,* 261–286. Adapted from Table 15, p. 277, with permission.

p. 364, Figure 8.7   A. T. Welford, Psychomotor performance. In J. E. Birren (Ed.), *Handbook of aging and the individual.* Chicago: University of Chicago Press, 1959. Adapted from Tables 22, 23, p. 598, with permission of the publisher.

p. 368, Table 8.2   S. J. Korchin & H. Basowitz. Age differences in verbal learning. *Journal of Abnormal and Social Psychology,* 1957, *54,* 64–69. Adapted from Table 1, p. 65. Copyright, 1957, by the American Psychological Association. Adapted with permission of the publisher and authors.

p. 369, Figure 8.9   F. L. Ruch. The differentiative effects of age upon human learning. *Journal of General Psychology,* 1934, *11,* 261–286. Adapted from Table 15, p. 277, with permission.

p. 371, Figure 8.10 (top)   S. J. Korchin & H. Basowitz. Age differences in verbal learning. *Journal of Abnormal and Social Psychology,* 1957, *54,* 64–69. Adapted from Figure 1, p. 66. Copyright, 1957, by the American Psychological Association. Adapted by permission of the publisher and authors.

p. 371, Figure 8.10 (bottom)   D. H. Kausler & J. M. Puckett. Frequency judgments and correlated cognitive abilities in young and elderly adults. *Journal of Gerontology,* 1980, *35,* 376–382. Adapted from data in study with permission.

p. 372, Figure 8.11   R. H. Monge. Studies of verbal learning from the college years through middle age. *Journal of Gerontology,* 1971, *26,* 324–329. Adapted from Table 3, p. 326, with permission.

p. 373, Figure 8.12   F. J. Winn, Jr., J. W. Elias, & P. H. Marshall. Meaningfulness and interference as factors in paired-associate learning. *Educational Gerontology,* 1976, *1,* 297–306. Adapted from Table 2, p. 302, with permission of Hemisphere Publishing Corporation.

p. 378, Figure 8.14   H. Zaretsky & J. Halberstam. Effects of aging, brain damage, and associative strength on paired-associate learning and relearning. *Journal of Genetic Psychology,* 1968, *112,* 149–163. Adapted from Figure 1, p. 154, with permission.

p. 381, Figure 8.16   R. E. Canestrari, Jr. Paced and self-paced learning in young and elderly adults. *Journal of Gerontology,* 1963, *18,* 165–168. Adapted from Table 2, p. 166, with permission.

p. 382 Figure 8.17   R. H. Monge & D. F. Hultsch. Paired-associate learning as a function of adult age and the length of the anticipation and inspection intervals. *Journal of Gerontology,* 1971, *26,* 157–162. Adapted from Table 2, p. 159, with permission.

p. 385, Figure 8.18   R. E. Canestrari, Jr. Age changes in acquisition. In G. A. Talland (Ed.), *Human aging and behavior.* Adapted from Figure 1, p. 179, with permission of Academic Press.

p. 387, Figure 8.19   D. Arenberg. Regression analysis of verbal learning on adult age differences at two anticipation intervals. *Journal of Gerontology,* 1967, *22,* 411–414. Adapted from Table 2, p. 412, with permission.

p. 395, Figure 8.22 (top)   R. E. Wimer & B. T. Wigdor. Age differences in retention of learning. *Journal of Gerontology,* 1958, *13,* 291–295. Adapted from Table 2, p. 293, with permission.

p. 395, Figure 8.22 (bottom)   I. M. Hulicka. Age differences in retention as a function of interference. *Journal of Gerontology,* 1967, *22,* 180–184. Adapted from Table 3, p. 182, with permission.

p. 398, Figure 8.23   D. Schonfield. In search of early memories. Paper presented at the

International Congress of Gerontology, Washington, D.C., July, 1969. Adapted from Table 1 with permission of the author.

p. 399, Figure 8.24 H. P. Bahrick. Maintenance of knowledge: Questions about memory we forgot to ask. *Journal of Experimental Psychology: General,* 1979, *108,* 296–308. Adapted from Figure 1, p. 305. Copyright, 1979, by the American Psychological Association. Adapted by permission of the publisher and author.

p. 405, Figure 8.26 (top) D. Arenberg. Age differences in retroaction. *Journal of Gerontology,* 1967, *22,* 88–91. Adapted from Table 1, p. 89, with permission.

p. 405, Figure 8.26 (bottom) I. M. Hulicka. Age differences in retention as a function of interference. *Journal of Gerontology,* 1967, *22,* 180–184. Adapted from Table 3, p. 182, with permission.

p. 406, Figure 8.27 J. S. Freund & K. L. Witte. Paired-associate transfer: Age of subjects, anticipation interval, association value, and paradigm. *American Journal of Psychology,* 1976, *89,* 695–705. Adapted from Figures 1 and 2, pp. 700, 701. Copyright, 1976, The University of Illinois Press. Adapted by permission of the publisher.

p. 421, Figure 9.2 G. Sperling. The information available in brief visual presentations. *Psychological Monographs,* 1960, *74* (11, Whole No. 498). Adapted from Figure 8, p. 11. Copyright 1960 by the American Psychological Association. Adapted with permission of the publisher and author.

p. 425, Figure 9.3 S. R. Parkinson & A. Perey. Aging, digit span, and the stimulus suffix effect. *Journal of Gerontology,* 1980, *35,* 736–742. Adapted from Figure 2, p. 739, with permission.

p. 426, Figure 9.4 S. A. Madigan. Modality and recall order interactions in short-term memory for serial order. *Journal of Experimental Psychology,* 1971, *87,* 294–296. Adapted from Figure 1, p. 295. Copyright, 1971, by the American Psychological Association. Adapted by permission of the publisher and author.

p. 427, Figures 9.5 D. Arenberg. The effects of input condition on free recall in young and old adults. *Journal of Gerontology,* 1976, *31,* 551–555. Adapted from Figure 1, p. 553, with permission.

p. 430, Figure 9.6 H. A. Taub. Coding for short-term memory as a function of age.

Journal of Genetic Psychology, 1974, *125,* 309–314. Adapted from Figure 1, p. 313, with permission of the publisher and author.

p. 432, Figure 9.8. B. J. Raymond. Free recall among the aged. *Psychological Reports,* 1971, *29,* 1179–1182. Adapted from Figure 1, p. 1180, with permission of the author and publisher.

p. 434, Figure 9.9 (top) L. R. Peterson & M. J. Peterson. Short-term retention of individual verbal items. *Journal of Experimental Psychology,* 1959, *58,* 193–198. Adapted from Figure 3, p. 195. Copyright 1959 by the American Psychological Association. Adapted with permission of the publisher and authors.

p. 434, Figure 9.9 (bottom) D. Schonfield. Age and remembering. Proceedings of Seminars, 1965–1969, Duke University Council on Aging and Human Development. Adapted from Table 3. Used with permission, Duke University Center for the Study of Aging and Human Development.

p. 435, Figure 9.10 C. S. Elias & N. Hirasuna. Age and semantic and phonological encoding. *Developmental Psychology,* 1976, *12,* 497–503. Adapted from Figure 1, p. 500. Copyright 1976, by the American Psychological Association. Adapted with permission of the publisher and authors.

p. 438, Figure 9.11 (top) S. Sternberg. High speed scanning in human memory. *Science,* 1966, *153,* 652–654. From Figure 1, p. 653. Copyright, 1966, by the American Association for the Advancement of Science. Reprinted by permission of publisher and author.

p. 438, Figure 9.11 (bottom) T. R. Anders, J. L. Fozard, & T. D. Lillyquist. Effects of age upon retrieval from short-term memory. *Developmental Psychology,* 1972, *6,* 214–217. Adapted from Figure 1, p. 216. Copyright, 1972, by the American Psychological Association. Adapted by permission of the publisher and authors.

p. 442, Figure 9.12 (top) D. Rundus & R. C. Atkinson. Rehearsal processes in free recall: A procedure for direct observation. *Journal of Verbal Learning and Verbal Behavior,* 1970, *9,* 99–105. Adapted from Figure 1, p. 102, with permission of Academic Press.

p. 442, Figure 9.12 (bottom) R. E. Sanders, M. D. Murphy, F. A. Schmitt, & K. K. Walsh. Age differences in free recall rehearsal strategies. *Journal of Gerontology,* 1980, *35,* 550–558. Adapted from Figure 2, p. 553, with permission.

p. 444, Figure 9.13   R. E. Sanders, M. D. Murphy, F. A. Schmitt, & K. K. Walsh. Age differences in free recall rehearsal strategies. *Journal of Gerontology,* 1980, *35,* 550–558. Adapted from Figure 1, p. 552, with permission.

p. 445, Figure 9.14   T. A. Salthouse. Aging and memory: Strategies for localizing the loss. In L. W. Poon, J. L. Fozard, L. S. Cermak, D. Arenberg, & L. W. Thompson (Eds.), New directions in memory and aging. Hillsdale, N.J.: Lawrence Erlbaum, 1980. Adapted from Figure 2.2, p. 57, with permission of the publisher and author.

p. 449, Figure 9.15   D. H. Kausler & D. M. Kleim. Age differences in processing relevant and irrelevant stimuli in multiple-item recognition learning. *Journal of Gerontology,* 1978, *33,* 87–93. Adapted from Table 1, p. 90, with permission.

p. 450, Figure 9.16   A. D. Smith. Aging and interference with memory. *Journal of Gerontology,* 1975, *30,* 319–325. Adapted from Figure 1, p. 322, with permission.

p. 452, Figure 9.17   T. S. Hyde & J. J. Jenkins. Differential effects of incidental tasks on the organization of recall of a list of highly associated words. *Journal of Experimental Psychology,* 1969, *82,* 472–481. Adapted from Table 1, p. 475. Copyright, 1969, by the American Psychological Association. Adapted with permission of the publisher and authors.

p. 454, Figure 9.18   M. W. Eysenck. Age differences in incidental learning. *Developmental Psychology,* 1974, *10,* 936–941. Adapted from Table 1, p. 938. Copyright 1974, by the American Psychological Association. Adapted with permission of the publisher and author.

p. 458, Figure 9.19 (top)   D. Drachman & J. Leavitt. Memory impairment in the aged: Storage versus retrieval deficit. *Journal of Experimental Psychology.* 1972, *93,* 302–308. Adapted from Figure 2, p. 305. Copyright 1972, by the American Psychological Association. Adapted with permission of the publisher and authors.

p. 458, Figure 9.19 (bottom)   A. D. Smith. Adult age differences in cued recall. *Developmental Psychology,* 1977, *13,* 326–331. Adapted from Figure 1, p. 329. Copyright,

1977, by the American Psychological Association. Adapted by permission of the publisher and author.

p. 460, Figure 9.20   G. Keppel & W. A. Mallory. Presentation rate and instruction to guess in free recall. *Journal of Experimental Psychology,* 1969, *79,* 269–275. Adapted from Figure 2, p. 272. Copyright, 1969, by the American Psychological Association. Adapted with permission of the publisher and author.

p. 461, Figure 9.21   R. E. Wright. Adult age similarities in free recall output order and strategies. *Journal of Gerontology,* in press. Adapted from Table 2 with permission.

p. 467, Figure 9.23   D. F. Hultsch. Adult age differences in retrieval: Trace-dependent and cue-dependent forgetting. *Developmental Psychology,* 1975, *11,* 197–201. Adapted from Tables 1, 2, and 3, pp. 198, 199. Copyright, 1975, by the American Psychological Association. Adapted with permission of the publisher and author.

p. 472, Table 9.2   G. A. Miller & J. A. Selfridge. Verbal context and the recall of meaningful material. *American Journal of Psychology,* 1950, *63* 176–185. Adapted from the Appendix, pp. 184, 185. Copyright, 1950, The University of Illinois Press. Adapted by permission of the publisher.

p. 473, Figure 9.24   F. I. M. Craik & P. A. Mesani. Age differences in the temporal integration of language. *British Journal of Psychology,* 1967, *58,* 291–299. Adapted from Table 2, p. 294, with permission of The British Psychological Society.

p. 474, Figure 9.25   S. K. Whitbourne & A. E. Slevin. Imagery and sentence retention in elderly and young adults. *Journal of Genetic Psychology,* 1978, *133,* 287–298. Adapted from Table 1, p. 293, with permission of the publisher and authors.

p. 474, Table 9.3   J. Botwinick & M. Storandt. *Memory, related functions and age.* Springfield, Illinois: Charles C. Thomas, 1974. Adapted from the text, p. 114, courtesy of Charles C. Thomas, Publisher, Springfield, Illinois.

p. 475, Figure 9.26   J. Botwinick & M. Storandt. *Memory, related functions and age.* Springfield. Illinois: Charles C. Thomas, 1974. Adapted from Figure 11, p. 116, courtesy of Charles C. Thomas, Publisher, Springfield, Illinois.

p. 478, Table 9.4   J. D. Bransford & J. J. Franks. The abstraction of linguistic ideas.

Cognitive Psychology, 1971, *2,* 331–350. Adapted from Table 1, p. 335, with permission of Academic Press.

p. 482, Figure 9.27   D. H. Kausler & J. M. Puckett. Adult age differences in recognition memory for a nonsemantic attribute. *Experimental Aging Research,* 1980, *6,* 349–355. Adapted from Table 1, p. 353, with permission of the authors and editor. Copyright, Beech Hill Enterprises, Inc., 1980.

p. 483, Figure 9.28   D. H. Kausler & J. M. Puckett. Adult age differences in memory for sex of voice. *Journal of Gerontology,* 1981, *36,* 44–50. Adapted from Table 1, p. 47, with permission.

p. 485, Figure 9.29   J. S. Freund & K. L. Witte. Recognition and frequency judgments in young and elderly adults. Paper presented at the annual meeting of the Psychonomic Society, San Antonio, Texas, November, 1978. Adapted from Figure 1 with permission of the authors.

p. 487, Figure 9.30   D. V. Howard, M. I. Lasaga, & M. P. McAndrews. Semantic activation during memory encoding across the adult life span. *Journal of Gerontology,* 1980, *35,* 884–890. Adapted from Table 3, p. 888, with permission.

p. 489, Figure 9.31   M. D. Murphy, R. E. Sanders, A. S. Gabriesheski, & F. A. Schmitt. Metamemory in the aged. *Journal of Gerontology,* 1981, *36,* 185–193. Adapted from Figure 1 and Table 1, pp. 188 and 189, with permission.

p. 500, Figure 10. 2   R. G. Bulgarella & E. J. Archer. Concept identification of auditory stimuli as a function of amount of relevant and irrelevant information. *Journal of Experimental Psychology,* 1962, *63,* 254–257. Adapted from Figure 1, p. 256. Copyright, 1962, by the American Psychological Association. Adapted by permission of the publisher and authors.

p. 510, Figure 10.5   V. G. Cicirelli. Categorization behavior in aging subjects. *Journal of Gerontology,* 1976, *31,* 676–680. Adapted from Table 1, p. 678, with permission.

p. 511, Figure 10.6   W. Wiersma & H. J. Klausmeier. The effect of age upon speed of concept attainment. *Journal of Gerontology,* 1965, *20,* 398–400. Adapted from Table 1, p. 399, with permission.

p. 516, Figure 10.8   J. F. Brinley, T. J. Jovick, & L. M. McLaughlin. Age, reasoning, and memory. *Journal of Gerontology,* 1974, *29,* 182–189. Adapted from Figure 1, p. 184, with permission.

p. 517, Table 10.3   D. Arenberg. Concept problem solving in young and old adults. *Journal of Gerontology,* 1968, *23,* 279–282. Adapted from Table 1, p. 280, with permission.

p. 519, Figure 10.9   W. J. Hoyer, G. W. Rebok, & S. M. Sved. Effects of varying irrelevant information on adult age differences in problem solving. *Journal of Gerontology,* 1979, *34,* 553–560. Adapted from Figure 2, p. 556, with permission.

p. 523, Figure 10.11   K. L. Witte. Optional shift behavior in children and young and elderly adults. *Psychonomic Science,* 1971, *25,* 329–330. Adapted from the text, p. 330, with permission of the publisher and author.

p. 525, Table 10.4   L. E. Bourne, Jr., R. L. Dominowski, & E. F. Loftus. *Cognitive processes.* Copyright, 1979, pp. 233, 262. Reprinted with permission of Prentice-Hall, Inc., Englewood Cliffs, N.J.

p. 532, Figure 10.14   H. J. A. Rimoldi & K. W. VanderWoude. Aging and problem solving. *Archives of General Psychiatry,* 1969, *20,* 215–225. Adapted from Figure 2, p. 221. Copyright, 1969, American Medical Association. Adapted with permission of publisher.

p. 533, Figure 10.15   J. M. Kleinman & D. M. Brodzinsky. Haptic explorations in young, middle-aged, and elderly adults. *Journal of Gerontology,* 1978, *33,* 521–527. Adapted from Figure 1, Tables 2, 6, pp. 523, 525, with permission.

p. 537, Figure 10.17   H. M. Clay. Changes of performances with age on tasks of varying complexity. *British Journal of Psychology,* 1954, *45,* 7–13. Adapted from Tables 2, 3, p. 9, with permission of the publisher.

p. 539, Figure 10.18   R. E. Wright. Aging, divided attention, and processing capacity. *Journal of Gerontology,* 1981, *36,* 605–614. Adapted from Table 4, p. 611, with permission.

p. 543, Figure 10.19   J. Botwinick. *Cognitive processes in maturity and old age.* New York: Springer, 1967. Adapted from Figures 20 and 21, pp. 178, 179, with permission of the publisher and author.

p. 549, Figure 10.20   C. M. Friend & J. P. Zubek. The effects of age on critical thinking ability. *Journal of Gerontology,* 1958, *13,* 407–413. Adapted from Figure 4, p. 410, with permission.

p. 551, Figure 10.21   R. E. Wright. Aging, divided attention, and processing capacity. *Journal of Gerontology,* 1981, *36,* 605–614. Adapted from Table 3, p. 609, with permission.

p. 553, Figure 10.22   R. N. Shepard & J. Metzler, Mental rotation of three-dimensional objects. *Science,* 1971, *171,* 701–703. Adapted from Figures 1 and 2, pp. 701, 702. Copyright, 1971, by the American Association for the Advancement of Science. Reprinted by permission of publisher and authors.

p. 555, Figure 10.23   S. A. Gaylord & G. R. Marsh. Age differences in the speed of a spatial cognitive process. *Journal of Gerontology,* 1975, *30,* 674–678. Adapted from Figure 2, p. 676, with permission.

p. 556, Figure 10.24   M. M. Jacewicz & A. A. Hartley. Rotation of mental images by young and old college students: The effects of familiarity. *Journal of Gerontology,* 1979, *34,* 396–403. Adapted from Figure 1, p. 399, with permission.

p. 559, Figure 10.25   N. R. Schultz & W. J. Hoyer. Feedback effects on spatial egocentrism is old age. *Journal of Gerontology,* 1976, *31,* 72–75. Adapted from Figure 1, p. 73, with permission.

p. 570, Table 11.1   R. J. Scheidt & K. W. Schaie. A taxonomy of situations for an elderly population: Generating situational criteria. *Journal of Gerontology,* 1978, *33,* 848–857. Adapted from Table 1, p. 851, with permission.

p. 571, Table 11.2   J. A. Demming & S. L. Pressey. Tests "indigenous" to the adult and older years. *Journal of Counseling Psychology,* 1957, *2,* 144–148. Adapted with permission of J. A. Demming from text, p. 173.

p. 571, Figure 11.1   E. F. Gardner & R. H. Monge. Adult age differences in cognitive abilities and educational background. *Experimental Aging Research,* 1977, *3,* 337–383. Taken from *Experimental Aging Research, 3,* 1977, Figures 3a and 5, pp. 352, 355, with permission of the authors and editor. Copyright, Beech Hill Enterprises, Inc., 1977.

p. 573, Figure 11.2   H. E. Jones. Intelligence and problem-solving. In J. E. Birren (Ed.), *Handbook of aging and the individual.* Chicago: University of Chicago Press, 1959. Adapted from Figures 1 and 3, pp. 702, 703. Copyright, 1959, by the University of Chicago. Adapted with permission of the publisher.

p. 574, Figure 11.3 (top)   H. E. Jones. Intelligence and problem-solving. In J. E. Birren (Ed.), *Handbook of aging and the individual.* Chicago: University of Chicago Press, 1959. Adapted from Figure 5, p. 705. Copyright, 1959, by the University of Chicago. Adapted by permission of the publisher.

p. 574, Figure 11.3 (bottom)   J. Botwinick. *Cognitive processes in maturity and old age.* New York: Springer, 1967. Adapted from Figure 3, p. 7, with permission of the publisher and author.

p. 575, Figure 11.4   K. W. Schaie. Cross-sectional methods in the study of psychological aspects of aging. *Journal of Gerontology,* 1959, *14,* 208–215. Adapted from Table 5 with permission.

p. 577, Figure 11.5   B. Berkowitz. The Wechsler-Bellevue performance of white males past 50. *Journal of Gerontology,* 1953, *8,* 76–80. Adapted from Table 2, p. 77, with permission.

p. 579, Figure 11.6   B. Berkowitz. The Wechsler-Bellevue performance of white males past 50. *Journal of Gerontology,* 1953, *8,* 76–80. Adapted from Table 3, p. 78, with permission.

p. 580, Figure 11.7 (top)   K. W. Schaie, F. Rosenthal, & R. M. Perlman. Differential mental deterioration of factorially "pure" functions in later maturity. *Journal of Gerontology,* 1953, *8,* 191–196. Adapted from Figure 2, p. 194, with permission.

p. 580, Figure 11.7 (bottom)   A. Heron & S. M. Chown. *Age and function.* London: Churchill, 1967. Adapted from Figure 28, p. 78. Copyright, 1967, Little, Brown, and Company. Adapted with permission of the publisher.

p. 585, Table 11.3   J. L. Horn & R. B. Cattell. Age differences in fluid and crystallized intelligence. *Acta Psychologica,* 1967, *26,* 107–129. Adapted from Table 1, p. 110, with permission of North-Holland Publishing Company.

p. 586, Figure 11.9 (bottom)   B. Hayslip, Jr. & H. L. Sterns. Age differences in relationships between crystallized and fluid intelligence and problem solving. *Journal of*

Gerontology, 1979, *34,* 404–414. Adapted from Table 2, p. 408, with permission.

p. 589, Figure 11.10   C. Eisdorfer & C. Service. Verbal rote learning and superior intelligence in the aged. *Journal of Gerontology,* 1967, *22,* 158–161. Adapted from Figures 1 and 2, pp. 159, 160, with permission.

p. 593, Table 11.4   B. Hayslip, Jr. & H. L. Sterns. Age differences in relationships between crystallized and fluid intelligence and problem solving. *Journal of Gerontology,* 1979, *34,* 404–414. Adapted from Table 3, p. 409, with permission.

p. 597, Figure 11.11   T. A. Salthouse. The role of memory in the age decline in digit-symbol substitution performance. *Journal of Gerontology,* 1978, *33,* 233–238. Adapted from Figure 1, p. 234, with permission.

p. 607, Figure 11.13   P. T. Costa, Jr., J. L. Fozard, R. R. McCrae, & R. Bosse. Relations of age and personality dimensions to cognitive ability. *Journal of Gerontology,* 1976, *31,* 663–669. Adapted from Figure 1, p. 665, with permission.

p. 609, Figure 11.14   K. W. Schaie, G. V. Labouvie, & B. U. Buech. Generational and cohort specific differences in adult cognitive functions. *Developmental Psychology,* 1973, *9,* 151–166. Adapted from Figure 9, p. 162. Copyright, 1973, by the American Psychological Association. Adapted with permission of the publisher and authors.

p. 611, Figure 11.15   P. E. Panek, G. V. Barrett, G. V. Sterns, & R. A. Alexander. Age differences in perceptual style, selective attention, and perceptual-motor reaction time. *Experimental Aging Research,* 1978, *4,* 377–387. Adapted from Table 1, p. 381, with permission of the authors and editor. Copyright, Beech Hill Enterprises, Inc., 1978.

p. 614, Table 11.6   M. A. Okun & F. J. DiVesta. Cautiousness in adulthood as a function of age and instructions. *Journal of Gerontology,* 1976, *31,* 571–576. Adapted from Table 1. Also, M. A. Okun & C. S. Elias. Cautiousness in adulthood as a function of age and payoff structure. *Journal of Gerontology,* 1977, *32,* 451–455. Adapted from Tables 2, 3, p. 453. Adapted with permission.

p. 617, Figure 11.16   S. Wolk & J. Kurtz. Positive adjustment and involvement during aging and expectancy for internal control. *Journal of Consulting and Clinical Psychology,* 1975, *43,* 173–178. Adapted from Table 2, p. 176. Copyright, 1975, by the American Psychological Association. Adapted with permission of the publisher and authors.

p. 620 Table 11.7   B. L. Neugarten, R. J. Havighurst, & S. S. Tobin. The measurement of life satisfaction. *Journal of Gerontology,* 1961, *16,* 134–143. Adaped from text, p. 141, with permission.

p. 623, Figure 11.17   J. R. Marshall. Changes in aged white male suicide: 1948–1972. *Journal of Gerontology,* 1978, *33,* 763–768. Adapted from Figure 1, p. 764, with permission.

p. 625, Table 11.8   R. Zemore & N. Eames. Psychic and somatic symptoms of depression among young adults, institutionalized aged and noninstitutionalized aged. *Journal of Gerontology,* 1979, *34,* 716–722. Adapted from Table 2 with permission.

p. 627, Figure 11.18   R. L. Klein. Age, sex and task difficulty as predictors of social conformity. *Journal of Gerontology,* 1972, *27,* 229–236. Adapted from Figure 1, p. 233, with permission.

p. 629, Figure 11.19   S. J. Cutler, S. A. Lentz, M. J. Muha, & R. N. Riter. Aging and conservation: Cohort changes in attitudes about legalized abortion. *Journal of Gerontology,* 1980, *35,* 115–123. Adapted from Figure 1, p. 119, with permission.

Author Index

Subject Index